Public Speaking Handbook

2nd Edition

D1298797

Steven A. Beebe

Texas State University–San Marcos

Susan J. Beebe

Texas State University–San Marcos

PEARSON

Allyn and Bacon

Boston   New York   San Francisco
Mexico City   Montreal   Toronto   London   Madrid   Munich   Paris
Hong Kong   Singapore   Tokyo   Cape Town   Sydney

Editor-in-Chief, Communication: Karon Bowers

Series Editorial Assistant: Jenny Lupica

Associate Development Editor: Deb Hanlon

Marketing Manager: Suzan Czajkowski

Production Editor: Beth Houston

Editorial Production Service: Lifland et al., Bookmakers

Composition Buyer: Linda Cox

Manufacturing Buyer: JoAnne Sweeney

Electronic Composition: Publishers' Design and Production Services, Inc.

Cover Administrator: Linda Knowles

For related titles and support materials, visit our online catalog at www.ablongman.com.

Copyright © 2007, 2005 Pearson Education, Inc.

All rights reserved. No part of the material protected by this copyright notice may be reproduced or utilized in any form or by any means, electronic or mechanical, including photocopying, recording, or by any information storage and retrieval system, without written permission from the copyright owner.

To obtain permission(s) to use material from this work, please submit a written request to Allyn and Bacon, Permissions Department, 75 Arlington Street, Boston, MA 02116 or fax your request to 617-848-7320.

Between the time Web site information is gathered and then published, it is not unusual for some sites to have closed. Also, the transcription of URLs can result in typographical errors. The publisher would appreciate notification where these errors occur so that they may be corrected in subsequent editions.

Library of Congress Cataloging-in-Publication Data
Beebe, Steven A., 1950-
    Public speaking handbook / Steven A. Beebe, Susan J. Beebe. — 2nd ed.
        p. cm.
    Includes bibliographical references and index.
    ISBN 0-205-50296-2
    1. Public speaking. 2. Oral communication. I. Beebe, Susan J. II. Title.

    PN4129.15.B44 2005
    808.5'1—dc22

                                                        2006050055

Printed in the United States of America

10 9 8 7 6 5 4 3 2   RRD-IN 10 09 08 07

Dedicated to our parents,
Russell and Muriel Beebe and
Herb and Jane Dye

And to our sons, Mark and Matthew Beebe

Contents

9 Supporting Your Speech   171

Crafting a Speech   191

10 Organizing Your Speech   199

Presentation Aids 315

16 Designing and Using Presentation Aids 321

17 Using Presentation Software 347

Preface

The *Public Speaking Handbook*, Second Edition is an adaptation of the successful sixth edition of *Public Speaking: An Audience-Centered Approach*. The goal of this edition of the *Public Speaking Handbook* is to be a practical and friendly resource to help students of public speaking connect their hearts and minds with those of their listeners. The distinguishing focus of the book is our audience-centered approach.

Audience-Centered Approach

The audience writes the speech. Although developed and delivered by the speaker, a good speech centers on the needs, values, and hopes of the audience. The audience should be first and foremost in a speaker's mind during every step of the process of developing and delivering a speech.

Our audience-centered model integrates the step-by-step process of speech preparation and delivery with the ongoing process of considering the audience. The model appears throughout the text to remind students of the steps involved in speech preparation and delivery, while simultaneously emphasizing the importance of considering the audience.

Focus on Ethics

Being audience-centered does not mean that a speaker tells an audience only what they want to hear. Audience-centered speakers give audience members free choice in responding to a message by articulating truthful messages while also using effective means of ensuring that messages are clear and credible.

From the first chapter onward, we link being an audience-centered speaker with being an ethical speaker. Not only have we devoted an entire chapter (Chapter 4) to being an ethical speaker, but we offer reminders, tips, and strategies for making ethical speaking and listening integral parts of human communication. Each chapter contains a question about ethics that can spark discussion and raise awareness of ethical issues in being an effective public speaker.

Focus on Diversity

To be audience-centered is to acknowledge the different ethnic and cultural backgrounds of audience members, their attitudes, beliefs, values, and a host of other factors that come into play when people assemble to hear a speech. It is rare to speak to an audience of like-minded people of your own age and gender and with cultural and ethnic backgrounds similar to your own. Being audience centered means that as a speaker, you are constantly aware of and striving to adapt to the cultural, gender, and experiential diversity of the people to whom you are speaking. The topic of adapting to diverse audiences is integrated into every step of our audience-centered approach.

Focus on Speaking with Confidence

To help students reduce their fear of public speaking, we have devoted an entire chapter (Chapter 2) to learning how to manage communication apprehension. Research findings help students understand why they may feel nervous about speaking in public. Techniques that can help manage speaker apprehension are included. In addition, students are encouraged not to procrastinate in preparing their speeches. Procrastination adds to a speaker's nervousness and decreases the effectiveness of a speech.

Focus on Listening

Chapter 5, Listening to Speeches, includes an expanded discussion of rhetorical principles to enhance students' critical thinking and listening skills. New theoretical information about emotional contagion theory in Chapter 15 and the elaboration likelihood model (ELM) of persuasion in Chapter 19 will provide richer theoretical scaffolding for skill development strategies.

Features

Tabs divide the *Public Speaking Handbook* into eight sections. For example, Part 3, Preparing a Speech, includes Chapter 7, Developing Your Speech; Chapter 8, Gathering Supporting Material; and Chapter 9, Supporting Your Speech. Each tab lists the chapters covered in that section and includes a brief table of contents for each chapter. Following each tab is At a Glance, which outlines the chapters in a bulleted list format and includes page numbers where content can be found.

Every chapter contains Quick Checks, which are lists that students can refer to as they prepare their speeches. Each chapter also concludes with a feature called A Question of Ethics to focus student attention on the need to conduct oneself ethically while preparing and delivering a speech.

Many chapters contain a new feature called How To. These sections provide step-by-step instructions for completing steps in the speech preparation process.

New to This Edition

In addition, we've updated examples and added new research applications to public speaking in every chapter. New sample speeches, both at the ends of selected chapters and in Appendix D, help students see full-text examples of effective speeches. Here's a more detailed look at what's new.

NEW EMPHASIS ON RHETORICAL ANALYSIS

Contemporary public-speaking instruction has its roots in classical rhetoric. To help students better analyze their own speeches and the speeches of others, we've added new material in Chapter 5 anchored in those classical rhetorical principles. We believe that an important goal of public-speaking instruction is to help students develop critical thinking and analysis skills, not only so they can evaluate their own speaking, but so they can be better consumers of the messages they hear. Our new discussion of rhetorical criticism achieves both of those goals.

NEW COVERAGE OF THEORY AND RESEARCH LINKED TO COMMUNICATION SKILL DEVELOPMENT

Although students typically clamor for strategies and techniques, they also need theory-based principles so they can apply the skills that they learn. We have consistently been praised for our balanced integration of theory with skill development. New to this edition is theoretical information about listening style (Chapter 5), emotions (Chapter 15), persuasion theory and use of fear appeals (Chapters 19 and 20), and use of metaphors and similes (Chapter 14). These references to contemporary communication theory are integrated into the text to give students a firm foundation for applying the skills we prescribe.

EXPANDED DISCUSSION OF USING HUMOR WISELY

As one sage put it, "Our five senses are incomplete without the sixth—a sense of humor." Skilled use of humor can help a speaker gain listener attention, maintain interest, and make a point. Ineffective humor can quickly cause a speech to implode. We've developed an expanded discussion of this often undeveloped area of public speaking in Chapter 21, Special-Occasion Speaking. We present both research-based and time-honed strategies for using humor wisely, to help students connect with listeners.

NEW TIPS AND STRATEGIES FOR EDITING SPEECHES

In this Internet age, students often suffer not from too little information, but too much. Among their biggest challenges in developing speech content is wending their way through a mound of data, information, and illustrations. They need help in editing their message. We've added new tips and techniques to help students achieve their speaking goals by editing out the superfluous and the unnecessary.

NEW TIPS AND STRATEGIES FOR USING PRESENTATION AIDS

The "PowerPointing" of public presentations has increased dramatically in the past decade. Especially in business and professional speaking contexts, audiences have come to expect a visual message along with the oral sound track. Yet speakers, especially novice speakers, sometimes overdo it. To ensure that students use presentation aids skillfully, we've added new information about the latest thinking on how to support a speech with visual messages.

NEW STUDENT SPEECHES

At the end of Chapters 3, 18, and 20, we've added new annotated student speeches. In addition, we've added many new speeches in our revised Appendix D to provide positive models of effective speeches. To make these speeches even more useful, students can see and hear the student speeches being delivered on video via MySpeechLab, an innovative Internet resource. Reading and hearing these student speeches offers implicit encouragement and good examples that beginning speakers can emulate.

NEW EXAMPLES

New examples throughout the book provide both classic and contemporary models to help students master the art of public speaking. As in the previous edition, we draw on both student speeches and speeches delivered by well-known people.

Our Partnership with Instructors and Students

Students rarely learn public speaking from reading a book. Students learn best in partnership with an experienced instructor who can offer encouragement as well as advice about being an audience-centered speaker.

INSTRUCTORS' SUPPLEMENTS

We offer an abundance of resources to supplement instructors' skill and experience in teaching public speaking and assist them in providing advice and guidance.

Print Materials

- *Instructor's Manual,* by Patricia A. Cutspec, East Tennessee State University. This manual provides resources for both new and experienced instructors. For each chapter in the text, the *Instructor's Manual* provides learning objectives, chapter outlines, review guides, lists of suggested videos, and activities and assignments.
- *Test Bank,* by Julie Weeks Simanski, Des Moines Area Community College. The *Test Bank* contains more than 1,000 questions, including multiple choice, true/false, short answer, and in-depth essay questions.

- *Allyn and Bacon Public Speaking Transparency Package, Version II.* This supplement includes 100 full-color transparencies created with PowerPoint® software that provide visual support for classroom lectures and discussions.

- *New Teacher's Guide to Public Speaking,* **Third Edition,** by Calvin L. Troup, Duquesne University. This guide helps new teachers teach the introductory public speaking course effectively. It covers such topics as preparing for the term, planning and structuring your course, evaluating speeches, utilizing the textbook, integrating technology into the classroom, and much more.

- *Great Ideas for Teaching Speech (GIFTS),* by Raymond Zeuschner, California Polytechnic State University. This instructional booklet provides descriptions of and guidelines for assignments that have been used successfully by experienced public speaking instructors in their classrooms.

Electronic Materials

- *Test Gen EQ: Computerized Test Bank* **(Download Only)** by Julie Weeks Simanski, Des Moines Area Community College. The questions in the print *Test Bank* are also available electronically through our computerized testing system, TestGen EQ. The fully networkable test-generating software is now available on a multiplatform CD-ROM. The user-friendly interface enables instructors to view, edit, and add questions, transfer questions to tests, and print tests in a variety of fonts. Search and sort features allow instructors to locate questions quickly and arrange them in a preferred order. Instructors can log on to the Instructor Resource Center at www.ablongman.com/irc to access the testing system.

- *PowerPoint® Presentation* **(Download Only),** by Nick Backus, Western Oregon University. This supplement includes a multitude of text-specific lecture outlines and graphic images. Instructors can log on to the Instructor Resource Center at www.ablongman.com/irc to access the presentation package.

- *Test Item File for Blackboard and CourseCompass* **(Download Only).** *Test Bank* questions can be accessed through the Instructor Resource Center and downloaded for Blackboard or Course Compass for use on quizzes.

- *Test Item File for WebCT* **(Download Only).** *Test Bank* questions can be accessed through the Instructor Resource Center and downloaded for WebCT for use on quizzes.

- *Allyn and Bacon Public Speaking Video.* This video includes excerpts of classic and contemporary speeches as well as student speeches to illustrate the public-speaking process. One speech is delivered two times under different circumstances by the same person to illustrate the difference between effective and ineffective delivery based on appearance, nonverbal communication, and verbal style. For adopters only; restrictions apply. See your Allyn and Bacon/Longman representative for details.

- *A&B Contemporary and Classic Speeches DVD.* This exciting supplement includes over 120 minutes of video footage in an easy-to-use DVD format. Each speech is accompanied by a biographical and historical summary that helps students understand the context and motivation behind it. For adopters only; restrictions apply. See your Allyn and Bacon/Longman representative for details.

- *A&B Video Library.* This collection of communication videos includes videos from the American Forensic Association highlighting award-winning student speeches, classroom-based student speeches, and a collection of videos produced by Film for the Humanities and Sciences. (FHS video topics include, but are not limited to, Business Presentations, Great American Speeches, and Conflict Resolution.) Separate video guides are available with selected A&B videos. For adopters only; restrictions apply. See your Allyn and Bacon/Longman representative for details.

- *A&B Communication Digital Media Archive, Version 3.0.* The Digital Media Archive CD-ROM contains electronic images of charts, graphs, maps, tables, and figures, along with media elements such as video, audio clips, and related Web links. These media assets are fully customizable to use with our pre-formatted PowerPoint® outlines or to import into the instructor's own lectures. All are both Windows and Mac compatible. For adopters only; restrictions apply. See your Allyn and Bacon/Longman representative for details.

- *Allyn and Bacon CourseCompass for Public Speaking, Professional Development Edition,* http://www.coursecompass.com (Access code required).

- *Allyn and Bacon Course Management.* Other course management options are available. Please contact your Allyn and Bacon representative for details.

- *VideoWorkshop for Public Speaking, Version 2.0,* by Tasha Van Horn, Citrus University, and Marilyn Reineck of Concordia University. *Student Learning Guide with CD-ROM* and *Instructor's Teaching Guide.* This complete teaching and learning system includes quality video footage on an easy-to-use CD-ROM plus a Student Learning Guide and an Instructor's Teaching Guide—both with text-specific Correlation Grids.

Technology Advantage

- *MySpeechLab or MySpeechLab CourseCompass with E-Book:* MySpeechLab is an interactive and instructive online solution for introductory public speaking. Designed to be used as a supplement to a traditional lecture course or to serve as a complete online course, MySpeechLab combines multimedia, video, speech preparation activities, research support, tests, and quizzes to make teaching and learning fun! Students benefit from a wealth of video clips that include student and professional speeches with running commentary, questions to consider, and helpful tips—all geared to help students learn to speak with confidence. http://www.myspeechlab.com (Access code required).

STUDENTS' SUPPLEMENTS

Students can take advantage of a selection of study and enrichment materials.

Print Materials

- *Study Cards for Public Speaking.* Colorful, affordable, and packed with useful information, Allyn and Bacon's Study Cards make studying easier, more efficient, and more enjoyable. Course information is distilled down to the basics, helping you quickly master the fundamentals, review a subject for understanding, or prepare for an exam. Because they're laminated for durability, you can keep these Study Cards for years to come and pull them out whenever you need a quick review. Sold separately or packaged with participating A&B texts.

- *Outlining Workbook,* by Reeze L. Hanson & Sharon Condon, Haskell Indian Nations University. This workbook includes activities, exercises, and answers to help students develop and master the critical skill of outlining.

- *Preparing Visual Aids for Presentations,* **Fourth Edition**, by Dan Cavanaugh. This brief booklet provides a host of ideas for using today's multimedia tools to improve presentations, including suggestions for planning a presentation, guidelines for designing visual aids and storyboarding, and a walkthrough that shows how to prepare a visual display using PowerPoint. Sold separately or packaged with participating A&B texts.

- *Speech Preparation Workbook,* by Jennifer Dreyer and Gregory H. Patton, San Diego State University. This workbook takes students through the stages of speech creation—from audience analysis to writing the speech—and includes guidelines, tips, and easy-to-fill-in pages. Sold separately or packaged with participating A&B texts.

- *Pathways to Careers in Communication,* by the National Communication Association. This booklet provides information about the discipline, its history and importance, information on career possibilities, and other resources for investigating communication studies. Valuepacked with any A&B communication text.

- *Public Speaking in the Multicultural Environment,* **Second Edition**, by Devorah Lieberman, Portland State University. This two-chapter essay focuses on speaking and listening to a culturally diverse audience and emphasizes preparation, delivery, and how speeches are perceived.

Electronic Materials

- *Speech Writer's Workshop CD-ROM, Version 2.0.* This speechwriting software includes a Speech Handbook that offers tips for researching and preparing speeches, a Speech Workshop that guides students step-by-step through the speechwriting process, a Topics Dictionary that gives students hundreds of ideas for speeches, and the Documentor citation database that helps them format bibliographic entries in either MLA or APA style. Sold separately or packaged with participating A&B texts.

- **ResearchNavigator.com Guide: Speech Communication,** by Steven L. Epstein, Suffolk County Community College, and Linda R. Barr, Texas Lutheran University. This updated booklet includes tips, resources, and Web sites to aid students conducting research on Pearson Education's Research Navigator Web site. The guide contains a student access code for the Research Navigator database, offering students free, unlimited access to a collection of more than 25,000 discipline-specific articles from top-tier academic publications and peer-reviewed journals, as well as *The New York Times* and popular news publications. The guide introduces students to the basics of the Internet and the World Wide Web and includes tips for searching for articles on the site and a list of journals useful for research in their discipline. Also included are hundreds of Web resources for the discipline, as well as information on how to correctly cite research. The guide is packaged with new copies of the text. http://www.researchnavigator.com

- **VideoWorkshop for Public Speaking, Version 2.0,** by Tasha Van Horn, Citrus University, and Marilyn Reineck, Concordia University. **Student Learning Guide with CD-ROM** and **Instructor's Teaching Guide.** This complete teaching and learning system includes quality video footage on an easy-to-use CD-ROM plus a Student Learning Guide and an Instructor's Teaching Guide—both with text-specific Correlation Grids.

- **A&B Public Speaking Web Site,** by Nan Peck, Northern Virginia Community College. This open access Web site contains six modules students can use along with their public speaking text to learn about the process of public speaking and help prepare for speeches. The Web site focuses on the six steps of speech preparation: Assess Your Speechmaking Situation, Analyze Your Audience, Research Your Topic, Organize and Write Your Speech, Deliver Your Presentation, and Discern Other Talks. In addition, interactive activities aid in speech preparation and Notes from the Instructor provide additional details on selected topics. Need some individual help with your speech? Ask the Speech Doctor lets you pose questions to a professor of speech communication via e-mail. Web links throughout are updated regularly and allow students to use and explore reliable Internet sites related to public speaking. www.ablongman.com/pubspeak

Acknowledgments

Writing a book is a partnership not only between authors but also with many people who have offered us the benefit of their experience and advice about how to make this the best possible teaching and learning resource. We appreciate all of the authors and speakers we have quoted or referenced; their words and wisdom have added resonance to our knowledge and richness to our advice. We are grateful for our students, colleagues, adopters, friends, and the editorial team at Allyn and Bacon.

Many reviewers have helped us shape the content and features of this text. These talented public-speaking teachers have supplemented our experience to help us make decisions about how to present and organize the content of this book. We express our sincere appreciation to the following reviewers who have shared their advice, wisdom, and expertise: Stephen Braden, Kennesaw State University; Josh Compton, Southwest Baptist University; Alan Hansen, Texas A & M University; Martin Mehl, California Polytechnic State University; and David E. Williams, Texas Tech University.

We thank Patricia Cutspec for sharing her wealth of teaching ideas and strategies in the *Instructor's Manual*. We thank Julie Weeks Simanski and Nick Backus for their work on the *Test Bank* and the PowerPoint Presentation package, respectively. Our editorial support team at Allyn and Bacon, Editor-in-Chief Karon Bowers and Development Editor Diane Durkee, have done another outstanding job of offering skilled advice to make this a better book.

Finally, we value the patience, encouragement, proud support, and love of our sons, Mark and Matthew Beebe. They offer many lessons in rhetorical criticism, listening, persuasion, ethos, logos, and pathos, and continue to be our most important audience.

Steven A. Beebe and Susan J. Beebe
San Marcos, Texas

1

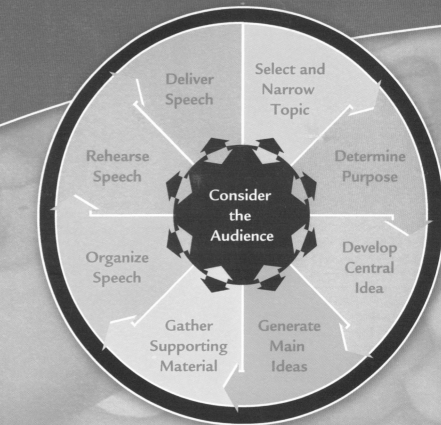

Deliver Speech

Select and Narrow Topic

Rehearse Speech

Consider the Audience

Determine Purpose

Organize Speech

Develop Central Idea

Gather Supporting Material

Generate Main Ideas

Introduction

Introduction

At a Glance

Introduction

1 Introduction to Public Speaking

➡ **Why Study Public Speaking?** (p. 7)
- As you study public speaking, you will learn and practice strategies for effective delivery and critical listening.
- The ability to speak with competence and confidence will provide empowerment.
- Being able to communicate effectively with others is key to success in any line of work.

➡ **Public Speaking and Conversation** (p. 8)
- Public speaking is more planned than conversation.
- Public speaking is also more formal than conversation.
- The roles of public speakers and audiences are clearly defined.

➡ **The Communication Process** (p. 11)
- Consider communication as action. A public speaker is a source of information and ideas for an audience.
- Consider communication as interaction; it involves feedback and takes place in a context.
- Consider communication as transaction, or a simultaneous process—we send and receive messages concurrently.
- The message in public speaking is the speech itself—both what is said and how it is said.
- A message is usually transmitted from sender to receiver via two channels: visual and auditory.
- Anything that interferes with the communication of a message is called noise.

➡ **The Rich Heritage of Public Speaking** (p. 14)
- The fourth century B.C. was a golden age for rhetoric in the Greek Republic.
- Nineteenth-century public speakers practiced the art of declamation—the delivery of an already famous address.

- From the mid-nineteenth to the early twentieth century, elocution manuals, providing elaborate and specific prescriptions for effective delivery, were standard references.
- In the twenty-first century, a new era of speechmaking begins, using rapidly evolving technology and media, but drawing on a rich heritage of providing information, influencing thought and action, entertaining, and paying tribute via the spoken word.

➡ **Public Speaking and Diversity (p. 16)**
- Gender, ethnicity, and culture of both speaker and audience are crucial components of the context of a speaking event.
- Diverse audiences have different expectations for appropriate and effective speech topics, argument structure, language style, and delivery.
- To be effective, public speakers need to understand, affirm, and adapt to diverse audiences.

2 Speaking with Confidence

➡ **Understand Your Nervousness (p. 19)**
- It's normal to be nervous.
- Your view of the speaking assignment, your perception of your speaking skill, and your self-esteem interact to create anxiety.
- Anxiety can be useful. Your heightened state of readiness can actually help you speak better, especially if you view the public-speaking event positively instead of negatively.

➡ **Build Your Confidence (p. 22)**
- Know to whom you will be speaking and learn as much about them as you can.
- Be prepared. The better prepared you are, the less anxiety you will experience.
- Re-create the speech environment when you practice. A realistic rehearsal will increase your confidence when your moment to speak arrives.
- Know your introduction and your conclusion.
- Visualize your success. Positive visualization is effective because it boosts your confidence by helping you see yourself as a more confident, accomplished speaker.

3 The Audience-Centered Speechmaking Process

➡ **An Audience-Centered Speechmaking Model (p. 29)**
- In designing and delivering your speech, always make choices with your audience in mind.

➡ **Consider Your Audience (p. 31)**
- Your selection of topic, purpose, and even major ideas should be based on a thorough understanding of your listeners.

➡ **Select and Narrow Your Topic (p. 31)**
- Determine what you will talk about and limit your topic to fit the constraints of your speaking assignment.
- Ask three questions: Who is the audience? What is the occasion? What are my interests, talents, and experiences?

➡ **Determine Your Purpose (p. 33)**
- There are three general purposes for speeches: to inform, to persuade, and to entertain.
- After making sure you understand your general purpose, formulate a specific purpose: a concise statement indicating what you want your listeners to be able to remember, do, or feel when you finish your speech.

➡ **Develop Your Central Idea (p. 34)**
- Your central idea identifies the essence of your message. Think of it as a one-sentence summary of your speech.

➡ **Generate the Main Ideas (p. 34)**
- Once you have an appropriate topic, a specific purpose, and a well-worded central idea down on paper, the next task is to identify the major divisions of your speech or key points that you wish to develop.
- To determine how to subdivide your central idea into key points, ask these three questions: Does the central idea have logical divisions? Can you think of several reasons why the central idea is true? Can you support the central idea with a series of steps?

➡ **Gather Verbal and Visual Supporting Material (p. 35)**
- With your main idea or ideas in mind, gather material to support them—facts, examples, definitions, and quotations from others that illustrate, amplify, clarify, and provide evidence.
- Supporting material should be personal and concrete, and it should appeal to your listeners' senses.

➡ **Organize Your Speech (p. 37)**
- A clearly and logically structured speech helps your audience remember what you say.
- Speakers need to present ideas, information, examples, illustrations, stories, and statistics in an orderly sequence so that listeners can easily follow what they are saying.
- Every well-prepared speech has three major divisions: the introduction, the body, and the conclusion.

➡ **Rehearse Your Speech (p. 41)**
- Rehearsing your speech is a way to "measure" your message so that you get it right when you present it to your audience.
- Rehearse your speech out loud.
- Practice making eye contact.
- Make decisions about the style of your speech.

➡ **Deliver Your Speech (p. 42)**
- Delivery is the final step in the preparation process.
- Concentrate on your message and your audience.
- Deliver your speech in a conversational style, and try to establish rapport with your listeners.

4 Ethics and Free Speech

➡ **Ethics (p. 47)**
- Ethics are the beliefs, values, and moral principles by which people determine what is right or wrong.
- Speakers who exercise their right to free speech have a responsibility to speak ethically.
- Ethical public speaking is inherently audience-centered, always taking into account the needs and rights of the listeners.

➡ **Free Speech** (p. 47)
- In a country in which free speech is protected by law, the right to speak freely must be balanced by the responsibility to speak ethically.

➡ **Speaking Freely** (p. 48)
- In 1791, the First Amendment to the U.S. Constitution was written to guarantee that "Congress shall make no law . . . abridging the freedom of speech."
- A few years later, Congress passed the Sedition Act, providing punishment for those who spoke out against the government.
- In 1920, the American Civil Liberties Union was the first organization formed to protect free speech.
- In 1940, Congress declared it illegal to urge the violent overthrow of the federal government.
- In 1964, the Supreme Court narrowed the definition of slander, or false speech that harms someone.
- In 1989, the Supreme Court defended the burning of the U.S. flag as a "speech act" protected by the First Amendment.
- In 1997, the Court struck down the highly controversial federal Communications Decency Act of 1996, which had imposed penalties for creating, transmitting, or receiving obscene material on the Internet.
- In 2001, the Patriot Act sparked new debate over the balance between national security and free speech.

➡ **Speaking Ethically** (p. 50)
- Have a clear, responsible goal.
- Use sound evidence and reasoning.
- Be sensitive to and tolerant of differences.
- Be honest.
- Avoid plagiarism.
- Do your own work.
- Acknowledge your sources.
- Take careful notes.
- Cite sources correctly.

➡ **Listening Ethically** (p. 56)
- Communicate your expectations and feedback.
- Be sensitive to and tolerant of differences.
- Listen critically.
- Consider diverse cultural norms and audience expectations as part of the context within which you listen to and evaluate the speaker.

Introduction to Public Speaking

Perhaps you think you have heard this speaker—or even taken a class from him: "His eyes were buried in his script. His words in monotone emerged haltingly from behind his mustache, losing volume as they were sifted through hair. Audiences rushed to see and hear him, and after they had satisfied their eyes, they closed their ears. Ultimately, they turned to small talk among themselves while the great man droned on."[1]

> *A journey of a thousand miles begins with a single step.*
> —**Chinese Proverb**

The speaker described here in such an unflattering way is none other than Albert Einstein. Sadly, although the great physicist could attract an audience with his reputation, he could not sustain their attention and interest because he lacked public-speaking skills.

Although you may not be blessed with his intellect, you have at least one distinct advantage over Einstein: the opportunity afforded by this text to study and practice public speaking. Right now, however, the experience may seem less like an opportunity and more like a daunting task. Why undertake it?

1.a Why Study Public Speaking?

As you study public speaking, you will learn and practice strategies for effective delivery and critical listening. You will discover new applications for skills you may already have, such as focusing and organizing ideas and gathering information from print and electronic sources. In addition to learning and applying these fundamental skills, you will gain long-term advantages related to *empowerment* and *employment*.

EMPOWERMENT

You will undoubtedly be called on to speak in public at various times in your life. The ability to speak with competence and confidence will provide **empowerment.** To be empowered is to have the resources, information, and attitudes that allow you to take action to achieve a desired goal.

Being a skilled public speaker will give you an edge that other, less skilled communicators lack—even those who may have superior ideas, training, or experience. It will position you for greater things. Former presidential speechwriter James Humes, who labels public speaking "the language of leadership," says, "Every time you have to speak—whether it's in an auditorium, in a company conference room, or even at your own desk—you are auditioning for leadership."[2] You feel truly empowered when you speak with confidence, knowing that your ideas are expressed with conviction and assurance. Being an empowered public speaker is within your grasp. And being an empowered speaker can open up leadership and career opportunities for you.

EMPLOYMENT

It was industrialist Charles M. Schwab who said, "I'll pay more for a person's ability to speak and express himself than for any other quality he might possess."[3] If you can speak well, you possess a skill that others will value highly. Whether you're currently employed as an entry-level employee or aspire to the highest rung of the corporate leadership ladder, being able to communicate effectively with others is key to success in any line of work. The skills you learn in a public-speaking course, such as how to ethically adapt information to listeners, organize your ideas, persuade others, and hold listeners' attention, are among the skills most sought after by any employer. In a nationwide survey, prospective employers of college graduates said they seek candidates with "public-speaking and presentation ability."[4] Other surveys of personnel managers, both in the United States and internationally, have confirmed that they consider communication skills the top factor in helping graduating college students obtain employment (see Table 1.1).[5]

1.b Public Speaking and Conversation

Public speaking has much in common with conversation, a form of communication in which you engage every day. Like conversation, public speaking requires you to focus and verbalize your thoughts:

> "Alicia, do you ever feel that people here are giving you trouble because you're Hispanic?" asks her roommate Sharon.
>
> Alicia wrinkles her brow in thought, then replies, "I guess once in a while, but not for the reasons you'd expect. Like I notice the white kids getting all nervous when I stand close to them when we talk. And they don't like to look me in the eye for a long time."

Alicia could easily build a speech about differences between Hispanics and Caucasians on these two nonverbal behaviors.

When you have a conversation, you have to make decisions "on your feet." If your friends look puzzled or interrupt with questions, you re-explain the idea you have been talking about. If they look bored, you insert a funny story or talk more animatedly. As a public speaker, you will learn to make similar adaptations based on your knowledge of who your listeners are, their expectations for your speech, and their reactions to what you are saying. In fact, the ability to adapt to your audience is so vital that this book focuses on public speaking as an audience-centered activity.

TABLE 1.1	Top Factors in Helping Graduating College Students Obtain Employment

Rank/Order	Factors/Skills Evaluated
1	Oral (spoken) communication
2	Written communication skills
3	Listening ability
4	Enthusiasm
5	Technical competence
6	Work experience
7	Appearance
8	Poise
9	Résumé
10	Part-time or summer employment
11	Specific degree held
12	Leadership in campus/community activity
13	Recommendations
14	Accreditation of program
15	Participation in campus/community activity
16	Grade point average

Source: Winsor, JB, Curtis, DB, Stephens, RD. "National Preferences in Business and Communication Education: A Survey Update," *Journal of the Association for Communication Administration* 3, September 1997: 174.

But if public speaking were exactly like conversation, Albert Einstein's lectures would have been more riveting, there would be no reason to take a public-speaking class, and there would be no need for this book. Let's take a look at some of the ways in which public speaking differs from conversation.

PUBLIC SPEAKING IS PLANNED

Public speaking is more planned than conversation. A public speaker may spend hours or even days planning and practicing his or her speech. Having already worked on his inaugural address for several weeks, president-elect John F. Kennedy rose before 8 a.m. on January 20, 1961, to review the speech and make final corrections. He practiced aloud while he took a bath, dressed, walked from room to room, and even while he ate breakfast.[6] Nearly forty years later, then–vice president Al Gore worked with speechwriters through 17 drafts of his August 2000 acceptance of the Democratic nomination for president. A few hours before he delivered the speech, an aide quipped, "It's in draft 625."[7] Both Kennedy's painstaking rehearsing and Gore's relentless revising reflect the forethought and planning typical of public speaking.

PUBLIC SPEAKING IS FORMAL

Public speaking is also more formal than conversation. The slang or casual language we often use in conversation is not appropriate for most public speaking. Audiences expect speakers to use standard English grammar and vocabulary.

The nonverbal communication of public speakers is also more formal than nonverbal behavior in ordinary conversation. People engaged in conversation often sit or stand close together, gesture spontaneously, and move about restlessly. The physical distance between public speakers and their audiences is usually greater than that between people in conversation. And although public speakers may certainly use extemporaneous gestures while speaking, they also plan and rehearse some gestures and movement to emphasize especially important parts of their speeches.

THE ROLES OF PUBLIC SPEAKERS AND AUDIENCES ARE CLEARLY DEFINED

Finally, public speaking is less fluid and interactive than conversation. People in conversation may alternately talk and listen, and perhaps even interrupt one another, but in public speaking the roles of speaker and audience are more clearly defined and remain stable. Rarely do audience members interrupt or even talk to speakers, although some cultures and contexts invite more speaker–audience interaction than do others.

QUICK CHECK: *Components of Effective Public Speaking*

- Plan your speech.
- Focus and vocalize your thoughts.
- Adapt your speaking to your listeners.
- Use standard English vocabulary and grammar.
- Use more formal nonverbal communication.

Even under these circumstances, however, the roles of speaker and audience are still clearly defined and stable.

Speaking in public requires you to sharpen existing communication skills and to learn and apply new ones. To better understand what is involved, let's look at several models of communication that illustrate the public-speaking process and its components.

1.c The Communication Process

Even the earliest communication theorists recognized that communication is a process. The models they formulated were linear, suggesting a simple transfer of meaning from a sender to a receiver, as shown in Figure 1.1. More recently, theorists have tried to create models that better demonstrate the complexity of the communication process. Let's explore what some of those models can teach us about what happens when we communicate.

COMMUNICATION AS ACTION

Although they were simplistic, the earliest linear models of communication as action identified most of the elements of the communication process. We will explain each element as it relates to public speaking.

Source A public speaker is a **source** of information and ideas for an audience. The job of the source or speaker is to **encode**, or translate, the ideas and images in his or her mind into verbal or nonverbal symbols (a **code**) that an audience can recognize. The speaker may encode into words (for example, "The fabric should be 2 inches square") or into gestures (showing the size with his or her hands).

Message The **message** in public speaking is the speech itself—both what is said and how it is said. If a speaker has trouble finding words to convey his or her ideas or

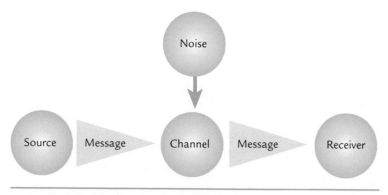

FIGURE 1.1 A Model of Communication as Action

sends contradictory nonverbal symbols, listeners may not be able to **decode** the speaker's verbal and nonverbal symbols back into a message.

Channels   A message is usually transmitted from sender to receiver via two **channels**: *visual* and *auditory*. Audience members see the speaker and decode his or her nonverbal symbols—eye contact (or lack of it), facial expressions, posture, gestures, and dress. If the speaker uses any visual aids, such as graphs or models, these too are transmitted along the visual channel. The auditory channel opens as the speaker speaks. Then the audience members hear words and such vocal cues as inflection, rate, and voice quality.

Receiver   The **receiver** of the message is the individual audience member, whose decoding of the message will depend on his or her own particular blend of past experiences, attitudes, beliefs, and values. As already emphasized, an effective public speaker should be receiver- or audience-centered.

Noise   Anything that interferes with the communication of a message is called *noise*. Noise may be physical and **external**. If your 8 a.m. public-speaking class is frequently interrupted by the roar of a lawn mower running back and forth under the window, it may be difficult to concentrate on what your instructor is saying. A noisy air-conditioner, a crying baby, or incessant coughing may make it difficult for audience members to hear or concentrate on a speech.

Noise may also be **internal**. It may stem from either *physiological* or *psychological* causes and may directly affect either the source or the receiver. A bad cold (physiological noise) may cloud a speaker's memory or subdue his or her delivery. An audience member who is worried about an upcoming exam (psychological noise) is unlikely to remember much of what the speaker says. Regardless of whether it is internal or external, physiological or psychological, or whether it originates in the sender or the receiver, noise interferes with the transmission of a message.

COMMUNICATION AS INTERACTION

Realizing that linear models were overly simplistic, later communication theorists designed models that depicted communication as a more complex process (see Figure 1.2). These models were circular, or interactive, and added two important new elements: feedback and context.

Feedback   As noted earlier, one way in which public speaking differs from casual conversation is that the public speaker does most or all of the talking. But public speaking is still interactive. Without an audience to hear and provide **feedback**, public speaking serves little purpose. Skillful public speakers are audience-centered. They depend on the nods, facial expressions, and murmurings of the audience to adjust their rate of speaking, volume, vocabulary, type and amount of supporting material, and other variables to communicate their message successfully.

Context   The **context** of a public-speaking experience is the environment or situation in which the speech occurs. It includes such elements as the time, the place, and

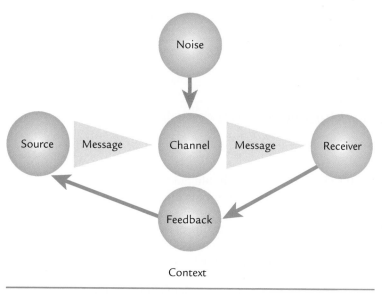

FIGURE 1.2 **An Interactive Model of Communication**

the speaker's and audience's cultural traditions and expectations. To paraphrase John Donne, no *speech* is an island—no speech occurs in a vacuum. Rather, each speech is a blend of circumstances that can never be replicated exactly again.

The person whose job it is to deliver an identical message to a number of different audiences at different times and in different places can attest to the uniqueness of each speaking context. If the room is hot, crowded, or poorly lit, these conditions affect both speaker and audience. The audience that hears a speaker at 10 a.m. is likely to be fresher and more receptive than a 4:30 p.m. audience. A speaker who fought rush-hour traffic for 90 minutes to arrive at his or her destination may find it difficult to muster much enthusiasm for delivering the speech.

Many of the skills that you will learn from this book relate not only to the preparation of effective speeches (messages), but also to the elements of feedback and context in the communication process. Our audience-centered approach focuses on "reading" your listeners' responses and adjusting to them as you speak.

COMMUNICATION AS TRANSACTION

The most recent communication models do not label individual components. Transactive models focus instead on communication as a simultaneous process. As the model in Figure 1.3 suggests, we send and receive messages concurrently. In a two-person communication transaction, both individuals are sending and receiving at the same time. When you are listening, you are simultaneously expressing your thoughts and feelings nonverbally.

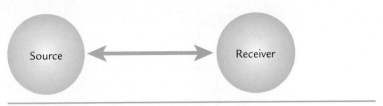

FIGURE 1.3 **A Transactive Model of Communication**

An effective public speaker should not only be focused on the message he or she is expressing, but also be tuned in to how the audience is responding to the message. A good public speaker shouldn't wait until a speech is over to gauge its effectiveness, but rather, because of the transactive nature of communication, should be scanning the audience during the speech for nonverbal clues to the audience's reaction.

Although communication models have been developed only recently, the elements of these models have long been recognized as the keys to successful public speaking. As you study public speaking, you will continue a tradition that goes back to the very beginnings of Western civilization.

QUICK CHECK: *Understand the Communication Process*

- The speaker is the source of information.
- The message is the speech.
- The message is transmitted through visual and auditory channels.
- The receiver decodes the message.
- Noise (external or internal) interferes with the message.

1.d The Rich Heritage of Public Speaking

Long before many people could read, they listened to public speakers. As you'll read in Appendix B, the study of *rhetoric* is ancient. **Rhetoric** is another term for the use of words and symbols to achieve a goal. Although rhetoric is often defined as the art of speaking or writing aimed at persuading others (changing or reinforcing attitudes, beliefs, values, or behavior), whether you're informing, persuading, or even entertaining listeners, you are using rhetoric, because you are trying to achieve a goal.

The fourth century B.C. was a golden age for rhetoric in the Greek Republic, where the philosopher Aristotle formulated guidelines for speakers that we still follow today. As politicians and poets attracted large followings in ancient Rome, Cicero and Quintilian sought to define the qualities of the "true" orator. On a lighter note, it is said that Roman orators invented the necktie. Fearing laryngitis, they wore "chin cloths" to protect their throats.[8]

In medieval Europe, the clergy were the most polished public speakers. People gathered eagerly to hear Martin Luther expound his Articles of Faith. In the eighteenth century, British subjects in the colonies listened to town criers and to the speeches of impassioned patriots of what was to become the United States.

Vast nineteenth-century audiences heard speakers such as Henry Clay and Daniel Webster debate states' rights; they listened to Frederick Douglass, Angelina Grimke, and Sojourner Truth argue for the abolition of slavery, and to Lucretia Mott plead for women's suffrage; they gathered for an evening's entertainment as Mark Twain traveled the lecture circuits of the frontier.

Students of nineteenth-century public speaking spent very little time developing their own speeches. Instead, they practiced the art of **declamation**—the delivery of an already famous address. Favorite subjects for declamation included speeches by Americans such as Patrick Henry and William Jennings Bryan and British orator Edmund Burke. Collections of speeches, such as Bryan's own ten-volume set of *The World's Famous Orations,* published in 1906, were extremely popular.

Hand in hand with declamation went the study and practice of **elocution**, the expression of emotion through posture, movement, gestures, facial expression, and voice. From the mid-nineteenth to the early twentieth century, elocution manuals, providing elaborate and specific prescriptions for effective delivery, were standard references not only in schools, but also in nearly every middle-class home in the United States.[9] Mark Twain was undoubtedly thinking back to the practitioners of declamation and elocution he had heard in his youth when he described the Reverend Mr. Sprague in *The Adventures of Tom Sawyer:*

> He was regarded as a wonderful reader. At church "sociables" he was always called upon to read poetry; and when he was through, the ladies would lift up their hands and let them fall helplessly in their laps, and "wall" their eyes, and shake their heads, as much as to say, "Words cannot express it; it is too beautiful, too beautiful for this mortal earth."[10]

In the first half of the twentieth century, radio made it possible for people around the world to hear Franklin Delano Roosevelt decry December 7, 1941, as "a date which will live in infamy." In the last half of the century, television provided the medium through which audiences saw and heard the most stirring speeches: Martin Luther King Jr. declaring "I have a dream"; Gerald Ford assuring a nation reeling from Watergate that "our long national nightmare is over"; George Bush affirming the American sense of community as "a thousand points of light"; and Charles Spencer of Britain eulogizing his sister, Princess Diana, as "the unique, the complex, the extraordinary and irreplaceable Diana."

With the twenty-first century dawned a new era of speechmaking. It was to be an era that would draw on age-old public-speaking traditions—an era in which the Declaration of Independence would be declaimed on July 4, 2001, at Philadelphia's Independence Hall by actors Michael Douglas, Morgan Freeman, Mel Gibson, Whoopi Goldberg, Kevin Spacey, and others. But it was also to be an era that would expand the parameters of public speaking—an era in which *Future Shock* author Alvin Toffler would address the 2004 graduates of Jones International University in Englewood, Colorado, via streaming video over the Internet. And it was to be an era that would summon public speakers to meet some of the most difficult challenges in history—an era in which a U.S. president would face a nation badly shocked by the events of September 11, 2001, and assure them that "terrorist attacks can shake the foundations of our biggest buildings, but they cannot touch the foundation of America. These acts shattered steel, but they cannot dent the steel of American resolve."[11] Speakers of the future will continue to draw on a long and rich heritage, in addition to forging new frontiers in public speaking.

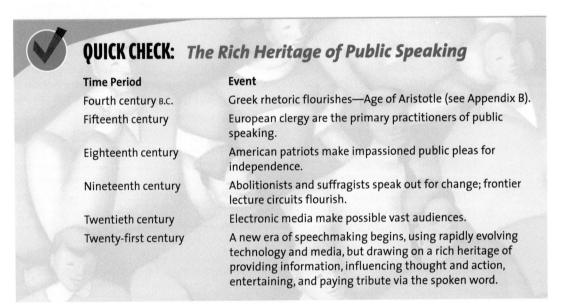

QUICK CHECK: *The Rich Heritage of Public Speaking*

Time Period	Event
Fourth century B.C.	Greek rhetoric flourishes—Age of Aristotle (see Appendix B).
Fifteenth century	European clergy are the primary practitioners of public speaking.
Eighteenth century	American patriots make impassioned public pleas for independence.
Nineteenth century	Abolitionists and suffragists speak out for change; frontier lecture circuits flourish.
Twentieth century	Electronic media make possible vast audiences.
Twenty-first century	A new era of speechmaking begins, using rapidly evolving technology and media, but drawing on a rich heritage of providing information, influencing thought and action, entertaining, and paying tribute via the spoken word.

1.e   Public Speaking and Diversity

Although the history of public speaking is as old as the history of civilization, only since the last half of the twentieth century has attention focused on the rhetorical implications of diversity. People are just beginning to understand that such factors as the gender, ethnicity, and culture of both speaker and audience are crucial components of the context of a speaking event.

DIVERSE AUDIENCES: A COHERENT FRAMEWORK

Diverse audiences have different expectations for appropriate and effective speech topics, argument structure, language style, and delivery. For example, a speech that may be quite persuasive to Native Americans may not have the same effect on White Americans, who do not share the beliefs and values underlying the message.

Similarly, a presentation that seems perfectly sensible and acceptable to a U.S. businessperson who is accustomed to straightforward, problem-oriented logic may seem shockingly rude to a Chinese businessperson who expects more circuitous, less overtly purposeful rhetoric. And some African American audiences "come to participate in a speech event,"[12] expecting the speaker to generate audience response through rhythmic "call response formulas"[13] from the African American oral tradition.

To be effective, then, public speakers need to understand, affirm, and adapt to diverse audiences. And it is with this acknowledgment of the critical role of the audience that we come full circle. Aristotle was right. The audience is the most important component in the communication process. It was true in the fifth century B.C., when students listened to the Greek rhetorician Gorgias. It was true in the nineteenth century, when parents of elocution students attended a school recital. And it was still true on May 28, 2004, when writer Toni Morrison told the graduating class of Wellesley College, "I see your life as already artful, waiting, just waiting and ready for you to make it art."[14] It is the focus on audience that provides a coherent framework for the history of public speaking, from classical rhetoric to the contemporary rhetoric of diversity.

DIVERSE AUDIENCES: A UNIFYING PRINCIPLE

Adapting to diverse audiences also provides the unifying principle of this text. In Chapter 2 we present a model of speech preparation that emphasizes the importance of the audience. Then, throughout the text, we illustrate how this focus on and consideration of audience can guide a speaker effectively through each stage of speech preparation and delivery.

Although our focus is on the audience, we also realize that as a student of public speaking, you have concerns and even fears about speaking in public. Focusing on your audience instead of on your anxiety is an audience-centered principle that can help you manage your apprehension. But you may need even more specific strategies and information to boost your confidence. In the next chapter we discuss strategies for speaking with confidence.

Summary

- Public speaking skill can empower you.
- Public speaking skill can also help you secure employment or advance your career.
- Public speaking is more planned and formal than conversation.
- The roles of speaker and audience are more clearly defined.
- Public speaking, like other forms of communication, is a process.
- Your study of public speaking will be guided by others' experience and knowledge, gained over centuries of making and studying speeches.

- The audience is the most important element in the communication process.
- Focus on and consideration of the audience help a speaker understand, affirm, and adapt to audiences whose expectations for appropriate and effective speech topics, argument structure, language style, and delivery may differ from his or her own.

Key Terms

channels (p. 12)
code (p. 11)
context (p. 12)
declamation (p. 15)
decode (p. 12)
elocution (p. 15)
empowerment (p. 7)
encode (p. 11)

external noise (p. 12)
feedback (p. 12)
internal noise (p. 12)
message (p. 11)
receiver (p. 12)
rhetoric (p. 14)
source (p. 11)

A QUESTION OF ETHICS

Declamation is defined as "the delivery of an already famous address." Is it ethical to deliver a speech that was written and/or already delivered by someone else? Explain your answer.

CHAPTER 2

Speaking with Confidence

Perhaps public speaking is a required class for you, but, because of the anxiety you feel when you deliver a speech, you've put it off as long as possible.

It's normal to be nervous. In a survey seeking to identify people's phobias, public speaking ranked as the most anxiety-producing experience most people face. Forty-one percent of all respondents reported public speaking as their most significant fear; fear of death ranked only sixth![1] Based on these statistics, comedian Jerry Seinfeld suggests, "Given a choice, at a funeral most of us would rather be the one in the coffin than the one giving the eulogy." Other studies have found that more than 80 percent of the population feels anxious when they speak to an audience.[2] Some people find that speaking is quite frightening; studies suggest that about 20 percent of all college students are highly apprehensive about speaking in front of others.[3]

You may find comfort in knowing you are not alone in experiencing speech anxiety. Even if your anxiety is not overwhelming, you can benefit from learning some positive approaches that allow your nervousness to work for you.[4] First, we will help you understand why you become nervous. Knowledge is power. Then we will offer specific strategies to help you speak with greater comfort and less anxiety.

> *The mind is a wonderful thing. It starts working the minute you're born and never stops . . . until you get up to speak in public.*
> **—Anonymous**

2.a Understand Your Nervousness

What makes you feel nervous about speaking in public? Why do your hands sometimes shake, your knees quiver, your stomach flutter, and your voice seem to go up an octave? What is happening to you? Believe it or not, your brain is signaling your body to help you with a difficult task. Sometimes, however, because your brain offers more "help" than you need, this assistance is not useful.

Your view of the speaking assignment, your perception of your speaking skill, and your self-esteem interact to create anxiety.[5] You want to do well, but you're not sure that you can or will. Presented with this conflict, your body responds by increasing your breathing rate, pumping more adrenaline, and causing more blood to rush through your veins. In short, your body summons more energy to deal with the conflict you are facing. Your brain switches to its default fight-or-flight mode: You can either fight to respond to the challenge or flee to avoid the cause of the anxiety. To put it more technically, you are experiencing physiological changes because of your psychological state, which explains why you may have a more rapid heartbeat, shaking knees and hands, a quivering voice, and increased perspiration. You may experience butterflies in your stomach because of changes in your digestive system. As a result of your physical discomfort, you may make less eye contact with your audience, use more vocalized pauses ("Um," "Ah," "You know"), and speak too rapidly. Although you see your physical responses as hindrances, your body is simply trying to help you with the task at hand.

WHAT MAKES PEOPLE NERVOUS WHEN SPEAKING IN PUBLIC?

A study by two communication researchers found that among the causes of anxiety about public speaking were fear of humiliation, concern about not being prepared, worry about one's looks, pressure to perform, personal insecurity, concern that the audience wouldn't be interested in oneself or the speech, lack of experience, fear of making mistakes, and an overall fear of failure.[6] Another study found that men are likely to experience more anxiety than women when speaking to people from a culture different from their own.[7] As you read the list, you'll probably find a reason that resonates with you—most people feel some nervousness when they speak before others. You're not alone if you are apprehensive about giving a speech.

Increasingly, researchers are concluding that communication apprehension may have a genetic or biological basis; some people may inherit a tendency to feel anxious about speaking in public.[8] You may wonder, "So if I have a biological tendency to feel nervous, is there anything I can do to help manage my fear?" The answer is yes. Even if you are predisposed to feel nervous because of your genetic makeup, there are strategies you can use to help manage your apprehension. A better understanding of why you feel apprehensive is a good starting point on the journey to speaking with greater confidence.[9]

WHEN ARE YOU MOST LIKELY TO FEEL NERVOUS ABOUT GIVING A SPEECH?

Research suggests that many people feel most nervous right before they give their speech. If you're typical, you'll feel the second-highest level of anxiety when your instructor explains the speech assignment. You'll probably feel the least anxiety when you're preparing your speech. One practical application of this research is that now you can understand when you'll need the most help managing your anxiety—right before you speak. It will also help to remember that as you begin speaking, anxiety begins to decrease—often dramatically. Another application of the research is to help you realize that you'll feel less anxious about your speech when you're doing something positive to prepare for it. Don't put off working on your speech; you'll not only have a better speech, you'll also feel less anxious about presenting it.

To identify patterns in how people experience communication apprehension, one researcher measured speakers' heart rates when they were delivering speeches and also asked them several questions about their fear of speaking.[10] After studying the results, he identified four styles of communication apprehension:

1. Average—you have a generally positive approach to communicating in public; your overall heart rate when speaking publicly is in the average range. Speakers with this style rated their own speaking performance the highest.

2. Insensitive—likely to be your style only if you have had previous experience in public speaking. Perhaps because of your experience, you tend to be less sensitive to apprehension when you speak; you have a lower heart rate when speaking and rate your performance as moderately successful.

3. Inflexible—you have the highest heart rate when speaking publicly. Some people use this high and inflexible level of anxiety to enhance their performance. Their fear motivates them to prepare and be at their best. For others, the anxiety of the inflexible style creates so much tension that their speaking performance is diminished.

4. Confrontational—you have a very high heart rate as you begin presenting a speech, and then your heart rate tapers off to more average levels. This style occurred in people who reported a strong emotional or affective response to speaking and was characteristic of more experienced speakers or people with at least some public-speaking background.

DOES YOUR STYLE OF COMMUNICATION APPREHENSION MAKE A DIFFERENCE?

First, it may help to know that you are not alone in how you experience apprehension and that others likely share your feelings. Although each person is unique, there are nonetheless general styles of apprehension. Second, having a general idea of your own style may give you greater insight in how to better manage your apprehension. For example, if you know that your apprehension tends to spike upward at the very beginning of speaking to an audience (the confrontational style), you will need to draw on strategies to help manage your anxiety at the outset of your talk. Finally, the research on apprehension styles lends support to the theory that communication apprehension may be a genetic trait or tendency.[11] That doesn't mean that there's nothing you can do to manage your anxiety; but it does mean that, depending on your own tendencies, you may need more information to help you develop constructive ways of managing the apprehension you may feel.

YOU ARE GOING TO FEEL MORE NERVOUS THAN YOU LOOK

When she finished her speech, Carmen sank into her seat and muttered, "Ugh, was I shaky up there! Did you see how nervous I was?"

"Nervous? You were nervous?" asked Kosta, surprised. "You looked pretty calm to me."

Realize that your audience cannot see evidence of everything you feel. If you worry that you are going to appear nervous to others, you may, in fact, increase your anxiety. Your body will exhibit more physical changes to deal with your self-induced state of anxiety.

ALMOST EVERY SPEAKER EXPERIENCES SOME DEGREE OF NERVOUSNESS

President Kennedy was noted for his superb public-speaking skills. When he spoke, he seemed perfectly at ease. Former British prime minister Winston Churchill was also hailed as one of the twentieth century's great orators. Amazingly, both Kennedy and Churchill were extremely fearful of speaking in public. The list of famous people who admit to feeling nervous before they speak may surprise you: Katie Couric, Conan O'Brien, Jay Leno, Carly Simon, and Oprah Winfrey have all reported feeling anxious and jittery before they speak in public.[12] Almost everyone experiences some anxiety when speaking. It is unrealistic to try to eliminate speech anxiety. Instead, your goal should be to manage your nervousness so that it does not create so much internal noise that it keeps you from speaking effectively.

ANXIETY CAN BE USEFUL

Extra adrenaline, increased blood flow, pupil dilation, increased endorphins to block pain, increased heart rate, and other physical changes caused by anxiety improve your energy level and help you function better than you might otherwise. Your heightened state of readiness can actually help you speak better, especially if you view the public-speaking event positively instead of negatively.

Speakers who label their increased feelings of physiological arousal as "nervousness" are more likely to feel anxious and fearful, but the same physiological feelings are experienced as enthusiasm or excitement by speakers who don't label the increased arousal as fear, anxiety, or nervousness. You are more likely to gain the benefits of the extra help your brain is trying to give you if you think positively rather than negatively about speaking in public. Don't let your initial anxiety convince you that you cannot speak effectively.

2.b Build Your Confidence

"Is there anything I can do to help manage my nervousness and anxiety when I give a speech?" you may wonder. Both contemporary research and centuries of experience from seasoned public speakers suggest some practical advice.

DON'T PROCRASTINATE IN PREPARING YOUR SPEECH

One research study confirmed what you probably already know: Speakers who are more apprehensive about speaking put off working on their speeches, in contrast to speakers who are less anxious about public speaking.[13] The fear of speaking often means that speakers delay preparing their speeches until the last minute. The lack of thorough preparation often results in a poorer speech performance, reinforcing the speaker's perception that public speaking is difficult. Realize that if you fear that you'll be nervous when speaking, you'll tend to put off working on your speech. Take charge by tackling the speech assignment early, giving yourself every chance to be successful. Don't let your fear freeze you into inaction. Prepare early.

KNOW YOUR AUDIENCE

Know to whom you will be speaking, and learn as much about your audience as you can. The more you can anticipate the kind of reaction your listeners will have to your speech, the more comfortable you will be in delivering your message. As you are preparing your speech, periodically visualize your listeners' response to your message. Consider their needs, goals, and hopes as you prepare your message. Be audience-centered rather than speaker-centered. Don't keep telling yourself how nervous you are going to be.[14] An audience-centered speaker focuses on connecting to listeners rather than focusing on fear.

SELECT AN APPROPRIATE TOPIC

You will feel less nervous if you talk about something with which you are familiar or with which you have some personal experience. Your comfort with the subject of your speech will be reflected in your delivery. In later chapters, we offer more detailed guidance about how to select a topic.

BE PREPARED

One formula applies to most speaking situations you are likely to experience: The better prepared you are, the less anxiety you will experience.[15] Being prepared means that you have researched your topic and practiced your speech several times before you deliver it. Being prepared also means that you have developed a logically coherent outline rather than one that is disorganized and difficult to follow. Transitional phrases and summaries can help you present a well-structured, easy-to-understand message.

DEVELOP AND DELIVER A WELL-ORGANIZED SPEECH

One of the key skills you'll learn in this handbook is the value of developing a well-organized message. For most North American listeners, speeches should have a beginning, middle, and end and should follow a logical outline pattern. Communication researcher Melanie Booth-Butterfield suggests that speakers can better manage their apprehension if they rely on the rules and structures of a speaking assignment, including following a clear outline pattern, when preparing and delivering a speech.[16]

Anxiety about a speech assignment decreased and confidence increased when speakers closely followed the directions and rules for developing a speech. So, to help manage your apprehension about speaking, listen carefully to what the specific assignment is, ask for additional information if you're unclear about the task, and develop a well-organized message.

KNOW YOUR INTRODUCTION AND YOUR CONCLUSION

You are likely to feel the most anxious during the opening moments of your speech. Therefore, it is a good idea to have a clear plan for how you will start your speech. We aren't suggesting memorizing your introduction word for word, but you should have it well in mind. Being familiar with your introduction will help you feel more comfortable about the entire speech. If you know how you will end your speech, you will have a safe harbor in case you lose your place. If you need to end your speech prematurely, a well-delivered conclusion can permit you to make a graceful exit.

RE-CREATE THE SPEECH ENVIRONMENT WHEN YOU PRACTICE

When you practice your speech, imagine that you are giving the speech to the audience you will actually address. Stand up. Imagine what the room looks like, or consider rehearsing in the room in which you will deliver your speech. What will you be wearing? Practice rising from your seat, walking to the front of the room, and beginning your speech. Practice aloud, rather than just saying the speech to yourself. A realistic rehearsal will increase your confidence when your moment to speak arrives.

USE DEEP-BREATHING TECHNIQUES

One of the symptoms of nervousness is a change in your breathing and heart rates. Nervous speakers tend to take short, shallow breaths. To help break the anxiety-induced breathing pattern, consider taking a few slow deep breaths before you rise to speak. No one will be able to detect that you are taking deep breaths if you just slowly inhale and exhale before beginning your speech. Besides breathing deeply, try to relax your entire body. Deep breathing and visualizing yourself as successful will help you relax.

CHANNEL YOUR NERVOUS ENERGY

One common symptom of being nervous is shaking hands and wobbly knees. What triggers this jiggling is the extra boost of adrenaline your body is giving you—and the resulting energy has to go somewhere. Your muscles may move whether you've asked them to move or not. Take control by channeling that energy.

As you are waiting to be introduced, focus on remaining calm. Act calm to feel calm. Give yourself a pep talk; tense and release your muscles to help you relax. Then, when your name is called, walk to the front of the room in a calm and collected manner. Before you present your opening, attention-catching sentence, take a moment to look for a friendly, supportive face. Think calm and act calm to feel calm.

HOW TO: *Channel Your Energy*

- To release tension, take a leisurely walk before you arrive wherever you will be speaking. Taking a slow, relaxing walk can help calm you down and use up some of your excess energy.
- Once you are seated, waiting to speak, grab the edge of your chair (without calling attention to what you are doing) and gently squeeze the chair to release tension; no one needs to know you're doing this. Unobtrusively, squeeze and relax, squeeze and relax.
- You can also purposely tense and then release your muscles in your legs and arms while you're seated. You don't need to look like you're going into convulsions; just imperceptibly tense and relax your muscles to burn energy.
- One more tip: You may want to keep both feet on the floor and gently wiggle your toes rather than sit with your legs crossed. Crossing your legs can sometimes cause one leg or foot to go to sleep. Keeping your feet on the floor and slightly moving your toes can ensure that all of you will be wide awake and ready to go when it's your turn to speak.

VISUALIZE YOUR SUCCESS

Studies suggest that one of the best ways to control anxiety is to imagine a scene in which you exhibit skill and comfort as a public speaker.[17] As you imagine giving your speech, picture yourself walking confidently to the front and delivering your well-prepared opening remarks. Visualize yourself giving the entire speech as a controlled, confident speaker. Imagine yourself calm and in command. Positive visualization is effective because it boosts your confidence by helping you see yourself as a more confident, accomplished speaker.[18]

GIVE YOURSELF A MENTAL PEP TALK

You may think that people who talk to themselves are slightly loony. But silently giving yourself a pep talk can give you confidence and take your mind off your nervousness. Here's a sample mental speech you could deliver to yourself right before you speak: "I know this stuff better than anyone else. I've practiced it. My message is well organized. I know I can do it. I'll do a good job." Research provides evidence that people who entertain thoughts of worry and failure don't do themselves any favors.[19] When you feel yourself getting nervous, use positive messages to replace negative thoughts that may creep into your consciousness. Examples include the following:

Negative Thought	**Positive Self-Talk**
I'm going to forget what I'm supposed to say.	I've practiced this speech many times. I've got notes to prompt me. If I lose my place, no one will know I'm not following my outline.

So many people are looking at me.	I can do this! My listeners want me to do a good job. I'll seek out friendly faces when I feel nervous.
People will think I'm dull and boring.	I've got some good examples. I can talk to people one-on-one, and people seem to like me.
I just can't go through with this.	I have talked to people all my life. I've given presentations in classes for years. I can get through this because I've rehearsed and I'm prepared.

FOCUS ON YOUR MESSAGE RATHER THAN YOUR FEAR

The more you think about being anxious about speaking, the more you will increase your level of anxiety. Instead, think about what you are going to say. In the few minutes before you address your listeners, mentally review your major ideas, your introduction, and your conclusion. Focus on your ideas rather than on your fear.

LOOK FOR POSITIVE LISTENER SUPPORT FOR YOUR MESSAGE

Evidence suggests that if you think you see audience members looking critical of you or your message, you may feel more apprehensive and nervous when you speak.[20] Stated more positively, when you are aware of positive audience support, you will feel more confident and less nervous. It is important to be audience centered. Although you may face some audiences that won't respond positively to you or your message, the overwhelming majority of listeners will be positive. Looking for positive, reinforcing feedback and finding it can help you feel more confident as a speaker. This has implications for you as a listener: When you're listening to speakers in your communication class, help them by being a positive, supportive listener: Provide eye contact and offer additional positive nonverbal support, such as nodding in agreement and maintaining a positive but sincere facial expression. You can help your fellow students feel more comfortable as speakers, and they can do the same for you; watch for their support.

SEEK SPEAKING OPPORTUNITIES

The more experience you gain as a public speaker, the less nervous you will feel. Researchers have found that those speakers who were the most nervous at the beginning of a public-speaking class experienced the greatest decreases in nervousness by the end of the class.[21] Another research study found that students who took a basic public-speaking course reported having less apprehension and more satisfaction about speaking than students who had not had such a course.[22] Consider joining clubs and organizations such as Toastmasters, an organization dedicated to improving public-speaking skills by providing a supportive group of people to help you polish your speaking and overcome your anxiety. As you develop a track record of successfully delivering speeches, you will have more confidence.[23]

This course in public speaking will give you opportunities to enhance both your confidence and your skill through frequent practice.

AFTER YOUR SPEECH, FOCUS ON YOUR ACCOMPLISHMENT, NOT YOUR ANXIETY

When you conclude your speech, you may be tempted to fixate on your fear. You might amplify in your own mind the nervousness you felt and think everyone could see how nervous you looked. Resist that temptation. When you finish your speech, tell yourself something positive to celebrate your accomplishment. Say to yourself, "I did it! I spoke and people listened." Don't replay your mental image of yourself as nervous and fearful. Instead, mentally replay your success in communicating with your listeners.

QUICK CHECK: *Build Your Confidence*

- View the public-speaking event positively.
- Know your audience.
- Be prepared and well organized.
- Select an appropriate topic.
- Rehearse out loud.
- Know your introduction and conclusion.
- Visualize your success.
- Use deep-breathing techniques.
- Focus on your message, not on your fear.
- Give yourself a mental pep talk.
- Channel your nervous energy.
- Seek additional speaking opportunities.
- Look for positive listener support.
- Prepare your speech early.

Summary

- It's normal to be nervous, and there are strategies you can use to help manage your apprehension.
- To help manage your apprehension, be prepared and know your audience; consider their needs, goals, and hopes as you prepare your message. Be audience-centered rather than speaker-centered.

- Imagine the speech environment when you rehearse, and use relaxation techniques, positive visualization, and positive verbal reinforcement.

- Don't put off working on your speech; the better prepared you are, the less anxiety you will experience.

- Be familiar with your introduction and conclusion.

- Focus on your ideas rather than on your fear.

- When you finish your speech, tell yourself something positive to celebrate your accomplishment.

A QUESTION OF ETHICS

One of your friends took public speaking last year and still has a file of speech outlines. Is it ethical to use one of your friend's outlines as the basis for one of your speeches? Explain your answer.

CHAPTER 3

The Audience-Centered Speechmaking Process

Unless you have some prior experience in higher mathematics, you may not have the foggiest notion of what calculus is when you first take a class in that subject. But when you tell people that you are taking a public-speaking class, most have at least some idea what a public speaker does.

A public speaker talks while others listen. You hear speeches almost every day. Each evening, when you turn on the news, you get a "sound bite" of some politician delivering a speech. Each day when you attend class, an instructor lectures. But even after hearing countless speeches, you may still have questions about how a speaker prepares and presents a speech.

In this chapter, we will preview the preparation and presentation skills that you will learn in this course. Undoubtedly you will be given a speech assignment early in your public-speaking course. Although it would be ideal to read this handbook from cover to cover before tackling your first speech, that would be impractical. To help you begin, we present a step-by-step overview designed to serve as the scaffolding on which to build your skill in public speaking.

> *If all my talents and powers were to be taken from me by some inscrutable Providence, and I had my choice of keeping but one, I would unhesitatingly ask to be allowed to keep the Power of Speaking, for through it, I would quickly recover all the rest.*
>
> **—Daniel Webster**

3.a An Audience-Centered Speechmaking Model

You've been speaking to others since you were 2 years old. Talking to people has seemed such a natural part of your life that you may never have stopped to analyze the process. But as you think about preparing your first speech, you may wonder, "What do I do first?" Your assignment may be to introduce yourself. Or your first assignment may be a brief informative talk—to describe something to your audience. Regardless of the specific assignment, however, you need some idea of how to begin.

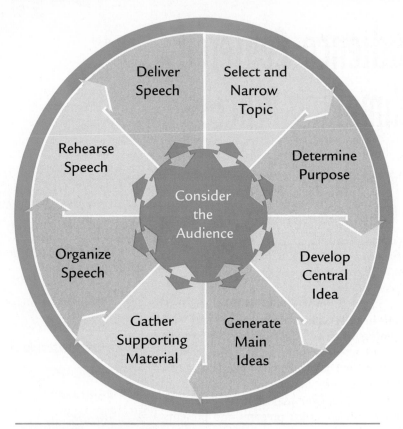

FIGURE 3.1 This model of the speechmaking process emphasizes the importance of considering your audience as you work on each task in the process of designing and presenting a speech.

You don't need to read this book cover to cover before you give your first speech. But it is useful to have an overview of the various steps and skills involved in giving a speech. To help you see this overview, Figure 3.1 diagrams the various tasks involved in the speechmaking process, emphasizing the audience as the central concern at every step of the process. We'll refer to this audience-centered model of public speaking throughout the text. In designing and delivering your speech, always make choices with your audience in mind.

We will begin our discussion of the speechmaking process with the central element: considering your audience. We will then discuss each step of the process, starting with selecting and narrowing a topic and moving clockwise around the model, examining each interrelated step.

3.b Consider Your Audience

Why should the central focus of public speaking be the audience? Why is it not topic selection, outlining, or research? The simple truth is, your audience influences the topic you choose and every later step of the speechmaking process. Your selection of topic, purpose, and even major ideas should be based on a thorough understanding of your listeners. In a very real sense, your audience "writes" the speech.[1]

As Figure 3.1 shows, considering your audience is an ongoing activity. The needs, attitudes, beliefs, values, and other characteristics of your audience should play a leading role at every step. After you select your topic, you need to consider how the audience will respond to your examples, organization, and delivery. That's why, in the model, arrows connect the center of the diagram with each step of the process. At any point during the process, you may need to revise your thinking or your material if you learn new information about your audience. So the model also has arrows pointing both ways across the boundaries of each step in the process.

Being audience-centered involves making decisions about the content and style of your speech before you speak, based on knowledge of your audience's values and beliefs. It also means being sensitive to your audience's responses during the speech so that you can make appropriate adjustments.

Different cultures have radically different conventions for public speaking. In Russia, for example, speakers have a "no frills" approach that emphasizes content over delivery. When one of this book's authors taught public speaking for several semesters in the Bahamas, however, he shocked students by suggesting that they try to achieve a conversational, informal manner. Bahamian audiences, he quickly discovered, expect formal oratory from their speakers, very much as U.S. audiences in the nineteenth century preferred the grandiloquence of Stephen A. Douglas to the quieter, homespun style of Abraham Lincoln. So your author had to embellish his own style when he taught the class.

You need not teach or give speeches in foreign countries to recognize the importance of adapting to the cultural expectations of different audiences. People in the United States are highly diverse in terms of their culture, age, ethnicity, sexual orientation, and religious tradition. You will want to adjust not only your delivery style but also your topic, pattern of organization, and even your dress, according to who your audience members are and what subject or subjects they are interested in. If you learn to analyze your audience and adapt to their expectations, you can apply these skills in numerous settings: at a job interview, during a business presentation or a city council election campaign—even while proposing marriage.

3.c Select and Narrow Your Topic

While keeping your audience foremost in mind, your next task is to determine what you will talk about and to limit your topic to fit the constraints of your speaking assignment. Pay special attention to the guidelines your instructor gives you for your assignment.

If your first speech assignment is to introduce yourself, your **speech topic** has been selected for you—*you* are the topic. It is not uncommon to be asked to speak on a specific subject. Often, though, you will be asked to speak but will not be given a topic. The task of selecting and narrowing a topic will be yours. Choosing or finding a topic on which to speak can be frustrating. "What should I talk about?" can become a haunting question.

Although there is no single answer to the question of what you should talk about, you may discover a topic by asking three standard questions: "Who is the audience?" "What is the occasion?" and "What are my interests, talents, and experiences?"

WHO IS THE AUDIENCE?

Your topic may grow from basic knowledge about your audience. For example, if you know that your audience members are primarily between the ages of 25 and 40, this information should help you select a topic of interest to people who are probably working and either seeking partners or raising families. An older audience may lead you to other concerns or issues: "Will Social Security be there when I need it?" or "The advantages of belonging to the American Association of Retired Persons."

WHAT IS THE OCCASION?

Besides your audience, you should consider the occasion for the speech when choosing a topic. A commencement address calls for a different topic, for example, than does a speech to a model railroad club. Another aspect of the occasion you'll want to consider is the physical setting of your speech. Will you be speaking to people seated in chairs arranged in a circle, or will you be standing in front of rows of people? The physical surroundings as well as the occasion affect the degree of formality your audience expects in your choice of topics.

WHAT ARE MY INTERESTS, TALENTS, AND EXPERIENCES?

Rather than racking your brain for exotic topics and outlandish ideas, examine your own background. Your choice of major in college, your hobbies, and your ancestry are sources for topic ideas. What issues do you feel strongly about? Reflect on jobs you've held, news stories that catch your interest, events in your hometown, your career goals, or interesting people you have met.

Once you have chosen your topic, narrow it to fit the time limits for your talk. If you've been asked to deliver a ten-minute speech, the topic "How to find counseling help on campus" would be more manageable than the topic "How to make the most of your college experience." Of course, as our model suggests, your audience should be foremost in your mind when you work on your topic.

3.d ## Determine Your Purpose

You might think that once you have your topic, you are ready to start the research process. Before you do that, however, you need to decide on both a general and a specific purpose There are three **general purposes** for speeches: to inform, to persuade, and to entertain. Even though we identify each purpose separately, they often overlap. For example, you may want to inform and entertain your audience while suggesting creative ways to avoid long lines during registration. In public-speaking classes, your general purpose will most often be set by your instructor.

The primary objective of class lectures, seminars, and workshops is to inform. When you inform, you teach, define, illustrate, clarify, or elaborate on a topic.

Ads on TV and radio, sermons, political speeches, and sales presentations are examples of speeches designed to persuade. They seek to change or reinforce attitudes, beliefs, values, or behavior. To be persuasive, you need to be sensitive to your audience's attitudes toward you and your topic.

The third general purpose for a speech is to entertain your audience. After-dinner speeches and comic monologues are mainly intended as entertainment. Often the key to an effective entertaining speech lies in your choice of stories, examples, and illustrations, as well as in your delivery. Appendix D has examples of informative, persuasive, and entertaining speeches.

After making sure you understand your general purpose, you need to formulate a **specific purpose:** a concise statement indicating what you want your listeners to be able to remember, do, or feel when you finish your speech. A statement of your specific purpose identifies the audience response you desire. Here again, we emphasize the importance of focusing on the audience as you develop your specific purpose. Perhaps you have had the experience of listening to a speaker and wondering, "What's the point? I know he's talking about education, but I'm not sure where he's going with this subject." You may have understood the speaker's general purpose, but the specific one wasn't clear. If you can't figure out what the specific purpose is, it is probably because the speaker does not know either.

Deciding on a specific purpose is not difficult once you have narrowed your topic: "At the end of my speech, the class will be able to identify three counseling facilities on campus and describe the best way to get help at each one." Notice that this purpose is phrased in terms of what you would like the audience to be able to do by the end of the speech. Your specific purpose should be a fine-tuned, audience-centered goal. For an informative speech, you may simply want your audience to restate an idea; define new words; or identify, describe, or illustrate something. In a persuasive speech, you may try to rouse your listeners to take a class, buy something, or vote for someone.

Once you have formulated your specific purpose, write it down on a piece of paper or note card, and keep it before you as you read and gather ideas for your talk. Your specific purpose should guide your research and help you choose supporting materials that are related to your audience. As you continue to work on your speech, you may even decide to modify your purpose. But if you have an objective in mind at all times as you move through the preparation stage, you will stay on track.

3.e Develop Your Central Idea

You should now be able to write the **central idea** of your speech. Whereas your statement of a specific purpose indicates what you want your audience to do when you have finished your speech, your central idea identifies the essence of your message. Think of it as a one-sentence summary of your speech. Here are two examples:

Topic:	DVD players
General Purpose:	To inform
Specific Purpose:	At the end of my speech, the audience will be able to identify the key reason digital video disk (DVD) players offer greater sound and picture fidelity than do videotape players.
Central Idea:	DVD players have greater sound and picture quality because they "read" the music and video information digitally, rather than analogically.

Topic:	Kachina dolls
General Purpose:	To inform
Specific Purpose:	At the end of my speech, the audience will be able to describe the significance of kachina dolls to the Hopi Indians.
Central Idea:	Kachina dolls, carved wooden figures used in Hopi Indian ceremonies, are believed to represent spirits of the dead that will help produce a good harvest.

3.f Generate the Main Ideas

In the words of H. V. Prochnow, "A good many people can make a speech, but saying something is more difficult." Effective speakers are good thinkers; they say something. They know how to play with words and thoughts to develop their **main ideas.** The ancient Romans called this skill **invention**—the ability to develop or discover ideas that result in new insights or new approaches to old problems. The Roman orator Cicero called this aspect of speaking the process of "finding out what [a speaker] should say."

Once you have an appropriate topic, a specific purpose, and a well-worded central idea down on paper, the next task is to identify the major divisions of your speech, or key points that you wish to develop. To determine how to subdivide your central idea into key points, ask these three questions:

1. Does the central idea have logical divisions?
2. Can you think of several reasons why the central idea is true?
3. Can you support the central idea with a series of steps?

Let's look at each of these questions along with examples of how to apply them.

DOES THE CENTRAL IDEA HAVE LOGICAL DIVISIONS?

If the central idea is "There are three ways to interpret the stock-market page of your local newspaper," your speech could be organized into three parts. You will simply identify the three ways to interpret the stock-market page and use each as a major point. A speech about the art of applying theatrical makeup could also be organized into three parts: eye makeup, face makeup, and hair color. Looking for logical divisions in your speech topic is the simplest way to determine key points.

CAN YOU THINK OF SEVERAL REASONS WHY THE CENTRAL IDEA IS TRUE?

If your central idea is "Medicare should be expanded to include additional coverage for individuals of all ages," each major point of your speech could be a reason you think Medicare should be expanded. For example, Medicare should be expanded because (1) not enough people are being served by the present system, (2) the people currently being served receive inadequate medical attention, and (3) the elderly cannot afford to pay what Medicare does not now cover. If your central idea is a statement that something is good or bad, you should focus on the reasons your central idea is true. Use these reasons as the main ideas of the speech.

CAN YOU SUPPORT THE CENTRAL IDEA WITH A SERIES OF STEPS?

Suppose your central idea is "Running for a campus office is easy to do." Your speech could be developed around a series of steps, telling your listeners what to do first, second, and third to get elected. Speeches describing a personal experience or explaining how to build or make something can usually be organized in a step-by-step progression.

Your time limit, topic, and information gleaned from your research will determine how many major ideas will be in your speech. A three- to five-minute speech might have only two major ideas. In a very short speech, you may develop only one major idea with examples, illustrations, and other forms of support. Don't spend time trying to divide a topic that does not need dividing.

3.8

Gather Verbal and Visual Supporting Material

With your main idea or ideas in mind, your next job is to gather material to support them—facts, examples, definitions, and quotations from others that illustrate, amplify, clarify, and provide evidence. Here, as always in preparing your speech, the importance of being an audience-centered speaker cannot be overemphasized. There's an old saying that an ounce of illustration is worth a ton of talk. If a speech is boring, it is usually because the speaker has not chosen supporting material that is relevant or interesting to the audience. Don't just give people data; connect facts to their lives. As one sage quipped, "Data is not information any more than 50 tons of cement is a skyscraper."[2]

CRITERIA FOR CHOOSING SUPPORTING MATERIAL

Supporting material should be personal and concrete, and it should appeal to your listeners' senses. Tell stories based on your own experiences, and provide vivid descriptions of things that are tangible so that your audience can visualize what you are talking about.

Besides sight, supporting material can appeal to touch, hearing, smell, and taste. The more senses you trigger with words, the more interesting your talk will be. Descriptions such as "the rough, splintery surface of weather-beaten wood" or "the sweet, cool, refreshing flavor of cherry Jell-O" evoke sensory images. In addition, relating abstract statistics to something tangible can help communicate your ideas more clearly. For example, if you say Frito-Lay sells 2.6 billion pounds of snack food each year, your listeners will have a hazy idea that 2.6 billion pounds is a lot of Fritos and potato chips; but if you add that 2.6 billion pounds is triple the weight of the Empire State Building, you've made your point more memorably.[3]

How does a public speaker find interesting and relevant supporting material? By developing good research skills. President Woodrow Wilson once admitted, "I use not only all the brains I have, but all that I can borrow." Although it is important to have good ideas, it is equally important to know how to build on existing knowledge. You can probably think of a topic or two about which you consider yourself an expert. Chances are that if you gave a short speech about a sport that you had practiced for years or about a recent trip that you took, you would not need to gather much additional information. But sooner or later, you will need to do some research on a topic in order to speak intelligently about it to an audience.

If your college classes up to this point have required only brief forays into the library, that experience is about to change! By the time you have given several speeches in this course, you will have learned to use a number of the following resources: your library's computerized card catalog, the *Social Sciences Index,* the *Directory of American Scholars, Bartlett's Familiar Quotations,* government document holdings, your library's periodical indexes, and an assortment of CD-ROM and Internet indexes. You would be wise to spend some time learning to use electronic databases such as LEXIS-NEXIS. To navigate the Internet, learn to use search engines such as Google and Yahoo!. There are also many Web sites that will help you both design and deliver your speeches.

In addition to becoming a skilled user of library and electronic resources, you will also learn to be on the lookout as you read, watch TV, and listen to the radio for ideas, examples, illustrations, and quotations that could be used in a speech. Finally, you will learn how to gather information through interviews and written requests for information on various topics.

Besides searching for verbal forms of supporting material, you can also seek visual supporting material. For many people, seeing is believing. Almost any presentation can be enhanced by reinforcing key ideas with visual aids. Often the most effective visual aids are the simplest: an object, a chart, a graph, a poster, a model, a map, or a person—perhaps you—to demonstrate a process or skill. Today there are many technologies for displaying visual aids. One of the most basic is an overhead projector that displays 8½-

by 11-inch acetate transparencies. Most classrooms now have video players, so you can show brief video segments to introduce or reinforce a point. The latest graphics packages for personal computers can help you generate colorful graphs, charts, signs, and banners. And with today's technology, you can project stunning video images with the proper equipment. Of course, using this high-tech equipment requires new skills and often extra rehearsal time.

Make your visual images large enough to be seen and allow plenty of time to prepare them; look at your audience, not your presentation aid; control your audience's attention by timing your visual displays; and keep your presentation aids simple. Always concentrate on communicating effectively with your audience, not on dazzling your listeners with glitzy presentation displays.

3.h Organize Your Speech

A wise person once said, "If effort is organized, accomplishment follows." A clearly and logically structured speech helps your audience remember what you say. A logical structure also helps you feel more in control of your speech, and greater control helps you feel more comfortable while delivering your message.

Classical rhetoricians—early students of speech—called the process of developing an orderly speech **disposition**. Speakers need to present ideas, information, examples, illustrations, stories, and statistics in an orderly sequence so that listeners can easily follow what they are saying.

DIVIDE YOUR SPEECH

Every well-prepared speech has three major divisions: the introduction, the body, and the conclusion. The introduction helps capture attention, serves as an overview of the speech, and provides your audience with reasons to listen to you. The body presents the main content of your speech. The conclusion summarizes your key ideas. You may have heard this advice on how to organize a speech: "Tell them what you're going to tell them (the introduction), tell them (the body of the speech), and tell them what you told them (the conclusion)."

As a student of public speaking, you will study and learn to apply variations of this basic pattern of organization (chronological, topical, cause–effect, problem–solution) that will help your audience understand your meaning. You will learn about previewing and summarizing—methods of oral organization that will help your audience retain your main ideas. In the outline of a sample speech, notice how the introduction catches the listener's attention, the body of the speech identifies the main ideas, and the conclusion summarizes the key ideas.

Because your introduction previews your speech and your conclusion summarizes it, most public-speaking teachers recommend that you prepare your introduction and conclusion after you have carefully organized the body of your talk.

OUTLINE YOUR SPEECH

If you have already generated your major ideas on the basis of logical divisions, reasons, or steps, you are well on your way to developing an outline. Indicate your major ideas by Roman numerals. Use capital letters for your supporting points. Use Arabic numerals if you need to subdivide your ideas further. Do not write your speech word for word. If you do, you will sound stilted and unnatural. It may be useful, however, to use brief notes—written cues on note cards—instead of a complete manuscript.

You may want to look at Chapters 10 through 12 for approaches to organizing a message and sample outlines. Chapters 11 and 12 provide more detailed suggestions for beginning and ending your speech. Some public-speaking teachers may require a slightly different outline format. For example, your teacher may want you to outline your speech introduction using a Roman numeral I for the introduction, a II for the body, and a III for your conclusion. Make sure you follow the precise guidelines your instructor provides for outlining your speech. For your first speech, you may want to adapt the following simple outline format.[4] Your instructor may want you to add more detailed information about your supporting material in outlines you submit in class.

Description	Example
TOPIC: Your instructor may assign a topic, or you may select it.	How to invest money
GENERAL PURPOSE: To inform, persuade, or entertain. Your instructor will probably specify your general purpose.	To inform
SPECIFIC PURPOSE: A clear statement indicating what your audience should be able to do after hearing your speech	At the end of my speech, the audience should be able to identify two principles that will help them better invest their money.
CENTRAL IDEA: A one-sentence summary of your talk	Knowing the source of money, how to invest it, and how money grows can lead to increased income from wise investments.
INTRODUCTION: Attention-catching opening line	Imagine for a moment that it is the year 2050. You are 65 years old. You've just picked up your mail and opened an envelope that contains a check for $100,000! No, you didn't win the lottery. You smile as you realize your own modest investment strategy over the last forty years has paid off handsomely.

PREVIEW MAJOR IDEAS

Today I'd like to answer three questions that can help you become a better money manager: First, where does money come from? Second, where do you invest it? And third, how does a little money grow into a lot of money?

TELL YOUR AUDIENCE WHY THEY SHOULD LISTEN TO YOU

Knowing the answers to these three questions can literally pay big dividends for you. With only modest investments and a well-disciplined attitude, you could easily have an annual income of $100,000 or more.

BODY:
  I. Major Idea
      A. Supporting idea
      B. Supporting idea
 II. Major Idea

      A. Supporting idea
      B. Supporting idea

      C. Supporting idea
III. Major Idea

      A. Supporting idea

      B. Supporting idea

  I. There are two sources of money.
      A. You already have some money.
      B. You will earn money in the future.
 II. You can do three things with a dollar.
      A. You can spend your money.
      B. You can lend your money to others.
      C. You can invest your money.
III. Two principles can help make you rich.
      A. The "magic" of compound interest can transform pennies into millions.
      B. Finding the best rate of return on your money can pay big dividends.

CONCLUSION:

Summarize main ideas and restate central idea.

Today I've identified three key aspects of effective money management: (1) knowing the sources of money, (2) knowing what you can do with money, and (3) understanding money-management principles that can make you rich. Now, let's go "back to the future"! Remember the good feeling you had when you received your check for $100,000? Recall that feeling again when you are depositing your first paycheck. Remember this simple secret for accumulating wealth: Part of all I earn is mine to keep. It is within your power to "go for the gold."

CONSIDER PRESENTATION AIDS

In addition to developing a written outline to use as you speak, consider using presentation aids to add structure and clarity to your major ideas. Developing simple visual reinforcers of your key ideas can help your audience retain essential points. For example, the first major idea in the outline just presented could be summarized on a visual aid such as the one in Figure 3.2.

The second major idea in our speech example could be emphasized with a visual like the one in Figure 3.3. The third major idea could be reinforced with a visual such as the one in Figure 3.4.

For all the steps we have discussed so far, your success as a speaker will ultimately be determined by your audience. That is why throughout the text we refer you to the audience-centered speechmaking model presented in this chapter.

Two Sources of Money:

1. $'s you currently have
2. $'s you will earn

FIGURE 3.2 Presentation Graphic for the First Major Idea in Your Speech

Three Things to Do with a $:

1. Spend it
2. Lend it
3. Invest it

FIGURE 3.3 Presentation Graphic for the Second Major Idea in Your Speech

How to Get Rich:

1. Use the "magic" of compound interest

2. Search for the best rate of return

FIGURE 3.4 **Presentation Graphic for the Third Major Idea in Your Speech**

Once you are comfortable with the structure of your talk and you have developed your visual aids, you are ready to rehearse.

3.i Rehearse Your Speech

Remember this joke? One man asks another, "How do you get to Carnegie Hall?" The answer: "Practice, man, practice." The joke may be older than Carnegie Hall itself, but it is still good advice to all beginners, including novice speakers. A speech is a performance. As with any stage performance, whether it is music, dance, or theater, you need to rehearse. Experienced carpenters know to "measure twice, saw once." Rehearsing your speech is a way to "measure" your message so that you get it right when you present it to your audience.

REHEARSE YOUR SPEECH ALOUD

The best way to practice is to stand just as you will when you deliver your speech to your audience. As you rehearse, try to find a comfortable way to phrase your ideas, but don't try to memorize your talk. In fact, if you have rehearsed your speech so many times that you are using exactly the same words every time, you have rehearsed long enough. Rehearse just enough so that you can discuss your ideas and supporting material without leaving out major parts of your speech. It is all right to use notes, but most public-speaking instructors limit the number of notes you may use.

PRACTICE MAKING EYE CONTACT

As you rehearse with your imaginary audience, practice making eye contact as often as you can. Also, be aware of the volume of your voice; you will need to practice speaking loudly enough for all in the room to hear. If you are not sure what to do with your hands when you rehearse, just keep them at your side. Focus on your message, rather than worrying about how to gesture. Avoid jingling change with your hand in your pocket or using other gestures that could distract your audience. If you practice your speech as if you were actually delivering it, you will be a more effective speaker when you talk to the audience.

MAKE DECISIONS ABOUT THE STYLE OF YOUR SPEECH

Besides rehearsing your physical delivery, you also will decide about the style of your speech. "Style," said novelist Jonathan Swift, "is proper words in proper places." The words you choose and your arrangement of those words make up the style of your speech. As we have said, some audiences respond to a style that is simple and informal. Others prefer a grand and highly poetic style. To be a good speaker, you must become familiar with the language your listeners are used to hearing and must know how to select the right word or phrase to communicate an idea. Work to develop an ear for how words will sound to your audience.

3.j Deliver Your Speech

The time has come, and you're ready to present your speech to your audience. Delivery is the final step in the preparation process. Before you walk to the front of the room, look at your listeners to see if the audience assembled is what you were expecting. Are the people out there of the age, race, and gender that you had predicted? Or do you

HOW TO: *Prepare for a Speech*

- Consider your audience before and during your speech.
- Consider the type of occasion.
- Determine what you will talk about.
- Choose a topic based on your interests, talents, experiences.
- Limit your topic to fit the constraints of your speaking assignment.
- Determine your general purpose (to inform, to persuade, to entertain).
- Determine the specific audience response you desire.
- Develop your central idea.
- Generate main ideas.
- Gather verbal and visual supporting material.
- Organize your speech.
- Rehearse your speech.
- Deliver your speech.

need to make last-minute changes in your message to adjust to a different mix of audience members?

When you are introduced, walk calmly and confidently to the front of the room, establish eye contact with your audience, smile naturally, and deliver your attention-catching opening sentence. Concentrate on your message and your audience. Deliver your speech in a conversational style, and try to establish rapport with your listeners. Deliver your speech just as you rehearsed it before your imaginary audience: Maintain eye contact, speak loudly enough to be heard, and use some natural variation in pitch. Finally, remember the advice of columnist Ann Landers: "Be sincere, be brief, and be seated."

Now that we have outlined what effective speakers must be able to do, let's look at a speech that illustrates these capabilities. The speech by public-speaking student Pao Yang Lee models many attributes of a well-crafted message that we have discussed.[5]

Summary

- To prepare for your first speaking assignment, follow the steps for preparing and presenting a speech, and make sure the audience is the central focus at each step.
- Throughout the speech-crafting and delivery process, make choices about the design and presentation of your message, guided by your knowledge of your audience.
- Based on information about your listeners, select and narrow your topic, determine your purpose, develop your central idea, and generate the main ideas.
- Gather and organize your supporting material, including visual aids.
- With a draft of your speech outline in hand, rehearse and deliver your speech.

Key Terms

central idea (p. 34)
disposition (p. 37)
general purpose (p. 33)
invention (p. 34)

main idea (p. 34)
specific purpose (p. 33)
speech topic (p. 32)

A QUESTION OF ETHICS

Your first assignment is to give a speech about something interesting that has happened to you. You have decided to talk about the joys and hassles of a train trip you took last year. Your sister recently returned from a cross-country train trip and had several interesting tales to tell. Would it be ethical to tell one of her experiences as if it had happened to you? Why or why not?

SAMPLE SPEECH *Our Immigration Story*

by Pao Yang Lee

Each one of us has our own story, a history of our lives that helps explain who we are and what motivates us to be the best we can be. My story starts with my parents. Most of our parents worked hard to raise us and get us an education. Today, I'm going to share with you a part of my story. I will tell you about my parents' struggle to leave Laos and a refugee camp in Thailand, and about our new life in America.

◀ Pao captures his listeners' attention by telling them about his parents' struggle to leave Laos.

I will start my story with my parents' struggle to leave Laos to make their way to Thailand. As most of you know, many Hmong people had escaped Laos because they were being persecuted by the Communists and had to escape for their lives and freedom. My parents, who hadn't met yet, each took their journey across the Mekong River on a bamboo raft. My parents were lucky. They made it across to Thailand. According to my Dad, about 1,000 Hmong people died making that exact journey. My parents' stories merged at a refugee camp in Thailand. In Thailand, although they had escaped with their lives, their lives did not improve much because the camp that the Hmong people were put in when they came to Thailand was in very poor condition. My parents met at the refugee camp in Bon Vinai a couple months later when they arrived in Thailand. My Dad asked my Mom's hand in marriage. At that time, my parents were very young. They didn't have any support from anybody. I was born in the refugee camp in Bon Vinai, February 18, 1980. Six months after I was born, we were sponsored by an American family, which allowed us to come to the United States.

◀ He sets the scene and provides a preview of what will be presented; audience members know that more details about the journey will be forthcoming, so they tune in to listen.
◀ The speech is organized chronologically. Pao uses a step-by-step arrangement to describe the events that occurred.

The next chapter in our story continues in America, where each of us has our own challenge. My Dad had the most responsibility when it came to supporting our family. He knew it was important to get an education, so he started attending college. However, shortly after our arrival, my sisters were born. Making ends meet, my Dad had to drop out of college and work full time to support us all. My Mom also struggled with all the new aspects of her life. For example, in Laos, where she used to live, there wasn't any machine that would wash your clothes. However, in the United States, there are machines that will wash clothes for you. Another thing that she struggled with was using other appliances as well. Being able to operate the machine and use it properly was the hardest thing for my Mom because she wasn't able to read the directions. Probably the biggest struggle for my Mom was learning how to speak English and understand the language. It is interesting when people can't understand you, they think you're stupid. But we are the people who speak the second language.

◀ Note how Pao signals a new idea by using the transition phrase "The next chapter in our story . . . ."
◀ Revealing personal details and information adds interest to a story and holds listeners' attention.

Like my Mother and Father, I had my own challenge. I had to live in both cultures at the same time. At school, I was trying to fit in by learning the rules about how to act. While at home, I was trying to be respectful to the Hmong custom and language. This is a very difficult thing to do. It was also difficult for me to be a translator for my parents. I was just a little kid and was expected to translate an adult conversation. I was also expected to be there for my parents whenever they needed me.

Now I'm able to see my life as a part of a bigger picture—a bigger story. I have learned that you have to work hard to succeed in life. Coming from a first-generation family in the United States, I have lived through and seen the struggle that my parents went through to raise my siblings and me.

◄ As Pao concludes his speech, he summarizes by noting the "bigger story," or the implications of what he has learned. Speeches based on personal experiences are enhanced if the speaker can draw some concluding point or idea from the story.

Well, today I told you a little bit about my story, a part of my ancestry that has helped make me who I am. It is a story that has been repeated by 90,000 Hmong people in the United States. As you have taken the journey with my parents from Laos, to Thailand, and to America, I hope you will be able to think of your own stories and how they have brought us to this present place and time, to learn and grow together.

◄ The speech ends with a concise summary of the major idea of the speech. Pao also invites the audience to relate his story to their own lives.

CHAPTER 4

Ethics and Free Speech

nly a few days after the September 11, 2001, terrorist attacks on the United States, Bill Maher, host of the intentionally controversial late-night television talk show *Politically Incorrect,* declared on the air that the terrorists were not cowards, but that it was cowardly for the U.S. military to launch retaliatory cruise missiles from thousands of miles away. Maher's remarks were sharply and publicly criticized by White House Press Secretary Ari Fleischer, who noted that at times like these, people should "watch what they say and watch what they do."[1] Fleischer was not questioning Maher's *right* to free speech, but his *ethics.*

> *Free speech not only lives, it rocks!*
> **—Oprah Winfrey**

4.a Ethics

Ethics are the beliefs, values, and moral principles by which people determine what is right or wrong. Ethics serve as criteria for many of the decisions we make in our personal and professional lives, and also for our judgments of others' behavior. The student who refuses to cheat on a test, the employee who will not call in sick to gain an extra day of vacation, and the property owner who does not claim more storm damage than she actually suffered have all made choices based on ethics. We read and hear about ethical issues every day in the media. Cloning and drug testing have engendered heated ethical debates among medical professionals. Advertising by some attorneys has incensed others, who believe that the overall increase in frivolous litigation is tarnishing the profession. And in the political arena, debates about reforms of social programs, fiscal responsibility, and the regulation of business and industry all hinge on ethical issues.

4.b Free Speech

Although you are undoubtedly familiar with many ethical issues, you may have given less thought to those that arise in public speaking. These issues center around one main concern: In a country in which **free speech** is protected by law, the right to speak freely must be balanced by the responsibility to speak ethically. In 1999, the National Communication Association developed a Credo for Communication Ethics, which emphasizes the fundamental nature and far-reaching impact of ethical communication:

> Ethical communication is fundamental to responsible thinking, decision making, and the development of relationships and communities within and across contexts, cultures, channels, and media. Moreover, ethical communication enhances human worth and dignity by fostering truthfulness, fairness, responsibility, personal integrity, and respect for self and others.[2]

Ethical considerations should guide every step of the public-speaking process. As you determine the goal of your speech, outline your arguments, and select your evidence, think about the beliefs, values, and morals of your audience, as well as your own. Ethical public speaking is inherently audience-centered, always taking into account the needs and rights of the listeners.

Any discussion of ethical public speaking is complicated by the fact that ethics are not hard-and-fast objective rules. Each person's ethical decisions reflect his or her individual values and religious beliefs, as well as cultural norms. Although we cannot, therefore, offer a universal definition of ethical public speaking, we can offer principles and guidelines that reflect the ethics of contemporary North American society and the legal guarantees granted under the U.S. Constitution, including the right to free speech. And as we offer guidelines for ethical speaking and listening, we will include suggestions for acknowledging and encouraging diversity.

We will turn first to a discussion of free speech and both its protection and its restriction by law and public policy. Then we will discuss the ethical practice of free speech by speakers and listeners, providing guidelines to help you balance your right to free speech with your responsibilities as an audience-centered speaker and as a critical listener. Within this framework, we will define and discuss plagiarism, one of the most troublesome violations of public-speaking ethics.

4.C   Speaking Freely

In 1791, the **First Amendment** to the U.S. Constitution was written to guarantee that "Congress shall make no law . . . abridging the freedom of speech." In the more than 200 years since then, entities as varied as state legislatures, colleges and universities, the American Civil Liberties Union, and the federal courts have sought to define through both law and public policy the phrase "freedom of speech."

Only a few years after the ratification of the First Amendment, Congress passed the Sedition Act, providing punishment for those who spoke out against the government. When both Thomas Jefferson and James Madison declared this act unconstitutional, however, it was allowed to lapse.

IN THE TWENTIETH CENTURY

During World War I, the U.S. Supreme Court ruled that it was lawful to restrict speech that presented "a clear and present danger" to the nation. This decision led to the founding, in 1920, of the American Civil Liberties Union, the first organization formed to protect free speech. In 1940, Congress declared it illegal to urge the violent over-throw of the federal government. However, even as they heard the hate speech em-ployed by Hitler and the Nazis, U.S. courts and lawmakers argued that only by *protecting* free speech could the United States protect the rights of minorities and the disenfran-chised. For most of the last half of the twentieth century, the U.S. Supreme Court con-tinued to protect rather than to limit free speech, upholding it as "the core aspect of democracy."[3]

In 1964, the Supreme Court narrowed the definition of slander, or false speech that harms someone. The Court ruled that before a public official can recover dam-ages for slander, he or she must prove that the slanderous statement was made with "actual malice."[4] Another 1964 boost for free speech occurred not in the courts, but on a university campus. In December of that year, more than 1,000 students at the University of California in Berkeley took over three floors of Sproul Hall to protest the recent arrest of outspoken student activists. The Berkeley Free Speech Move-ment that arose from the incident permanently changed the political climate of U.S. college campuses. In a written statement on the thirty-year anniversary of the protest, Berkeley's vice chancellor, Carol Christ, wrote, "Today it is difficult to imagine life in a university where there are serious restrictions on the rights of po-litical advocacy."[5]

IN RECENT HISTORY

Free speech gained protection in the last two decades of the twentieth century, during which the Supreme Court found "virtually all attempts to restrain speech in advance . . . unconstitutional," regardless of how hateful or disgusting the speech may seem to some.[6] In 1989, the Supreme Court defended the burning of the U.S. flag as a **"speech act"** protected by the First Amendment. In 1997, the Court struck down the highly controversial federal Communications Decency Act of 1996, which had imposed penal-ties for creating, transmitting, or receiving obscene material on the Internet. The Court ruled that "the interest in encouraging freedom of expression in a democratic society outweighs any theoretical but unproven benefit of censorship."[7]

Perhaps no recent test of free speech received more publicity than the sensational 1998 lawsuit brought by four Texas cattlemen against popular talk-show host Oprah Winfrey. In a 1996 televised show on "mad cow disease," Winfrey had declared that she would never eat another hamburger. Charging that her statement caused cattle prices to plummet, the cattlemen sued for damages; however, Winfrey's attorneys successfully argued that the case was an important test of free speech. Emerging from the court-room after the verdict in her favor, Winfrey shouted, "My reaction is that free speech not only lives, it rocks!"[8]

One month after the September 11, 2001, terrorist attacks on the United States, the pendulum again swung toward restriction of free speech, with the passage of the Patriot Act, which broadened the investigative powers of government agencies. Not surpris-ingly, the Patriot Act has been roundly criticized by various civil-rights, free speech, and publishing groups. One coalition of such groups described the Patriot Act as "the latest in a long line of abuses of rights in times of conflict."[9] There can be little doubt that in the months and years to come, the United States will continue to debate "the balance among national security, free speech, and patriotism."[10]

QUICK CHECK: *History of Free Speech in the United States*

1791	First Amendment guarantees that "Congress shall make no law ... abridging the freedom of speech."
1798	Sedition Act is passed.
1919	U.S. Supreme Court suggests that speech presenting "a clear and present danger" may be restricted.
1920	American Civil Liberties Union is formed.
1940	Congress declares it illegal to urge the violent overthrow of the federal government.
1964	U.S. Supreme Court restricts definition of slander; Berkeley Free Speech Movement is born.
1989	U.S. Supreme Court defends the burning of the U.S. flag as a "speech act."
1997	U.S. Supreme Court strikes down Communications Decency Act of 1996, in defense of free speech on the Internet.
1998	Oprah Winfrey successfully defends her right to speak freely on television.
2001	September 11 terrorist attacks spark passage of the Patriot Act and new debate over the balance between national security and free speech.

4.d   Speaking Ethically

As the boundaries of free speech expand, the importance of ethical speech increases. As we have said, there is no definitive ethical creed for a public speaker. But teachers and practitioners of public speaking generally agree that an ethical speaker is one who has a clear, responsible goal; uses sound evidence and reasoning; is sensitive to and tolerant of differences; is honest; and avoids plagiarism. In the discussion that follows, we offer suggestions for observing these ethical guidelines.

HAVE A CLEAR, RESPONSIBLE GOAL

The goal of a public speech should be clear to the audience. For example, if you are trying to convince the audience that your beliefs on abortion are more correct than those of others, you should say so at some point in your speech. If you keep your true agenda hidden, you violate your listeners' rights. In addition, an ethical goal should be socially responsible. A socially responsible goal is one that gives the listener choices, whereas an irresponsible, unethical goal is psychologically coercive. Adolf Hitler's speeches, which incited the German people to hatred and genocide, were coercive, as were those of Chinese leader Deng Xiaoping, who tried to intimidate Chinese citizens into revealing the whereabouts of leaders of the unsuccessful 1989 student uprising in Tiananmen Square.

If your overall objective is to inform or persuade, it is probably ethical; if your goal is to coerce or corrupt, it is unethical. But lawyers and ethicists do not always agree on this distinction. As we have pointed out, Congress and the U.S. Supreme Court have at times limited speech that incites sedition, violence, and riot, but they have also protected free speech rights "for both the ideas that people cherish and the thoughts they hate."[11] Even those who defend a broad legal right to free speech recognize that they are defending the right to unethical, as well as ethical, speech. For example, in 2003, Indiana University chancellor Sharon Brehm called a professor's anti-homosexual blog "deeply offensive, hurtful, and very harmful stereotyping."[12] But she went on to support the professor's right to free speech.

USE SOUND EVIDENCE AND REASONING

Ethical speakers use critical-thinking skills such as analysis and evaluation to draw conclusions and formulate arguments. Unethical speakers substitute false claims and manipulation of emotion for evidence and logical arguments. In the early 1950s, Wisconsin senator Joseph McCarthy incited national panic by charging that Communists were infiltrating every avenue of American life. Thousands of people came under suspicion, many losing jobs and careers because of the false accusations. Never able to substantiate his claims, McCarthy nevertheless succeeded in his witch-hunt by exaggerating and distorting the truth. One United Press reporter noted, "The man just talked in circles. Everything was by inference, allusion, never a concrete statement of fact. Most of it didn't make sense."[13] Although today we recognize the flimsiness of McCarthy's accusations, in his time the man wielded incredible power. Like Hitler, McCarthy knew how to manipulate emotions and fears to produce the results he wanted. It is sometimes tempting to resort to false claims to gain power over others, but it is always unethical to do so.

It can also be tempting simply to bypass sound evidence and reasoning. In the current U.S. political environment, both media "sound bites" and presidential debates have come under fire as shallow forums. Former CBS anchor Walter Cronkite has called the presidential debates "part of the unconscionable fraud that our political campaigns have become," because "substance is to be avoided if possible. Image is to be maximized."[14] Although using clever phrases and emphasizing positive images are not in themselves unethical, if they substitute for sound evidence and reasoning, then these tactics can become unethical practices.

One last, but important, requirement for the ethical use of evidence and reasoning is to share with an audience all information that might help them reach a sound decision, including information that may be potentially damaging to your case. Even if you proceed to refute the opposing evidence and arguments, you have fulfilled your ethical responsibility by presenting the perspective of the other side. And you can actually make your own arguments more convincing by anticipating and answering counter-arguments and evidence.

BE SENSITIVE TO AND TOLERANT OF DIFFERENCES

Being audience-centered requires that you become as aware as possible of others' feelings, needs, interests, and backgrounds. Former New Jersey senator Bill Bradley has described this ethical dimension as "tolerance, curiosity, civility—precisely the qualities we need to allow us to live side by side in mutual respect."[15] Sometimes called **accommodation**, sensitivity to differences does not mean that speakers must abandon their own convictions for those of their audience members. It does mean that speakers should demonstrate a willingness to listen to opposing viewpoints and learn about different beliefs and values. Such willingness not only communicates respect; it can also help a speaker to select a topic, formulate a purpose, and design strategies to motivate an audience.

Your authors are currently involved in an informal educational exchange with a professor from the St. Petersburg Cultural Institute in Russia, and we recently had a chance to visit the professor and her family in St. Petersburg. In talking with the professor's talented teenage daughter, we inquired about her plans after she finished her university education. Smiling at us in both amusement and amazement, she replied, "Americans are always planning what they are going to do several years in the future. In Russia, we do not plan beyond two or three weeks. Life is too uncertain here." Having gained this insight into Russian life, we know now that it would raise false hopes to attempt to motivate Russian audiences with promises of benefits far in the future. Our new understanding not only helps us see that speaking of immediate, deliverable rewards is a more realistic and ethical approach to communication with our Russian friends, but it has broader implications as well. DePaul University communication professor Kathy Fitzpatrick notes,

> Our success in public diplomacy will turn on our ability to speak in ways that recognize and appreciate how [our audiences] will interpret our messages.[16]

A speaker who is sensitive to differences also avoids language that might be interpreted as in any way biased or offensive. Although it may seem fairly simple and a matter of common sense to avoid overtly abusive language, it is not so easy to avoid language that discriminates more subtly.

BE HONEST

Knowingly offering false or misleading information to an audience is an ethical violation. In 2003, President George W. Bush and members of his staff accepted responsibility for telling the public that Iraq was getting nuclear fuel from Africa, even after intelligence reports several months earlier had discredited the claim. In 1999, Toronto Blue Jays manager Tim Johnson was fired after it was revealed that the stories he had told to his team about his combat experiences in Vietnam were false. During the war, it turned out, he actually played ball while serving with the Reserves in California.[17]

Perhaps most famously, in January 1998, then-President Bill Clinton's finger-wagging declaration that "I did not have sexual relations with that woman—Miss Lewinsky" was a serious breach of ethics that came back to haunt him. Many Americans were willing to forgive the inappropriate relationship; fewer could forgive the dishonesty.

A seeming exception to the dictum to avoid false information is the use of hypothetical illustrations—illustrations that never actually occurred but that might happen. Many speakers rely on such illustrations to clarify or enhance their speeches. As long as a speaker makes clear to the audience that the illustration is indeed hypothetical—for example, prefacing the illustration with a phrase such as "Imagine that . . ."—such use is ethical.

Honesty also requires that speakers give credit for ideas and information that are not their own. The *Publication Manual of the American Psychological Association* states that "an author does not present the work of another as if it were his or her own work. This can extend to ideas as well as written words."[18] Presenting the words and ideas of others without crediting them is called *plagiarism*. This ethical violation is both serious enough and widespread enough to warrant a separate discussion.

AVOID PLAGIARISM

Most people are taught from earliest childhood that it is wrong to steal. Yet even those who would never think of stealing money or shoplifting may be tempted to **plagiarize** —to steal ideas. Perhaps you can remember copying a grade-school report directly from the encyclopedia, or maybe you've even purchased or "borrowed" a paper to submit for an assignment in high school or college. These are obvious forms of plagiarism.

A less obvious form is **plagiaphrasing**—lacing a speech with compelling phrases you find in a source that you do not credit. Whether your lapse is intentional or due merely to careless or hasty note-taking, it is a serious offense. Yet one study reported that more than 50 percent of 300 students surveyed acknowledged cheating in some way in a public-speaking class.[19]

Most colleges impose stiff penalties on students who plagiarize. Plagiarists almost always fail the assignment in question, frequently fail the course, and are sometimes put on academic probation or even expelled. Penalties for plagiarism outside the classroom are severe as well, costing one U.S. senator his bid for the Democratic nomination for president. In August 1987, Delaware Senator Joseph Biden plagiarized the words of former British Labor Party leader Neil Kinnock, in a speech in Des Moines, Iowa. When the plagiarism was exposed, along with evidence of a previous plagiarism from a speech by Robert Kennedy, Biden was forced to withdraw from the presidential race. Publicized evidence of plagiarism also haunted Hamilton College (New York) president Eugene Tobin, who in September 2002 delivered to the college's freshman class a convocation speech that was later discovered to have been plagiarized from Amazon.com. And more recently, a school board president in North Carolina delivered to the 2004 graduating class of Orange High School a speech given some six years earlier by Donna Shalala, at the time President Clinton's Secretary of Health and Human Services. Biden, Tobin, and the board president violated their ethical responsibilities and paid the price for that violation with their reputations and careers.

Do Your Own Work   The most flagrant cases of plagiarism result from not doing your own work. For example, while you are poking around the library for ideas to use in a speech assignment, you may discover an entire speech or perhaps an article that could easily be made into a speech. However tempting it may be to use this material, and however certain you are that no audience member could possibly have seen it, resist the urge to plagiarize. First, you will be doing yourself a disservice if you do not learn how to compose a speech on your own. After all, you are in college to acquire new skills. In addition, the risk may be much greater than you suspect.

A few years ago, one of your authors heard an excellent student speech on the importance of detecting cancer early. The only problem was, she heard the same speech again in the following class period! On finding the "speech"—actually a *Reader's Digest* article that was several years old—both students were certain that they had discovered a surefire shortcut to an A. Instead, they failed the assignment, ruined their course grades, and lost your author's trust. The consequences of academic plagiarism can be even more dire, including expulsion in many schools.

Another way speakers sometimes attempt to shortcut the speech preparation task is to ask another person to edit a speech so extensively that it becomes more that other person's work than their own. This is another form of plagiarism, as well as another way that novice speakers can cheat themselves out of the skills they need to develop.

Acknowledge Your Sources   Our admonition to do your own work in no way suggests that you should not research your speeches and then share the results with audience members. In fact, an ethical speaker is responsible for doing just that. Furthermore, some information is so widely known that you do not have to acknowledge a source for it. For example, you need not credit a source if you say that a person must be infected with the HIV virus in order to develop AIDS, or that the Treaty of Versailles was signed on June 28, 1919. This information is widely available in a variety of reference sources. However, if you decide to use any of the following in your speech, you must give credit to the source:

- Direct quotations, even if they are only brief phrases
- Opinions, assertions, or ideas of others, even if you paraphrase them rather than quote them verbatim
- Statistics
- Any nonoriginal visual materials, including graphs, tables, and pictures

Take Careful Notes   To be able to acknowledge your sources, you must first practice careful and systematic note-taking. Indicate with quotation marks any phrases or sentences that you photocopy or copy by hand verbatim from a source, and be sure to record the author, title, publisher or Web site, publication date, and page numbers for all sources from which you take quotations, ideas, statistics, or visual materials.

Cite Sources Correctly   In addition to keeping careful records of your sources, you must also know how to cite sources for your audience, both orally and in writing. Perhaps you have heard a speaker say, "Quote," while holding up both hands with index and middle fingers curved to indicate quotation marks. This is an artificial

HOW TO: *Incorporate an Oral Citation into Your Speech*

In a May 2004	◀ Provide the date.
online fact sheet	◀ Specify the type of resource.
entitled *Mold*, the	◀ Give the title.
National Center for Environmental Health	◀ Provide the author or source.
describes *Stachybotrys chartarum* as	◀ Pause briefly to signal that you are about to begin quoting.
"a greenish-black mold. It can grow on material with a high cellulose and low nitrogen content, such as fiberboard, gypsum board, paper, dust, and lint. Growth occurs when there is moisture from water damage, excessive humidity, water leaks, condensation, water infiltration, or flooding."	◀ Quote the source. ◀ Pause again to indicate that you are ending the quoted passage.

and distracting way to cite a source; an **oral citation** can be integrated more smoothly into a speech.

You can also provide a written citation for a source. In fact, your public-speaking instructor may ask you to provide a bibliography of sources along with the outline or other written materials he or she requires for each speech. Instructors who require a bibliography will usually specify the format in which they want the citations; if they do not, you can use a style guide such as those published by the MLA (Modern Language Association) or the APA (American Psychological Association), both of which are available online as well as in traditional print format. Here is an example of a written citation in MLA format for the source cited orally in the earlier example. Notice that the citation provides two dates: the date the material was posted online and the date it was accessed by the researcher. If you are unable to find the date the material was posted—or any other single element of information—proceed directly to the next item in the citation.

National Center for Environmental Health. "Mold." 19 May 2004. 14 June 2004 <www.cdc.gov/nceh/airpollution/mold/stachy.htm>.

Perhaps now you are thinking, "What about those 'gray areas,' those times when I am not certain whether information or ideas I am presenting are common knowledge?" A good rule is this: When in doubt, document. You will never be guilty of plagiarism if you document something you didn't need to, but you could be committing plagiarism if you do not document something you really should have.

QUICK CHECK: *The Ethical Public Speaker...*

- Has a clear, responsible goal.
- Uses sound evidence and reasoning.
- Is sensitive to and tolerant of differences.
- Is honest.
- Avoids plagiarism.

4.e   Listening Ethically

Until now, we have been focusing primarily on the ethical exercise of free speech by the speaker. But audience members also share responsibility for ethical communication. In the fourth century B.C., Aristotle warned, "Let men be on their guard against those who flatter and mislead the multitude." And contemporary rhetorician Harold Barrett has said that the audience is the "necessary source of correction" for the behavior of a speaker.[20] The following guidelines for ethical listening incorporate what Barrett calls "attributes of the good audience."

COMMUNICATE YOUR EXPECTATIONS AND FEEDBACK

As an audience member, you have the right—even the responsibility—to enter a communication situation with expectations about both the message and how the speaker will deliver it. Know what information and ideas you want to get out of the communication transaction. Expect a coherent, organized, and competently delivered presentation.

Communicate your objectives and react to the speaker's message and delivery through appropriate nonverbal and verbal feedback. For example, maintain eye contact with the speaker. Nod in agreement when you support something the speaker says; look puzzled if you do not understand the speaker's point. Turn your head to one side and tilt it slightly forward to communicate that you are having trouble hearing. If a question-and-answer period follows the speech, ask questions you may still have about the speaker's topic or point of view. Perhaps no public-speaking situation better illustrates the effectiveness of audience feedback than the traditional African American sermon, during which the congregation's willingness to "finish the preacher's sentence, shout encouragement or warn the preacher that he's wandered off the point . . . lets a preacher know whether he is misfiring or connecting from the pulpit."[21] Although such outspokenness is not appropriate to many public-speaking settings, the African American congregation's enthusiastic involvement is a good example of how listener feedback can affect the communication process.

BE SENSITIVE TO AND TOLERANT OF DIFFERENCES

We have already discussed the importance of being a sensitive and tolerant speaker. But it is equally important for you to exercise social and cultural awareness and tolerance as a member of the audience. For example, suppose you were to attend a high-school baccalaureate ceremony at which the speaker was a dynamic African American minister used to the duet-style preaching described in the preceding section. If you were to dismiss the minister's delivery as too flamboyant, you might miss out on a powerful message.

Understanding diverse cultural norms can sometimes pose quite a complex ethical-listening challenge. For example, Jesse Jackson has in the past been accused of making dishonest claims in some of his speeches about his background and behavior. He has said that he left the University of Illinois because of racism on the football team, which caused him to be passed over for starting quarterback—yet former teammates insist that he did not become starting quarterback simply because he was not the strongest player. Jackson has also overstated the poverty he experienced as a child, when in fact he grew up in a fairly comfortable middle-class home. Although many have criticized such exaggeration, at least one communication researcher has defended Jackson, arguing that although his "tall tales" are not necessarily "the truth" in a strictly objective sense, they are part of a valid African American oral tradition that focuses on the "symbolic import of the story" and in which speakers traditionally exaggerate to enhance the impact of their illustrations.[22]

Be attentive and courteous. Consider diverse cultural norms and audience expectations as part of the context within which you listen to and evaluate the speaker. Making an effort to understand the needs, goals, and interests of both the speaker and other audience members can help you judge how to react appropriately and ethically as a listener.

LISTEN CRITICALLY

Courtesy and tolerance are not the same as approval or agreement. In fact, the necessary check on free speech is the listener who recognizes and refuses to license abusive or dangerous ideas or plans. As University of Chicago professor and ethicist Richard M. Weaver explains, "It is the principle of our society that we can listen to propaganda from all the special interests . . . and do a pretty fair job of sifting the true claims from the false."[23] In other words, it is the audience members' job to listen critically.

To listen critically is to hold a speaker to his or her ethical responsibilities. Is the speaker presenting both sides of the issue? Is the speaker disclosing all the information to which he or she has access, or is the speaker trying to hide something? Is the speaker being honest about the purpose of the speech? As already noted, you can communicate to the speaker through nonverbal feedback during a speech. Frowning, shaking your head, or looking away can signal to the speaker that you do not approve of his or her message. If there is a chance that you may have misunderstood the speaker, take advantage of opportunities after the speech to question him or her. Read more about the topic for yourself, to check the speaker's facts. And if you conclude that the speaker's message or motives are indeed unethical, discuss your opinion with others, and seek out or create a forum through which you can express your dissent. Although you can and should refuse to sanction unethical messages and tactics, seek ways to question and refute ideas and arguments without being discourteous or resorting to unethical tactics yourself.

QUICK CHECK: *The Ethical Listener...*

- Communicates expectations and feedback.
- Is sensitive to and tolerant of differences.
- Listens critically.

Summary

- Ethical speaking and listening are very important in a society that protects free speech. Although Congress and the courts have occasionally limited free speech by law and policy, more often they have protected and broadened its application.

- The right to free speech has also been upheld by such organizations as the American Civil Liberties Union and by colleges and universities.

- Speakers who exercise their right to free speech are responsible for tempering what they say by applying ethics, or moral principles and values.

- Although there is no definitive standard of ethics, most people agree that public speakers must be responsible, honest, and tolerant in order to be ethical.

- Plagiarism is one of the most common violations of speech ethics. You can usually avoid plagiarism by understanding what it is, doing your own work, and acknowledging the sources for any quotations, ideas, statistics, or visual materials you use in a speech.

- Ethical listeners should provide feedback; be sensitive to and tolerant of differences; and listen critically, refusing to sanction unethical messages and tactics.

Key Terms

accommodation (p. 52)   oral citation (p. 55)
ethics (p. 47)   plagiaphrasing (p. 53)
First Amendment (p. 48)   plagiarize (p. 53)
free speech (p. 47)   speech act (p. 49)

A QUESTION OF ETHICS

It has been openly acknowledged that George Bush's speech to Congress and the nation on Thursday, September 20, 2001, "was a collaboration by administration wordsmiths." Is the use of such "ghostwriters" unethical? Why or why not?

2

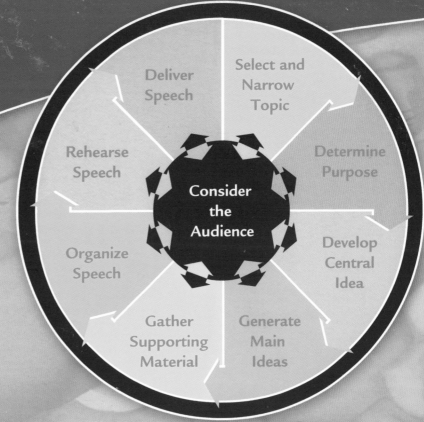

Deliver Speech

Select and Narrow Topic

Rehearse Speech

Determine Purpose

Consider the Audience

Organize Speech

Develop Central Idea

Gather Supporting Material

Generate Main Ideas

Analyzing an Audience

Analyzing an Audience

Analyzing an Audience

5 Listening to Speeches

➡ **Barriers to Effective Listening (p. 64)**
- Listening barriers are created when we fail to select, attend to, or understand a message or remember what was said.
- Other barriers include information overload, personal concerns, outside distractions, prejudice, differences between speech rate and thought rate, and receiver apprehension.

➡ **Becoming a Better Listener (p. 69)**
- Focus on a speaker's message, not on his or her delivery style.
- Listen with your eyes as well as your ears. A speaker's posture and gestures can reinforce the intensity of the emotion.
- Keep your emotions under control; heightened emotions can affect your ability to understand a message.
- Avoid jumping to conclusions.
- Find ways to benefit from the information you are listening to and to connect it with your own experiences and needs.
- Listen for major ideas, and try to summarize the major idea that the specific facts support.
- Identify your listening style. Is it people oriented, action oriented, content oriented, or time oriented?

➡ **Improving Your Note-Taking Skills (p. 75)**
- Come prepared to take notes.
- Determine whether you need to take notes.
- Decide on the type of notes you need to take.
- Make your notes meaningful. The goal is to remember the message, not to transcribe it.

➡ **Listening and Critical Thinking (p. 77)**
- The ability to separate facts from inferences is one of the most basic critical thinking and listening skills.
- An effective critical listener listens not only for evidence, but also for the overall structure of the logic or argument the speaker uses to reach a conclusion.

➡ **Analyzing and Evaluating Speeches (p. 79)**
- The message should be effective.
- The message should achieve its intended purpose.
- The message should be ethical. An ethical public speaker tells the truth, gives credit for ideas and words where credit is due, and doesn't plagiarize.
- Rhetorical strategies are methods and techniques that speakers employ to achieve their speaking goals. Be aware of how some speakers may use rhetorical techniques to deceive or manipulate you.
- When giving feedback to others, identify both strengths of a speech and aspects that could be improved; be descriptive; be specific; be positive; be constructive; be sensitive; and be realistic.
- When giving feedback to yourself, look for and reinforce your skills and speaking abilities, evaluate your effectiveness based on your specific speaking situation and audience, and identify one or two areas for improvement.

6 Analyzing Your Audience

➡ **Becoming an Audience-Centered Speaker (p. 89)**
- At each stage in crafting your speech, you must be mindful of your audience.
- When you think of your audience, think of individuals.

➡ **Gathering Information About Your Audience (p. 91)**
- As an audience-centered speaker, try to find out as much as you can about your audience before planning your speech.
  - Gather information informally by observing your listeners or asking general questions about them.
  - Gather information formally by administering a survey to obtain more specific information about your audience.

- Analyze the information you have gathered.
  - How are audience members similar to one another?
  - How are audience members different from one another?
  - Based on their similarities and differences, how can I establish common ground with the audience?
- Adapt to your audience by ethically using information you have gathered to help your audience clearly understand your message and to achieve your speaking objective.

➡ Analyzing Your Audience Before You Speak (p. 96)
- Learn about your audience members' backgrounds and attitudes. These can help you in selecting a topic, defining a purpose, and developing an outline.
- Identify your audience's demographic makeup, such as age; gender; educational level; religious views; sexual orientation; culture, ethnicity, and race; group membership; and socioeconomic status.
- Adapt to diverse listeners.
  - Focus on a target audience.
  - Use diverse strategies for a diverse audience.
  - Identify common values.
  - Rely on visual materials that transcend language differences.
- A psychological audience analysis explores an audience's attitudes toward a topic, purpose, and speaker, while probing the underlying beliefs and values that might affect these attitudes.
  - An attitude reflects likes or dislikes.
  - A belief is what you hold to be true or false.
  - A value is an enduring concept of good and bad, right and wrong.
- The topic of a speech provides one focus for an audience's attitudes, beliefs, and values. When you are analyzing your audience, it may help to categorize the group along three dimensions: interested–uninterested, favorable–unfavorable, and captive–voluntary.
- Your speech class is a captive audience rather than a voluntary one. A captive audience has externally imposed reasons for being there (such as a requirement to attend class).
- Audience members' attitude toward you in your role as speaker is another factor that can influence their reaction to your speech. If members of an audience regard you as credible, they will be much more likely to be interested in, and supportive of, what you have to say.
- Situational audience analysis includes an examination of the time and place of your speech, the size of your audience, and the speaking occasion.

➡ **Adapting to Your Audience as You Speak (p. 111)**
- Once a speech is in progress, the speaker must rely on nonverbal clues from the audience to judge how people are responding to the message.
- Identify nonverbal audience cues. Although it's not possible to read your listeners' minds, it is important to analyze and adapt to cues that can enhance the effectiveness of your message.
  - Eye contact. The more eye contact audience members make, the more likely it is that they are listening to your message.
  - Facial expression. Members of an attentive audience not only make direct eye contact but also have attentive facial expressions.
  - Movement. An attentive audience doesn't move much.
- Interested audience members respond verbally and nonverbally when encouraged or invited by the speaker.
- Not only will audiences indicate agreement nonverbally, some will also indicate their interests verbally.
- The value in recognizing nonverbal clues from your listeners is that you can respond to them appropriately.

➡ **Analyzing Your Audience After You Speak (p. 116)**
- Nonverbal responses. The most obvious nonverbal response is applause. Responsive facial expressions, smiles, and nods are other nonverbal signs that the speech has been well received.
- Verbal responses. What do members of the audience say to you about your speech? General comments are not of much analytic help. Specific comments can indicate where you succeeded and where you failed.
- Survey responses. Develop survey questions that will help you determine the general reactions to you and your speech, as well as specific responses to your ideas and supporting materials.
- Behavioral responses. Your listeners' actions are the best indicators of your speaking success.

CHAPTER 5

Listening to Speeches

Are you a good listener? Considerable evidence suggests that your listening skills could be improved. Within twenty-four hours after listening to a lecture or speech, you will recall only about 50 percent of the message. Forty-eight hours later, you are above average if you remember more than 25 percent of the message. (And in a recent survey of adult listeners, only 15 percent reported that they were above-average listeners.)

> *Learn how to listen and you will prosper— even from those who talk badly.*
>
> **—Plutarch**

A psychology professor had dedicated his life to teaching and worked hard to prepare interesting lectures, yet he found his students sitting through his talks with glassy-eyed expressions.[1] To learn what was wrong, and also find out what was on his students' minds if they were not focusing on psychology, he would, without warning, fire a blank from a gun and then ask his students to record their thoughts at the instant they heard the shot. Here is what he found:

20 percent were pursuing erotic thoughts or sexual fantasies.

20 percent were reminiscing about something (they weren't sure what they were thinking about).

20 percent were worrying about something or thinking about lunch.

8 percent were pursuing religious thoughts.

20 percent were reportedly listening.

12 percent were able to recall what the professor was talking about when the gun fired.

You hear more than one billion words each year. Yet how much information do you retain? In this chapter, we are going to focus on improving your listening skills. If you apply the principles and suggestions we offer, we believe you will become not only a better listener but also a better public speaker. In addition, improving your listening skills will strengthen your ability to think critically and evaluate what you hear and also enhance your listening in one-on-one interpersonal interactions.

In this chapter, we will discuss how people listen and identify barriers and pitfalls that keep both speakers and audiences from listening effectively. We will also make some suggestions for improving your listening and note-taking skills. Finally, we will discuss how you can enhance your ability to listen critically and evaluate speeches.

Barriers to Effective Listening

Listening barriers are created when we fail to select, attend to, or understand a message or remember what was said.

SELECT

To **select** a sound is to single out a message from several competing messages. A listener has many competing messages to sort through, including personal thoughts. Your job as a public speaker is to develop a message that motivates listeners to focus on *your* message.

ATTEND

The sequel to selecting is attending. To **attend** to a sound is to focus on it. Most people's average attention span while listening to someone talk is about 8 seconds.[2] One of your key challenges as a public speaker is to capture and hold the attention of your audience. Your choice of supporting material is often the key to gaining and maintaining attention; we'll talk much more about strategies for gathering and using supporting material in the chapters ahead.

UNDERSTAND

Boiled down to its essence, communication is the process of making sense out of the world and sharing that sense with others.[3] Understanding is the process of making sense out of our experiences. To **understand** something, people assign meaning to the stimuli that come their way. Although no single theory explains how people make sense of words, we do know that you understand what you hear by relating it to something you have already seen or heard. As a speaker, your job is to facilitate listener understanding by making sure you clearly explain your ideas in terms and images to which your listeners can relate. Again, the challenge of being understood comes back to a focus on the audience.

REMEMBER

The final stage in the listening process is remembering. To **remember** is to recall ideas and information. Most listening experts believe that the main way to determine if audience members have been listening is to determine what they remember. Your geography professor determines how well you understand geography by testing you on the content of his or her lecture. But intentionally or not, the professor is testing your listening skill as well as your knowledge of geography.

Your goal as a public speaker is to develop and deliver a speech that audience members will listen and respond to. The more you know about potential obstacles that keep your listeners from listening, the better able you will be to develop messages that hold their interest. Let's look at specific barriers that keep listeners from selecting, attending to, understanding, and remembering a message; we'll also suggest how you can overcome these barriers, both as a speaker and as an audience member.

INFORMATION OVERLOAD

We all spend a large part of each day listening. That's good news and bad news. The good news is that because we listen a lot, we have the potential to become very effective listeners. The bad news is that instead of getting better at it, we often "tune out," because we hear so much information that we get tired of listening.

As a public speaker, you can keep your audience from tuning you out by making sure your speech has a good balance between new information and supporting material, such as stories and examples. A speech that is too dense—chock-full of facts, new definitions, and undeveloped ideas—can make listening a tedious process. On the other hand, listeners don't want to listen to a bare bones outline of ideas; they need ideas that are fleshed out with illustrations.

HOW TO: *Prevent Information Overload*

- Pace the flow of new ideas and information. Communication expert Frank E. X. Dance recommends a 30/70 balance: 30 percent of your speaking time should be spent presenting new ideas and information, and 70 percent of your time should be spent supporting the ideas with vivid examples and interesting stories.[4]
- Build redundancy into your message. If listeners miss the idea the first time you present it, perhaps they will catch it during your concluding summary. Repeating key ideas can be part of that 70 percent of your message that extends the new information you present.

PERSONAL CONCERNS

You are sitting in your African history class on a Friday afternoon. It's a beautiful day. You slump into your seat, open your notebook, and prepare to take notes on the lecture. As the professor talks about an upcoming assignment, you begin to think about how you are going to spend your Saturday. One thought leads to another as you mentally plan your weekend. Suddenly you hear your professor say, "For Monday's test, you will be expected to know the principles I've just reviewed." What principles? What test? You were present in class, and you did *hear* the professor's lecture, but you're not sure what was said.

Your own thoughts are among the biggest competitors for your attention when you are a member of an audience. Most of us would rather listen to our own inner speech than to the message of a public speaker. As the psychology professor with the gun found, sex, lunch, worries, and daydreams are major distractions for the majority of listeners.

To counteract this problem, as a speaker you can focus on maintaining your audience's attention, using occasional "wake-up" messages such as "Now listen carefully, because this will affect your future grade (or family, or employment)." As a listener, you can learn to recognize when your own agenda is keeping you from listening, then force yourself to focus on the speaker's message. Later in this chapter, we will offer specific suggestions for what to do when you find your attention flagging.

OUTSIDE DISTRACTIONS

While sitting in class, you notice that a fluorescent light is flickering overhead. Two classmates behind you are swapping stories about their favorite soap opera plots. Out the window you see a varsity football hero struggling to break into his car to retrieve the keys he left in the ignition. As your history professor drones on about the Bay of Pigs invasion, you find it difficult to focus on his lecture. Most of us don't listen well when physical distractions are competing with the speaker.

HOW TO: *Minimize Outside Distractions*

- When you are the speaker, try to control the physical arrangements of the speaking situation before you begin your speech.
- Try to empathize with your listeners.
- Check out the room ahead of time: Sit where your audience will be seated, and look for possible distractions. Then do the best you can to reduce or eliminate distractions (close windows and window shades to limit visual and auditory distractions; turn off blinking fluorescent lights if you can; try to discourage whispering in the audience).
- As a listener, you also need to do your best to control the listening situation.
- If you must, move to another seat.
- If the speaker has failed to monitor the listening environment, you may need to close the blinds, turn up the heat, turn off the lights, close the door, or do whatever is necessary to minimize distractions.

PREJUDICE

Your buddy is a staunch Democrat. He rarely credits a Republican with any useful ideas. So it's not surprising that when the Republican governor from your state makes a major televised speech outlining suggestions for improving the state's sagging economy, your friend finds the presentation ludicrous. As the speech is broadcast, your buddy constantly argues against each suggestion, mumbling comments about Republicans, business interests, and robbing the poor. The next day he is surprised to see editorials in the press praising the governor's speech. "Did they hear the same speech I did?" your friend wonders. Yes, they heard the same speech, but they listened differently. When you prejudge a message, your ability to understand it decreases.

Another way to prejudge a speech is to decide that the topic has little value for you before you even hear the message. Most of us at one time or another have not given our full attention to a speech because we decided beforehand that it was going to bore us.

Sometimes we make snap judgments about a speaker based on his or her appearance and then fail to listen because we dismissed his or her ideas in advance as inconsequential or irrelevant. Female speakers often complain that males in the audience do not listen to them as attentively as they would to another male; members of ethnic and racial minorities may feel slighted in a similar way. On the flip side, some people too readily accept what someone says just because they like the way the person looks, sounds, or dresses. For example, Tex believes that anyone with a Texas drawl must be an honest person. Such positive prejudices can also inhibit your ability to listen accurately to a message. What can be done to counteract audience members' **prejudices**?

HOW TO: *Counteract Prejudice*

- As a speaker, the most effective strategy is to use your opening statements to grab the audience's attention. Focus on your particular listeners' interests, needs, hopes, and wishes.

- When addressing an audience that may be critical of or hostile toward your message, use arguments and evidence that your listeners will find credible.

- If you think audience members are likely to disagree with you, strong emotional appeals will be less successful than careful language, sound reasoning, and convincing evidence.

- As a listener, you need to guard against becoming so critical of a message that you don't listen to it or so impressed that you decide too quickly that the speaker is trustworthy.

DIFFERENCES BETWEEN SPEECH RATE AND THOUGHT RATE

Ralph Nichols, a pioneer in listening research and training, has identified a listening problem that centers on the way you process the words you hear.[5] Most people talk at a rate of 125 words a minute. But you have the ability to listen to up to 700 words a minute; some studies suggest that you may even be able to listen to 1,200 words a minute. Regardless of the exact numbers, you have the ability to process words much faster than you generally need to. The problem is that the difference gives you time to ignore a speaker periodically. Eventually, you stop listening. Your "extra" time allows you to daydream and drift from the message.

Nichols suggests that the different rates of speech and thought need not be a listening liability. Instead of drifting away from the speech, you can enhance your listening effectiveness by mentally summarizing what the speaker is saying from time to time.

As a speaker, you need to be aware of your listeners' tendency to stop paying attention. If they can process your message much faster than you can say it, you need to build in message redundancy, be well organized, and make your major ideas clear. Just talking faster won't do much good. Even if you could speak as fast as 200 words a minute, your listeners would still want to go about four times faster than that.

RECEIVER APPREHENSION

You already know about speaker apprehension, or the fear of speaking to others, but did you know that some people may be fearful of *listening* to information? Researchers have discovered a listening barrier called receiver apprehension. **Receiver apprehension** is fear of misunderstanding or misinterpreting, or of not being able to adjust psychologically to, messages spoken by others.[6] Some people are just uncomfortable or nervous about hearing new information; their major worry is that they won't be able to understand the message. If you are one of those people, you may have difficulty understanding all you hear because your anxiety about listening creates "noise" that may interfere with how much information you comprehend.

HOW TO: *Overcome Receiver Apprehension*

- If you experience receiver apprehension, work harder to comprehend the information presented by others.
- Use a tape recorder to record a lecture; this may help you feel more comfortable and less anxious about trying to remember each point made by the speaker.[7]
- Summarize mentally what you hear a speaker saying during a speech.
- Take accurate notes; doing so can help you feel more comfortable about being a listener.
- As a speaker, be mindful that some listeners may be anxious about understanding your message.
- You can help people with receiver apprehension by being more redundant.
- Offer clear preview statements that give an overview of your main ideas.
- Include appropriate internal summaries while you're making a transition from one point to the next.
- Summarize major ideas at the end of your talk.[8]
- Use presentation aids to summarize key ideas—such as listing major ideas on an overhead transparency, PowerPoint® slide, chalkboard, or flipchart—which can also help increase comprehension and decrease receiver apprehension.

5.b Becoming a Better Listener

Now that we have examined barriers to effective listening, we will offer some additional suggestions for improving your listening skill.

ADAPT TO THE SPEAKER'S DELIVERY

Good listeners focus on a speaker's message, not on his or her delivery style. To be a good listener, you must adapt to the particular idiosyncrasies some speakers have. You may have to ignore or overlook a speaker's tendency to mumble, speak in a monotone, or fail to make eye contact. Perhaps more difficult still, you may even have to forgive a speaker's lack of clarity or coherence. Rather than mentally criticizing an unpolished speaker, you may need to be sympathetic and try harder to concentrate on the message. Good listeners focus on the message, not the messenger.

Poor speakers are not the only challenge to good listening. You also need to guard against glib, well-polished speakers. Just because a speaker has an attractive style of delivery does not necessarily mean that his or her message is credible. Don't let a smooth-talking salesperson convince you to buy something without carefully considering the content of his or her message.

LISTEN WITH YOUR EYES AS WELL AS YOUR EARS

Even though we have cautioned you against letting a speaker's style of delivery distract you, don't totally ignore a speaker's body language. Nonverbal clues play a major role in communicating a message. One expert has estimated that as much as 93 percent of the emotional content of a speech is conveyed by nonverbal clues.[9] Even though this statistic does not apply in every situation, emotion is primarily communicated by unspoken messages. For example, facial expressions help identify the emotions being communicated; a speaker's posture and gestures can reinforce the intensity of the emotion.[10]

If you have trouble understanding a speaker, either because he or she speaks too softly or because he or she speaks in an unfamiliar dialect, get close enough so that you can see the speaker's mouth. A good view can increase your level of attention and improve your understanding.

MONITOR YOUR EMOTIONAL REACTION TO A MESSAGE

Heightened emotions can affect your ability to understand a message. If you become angry at a word or phrase a speaker uses, your listening comprehension decreases. Depending on their cultural backgrounds, religious convictions, and political views, listeners may become emotionally aroused by certain words. For most listeners, words that connote negative opinions about their ethnic origin, nationality, or religious views can trigger strong emotions. Cursing and obscene language are red flags for other listeners.

Yin Ping is an Asian American who has distinguished himself as a champion debater on the college debate team. One sly member of an opposing team sought to distract him by quoting a bigoted statement that disparaged Asian Americans for "taking over the country." It was tempting for Yin Ping to respond emotionally to the insult, but he kept his wits, refuted the argument, and went on to win the debate. When someone uses a word or phrase you find offensive, it's important to overcome your repugnance and continue to listen. Don't let a speaker's language close down your mind.

How can you keep your emotions in check when you hear something that sets you off? First, recognize when your emotional state is affecting your rational thoughts. Second, use the skill of self-talk to calm yourself down. Say to yourself, "I'm not going to let this anger get in the way of listening and understanding." You can also focus on your breathing for a moment to calm down.

AVOID JUMPING TO CONCLUSIONS

"Not another speech about religion," you groan to yourself as your classmate, Frank Fuller, a divinity student, gets up to speak. "He's always preaching to us." As Fuller begins his slide lecture, you slump down in your seat, prepared to be bored and bothered. Sure enough, his opening line is "The Bible: It's not what you think!" But about halfway through the speech, you start listening to Fuller and realize that he is presenting some fascinating historical evidence connected with Noah's Ark. He's not trying to convert you; he's just describing some of the archaeological evidence related to one of the stories in the Bible. At the end of the speech, your classmates give him a hearty round of applause. Now you're sorry you missed the first part of the speech.

Don't jump to conclusions prematurely. Give a speaker time to develop and support his or her main point before you decide whether you agree or disagree or whether the message has any value. As we've already noted, if you mentally criticize a speaker's style or message, your listening efficiency will decline.

BE A SELFISH LISTENER

Although it may sound crass to suggest it, being a selfish listener can help you maintain your powers of concentration. If you find your attention waning, ask yourself questions such as "What's in this for me?" and "How can I use information from this talk?" Granted, you will find more useful information in some presentations than others, but be alert to the possibility in all speeches. Find ways to benefit from the information you are listening to, and try to connect it with your own experiences and needs.

LISTEN FOR MAJOR IDEAS

In a classic study, Ralph Nichols asked both good and poor listeners what their listening strategies were.[11] The poor listeners indicated that they listened for facts, such as names and dates. The good listeners reported that they listened for major ideas and principles. Facts are useful only when you can connect them to a principle or concept. In speeches, facts as well as examples are used primarily to support major ideas. Try to mentally summarize the major idea that the specific facts support.

If you had been present on that brisk March morning in 1933 to hear Franklin Delano Roosevelt deliver his first inaugural address, you would have heard him introduce his key idea in the fourth sentence of the speech: "This great Nation will endure as it has endured, will revive and will prosper. So, first of all, let me assert my firm belief that the only thing we have to fear is fear itself." A good listener would recognize this immediately as the core of the speech.

How can you tell what the major ideas in a speech are? A speaker who is well organized or familiar with good speaking techniques will offer a preview of the major ideas early in the speech. If no preview is provided, listen for the speaker to enumerate major points: "My first point is that the history of Jackson County is evident in its various styles of architecture." Transitional phrases and a speaker's internal summaries are other clues that can help you identify the major points. If your speaker provides few overt indicators, you may have to discover them on your own. In that event, mentally summarize the ideas that are most useful to you. As suggested earlier, be a selfish listener. Treat a disorganized speech as a river with gold in the sands. Take your mental mining pan and search for the meaningful nuggets.

IDENTIFY YOUR LISTENING GOAL

If you are a typical student, you spend over 80 percent of your day involved in communication-related activities.[12] You spend about 9 percent of your communication time writing, 16 percent reading, 30 percent speaking, and at least 45 percent listening (see Figure 5.1). You listen a lot. Your challenge is to stay on course and keep your listening focused.

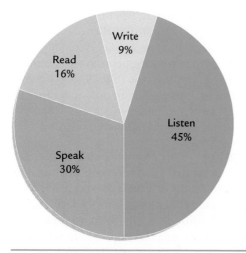

FIGURE 5.1 **What You Do with Your Communication Time**

One way to stay focused is to determine your listening purpose. There are at least four major listening goals: listening for pleasure, to empathize, to evaluate, and to gain information. Being conscious of your listening goal can help you listen more effectively. If, for example, your listening goal is simply to enjoy what you hear, you need not listen at the same intensity as when you are trying to remember what you are hearing.

Listening for Pleasure   You listen to some things just for the fun of it. You might watch TV, listen to music, go to a movie, or chitchat with a friend. You won't be tested on *Friends* reruns. Nor will you be asked to remember every joke in David Letterman's monologue. So, when listening for pleasure, just enjoy what you hear. You can, however, observe how effective speakers or entertainers gain and maintain your attention and keep you interested in their messages.

Listening to Empathize   To have empathy means to make an attempt to feel what the speaker is feeling. Usually, empathic listening occurs in one-on-one listening situations with a good friend. Sometimes, in your job, you may need to listen empathically to a client, customer, or coworker. Listening to empathize requires these essential steps:

1. **Stop.** Stop what you are doing and give your complete attention to the speaker.
2. **Look.** Make eye contact and pay attention to nonverbal cues that reveal emotions.
3. **Listen.** Pay attention to both the details of the message and the major ideas.
4. **Imagine.** Visualize how you would feel if you had experienced what the speaker experienced.
5. **Check.** Check your understanding of the message by asking questions to clarify what you heard and by summarizing what you think you heard.

Listening to Evaluate   When you evaluate a message, you are making a judgment about its content. You are interested in whether the information is reliable, true, or useful. When evaluating what you hear, the challenge is to not become so critical of the message that you miss a key point the speaker is making. Rather, you must juggle two very difficult tasks: You must make judgments as well as understand and recall the information you are hearing. Our point is this: When you are listening to a message and also evaluating it, you have to work harder than at other times to understand the speaker's message. Your biases and judgments act as noise, sometimes causing you to misunderstand the intended meaning of the message.

Listening for Information   Since elementary school, you have been in listening situations in which someone wanted you to learn something. Keys to listening for information are listening for the details of a message and making certain you link the details to major ideas. Poor listeners either listen only for facts and pieces of a message or are interested only in "the bottom line." By concentrating on both facts and major ideas, while also mentally summarizing the information you hear, you can dramatically increase your ability to remember messages. Also, remember to compare unfamiliar information to ideas and concepts with which you are familiar.

Knowing your listening goal can help you develop an appropriate listening strategy. Be conscious of what you are seeking from a message.

As a speaker, it is also important for you to know your audience's objectives. If you planned to deliver an educational lecture, but it turns out your listeners are there only for pleasure, you will have to make some quick adjustments to meet your audience's needs. Audience-centered speakers consider the listening goals of their audiences.

PRACTICE LISTENING

Because we've noted that you spend at least 45 percent of your day listening, you may wonder why we suggest that you practice listening. The reason is that listening skills do not develop automatically. You learn to swim by getting proper instruction; you're unlikely to develop good aquatic skills by just jumping in the water and flailing around. Similarly, you will learn to listen by practicing the methods we recommend.

Researchers believe that poor listeners avoid challenge. For example, they listen to and watch TV situation comedies rather than documentaries or other informative programs. Skill develops as you practice listening to speeches, music, and programs with demanding content.

UNDERSTAND YOUR LISTENING STYLE

New research suggests that not everyone listens to information the same way. There are at least four different **listening styles**—preferred ways of making sense out of spoken messages. Listening researchers Kitty Watson, Larry Barker, and James Weaver discovered that listeners tend to be either people-oriented, action-oriented, content-oriented, or time-oriented.[13] Understanding your listening style can help you become a better and more flexible listener.[14]

People-Oriented Listeners   You're a people-oriented listener if you are comfortable listening to people express feelings and emotions. It's likely that you are highly empathic and that you seek common ground with the person you are listening to. You are easily moved by poignant illustrations and anecdotes.

Action-Oriented Listeners   If you like information that is well organized, brief, and accurate, but don't like long stories or digressions from the main ideas, you're likely an action-oriented listener. The action-oriented listener wants people to get to the point and listens for actions that need to be taken. Action-oriented listeners also seem to be more skeptical than people who use other listening styles. They prefer being given evidence to support the recommendations for action.

Content-Oriented Listeners   Content-oriented listeners prefer to listen to complex information that is laced with facts and details. You're a content-oriented listener if you reject messages because they don't have adequate support. Content-oriented listeners make good judges or lawyers, because they enjoy listening to debates and hearing arguments for and against ideas.[15]

Time-Oriented Listeners You're a time-oriented listener if you like your messages delivered succinctly. Time is important to you; you want the information you hear to be presented briefly because you are busy. Time-oriented listeners don't like rambling, long-winded messages with lots of fillers. Like action-oriented listeners, they want the speaker to get to the point, but they are even more interested in saving time and getting the essential ideas in brief sound bites.

Knowing your listening style can help you better adapt to speakers who are not speaking in your preferred style. For example, if you are a time-oriented listener, and a speaker is spending more time than you'd like telling stories and meandering through the material, you'll have to tell yourself to concentrate harder on the message. If you are a people-oriented listener, and you're listening to a message that's primarily facts, principles, and ideas, you can be a better listener if you are conscious of why the message may not be holding your attention and work to focus on the message.

We've emphasized the importance of being an audience-centered speaker, but the opposite is true as well: As a listener you can increase your concentration if you adjust and adapt your listening style to the speakers you hear. The key, whether you are speaker or listener, is to ethically adapt and adjust to enhance the quality of communication.

BECOME AN ACTIVE LISTENER

An active listener is one who remains alert and mentally re-sorts, rephrases, and repeats key information when listening to a speech. You can listen to words much faster than

QUICK CHECK: *Enhance Your Listening Skills*

The Good Listener . . .	The Poor Listener . . .
Adapts to the speaker's delivery	Is easily distracted by the delivery of the speech
Looks for nonverbal clues to aid understanding	Focuses only on the words
Controls emotions	Erupts emotionally when listening
Listens before making a judgment about the value of the content	Jumps to conclusions about the value of the message
Mentally asks, "What's in this for me?"	Does not attempt to relate to the information personally
Listens for major ideas	Listens for isolated facts
Remains focused	Does not mentally summarize
Seeks opportunities to practice listening skills	Avoids listening to difficult information
Understands and adapts his or her listening style to the speaker	Is not aware of how to capitalize on his or her listening style

a speaker can speak them. Therefore, it's natural for your mind to wander. But you can use the extra time to focus on interpreting what the speaker says.

First, use your listening time to re-sort disorganized or disjointed ideas. If the speaker is rambling and throwing out unorganized ideas, seek ways to rearrange them into a new, more logical pattern. You can also rephrase or summarize what the speaker is saying. This mental activity will help stay alert so you can follow the speaker's flow of ideas. Listen for main ideas, and then put them into your own words. You are more likely to remember your mental paraphrase than the speaker's exact words.

An additional active listening strategy is to listen for "information handles" provided by the speaker. In the opening few minutes of the speech, an effective speaker should give a preview of the message; listen for this preview. During the speech, listen for the speaker to identify major ideas by using transition phrases or signposts; *signposts* occur when a speaker says, "My first point is . . . . Now, here's my second point," and so on. Finally, concentrate on the conclusion of the speech. Does the speaker clearly summarize the major ideas? Listening for the overall structure of the message as evidenced through preview, transitions, signposts, and summary statements can help you remain actively involved as a listener.

Finally, do more than just rephrase the information as you listen to it. Periodically, repeat key points you want to remember. Go back to essential ideas and restate them to yourself. If you follow these steps for active listening, you will find yourself feeling stimulated and engaged instead of tired and bored as you listen to even the dullest of speakers.

5.C Improving Your Note-Taking Skills

"What's everyone taking notes for?" wondered Carolyne, scanning the lecture hall during her U.S. history class. "Can't they remember the key points without trying to scribble them in their notebooks?" At the end of the lecture, however, Carolyne found that she was getting confused about the dates and events her professor had mentioned, and she ended up having to borrow some notes from one of her classmates.

So far, we have suggested ways to improve your listening skills. But we also recognize that you will not remember everything you listen to. It is difficult to recall the details of a lengthy speech unless you have taken notes. Coupling improved listening skills with better skill in taking notes can greatly enhance your ability to retrieve information. Try the following suggestions to improve your note-taking skills.

PREPARE

Come prepared to take notes, even if you're not sure you need to. Bring a pencil or pen and paper to every class, lecture, or meeting.

DETERMINE WHETHER YOU NEED TO TAKE NOTES

After the presentation has started, decide whether you need to take notes. If you receive a handout that summarizes the content of the message, it may be best to pay attention, concentrate on the message, and take very few notes.

DECIDE ON THE TYPE OF NOTES YOU NEED TO TAKE

If notes seem necessary, decide whether you need to outline the speech, identify facts and principles, jot down key words, or just record major ideas. Some speakers do not follow organized outline patterns, in which case it is tricky to outline the message. If you are going to take an objective test on the material, you may need to note only facts and principles. Noting key words may be enough to help you recall what was said if you are going to prepare a report for someone else to read. Or you may want to write down just major ideas. The type of notes you take will depend on how you intend to use the information you get from the speech.

MAKE YOUR NOTES MEANINGFUL

Beware of taking too many notes; the goal is to remember the message, not to transcribe it. Instead, use the re-sorting and rephrasing techniques we discussed earlier and write down only what will be meaningful to you later.

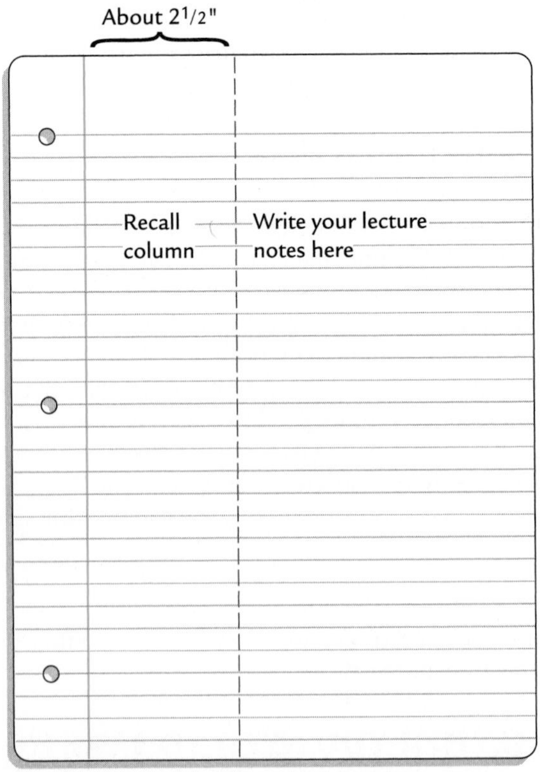

FIGURE 5.2 **Sample Page for Note-Taking**

Leave a blank area in your notes to use as a recall column.[16] A recall column is a blank margin between 2 and 3 inches wide that you leave to one side of your notes (see Figure 5.2). Don't fill this column in while you are taking notes. Use it when reviewing your notes to sift through the ideas you have written down and pull out the key material you want to remember. After you have heard the entire message, you may have a better idea of the most significant content you want to recall later.

5.d Listening and Critical Thinking

Effective listening also requires the ability to listen critically. Listening critically and thinking critically both involve a variety of skills we return to throughout this text. **Critical listening** is the process of listening to evaluate the quality, appropriateness, value, or importance of the information you hear. Related to being a critical listener is being a critical thinker. **Critical thinking** is a mental process of making judgments about the conclusions presented by what you see, hear, and read. The goal of a critical listener or critical thinker is to evaluate information to make a choice. Whether you are listening to a political candidate giving a persuasive presentation to get your vote, a radio announcer extolling the virtues of a new herbal weight-loss pill, or someone asking you to invest in a new dot.com technology company, your goal as a critical listener is to assess the quality of the information and the validity of the conclusions presented.

Effective critical listeners use not just one skill but a set of skills that help them evaluate messages. In your public-speaking class you may well listen to more than 100 speeches during your semester or term. Rather than merely listening to your classmates' speeches because that's what you're supposed to do, make an effort to practice being a critical listener. We should emphasize that being a critical listener does not mean you're only looking for what the speaker says that is wrong; we're not suggesting that you listen to a speaker only to pounce on the message and the messenger at the conclusion of the speech. Listen to identify what the speaker does that is effective, as well as to identify which conclusions don't hold up. Specifically, what does a critical listener do? Consider the following skills.

SEPARATE FACTS FROM INFERENCES

The ability to separate facts from inferences is one of the most basic critical thinking and listening skills. **Facts** are based on something that has been proven true by direct observation. For example, it has been directly observed that water boils at 212 degrees Fahrenheit, that the direction of the magnetic north pole can be found by consulting a compass, and that U.S. presidents have been inaugurated on January 20 every four years for several decades. An **inference** is a conclusion based on partial information, or an evaluation that has not been directly observed. You infer that your favorite sports team will win the championship or that it will rain tomorrow. You can also infer, if more Republicans than Democrats are elected to Congress, that the next president might be a Republican. But you can only know this for a *fact* after the presidential election. Facts are in the realm of certainty; inferences are in the realm of probability and opinion—where most arguments advanced by public speakers reside. A critical listener knows that when a politician running for office claims, "It's a fact that my opponent is not qualified to be elected," this statement is *not* a fact, but an inference.

EVALUATE THE QUALITY OF EVIDENCE

Evidence consists of the facts, examples, opinions, and statistics that a speaker uses to support a conclusion. Researchers have documented that the key element in swaying a jury is the quality and quantity of the evidence presented to support a case.[17] Without credible supporting evidence, it would not be wise to agree with a speaker's conclusion.

What should you listen for when trying to decide if evidence is credible? If, for example, a speaker says, "It's a fact that this herbal weight-loss pill helps people lose weight," your job as a listener is to determine if that statement is, in fact, a fact. As we've just discussed, a fact is something that has been proven with direct observation to be true. The speaker has an obligation to provide evidence to support the statement asserted.

Some speakers support a conclusion with examples. But if the examples aren't typical, or only one or two examples are offered, or other known examples differ from the one the speaker is using, then you should question the conclusion.

Another form of evidence a speaker might use to convince you is an opinion. Simply stated, an opinion is a quoted comment from someone. The best opinions come from reliable, credible sources. What makes a source credible? A credible source is someone who has the credentials, experience, and skill to make an observation about the topic at hand. Listen for whom a speaker cites when quoting an expert on a subject.

A fourth kind of evidence often used, especially with a skeptical listener, is statistics. A statistic is a number that summarizes a collection of examples. Some of the same kinds of questions that should be raised about other forms of evidence should be raised about statistics: Are the statistics reliable, unbiased, recent, representative, and valid?

Here we've introduced you to the importance of *listening for* good evidence. Because evidence is an important element of public speaking, we'll provide more detailed information about how to *use* evidence when we discuss using supporting material and using evidence to persuade.

EVALUATE THE UNDERLYING LOGIC AND REASONING

An effective critical listener listens not only for evidence, but also for the overall structure of the logic, or argument, the speaker uses to reach a conclusion. **Logic** is a formal system of rules applied to reach a conclusion. A speaker is logical if he or she offers appropriate evidence to reach a valid, well-reasoned conclusion. For example, Angela was trying to convince her listeners to take Slimlean as a weight-loss herb by pointing out that many stores sell this diet product, but that is not a strong logical framework for her conclusion. Just because Slimlean is readily available does not mean that it's effective and safe.

Reasoning is the process of drawing a conclusion from evidence within the logical framework of the arguments. Can we reasonably conclude that anyone can lose weight by taking Slimlean, simply because it's available in many stores? The evidence very likely does not support this conclusion. When a speaker is seeking to change your behavior, listen especially carefully to the logic or structure of the arguments presented. Is the speaker trying to convince you to do something by offering one or two specific examples? Or is the speaker reaching a conclusion based on a fundamental principle such as "All herbal diet medicine will cause you to lose weight"? The critical listener appropriately reviews the logic and reasoning used to reach a conclusion. When we discuss reasoning fallacies, we will elaborate on different types of reasoning and identify several ways speakers misuse logic, reasoning, and evidence.

You might reasonably suspect that a primary goal of a public-speaking class would be to enhance your speaking skill, and you'd be right. But in addition to becoming a better speaker, a study of communication principles and skills should also help you become a better *consumer* of messages. Becoming a critical listener and thinker is an important benefit you will enjoy by learning about how messages are constructed. But is there evidence that learning about critical listening and thinking will be beneficial? In fact, researchers have found that students who complete any communication course, such as debate, argumentation, or public speaking, are likely to show improved critical thinking ability. The introduction to critical listening and thinking skills presented here is reinforced throughout the rest of the book by discussions of how to become an audience-centered public speaker.

5.e Analyzing and Evaluating Speeches

Your critical thinking and listening skills will help you evaluate not only the speeches of others but also your own speeches. When you evaluate something, you judge its value and appropriateness. To make a judgment about the value of something, it's important to use criteria for what is and is not effective or appropriate.

Rhetorical criticism is the process of using a method or standards to evaluate the effectiveness and appropriateness of messages. Rhetorical critics often point to educator and philosopher John Dewey's description of criticism: "Criticism . . . is not fault-finding. It is not pointing out evils to be reformed. It is judgment engaged in discriminating among values. It is talking through as to what is better and worse . . . with some consciousness of why the worse is worse."[18] A critic not only evaluates a message but also helps *illuminate* it.[19] To illuminate is to shine a metaphorical light on the message to help others better interpret it. We'll first suggest criteria for evaluating messages and then offer specific strategies for sharing your evaluations with others.

UNDERSTANDING CRITERIA FOR EVALUATING SPEECHES

What makes a speech good? For more than 2,000 years, rhetorical scholars have been debating this question. Our purpose here is not to take you through the centuries of dialogue and debate about this issue but to offer some practical ways to help you evaluate your own messages as well as the messages of others.

Your public-speaking teacher will probably have you use an evaluation form that lists the precise criteria for evaluating your speeches. Figure 5.3 lists key questions to use in evaluating any speech. The questions reflect the audience-centered model of public speaking.

Underlying any list of what a good speaker should do are two fundamental goals: *Any speech should be both effective and ethical.* The mission of the National Communication Association mirrors these two goals—to promote effective and ethical communication. These two requirements can translate into general criteria for evaluating speeches you give as well as those you hear.

The Message Should Be Effective   To be effective, the message of a speech should be understandable to listeners and should achieve its intended purpose.[20] Public speaking is sometimes called *public communication*. A goal of any communication effort is to create a common understanding of the message on the part of both the sender and the receiver. The words *common* and *communication* resemble each other.

If listeners fail to comprehend the speaker's ideas, the speech fails. Even more difficult than saying something is saying something a listener understands. In this course you'll learn an array of principles and strategies to help you develop a common understanding between you and your audience. The process of communicating to be understood is anchored first and foremost in considering the needs of your listeners. As you listen to speeches, a fundamental criterion for determining whether the message is a good one is whether you understand the message.

Another way to evaluate the effectiveness of a message is to assess whether it achieved its intended goal. When you communicate with an audience, you want to achieve a goal or accomplish something. Typical general goals of public speaking are to inform, to persuade, and to entertain. The challenge in using this criterion in evaluating speeches is that you may not always know the speaker's true intent. Often the best you can do is try to determine the purpose by being a careful listener.

The Message Should Be Ethical   A good speaker is an ethical speaker. Ethics are the beliefs, values, and moral principles by which people determine what is right or wrong. An ethical public speaker tells the truth, gives credit for ideas and words where credit is due, and doesn't plagiarize. If a speaker's message is clearly understood by the audience and also gets the reaction the speaker desired but uses unethical means to achieve the goal, it may be an effective message, but it is not an appropriate message.

You will probably speak to audiences with a wide array of cultural backgrounds. Regardless of their cultural tradition, your listeners hold an underlying ethical code. Although not every culture has the same ethical rules, some generalizations about ethics seem to transcend culture. All religions of the world, for example, have a moral code that provides a framework for how to respect the rights of others. Christians and Jews share the values described in the Ten Commandments. Christians rely on the Golden Rule, "Do unto others what you would have others do unto you." Buddhists value the admonition that "One should seek for others the happiness one desires for one's self."

Audience Orientation
- [ ] Did the speaker make a specific effort to adapt to the audience?

Topic Selection
- [ ] Was the topic appropriate for the audience, the occasion, and the speaker?
- [ ] Was the speech narrowed to fit the time limits?

Purpose
- [ ] Was the general purpose clear?
- [ ] Was the specific purpose appropriate for the audience?
- [ ] Was the purpose achieved?

Central Idea
- [ ] Was the central idea clear enough to be summarized in one sentence?

Main Ideas
- [ ] Were the main ideas clearly identified in the introduction of the speech, developed in the body of the speech, and summarized in the conclusion of the speech?

Supporting Material
- [ ] Did the speaker use varied and interesting supporting material?
- [ ] Did the speaker use effective and appropriate evidence to support conclusions?
- [ ] Did the speaker use credible supporting material?

Organization
- [ ] Did the speech have a clear introduction that caught attention, provided a preview of the speech, and established the speaker's credibility?
- [ ] Did the speaker organize the body of the speech in a logical way?
- [ ] Did the speaker use transitions, summaries, and signposts to clarify the organization?
- [ ] Did the speaker appropriately summarize the major ideas and provide closure to the speech during the conclusion?

Speech Rehearsal
- [ ] Did the speech sound as though it was well rehearsed?
- [ ] Did the speaker seem familiar with the speech content?

Speech Delivery
- [ ] Did the speaker make appropriate eye contact with the audience?
- [ ] Did the speaker use appropriate volume and vocal variation?
- [ ] Did the speaker use gestures and posture appropriately?
- [ ] Did the speaker use presentation aids that were easy to see and handled effectively?
- [ ] Did the speaker use presentation aids that were of high quality?

FIGURE 5.3 **A Checklist of Effective Public-Speaking Characteristics**

For Hindus, "Do nothing to others that would cause pain if done to you" and for Muslims, "No one of you is a believer until he desires for his brother that which he desires for himself" express a similar perspective on considering the needs of others. In essence, these precepts state the value of being audience-centered by considering how others would like to be treated. An ethical public speaker focuses not only on achieving the goal of the message but on doing so while being sensitive and responsive to listeners.

IDENTIFYING AND ANALYZING RHETORICAL STRATEGIES

Rhetoric is the use of symbols to achieve goals. **Symbols** are words, images (a flag, a cross, a six-pointed star), and behaviors that create meaning for others. Whether you use them in an interview to convince an employer to hire you for a job or hear them in a TV commercial to persuade you to vote for a presidential candidate, words and images that symbolically inform and persuade are all around you. Public speakers, too, are rhetoricians who use symbols to achieve their goals. The study of rhetoric is centuries old. Appendix B provides a brief history of the classical origins of rhetorical study.

Studying public speaking not only can make you a better speaker but can help you be a better consumer of the speeches you hear. One way to enhance your listening skill and become more mindfully aware of how messages influence your behavior is to analyze the rhetorical strategies a speaker is using. **Rhetorical strategies** are methods and techniques that speakers employ to achieve their speaking goals. It's especially important to be aware of how some speakers may use rhetorical techniques to deceive or manipulate you. Speakers sometimes use unethical strategies to achieve their goals, such as misusing evidence, relying too heavily on emotion to persuade, or fabricating information.

Rhetorician Robert Rowland offers a simple but comprehensive framework for describing and analyzing rhetorical messages: Be conscious of the goal of the message, its organization, the speaker's role, the overall tone of the message, the intended audience, and the techniques the speaker uses to achieve the goal.[21] By considering the questions in Table 5.1, you can begin to understand how any speaker is using rhetorical strategies to achieve his or her goal. Using these questions will help you figure out what any speaker is really saying and better understand the techniques he or she is using. Whether it's a speaker in your public-speaking class, the president delivering a State of the Union address, a member of the clergy delivering a sermon, or a parent addressing the school board, each speaker is using rhetorical strategies to achieve a goal. The more clearly you can identify and analyze the speaker's methods, the more effectively you can assess whether the message and the messenger are worthy of your support. Although this particular chapter focuses on being a better listener or consumer of rhetoric, the entire book is designed to help you be a more discerning rhetorical critic of the messages you hear.

TABLE 5.1	Evaluating a Speaker's Rhetorical Strategies
Speech Goal	What is the overall goal of the message? What are the main points or themes of the message? What is the speaker asking the audience to do?
Speech Organization	What is the overall organizational structure of the message? How does the introduction set the tone for the message? How does the conclusion summarize the message and point listeners to what the speaker wants to happen next? How does the body of the speech support the primary objective of the speech?
Speaker Role	What is the role of the speaker? Is the speaker assuming either an explicit or an implied role, such as authority figure or expert on the topic addressed? What kind of relationship has the speaker established with the audience?
Speaker Tone	What is the overall tone, or "feel," of the message? How does the speaker use language to establish a tone? How does the speaker use stories and other illustrations to establish a tone? How does the speaker deliver the message to establish a tone?
Audience	Who is the intended audience of the message? Who is present to hear the message? Is the message aimed at others who are not present?
Speaker Techniques	What strategies or techniques does the speaker use to achieve the speech goals? • Does the speaker use rational, logical arguments? Stories? Artistic language? • Does the speaker appeal to the needs and values of the listeners? • Does the speaker develop high credibility? • Does the speaker attempt to move listeners by confronting them?

GIVING FEEDBACK TO OTHERS

As you enhance your skills of listening to messages and identifying the rhetorical strategies a speaker uses, you may be asked to evaluate the speeches of others and provide feedback to them. Both the checklist of speech evaluation criteria in Figure 5.3 and the framework of questions to use in analyzing rhetorical strategies in Table 5.1 can serve you well as you evaluate others' messages. Your instructor may provide you with a speech evaluation form that will also help you focus on and evaluate essential elements of public speechmaking.

When you're invited to critique your classmates, your feedback will be more effective if you keep some general principles in mind. The word *criticism* comes from a Greek word meaning "to judge or discuss." Therefore, as noted earlier, to criticize a speech is to discuss the speech—identifying both strengths and aspects that could be improved. Effective criticism stems from developing a genuine interest in the speaker rather than from seeking to find fault. When given the opportunity to critique your classmates, supplement the evaluations you provide on your evaluation form with the following kinds of feedback.

1. Be descriptive. In a neutral way, describe what you saw the speaker doing. Act as a mirror for the speaker to help him or her become aware of gestures and other nonverbal signals of which he or she may not be aware. (If you are watching a videotape of the speech together, you can help point out behaviors.) Avoid providing a list of only your likes and dislikes; describe what you observe.

> Effective: Stan, I noticed that about 50 percent of the time you had direct eye contact with your listeners.
>
> Less Effective: Your eye contact was lousy.

2. Be specific. When you describe what you see a speaker doing, make sure your descriptions are precise enough to give the speaker a clear image of your perceptions. Saying that a speaker had "poor delivery" doesn't give him or her much information—it's only a general evaluative comment. Be as specific and thoughtful as you can.

> Effective: Dawn, your use of color on your overhead transparency helped to keep my attention.
>
> Less Effective: I liked your visuals.

3. Be positive. Begin and end your feedback with positive comments. Beginning with negative comments immediately puts the speaker on the defensive and can create so much internal noise that he or she stops listening. Starting and ending with positive comments engender less defensiveness. Some teachers call this approach the "feedback sandwich." First, tell the speaker something he or she did well. This will let the speaker know you're not an enemy who's trying to shoot holes in his or her performance. Then share a suggestion or two that may help the speaker improve the presentation. End your evaluation with another positive comment or restate what you liked best about the presentation.

| Effective: | Gabe, I thought your opening statistic was very effective in catching my attention. You also maintained direct eye contact when you delivered it. Your overall organizational pattern would have been clearer to me if you had used more signposts and transition statements. Or perhaps you could use a visual aid to summarize the main points. You did a good job of summarizing your three points in your conclusion. I also liked the way you ended your speech by making a reference to your opening statistics. |
| Less Effective: | I got lost when you were in the body of your speech. I couldn't figure out what your major ideas were. I also didn't know when you made the transition between the introduction and the body of your speech. Your intro and conclusion were good, but the organization of the speech was weak. |

4. Be constructive. Give the speaker some suggestions or alternatives for improvement. It's not especially helpful to rattle off a list of things you don't like, without providing some suggestions for improvement. As a student of public speaking, your comments should reflect your growing skill and sophistication in the speech-making process.

| Effective: | Jerry, I thought your speech had several good statistics and examples that suggest you spent a lot of time in the library researching your topic. I think you could add credibility to your message if you shared your sources with the listener. Your vocal quality was effective, and you had considerable variation in your pitch and tone, but at times the speech rate was a little fast for me. A slower rate would help me catch some of the details of your message. |
| Less Effective: | You spoke too fast. I had no idea whom you were quoting. |

5. Be sensitive. "Own" your feedback by using *I*-statements rather than *you*-statements. An *I-statement* is a way of phrasing your feedback so that it is clear that your comments reflect your personal point of view. "I found my attention drifting during the body of your speech" is an example of an I-statement. A *you-statement* is a less sensitive way of describing someone's behavior by implying that the other person did something wrong. "You didn't summarize very well in your conclusion" is an example of a you-statement. A better way to make the same point is to say, "I wasn't sure I understood the key ideas you mentioned in your conclusion." Here's another example:

| Effective: | Mark, I found myself so distracted by your gestures that I had trouble focusing on the message. |
| Less Effective: | Your gestures were distracting and awkward. |

6. Be realistic. Provide usable information. Provide feedback about aspects of the presentation that the speaker can improve rather than about things he or she cannot control. Maybe you have heard this advice: "Never try to teach a pig to sing. It wastes your time. It doesn't sound pretty. And it annoys the pig." Saying "You're too short to be seen over the lectern," "Your lisp doesn't lend itself to public speaking," or "You looked nervous" is not constructive—comments like these will just annoy or frustrate the speaker, because they refer to things the speaker can't do much to change. Concentrate on behaviors over which the speaker has control.

Effective: Taka, I thought your closing quote was effective in summarizing your key ideas, but it didn't end your speech on an uplifting note. Another quote from Khalil Gibran that I'll share with you after class would also summarize your key points and provide a positive affirmation of your message. You may want to try it if you give this speech again.

Less Effective: Your voice isn't well suited to public speaking.

As you provide feedback, whether in your public-speaking class or to a friend who asks you for a reaction to his or her speech, remember that the goal of feedback is to offer descriptive and specific information that helps a speaker build confidence and skill.

GIVING FEEDBACK TO YOURSELF

While you are collecting feedback from your instructor, classmates, family, and friends, keep in mind that you are the most important critic of your speeches. The ultimate goal of public-speaking instruction is to learn principles and skills that enable you to be your own best critic. As you rehearse your speech, use self-talk to comment about the choices you make as a speaker. Learn to recognize when to make changes on your feet, in the middle of a speech. For example, if you notice that your audience just isn't interested in the facts and statistics you are sharing, you may decide to support your points with a couple of stories instead. After your speech, take time to reflect on both the speech's virtues and the areas for improvement in your speechmaking skill. We encourage you to consider the following principles to enhance your own self-critiquing skills.

Look for and Reinforce Your Skills and Speaking Abilities   Try to recognize your strengths and skills as a public speaker. Note how your audience analysis, organization, and delivery were effective in achieving your objectives. Such positive reflection can reinforce the many skills you are learning in this course. Resist the temptation to be too harsh or critical of your speaking skill.

Evaluate Your Effectiveness Based on Your Specific Speaking Situation and Audience   Throughout the book we offer many suggestions and tips for improving your speaking skill. We also stress, however, that these prescriptions should be considered in light of your specific audience. Don't be a slave to rules. If you are giving a pep talk to the Little League team you are coaching, you might not have to construct an attention-getting opening statement. Be flexible. Public speaking is an art as well as a science. Give yourself permission to adapt principles and practices to specific speech situations.

Identify One or Two Areas for Improvement   After each speaking opportunity, identify what you did right, then give yourself a suggestion or two for ways to improve. You may be tempted to overwhelm yourself with a long list of things you need to do as a speaker. Rather than trying to work on a dozen goals, concentrate on two or three, or maybe even just one key skill you would like to develop. To help you make your decision, keep in mind the audience-centered model of public speaking.

Ultimately, the goal of this course is to teach you how to listen to your own commentary and become your own expert in shaping and polishing your speaking style.

Summary

- Listening is a process that involves selecting, attending, understanding, and remembering.

- Some of the barriers that keep people from listening at peak efficiency include information overload, personal concerns, outside distractions, prejudice, differing speech and thought rates, and receiver apprehension.

- To overcome these barriers and improve your listening skill: Adapt to the speaker's delivery, listen with your eyes as well as your ears, monitor your emotional reaction, avoid jumping to conclusions, be a selfish listener, listen for major ideas, identify your listening goal, practice listening, and become an active listener.

- Effective notes can help you retain information that you hear.

- Learn the criteria for good speeches, and learn to give and receive evaluative feedback on speeches and exchanges with your peers and instructors.

Key Terms

attend (p. 64)
critical listening (p. 77)
critical thinking (p. 77)
evidence (p. 78)
fact (p. 77)
inference (p. 77)
listening style (p. 73)
logic (p. 78)
prejudice (p. 67)

reasoning (p. 79)
receiver apprehension (p. 68)
remember (p. 64)
rhetorical criticism (p. 79)
rhetorical strategy (p. 82)
select (p. 64)
symbol (p. 82)
understand (p. 64)

A QUESTION OF ETHICS

As an ethical listener, what can you do to be less distracted by the delivery and emotional elements of a speaker's message and more focused on the substance or content of the message? Explain your answer.

CHAPTER 6

Analyzing Your Audience

I t seemed harmless enough. Charles Williams was asked to speak to the Cub Scout pack about his experience as a young cowboy in Texas. The boys were learning to tie knots, and Williams, a retired rancher, could tell them how to make a lariat and how to make and use other knots.

His speech started out well. He seemed to be adapting to his young audience. However, for some reason, Williams thought the boys might also enjoy learning how to exterminate the screw worm, a pesky parasite of cattle. In the middle of his talk about roping cattle, he launched into a presentation about the techniques for sterilizing male screw worms. The parents in the audience fidgeted in their seats. The 7- and 8-year-olds didn't have the foggiest idea what a screw worm was, what sterilization was, or how male and female screw worms mate.

For of the three elements in speechmaking—speaker, subject, and person addressed—it is the last one, the hearer, that determines the speech's end and object.

—Aristotle

It got worse; his audience analysis skills deteriorated even more. Williams next talked about castrating cattle. Twenty-five minutes later, he finally finished the screw-worm–castration speech. The parents were relieved. Fortunately, the boys hadn't understood it.

Williams's downfall resulted from his failure to analyze his audience. He may have had a clear objective in mind, but he hadn't considered the background or knowledge of his listeners. Audience analysis is essential for any successful speech.

6.a Becoming an Audience-Centered Speaker

The key elements in communication are source, receiver, message, and channel. All four elements are important, but perhaps the most important is the receiver. In public speaking, the receiver is the audience, and the audience is the reason for a speech event.

The model shown in Figure 6.1 provides an overview of the entire process of speech preparation and delivery. We re-emphasize here the concept of public speaking as an audience-centered activity. At each stage in crafting your speech, you must be mindful of your audience. The audience-analysis skills and techniques that we present in this chapter will help you throughout the public-speaking process. Consciousness of your audience will be important as you select a topic, determine the purpose of your speech, develop your central idea, generate main ideas, gather supporting material, firm up your organization, rehearse, and deliver your speech.

When you think of your audience, don't think of some undifferentiated mass of people waiting to hear your message. Instead, think of individuals. Public speaking is the process of speaking to a group of individuals, each with a unique point of view. Your challenge as an audience-centered public speaker is to find out as much as you can about these individuals. From your knowledge of the individuals, you can then develop a general profile of your listeners.

FIGURE 6.1　**Audience analysis is central to the speechmaking process.**

HOW TO: *Become an Audience-Centered Speaker*

- Gather information about your audience. You can gather some information informally just by observing your listeners or asking general questions about them. Or you can take a more formal approach and administer a survey to obtain more specific information about them.
- Analyze the information you have gathered. To analyze information is to categorize and evaluate what you have gathered to determine your listeners' psychological profile, as well as to consider the occasion at which you are speaking.
- Once you have gathered and analyzed information about your audience, use the information to ethically adapt to your listeners. As our audience-centered model illustrates, each decision you make when designing and delivering your message should consider the needs and backgrounds of your audience. We'll talk about these three steps in more detail and discuss the process of analyzing your audience before, during, and after you speak.

6.b Gathering Information About Your Audience

As an audience-centered speaker, you should try to find out as much as you can about your audience before planning your speech. You may wonder, "How do I go about gathering information about my audience?" There are two approaches you can take: an informal one and a formal one.

GATHERING INFORMATION INFORMALLY

The simplest way to gather information about your audience informally is just to observe them and ask questions before you speak. Informal observations can be especially important in helping you assess obvious demographic characteristics. **Demographics** are statistical information on population characteristics such as age, race, gender, sexual orientation, educational level, and ideological or religious views of an audience. For example, you can observe how many members of your audience are male or female, and you can also make some inferences from their appearance about their education level, ethnic or cultural traits, and approximate age.

If, for example, you were going to address your local PTA meeting about a new store you were opening to help students and parents develop science projects, you could attend a meeting before your speaking date. You might note the general percentage of men and women in the audience and the ages of the parents who attended. You could also ask whether most parents who show up for PTA meetings are parents of elementary, middle-school, or high-school students. Knowing these key pieces of information would help you tailor your speech to address your listeners' interests. Also, talk with people who know something about the audience you will be addressing. If you are invited to speak to a group you have not spoken to before, ask the person who invited you some general questions about the audience members: What is their average age? What are their political affiliations? What are their religious beliefs? What are their attitudes toward your topic? Try to get as much information as possible about your audience before you give your speech.

GATHERING INFORMATION FORMALLY

Rather than relying only on inferences drawn from casual observation and conversations with others, you may, if time and resources permit, want to conduct a more formal survey of your listeners. A survey allows you to gather both demographic information and information about what audience members like or dislike, believe to be true or false, or think is good or bad about the topic or issues you are discussing. To gather information formally requires developing a well-written survey or questionnaire (see Figure 6.2).

How do you develop a formal survey? First, decide what you want to know about your audience that you don't already know. Let your topic and the speaking occasion help you determine the kinds of questions you should pose. Once you have an idea of what you would like to know, you can ask your potential audience straightforward questions about such demographic information as age, sex, occupation, and member-

---

Demographic Audience-Analysis Questionnaire

1. Name (optional): _____

2. Sex: Male ☐   Female ☐

3. Occupation: _____

4. Religious affiliation: _____

5. Marital status: Married ☐   Single ☐   Divorced ☐

6. Major in school: _____

7. Years of schooling beyond high school: _____

8. Annual income: _____

9. Age: _____

10. Ethnic background: _____

11. Hometown and state: _____

12. Political affiliation: Republican ☐   Democrat ☐   Other ☐   None ☐

13. Membership in professional or fraternal organizations: _____

FIGURE 6.2 **Demographic Audience-Analysis Questionnaire**

ships in professional organizations. You can modify the sample questionnaire in Figure 6.2 according to your audience and topic. If your topic is the best approach to finding a rental apartment and you are speaking in a suburban area, find out how many members of your audience own a home and how many are presently living in an apartment. You may also want to ask how they found their current apartment, how many are now searching for an apartment, and how many anticipate searching for one. Answers to these questions can give you useful information about your audience and may also provide examples to use in your presentation.

Although knowing your audience's demographics can be helpful, again we caution you that inferences based on generalized information may lead to faulty conclusions. For example, it might seem reasonable to infer that if your audience consists mainly of 18- to 22-year-olds, they will not be deeply interested in retirement programs. But unless you have talked to them specifically about these topics, your inference may be incorrect. Whenever possible, ask specific questions about audience members' attitudes.

To gather useful information about audience members' attitudes, beliefs, and values, you can ask two basic types of questions. Open-ended questions allow for unrestricted answers, without limiting answers to choices or alternatives. Use open-ended questions when you want more detailed information from your audience. Essay questions, for example, are open-ended. Closed-ended questions offer several alternatives from which to choose. Multiple-choice, true/false, and agree/disagree questions are examples of closed-ended questions.

After you develop the questions, it is wise to test them on a small group of people to make sure they are clear and will encourage meaningful answers. Suppose you plan to address an audience about in-school health clinics that dispense birth-control pills to high-school students. The sample questions in Figure 6.3 on page 94 illustrate various open and closed questions that might yield useful audience information.

ANALYZE INFORMATION ABOUT YOUR AUDIENCE

Audience analysis is the process of examining information about the listeners who will hear your speech. That analysis helps you adapt your message so that your listeners will respond as you wish. You analyze audiences every day as you speak to others or join in group conversations. For example, most of us do not deliberately make offensive comments to family members or friends. Rather, we analyze our audience (often very quickly), and then we adapt our messages to the individuals with whom we are speaking. Public speaking involves the same sort of process.

Precisely what do you look for when analyzing the information that you have gathered about your audience? Consider answering the following questions:

- How are audience members similar to one another?

- How are audience members different from one another?

- Based on their similarities and differences, how can I establish common ground with the audience?

To establish common ground, look for what you and your audience members have in common, and then find ways to maximize similarities and minimize differ-

Open-Ended Questions

1. What are your feelings about having high-school health clinics dispense birth-control pills?
2. What are your reactions to the current rate of teenage pregnancy?
3. What would you do if you discovered your daughter was receiving birth-control pills from her high-school health clinic?

Closed-Ended Questions

1. Are you in favor of school-based health clinics dispensing birth-control pills to high-school students?
   Yes ☐   No ☐
2. Birth-control pills should be given to high-school students who ask for them in school-based health clinics. (Circle the statement that best describes your feeling.)
   Agree strongly   Agree   Undecided   Disagree   Disagree strongly
3. Check the statement that most closely reflects your feelings about school-based health clinics and birth-control pills.
   ☐ Students should receive birth-control pills in school-based health clinics whenever they want them, without their parents' knowledge.
   ☐ Students should receive birth-control pills in school-based health clinics whenever they want them, as long as they have their parents' permission.
   ☐ I am not certain whether students should receive birth-control pills in school-based health clinics.
   ☐ Students should not receive birth-control pills in school-based health clinics.
4. Rank the following statements from most desirable (1) to least desirable (5).
   ☐ Birth-control pills should be available to all high-school students in school-based health clinics, whenever students want them, and even if their parents are not aware that their daughters are taking the pills.
   ☐ Birth-control pills should be available to all high-school students in school-based health clinics, but only if their parents have given permission.
   ☐ Birth-control pills should be available to high-school students without their parents' knowledge, but not in school-based health clinics.
   ☐ Birth-control pills should be available to high-school students, but not in school-based health clinics, and only with their parents' permission.
   ☐ Birth-control pills should not be available to high-school students.

FIGURE 6.3   Sample Questions

ences between you and your listeners. Keep in mind that although each audience member is a unique individual with his or her own characteristics and preferences, when analyzing your audience, you are seeking to identify major trends in similarities or dissimilarities.

When looking for similarities, consider the following questions. What ethnic and cultural characteristics do audience members have in common? Are they all about the same age? Are they all from the same geographic region? Do they (or did they) attend the same college or university? Do they have similar levels of education? Do they all like the same kinds of things? Answering these and other questions will help you develop your own ideas and relate your message to your listeners.

Besides noting similarities, you can also note differences among your audience members. It is unlikely that audience members for the speeches you give in class will have similar backgrounds. The range of cultural backgrounds, ethnic ties, and religious traditions among students at most colleges and universities is rapidly expanding. You can also note a range of differences in age and gender, as well as perspectives about your topic.

Similarities between you and your audience can help you establish common ground—but sometimes the only common ground you may find is that both you and your listeners believe the issue you are addressing is a serious problem; you may have different views about the best solution. If, for example, you were addressing a group of people who were mostly in favor of increasing taxes to pay teachers a higher salary, but you were opposed to tax increases, you could establish common ground by noting that both you and your listeners value education and want high-quality teachers in the classroom. Use the information from your audience analysis to build bridges between you and your audience. In the discussion ahead, we'll offer additional strategies for establishing common ground with your listeners.

ADAPT TO YOUR AUDIENCE

Audience adaptation is the process of ethically using information you've gathered when analyzing your audience to help your audience clearly understand your message and to achieve your speaking objective. If you only analyze your audience but don't use the information to customize your message, the information you've gathered will be of little value. Using your skill to learn about your listeners and then to adapt to them can help you maintain your listeners' attention and make them more receptive to your ideas.

Here's an example of how analyzing and adapting to others works: Mike spent a glorious spring break at Daytona Beach. He and three friends piled in a car and headed for a week of adventure. When he returned from the beach, sunburned and fatigued from merrymaking, people asked how his holiday went. He described his escapades to his best friend, his mother, and his communication professor.

To his best friend, he bragged, "We partied all night and slept on the beach all day. It was great!" He informed his mother, "It was good to relax after the hectic pace of college." And he told his professor, "It was mentally invigorating to have time to think things out." It was the same vacation—but how different the messages were! Mike adapted his message to the people he addressed; he had analyzed his audiences.

When you are speaking in public, you should use the same process Mike used in reporting on his spring break. The principle is simple, yet powerful: An effective public speaker is audience-centered. Several key questions can help you formulate an effective approach to your audience:

To whom am I speaking?

What does my audience expect from me?

What topic would be most suitable to my audience?

What is my objective?

What kind of information should I share with my audience?

How should I present the information to them?

How can I gain and hold their attention?

What kind of examples would work best?

What language or linguistic differences do audience members have?

What method of organizing information will be most effective?

Being audience-centered does not mean you should tell your listeners only what they want to hear, or that you should fabricate information simply to please your audience or achieve your goal. If you adapt to your audience by abandoning your own values and sense of truth, then you will become an unethical speaker rather than an audience-centered one. It was President Truman who pondered, "I wonder how far Moses would have gone if he'd taken a poll in Egypt?" The audience-centered speaker adjusts his or her topic, purpose, central idea, main ideas, supporting materials, organization, and even delivery of the speech so as to encourage the audience to listen to his or her ideas. The goal is to make the audience come away from the speaking situation, if not persuaded, then at least feeling thoughtful rather than offended or hostile.

In this overview of how to become an audience-centered speaker, we've pointed out the importance of gathering information, analyzing it to establish common ground, and then using the information to ethically adapt to your listeners. Now we'll discuss these ideas in more detail. You'll want to gather and analyze information and use it to adapt to your listeners at three stages of the speechmaking process: before you speak, as you speak, and after you speak.

6.c Analyzing Your Audience Before You Speak

Learning about your audience members' backgrounds and attitudes can help you in selecting a topic, defining a purpose, and developing an outline, and in other speech-related activities. It is important to analyze your audience before doing anything else. We will discuss three basic dimensions you can use for prespeech analysis:

1. Demographic audience analysis
2. Psychological audience analysis
3. Situational audience analysis

DEMOGRAPHIC AUDIENCE ANALYSIS

A basic approach to analyzing an audience is to identify its demographic makeup. *Demographics* are statistics on population characteristics such as age, race, gender, educational level, and religious views. In essence, demographic information provides clues to help you determine how to adapt to your listeners. Let's consider how **demographic audience analysis** can help you better understand your audience.

Age   Although you must use caution in generalizing from only one factor such as age, that information can suggest the kinds of examples, humor, illustrations, and other types of supporting material to use in your speech. For example, many students in your public-speaking class will probably be in their late teens or early twenties. Some, however, may be older. The younger students may know the latest rap performers or musicians, for example, but the older ones may not be familiar with Ludacris, UGK, or OutKast. If you are going to give a talk on rap music, you will have to explain who the performers are and describe or demonstrate their style if you want all the members of your class to understand what you are talking about.

Gender   Josh began his speech by thanking his predominantly female audience for taking time from their busy schedules to attend his presentation on managing personal finances. Not a bad way to begin a talk. He continued, however, by noting that their job of raising children, keeping their homes clean, and feeding their families was among the most important tasks in America. Josh thought he was paying his audience a compliment. He did not consider that today most women work outside the home as well as in it. Many of his listeners were insulted. Many of his listeners stopped being listeners.

AVOID GENDER STEREOTYPES.   A key question to ask when considering your audience is, "What is the ratio of males to females?" No matter what the mix, avoid making sweeping judgments based on gender stereotypes. A person's sex is determined by biology, as reflected in his or her anatomy and reproductive systems; someone is born either male or female. **Gender** is the culturally constructed and psychologically based perception of one's self as feminine or masculine. A person's gender-role identity, which falls somewhere on the continuum from masculine to feminine, is learned or socially reinforced by others as well as by the person's own personality and life experiences; genetics also plays a part in shaping gender-role identity. Try to ensure that your remarks reflect sensitivity to diversity in your listeners' point of view.

AVOID SEXIST LANGUAGE.   One goal of an audience-centered speaker is to avoid sexist language or remarks. A sexist perspective stereotypes or prejudges how someone will react based on his or her sex. Take time to educate yourself about what words, phrases, or perspectives are likely to offend or create psychological noise for your listeners. Think carefully about the implications of words or phrases you take for granted. For example, many people still use the words *ladies* or *matrons* without thinking about their connotations in U.S. culture. Be especially wary about jokes. Many are derogatory to one sex or the other. Avoid stereotypes in your stories and examples as well.

BE INCLUSIVE. Make your language and your message as inclusive as possible. If you are speaking to a mixed audience, make sure your speech relates to all your listeners, not just to one gender. If, for example, you decided to discuss breast cancer, you could note that men, too, can be victims of breast cancer and that the lives of husbands, fathers, and brothers of victims are affected by the disease.

AVOID MAKING ASSUMPTIONS ABOUT GENDER. Be cautious about assuming that men and women will respond differently to your message. Early social science research found some evidence that females were more susceptible to efforts to persuade them than were males.[1] For many years textbooks and communication teachers presented this conclusion to students. More contemporary research, however, suggests there may be no major differences between men and women in susceptibility to persuasive messages.[2]

Moreover, although some research suggests women are socialized to be more emotional and empathic than men, other evidence suggests men can be equally sensitive.[3] It is clear there are learned sex differences in language usage and nonverbal behavior, but we caution against making sweeping gender-based assumptions about your audience.

Sexual Orientation An audience-centered speaker is sensitive to contemporary issues and attitudes related to sexual orientation. The audience-centered speaker's goal is to enhance understanding rather than create noise that may distract an audience from becoming listeners, regardless of the attitudes or beliefs audience members may hold about sexual orientation. Stories, illustrations, and humor whose point or punch line rely on ridiculing a person because of his or her sexual orientation may lower perceptions of your credibility, not only among gay and lesbian members of your audience, but also among audience members who disdain bias against gays and lesbians.

People evaluate credibility by behavior, not by intentions. Sometimes we unintentionally offend someone through more subtle misuse of language. For example, gays and lesbians typically prefer to be referred to as "gay" or "lesbian" rather than as "homosexual." Further, it is not appropriate to single out gays and lesbians as separate categories of people who are assumed to hold political, ideological, or religious views consistently different from those of straight people. Monitor your language choice and use of illustrations and humor so you don't alienate members of your audience.[4]

Culture, Ethnicity, and Race **Culture** is a learned system of knowledge, behavior, attitudes, beliefs, values, and norms shared by a group of people. **Ethnicity** is that portion of a person's cultural background that relates to a national or religious heritage. A person's **race** is his or her biological heritage—for example, Caucasian or Latino/Latina. The cultural, ethnic, or racial background of your audience influences the way they perceive your message. An effective speaker adapts to differences in culture, race, and ethnicity.

As you approach any public-speaking situation, avoid an ethnocentric mindset. **Ethnocentrism** is an assumption that your own cultural approaches are superior to those of other cultures. The audience-centered speaker is sensitive to cultural differences and avoids saying things that would disparage the cultural background of the audience. You need not have international students in your class to have a culturally diverse audience. Unique ethnic and cultural traditions thrive among people who have lived in the United States all their lives. Students from a Polish family in Chicago, a German family in Texas, or a Haitian family in Brooklyn may be native U.S. citizens with cultural traditions different from your own. Effective public speakers seek to learn as much as possible about the cultural values and knowledge of their audience so that they can understand the best way to deliver their message.

Researchers classify or describe cultural differences along several lines.[5] Understanding these classifications may provide clues to help you adapt your message when you speak before diverse audiences.

INDIVIDUALISTIC AND COLLECTIVISTIC CULTURES.   Some cultures place greater emphasis on individual achievement, whereas others place more value on group or collective achievement. Among the countries that tend to value individual accomplishment are Australia, Great Britain, the United States, Canada, Belgium, and Denmark. Japan, Thailand, Colombia, Taiwan, and Venezuela are among those that have more collectivistic cultures. Audience members from individualistic cultures tend to value and respond to appeals that encourage personal accomplishment and single out individual achievement. Audience members from collectivistic cultures may be more likely to value group or team rewards and achievement.

HIGH-CONTEXT AND LOW-CONTEXT CULTURES.   The terms *high-context* and *low-context* refer to the importance of unspoken or nonverbal messages. In high-context cultures, people place considerable importance on such contextual factors as tone of voice, gestures, facial expression, movement, and other nonverbal aspects of communication. People from low-context traditions are just the opposite. They place greater emphasis on the words themselves; the surrounding context has a relatively low impact on the meaning of the message. Arab cultures are a high-context cultures, as are those of Japan, Asia, and southern Europe. Low-context cultures, which place a high value on words, include those of Switzerland, Germany, the United States, and Australia.

Listeners from low-context cultures will need and expect more detailed and explicit information from you as a speaker. Subtle and indirect messages are less likely to be effective. People from high-context cultures will pay particular attention to your delivery and to the communication environment when they try to interpret your meaning. These people will be less impressed by a speaker who boasts about his or her own accomplishments; such an audience will expect and value more indirect ways of establishing credibility.

TOLERANCE OF UNCERTAINTY AND NEED FOR CERTAINTY.   Some cultures are more comfortable with ambiguity and uncertainty than others. Those cultures in which people prefer to have details "nailed down" tend to develop very specific regulations and rules. People from cultures with a greater tolerance of uncertainty are more comfortable with vagueness and are not upset when all the details aren't spelled out.

Cultures with a high need for certainty include those of Russia, Japan, France, and Costa Rica. Cultures that have a higher tolerance for uncertainty include those of Great Britain and Indonesia. If you are speaking to an audience with many people who have a high need for certainty, make sure you provide concrete details when you present ideas.

QUICK CHECK: *Describing Cultural Differences*

Individualistic cultures	Individual achievement is emphasized more than group achievement.
Collectivistic cultures	Group or team achievement is emphasized more than individual achievement.
High-context cultures	The context of a message—including nonverbal cues, tone of voice, posture, and facial expression—is often more important than the words.
Low-context cultures	The words in a message are given more attention than the surrounding context.
Tolerance of uncertainty	People can accept ambiguity and are not bothered if they do not know all the details.
Need for certainty	People dislike ambiguous messages and want specifics.
High-power cultures	Status and power differences are emphasized; roles and chains of command are clearly defined.
Low-power cultures	Status and power differences receive less emphasis; people strive for equality rather than exalting those in positions of leadership.

HIGH-POWER AND LOW-POWER CULTURES. Power is the ability to influence or control others. Some cultures prefer clearly defined lines of authority and responsibility; these are said to be high-power cultures. People in low-power cultures are more comfortable with blurred lines of authority and less formal titles. Austria, Israel, Denmark, Norway, Switzerland, and Great Britain typically have an equitable approach to power distribution. Cultures that are high on the power dimension include those of the Philippines, Mexico, Venezuela, India, Brazil, and France; people from these cultural traditions tend to respond positively to clearly defined power roles and structures. Those from low-power cultures often favor more shared approaches to leadership and governance.

Group Membership It's said we are each members of a gang—it's just that some gangs are more socially acceptable than others. We are social creatures; we congregate in groups to gain an identity, to help accomplish projects we support, and to have fun. So it's reasonable to assume that many of your listeners belong to groups, clubs, or organizations. Knowing what groups your listeners belong to can help you make inferences about their likes, dislikes, beliefs, and values.

RELIGIOUS GROUPS. Marsha is a follower of Scientology, and she believes that the philosophy outlined in *Dianetics* (the book that is the basis of Scientology) is as important as the religious precepts in the Bible. Planning to speak about scientology to a Bible-belt college audience, many of whose members view Scientology as a cult, Marsha would be wise to consider how her listeners will respond to her message. This is not to suggest that she should refuse the speaking invitation. She should, however, be aware of her audience's religious beliefs as she prepares and presents her speech. When touching on religious beliefs or an audience's values, use great care in what you say and how you say it. Remind yourself that some members of your audience will undoubtedly not share your beliefs and that few beliefs are held as intensely as religious ones. If you do not wish to offend your listeners, plan and deliver your speech with much thought and sensitivity.

POLITICAL GROUPS.   Are members of your audience active in politics? Knowing whether your listeners are active in such groups as Young Republicans or Young Democrats can help you address political topics. Members of environmental or other special-interest groups may also hold strong political opinions on various topics and political candidates.

WORK GROUPS.   Most professions give rise to organizations or associations to which professional people can belong. If you are speaking to an audience of professionals, it's important to be aware of professional organizations they may belong to (there may be several) and to know, for example, if such organizations have taken formal stands that may influence audience members' views on certain issues. Work groups also may use abbreviations or acronyms that may be useful to know. Your communication instructor, for example, may be a member of the National Communication Association (NCA) and may belong to a specific division of the NCA, such as the IDD (Instructional Development Division).

SOCIAL GROUPS.   Some groups exist just so that people can get together and enjoy a common activity. Book clubs, film clubs, cycling clubs, cooking groups, dancing groups, and bowling teams exist to bring people with similar ideas of fun together to enjoy the activity. Knowing whether members of your audience belong to such groups may help you adapt your topic to them or, if you are involved in similar groups, establish common ground with them.

SERVICE GROUPS.   Many people are actively involved in groups that emphasize community service as their primary mission. If you are speaking to a service group such as the Lions Club or the Kiwanis Club, you can reasonably assume that your listeners value community service and will be interested in how to make their community a better place.

Socioeconomic Status   **Socioeconomic status** is a person's perceived importance and influence based on such factors as income, occupation, and education level. In Europe, Asia, the Middle East, and other parts of the world, centuries-old traditions of acknowledging status differences still exist today. Status differences exist in the United States but are often more subtle. Having an idea about audience members' incomes, occupations, and education levels can be helpful as you develop a message that connects with listeners.

INCOME.   It's considered rude to ask people how much money they make, yet having some general idea of the income level of your listeners can be of great value to you as a speaker. For example, if you know that most audience members are struggling to meet weekly expenses, it is unwise to talk about how to see the cultural riches of Europe by traveling first class. But talking about how to get paid to travel to Europe by serving as a courier may hold considerable interest.

OCCUPATION.   Knowing what people do for a living can give you useful information about how to adapt your message to them. Speaking to teachers gives you an opportunity to use different examples and illustrations than if you were speaking to lawyers, ministers, or automobile assembly-line workers. Many college-age students may hold jobs, but don't yet hold the jobs they aspire to after they graduate from college. Knowing their future career plans can help you adjust your topic and supporting material to your listeners' professional goals.

EDUCATION.   About one-third of U.S. high-school graduates obtain a college diploma. Less than 10 percent of the population earns graduate degrees. The educational background of your listeners is yet another component of socioeconomic status that can help you plan your message. For example, you have a good idea that your classmates in your college-level public-speaking class value education, because they are striving, often at great sacrifice, to advance their education. Knowing the educational background of your audience can help you make decisions about your choice of vocabulary, your language style, and your use of examples and illustrations. For example, Mary White Eagle, a Native American from Roswell, New Mexico, was invited to speak to her daughter's grade-school class. Although she could have talked about the oppression of her ancestors by whites, she instead selected a topic more appropriate to her listeners: She spoke about the houses that Native Americans had to build and rebuild to follow the herds of buffalo that roamed the Southwest. As an audience-centered speaker, she used her knowledge of the education level of her listeners to guide her in her selection of a topic.

Adapting to Diverse Listeners   The most recent U.S. census figures document what you already know from your own life experiences: We all live in an age of diversity. For example,

- Two-thirds of immigrants worldwide come to the United States.[6]

- It is estimated that more than 40 million U.S. residents speak something other than English as their first language, including 18 million people whose first language is Spanish.[7]

- Whites are the minority ethnic group in nearly half of the largest cities in the United States.[8]

- For the first time in modern U.S. history, non-Hispanic whites are in the minority in California.[9]

Virtually every state in the United States has experienced a dramatic increase in foreign-born residents. If trends continue as they have during the past quarter-century, cultural and ethnic diversity will continue to grow during your lifetime. This swell of immigrants translates to increased diversity in all aspects of society, including in most audiences you'll face—whether in business, at school-board meetings, or in your college or university classes.

Audience diversity, however, involves more factors than just ethnic and cultural differences. Central to our point about considering your audience is examining the full spectrum of audience diversity, not just cultural differences. Each topic we've reviewed when discussing demographic and psychological aspects of an audience contributes to overall audience diversity. Diversity simply means differences. Audience members are diverse. The question and challenge for a public speaker is, "How do I adapt to listeners with such different backgrounds and experiences?" We offer several general strategies. You could decide to focus on a target audience, consciously use a variety of methods of adapting to listeners, seek common ground, or consider using powerful visual images to present your key points.

FOCUS ON A TARGET AUDIENCE. A **target audience** is a specific segment of your audience that you most want to address or influence. You've undoubtedly been a target of skilled communicators and may not have been aware that messages had been tailored just for you. For example, most colleges and universities spend a considerable amount of time and money encouraging students to apply for admission. You probably received some of this recruitment literature in the mail during your high-school years. But not every student in the United States receives brochures from the same colleges. Colleges and universities targeted you based on your test scores, your interests, where you live, and your involvement in school-sponsored or extracurricular activities. Likewise, as a public speaker, you may want to think about the portion of your audience you most want to understand or be convinced of your message. The challenge when consciously focusing on a target audience is not to lose or alienate the rest of your listeners—to keep the entire audience in mind while simultaneously making a specific attempt to hit your target segment. For example, Sasha was trying to convince his listeners to invest in the stock market instead of relying on the Social Security system. He wisely decided to focus on the younger listeners; those approaching retirement age have already made their major investment decisions. Although he focused on the younger members of his audience, however, Sasha didn't forget the mature listeners. He suggested that older listeners encourage their children or grandchildren to consider his proposal. He focused on a target audience, but didn't ignore others.

USE DIVERSE STRATEGIES FOR A DIVERSE AUDIENCE. Another approach you can adopt, either separately or in combination with a target audience focus, is to use a variety of strategies to reflect the diversity of your audience. Based on your efforts to gather information about your audience, you should know the various constituencies that will likely be present for your talk. Consider using several methods of reaching the different listeners in your audience.

IDENTIFY COMMON VALUES. People have debated for a long time whether there are universal human values. Several scholars have made strong arguments that common human values do exist. Communication researcher David Kale suggests that all people can identify with the individual struggle to enhance one's own dignity and worth, although different cultures express that in different ways.[10] A second common value is the search for a world at peace. Underlying that quest is a fundamental desire for equilibrium, balance, and stability. Although there may always be a small but corrosive

HOW TO: *Use Diverse Strategies*

- Use a variety of different types of supporting materials (illustrations, examples, statistics, opinions).
- Remember the power of stories. People from most cultures appreciate a good story. And some people, such as those from Asian and Middle Eastern cultures, prefer hearing stories and parables used to make a point or support an argument, rather than facts and statistics.
- If you're very uncertain about cultural preferences, use a balance of both logical support (statistics, facts, specific examples) and emotional support (stories and illustrations).
- Consider showing the audience an outline of your key ideas using an overhead transparency or computer-generated graphic. If there is a language barrier between you and your audience, being able to read portions of your speech as they hear you speaking may improve audience members' comprehension. If an interpreter is translating your message, an outline can also help ensure that your interpreter will communicate your message accurately.

minority of people whose actions do not support the universal value of peace, the prevailing human values in most cultures ultimately do support peace. Cultural anthropologists specialize in the study of behavior that is common to all humans. Cultural anthropologist Donald Brown has compiled a list of hundreds of "surface" universals of beliefs, emotions, or behavior. According to Brown, people in all cultures[11]

- Have beliefs about death
- Have a childhood fear of strangers
- Have a division of labor by sex
- Experience certain emotions and feelings, such as envy, pain, jealousy, shame, and pride
- Use facial expressions to express emotions
- Have rules for etiquette
- Experience empathy
- Value some degree of collaboration or cooperation
- Experience conflict and seek to manage or mediate conflict

Of course, not all cultures have the same beliefs about death or the same way of dividing up labor—but people in all cultures address these issues.

Intercultural communication scholars Larry Samovar and Richard Porter suggest other commonalities among people from all cultures. They propose that all humans seek physical pleasure as well as emotional and psychological pleasure and confirmation and seek to avoid personal harm.[12] Although each culture defines what constitutes pleasure and pain, it may be useful to interpret human behavior with these general assumptions in mind. People also realize that their biological lives will end, that to some degree each person is isolated from all other human beings, that we each make choices, and that each person seeks to give life meaning. These similarities offer some basis for developing common messages with universal meaning.

Identifying common cultural issues and similarities can help you establish common ground with your audience. If you are speaking about an issue on which you and your audience have widely different views, identifying a larger common value that is relevant to your topic (such as the importance of peace, prosperity, or family) can help you find a foothold so that your listeners will at least listen to your ideas.

RELY ON VISUAL MATERIALS THAT TRANSCEND LANGUAGE DIFFERENCES. Pictures and images can communicate universal messages—especially emotional ones. Although there is no universal language, most listeners, regardless of culture and language, can comprehend visible expressions of pain, joy, sorrow, and happiness. An image of a mother holding the frail, malnourished body of her dying child communicates the ravages of famine without elaborate verbal explanations. The more varied your listeners' cultural experiences, the more effective it can be to use visual materials to illustrate your ideas.

QUICK CHECK: *Adapting to Diverse Listeners*

- Focus on a target audience without losing or alienating the rest of your listeners.
- Use diverse supporting materials that reflect a balance of logical and emotional support.
- Use visual aids.
- Appeal to such common values as peace, prosperity, and family.

PSYCHOLOGICAL AUDIENCE ANALYSIS

Demographic information lets you make some useful inferences about your audience and predict likely responses. Learning how the members of your audience feel about your topic and purpose may provide specific clues about possible reactions. A **psychological audience analysis** explores an audience's attitudes toward a topic, purpose, and speaker, while probing the underlying beliefs and values that might affect these attitudes.

It is important for a speaker to distinguish among attitudes, beliefs, and values. The attitudes, beliefs, and values of an audience may greatly influence a speaker's selection of a topic and specific purpose, as well as various other aspects of speech preparation and delivery.

Attitudes An **attitude** reflects likes or dislikes. Do you like health food? Are you for or against capital punishment? Should movies be censored? What are your views on nuclear energy? Your answers to these widely varied questions reflect your attitudes.

Beliefs   A **belief** is what you hold to be true or false. If you think the sun will rise in the east in the morning, you hold a belief about the sun based on what you perceive to be true or false.

Beliefs underlie attitudes. Why do you like health food? You may believe that natural products contain more vitamins and minerals than more processed food. That belief about health food explains your positive attitude. Why do you not like to travel on airplanes? You may believe that you are less safe traveling by airplane than you are in a car. Once your belief changes (for example, when someone gives you credible evidence that you are really safer traveling by plane than by car), then your attitudes about plane travel may change as well. If you can understand the underlying beliefs that explain why audience members like or dislike something, then you may be able to address those underlying beliefs. How do you change beliefs? You use credible evidence. Using evidence to prove that plane travel is less likely to result in personal injury than traveling by car is a way to address both beliefs about plane travel (what the listener believes to be true or false) and attitudes (what the listener likes or dislikes) toward it.

Values   A **value** is an enduring concept of good and bad, right and wrong. More deeply ingrained than either attitudes or beliefs, values are therefore more resistant to change. Values support both attitudes and beliefs. For example, you like health food because you believe that natural products are more healthful. And you value good health. You are against capital punishment because you believe that it is wrong to kill people. You value human life. As with beliefs, a speaker who has some understanding of an audience's values is better able to adapt a speech to them.

Analyzing Attitudes Toward a Topic   The topic of a speech provides one focus for an audience's attitudes, beliefs, and values. It is useful to know how members of an audience feel about your topic. Are they interested or apathetic? How much do they already know about the topic? If the topic is controversial, are their attitudes toward it positive or negative? Knowing the answers to these questions from the outset lets you adjust your message accordingly. For example, if you plan to talk about increasing taxes to improve education in your state, you probably want to know how your listeners feel about taxes and education.

When you are analyzing your audience, it may help to categorize the group along three dimensions: interested–uninterested, favorable–unfavorable, and captive–voluntary. With an interested audience, your task is simply to hold and amplify interest throughout the speech. If your audience is uninterested, you need to find ways to "hook" the members. Given our visually oriented culture, consider using visual aids to gain and maintain the attention of apathetic listeners.

You may also want to gauge how favorable or unfavorable your audience may feel toward you and your message before you begin to speak. Some audiences, of course, are neutral, apathetic, or simply uninformed about what you plan to say. But even if your objective is simply to inform, it is useful to know whether your audience is predisposed to respond positively or negatively toward you or your message. Giving an informative talk about classical music would be quite challenging, for example, if you were addressing an audience full of die-hard punk-rock fans. You might decide to show the connections between classical music and punk to arouse their interest.

Your Speech Class as Audience You may think that your public-speaking class is not a typical audience because class members are required to attend. Your speech class is a captive audience rather than a voluntary one. A captive audience has externally imposed reasons for being there (such as a requirement to attend class).

✔ **QUICK CHECK:** *Adapting Your Message to Different Types of Audiences*

Type of Audience	Example	How to Be Audience-Centered
Interested	Mayors who attend a talk by the governor about increasing security and reducing the threat of terrorism	Acknowledge audience interest early in your speech; use the interest they have in you and your topic to gain and maintain their attention.
Uninterested	Junior high students attending a lecture about retirement benefits	Make it a high priority to tell your listeners why your message should be of interest to them. Remind your listeners throughout your speech how your message relates to their lives.
Favorable	A religious group that meets to hear a group leader talk about the importance of their beliefs	Use audience interest to move them closer to your speaking goal; you may be more explicit in telling them in your speech conclusion what you would like them to do.
Unfavorable	Students who attend a lecture by the university president explaining why tuition and fees will increase 15 percent next year	Be realistic in what you expect to accomplish; acknowledge their opposing point of view; consider using facts to refute misperceptions they may hold.
Voluntary	Parents attending a lecture by the new principal at their children's school	Anticipate why they are coming to hear you, and speak about the issues they want you to address.
Captive	Students in a public-speaking class	Find out who will be in your audience, and use this knowledge to adapt your message to them.

Because class members must show up to earn credit for class, you need not worry that they will get up and leave during your speech. However, your classroom speeches are still real speeches. Your class members are certainly real people with likes, dislikes, beliefs, and values.

Your classroom speeches should connect with your listeners so they forget they are required to be in the audience. Class members should listen because your message has given them new, useful information; touched them emotionally; or persuaded them to change their opinion or behavior in support of your position.

You will undoubtedly give other speeches to other captive audiences. Audiences at work or at professional meetings are often captive in the sense that they may be required to attend lectures or presentations to receive continuing-education credit or as part of their job duties. Your goal with a captive audience is the same as with other types of audiences. You should make your speech just as interesting and effective as one designed for a voluntary audience. You still have an obligation to address your listeners' needs and interests and to keep them engaged in what you have to say. A captive audience gives you an opportunity to polish your speaking skills.

Analyzing Attitudes Toward You, the Speaker   Audience members' attitude toward you in your role as speaker is another factor that can influence their reaction to your speech. Regardless of how they feel about your topic or purpose, if members of an audience regard you as credible, they will be much more likely to be interested in, and supportive of, what you have to say.

Your **credibility**—others' perception of you as trustworthy, knowledgeable, and interesting—is one of the main factors that will shape your audience's attitude toward you. If you establish your credibility before you begin to discuss your topic, your listeners will be more likely to believe what you say and to think that you are knowledgeable, interesting, and dynamic.

For example, when a high-school health teacher asks a former drug addict to speak to a class about the dangers of cocaine addiction, the teacher recognizes that the speaker's experiences make him credible and that his message will be far more convincing than if the teacher just lectured on the perils of cocaine use.

An audience's positive attitude toward a speaker can overcome negative or apathetic attitudes they may have toward the speaker's topic or purpose. If your analysis reveals that your audience does not recognize you as an authority on your subject, you will need to build your credibility into the speech. If you have had personal experience with your topic, be sure to let the audience know. You will gain credibility instantly.

SITUATIONAL AUDIENCE ANALYSIS

So far we have concentrated on the people who will be your listeners as the primary focus of being an audience-centered speaker. You should also consider your speaking situation. **Situational audience analysis** includes an examination of the time and place of your speech, the size of your audience, and the speaking occasion. Although these elements are not technically characteristics of the audience, they can have a major effect on how your listeners respond to you.

Time   You may have no control over when you will be speaking, but when designing and delivering a talk, a skilled public speaker considers the time of day as well as audience expectations about the speech length. If you are speaking to a group of exhausted parents during a midweek evening meeting of the band-boosters club, you can bet they will appreciate a direct, to-the-point presentation more than a long oration. If you are on a program with other speakers, speaking first or last on the program carries a slight edge, because people tend to remember what comes first or last. Speaking early in the morning when people may not be quite awake, after lunch when they may feel a bit drowsy, or late in the afternoon when they are tired may mean you'll have to strive consciously for a more energetic delivery to keep your listeners' attention.

Another aspect of time: Be mindful of your time limits. If your audience expects you to speak for 20 minutes, it is usually better to end either right at 20 minutes or even a little earlier; most North Americans don't appreciate being kept overtime for a speech. In your public-speaking class you will be given time limits, and you may wonder whether you will encounter such strict time-limit expectations outside of public-speaking class. The answer is a most definite yes. Whether it's a business presentation or a speech to the city council or school board, time limits are often strictly enforced.

Location   In your speech class, you have the advantage of knowing what the room looks like, but in a new speaking situation, you may not have that advantage. If at all possible, visit the place where you will speak to examine the physical setting and find out, for example, how far the audience will be from the lectern. Physical conditions such as room temperature and lighting can affect your performance, audience response, and the overall success of the speech.

Room arrangement and decor may affect the way an audience responds. Be aware of the arrangement and appearance of the room in which you will speak. If your speaking environment is less than ideal, you may need to work especially hard to hold your audience's attention. Although you probably will not be able to make major changes in the speaking environment, it is ultimately up to you to obtain the best speaking environment you can. The arrangement of chairs, placement of audiovisual materials, and opening or closing of drapes should all be in your control.

Size of Audience   The size of your audience directly affects speaking style and audience expectations about delivery. As a general rule, the larger the audience, the more likely they are to expect a more formal style. With an audience of ten or fewer, you can punctuate a very conversational style by taking questions from your listeners. If you and your listeners are so few that you can be seated around a table, they may expect you to stay seated for your presentation. Many business "speeches" are given around a conference table.

A group of between 20 to 30 people—the size of most public-speaking classes—will expect more formality than the audience of a dozen or less. Your speaking style can still be conversational, but your speech should be appropriately structured and well organized; your delivery may include more expansive gestures than you display during a one-on-one chat with a friend or colleague.

Audiences that fill a lecture hall will still appreciate a direct, conversational style, but your gestures may increase in size, and, if your voice will be unamplified, you will be expected to speak with enough volume and intensity that people in the last row can hear you.

Occasion   Another important way to gain clues about your listeners is to consider the reason this audience is here. What occasion brings this audience together? The mindset of people gathered for a funeral will obviously be different from that of people who've asked you to say a few words after a banquet. Knowing the occasion helps you predict both demographic characteristics of the audience and the members' psychological state of mind.

If you're presenting a speech at an annual or monthly meeting, you have the advantage of being able to ask those who've attended previous presentations what kind of audience typically gathers for the occasion. Your best source of information may be either the person who invited you to speak or someone who has attended similar events. Knowing when you will speak on the program or whether a meal will be served before or after you talk will help you gauge what your audience expects from you. In preparing for a speaking assignment, ask the following questions, and keep the answers in mind:

- How many people are expected to attend the speech?
- How will the audience seating be arranged?
- How close will I be to the audience?
- Will I speak from a lectern?
- Will I be expected to use a microphone?
- What time of day will I be speaking?
- What is the room lighting like? Will the audience seating area be darkened beyond a lighted stage?
- Will I have adequate equipment for my visual aids?
- Where will I appear on the program?
- Will there be noise or distractions outside the room?
- What is the occasion that brings the audience together?

Advance preparation will help you avoid last-minute surprises about the speaking environment and the physical arrangements for your speech. A well-prepared speaker adapts his or her message not only to the audience but also to the speaking environment.

Also keep in mind that when you arrive to give your speech, you can make changes in the previous speaker's room arrangements. For example, the purpose of the speaker immediately before Yue Hong was to generate interest in a memorial for Asian Americans who fought in Vietnam. Because the previous speaker wanted to make sure the audience felt free to ask questions, the chairs were arranged in a semicircle and the lights were turned on. But Yue Hong was giving a more formal presentation on the future of the Vietnamese population, which included a brief slide show. So when the preceding speaker had finished, Yue Hong rearranged the chairs and darkened the room.

6.d   Adapting to Your Audience as You Speak

So far, we have focused on discovering as much as possible about an audience before the speaking event. Prespeech analyses help with each step of the public-speaking process: selecting a topic, formulating a specific purpose, gathering supporting material, identifying major ideas, organizing the speech, and planning its delivery. Each of these components depends on understanding your audience. But audience analysis and adaptation do not end when you have crafted your speech. They continue as you deliver your speech. Generally, a public speaker does not have an exchange with the audience unless the speech is part of a question-and-answer or discussion format. Once the speech is in progress, the speaker must rely on nonverbal clues from the audience to judge how people are responding to the message.

Once, when speaking in India, Mark Twain was denied eye contact with his listeners by a curtain separating him from his audience. Mark Twain's daughter, Clara, recalled this experience:

> One of Father's first lectures was before a Purdah audience; in other words, the women all sat behind a curtain through which they could peek at Mark Twain without being seen by him . . . a deadly affair for the poor humorist, who had not even the pleasure of scanning the faces of his mute audience.[13]

Mark Twain missed learning how well his speech was being received as he was speaking. You could experience the same disadvantage if you fail to look at your listeners while you're speaking.

IDENTIFYING NONVERBAL AUDIENCE CUES

Many beginning public speakers may find it challenging at first not only to have the responsibility of presenting a speech they have rehearsed but also to have to change or modify the speech on the spot. We assure you that with experience you can develop the sensitivity to adapt to your listeners, much as a jazz musician adapts to the other musicians in the ensemble, but it will take practice. Although it's not possible to read your listeners' minds, it is important to analyze and adapt to cues that can enhance the effectiveness of your message. The first step in developing this skill is to be aware of the often unspoken clues that let you know whether your audience is hanging on every word or is bored. After learning to "read" your audience, you then need to consider developing a repertoire of behaviors to help you connect with your listeners.

Eye Contact   Perhaps the best way to determine whether your listeners are maintaining interest in your speech is to note the amount of eye contact they have with you. The more contact they have, the more likely it is that they are listening to your message. If you find them repeatedly looking at their watches, looking down at the program (or, worse yet, closing their eyes), you can reasonably assume that they have lost interest in what you're talking about.

Facial Expression   Another clue to whether an audience is "with you" is facial expression. Members of an attentive audience not only make direct eye contact but also have attentive facial expressions. Beware of a frozen, unresponsive face. We call this sort of expression the "in-a-stupor" look. The classic in-a-stupor expression consists of a slightly tilted head, a faint, frozen smile, and often, a hand holding up the chin. This expression may give the appearance of interest, but it more often means that the person is daydreaming or thinking of something other than your topic.

Movement   An attentive audience doesn't move much. An early sign of inattentiveness is fidgeting fingers, which may escalate to pencil wagging, leg jiggling, and arm wiggling. Seat squirming, feet shuffling, and general body movement often indicate that members of the audience have lost interest in your message.

Nonverbal Responsiveness   Interested audience members respond verbally and nonverbally when encouraged or invited by the speaker. When you ask for a show of hands and audience members sheepishly look at one another and eventually raise a finger or two, you can reasonably infer lack of interest and enthusiasm. Frequent applause and nods of agreement with your message are indicators of interest and support.

Verbal Responsiveness   Not only will audiences indicate agreement nonverbally, some will also indicate their interest verbally. Audience members may shout out a response or more quietly express agreement or disagreement to people seated next to them. A sensitive public speaker is constantly listening for verbal reinforcement or disagreement.

RESPONDING TO NONVERBAL CUES

The value in recognizing nonverbal clues from your listeners is that you can respond to them appropriately. If your audience seems interested, supportive, and attentive, your prespeech analysis has clearly led you to make good choices in preparing and delivering your speech.

If your audience becomes inattentive, however, you may need to make some changes while delivering your message. If you think audience members are drifting off into their own thoughts or disagreeing with what you say, or if you suspect that they don't understand what you are saying, then a few spontaneous changes may help. It takes experience and skill to make on-the-spot changes in your speech. Consider the following tips from seasoned public speakers for adapting to your listeners.[14]

If your audience seems inattentive or bored:

- Tell a story.
- Use an example to which the audience can relate.
- Use a personal example.
- Remind your listeners why your message should be of interest to them.
- Eliminate some abstract facts and statistics.
- Use appropriate humor.

- Make direct references to the audience, using members' names or mentioning something about them.
- Encourage the audience to participate by asking questions or asking them for an example.
- Ask for a direct response, such as a show of hands, to see whether they agree or disagree with you.
- Pick up the pace of your delivery.
- Pause for dramatic effect.

If your audience seems confused or doesn't seem to understand your point:

- Be more redundant.
- Try phrasing your information in another way, or think of an example you can use to illustrate your point.
- Use a visual aid such as a chalkboard or flipchart to clarify your point.
- If you have been speaking rapidly, slow your speaking rate.
- Clarify the overall organization of your message for your listeners.
- Ask for feedback from an audience member to help you discover what is unclear.
- Ask someone in the audience to summarize the key point you are making.

If your audience seems to be disagreeing with your message:

- Provide additional data and evidence to support your point.
- Remind your listeners of your credibility, credentials, or background.
- Rely less on anecdotes and more on facts to present your case.
- Write facts and data on a chalkboard, overhead transparency, or flipchart if one is handy.
- If you don't have the answers and data you need, tell listeners you will provide more information by mail, telephone, or e-mail (and make sure you get back in touch with them).

Remember, it is not enough to note your listeners' characteristics and attitudes. You must also respond to the information you gather by adapting your speech to retain their interest and attention. Moreover, you have a responsibility to ensure that your audience understands your message. If your approach to the content of your speech is not working, alter it and note whether your audience's responses change. If all else fails, you may need to abandon a formal speaker–listener relationship with your audience and open up your topic for discussion. Of course, in your speech class, your instructor may expect you to keep going, to fulfill the requirements for your assignment. With other audiences, however, you may want to consider switching to a more interactive question-and-answer session to ensure that you are communicating clearly. Later chapters on supporting material, speech organization, and speech delivery will discuss other techniques for adjusting your style while delivering your message.

QUICK CHECK: *Analyzing and Adapting to Your Audience as You Speak*

Signs That You Are Connecting with Your Audience	Signs That You Are Not Connecting with Your Audience	Strategies for Adapting to an Unsupportive Audience
Audience members make eye contact; most audience members look you in the eye while you are speaking.	Audience members don't make eye contact with you.	• Tell a story. • Use more personal examples or illustrations. • Consider making direct references to your listeners by mentioning some people by name.
Audience members have sincere smiles or pleasant facial expressions.	Audience members frown or display blank or unresponsive facial expressions.	• Ask audience members whether they understand your message. • Increase your speaking energy. • Remind your listeners why your message is important to them. • Consider clarifying your message by using a chalkboard or other visual aid.
Audience members are quiet.	Audience members are talking to other audience members.	• Pause to gain listeners' attention. • Ask the audience either a rhetorical question (one you don't expect them to actually answer) or a question to which you do expect a response.
Audience members are sitting quietly; there is little audience movement.	Audience members are restless; their hands and feet are moving.	• Pick up the pace of your delivery. • Use appropriate humor. • Use more concrete examples.
Audience members respond to your requests for information or your questions by raising their hands when you ask.	Audience members do not respond to your questions or do not show interest in your message.	• Ask audience members if they understand the question you've asked. • Repeat your question, and make it clear that you'd like their response and participation.
Audience members make appropriate verbal responses; they laugh when you use humor.	Audience members don't respond to your questions; they don't laugh at your humor.	• If listeners are not responsive to your humor, rely less on jokes and use more stories or personal illustrations.

STRATEGIES FOR CUSTOMIZING YOUR MESSAGE TO YOUR AUDIENCE

Many people value having something prepared especially for them. Perhaps you've bought a computer that you ordered to your exact specifications. In a restaurant you order food prepared to your specific taste. Audiences, too, prefer messages that are adapted just to them; they don't like hearing a "canned" message. As a speaker, you may have worked hard to adapt your message to your audience, but your audience won't give you credit for adapting your message to them unless you let them know that you've done so. What are some ways to communicate to your listeners that your message is designed specifically for them? Here are a few suggestions:

Appropriately Use Audience Members' Names   Consider using audience members' names in your talk to relate specific information to individual people. Obviously, you don't want to embarrass people by using them in an example that would make them feel uncomfortable. But you can selectively mention people you know who are in the audience. It's become a standard technique in many State of the Union speeches for the president to have someone sitting in the balcony who can be mentioned in his talk. That person becomes a living "visual aid" to provide focus for an idea or point made in the address. If you are uncertain whether you should mention someone by name, before you speak, ask the person for permission to use his or her name in your talk.

Refer to the Town, City, or Community   Make a specific reference to the place where you are speaking. If you are speaking to a college audience, relate your message and illustrations to the school where you are speaking. Many politicians use this technique: They have a standard stump speech to tout their credentials but adapt the opening part of their message to the specific city or community in which they are speaking.

Refer to a Significant Event That Happened on the Date of Your Speech   Most libraries have books (such as the *Speaker's Lifetime Library*) that identify significant events in world or national history.[15] For example, on the day this paragraph was written, Julius Caesar was assassinated in 44 B.C. It's also known as the Ides of March—a day Caesar was warned about in Shakespeare's famous play. If you were giving a speech on this day, a reference to the Ides of March might be especially apropos if your goal was to encourage your audience to beware of whatever issue or topic you were discussing.

Many local papers keep records of local historical events and list what happened 10, 25, or 50 years ago on a certain date. Relating your talk to a historical event that occurred on the same date as your talk can give your message a feeling of immediacy. It tells your audience that you have thought about this specific speaking event.

Refer to a Recent News Event   Always read the local paper to see whether there is a local news story that you can connect to the central idea of your talk. Or, perhaps you can use a headline from your university newspaper or a recent story that appeared on your university Web site. If there is a newspaper headline that connects with your talk, consider holding up the paper as you refer to it—not so that people will be able to read the headline, but to emphasize the immediacy of your message.

Refer to a Group or Organization   If you're speaking to an audience of service, religious, political, or work group members, by all means make specific positive references to the group. But be honest—don't offer false praise; audiences can sniff out phony flattery. A sincere compliment about the group will be appreciated, especially if you can link the goals of the group to the goal of your talk.

Relate Information Directly to Your Listeners   Find ways to apply facts, statistics, and examples to the people in your audience. If, for example, you know that four out of ten women are likely to experience gender discrimination, customize that statistic by saying, "Forty percent of women listening to me now are likely to experience gender discrimination. That means of the twenty women in this audience, eight of you are likely to be discriminated against." Or, if you live in a city of 50,000 people, you can cite the statistic that 50,000 people on our nation's highways become victims of drunk driving each year, and then point out that that number is equivalent to killing every man, woman, and child in your city. Relating abstract statistics and examples to your listeners communicates that you have them in mind as you develop your message.

6.e Analyzing Your Audience After You Speak

After you have given your speech, you're not finished analyzing your audience. It is important to evaluate your audience's positive or negative response to your message. Why? Because this evaluation can help you prepare your next speech. Postspeech analysis helps you polish your speaking skill, regardless of whether you will face the same audience again. From that analysis you can learn whether your examples were clear and whether listeners accepted your message. Let's look at some specific methods for assessing your audience's response to your speech.

NONVERBAL RESPONSES

The most obvious nonverbal response is applause. Is the audience simply clapping politely, or is the applause robust and enthusiastic, indicating pleasure and acceptance? Responsive facial expressions, smiles, and nods are other nonverbal signs that the speech has been well received.

Realize, however, that audience members from different cultures respond to speeches in different ways. Japanese audience members, for example, are likely to be restrained in their response to a speech and to show little expression. Some Eastern European listeners may not maintain eye contact with you; they may look down at the floor when listening. In some contexts, African American listeners may enthusiastically voice their agreement or disagreement with something you say during your presentation.[16]

Nonverbal responses at the end of the speech may express some general feeling of the audience, but they are not much help in identifying which strategies were the most effective. Also consider what the members of the audience say, both to you and to others, after your speech.

VERBAL RESPONSES

What might members of the audience say to you about your speech? General comments, such as "I enjoyed your talk" or "Great speech," are good for the ego—which is important—but are not of much analytic help. Specific comments can indicate where you succeeded and where you failed. If you have the chance, try to ask audience members how they responded to the speech in general as well as to points you are particularly interested in.

SURVEY RESPONSES

You are already aware of the value of conducting audience surveys before speaking publicly. You may also want to survey your audience after you speak. You can then assess how well you accomplished your objective. Use the same survey techniques discussed earlier. Develop survey questions that will help you determine the audience's general reactions to you and your speech, as well as specific responses to your ideas and supporting materials. Professional speakers and public officials often conduct such surveys. Postspeech surveys are especially useful when you are trying to persuade an audience. Comparing prespeech and postspeech attitudes can give you a clear idea of your effectiveness. A significant portion of most political-campaign budgets goes toward evaluating how a candidate is received by his or her constituents. Politicians want to know what portions of their messages are acceptable to their audiences so they can use this information in the future.

If your objective was to teach your audience about some new idea, a posttest can assess whether you expressed your ideas clearly. In fact, classroom exams are posttests that determine whether your instructor presented information clearly.

BEHAVIORAL RESPONSES

If the purpose of your speech was to persuade your listeners to do something, you will want to learn whether they ultimately behave as you intended. If you wanted them to vote in an upcoming election, you might survey your listeners to find out how many did vote. If you wanted to win support for a particular cause or organization, you might ask them to sign a petition after your speech. The number of signatures would be a clear measure of your speech's success. Some religious speakers judge the success of their ministry by the amount of contributions they receive. Your listeners' actions are the best indicators of your speaking success.

Summary

- It is important to become an audience-centered speaker.
- To be an effective speaker, learn as much as you can about your listeners before, during, and after your speech.

- Before your speech, perform three kinds of analysis: demographic, psychological, and situational. You can use informal and formal approaches to gather information about your listeners for your analyses.

- While speaking, look for feedback from your listeners. Audience eye contact, facial expression, movement, and general verbal and nonverbal responsiveness provide clues to how well you are doing.

- Evaluate audience reaction after your speech. Nonverbal clues as well as verbal ones will help you judge your speaking skill.

- The best indicator of your speaking success is whether your audience is actually able or willing to follow your advice or remembers what you have told them.

Key Terms

attitude (p. 105)
audience adaptation (p. 95)
audience analysis (p. 93)
belief (p. 106)
credibility (p. 108)
culture (p. 98)
demographic audience analysis (p. 97)
demographics (p. 91)
ethnicity (p. 98)

ethnocentrism (p. 98)
gender (p. 97)
psychological audience analysis (p. 105)
race (p. 98)
situational audience analysis (p. 108)
socioeconomic status (p. 101)
target audience (p. 103)
value (p. 106)

A QUESTION OF ETHICS

Marianne strongly believes that the drinking age should be raised to 22 in her state. When she surveyed her classmates, the overwhelming majority thought the drinking age should be lowered to 18. Should Marianne change the topic and purpose of her speech to avoid facing a hostile audience? Why or why not?

3

Preparing a Speech

Preparing a Speech

At a Glance ➤

Preparing a Speech

7 Developing Your Speech

➡ **Select and Narrow Your Topic (p. 128)**
- Choose a topic to speak about and narrow this topic to fit your time limits.
- When selecting a topic:
  - Consider the audience. Not only should a speaker's choice of topic be relevant to the interests and expectations of his or her listeners, it should also take into account the knowledge listeners already have about the subject.
  - Consider the occasion. To be successful, a topic must be appropriate to both audience and occasion.
  - Consider yourself. The best public-speaking topics are those that reflect your personal experience or that especially interest you.
- There are several strategies that can help generate speech topics.
  - Brainstorming is a widely used problem-solving technique that can easily be used to generate ideas for speech topics.
  - Listen and read for topic ideas.
  - Access a Web directory such as Yahoo! (www.yahoo.com).
- To narrow the topic so that it fits within the time limits set by your assignment:
  - Create categories. Write your general topic at the top of a list, and make each succeeding word in the list a more specific or concrete topic.
  - Find the right level. Be careful not to narrow your topic so much that you cannot find enough information for even a three-minute talk.

➡ **Determine Your Purpose (p. 134)**
- The general purpose of virtually any speech is either to inform, to persuade, or to entertain.
- Speaking to inform gives listeners information.
- Speaking to persuade uses the information to try to change or reinforce an audience's convictions and often to urge some sort of action.
- Speaking to entertain gets the members of an audience to relax, smile, perhaps laugh, and generally enjoy themselves.
- To arrive at a specific purpose for your speech, think in precise terms of what you want your audience to be able to do at the end of your speech.
  - Identify a behavioral objective by specifying the behavior you seek from the audience.
  - Formulate the specific purpose—an observable, measurable action that the audience should be able to take by the end of the speech.
  - Use the specific purpose to help you assess the information you are gathering for your speech.

➡ **Develop Your Central Idea (p. 138)**
- Your central idea should be a one-sentence summary of your speech.
  - Express the central idea in a complete declarative sentence.
  - Use direct, specific language rather than qualifiers and vague generalities.
  - The central idea should be a single idea.
  - The central idea should reflect consideration of the audience.

➡ **Generate and Preview Your Main Ideas (p. 141)**
- Write the central idea at the top of a sheet of paper. Then ask these three questions:
  - Does the central idea have logical divisions?
  - Can you think of several reasons why the central idea is true?
  - Can you support your central idea with a series of steps or a chronological progression?
- Create a blueprint for your speech by combining the central idea and a preview of the main ideas.

➡ **Meanwhile, Back at the Computer . . . (p. 143)**
- Once you have narrowed the topic, write your purpose statement.

8 Gathering Supporting Material

➡ **Personal Knowledge and Experience (p. 147)**
- You may be able to provide an effective illustration, explanation, definition, or other type of support from your own knowledge and experience.
- Personal knowledge often has the additional advantage of heightening your credibility in the minds of your listeners.

➡ **The Internet (p. 148)**
- The World Wide Web is of primary interest when you are searching for supporting materials for a speech.
- Use directories and search engines such as those provided by Yahoo!, Google, Alta Vista, or a number of other sites.
- To narrow your search, do an advanced, or Boolean, search.
- Evaluate Web resources according to a consistent standard that assesses accountability, accuracy, objectivity, date, usability, and diversity.

➡ **Library Resources (p. 152)**
- Books: Libraries' collections of books are called the stacks. Stacks may be either open or closed, depending on library policy.
- Periodicals: The term *periodical* refers to both general-interest magazines and trade and professional journals, which are timelier than books.
- Full-text databases combine both an index and text, allowing you to locate not only bibliographic information but the resources themselves through a key word or subject search.
- Newspapers are more current than periodicals.
- Reference resources are indexed in the card catalog with a *Ref* prefix or suffix on their call numbers, to show that they are housed in the reference section of the library.
- Government documents can be a rich source of support material. The federal government researches and publishes information on almost every conceivable subject, as well as keeping exhaustive records of almost all official federal proceedings.
- Special services: Most libraries offer a number of special services. These include interlibrary loan and reciprocal borrowing privileges with other area libraries.

➡ **Interviews (p. 159)**
- Consider interviewing someone to get material for your speech.
- Establish a purpose or objective for the interview. Decide just what you want to have or know when the interview is over.
- Once you have a specific purpose for the interview and have decided whom you need to speak with, arrange a meeting.
- Find out as much as you can about both your subject and the person you are interviewing.
- Prepare questions that take full advantage of the interviewee's specific knowledge of your subject.
  - Plan specific questions, both closed-ended and open-ended ones.
  - Plan a sequence of questions.
- Plan a recording strategy. Audio and video recorders can free you from having to take copious notes.
- Conduct the interview.
  - Dress appropriately. Take paper and pen or pencil for note taking.
  - Arrive a few minutes ahead of the scheduled hour. Once you are settled with the person, remind him or her of your purpose.
  - Use the questions you have prepared as a guide but not a rigid schedule. Do not prolong the interview beyond the time limits of your appointment. Thank your interviewee for his or her contribution, and leave.
- Follow up the interview.
  - Read through your notes carefully, and rewrite any portions that may be illegible.
  - If you recorded the interview, label the tape with the date and the interviewee's name.

➡ **Resources from Special-Interest Groups and Organizations (p. 162)**
- Business and industrial groups, nonprofit organizations, and professional societies produce pamphlets, books, fact sheets, and other information about an extraordinarily wide variety of subjects.

➡ **Research Strategies (p. 163)**
- Develop a preliminary bibliography.
- Keep track of resources.
- Use a consistent format.
- Choose an appropriate number.
- Evaluate the usefulness of resources.

- Take notes.
  - Start with the most useful resources.
  - Create a record of resource notes.
  - Use a notebook, disk, or note cards.
  - Write one idea per card or page.
  - Indicate the source.
  - Summarize the idea.
- Identify possible presentation aids.

9 Supporting Your Speech

➡ **Illustrations (p. 171)**
- An illustration—a story or anecdote that provides an example of an idea, issue, or problem the speaker is discussing—almost always ensures audience interest.
  - Brief illustrations are often no longer than a sentence or two.
  - Extended illustrations resemble a story. They are more descriptive than brief illustrations and have a plot—which includes an opening, complications, a climax, and a resolution.
  - Hypothetical illustrations may be either brief or extended. They describe situations or events that have not actually occurred.
- Use illustrations effectively:
  - Be sure your illustrations are relevant to what they are supposed to support.
  - Choose illustrations that represent a trend.
  - Make your illustrations vivid and specific.
  - Use illustrations with which your listeners can identify.
  - Remember that the best illustrations are personal ones.

➡ **Descriptions and Explanations (p. 175)**
- To describe is to produce word pictures—detailed information that allows an audience mentally to see, hear, smell, touch, or taste what you are describing.
- Explaining how is used by speakers who discuss or demonstrate processes of any kind.

- Explaining why involves giving reasons for or consequences of a policy, principle, or event.
- Use descriptions and explanations effectively:
  - Keep your descriptions and explanations brief.
  - Use language that is as specific and concrete as possible.
  - Avoid too much description and explanation.

➡ **Definitions (p. 176)**

- A speaker should be sure to define any and all specialized, technical, or little-known terms in his or her speech. A speaker may define a term by showing how it works or how it is applied in a specific instance.
  - To explain the meaning of a term, you may use a definition by classification from the *Oxford English Dictionary, Webster's,* or another reputable general dictionary, or you may turn to a specialized dictionary, such as *Black's Law Dictionary.*
  - Operational definitions are more concrete, explaining how something works or what it does.
- To use definitions effectively:
  - Use a definition only when needed.
  - Be certain that your definition is understandable.
  - Be certain that your definition and your use of a term are consistent throughout a speech.

➡ **Analogies (p. 178)**

- An analogy is a comparison.
  - A literal analogy is a comparison between two similar things.
  - A figurative analogy, because it relies not on facts or statistics but rather on imaginative insights, is not considered "hard" evidence.
- To use analogies effectively:
  - Be sure that the two things you compare in a literal analogy are very similar.
  - Be sure that the essential similarity between the two objects of a figurative analogy is readily apparent.

➡ **Statistics (p. 180)**

- Statistics are considered by most people to be the ultimate "hard" evidence—firm, convincing fact. Just as three or four brief examples may be more effective than just one, a statistic that represents hundreds or thousands of individuals may be more persuasive still.

- To use statistics effectively:
  - Use reliable sources that are reputable, authoritative, and unbiased.
  - Interpret statistics accurately.
  - Make your statistics understandable and memorable by compacting them, exploding them, or comparing them.
  - Round off numbers.
  - Use visual aids to present your statistics.

➡ Opinions (p. 184)
  - Three types of opinions may be used as supporting material in speeches: the testimonies of expert authorities, the testimonies of ordinary (lay) people with firsthand or eyewitness experience, and quotations from literary works.
    - Expert testimony can add a great deal of weight to your arguments. You may quote experts directly or paraphrase their words, as long as you are careful not to alter the intent of their remarks.
    - Lay testimony can stir an audience's emotions. And, although lay testimony is neither as authoritative nor as unbiased as expert testimony, it is often more memorable.
    - Literary quotations provide another way to make a point memorable.
  - Use opinions effectively:
    - Be certain that any authority you cite is an expert on the subject.
    - Identify your sources.
    - Cite unbiased authorities.
    - Cite opinions that are representative of prevailing opinion.
    - Quote your sources accurately.
    - Use literary quotations sparingly.

➡ Selecting the Best Supporting Material (p. 187)
  - You should use accountability, accuracy, objectivity, date, usability, and diversity as criteria in evaluating supporting material you hope to use. In addition, consider
    - Magnitude. Bigger is better. The larger the numbers, the more convincing your statistics.
    - Proximity. The best supporting material is whatever is the most relevant to your listeners, or "closest to home."
    - Concreteness. By themselves, abstract assertions and explanations bore an audience. If you need to discuss principles and theories, explain them with concrete examples and specific statistics.

At a Glance *(continued)*

- Variety. Even if your supporting material meets the first four requirements, if it is all of the same type, your audience may lose interest or question your research. A mix of illustrations, opinions, definitions, and statistics is much more interesting and convincing than the exclusive use of any one type of supporting material.
- Humor. Audiences usually appreciate a touch of humor in an example or opinion.
- Suitability. Your final decision about whether to use a certain piece of supporting material will depend on its suitability to you, your speech, the occasion, and your audience.

CHAPTER 7

Developing Your Speech

Ed Garcia has arranged the books and papers on his desk into neat, even piles. He has sharpened his pencils and laid them out parallel to one another. He has even dusted his desktop and cleaned the computer monitor's screen. Ed can think of no other task to delay writing his speech. He opens a new word-processing document, carefully centers the words "Informative Speech" at the top of the first page, and then slouches in his chair, staring glumly at the blank expanse that threatens his well-being. Finally, he types the words "College Football" under the words "Informative Speech." Another long pause. Hesitantly, he begins his first sentence: "Today I want to talk to you about college football." Rereading his first ten words, Ed decides that they sound moronic. He deletes the sentence and tries again. This time the screen looks even blanker than before. He writes—deletes—writes—deletes. Half an hour later, Ed is exhausted and still mocked by a blank screen. And he is frantic—this speech has to be ready by 9 in the morning.

In all matters, before beginning, a diligent preparation should be made.

—Cicero

Getting from a blank screen or sheet of paper to a speech outline is often the biggest hurdle you will face as a public speaker. Fortunately, however, it is one that you can learn to clear. If your earlier efforts at speech writing have been like Ed Garcia's, take heart. Just as you learned to read, do long division, drive a car, and get through college registration, so, too, can you learn to prepare a speech.

There are four first steps in preparing a speech:

1. Select and narrow your topic.
2. Determine your purpose.
3. Develop your central idea.
4. Generate your main ideas.

At the end of step 4, you will have a plan for the speech and be ready to develop and polish your main ideas further.

For most brief classroom speeches (under ten minutes), you should allow at least one week between selecting a topic and delivering your speech. A week gives you enough time to develop and research your speech. Many habitual procrastinators like Ed Garcia, who grudgingly decide to begin an assignment a week in advance, learn to their surprise that the whole process is far easier than it would be if they put off working until the night before they are supposed to deliver their speech.

Audience-centered speakers consider the needs, interests, and expectations of their audience during the entire speech-preparation process—needs, interests, and expectations that will be as diverse as the audiences themselves. As you move from topic selection to speech plan, remember that you are preparing a message for your listeners. Always keep the audience as your central focus.

7.a Select and Narrow Your Topic

Your first task, as illustrated in Figure 7.1, is to choose a topic to speak about. You will need to narrow this topic to fit your time limits. Sometimes you can eliminate one or both of these steps because the topic has been chosen and properly defined for you. For

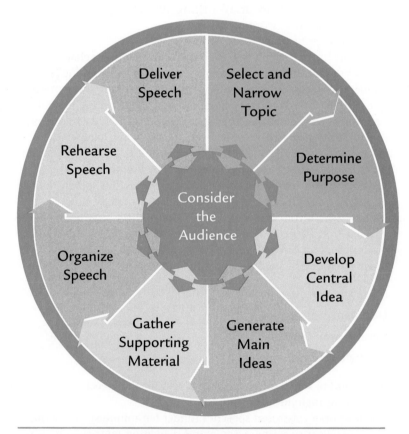

FIGURE 7.1 Selecting and narrowing the topic and determining the general and specific purpose of the speech are early speechmaking tasks.

example, knowing that you visited England's Lake District on your tour of Great Britain last summer, your English literature teacher asks you to speak about the mountains and lakes of that region before your class studies the poetry of Wordsworth and Coleridge. Or imagine that the Lions Club asks you to speak at its weekly meeting about the goals of the local drug-abuse task force, which you chair. In both cases, your topic and its scope have been decided for you.

In other instances, the choice of topic may be left entirely to you. In your public-speaking class, your instructor may provide such guidelines as time limits and type of speech (informative, persuasive, or entertaining) but allow you to choose your topic. In this event, you should realize that the success of your speech may rest on this decision. But how do you go about choosing an appropriate, interesting topic?

GUIDELINES FOR SELECTING A TOPIC

> Davy Crockett was scheduled to speak first on a platform with a political opponent known always to deliver the same standard speech. So Davy memorized that speech, gave it, and left the opponent speechless.[1]

Consider the Audience The downfall of Crockett's literally speechless opponent was that he relied on a standard spiel, rather than tailoring his speeches to each specific audience. "What interests and needs do the members of this audience have in common?" and "Why did they ask me to speak?" are important questions to ask yourself as you search for potential speech topics. Keep in mind each audience's interests and expectations; for example, a university president invited to speak to a civic organization should talk about some new university program or recent accomplishment; a police officer speaking to an elementary school's PTA should address the audience's concern for the safety of young children.

Not only should a speaker's choice of topic be relevant to the *interests* and *expectations* of his or her listeners, it should also take into account the *knowledge* listeners already have about the subject. For example, the need for a campuswide office of disability services would not be a good topic for a group of students with disabilities, who would already be well aware of such a need. The speech would offer them no new information.

Finally, speakers should choose topics that are important—topics that matter to their listeners, as well as to themselves. Student speaker Roger Fringer explains the stakes for students in a public-speaking class:

> We work hard for our tuition, so we should spend it wisely. Spending it wisely means . . . we don't waste our classmates' time who have to listen to our speeches.[2]

In November 1994, Bruce Gronbeck, then-president of the Speech Communication Association (now the National Communication Association), reminded an audience of communication instructors that students should be giving "the important kinds of . . . speeches that show . . . people how to confront the issues that divide them . . . ."[3] Table 7.1 on page 130 offers examples of topics appropriate for the interests, expectations, knowledge, and concerns of given audiences.

TABLE 7.1	Sample Audience-Centered Topics
Audience	**Topic**
Retirees	Preserving Social Security benefits
Civic organization	The Special Olympics
Church members	Starting a community food bank
First graders	What to do in case of a fire at home
Teachers	Building children's self-esteem
College fraternity	Campus service opportunities

Consider the Occasion   On December 17, 1877, Mark Twain was invited to be one of the after-dinner speakers for American poet John Greenleaf Whittier's seventieth-birthday celebration.[4] The guest list included such dignitaries as Oliver Wendell Holmes, Ralph Waldo Emerson, William Dean Howells, and Henry Wadsworth Longfellow.

When it was Twain's turn to speak, he began with a burlesque in the style of *Saturday Night Live,* featuring Longfellow, Emerson, and Holmes as drunken card-playing travelers in Nevada. Used to laughter and applause from his audiences, Twain was stunned by the silence that descended and seemed to grow as he continued.

What had gone wrong? Was Mark Twain's topic of *interest* to his listeners? Undoubtedly. Did they *expect* to hear someone talk about the distinguished guests? Yes. Could Twain *add to their knowledge of the subject?* Probably. Was his topic *appropriate to the occasion?* Definitely not!

Although after-dinner speeches are usually humorous, Twain's irreverence was inappropriate to the dignity of the birthday observance. Even though he had considered his audience, he had not considered carefully enough the demands of the occasion. Twain's irreverent talk aroused quite a commotion at the time and is said to have embarrassed him for years afterward. To be successful, a topic must be appropriate to both audience and occasion.

Consider Yourself   What do you talk about with good friends? You probably discuss school, mutual friends, political or social issues, hobbies or leisure activities, or other topics of interest and importance to you. Like most people, your liveliest, most animated conversations revolve around topics of personal concern that arouse your deepest convictions.

The best public-speaking topics are also those that reflect your personal experience or especially interest you. Where have you lived? Where have you traveled? Describe your family or your ancestors. Have you held any part-time jobs? Describe your first days at college. What are your favorite classes? What are your hobbies or interests?

What is your favorite sport? What social issues especially concern you? Here is one list of topics that was generated by such questions:

Blues music

"Yankee, go home": the American tourist in France

Why most diets fail

Behind the counter at McDonald's

My first day at college

Maintaining family ties while living a long distance from home

Getting involved in political campaigns

An alternative to selecting a topic with which you are already familiar is to select one you would like to know more about. Your interest will motivate both your research and your eventual delivery of the speech.

STRATEGIES FOR SELECTING A TOPIC

All successful topics reflect audience, occasion, and speaker. But just contemplating those guidelines does not automatically produce a good topic. Sooner or later, we all find ourselves unable to think of a good speech topic, whether it is for the first speech of the semester, for that all-important final speech, or for a speaking engagement long after your school years are over. Nothing is as frustrating to a public speaker as floundering for something to talk about!

Fortunately, there are several strategies that can help generate speech topics. They are somewhat more artificial than considering audience, occasion, and yourself to produce a "natural" topic choice. Nevertheless, they can yield good topics.

Brainstorming   A problem-solving technique widely used in such diverse fields as business, advertising, writing, and science, **brainstorming** can easily be used to generate ideas for speech topics as well.[5] To brainstorm a list of potential topics, get a sheet of paper and a pencil or pen. Set a minimum time limit of, say, three to five minutes. Write down the first topic that comes to mind. Do not allow yourself to evaluate it. Just write it down in a word or a phrase, whether it is a vague idea or a well-focused one.

Now jot down a second idea—again, anything that comes to mind. The first topic may remind you of a second possibility. Such "piggybacking" of ideas is perfectly okay. Continue without any restraints until your time is up. At this stage, anything goes. Your goal is quantity—as long a list as you can think up in the time you have.

The following list of twenty-one possible topics came from a brainstorming session of about three minutes:

Music	Retro music
Reggae	Buddy Holly
Bob Marley	Censorship of music
Sound-recording technology	Movie themes

Oscar-winning movies of the 1990s	Popular rock bands
Great epic movies	MTV
Titanic (the movie)	Treasure hunting
Salvaging the *Titanic* (the ship)	Key West, Florida
The Beatles	Ernest Hemingway
John Lennon	Cats
Alternative music	

If your brainstorming yields several good topics, so much the better. Set aside a page or two in your class notebook where you list topic ideas you don't end up choosing. You can then reconsider them when you get your next assignment.

HOW TO: *Brainstorm for a Topic*

- Start with a blank sheet of paper.
- Set a time limit for brainstorming.
- Begin writing as many possible topics for a speech as you can.
- Do not stop to evaluate your topics; just write them down.
- Let one idea lead to another—free-associate; piggyback off your own ideas.
- Keep writing until your time is up.

Listening and Reading for Topic Ideas   Very often something you see, hear, or read triggers an idea for a speech. A current story on the evening news or in your local paper may suggest a topic. The following list of topics was brought to mind by recent headline stories in a large daily newspaper:

How to read and interpret stock-market indicators

Prison overcrowding

Health codes and restaurants

The Nobel Prizes

How record prices for art and artifacts are affecting museum acquisitions

Television evangelism

Deteriorating interstate highways

Mothers Against Drunk Driving

In addition to discovering topics in news stories, you might find them in an interesting segment of *60 Minutes, 20/20, Dateline,* or *Oprah.* Chances are that a topic covered in one medium has been covered in another as well, allowing extended research on the topic. For example, Oprah's interview of the parents of a child suffering from a genetic disease may be paralleled by *Newsweek's* report on stem-cell research.

You may also find speech topics in one of your other classes. A lecture in an economics or political science class may arouse your interest and provide a good topic for your next speech. The instructor of that class could probably suggest additional references on the subject.

Sometimes even a subject you discuss casually with friends can be developed into a good speech topic. You have probably talked with classmates about such campus issues as dormitory regulations, inadequate parking, or your frustration with registration and advisers. Campuswide concerns would be relevant to the student audience in your speech class, as would such matters as how to find a good summer job or the pros and cons of living on or off campus.

Just as you jotted down possible topics generated by brainstorming sessions, remember to write down topic ideas you get from media, class lectures, or informal conversations. If you rely on memory alone, what seems like a great topic today may be only a frustrating blank tomorrow.

Scanning Web Directories   By now, you probably have a list of topics from which to choose. But if all your efforts have failed to produce any ideas that satisfy you, try the following strategy.

Access a **Web directory** such as Yahoo! (www.yahoo.com). Select a category at random. Click on it, and look through the subcategories that come up. Click on one of them. Continue to follow the chain of categories until you see a topic that piques your interest—or until you reach a dead end, in which case you can return to the Yahoo! homepage and try again.

A recent random directory search yielded the following categories, listed from general to specific:

Health

Alternative medicine

Homeopathy

National Center for Homeopathy

Introduction to homeopathy

Healthy pets and homeopathy

QUICK CHECK: *Selecting a Topic*

Guidelines:	Consider the audience.
	Consider the occasion.
	Consider yourself.
Strategies:	Brainstorm.
	Listen and read.
	Scan Web directories.

This search took only a few minutes (as will yours, as long as you resist the temptation to begin surfing the Web) and yielded one or two possible topics: homeopathy and alternative veterinary medicine. An additional advantage of this strategy is that you begin to develop your preliminary bibliography while you are searching for a topic. In Chapter 8, we talk in more detail about Web directories and about gathering supporting materials.

NARROWING THE TOPIC

After brainstorming, reading the newspaper, surfing the Web, and talking to friends, you have come up with a topic. For some students, the toughest part of the assignment is over at this point. But others soon experience additional frustration because their topic is so broad that they find themselves overwhelmed with information. How can you cover all aspects of a topic as large as "television" in three to five minutes? Even if you trained yourself to speak as rapidly as an auctioneer, it would take days to get it all in!

Create Categories   The solution is to narrow your topic so that it fits within the time limits set by your assignment. The challenge lies in how to do this. If you have a broad, unmanageable topic, you might first try narrowing it by constructing categories similar to those created by Web directories. Write your general topic at the top of a list, and make each succeeding word in the list a more specific or concrete topic. Megan uses categories to help her narrow her general topic, music. She writes "Music" at the top of a sheet of paper, and constructs a categorical hierarchy:

Music

Folk music

Irish folk music

The popularity of Irish folk music in the United States

Find the Right Level   Megan soon discovers her topic is still a bit too broad. She simply cannot cover all the forms of Irish folk music popular in the United States in a talk of no more than five minutes. So she chooses one form of music—dance—and decides to talk about the kind of Irish hard-shoe dance music featured in *Riverdance*.

Be careful not to narrow your topic so much that you cannot find enough information for even a three-minute talk. If you do, just go back a step. In our example, Megan could return to the broader topic of the popularity of Irish folk music in the United States.

7.b   Determine Your Purpose

Now that you have selected and narrowed your topic, you need to decide on a purpose (as shown in Figure 7.1). If you do not know what you want your speech to achieve, chances are your audience won't either. Ask yourself, "What is really important for the audience to hear?" and "How do I want the audience to respond?" Clarifying your objectives at this stage will ensure a more interesting speech and a more successful outcome.

GENERAL PURPOSE

The **general purpose** of virtually any speech is either to inform, to persuade, or to entertain. The speeches you give in class will generally be either informative or persuasive. It is important that you fully understand what constitutes each type of speech so you do not confuse them and fail to fulfill an assignment. You certainly do not want to deliver a first-rate persuasive speech when an informative one was assigned!

Speaking to Inform An informative speaker is a teacher. Informative speakers give listeners information. They define, describe, or explain a thing, person, place, concept, process, or function. In this excerpt from a student's informative speech on anorexia nervosa, the student describes the disorder for her audience:

> Anorexia nervosa is an eating disorder that affects 1 out of every 200 American women. It is a self-induced starvation that can waste its victims to the point that they resemble victims of Nazi concentration camps.
>
> Who gets anorexia nervosa? Ninety-five percent of its victims are females between the ages of 12 and 18. Men are only rarely afflicted with the disease. Anorexia nervosa patients are usually profiled as "good" or "model" children who have not caused their parents any undue concern or grief over other behavior problems. Anorexia nervosa is perhaps a desperate bid for attention by these young women.[6]

Most lectures you hear in college are informative. The university president's annual "state of the university" speech is also informative, as is the colonial Williamsburg tour guide's talk. Such speakers are all trying to increase the knowledge of their listeners. Although they may use an occasional bit of humor in their presentations, their main objective is not to entertain. And although they may provoke an audience's interest in the topic, their main objective is not to persuade.

Speaking to Persuade Persuasive speakers may offer information, but they use the information to try to change or reinforce an audience's convictions and often to urge some sort of action. For example, Brian offered compelling statistics to help persuade his audience to take steps to prevent and alleviate chronic pain:

> A hundred million Americans, nearly a third of the population, [suffer] from chronic pain due to everything from accidents to the simple daily stresses on our bodies.[7]

The representative from Mothers Against Drunk Driving (MADD) who spoke at your high-school assembly urged you not to drink and drive and to help others realize the inherent dangers of the practice. The fraternity president talking to your group of rushees tried to convince you to join his fraternity. Appearing on television during the last election, the candidates for president of the United States asked for your vote. All these speakers gave you information, but they used that information to try to get you to believe or do something.

Speaking to Entertain   The entertaining speaker tries to get the members of an audience to relax, smile, perhaps laugh, and generally enjoy themselves. Storyteller Garrison Keillor spins tales of the town and residents of Lake Wobegon, Minnesota, to amuse his listeners. Comedian Whoopi Goldberg delivers comic patter to make her audience laugh. Most after-dinner speakers talk to entertain the banquet guests. Like persuasive speakers, entertaining speakers may inform their listeners, but providing knowledge is not their main goal. Rather, their objective is to produce at least a smile and at best a belly laugh.

Early on, you need to decide which of the three general purposes your speech is to have. This decision keeps you on track throughout the development of your speech. The way you organize, support, and deliver your speech depends, in part, on your general purpose.

QUICK CHECK: *General Purposes for Speeches*

To inform	To share information with listeners by defining, describing, or explaining a thing, person, place, concept, process, or function
To persuade	To change or reinforce a listener's attitude, belief, value, or behavior
To entertain	To help listeners have a good time by getting them to relax, smile, and laugh

SPECIFIC PURPOSE

Now that you have a topic and you know generally whether your speech should inform, persuade, or entertain, it is time you decided on its **specific purpose**. Unlike the general purpose, which can be assigned by your instructor, you alone must decide on the specific purpose of your speech, because it depends directly on the topic you choose.

Identify a Behavioral Objective   To arrive at a specific purpose for your speech, you must think in precise terms of what you want your audience to be able to *do* at the end of your speech. This kind of goal or purpose is called a **behavioral objective**, because you specify the behavior you seek from the audience.

For a speech on how television comedy represents the modern family, you might write, "At the end of my speech, the audience will be able to explain how comedy portrays American family life today." The specific-purpose statement for a how-to speech using visual aids might read, "At the end of my speech, the audience will be able to use an online periodical index." For a persuasive speech on universal health care, your specific-purpose statement could say, "At the end of my speech, the audience will be able to explain why the United States should adopt a plan of national health insurance." A speech to entertain has a specific purpose, too. A stand-up comic may have a simple specific purpose: "At the end of my speech, the audience will laugh and applaud." An after-dinner speaker whose entertaining message has more informative value than that of the stand-up comic may say, "At the end of my speech, the audience will list four characteristics that distinguish journalists from the rest of the human species."

Formulate the Specific Purpose Note that almost all of our sample specific-purpose statements begin with the same twelve words: "At the end of my speech, the audience will be able to . . . ." The next word should be a verb that names an observable, measurable action that the audience should be able to take by the end of the speech.

Use verbs such as *list, explain, describe,* or *write.* Do not use words such as *know, understand,* or *believe.* You can discover what your listeners know, understand, or believe only by having them show their increased capability in some measurable way.

A statement of purpose does not say what you, the *speaker,* will do. The techniques of public speaking help you achieve your goals, but they are not themselves goals. To say, "In my speech, I will talk about the benefits of studying classical dance" emphasizes your performance as a speaker. This goal statement is centered on you, rather than on the audience. Other than restating your topic, this statement of purpose provides little direction for the speech. But to say, "At the end of my speech, the audience will be able to list three ways in which studying classical dance can benefit them" places the audience and their behavior at the center of your concern. This latter statement provides a tangible goal that can guide your preparation and by which you can measure the success of your speech.

The following guidelines will help you prepare your statement of purpose.

- Use words that refer to observable or measurable behavior.

    Not Observable: At the end of my speech, the audience will know some things about Hannibal, Missouri.

    Observable: At the end of my speech, the audience will be able to list five points of interest in the town of Hannibal, Missouri.

- Limit the specific purpose to a single idea. If your statement of purpose has more than one idea, you will have trouble covering the extra ideas in your speech. You will also run the risk of having your speech "come apart at the seams." Both unity of ideas and coherence of expression will suffer.

    Two Ideas: At the end of my speech, the audience will be able to write a simple computer program in BASIC and play the video game Halo.

    One Idea: At the end of my speech, the audience will be able to write a simple computer program in BASIC.

- Make sure your specific purpose reflects the interests, expectations, and knowledge level of your audience. Also be sure that your specific purpose is important. Earlier in this chapter, we discussed these criteria as guidelines for selecting a speech topic. Consider them again as you word your specific purpose statement.

Behavioral statements of purpose help remind you that the aim of public speaking is to win a response from the audience. In addition, using a specific purpose to guide the development of your speech helps you focus on the audience during the entire preparation process.

QUICK CHECK: *Specific Purposes for Speeches*

Your specific purpose should . . .

- Use words that refer to observable or measurable behavior
- Be limited to a single idea
- Reflect the needs, interests, expectations, and level of knowledge of your audience

Use the Specific Purpose   Everything you do while preparing and delivering the speech should contribute to your specific purpose. The specific purpose can help you assess the information you are gathering for your speech. For example, you may find that an interesting statistic, although related to your topic, does not help achieve your specific purpose. In that case, you can substitute material that directly advances your purpose.

As soon as you have decided on it, write the specific purpose on a 3-by-5-inch note card. That way you can refer to it as often as necessary while developing your speech.

7.C   Develop Your Central Idea

Having stated the specific purpose of your speech, you are ready to develop your *central idea,* the first step highlighted in Figure 7.2. The **central idea** is a one-sentence summary of the speech. The central idea (sometimes called the *thesis*), like the purpose statement, restates the speech topic. But whereas a purpose statement focuses on audience behavior, the central idea focuses on the content of the speech.

Professional speech coach Judith Humphrey explains the importance of a central idea:

> Ask yourself before writing a speech . . . "What's my point?" Be able to state that message in a single clear sentence. Everything else you say will support that single argument.[8]

The guidelines in the following sections can help you put your central idea into words.

A COMPLETE DECLARATIVE SENTENCE

The central idea should be a complete declarative sentence—not a phrase or clause, and not a question.

Phrase:	Car maintenance
Question:	Is regular car maintenance important?
Complete Declarative Sentence:	Maintaining your car regularly can ensure that it provides reliable transportation.

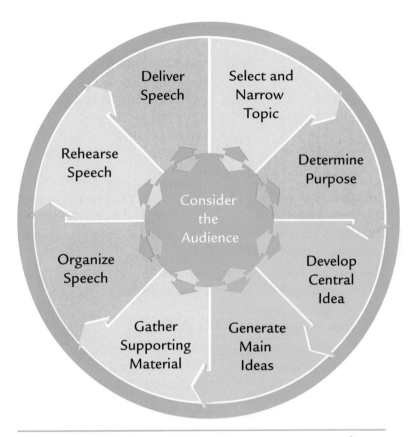

FIGURE 7.2 **State your central idea as a one-sentence summary of your speech, and then generate main ideas by looking for natural divisions, reasons, or steps to support your central idea.**

The phrase "car maintenance" is really not a central idea, but a topic. It does not say anything about car maintenance. The question "Is regular car maintenance important?" is more complete but does not reveal whether the speaker is going to support the affirmative or the negative answer. By the time you word your central idea, you should be ready to summarize your stand on your topic in a complete declarative sentence.

DIRECT, SPECIFIC LANGUAGE

The central idea should use direct, specific language rather than qualifiers and vague generalities.

Qualified Language: In my opinion, censorship of school textbooks threatens the rights of schoolchildren.

Direct Language:	Censorship of school textbooks threatens the rights of schoolchildren.
Vague:	Tropical Storm Allison affected Houston, Texas.
Specific:	Killing 22 people and inflicting more than $5 billion in damage, Tropical Storm Allison changed forever the lives of the citizens of Houston, Texas.

A SINGLE IDEA

The central idea should be a single idea.

| Two Ideas: | Deforestation by lumber interests and toxic-waste dumping are major environmental problems in the United States today. |
| One Idea: | Toxic-waste dumping is a major environmental problem in the United States today. |

More than one central idea, like more than one idea in a purpose statement, only leads to confusion and lack of coherence in a speech.

AN AUDIENCE-CENTERED IDEA

The central idea should reflect consideration of the audience. You considered your audience when selecting and narrowing your topic and when composing your purpose statement. In the same way, you should consider your audience's needs, interests, expectations, and knowledge when stating your central idea. If you do not consider your listeners, you run the risk of losing their attention before you even begin developing the speech. If your audience consists mainly of college juniors and seniors, the second of the central ideas at the top of the facing page would be better suited to your listeners than the first.

QUICK CHECK: *Purpose Statement Versus Central Idea*

The Purpose Statement . . .

- Indicates what the audience should be able to do by the end of the speech
- Guides the speaker's choices throughout the preparation of the speech

The Central Idea . . .

- Summarizes the speech
- Guides the audience in their understanding of the speech
- Is complete declarative sentence
- Uses direct, specific language
- Is a single idea
- Is an audience-centered idea

Inappropriate:	Scholarships from a variety of sources are readily available to first-year college students.
Appropriate:	Although you may think of scholarships as a source of money for freshmen, a number of scholarships are available only to students who have completed their first year of college.

7.d Generate and Preview Your Main Ideas

Next to selecting a topic, probably the most common stumbling block in developing speeches is coming up with a speech plan. Trying to decide how to subdivide your central idea into two, three, or four **main ideas** can make you chew your pencil, scratch your head, and end up as you began, with a blank sheet of paper. The task will be much easier if you use the following strategy.

GENERATING YOUR MAIN IDEAS

Write the central idea at the top of a sheet of paper. Then ask these three questions:

- Does the central idea have *logical divisions?* (These may be indicated by such phrases as "three types" or "four means.")
- Can you think of several *reasons* why the central idea is true?
- Can you support your central idea with a series of *steps* or a chronological progression?

You should be able to answer yes to one or more of these questions. With your answer in mind, write down the divisions, reasons, or steps you thought of. Let's see this technique at work with several central idea statements.

Finding Logical Divisions   Suppose your central idea is "A liberal arts education benefits the student in three ways." You now turn to the three questions. But for this example, you needn't go beyond the first one. Does the central idea have logical divisions? The phrase "three ways" indicates that it does. You can logically divide your speech into ways in which the student benefits:

1. Job opportunities
2. Appreciation of culture
3. Concern for humankind

A brief brainstorming session then could help you come up with more specific examples of ways in which a liberal arts education might benefit students. At this stage, you needn't worry about Roman numerals, parallel form, or even the order in which the main ideas are listed. Your goal now is simply to generate ideas. Moreover, just because you write them down, don't think that the ideas you come up with now are engraved in stone. They can—and probably will—change. After all, this is a *preliminary* plan. It may undergo many revisions before you actually deliver your speech. In our example, three points may well prove to be too many to develop in the brief time allowed for most classroom speeches. But because it is much easier to eliminate ideas than to invent them, list them all for now.

Establishing Reasons   Suppose your central idea is "Upholstered furniture fires are a life-threatening hazard."[9] Asking yourself whether this idea has logical divisions is no help at all. There are no key phrases indicating logical divisions—no "ways," "means," "types," or "methods" appear in the wording. The second question, however, is more productive: Having done some initial reading on the topic, you can think of reasons this central idea is true. Asking yourself, "Why?" after stating your central idea yields three answers:

1. Standards to reduce fires caused by smoldering cigarettes have lulled furniture makers into a false sense of security.
2. Government officials refuse to force the furniture industry to reexamine its standards.
3. Consumers are largely ignorant of the risks.

Notice that these main ideas are expressed in complete sentences, whereas the ones in the preceding example were in phrases. At this stage, it doesn't matter. What does matter is getting your ideas down on paper. You can rewrite and reorganize them later.

Tracing Specific Steps   "NASA's space shuttle program has known both great achievement and tragic failure." You stare glumly at the central idea you so carefully formulated yesterday. Now what? You know a lot about the subject; your aerospace science professor has covered it thoroughly this semester. But how can you organize all the information you have? Again, you turn to the three-question method.

Does the main idea have logical divisions? You scan the sentence hopefully, but you can find no key phrases suggesting logical divisions.

Can you think of several reasons the central idea is true? You read the central idea again and ask "Why?" at the end of it. Answering that question may indeed produce a plan for a speech, one in which you would talk about the reasons for the achievements and failures. But your purpose statement reads, "At the end of my speech, the audience will be able to trace the history of the space shuttle." Giving reasons for the space shuttle program's achievements and failures would not directly contribute to your purpose. So you turn to the third question.

Can you support your central idea with a series of steps? Almost any historical topic, or any topic requiring a chronological progression (for example, topics of how-to speeches), can be subdivided by answering the third question. You therefore decide that your main ideas will be a chronology of important space shuttle flights:[10]

1. April 1981: Test flight of the space shuttle.
2. January 1986: Shuttle *Challenger* explodes on launch.
3. April 1990: Deployment of the Hubble space telescope.
4. October–November 1998: Flight of John Glenn, age 77, who had been the first American in orbit in 1962.

5. May–June 1999: Shuttle *Discovery* docks with the International Space Station

6. February 2003: Shuttle *Columbia* disintegrates on re-entry.

You know that you can add to, eliminate, or reorganize these ideas later. But you have a start.

Notice that for this last example, you consulted your purpose statement as you generated your main ideas. If these main ideas do not help achieve your purpose, you need to rethink your speech. You may finally change either your purpose or your main ideas; but whichever you do, you need to synchronize them. Remember, it is much easier to make changes at this point than after you have done your research and produced a detailed outline.

PREVIEWING YOUR MAIN IDEAS

Once you have generated your main ideas, you can add a preview of those main ideas to your central idea to produce a **blueprint** for your speech. Preview the ideas in the same order you plan to discuss them in the speech.

Some speakers, like Nicole, integrate their central idea and preview into one blueprint sentence:

> Obsolete computers are straining landfills because they contain hazardous materials and take a distinctively long time to decay.[11]

In this example, Nicole started with a central idea: "Obsolete computers are straining landfills." Asking herself "Why?" yielded two reasons, which became her two main points: "They contain hazardous materials" and "They take a distinctively long time to decay." Combining these reasons with her central idea produced a blueprint.

Other speakers, like Erin, state their blueprints in several sentences:

> Today I would like to expose the myth that owning a gun guarantees your personal safety. First, I will discuss the fact that guns are rarely reached in time of need. Then I will address the risk of accidental shootings and how this is greatly increased by people's failure to receive proper gun-handling training. And finally, I will propose an alternative solution, self-defense.[12]

Erin also started with a central idea: "Owning a gun does not guarantee your personal safety." Like Nicole, she generated reasons for her central idea, which in this case were that "guns are rarely reached in time of need" and that "the risk of accidental shootings is increased." She decided also to discuss martial-arts "self-defense" as a solution to the problem. Thinking that a single sentence might become unwieldy, Erin decided to use four shorter sentences for her blueprint.

7.e Meanwhile, Back at the Computer . . .

It's been a while since we abandoned Ed Garcia, the student in the opening paragraphs of this chapter who was struggling to write a speech on college football. Even though he has procrastinated, if he follows the steps we have discussed, he should still be able to plan a successful informative speech.

Ed has already chosen his topic. His audience is likely to be interested in his subject. Because Ed is a varsity defensive tackle, the audience will probably expect him to talk about college football. And he himself is passionately interested in and knowledgeable about the subject. It meets all the requirements of a successful topic.

But "college football" is too broad for a three- to five-minute talk. Ed needs to narrow his topic to a manageable size. He goes online to Yahoo! and clicks on the category Sports. This search yields a fairly long list of subcategories. He is just about to select College and University when another category catches his eye: Medicine. Sports medicine? Hmmmm. . . . Ed has suffered several injuries and feels qualified to talk about this aspect of football. Ed doesn't need to go further. He has his topic: "Injuries in college football."

Now that he has narrowed the topic, Ed needs a purpose statement. He decides that his audience may know something about how players are injured, but they probably do not know how these injuries are treated. He types, "The audience will be able to explain how the three most common injuries suffered by college football players are treated."

A few minutes later, Ed derives his central idea from his purpose: "Sports medicine specialists have developed specific courses of treatment for the three most common kinds of injuries suffered by college football players."

Generating main ideas is also fairly easy now. Because his central idea mentions three kinds of injuries, he can plan his speech around those three ideas (logical divisions). Under the central idea Ed lists three injuries:

1. Bruises
2. Broken bones
3. Ligament and cartilage damage

Now Ed has a plan and is well on his way to developing a successful three- to five-minute informative speech.

Summary

- The four main steps in getting from a blank piece of paper to a speech plan are to (1) select and narrow your topic, (2) determine your purpose, (3) develop your central idea, and (4) generate your main ideas.

- Selecting a topic may or may not be difficult, depending on the requirements of the speech. You may be asked to address a specific topic or you may be given only broad guidelines, such as a time limit and an idea of the occasion.

- As you consider possible topics, keep in mind your audience's interests, expectations, and knowledge levels.

- Select topics of importance, and consider the special demands of the occasion.

- Take into account your own interests, abilities, and experiences. Usually these help you select appropriate topics. If you are still undecided, you may try such strategies as brainstorming, consulting the media, or scanning Web directories for potential topics.

- Narrow the topic so that it fits within the time limits that have been set.

- Decide on general and specific purposes. Consider whether a speech is going to be informative, persuasive, or entertaining.

- With a general purpose in mind, write a specific-purpose statement. A specific-purpose statement should be worded behaviorally, in terms of what you want the audience to be able to do at the end of the speech.

- The specific purpose serves as a yardstick by which you can measure the relevance of ideas and supporting materials while developing the speech.

- Specific-purpose statements indicate what you hope to accomplish.

- Central ideas summarize what you will say. The central idea should be stated in a complete declarative sentence. From the central idea, you can generate main ideas.

- To generate main ideas, determine whether the central idea has logical divisions, can be supported by several reasons, or can be traced through a series of steps. These divisions, reasons, or steps become the speech plan, which you will probably preview in the introduction and summarize in the conclusion.

Key Terms

behavioral objective (p. 136)
blueprint (p. 143)
brainstorming (p. 131)
central idea (p. 138)

general purpose (p. 135)
main ideas (p. 141)
specific purpose (p. 136)
Web directory (p. 133)

A QUESTION OF ETHICS

Steven has decided to develop a speech about socialized medicine, a topic with which he is unfamiliar. He reasons that he has several friends who are knowledgeable and feel strongly about the topic and that he will learn more about the topic through his research to support his speech. Is it ethical for Steven to adopt his friends' opinions about the topic and then find material to support their opinions? Why or why not?

CHAPTER 8

Gathering Supporting Material

Apple pie is your family and friends relish your flaky crust, spicy filling, and crunchy crumb topping. Fortunately, not only do you have a never-fail recipe and technique, but you also know where to go for the best ingredients. Fette's Orchard has the tangiest pie apples in town. For your crust, you use only Premier shortening, which you buy at Meyer's Specialty Market. Your crumb topping requires both stone-ground whole-wheat flour and fresh creamery butter, available on Tuesdays at the farmer's market on the courthouse square.

> *Learn, compare,*
> *collect the facts! . . .*
> *Always have the*
> *courage to say to*
> *yourself—I am*
> *ignorant.*
>
> **—Ivan Petrovich**
> **Pavlov**

Just as making your apple pie requires that you know where to find specific ingredients, creating a successful speech requires knowledge of both sources of and types of supporting material that speechmakers typically use; as Figure 8.1 on page 148 illustrates, gathering supporting material is a key step in the crafting of any speech. In this chapter we will identify various sources of information and discuss ways to access them. In a later chapter we will focus on recognizing and effectively using various types of supporting material.

8.a Personal Knowledge and Experience

Because you will probably give speeches on topics you are particularly interested in, you may find that you are your own best source. Your speech may be on a skill or hobby in which you are expert, such as raising tropical fish, stenciling, or stamp collecting. Or you may talk on a subject with which you have had some personal experience, such as buying a used car, deciding whether to join a club, or seeking assisted living for an elderly relative. Don't automatically run to your computer or the library to find every piece of supporting material for every topic on which you speak.

It is true that most well-researched speeches include some objective material gathered from outside sources. But you may also be able to provide an effective illustration, explanation, definition, or other type of support from your own knowledge and expe-

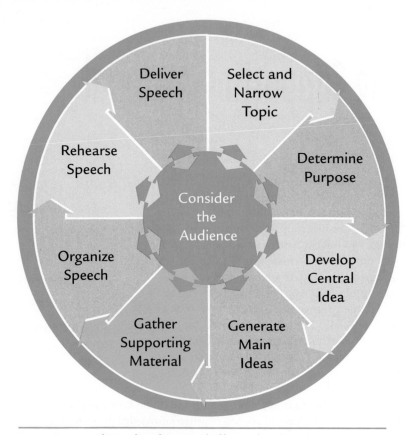

FIGURE 8.1 **Finding, identifying, and effectively using supporting material are activities that comprise an essential step of the speech-preparation process.**

rience. As an audience-centered speaker, you should realize, too, that personal knowledge often has the additional advantage of heightening your credibility in the minds of your listeners. They will accord you more respect as an authority when they realize that you have firsthand knowledge of a topic.

8.b ## The Internet

Originating as a modest network of four computers in 1969, the **Internet** today is a vast collection of computers accessible to millions of people all over the world. In the decades since its inception, the Internet has gone from a novel, last-resort resource to the first place most people turn when faced with a research task. More specifically, it is the World Wide Web, the most popular information-delivery system of the Internet, that is of primary interest when you are searching for supporting material for a speech. Understanding the World Wide Web, the tools for accessing it, and some of the amazing types of information available can help make research easier, more productive, and even more fun.

THE WORLD WIDE WEB

Web sites and **Web pages** may include personal and company pages, periodicals, newspapers, reference material, and government documents, as well as indexes and catalogs of these resources. Each Web site and Web page has its own address, or uniform resource locator (**URL**), the line of characters that will access the site when typed into the designated space on your **browser** software. Netscape Navigator and Microsoft Internet Explorer are the most commonly used Web browsers.

As well as being accessible by address, Web pages are connected by **hyperlinks**, indicated on screen by colored and underlined text or images. Clicking with your mouse on a hyperlink automatically calls up the linked page, without your having to know its address. Your browser lets you set an electronic **bookmark** on any interesting page so that you can return to it directly in the future without beginning a new search or going through other links.

DIRECTORIES AND SEARCH ENGINES

When you are just beginning to research a topic, you may not know an address for a relevant Web site. Even if you do, you may not find the hyperlinks there particularly useful for continuing your research. You need a **Web directory** or **search engine**, such as those provided by Yahoo!, Google, or another of the sites listed below.

Alta Vista	http://www.altavista.com
Google	http://www.google.com
Lycos	http://www.lycos.com
Yahoo!	http://www.yahoo.com

Browsing Broad Categories Regardless of whether you have spent countless hours surfing the Web or are a relative newcomer to its remarkable array of resources, today's directories and search engines make the Web easy to use. At times, you might want to browse broad categories of information on the Web, just as you would browse a section of library shelves for books all on the same subject. Directories work by setting up broad categories that are subdivided into ever-more-specific categories. When you call up a directory, you see a list of broad categories such as education, entertainment, government, reference, and science. Simply click on the category that seems most appropriate to your needs. You will likely be taken to a second level of categories; again, click on the most likely subcategory. Eventually, you will get a list of hits, or Web sites and Web pages that deal with the category you have selected.

Using Key Words At other times, you might prefer to access Web sites and Web pages by key words or subjects, much as you would search a traditional library card catalog. Search engines index the World Wide Web in this manner. At one time, most Web sites specializing in Internet searches were either directories or search engines; most now offer both functions.

Doing Advanced Searches Only a few years ago, students struggled to find enough information for speeches and papers. One of the ways in which the World Wide Web has changed research is that today, students often find themselves overwhelmed by too much material. One strategy that can help you narrow your search is called an advanced, or Boolean, search. A **Boolean search** lets you enclose phrases in quotation marks or parentheses so that a search yields only those sites on which all words of the phrase appear in that order, rather than sites that contain the words at random. Boolean searches also permit you to insert "AND" or "+" between words and phrases to indicate that you wish to see results that contain both phrases. Conversely, Boolean searches let you exclude certain words and phrases from your search. And they let you restrict the dates of your hits, so that you see only documents posted within a specified time frame. These relatively simple strategies can help you narrow a list of hits from, in some cases, millions of sites, to a more workable number.

HOW TO: *Do an Advanced Search*

The following steps illustrate how use Google's advanced search capabilities to limit a search for information—in this case, for your speech on the Volkswagen Beetle:

1. Type the key word *beetle* in the search box, and click on Google Search. Google finds 2,410,000 sites.

2. Click on the *Advanced Search* option. In the box labeled *Find results without the words*, type in *insect* to communicate that you are interested only in sites on beetles that are not about the insect known as a beetle. Google Search yields 1,380,000 sites, cutting the original number almost in half.

3. Clarify that you want only sites about the Volkswagen Beetle. Return to *Advanced Search*. This time, in the box labeled *Find results with **all** of the words*, type in *Beetle + Volkswagen*. Google Search finds 611,000 sites.

4. Return once again to *Advanced Search*. Scroll down to *Language*, and select *English*. Under *Date*, select *past 3 months*. Under *Occurrences*, select *in the title of the page*. And under *Domain*, type in *.gov*. Now you are searching for government sites in English that have been updated in the past three months and that have "Volkswagen Beetle" in their titles. Google Search yields 73 sites—a more reasonable number of sources with which to begin your research.

Different search engines use slightly different syntaxes for advanced searches. Most provide search tips that can help you format searches and interpret results.

EVALUATING WEB RESOURCES

The World Wide Web is an unparalleled experiment in free speech. Never before have so many people and organizations been able to publish their ideas, opinions, and information as readily as they now can on the World Wide Web. Although the Web is a great victory for those who support free speech, the lack of legal, financial, or editorial restriction on what is published presents both a logistical and an ethical challenge to researchers.

As you begin to explore the sites you discover, you need to evaluate them according to a consistent standard. The following six criteria can serve as such a standard:[1]

Accountability   Find out what individual or organization is responsible for the Web site. First, look to see whether the page is signed. If you find the name of the author, but not his or her qualifications, you need to seek further information in order to be able to assess the author's expertise and authority. You may be able to get such information by following hyperlinks from the page you found to other documents.

Another way to get information is to enter the author's name in a search engine. You may find either information about, or other pages by, this author.

If the Web site is unsigned, you may still be able to find out what organization sponsors it. Look for a header or footer that indicates affiliation. Or you may be able to follow a hyperlink at the top or bottom of the page to the homepage of which this document is a part. If you can identify an organization but still do not know anything about its reputation, the domain, indicated by the last three letters of a site's URL, can give you additional information. The following domains are used by the types of organizations indicated:

.com or **.net**	commercial sites
.org	nonprofit groups
.edu	educational institutions
.gov	government agencies
.mil	military groups

You can also try entering the name of the organization, enclosed in quotation marks, in a search engine. If you have tried these strategies and still cannot identify or verify the author or sponsor of a Web site, be extremely wary of the site. If no one is willing to be accountable for the information it contains, you cannot be accountable to your audience for using the information in a speech. Continue your search elsewhere.

Accuracy   Unless you are an expert in the area a particular Web site addresses, it may be difficult to determine whether the information it contains is accurate. However, two considerations can help you assess accuracy. First, realize that accuracy is closely related to accountability. If the author or sponsoring organization of a Web site is a credible authority on the subject, the information posted on the site is more likely to be accurate than is information on an anonymous or less thoroughly documented site.

Second, assess the care with which the Web site has been written. References or hyperlinks should be provided for any information that comes from a secondary source.

The site should also be relatively free of common writing errors in usage and mechanics. A site laden with such errors may contain content errors, as well.

If you find yourself still somewhat uncertain about the accuracy of information you find on a Web site, conduct further research. You may be able to verify or refute the information by consulting another site or a print resource.

Objectivity   Like accuracy, objectivity is related to accountability. Once you know who is accountable for a site, consider the interests, philosophical or political biases, and source of financial support of that individual or organization. Are these interests or biases likely to slant the information presented? The more objective the author, the more credible the facts and information presented.

Date   Look for evidence that the site was posted recently or is kept current. At the bottom of many sites you will find a statement of when the site was posted and when it was last updated. If you do not find a date there, click on the View menu at the top of your browser screen and go down to Page Info. When you click on Page Info, you will open a screen that includes a Last Modified date. Still another strategy is to search for the title of the Web site on a search engine. The information that comes up should include a date. When you are concerned with factual data, the more recent, the better.

Usability   The layout and design of the site should facilitate its use. Frames, graphics, and multimedia resources can enhance a site but may also slow down the rate at which it loads or cause your computer to freeze. Some sites offer a "text-only" or "non-tables" option. Also consider whether there is a fee to gain access to any of the information on the site. Balance the graphics features and any possible cost against practical efficiency.

Diversity   A diversity-sensitive Web site will be free of material that communicates bias against either gender; against any ethnic, racial, or sexual-preference subgroup; or against people with disabilities.[2] Such a site may also offer divergent perspectives through hyperlinks or invite divergent perspectives through interactive forums. A site friendly to people with disabilities may offer a large-print option or an audio alternative to printed text.

As of June 2001, U.S. government Web sites were required to comply with a set of standards that include such requirements as making sure hyperlinks can be detected by color-blind users and supplying written captions for audio and video clips for people with hearing impairment.[3]

8.c Library Resources

Despite the rapid development of the World Wide Web, you should not rely solely on Internet resources to support your speech. The more traditional holdings of libraries remain rich sources of supporting material. Although your college or university library may seem a forbidding maze, all libraries, from the smallest village library to the huge Library of Congress, house the same sorts of material and are organized in a similar way.

Become familiar with your library's layout and services. Some libraries offer staff-guided tours; most others will at least have floor plans and location guides available. Before you have to do research under pressure, explore the library at a leisurely pace. Find out what electronic resources are available and where you can access them. In addition, determine where and how to find the following resources and services:

Books

Periodicals

Full-text databases

Newspapers

Reference resources

Government documents

Special services

BOOKS

When you think of libraries, you generally think of books. And with good reason: Most of the floor space of a library is devoted to books.

Stacks   Libraries' collections of books are called the **stacks**. Stacks may be either open or closed, depending on library policy. In an open-stack library, collections are on open shelves and available to anyone who wishes to browse through them. Open stacks give researchers the chance to make lucky finds, because books on a particular subject are shelved next to one another. For example, if you are looking for a specific book on play therapy, you may, on the same shelf, find two or three other books on the same subject. The main drawback to open stacks is that they are vulnerable to both loss of materials and misplacement of books by careless users.

The closed-stack library is one in which only people granted certain privileges are allowed in the stacks—most generally, librarians, library aides, faculty, and graduate students. Undergraduates and others must consult the card catalog and copy onto a retrieval card or call slip the title, author, and call number of the book they want. This card or slip is then given to a librarian at the circulation desk, who sends it to the appropriate area of the stacks. A library worker there finds the desired book and sends it to circulation, where the borrower can either check it out or use it in the study area of the library.

Card Catalog   Just how do you find what you want from among those several floors in your college library? You probably have used a **card catalog** in a smaller public or school library. College libraries are no different. Even though their holdings are much larger than those of the average public library, college libraries also contain card catalogs.

Today even very small community and school libraries are likely to have computerized card catalogs. Instead of checking a huge number of filing cabinets, trying to find the drawers you need, you go to a computer and follow the directions given. Many libraries' card catalogs are now available online, allowing researchers to build prelimi-

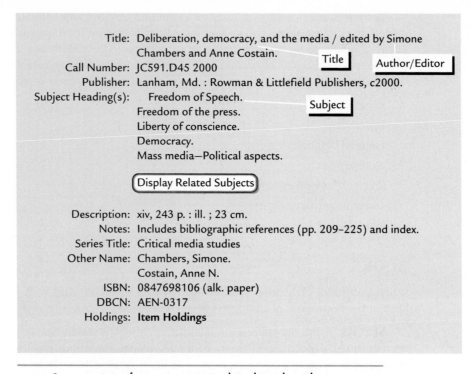

Title: Deliberation, democracy, and the media / edited by Simone Chambers and Anne Costain.

Call Number: JC591.D45 2000

Publisher: Lanham, Md. : Rowman & Littlefield Publishers, c2000.

Subject Heading(s): Freedom of Speech.
Freedom of the press.
Liberty of conscience.
Democracy.
Mass media—Political aspects.

Display Related Subjects

Description: xiv, 243 p. : ill. ; 23 cm.
Notes: Includes bibliographic references (pp. 209–225) and index.
Series Title: Critical media studies
Other Name: Chambers, Simone.
Costain, Anne N.
ISBN: 0847698106 (alk. paper)
DBCN: AEN-0317
Holdings: **Item Holdings**

FIGURE 8.2 **An Entry from a Computerized Card Catalog. The same entry appears on the screen regardless of whether the book is accessed using title, author, or subject.**

nary bibliographies of books and call numbers before they ever go to the library building. Figure 8.2 illustrates a sample entry from a computerized card catalog.

Books can provide in-depth coverage of topics, which is simply not possible in shorter publications. However, remember that most books are written two or three years before they are published. If your speech addresses a current topic or if you want to use current examples, turn to periodicals and newspapers.

PERIODICALS

The term **periodicals** refers to both general-interest magazines, such as *Newsweek, Consumer Reports,* and *Sports Illustrated,* and trade and professional journals, such as *Communication Monographs,* the *Quarterly Journal of Economics,* and *American Psychologist.* Both types of periodicals are useful to researchers. As we just observed, periodicals are timelier than books. Current periodicals may be only a few days old. Many periodicals are available online as well as in hard copy.

Just as you need a card catalog to help you find books, you need help to decide what periodicals might be useful. A large number of **periodical indexes** are published,

Public speaking
> *See also*
> Debates and debating
> Don't Shy Away from Public Speaking Class. H. Geshelin. il
> *Career World* v32 no4 p4–5 Ja 2004

FIGURE 8.3 A Typical Subject Entry from the *Reader's Guide*. A key to abbreviations can be found in each volume.

covering a vast range of subject areas and listing most of the thousands of periodicals published on a regular basis. Many of these indexes are available online or on CD-ROM. If your library subscribes to the electronic formats, you may be able to access the indexes from remote locations via the library's Web site. Some of the best-known indexes include the following:

- The *Reader's Guide to Periodical Literature* is the oldest and most frequently consulted periodical index. It lists both popular magazines and a few trade and professional journals. Articles are alphabetized according to both subject and author. The most convenient way to use the *Reader's Guide* is to search for subjects or key words, much as you would when using a World Wide Web search engine or a card catalog.

  Figure 8.3 illustrates a typical subject entry in the *Reader's Guide*. The *Reader's Guide* is a cumulative index, published every two weeks. The indexes are combined into quarterly and annual volumes. Its cumulative structure allows the *Reader's Guide* to list very current material, as well as information from past years. Some libraries now subscribe to the *Reader's Guide* in the form of electronic databases.

- *InfoTrac* is not a single periodical index, but a collection of indexes available from a single company. Examples of specific *InfoTrac* indexes include the *Health Reference Center, Expanded Academic Index, General BusinessFile,* and *Business Index Backfile.*

- The *Social Sciences Index* and the *Humanities Index* list professional, trade, and specialty publications dealing with the social sciences and the humanities. Originally published as the *Reader's Guide Supplement,* the *Social Sciences Index* and the *Humanities Index* are organized and cumulated like the *Reader's Guide.* Like the *Reader's Guide,* these indexes are now available on CD-ROM. In addition, some libraries subscribe to Web-based versions that include full-text articles dating from the early 1980s to the present. These versions are called *Social Sciences Full Text* and *Humanities Full Text.* (Other full-text databases are discussed in the next section.)

- The *Education Index* lists articles not only about education but also on various subjects that are taught (think about the wide range of departments within a university, and you will have some idea of the scope). Its format is similar to that of the other periodical indexes.

- The *Public Affairs Information Service (PAIS) Bulletin* indexes both periodicals and books in such fields as sociology, political science, and economics. Entries are listed alphabetically by subject, in much the same format as the other indexes. An electronic *PAIS* is also available.

• Other specialized indexes may also prove valuable, depending on your topic and purpose. The *Business Periodicals Index,* the *Psychology Index,* the *Music Index,* the *Art Index,* and the *Applied Science and Technology Index* are a few of these specialized publications that you may wish to explore at one time or another.

FULL-TEXT DATABASES

Another contribution made by the electronic age to research is the **full-text database**. Periodicals are the most common type of resource available in this format, although newspapers and government documents are included in some databases. Full-text databases combine both an index and text, allowing you to locate not only bibliographic information but the resources themselves through a key word or subject search.

Among the rapidly increasing number of full-text databases that you may find useful is *Academic Search Premier,* the largest multidisciplinary database, which provides full text of more than 4,600 scholarly publications in virtually every academic field. Coverage is updated daily and currently dates back to 1975.

Other, more specialized full-text databases include *ABI/Inform,* which indexes more than 1,000 business and trade periodicals, and ERIC, which focuses on education. Your university library's Web page probably has a link to online databases. Use this link, or contact your library directly, to find out what full-text databases are available to you, as well as how to access them from remote (off-campus) sites.

NEWSPAPERS

Just as periodicals are more up-to-date than books, so newspapers are more current than periodicals. By reading the latest edition of a daily newspaper, you may be able to find information that is only hours old. Newspapers also offer more detailed coverage of events and special stories than do periodicals, simply because they are published more often. Finally, newspapers usually cover stories of local significance that most often would not appear in national news magazines.

Back Issues   Generally, libraries have only the latest newspapers in their racks. Back issues are quickly transferred to microfilm for more efficient and permanent storage. Don't let microfilm intimidate you. Microfilm readers are easy to use, and most librarians or aides working in the newspaper section will be glad to show you how to set up the reader with the film you need. In recent years, newspapers ranging in size and circulation from major national newspapers to local and college newspapers have also become available online.

Indexes   As with any research, before you can consult a newspaper, you have to know where to look. To find relevant information on your subject, you need to consult a newspaper index. The electronic *National Newspaper Index* indexes *The New York Times, The Wall Street Journal, The Christian Science Monitor, The Washington Post,* and *The Los Angeles Times* from 1997 to the present. Another electronic resource, *Newspaper*

Source, provides not only citations but also selected full text for 25 national and international newspapers and more than 200 regional U.S. newspapers, as well as transcripts of television and radio news shows. In addition, a number of medium-sized and large newspapers publish their own electronic indexes, and most newspapers that are available online include an index function.

REFERENCE RESOURCES

All major libraries contain reference resources. Reference resources are indexed in the card catalog with a *Ref* prefix or suffix on their call numbers, to show that they are housed in the reference section of the library. Like periodicals, newspapers, and microfilms, they are usually available only for in-house research and cannot be checked out.

Reference resources include encyclopedias, dictionaries, directories, atlases, almanacs, yearbooks, books of quotations, and biographical dictionaries. All may, at one time or another, prove useful to a speaker. Let's examine a few of the most frequently consulted reference works, many of which today are available online or in CD-ROM versions.

- **Encyclopedias.** The standard general encyclopedia has for many years been the *Encyclopedia Britannica.* Nearly every library has a fairly recent set of *Britannica,* as well as several other general encyclopedias, such as the *Encyclopedia Americana.* An online version of the *Encyclopedia Britannica* is now available at www.britannica.com/. Your library may provide access to other online or CD-ROM encyclopedias, in addition to having bound sets.

A number of specialized encyclopedias are also available. Art, philosophy, psychology, and music are just a few of the fields covered by specialty encyclopedias.

- **Dictionaries.** The foremost dictionary of the English language is the *Oxford English Dictionary,* or *OED.* Published in twelve large volumes or available on CD-ROM or via Web subscription at www.oed.com/, the *OED* provides definitions, pronunciations, etymologies, and usage histories for every word in the dictionary. No other dictionary is this comprehensive. Realistically, however, you will rarely need as much information about a word as the *OED* provides. A good desktop dictionary, such as *Webster's Collegiate Dictionary,* will serve most purposes.

Specialty dictionaries also exist. *Black's Law Dictionary,* which provides legal definitions, is one example. Such diverse fields as geography, music, and economics also have their own special dictionaries.

- **Directories.** The *Encyclopedia of Associations,* the *Directory of Nonprofit Organizations,* and other directories, including telephone directories, are usually available in the reference section.

- **Atlases.** An atlas is a geographical tool that provides maps, tables, pictures, and facts about the people and resources of various regions. Frequently used atlases include *Goode's World Atlas,* the *Rand McNally College World Atlas,* and the *Township Atlas of the United States.* There are also specialized atlases of history and politics.

- **Almanacs and yearbooks** are compilations of facts. The *Statistical Abstract of the United States* is published annually by the Census Bureau and contains statistics on nearly every facet of life in the United States, including birth and mortality rates, income, education, and religion. An abridged version is available online at www.census.gov/statab/www/. The *World Almanac* contains factual information about almost every subject imaginable—anything from facts about monarchs of the eighteenth century to a list of every winner of the Kentucky Derby.

• **Books of quotations** are compilations of quotes on almost every conceivable subject. Most of these books are arranged alphabetically by subject; a few are arranged according to author, with the subject entered in an index. The *Oxford Dictionary of Quotations* and *Bartlett's Familiar Quotations* are two widely consulted works. An early edition of *Bartlett's* is now available online at www.bartleby.com/100/.

• **Biographical dictionaries** are reference works that contain biographical articles— some short, others not—on people who have achieved some recognition. Biographical dictionaries are usually organized alphabetically. Probably the best-known general works of this kind are the *Who's Who* series, which includes brief biographies of international, national, and regional figures of note. The *Dictionary of National Biography* provides biographies of famous British citizens who are no longer living; the *Dictionary of American Biography* does the same for deceased Americans of note. The *Directory of American Scholars* provides information about American academicians. (You can probably find profiles of some of your current professors in this work.) And if none of the resources just mentioned has the biography you are seeking, you might try the *Biography Index,* a quarterly publication that lists current articles and books containing biographical sketches. One of these directories or indexes might be especially useful to the speaker who wants to quote a reputed expert but does not know anything about the expert's credentials.

Reference librarians are specialists in the field of library science. They are often able to suggest additional print or electronic resources that you might otherwise overlook. A suggestion: If you plan to use the reference section, visit the library during daytime working hours. A full-time reference librarian is more likely to be on hand and available to help you at that time than in the evenings or on weekends.

GOVERNMENT DOCUMENTS

Government documents can be a rich source of support material. The federal government researches and publishes information on almost every conceivable subject, as well as keeping exhaustive records of almost all official federal proceedings. Documents published by the government are usually housed together in a special area of the library called the Government Documents Section.

The most important index of government documents is the *Catalog of U.S. Government Publications,* available online at www.access.gpo.gov/su_docs/locators/cgp/index.html. Also useful to speakers is the *American Statistics Index,* which indexes government statistical publications exclusively and is also available through some libraries online.

The huge number and wide variety of formats of government pamphlets, reports, and other publications have long presented a challenge, both to library archivists and to researchers. The World Wide Web has made these resources much more easily accessible.

SPECIAL SERVICES

In addition to the resources just described, most libraries offer a number of special services. These include interlibrary loan and reciprocal borrowing privileges with other area libraries.

Interlibrary loan is one way to obtain resources that you have found indexed, but that are not owned by your library. You might, for example, discover in an article you are reading a reference to a book that you might also want to read. But your library does not have the book in its collection. Interlibrary loan can locate the book at another library and get it to you, usually within a few days. Some libraries charge a small fee for this service.

Many libraries also have reciprocal borrowing arrangements with libraries of neighboring colleges and universities. You may find that in addition to your own college library, two or three others within a fairly convenient radius are available for your use.

QUICK CHECK: *Supporting Material in the Library*

Library resources may include:

- Books
- Periodicals
- Full-text databases
- Newspapers
- Reference resources
- Government documents
- Special services

8.d Interviews

If you don't know the answers to some of the important questions raised by your speech topic, but you can think of someone who might, consider interviewing that person to get material for your speech. For example, if you are preparing a speech on the quality of food in the dining hall, who better to ask about the subject than the director of food services? If you want to discuss the pros and cons of building a new prison in an urban area, you might interview an official of the correctional service, a representative of the city administration, and a resident of the area. Or if you want to explain why Al Gore lost the 2000 presidential election even though he won the popular vote, you might consult your professor of political science or American history.

Consider a word of caution, however, before you decide that an interview is necessary: Be sure that your questions cannot be answered easily by looking at a Web site or reading a newspaper article or a book. Do some preliminary reading on your subject before you decide to take up someone's valuable time in an interview. If you decide that only an interview can give you the material you need, you should prepare for it in advance.

DETERMINING THE PURPOSE OF THE INTERVIEW

The first step in preparing for an interview is to establish a purpose or objective for it. Specifically, what do you need to find out? Do you need hard facts that you cannot obtain from other sources? Do you need the interviewee's expert testimony on your subject? Does the person you are going to interview have a particularly significant personal experience that you wish to hear described firsthand? Or do you need an explanation of some of the information you have found in print sources? Before you begin preparing for the interview, decide just what information you want to have or what you want to know when the interview is over.

SETTING UP THE INTERVIEW

Once you have a specific purpose for the interview and have decided whom you need to speak with, arrange a meeting. It is unwise to arrive unannounced at the office of a businessperson, public official, educator, or other professional and expect an on-the-spot interview. Even veteran journalist Mike Wallace has been refused under such circumstances!

Instead, several days in advance, telephone the person you hope to interview, explain briefly who you are and why you are calling, and ask for an appointment. Most people are flattered to have their authority and knowledge recognized and willingly grant interviews to serious students if schedules permit.

If you are considering recording the interview on audio- or videotape, ask for the interviewee's okay during this initial contact. If the person does not grant permission, you will need to be prepared to gather your information without electronic assistance.

PLANNING THE INTERVIEW

Now that you know what you need to find out, whom you will see, and when the meeting will take place, your next step is to prepare for the interview itself. Do not try to "wing it" and let the interviewee ramble at will. To ensure the results you want, you need to plan your questions.

Gather Background Information   Experienced interviewers are successful largely because they prepare so thoroughly for their interviews. Likewise, before you interview someone, find out as much as you can about both your subject and the person you are interviewing.

Prepare questions that take full advantage of the interviewee's specific knowledge of your subject. You can do this only if you already know a good deal about your subject. Build your line of questioning on facts, statements the interviewee has made, or positions he or she has taken publicly.

Plan Specific Questions   In addition to learning something about your subject and the person you are going to interview, it is helpful to think about how you should combine the two basic types of interview questions: closed-ended and open-ended.

Closed-ended questions call for a yes or no answer or some brief statement of fact. "How many years have you served in the job?" and "Do you think that next month's tax referendum will pass?" are examples of closed-ended questions.

If you ask only closed-ended questions, however, you will limit and possibly frustrate your interviewee. You may also frustrate yourself. Open-ended questions allow the interviewee to express a personal point of view more fully. The interviewee may also give you more of the kind of information you probably want: expert testimony and personal experience. "Why do you think the asbestos should not be removed?" and "What, in your opinion, are the most serious potential consequences if it is removed?" are examples of open-ended questions. Open-ended questions often follow closed-ended questions. If the person you are interviewing answers a closed-ended question with a simple yes or no, you may wish to follow up by asking, "Why?"

Plan a Sequence of Questions   Once you have designed your questions to yield the information you want, you need to consider the order in which to ask them. You may want to organize questions according to subject categories, with three or four questions on one topic followed by three or four on another. You may want to arrange them according to complexity of information, with the easiest questions first, in part to ensure that you understand the subject. Or you may want to order them by the sensitivity of the content, building some rapport with your interviewee and ensuring that you get at least some information, should he or she decline to answer the more sensitive or difficult questions.

Plan a Recording Strategy   Audio and video recorders can free you from having to take copious notes; you can concentrate instead on processing and analyzing the ideas and information being presented. Another advantage of recording an interview is that doing so gives you a complete record of the entire interview. You will not have to decipher hastily scribbled notes a day or two after the interview.

The main disadvantage of using an electronic recorder is that it makes some people more self-conscious and nervous than if you were scribbling notes. You want the person being interviewed to concentrate on your questions, not on his or her own facial expression or vocal inflection. As we noted earlier, you should ask in advance whether the person you are interviewing will allow you to tape the session. Even if he or she gives permission, be prepared to turn off the device and switch to manual note taking if you sense at any time that the interviewee is distracted by the recorder.

Before taping an interview, there are a number of questions that you should consider. What kind of recorder should you use? Would a simple tape recorder with a built-in mike be less intimidating than a video camera on a tripod? Although the person you are interviewing is aware that you are taping the interview, would he or she be more comfortable if the machine were out of sight? Ask the interviewee. You might also want to ask some casual questions before turning on the recorder so that both of you can ease into the actual interview.

CONDUCTING THE INTERVIEW

On Your Mark . . .   Dress appropriately for the interview. For most interviews, conservative, businesslike clothes show that you are serious about the interview and that you respect the norms of your interviewee's world.

Take paper and pen or pencil for note taking. Even if you are planning to use a tape recorder, you may want to turn it off at some point during the interview, so you'll need an alternative. Or Murphy's Law may snarl your tape or break your recorder. Ensure that the interview can continue, in spite of any mishaps.

Get Set . . .   Arrive for the interview a few minutes ahead of the scheduled hour. Be prepared, however, to wait patiently, if necessary. Although the interview may be a high priority for you, the person you will interview has granted it as a courtesy and may need to complete something else before speaking with you.

Once you are settled with the person you will interview, remind him or her of your purpose. If you are familiar with and admire the work the interviewee has done or published, don't hesitate to say so. Sincere flattery can help set a positive tone for the exchange. If you have decided to use a recorder, set it up. You may keep it out of sight once the interviewee has seen it, but never try to hide a recorder at the outset—such a ploy is unethical. If you are going to take written notes, get out your paper and pen. Now you are ready to begin asking your prepared questions.

Go!   As you conduct the interview, use the questions you have prepared as a guide but not a rigid schedule. If the person you are interviewing mentions an interesting angle you did not think of, don't be afraid to pursue the point. Listen carefully to the person's answers, and ask for clarification of any ideas you don't understand.

Do not prolong the interview beyond the time limits of your appointment. The person you are interviewing is probably very busy and has been courteous enough to fit you into a tight schedule. Ending the interview on time is simply returning the courtesy. Thank your interviewee for his or her contribution, and leave.

FOLLOWING UP THE INTERVIEW

As soon as possible after the interview, read through your notes carefully and rewrite any portions that may be illegible. If you recorded the interview, label the tape with the date and the interviewee's name. You will soon want to transfer any significant facts, opinions, or anecdotes from either notes or tape to index cards or to a word-processing file. You will find a format for transcribing notes later in this chapter.

8.e ## Resources from Special-Interest Groups and Organizations

Business and industrial groups, nonprofit organizations, and professional societies produce pamphlets, books, fact sheets, and other information about an extraordinarily wide variety of subjects. How do you find out about such resources? Those available online may be discovered through Web searches. Others may be found by consulting some of the reference works we have already discussed, such as the *Encyclopedia of Associations* and the *Directory of Nonprofit Organizations*. Although these reference works do not indicate specific publications, they provide the names, addresses, and telephone numbers of businesses and organizations that may have a special interest in, and produce resources related to, your topic. Such resources may be available online or by mail at little or no cost.

Remember that private companies and organizations set up Web sites and produce printed resources because they have a vested interest in the topic. You can expect resources produced by oil companies, for example, to minimize the harm oil spills can do to an environment. The criteria offered earlier in this chapter for evaluating Web sites should be applied to all kinds of resources obtained from special-interest groups and organizations.

8.f Research Strategies

You have access to a computer with an Internet connection and Web browser software. You know the kinds of materials and services your library offers and how to use them. In short, you're ready to begin researching your speech. But unless you approach this next phase of speech preparation systematically, you may find yourself wasting a good deal of time and energy retracing steps to find bits of information you remember seeing but forgot to bookmark, print out, or write down the first time.

Well-organized research strategies can make your efforts easier and more efficient. You need to develop a preliminary bibliography; evaluate the usefulness of resources; take notes; and identify possible presentation aids.

DEVELOP A PRELIMINARY BIBLIOGRAPHY

Creating a **preliminary bibliography**, or list of promising resources, should be your first research goal. The preliminary bibliography should include electronic resources as well as print materials. You will probably discover more resources than you actually look at or refer to in your speech; at this stage, the bibliography simply serves as a menu of possibilities.

Keep Track of Resources You will need to develop a system for keeping track of your resources. As we mentioned earlier in this chapter, Web browsers let you bookmark pages for future reference and ready access. Your bookmarks can serve as one part of your preliminary bibliography. If you are using a CD-ROM index connected to a printer, you may be able to print out the references you discover. These printouts can be a second part of your preliminary bibliography.

If you are using more traditional catalogs and indexes, you will need to copy down the necessary bibliographical information, a process we will discuss in more detail shortly. Using 3- by 5-inch note cards will give you the greatest flexibility. Later you can omit some of the cards, add others, write comments on them, or alphabetize them much more easily than if you had made a list on a sheet of paper.

Use a Consistent Format   The key to developing a useful bibliography is to establish a consistent format so that you can easily find and cite the page number, title, publisher, or some other vital fact about a publication. The two most common formats, or documentation styles, are those developed by the MLA (Modern Language Association) and the APA (American Psychological Association). MLA style is usually used in the humanities, APA style in the natural and social sciences. Although we describe and use the MLA format here, check with your instructor about which format he or she prefers.

- **Books, articles:** For a book, you should record the author's name, the title of the book, the name of the publisher and date of publication, and the library's call number. Figure 8.4 illustrates how to transfer information from an electronic catalog entry to a bibliography card. For an article in a periodical or newspaper, you should document the author's name, the title of the article, the title of the periodical, the date of publication, and inclusive page numbers of the article.

- **Government and specialized information formats:** For government publications, pamphlets, newsletters, fact sheets, or other specialized information formats, as long as you record the title, author, publisher, date, and page number, you will probably have at hand the information you need to locate any print material. For a government document, you will also need to record the Superintendent of Documents classification number, available in the *Catalog of U.S. Government Publications.*

- **Electronic resources:** Documentation formats for Web pages and other electronic resources are still evolving, although they are similar to the formats for other kinds of material.

HOW TO: *Document an Electronic Resource in MLA Format*

Author's name (last name first). "**Title of article**" (if any; enclosed in quotation marks). <u>Title of Web site</u> (underlined) or a **description such as Homepage** (not underlined). **Date of Internet publication. Date of your access <URL>.** (The URL should be enclosed in angle brackets, as illustrated here. Break a URL from one line to the next only after a slash.)

If you cannot find one element of information about an electronic source (such as author or date of Internet publication), simply skip it and go directly to the next item. The most distinctive features of Web documentation are, of course, the address of the Web page and the date you accessed the page.

If you have additional questions about how to format electronic resources, the Web itself can be your best ally. A number of sites provide instructions on how to cite electronic resources according to various style guides. For example, a page from *Purdue University's On-Line Writing Lab (OWL)* at owl.english.purdue.edu/handouts/research/

Title: Cyber rights : defending free speech in the digital age / Mike Godwin.
Author: Godwin, Mike, 1956-
Call Number: KF4772.G63 2003
Publisher: Cambridge, Mass. : MIT Press, c2003.
Subject Heading(s): Freedom of Speech--United States.
Internet--Law and legislation--United States.
0453F

(Display Related Subjects)

Description: xxiii, 402 p. ; 23 cm.
Notes: Includes bibliographic references and index.
A new frontier for free speech and society -- Where the "virtual" meets the "real" : free speech, community, and ethics on the Net -- The Net backlash : fear of freedom -- Libel on the Net -- When words hurt : two hard cases about online speech -- Privacy versus society? -- The battle over copyright on the Net (and other intellectual property encounters) -- A bad spin and a cyberporn primer -- Fighting a cyberporn panic -- Courting the future : the Communications Decency Act of 1996 -- Free speech and communities : what the lawyers know.
ISBN: 0262571684 (pbk. : alk. paper)
DBCN: AFF-6250
Holdings: **Item Holdings**

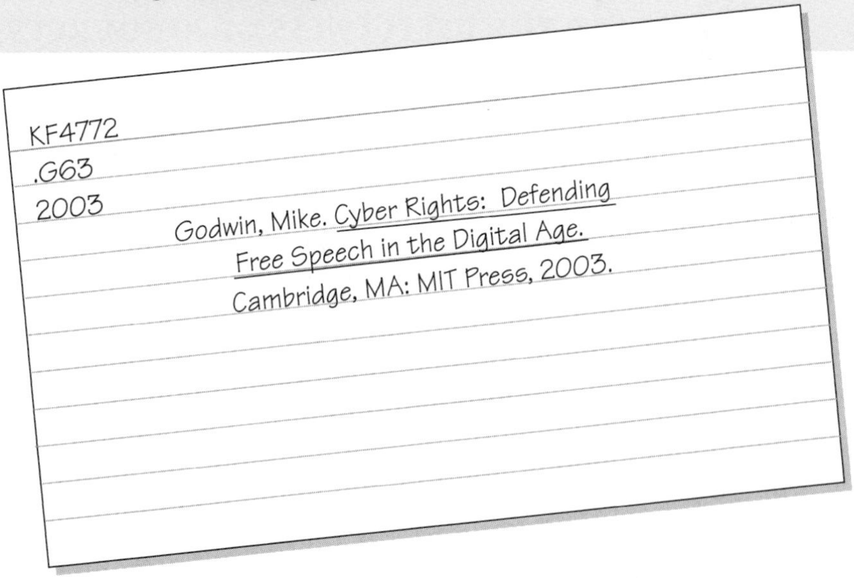

KF4772
.G63
2003
Godwin, Mike. Cyber Rights: Defending
Free Speech in the Digital Age.
Cambridge, MA: MIT Press, 2003.

FIGURE 8.4   **Transferring Information from an Electronic Catalog Entry to a Bibliography Card**

Jehl, Douglas. "Questioning Nearly Every Aspect of the Responses to Sept. 11."
The New York Times on the Web. 18 June 2004. 18 June 2004 <www.nytimes.com>.

FIGURE 8.5   A Bibliography Entry in MLA Style for an Article in *The New York Times on the Web*

r_docElectric.html/ provides links to both MLA and APA documentation formats for electronic resources. Figure 8.5 illustrates a bibliography entry in MLA style for an article in *The New York Times on the Web*.

Choose an Appropriate Number   How many resources should you list in a preliminary bibliography for, say, a ten-minute speech? A reasonable number might be ten or twelve that look promising. If you have many more than that, you may feel overwhelmed. If you have fewer, you may have too little information. Out of a list of three books, three articles, three Web pages, and a pamphlet, you might find that two of the Web pages are not really very useful, your library does not have a couple of the articles, and one of the books is checked out. If you are left with three or four good resources, you are doing well.

EVALUATE THE USEFULNESS OF RESOURCES

It makes sense to gauge the potential usefulness of your resources before you begin to read more closely and take notes. Think critically about how the various resources you have found are likely to help you achieve your purpose and about how effective they are likely to be with your audience. Glance over the tables of contents of books, and flip quickly through the texts to note any charts, graphs, or other visual materials that might be used as visual aids. Skim a key chapter or two. Skim shorter articles, pamphlets, and fact sheets as well.

You may wish to devise a number or letter system to rank your resources according to their potential. You can write this code on your bibliography card or printout. If none of the resources looks particularly good, you may need to return to the bibliography-building stage to try to locate more potential resources.

TAKE NOTES

Once you have located, previewed, and ranked your resources, you are ready to begin more careful reading and note-taking.

Start with the Most Useful Resources   Start with the resources that you think have the greatest potential. If you are looking at a Web page, an article, a pamphlet, an encyclopedia entry, or another kind of short document, you can read the whole text fairly quickly. But you probably do not have time to read entire books, so read only those chapters or sections that seem particularly relevant and potentially useful to your speech.

Create a Record of Resource Notes   When you find an example, a statistic, an opinion, or other material that might be useful to your speech, write it down, photocopy it, download it into a computer file, or print it. Be sure to identify the source.

Use a Notebook, Disk, or Note Cards   Don't create extra work for yourself by scribbling notes on scratch paper, the inside of a book cover, a checkbook, or a printout of the latest e-mail from Mom. Instead, have on hand a notebook, storage disk if you are using a computer, or note cards.

Even if you plan to photocopy or enter most of your notes into a word-processing file, it is a good idea to carry a few note cards with you whenever you are working on a speech. You can use one to jot down an idea that comes to mind while you are sipping coffee or to record a fact you discover in a magazine article you read in a doctor's office or at a friend's house. Another advantage of using note cards is that you can later arrange them in the order of your speech outline, simplifying the integration of your ideas and supporting material into the speech.

Write One Idea per Card or Page   What should you include in your notes? First, put only one item of supporting material or one idea on each card or each page of your speech notebook or word-processing file. If you are photocopying your sources or printing out Web pages and you find a single page with several pieces of supporting material, you may want to "cut and paste"—literally cut the page apart and paste the separate items onto separate note cards.

There is no rule as to how many note cards or pages you will have for each source. You may write only one note from one article you read, five from another, and twenty from a third. The amount of useful supporting material you find will vary widely from one source to another.

If you copy a phrase, sentence, or paragraph verbatim from a source, be sure to put quotation marks around it when you write it down or enter it. You may need to know later in the preparation process whether it was a direct quote or a paraphrase. This information will be obvious, of course, on printouts or photocopies.

Indicate the Source   In addition to copying the information itself, you need to indicate its source. If you consistently record your sources when you take notes, you will avoid the possibility of committing unintentional plagiarism later.

You may wish to number the entries in your bibliography and then place the source number at the top of each note card or page of information or quotes from that source. Then you will need to add only the page number of each note. A somewhat more elaborate option is to use only the author's last name, title, and page number or Web address on the note card. Or you may wish to write a complete bibliographic reference on each card or page. This procedure takes more time but ensures that you will have vital reference information immediately at hand as you work on your speech later.

Paraphrased Note

Crossburning as Free Speech

Russomanno, Joseph. *Speaking Our Minds: Conversations with the People Behind Landmark First Amendment Cases.* Mahwah, NJ: Lawrence Erlbaum, 2002. 45.

R.A.V. v. city of St. Paul, MN, a case that involved a crossburning, resulted in a Supreme Court decision declaring unconstitutional a St. Paul ordinance limiting free speech acts.

Direct Quotation

Government Backlash against Internet Free Speech

Godwin, Mike. *Cyber Rights: Defending Free Speech in the Digital Age.* Cambridge, MA: MIT Press, 2003. 22.

"Here in the United States, the government has frequently used the fear of Net crimes and Net criminals as justification for imposing greater control on the Net as a whole."

FIGURE 8.6   **Sample Note Cards**

Summarize the Idea   Finally, leave enough space at the top of each note card or page to summarize the idea expressed in the note. Such headings make it easier to find a particular bit of material quickly when you are ready to assemble the speech. Figure 8.6 illustrates two note cards—one with a paraphrased note and one with a direct quotation.

IDENTIFY POSSIBLE PRESENTATION AIDS

As we noted earlier in this chapter, in addition to discovering verbal supporting material in your sources, you may also find charts, graphs, photographs, and other potentially valuable visual material. You may think you will be able to remember what visuals were in which sources. But many speakers have experienced frustrating searches for that "perfect" presentation aid they remember seeing somewhere while they were taking notes for their speech.

Even if you are not certain at this point that you will even use presentation aids in your speech, it can't hurt to print out, photocopy, or sketch on a note card any good possibilities, recording sources of information just as you did for your written materials. Then, when the time comes to consider if and where presentation aids might enhance the speech, you will have some readily at hand.

QUICK CHECK: *Research Strategies*

- Develop a preliminary bibliography.
- Consider the potential usefulness of sources.
- Take notes.
- Identify possible presentation aids.

Summary

- Public speakers need to know where and how to find supporting material to use in their speeches.

- There are five sources of supporting material: personal knowledge and experience; the Internet; library resources; interviews; and resources from special-interest groups and organizations.

- Using illustrations, explanations, definitions, or other supporting material from your own knowledge and experience has the advantage of increasing the audience's respect for your authority.

- Although the Internet provides a vast collection of resources, which are easily accessible on the World Wide Web through directories and search engines, you need to evaluate who is accountable for the resources and whether they are accurate, objective, current, usable, and sensitive to diversity.

- You may also want to use library resources—books, periodicals, full-text databases, newspapers, reference resources, and government documents—as sources of supporting material.

- Interviewing someone who is an expert on the subject of your speech or who has a unique point of view about the subject is a fourth way to gather supporting material. You may take written notes or tape your interview; later, you can transcribe the information you have gathered onto note cards.

- Information about many topics is available from various special-interest groups and organizations; however, because many such entities produce printed resources primarily to support their vested interests, you should consider how accountable, accurate, objective, and current such resources are.

- Once you discover possible resources, you should develop a preliminary bibliography of those resources, consider their potential usefulness, take notes, and identify possible presentation aids.

Key Terms

bookmark (p. 149)
Boolean search (p. 150)
browser (p. 149)
card catalog (p. 153)
full-text database (p. 156)
hyperlink (p. 149)
Internet (p. 148)
periodical (p. 154)

periodical index (p. 154)
preliminary bibliography (p. 163)
search engine (p. 149)
stacks (p. 153)
URL (p. 149)
Web directory (p. 149)
Web page (p. 149)
Web site (p. 149)

A QUESTION OF ETHICS

While in the library gathering material for a speech, you find a wonderful magazine article from which you plan to quote extensively, and you take copious notes. In your excitement about finding the article, you neglect to record the bibliographic information on your note cards. As you compose your speech the night before you will deliver it, you discover your omission and have no time to return to the library. How can you solve your problem in an ethical way?

CHAPTER 9

Supporting Your Speech

obacco heir Patrick Reynolds speaks frequently at universities, youth assemblies, and corporate seminars around the country.[1] He has appeared on most of the major network and cable news and talk shows, including *Good Morning, America* and *Oprah*. Reynolds's objective is not, as one might suppose, to defend the tobacco industry, but to campaign aggressively *against* it.

> *I use not only all the brains I have, but all I can borrow.*
>
> —**Woodrow Wilson**

Citing information from the American Cancer Society, the American Lung Association, and the federal government, Reynolds points out that one out of every five deaths in the United States is caused by smoking, making it the leading killer in this country. He tells his audiences that 60 percent of all smokers start by age 14, with 90 percent becoming addicted by the age of 19. And then Reynolds adds his own personal, tragic, and ironic illustrations: His father, mother, aunt, and half-brother all died of smoking-related causes.

Patrick Reynolds has been described as a "compelling" speaker. Why? He is compelling, at least in part, because of the skill with which he combines explanations, illustrations, and statistics to capture and maintain the attention of his audiences. Without effective supporting material, Reynolds—like any speaker—would find his plea dismissed as only so much hot air.

Gathering appropriate supporting material is an essential step in the speech-preparation process. And once you have gathered a variety of material, you will need to make decisions about how to use your information to best advantage. You will need to look at your speech from your audience's perspective and decide where an explanation might help them understand a point, where statistics might convince them of the significance of a problem, and where an illustration might stir their emotions. In this chapter, we will discuss these and other types of supporting material and present guidelines for using them effectively.

9.a   Illustrations

Hugh Stuart-Buttle was preparing a speech to the news media to introduce the products made by his company, Ciba Specialty Chemicals, for protection against the sun's ultraviolet rays. He remembered that, when he was a little boy, his mother insisted that he cover up before he went out in the sun. He decided to draw on this memory in his presentation. His speech coach, communication consultant Karen Berg, approved. "Anything that engages the mind's eye is more memorable than just getting up and spouting off data," she says. "[The audience] will remember the visual images."[2]

Stuart-Buttle's use of a personal anecdote is hardly a revolutionary public-speaking strategy. Politicians and after-dinner speakers have always told stories to help make their points and keep their listeners' attention. Until recently, however, business speakers rarely did so. Now they are beginning to discover what speakers in other contexts have always known: *Everybody likes to hear a story.* If you remember nothing else from this chapter, remember that one principle. An **illustration**—a story or anecdote that provides an example of an idea, issue, or problem the speaker is discussing—almost always ensures audience interest. Let's look more closely at different kinds of illustrations and examine some guidelines for using them.

BRIEF ILLUSTRATIONS

Brief illustrations are often no longer than a sentence or two. To drive home a point about the dangers faced by journalists in politically volatile countries, one speaker offered the following brief illustrations:

* In Kosovo, Aferdita Kelmendi saw her radio station destroyed, learned she was on a Serbian hit list—and finally fled the country with her family.

* In Ukraine, Tatyana Goryachova, editor of an independent newspaper there, covered stories on government corruption and malfeasance. She was harassed and threatened by the government, and in 2002 somebody threw sulfuric acid into her face.

* In Colombia, Jineth Lima covered the conflict between the government and paramilitary groups. In May 2000 she went to interview someone she thought was a paramilitary leader in a Colombian prison, but it was a trap. She was instead kidnapped at gunpoint, beaten, and raped by suspected military gunmen.[3]

Why use multiple brief illustrations? Sometimes a series of brief illustrations can have more impact than either a single brief illustration or a more detailed extended illustration. In addition, although an audience could dismiss a single illustration as an exception, two or more strongly suggest a trend or norm.

EXTENDED ILLUSTRATIONS

Longer and more detailed than the brief illustration, the **extended illustration** resembles a story. It is more vividly descriptive than a brief illustration, and it has a plot—which includes an opening, complications, a climax, and a resolution.

In a speech entitled "Middle Earth, Motown and Mo' Better Blues," Kathleen Ligocki, President and CEO of Tower Automotive, offered the following extended illustration of her point that success depends on a clear vision:

Back in 1952, Florence Chadwick became the first woman to ever swim the Catalina Channel. She had to make two attempts before she achieved her goal. On her first try, she quit—after swimming $21\frac{1}{2}$ miles—only a half-mile from shore.

The reason? It wasn't the freezing cold water. Or the fear of the sharks circling around her. Or even her fatigue. She told reporters later that it was because she couldn't see the shore through the fog. She had lost sight of her goal. Two months later, she swam the channel again—this time with a clear mental picture of the shore that lay beyond the fog. She not only became the first woman to swim the channel, she beat the existing world's record by two hours![4]

To use an extended illustration takes more time than to cite a brief example, but longer stories can be more dramatic and emotionally compelling. Extended illustrations can work well as speech introductions.

HYPOTHETICAL ILLUSTRATIONS

Hypothetical illustrations may be either brief or extended. They are different from the illustrations we have discussed so far, because they describe situations or events that have not actually occurred. Rather, they are scenarios that *might* happen. Plausible hypothetical illustrations may serve your purpose better than any real examples by enabling your audience to imagine themselves in a particular situation.

The following hypothetical illustration introduced a speech on how universities profit from sweatshop labor:

Imagine one day walking into class, only to find children chained to desks, sewing T-shirts, jackets, and other products representing your school.[5]

Notice the word *imagine* in this illustration. The purpose of a hypothetical illustration is not to trick your listeners into believing a bogus story. They should be aware from the beginning that the illustration is hypothetical.

USING ILLUSTRATIONS EFFECTIVELY

Illustrations are almost guaranteed attention getters, as well as a way to support your statements. But even this excellent form of support can be ineffective if not used to its best advantage. The following suggestions can help you use illustrations more effectively in your speeches.

Be Sure Your Illustrations Are Relevant to What They Are Supposed to Support   As obvious as this principle seems, many student speakers, learning of the value of illustrations, go to great lengths to use as many of them as they can in their speeches. They are so eager, in fact, that some of their illustrations have little bearing on the specific point they are trying to make. Their listeners become confused.

Never leave your audience in doubt as to why you used a certain illustration. Be sure that illustrations are obviously related to the idea they support.

Choose Illustrations That Represent a Trend   It is not ethical to find one or two isolated illustrations and use them as though they were typical. If your illustrations are rare instances, you owe it to your listeners to tell them so.

Make Your Illustrations Vivid and Specific   You probably know people who cannot tell a joke. They just can't relate a story or deliver a punch line. Or they lack the sense of timing needed to make a joke funny. Unfortunately, some speakers bumble their best illustrations in a similar way. Some years ago, a speech professor was fascinated to discover that one of his students had been on the last voyage of the ill-fated Italian ship *Andrea Doria*. Early in the semester, he urged the young man to relate his experience as part of an informative speech on how humans respond to danger. The professor expected a speech with great dramatic impact. Instead, much to his surprise, the student's narrative went something like this: "Well, there was a loud noise and then the sirens went off and we all got in lifeboats and the ship sank."[6] Hardly the stuff great drama is made of!

If you have chosen to tell a poignant story, give it enough detail to make it come alive in the minds of your listeners. Paint a mental picture of the people, places, and things involved.

Use Illustrations with Which Your Listeners Can Identify   Just as you should use illustrations that are typical, so, too, should you use audience-centered illustrations—ones the members of your audience can relate to. If, on hearing your illustration, your listeners mentally shrug and think, "That could never happen to me," the power of your story is considerably lessened. The best illustrations are the ones that your listeners can imagine experiencing themselves. Other compelling stories, like the sinking of the *Andrea Doria,* can illustrate such great human drama that everyone listening will be immediately interested and attentive.

If you cannot find a plausible example, you may want to invent a hypothetical one, which you can gear specifically to your audience. You can then be sure of its pertinence to your listeners.

Remember That the Best Illustrations Are Personal Ones
Speakers gain conviction and enthusiasm when they talk about personal experiences. Patrick Reynolds, for example, introduced at the beginning of this chapter, is a compelling speaker in large part because he shares his own tragic personal experiences of

QUICK CHECK: *Choose the Right Illustrations*

- Do they represent a trend?
- Are they vivid and specific?
- Can your listeners identify with your illustrations?
- Are any of them based on your personal experience?

the results of smoking. Of course, you will not have had personal experience with every topic on which you may speak. In a speech on the conflict between the legislative and executive branches of government, a good illustration might focus on the working relationship between the president and the speaker of the House. The best illustrations for a speech on American military strategy during the Revolutionary War might come from the letters of George Washington. But if you *have* had personal experience with the subject on which you are speaking, be sure to describe that experience to the audience.

9.b Descriptions and Explanations

Probably the most commonly used forms of support are descriptions and explanations. A **description** tells you what something is like. Descriptions provide the details that allow audience members to develop mental pictures of what speakers are talking about. An **explanation** is a statement that makes clear how something is done or why it exists in its present form or existed in its past form.

DESCRIBING

To describe is to produce word pictures—detailed information that allows an audience mentally to see, hear, smell, touch, or taste what you are describing. The more senses you appeal to with your word pictures, the better. Good descriptions are vivid, accurate, and specific; they make people, places, and events come alive for the audience.

Description may be used in a brief example, an extended illustration, a hypothetical instance, or by itself. In his June 2004 speech commemorating the 60th anniversary of D-Day, President George W. Bush described the crossing of the English Channel by Allied Forces on June 6, 1944:

> Only the ones who made that crossing can know what it was like. They tell of the pitching deck, the whistles of shells from the battleships behind them, the white jets of water from enemy fire around them, and then the sound of bullets hitting the steel ramp that was about to fall.[7]

EXPLAINING HOW

Edwin Pittock, president of the Society of Certified Senior Advisors, explained to a group of businesspeople how depression develops in the elderly:

> Bad things happen, they layer, and you become more depressed as time goes along. You come to expect that bad things will happen to you, and your attitude becomes a self-fulfilling prophecy.[8]

Speakers who discuss or demonstrate processes of any kind rely at least in part on explanations of how those processes work.

EXPLAINING WHY

Explaining why involves giving reasons for or consequences of a policy, principle, or event. In her speech on the nursing shortage, Dayna explained why the nursing short-age harms patients:

> Fewer nurses equal less time spent with each patient, which in turn equals less quality care.[9]

Often, having explained causes or reasons, a speaker can then tailor a solution to those specific causes. A student seeking to reverse a university policy forbidding fresh-men to have cars on campus can first explain why that policy was adopted and then point out why it is no longer needed. In short, explaining *why* some condition or situation exists provides an analysis that often leads to solutions to problem sitations.

USING DESCRIPTIONS AND EXPLANATIONS EFFECTIVELY

Perhaps because they are the most commonly used forms of support, descriptions and explanations are also among the most frequently abused. When large sections of a speech contain long, nonspecific explanations, audience eyelids are apt to fall. The following suggestions can help you use descriptions and explanations effectively in your speeches.

Keep Your Descriptions and Explanations Brief   Lengthiness is often the reason audiences become bored with many descriptions and explanations. An explanation should supply only as many details as necessary for an audience to understand how or why something works or exists. Too many details may make your listeners say your speech was "everything I *never* wanted to know about the subject."

Use Language That Is as Specific and Concrete as Possible Explanations tend to be general and thus somewhat deadly. Vivid and specific language brings your explanations alive. Liveliness helps you hold the audience's attention and paint in your listeners' minds the image you are trying to communicate.

Avoid Too Much Description and Explanation   Even brief, specific explanations are boring if used alone, without other kinds of support. You can hold your audience's attention more effectively if you alternate explanations and descriptions with other types of supporting material, such as brief examples or statistics.

9.c   Definitions

Steve thought and thought but couldn't come up with a good opening for his speech. In desperation, he turned to the dictionary. To introduce his speech on modern legal training in the United States, he decided to define *lawyer*. Much to Steve's disappointment, his introduction only succeeded in putting his 8 a.m. class soundly back to sleep. Steve's problem? He had misused a perfectly legitimate form of support. He did not need to define *lawyer* for a college class—or for any class beyond elementary school, for that matter. Steve had resorted to an unnecessary definition as a crutch, and it didn't hold up.

Definitions have two justifiable uses in speeches. First, a speaker should be sure to define any and all specialized, technical, or little-known terms in his or her speech. If Steve had discussed "tort reform," he would have needed to define that phrase early in his speech. Such definitions are usually achieved by *classification,* the kind of definition you would find in a dictionary. Second, a speaker may define a term by showing how it works or how it is applied in a specific instance—what we call an *operational definition.* Let's look at examples of both types of definitions.

DEFINITIONS BY CLASSIFICATION

If you have to explain the meaning of a term, you may use a **definition by classification** from the *Oxford English Dictionary, Webster's,* or another reputable general dictionary, or you may turn to a specialized dictionary, such as *Black's Law Dictionary.* Any of these references defines words by classification—that is, by first placing a term in the general class, group, or family to which it belongs and then differentiating it from all the other members of that class.

A dictionary definition has authority. This can be an important advantage, especially when you are discussing a controversial subject. If you quote a reputable dictionary, the audience usually accepts without question the definition you are using.

In simpler or less controversial instances, it is also possible to define by classification in your own words, as Shannon did in her speech on the dangers of vaccines: "A vaccine is basically a dead viral cell that is injected into the patient's body."[10] Note how this definition fits our explanation of how to define by classification: Generally speaking, a vaccine fits into the class of "dead viral cell," but it differs from other dead viruses by being "injected into the patient's body."

OPERATIONAL DEFINITIONS

As noted earlier, sometimes a word or phrase may not be totally unfamiliar to an audience, but you as a speaker may be applying it in a unique or specific way that needs to be clarified. At other times, defining a word by classification may result only in an abstract notion that does not particularly clarify the word's meaning. In such cases, you would be better off providing a more concrete **operational definition**, explaining how something works or what it does.

In his speech on hazing, Manuel Goni defined hazing operationally:

> The term hazing is not merely verbal abuse or bullying. . . . Hazing activities include eating excrement, receiving physical beatings, coerced consumption of alcohol, using illegal drugs, vandalizing property, stealing, and even sexual attacks like rape.[11]

Operational definitions are usually original; they are not found in dictionaries. Although they may lack the credibility of dictionary definitions by classification, they can be specifically tailored to a speech.

USING DEFINITIONS EFFECTIVELY

The following suggestions can help you use definitions more effectively in your speeches.

Use a Definition Only When Needed   As we mentioned, novice speakers too often use a definition as an easy introduction or a time-filler. Resist the temptation to provide a definition unless you are using a relatively obscure term or one with several definitions. Unnecessary definitions are boring and, more serious still, insulting to the listeners' intelligence.

Be Certain That Your Definition Is Understandable   You probably have had the frustrating experience of looking up a word in the dictionary, only to find that the full definition is as confusing as the word itself. The word *dogmatic,* for example, may be defined as "characterized by or given to the use of dogmatism." To find a more satisfactory definition, you can look down the column until you find *dogmatism.* Your listeners do not have that capability, so make certain you give them definitions that are immediately and easily understandable—or you will have wasted your time and perhaps even lost your audience.

Be Certain That Your Definition and Your Use of a Term Are Consistent Throughout a Speech   Even seemingly simple words can create confusion if not defined and used consistently. For example, Roy opened his speech on the potential hazards of abusing nonprescription painkillers by defining *drugs* as nonprescription painkillers. A few minutes later, he confused his audience by using the word *drug* to refer to cocaine. Once he had defined the term, he should have used it only in that context throughout the speech.

9.d   Analogies

An **analogy** is a comparison. Like a definition, it increases understanding; unlike a definition, it deals with relationships and comparisons—between the new and the old, the unknown and the known, or any other pairs of ideas or things. In her speech to the 1990 graduating class of Wellesley College, Barbara Bush found the concept of color a unifying analogy for the speaker, the occasion, and school tradition:

> Now I know your first choice for today was Alice Walker, known for *The Color Purple.* Instead you got me—known for the color of my hair! Of course, Alice Walker's book has a special resonance here. At Wellesley, each class is known by a special color, and for four years the class of '90 has worn the color purple. Today you meet on Severance Green to say goodbye to all that, to begin a new and very personal journey, a search for your own true colors.[12]

Analogies can help your listeners understand unfamiliar ideas, things, and situations by showing how these matters are similar to something they already know.

There are two types of analogies. A *literal* analogy compares things that are actually similar (two sports, two cities, two events). A *figurative* analogy may take the form of a simile or a metaphor. It compares things that at first seem to have little in common (such as the West Wind and revolution, in Percy Bysshe Shelley's poem "Ode to the West Wind") but that share some vital feature (a fierce impetus for change).

LITERAL ANALOGIES

Attorney Stephen Dannhauser, speaking to the European Banking and Financial Forum in Prague, compared traveling across the United States and traveling across Western Europe, now that Western European countries all use a single currency:

> As an American accustomed to traveling 3,000 miles from coast to coast in the United States without having to concern myself with a diversity of currencies, enjoying a similar experience across much of Western Europe is welcome.[13]

Dannhauser's comparison of the two experiences is a **literal analogy**—a comparison between two similar things. If your listeners are from a culture or group other than your own or the one from which the speech derives, literal analogies that draw on the listeners' culture or group may help them understand more readily the less familiar places, things, and situations you are discussing. Literal analogies are often employed by people who want to influence public policy. For example, proponents of trade restrictions argue that because Japan maintains its trade balance through stringent import controls, so should the United States. Or, if Columbia, Missouri, solved both ecological and financial woes by successfully instituting an aluminum can tax, why not try the same approach in Lawrence, Kansas? The more similarities a policymaker can show between the policies or situations being compared, the better his or her chances of being persuasive.

FIGURATIVE ANALOGIES

On a warm July afternoon in 1848, feminist Elizabeth Cady Stanton delivered the keynote address to the first women's-rights convention in Seneca Falls, New York. Near the end of her speech, she offered this impassioned analogy:

> Voices were the visitors and advisers of Joan of Arc. Do not "voices" come to us daily from the haunts of poverty, sorrow, degradation, and despair, already too long unheeded? Now is the time for the women of this country, if they would save our free institutions, to defend the right, to buckle on the armor that can best resist the keenest weapons of the enemy—contempt and ridicule.[14]

A literal analogy might have compared the status of women in medieval France to that of women in nineteenth-century America. But the **figurative analogy** Stanton employed compared the voices that moved Joan of Arc to the social ills faced by nineteenth-century women.

Because it relies not on facts or statistics, but rather on imaginative insights, the figurative analogy is not considered "hard" evidence. But because it is creative, it is inherently interesting and should help grab an audience's attention. Speakers often employ figurative analogies in their introductions and conclusions. Eric opened his speech on the National Flood Insurance Program with this figurative analogy between gambling on horse races and gambling with nature:

> If someone were to lose thousands of dollars gambling on horse races, would you want your tax dollars to bail them out? Probably not. What if they lost those thousands of dollars without having any knowledge they were even gambling? What if I told you sooner or later you might find yourself or someone you know in a similar predicament? Currently in the United States there are millions of people gambling not on horse races, but on Mother Nature by living on flood plains or coasts. When these people lose, they lose big: beach houses, farm houses, and apartment houses go out to sea, down the river, or simply soak up catastrophic damages.[15]

USING ANALOGIES EFFECTIVELY

These suggestions can help you use literal and figurative analogies more effectively.

Be Sure That the Two Things You Compare in a Literal Analogy Are Very Similar   If you base your speech on a literal analogy, it is vital that the two things you compare be very much alike. One reason socialized medicine has not been adopted in the United States is that critics of the idea have pointed out how dissimilar the United States is to most of the countries that have adopted such programs. What works in those nations would not work here, they argue. The more alike the two things being compared, the more likely it is that the analogy will stand up under attack.

Be Sure That the Essential Similarity Between the Two Objects of a Figurative Analogy Is Readily Apparent   When you use a figurative analogy, it is crucial to make clear the similarity on which the analogy is based. If you do not, your audience will end up wondering what in the world you are talking about. And you will only confuse your listeners further if you try to draw on that same analogy later in your speech.

It may be a good idea to try out a figurative analogy on an honest friend before using it during a speech. Then you can be certain that your point is clear.

9.e   Statistics

Many of us live in awe of numbers, or **statistics**. Perhaps nowhere is our respect for statistics so evident—and so exploited—as in advertising. If three out of four doctors surveyed recommend Pain Away aspirin, it must be the best. If Sudsy Soap is 99.9 percent pure (whatever that means), surely it will help our complexions. And if nine out of ten people like Sloppy Catsup in the taste test, we will certainly buy some for this weekend's barbecue. How can the statistics be wrong?

The truth about statistics lies somewhere between such unconditional faith in numbers and the wry observation that "There are three kinds of lies: lies, damned lies, and statistics."

USING STATISTICS AS SUPPORT

Just as three or four brief examples may be more effective than just one, a statistic that represents hundreds or thousands of individuals may be more persuasive still.

> As a company with 360,000 employees, 88,000 vehicles, and 2,850 operating facilities worldwide, UPS has a significant impact on society, the global economy, and the environment.[16]

Or statistics can express the relationship of a part to the whole:

> The National Highway Traffic Safety Administration reports that a whopping 40 percent of car repair costs last year were either fraudulent or unnecessary.[17]

Whatever their purpose, statistics are considered by most people to be the ultimate "hard" evidence—firm, convincing fact.

USING STATISTICS EFFECTIVELY

The following discussion can help you analyze and use statistics effectively and correctly.

Use Reliable Sources   It has been said that figures don't lie, but liars figure! And indeed, statistics can be produced to support almost any conclusion desired. Your goal is to cite *reputable, authoritative,* and *unbiased* sources.

REPUTABLE.   The most reputable sources of statistics are usually government agencies, independent survey organizations, scholarly research reports, and such statistical reference works as the *World Almanac* and the *Statistical Abstract of the United States*. Private businesses may also be reputable, but you should view their statistics with a bit more caution. These organizations may use questionable data collection methods, or their data may be biased by special interests.

AUTHORITATIVE.   Statistical sources should also be authoritative. No source is an authority on everything and thus cannot be credible on all subjects. For example, we expect the U.S. Surgeon General's office to gather and release statistics on smokers' risks of developing lung cancer. But we would look askance at statistics from that same office that dealt with the numbers of hurricanes that have hit the coastal United States in the last 100 years.

The most authoritative source is the **primary source**—the original collector and interpreter of the data. If you find an interesting statistic in a newspaper or magazine article, look closely to see whether a source is cited. If it is, try to find that source and the original report of the statistic. Do not just assume that the secondhand account, or **secondary source**, has reported the statistic accurately and fairly. As often as possible, go to the primary source.

UNBIASED.   As well as being reputable and authoritative, sources should be as unbiased as possible. We usually extend to government research and various independent sources of statistics the courtesy of thinking them unbiased. Because they are, for the most part, supposed to be unaffiliated with any special interest, statistics from such sources are presumed to be less biased than those coming from such organizations as the American Tobacco Institute, the AFL-CIO, or the Burger King Corporation. All three organizations have some special interest at stake, and data they gather are more likely to reflect their biases.

As you evaluate your sources, try to find out how the statistics were gathered. For example, if a statistic relies on a sample, how was the sample taken? A Thursday afternoon telephone poll of 20 registered voters in Brooklyn is not an adequate sample of New York City voters. The sample is too small and too geographically limited. In addition, it excludes anyone without a telephone or anyone unlikely to be at home when the survey was conducted. Sample sizes and survey methods do vary widely, but most legitimate polls involve samples of 500 to 2,000 people, selected at random from a larger population. Of course, finding out about the statistical methodology may be more difficult than discovering the source of the statistic, but if you can find it, the information will help you to analyze the value of the statistic.

Interpret Statistics Accurately   People are often swayed by statistics that sound good but have in fact been wrongly calculated or misinterpreted. In an interview for *The New York Times,* Joel Best, author of *Damned Lies and Statistics: Untangling Numbers from the Media, Politicians, and Activists,* offered his favorite "bad statistic":

> A student of mine quoted an article that contained the sentence, "Every year since 1950, the number of American children gunned down has doubled." This is [a] mutant statistic. If one child were gunned down in 1950, and two in 1951, then by 1995, the year that the article was written, there would have been 35 trillion children gunned down, more than the total number of people who ever lived.[18]

A misrepresentation of statistics became a national issue with the appointment of former Houston, Texas, school superintendent Rod Paige as secretary of education. It was later revealed that Houston's amazing gains on such education indicators as dropout rates had actually resulted, not from visionary leadership, but from

> classifying, or coding [dropouts] as leaving for acceptable reasons: transferring to another school or returning to their native country.[19]

Both as a user of statistics in your own speeches and as a consumer of statistics in articles, books, and speeches, be constantly alert to what the statistics actually mean.

Make Your Statistics Understandable and Memorable   You can make your statistics easier to understand and more memorable in several ways.

COMPACTING STATISTICS.   You can *compact* a statistic, or express it in limits that are more meaningful or more easily understandable to your audience. When he outlined his first budget to a joint session of Congress on February 27, 2001, President George W. Bush compacted a statistic to help his listeners understand what a $1,600 tax savings could mean to an average American family:

Now $1,600 may not sound like a lot to some, but it means a lot to many families: $1,600 buys gas for two cars for an entire year. It pays tuition for a year at a community college. It pays the average family grocery bill for three months. That's real money.[20]

EXPLODING STATISTICS.   You might also make your statistics more memorable by exploding them. Exploded statistics are created by adding or multiplying related numbers—for example, cost per unit times number of units. Because it is larger, the exploded statistic seems more significant than the original figures from which it was derived. Soprano Renée Fleming, a professional opera singer, used an exploded statistic in her speech to the 2003 graduating class of the Juilliard School:

> Those of you who perform—musicians and dancers—will have by now practiced perhaps 3,000 hours a year, times 15 years, which equals 45,000 hours. Which means collectively that you as a group will have practiced 11 million hours.[21]

COMPARING STATISTICS.   Finally, you can compare your statistic with another that heightens its impact. Having offered the statistic that 11 percent of the elderly live at the poverty level, one speaker went on to say,

> Eleven percent—that's 3.8 million people, or the equivalent of the population of Los Angeles and Denver combined.[22]

Round Off Numbers   It is much easier to grasp and remember "2 million" than 2,223,147. Percentages, too, are more easily remembered if they are rounded off. And most people seem to remember percentages even better if they are expressed as fractions. "About 30 percent" is a better way to express "31.69 percent," and "about one third" is even easier to understand and remember. However, do not round off a statistic unless you can do so without distorting or falsifying the statistic.

Use Visual Aids to Present Your Statistics   Most audience members have difficulty remembering a barrage of numbers thrown at them during a speech. But if the numbers are displayed in a table or graph in front of your listeners, they can more

QUICK CHECK: *Select Effective Statistics*

- Are your sources reputable, unbiased, and authoritative?
- Are the data from a primary source?
- Are the data from a secondary source?
- Did you interpret the statistics accurately?
- Are your statistics easy to understand?
- Are they memorable?
- Can you present the statistics with visual aids?

Country of Origin	Preferred Family Size	
	0–2	3 or more
Iceland	26%	69%
United States	50%	41%
Mexico	56%	42%
Thailand	69%	30%
Germany	77%	17%
India	87%	12%

Note: "No opinion" omitted.

FIGURE 9.1   **Example of a Table of Statistics**

easily grasp the statistics. Figure 9.1 illustrates how a speaker could lay out a table of statistics regarding what people from various countries perceive to be an ideal number of children for a family to have. Using such a table, you would still need to explain what the numbers mean, but you wouldn't have to recite them.

9.f   Opinions

Three types of **opinions** may be used as supporting material in speeches: the testimonies of expert authorities, the testimonies of ordinary (lay) people with firsthand or eyewitness experience, and quotations from literary works.

If the person you quote is a recognized authority on your topic, citing his or her opinion may add credibility to your own arguments. Or the person you quote may have "said it in a nutshell"—phrased an argument or observation clearly, succinctly, and memorably. Let's look at the specific purposes and advantages of both expert testimonies and literary quotations.

EXPERT TESTIMONY

Having already offered statistics on the number of cigars Americans consume annually, Dena emphasized the danger to both smoker and secondhand recipient by providing **expert testimony** from a National Cancer Institute adviser:

> James Repace, an adviser to the National Cancer Institute, states, "If you have to breathe secondhand smoke, cigar smoke is a lot worse than cigarette smoke."[23]

Whether your topic is controversial or not, the testimony of a recognized authority can add a great deal of weight to your arguments. Or if your topic requires that you make predictions—statements that can be supported only in a marginal way by statistics or examples—the statements of expert authorities may prove to be your most convincing support. You may quote experts directly or paraphrase their words, as long as you are careful not to alter the intent of their remarks.

LAY TESTIMONY

You are watching the nightly news. Newscasters, reporting on the fires that continue to rage in California, explain how these fires started. They provide statistics on how many thousands of acres have burned and how many hundreds of homes have been destroyed. They describe the intense heat and smoke at the scene of one of the fires and ask an expert—a veteran firefighter—to predict the likelihood that the fires will be brought under control soon. But the most poignant moment of this news story is an interview with a woman who has just been allowed to return to her home and has found it in smoldering ashes. She is a layperson—not a firefighter or an expert on forest fires, but someone who has experienced the tragedy firsthand.

Like illustrations, **lay testimony** can stir an audience's emotions. And, although neither as authoritative nor as unbiased as expert testimony, lay testimony is often more memorable.

LITERARY QUOTATIONS

Another way to make a point memorable is to include a **literary quotation** in your speech. Speaking on the complex issue of using race as a factor in college admissions, University of Hartford President Walter Harrison turned to writer F. Scott Fitzgerald:

> The use of race as a factor in selective college admissions processes . . . is complex and emotionally charged. In 1935, the American novelist F. Scott Fitzgerald wrote, "The test of a first-rate intelligence is the ability to hold two opposed ideas in the mind at the same time, and still retain the ability to function."[24]

Fitzgerald's words are especially appropriate because they appeal to the intelligence of the listeners. Note, too, that the quotation is short. Brief, pointed quotations usually have greater audience impact than longer, more rambling ones. As Shakespeare said, "Brevity is the soul of wit" (*Hamlet,* II:2).

Literary quotations have the additional advantage of being easily accessible. You'll find any number of quotation dictionaries on the Web and in the reference sections of most libraries. Arranged alphabetically by subject, these compilations are easy to use.

USING OPINIONS EFFECTIVELY

Here are a few suggestions for using opinions effectively in your speeches.

Be Certain That Any Authority You Cite Is an Expert on the Subject Unless the authority you are calling on has expertise in the subject on which he or she is expressing an opinion, your quote will have little value. Quoting the opinions of an atomic scientist about works of art, for example, is to do little more than accept the opinions of the average person.

Be sure, then, that the sources you quote are not merely recognized authorities but recognized in the particular subject area they are talking about. Advertisements, especially, ignore this rule when they use well-known athletes to endorse such items as flashlight batteries, breakfast cereals, and cars. Athletes may indeed be experts on athletic shoes, tennis rackets, or stopwatches, but they lack any specific qualifications to talk about most of the products they endorse.

Identify Your Sources   Perhaps you chose an eminently qualified authority on your subject. Unless the audience, too, is aware of the qualifications of your authority, they may not grant him or her any credibility. If a student quotes the director of Literacy Services of Wisconsin but identifies that person only as Vyvyan Harding, no one will recognize the name, let alone acknowledge her authority.

In the course of citing your sources orally, you can provide additional information about the qualifications of those sources. Note how the student speakers in the following examples use a variety of phrases and sentence structures to help them identify their sources for their audiences in a fluent way:

> Casper Bowden of the Foundation for Information Policy Research says in the May 25, 2002, *New Scientist:* "Privacy is paradoxical . . . without it, people may fear to participate in a public life or support unpopular causes."[25]

> Mark Finney, research assistant at the Forest Service Fire Sciences Laboratory, reported the success of [selective forestry] to *Fox News* on August 26, 2002. He said, "Strategically thinning in a herringbone pattern forces the fire to move perpendicularly to the prevailing wind. It can have a huge effect."[26]

> As explained on June 3, 2002 in *Wired Magazine,* David Wood, program director of the GrassRoots Recycling Network, says, "It is simply cheaper to put electronic junk on a container ship to China."[27]

Cite Unbiased Authorities   Just as the most reliable sources of statistics are unbiased, so, too, are the most reliable sources of opinion. The chairman of General Motors may offer an expert opinion that the Chevrolet Lumina is the best midsized car on the market today. His expertise is unquestionable, but his bias is obvious and makes him a less-than-trustworthy source of opinion on the subject. A better source would be the *Consumer Reports* analyses of the reliability and repair records of midsized cars.

Cite Opinions That Are Representative of Prevailing Opinion
Perhaps you have found a bona fide expert who supports your conclusions. Unless most of the experts in the field share his or her opinion, its value is limited. Citing such opinion only leaves your conclusions open to easy rebuttal.

Quote Your Sources Accurately   If you quote or paraphrase either an expert or a layperson, be certain that your quote or paraphrase is accurate and presented in the context in which the remarks were originally made. Major misunderstandings may result from someone's being quoted inaccurately. "Letters to the Editor" columns in major news publications often include letters from irate readers who have found themselves misquoted in recent articles.

Use Literary Quotations Sparingly   Even though a relevant literary quote may be just right for a speech, use it with caution. Overuse of such quotations often bores an audience and causes them to doubt your creativity and research ability and to view you as somewhat pretentious. It is sometimes better not to use any quotation than to use literary quotations out of desperation, just because you can't find anything better. Be sure that you have a valid reason for citing a literary quotation, and then use only one or two such quotations at most in a speech.

QUICK CHECK: *Types of Supporting Material*

Illustrations	Relevant stories
Explanations	Statements that make clear how something is done or why it exists in its present form or existed in a past form
Descriptions	Word pictures
Definitions	Concise explanations of a word or concept
Analogies	Comparisons between two things
Statistics	Numbers that summarize data or examples
Opinions	Testimony or quotations from someone else

9.8 Selecting the Best Supporting Material

The six criteria for evaluating Web sites are accountability, accuracy, objectivity, date, usability, and diversity. You should use the same criteria in evaluating any supporting material you hope to use. Throughout this chapter, we have presented guidelines for using each of six types of supporting material effectively. However, even after you have applied these criteria and guidelines and eliminated some material, you may still have more supporting material than you can possibly use for a short speech.

HOW TO: *Decide Which Is Your Best Supporting Material*

- **Magnitude.** Bigger is better. The larger the numbers, the more convincing your statistics. The more experts who support your point of view, the more your expert testimony will command your audience's attention.

- **Proximity.** The best supporting material is whatever is the most relevant to your listeners, or "closest to home." If you can demonstrate how an incident could affect audience members themselves, that illustration will have far greater impact than a more remote one.

- **Concreteness.** By themselves, abstract assertions and explanations bore an audience. If you need to discuss principles and theories, explain them with concrete examples and specific statistics.

- **Variety.** Even if your supporting material meets the first three requirements, if it is all of the same type, your audience may lose interest or question your research. A mix of illustrations, opinions, definitions, and statistics is much more interesting and convincing than the exclusive use of any one type of supporting material.

- **Humor.** Audiences usually appreciate a touch of humor in an example or opinion. Only if your audience is unlikely to understand the humor or if your speech is on a very somber and serious topic is humor not appropriate.

- **Suitability.** Your final decision about whether to use a certain piece of supporting material will depend on its suitability to you, your speech, the occasion, and—as we continue to stress throughout the book—your audience. For example, you would probably use more statistics in a speech to a group of scientists than in an after-luncheon talk to the local Rotary Club.

Summary

- Interesting, convincing supporting material is essential to making a speech successful.

- Choose from various types of supporting material, including illustrations, descriptions and explanations, definitions, analogies, statistics, and opinions.

- Follow the suggestions presented in this chapter to gauge the validity and reliability of your evidence.

- Six additional criteria—magnitude, proximity, concreteness, variety, humorousness, and suitability—can help you choose the most effective support for your speech.

Key Terms

analogy (p. 178)
brief illustration (p. 172)
definition (p. 177)
definition by classification (p. 177)
description (p. 175)
expert testimony (p. 184)
explanation (p. 175)
extended illustration (p. 172)
figurative analogy (p. 179)
hypothetical illustration (p. 173)

illustration (p. 172)
lay testimony (p. 185)
literal analogy (p. 179)
literary quotation (p. 185)
operational definition (p. 177)
opinion (p. 184)
primary source (p. 181)
secondary source (p. 181)
statistics (p. 180)

A QUESTION OF ETHICS

You have decided on a topic for your speech and have been conducting a great deal of research. However, you have not been able to find enough material to support your speech. Is it ethical to create supporting material or to distort facts to make your point if you have been unable to find what you need? Explain your answer.

4

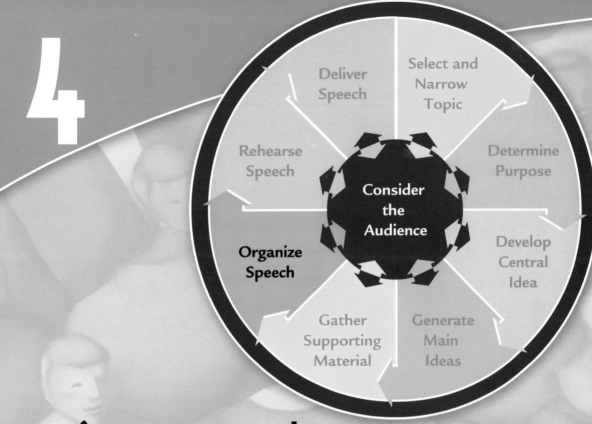

Deliver Speech

Select and Narrow Topic

Rehearse Speech

Determine Purpose

Consider the Audience

Organize Speech

Develop Central Idea

Gather Supporting Material

Generate Main Ideas

Crafting a Speech

Crafting a Speech

Crafting a Speech

10 Organizing Your Speech

➡ **Organizing Your Main Ideas (p. 200)**

- You can choose from among five organizational patterns: (1) chronological, (2) topical, (3) spatial, (4) causal, and (5) problem–solution. Or, you can combine several of these patterns.
- Chronological organization is organization by time—from earliest to most recent (forward in time) or from recent events back into history (backward in time).
  - How-to explanations are chronological—following a sequence or series of steps arranged from beginning to end, from the first step to the last—forward in time.
- If your central idea has natural divisions, you can organize your speech topically.
  - It may not matter which point you discuss first, second, or third. You can simply arrange your main points as a matter of personal preference.
  - If you want to emphasize one point more than the others, consider the principle of recency. Audiences tend to remember best what they hear last.
  - If your topic is controversial, you may want to organize your main ideas according to the principle of primacy, or putting the most important or convincing idea first.
  - If your main points range from simple to complicated, arrange them in order of complexity, progressing from the simple to the more complex.
- Use spatial organization to arrange items according to their location and direction.
- Use cause and effect to identify a situation and then discuss the effects that result from it (cause ➝ effect). Or, present a situation and then seek its causes (effect ➝ cause).
- To emphasize how best to solve a problem, use a problem-and-solution pattern of organization.

➡ **Subdividing Your Main Ideas (p. 208)**
- After you decide how to organize your main ideas, you may need to subdivide some of them. You can arrange your main ideas according to one pattern and your subpoints according to another.

➡ **Integrating Your Supporting Material (p. 209)**
- If you are using a word-processing file, print out a hard copy of this file so that you can have it in front of you while you work on your speech plan.
- Arrange note cards in the order in which you have organized your speech. Then go through the cards, one by one, and decide where in the speech you will use each one.
- Search photocopies for what you need, and then write or type this supporting material into your speech plan.
- Once your supporting material is logically placed into your plan, your next goal is to incorporate it smoothly into your speech so as not to interrupt the flow of ideas.

➡ **Organizing Your Supporting Material (p. 210)**
- If none of the five standard organizational patterns seem suited to your supporting materials, you may want to try these strategies: (1) primacy or recency, (2) specificity, (3) complexity, or (4) "soft" to "hard" evidence.
  - The principles of primacy and recency can determine whether you put material at the beginning or the end of your speech.
  - You may offer your specific information first and end with your general statement, or make the general statement first and support it with specific evidence.
  - Start with the simplest ideas that are easy to understand and work up to more complex ones.
  - Supporting material can also be arranged from "soft" to "hard." Soft evidence rests on opinion or inference. Hard evidence includes factual examples and statistics.

➡ **Developing Signposts (p. 213)**
- Develop signposts—words and gestures that allow you to move smoothly from one idea to the next throughout your speech, showing relationships between ideas and emphasizing important points.
  - Transitions indicate that a speaker has finished discussing one idea and is moving to another. Transitions may be either verbal or nonverbal.
  - One type of signpost that can occasionally backfire and do more harm than good is one that signals the end of a speech.

- Previews help to ensure that audience members will first anticipate and later remember the important points of a speech.
- Summaries provide additional exposure to a speaker's ideas and can help ensure that audience members will grasp and remember them.

➡ **Supplementing Signposts with Presentation Aids (p. 217)**
- One way you can increase the likelihood of your listeners' attending to your signposting is to prepare and use presentation aids to supplement your signposts.

11 Introducing Your Speech

➡ **Purposes of Introductions (p. 221)**
- A good introduction must perform five important functions: get the audience's attention, introduce the subject, give the audience a reason to listen, establish your credibility, and preview your main ideas.
  - A key purpose of the introduction is to gain favorable attention for your speech.
  - The best way to ensure that your introduction does introduce the subject of your speech is to include a statement of your central idea in the introduction.
  - Give the audience a reason to listen by showing them how the topic affects them directly.
  - Establish your credibility in your introduction so that your audience will be motivated to listen.
  - Preview the main ideas of your speech. The preview statement allows your listeners to anticipate the main ideas of your speech, which in turn helps ensure that they will remember those ideas after the speech.

➡ **Effective Introductions (p. 225)**
- There are many effective ways of introducing a speech.
  - Use an illustration or anecdote.
  - Use a personal anecdote to establish your credibility.
  - Use a startling fact or statistic.

- Use an appropriate quotation.
- Use humor; however, if your audience is linguistically diverse or composed primarily of listeners whose first language is not English, you may want to choose a strategy other than humor.
- Ask a rhetorical question—the kind you don't expect an answer to.
- Refer to an historic event.
- If your topic is timely, refer to a recent event.
- Refer to yourself or a personal experience.
- Refer to the occasion.
- Refer to a preceding speech.

12 Concluding your Speech

➡ **Purposes of Conclusions (p. 235)**
- An effective conclusion summarizes the speech, reemphasizes the main idea in a memorable way, motivates the audience to respond, and provides closure.
  - Your conclusion is your last chance to summarize your main ideas for the audience.
  - Your conclusion should restate the central idea of the speech in a memorable way.
  - Create motivation—not motivation to listen, but motivation to respond to the speech in some way.
  - Let the audience know that the speech has ended.

➡ **Effective Conclusions (p. 238)**
- Effective conclusions may employ illustrations, quotations, personal references, or any of the other methods used for introductions.
  - An illustration or anecdote can help the audience focus on the main point of your speech and hold their attention.
  - Startling facts and statistics can help your audience remember afterward what you had to say.
  - Use a quotation to conclude a speech.
  - Give a humorous conclusion that puts the audience in a relaxed frame of mind so that they leave with a sense of enjoyment and goodwill toward you as the speaker.

- Using a rhetorical question keeps your speech in the audience's mind as they try to answer the question.
- Issue an inspirational appeal or challenge to your listeners, rousing them to a high emotional pitch at the conclusion of the speech.
- Include an appeal to action in your conclusion if you give a persuasive speech.

13 Outlining and Editing Your Speech

➡ **Developing a Preparation Outline (p. 244)**
- A detailed preparation outline should include main ideas, subpoints, and supporting material. It may also include the specific purpose, introduction, blueprint, conclusion, and signposts.
- To begin outlining, try a technique known as mapping, or clustering. Write on a sheet of paper all the main ideas, subpoints, and supporting material for the speech.
  - Write your preparation outline in complete sentences, like those you will use when delivering your speech.
  - Use standard outline form.
  - Use standard outline numbering.
  - Use at least two subdivisions, if any, for each point.
  - Indent main ideas, points, subpoints, and supporting material properly.
  - Write and label your specific purpose at the top of your preparation outline.
  - Add the blueprint, key signposts, and an introduction and conclusion to your outline.
- Use your preparation outline to help analyze and possibly revise the speech.
  - Does the speech as outlined fulfill the purpose you have specified? Are the main ideas logical extensions (natural divisions, reasons, or steps) of the central idea?
  - Do the signposts enhance the comfortable flow of each idea into the next?
  - Does each subpoint provide support for the point under which it falls?
  - Is your outline form correct?

At a Glance *(continued)*

➡ **Editing Your Speech (p. 252)**
- When you rehearse using your preparation outline, you may discover that your speech is too long. To edit your speech to shorten it:
  - Review your specific purpose.
  - Consider your audience.
  - Simply say it.
  - Keep only the best supporting material.
  - Ask a listener to help you cut.
  - Look at your introduction and conclusion.

➡ **Developing Your Delivery Outline and Speaking Notes (p. 254)**
- A delivery outline is meant to give you all you will need to present your speech in the way you have planned and rehearsed. It should not be so detailed that it encourages you to read it rather than speak to your audience.
- Your delivery outline, with slight adjustments, serves as the basis for your final speaking notes.
  - Make the outline as brief as possible, and write in single words or short phrases rather than complete sentences.
  - Include the introduction and conclusion in much shortened form.
  - Include supporting material and signposts. Write out statistics, direct quotations, and key signposts.
  - Do not include your purpose statement in your delivery outline.
  - Use standard outline form.
- Instead of using an outline, you might use an alternative format for your speaking notes. For example, you could use a map. Or you could use a combination of words, pictures, and symbols. Whatever form your notes take, they should make sense to you.

14 Using Words Well: Speaker Language and Style

➡ **Oral versus Written Language Style (p. 262)**
- There are at least three major differences between oral and written language styles.

- Oral style is more personal.
- Oral style is less formal.
- Oral style is more repetitious.

➡ **Using Words Effectively (p. 264)**
- Use specific, concrete words.
- Use simple words.
- Use words correctly.

➡ **Adapting Your Language Style to Diverse Listeners (p. 266)**
- Use language that your audience can understand.
- Use appropriate language.
- Use unbiased language.

➡ **Crafting Memorable Word Structures (p. 269)**
- Memorable speeches are stylistically distinctive. They create arresting images.
- One way to make your message memorable is to use figures of speech to create arresting images. A figure of speech deviates from the ordinary, expected meanings of words to make a description or comparison unique, vivid, and memorable.
  - A metaphor is an implied comparison. A simile is a comparison that includes the word *like* or *as*.
  - Personification is the attribution of human qualities to inanimate things or ideas.
- Another way you can make phrases and sentences memorable is to use them to create drama in your speech—to keep the audience in suspense or to catch them slightly off guard by saying something in a way that differs from the way they expected you to say it.
  - Use a short sentence to express a vitally important thought.
  - Use omission—leave out a word or phrase that the audience expects to hear.
  - Use inversion—reverse the normal word order of a phrase or sentence.
  - Use suspension—place a key word or phrase at the end of a sentence, rather than at the beginning.
- Create cadence by taking advantage of language rhythms, not by speaking in singsong patterns, but by using such stylistic devices as parallelism, antithesis, repetition, and alliteration.
  - Parallelism occurs when two or more clauses or sentences have the same grammatical pattern.

- The word *antithesis* means "opposition." In language style, a sentence that uses antithesis has two parts with parallel structures but contrasting meanings.
- Repetition of a key word or phrase gives rhythm and power to your message and makes it memorable.
- Alliteration is the repetition of a consonant sound (usually an initial consonant) several times in a phrase, clause, or sentence. Alliteration adds cadence to a thought.

➡ **Tips for Using Language Effectively (p. 274)**
- Use distinctive stylistic devices sparingly.
- Use stylistic devices at specific points in your speech.
- Short words are more forceful than long ones.
- Use stylistic devices to economize.

CHAPTER 10

Organizing Your Speech

aria went into the lecture hall feeling exhilarated. After all, Dr. Anderson was a Nobel Laureate in literature. He would be teaching and lecturing on campus for at least a year. What an opportunity!

Maria took a seat in the middle of the fourth row, where she had a clear view of the podium. She opened the notebook she had bought just for this lecture series, took out one of the three pens she had brought with her, and waited impatiently for Dr. Anderson's appearance. She didn't have to wait long. Dr. Anderson was greeted by thunderous applause when he walked onto the stage. Maria was aware of an almost electric sense of expectation among the audience members. Pen poised, she awaited his first words.

Five minutes later, Maria still had her pen poised. He had gotten off to a slow start. Ten minutes later, she laid her pen down and decided to concentrate just on listening. Twenty minutes later, she still had no idea what point Dr. Anderson was trying to make. And by the time the lecture was over, Maria was practically asleep. Disappointed, she gathered her pens and her notebook (which now contained one page of doodles) and promised herself she would skip the remaining lectures in the series.

Dr. Anderson was not a dynamic speaker. But his motivated audience of young would-be authors and admirers might have forgiven that shortcoming. What they were unable to do was to unravel his hour's worth of seemingly pointless rambling—to get some sense of direction or some pattern of ideas from his talk. Dr. Anderson had simply failed to organize his thoughts.

The scenario described above actually happened. Dr. Anderson (not his real name) disappointed many who had looked forward to his lectures. His inability to organize his ideas made him an ineffectual speaker. You, too, may have had an experience with a teacher who possessed awesome knowledge and ability in his or her field but could not organize his or her thoughts well enough to lecture effectively. No matter how knowledgeable speakers may be, they must organize their ideas in logical patterns to ensure that their audience can follow, understand, and remember what is said. Our model of audience-centered communication emphasizes that speeches are organized for audiences, with decisions about organization based in large part on an analysis of the audience.

> *Organized thought is the basis of organized action.*
>
> —**Alfred North Whitehead**

In preceding chapters of this book, you learned how to plan and research a speech based on audience needs, interests, and expectations. The planning and research process has taken you through five stages of speech preparation:

- Selecting and narrowing a topic
- Determining your purpose
- Developing your central idea
- Generating main ideas
- Gathering supporting material

As the arrows on the model in Figure 10.1 suggest, you may have moved *recursively* through these first five stages, returning at times to earlier stages to make changes and revisions based on your consideration of the audience. Now, with the results of your audience-centered planning and research in hand, it is time to begin to put the speech together—in other words, to organize your ideas and information. The next stage in the audience-centered public-speaking process is simply that: Organizing your speech

In this chapter, we will discuss the patterns of organization commonly used to arrange the main ideas of a speech. Then we will discuss how to organize subpoints and supporting materials. Finally, we will talk about transitions, previews, and summaries. Creating introductions and conclusions and outlining, the final components of the organizational stage of the preparation process, will be discussed in later chapters.

10.a Organizing Your Main Ideas

We discussed earlier how to generate a preliminary plan for your speech by determining whether your central idea had logical divisions, could be supported by several reasons, or could be explained by identifying specific steps. These divisions, reasons, or steps became the main ideas of the body of your speech and the basis for the organization task highlighted in Figure 10.1.

Now you are ready to decide which of your main ideas to discuss first, which one second, and so on. You can choose from among five organizational patterns: (1) chronological, (2) topical, (3) spatial, (4) causal, and (5) problem–solution. Or, you can combine several of these patterns. One additional variation of the problem–solution pattern is the motivated sequence.

ORDERING IDEAS CHRONOLOGICALLY

If you decide that your central idea could be explained best by a number of steps, you will probably organize those steps chronologically. **Chronological organization** is organization by time; that is, your steps are ordered according to when each occurred or should occur. Historical speeches and how-to speeches are the two kinds of speeches usually organized chronologically.

Examples of topics for historical speeches might include the history of the women's movement in the United States, the sequence of events that led to the 1974

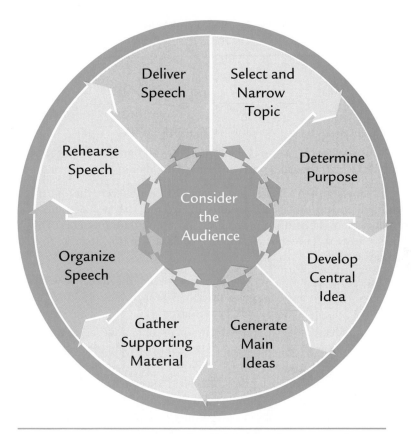

FIGURE 10.1 **Organize your speech to help your audience remember your key ideas and to give your speech clarity and structure.**

resignation of President Richard Nixon, or the development of the modern Olympic Games.

You can choose to organize your main points either from earliest to most recent (forward in time) or from recent events back into history (backward in time). The progression you choose depends on your personal preference and on whether you want to emphasize the beginning or the end of the sequence. According to the principle of **recency**, the event discussed last is usually the one the audience will remember best.

Forward in Time   In the following outline of a speech on the nation's 911 system, the speaker moves forward in time, making his last point the one that remains fresh in the minds of his audience at the end of his speech.

Purpose Statement: At the end of my speech, the audience will be able to trace the decline in the effectiveness of the 911 emergency system in the United States. The 911 system has decreased in effectiveness since its inception in 1967.

Central Idea:	I. In 1967, Lyndon Johnson signed legislation creating the 911 system.
Main Ideas:	II. In 1987, the average 911 response time was 6 minutes.
	III. By 1998, the average 911 response time was 12 minutes.
	IV. By 2001, 911 was struggling to handle the booming mobile-phone industry.[1]

Note that in this example, the central idea and main ideas together form a kind of blueprint, which we will discuss in more detail later in this chapter.

Backward in Time   In another historical speech, this one discussing the factors that led to the literary Renaissance in England, the speaker wants to emphasize the introduction of the printing press as the most important influence. Thus, as the outline shows, the speaker organizes the speech backward in time in order to discuss the printing press last.

Purpose Statement:	At the end of my speech, the audience will be able to list and explain the two forces that prompted the English literary Renaissance.
Central Idea:	Two powerful forces for change led to the English literary Renaissance, which began late in the fifteenth century.
Main Ideas:	I. 1485—Henry VII defeated Richard III at the Battle of Bosworth Field, ascended the throne, and began the Tudor dynasty.
	II. 1476—William Caxton brought the printing press to England.

Chronological organization, then, involves either forward or backward progression, depending on which end of a set of events the speaker intends to emphasize. The element common to both movements is that dates and events are discussed in sequence rather than in random order.

How-To Explanations   How-to explanations usually follow a sequence or series of steps arranged from beginning to end, from the first step to the last—forward in time. A speech explaining how to strip painted furniture might be organized as follows:

Purpose Statement:	At the end of my speech, the audience will be able to list the four steps involved in stripping old paint from furniture.
Central Idea:	Stripping old paint from furniture requires four steps.
Main Ideas:	I. Prepare work area and gather materials.
	II. Apply chemical stripper.
	III. Remove stripper with scrapers and steel wool.
	IV. Clean and sand stripped surfaces.

ORGANIZING IDEAS TOPICALLY

If your central idea has natural divisions, you can often organize your speech topically. Speeches on such diverse topics as factors to consider when selecting a mountain bike, types of infertility treatments, and the various classes of ham-radio licenses all could reflect **topical organization**.

Personal Preference   Natural divisions are often basically equal in importance. It may not matter which point you discuss first, second, or third. You can simply arrange your main points as a matter of personal preference.

Recency   At other times, you may wish to emphasize one point more than the others. If so, you will again need to consider the principle of recency. As we observed earlier, audiences tend to remember best what they hear last. For example, if your speech is on the various living arrangements available to college students, you may decide to discuss living at home, rooming in a dorm, joining a fraternity or sorority, and renting an apartment. If you want your audience of fellow students to consider living at home because of the savings involved, you would probably discuss that possibility as the fourth and last option. Your speech might have the following structure:

Purpose Statement: At the end of my speech, the audience will be able to discuss the pros and cons of four living arrangements for college students.

Central Idea: College students have at least four living arrangements available to them.

Main Ideas: I. Living in a dormitory

II. Renting an apartment

III. Joining a fraternity or sorority

IV. Living at home

Primacy   By contrast, if your topic is controversial and you know or suspect that your audience will be skeptical of or hostile to your ideas, you may want to organize your main ideas according to the principle of **primacy**, or putting the most important or convincing idea first. This way you do not risk losing or alienating your audience before you can reach your most significant idea. Further, your strongest idea may so influence your listeners' attitudes that they will be more receptive to the rest of your speech.

Purpose Statement: At the end of my speech, the audience will be able to explain the applications of stem cell research.

Central Idea: Stem cell research has three important applications.

Main Ideas: I. At the most fundamental level, understanding stem cells can help us to understand better the process of human development.

    II. Stem cell research could streamline the way we develop and test drugs.

   III. Stem cell research can generate cells and tissue that could be used for "cell therapies."[2]

In this example, the speaker realizes the controversial nature of stem cell research. The three main points of the speech are therefore arranged according to primacy, advancing the most persuasive argument first.

    Complexity   One other set of circumstances may dictate a particular order of the main points in your speech. If your main points range from simple to complicated, it makes sense to arrange them in order of **complexity**, progressing from the simple to the more complex. If, for example, you were to explain to your audience how to compile a family health profile and history, you might begin by discussing the most easily accessible source of health information and proceed to the more involved.

Purpose Statement: At the end of my speech, the audience will be able to compile a family health profile and history.

Central Idea: Compiling a family health profile and history can be accomplished with the help of three sources.

Main Ideas: I. Elderly relatives

    II. Old hospital records and death certificates

   III. National health registries[3]

Teachers, from those in the very early elementary grades on up, use order of complexity to organize their courses and lessons. The kindergartner is taught to trace circles before learning to print a lowercase *a*. The young piano student practices scales and arpeggios before playing Beethoven sonatas. The college student practices writing 500-word essays before attempting a major research paper. You have learned most of your skills in order of complexity.

ARRANGING IDEAS SPATIALLY

When you say, "As you enter the room, the table is to your right, the easy chair to your left, and the kitchen door straight ahead," you are organizing your ideas spatially.

    Location and Direction   A speaker who relies on **spatial organization** arranges items according to their location and direction. It does not usually matter whether the speaker chooses to progress up or down, east or west, forward or back, as long as ideas are developed in a logical order. If the speaker skips up, down, over, and back, he or she will only confuse the audience rather than paint a distinct word picture for it.

    Speeches on such diverse subjects as the Heard Museum in Phoenix, the travels of Robert Louis Stevenson, and the makeup of an atom can all be organized spatially. Here is a sample outline for the first of those topics:

Purpose Statement:	At the end of my speech, the audience will be able to list and describe the four permanent exhibits of the Heard Museum.
Central Idea:	The Heard Museum in Phoenix has four large permanent exhibits on Native American anthropology and culture.
Main Ideas:	I. Ethnological and historical materials of southwestern Native Americans
	II. Basketry
	III. Jewelry and pottery
	IV. Kachina dolls

The organization of this outline is spatial, progressing from the front entrance through the Heard Museum.

ORGANIZING IDEAS TO SHOW CAUSE AND EFFECT

A speech organized to show **cause and effect** may first identify a situation and then discuss the effects that result from it (cause ⟶ effect). Or, the speech may present a situation and then seek its causes (effect ⟶ cause). As the recency principle would suggest, the cause–effect pattern emphasizes the effects; the effect–cause pattern emphasizes the causes.

Cause–Effect   In the following example, Vonda organizes her speech according to cause–effect, discussing the cause (widespread adult illiteracy) as her first main idea, and its effects (poverty and social costs) as her second and third main ideas:

Purpose Statement:	At the end of my speech, the audience will be able to identify two effects of adult illiteracy.
Central Idea:	Adult illiteracy affects everyone.
Main Ideas:	I. (*Cause*): Adult illiteracy is widespread in America today.
	II. (*Effect*): Adult illiterates often live in poverty.
	III. (*Effect*): Adult illiteracy is costly to society.[4]

Effect–Cause   In contrast, Laurel organizes her speech on writing wills according to an effect–cause pattern, discussing the effect (people not writing wills) as her first main idea, and its causes (having to face mortality and being ignorant of how to prepare a will) as her second and third main ideas:

Purpose Statement:	At the end of my speech, the audience will be able to explain the reasons people don't write wills.
Central Idea:	People fail to prepare wills for several reasons.
Main Ideas:	I. (*Effect*): People are hesitant to write wills.
	II. (*Cause*): Writing a will brings people face to face with their own mortality.

    III. (*Cause*): Many people don't know how to prepare a will.[5]

In both of the preceding examples, the speakers may decide in what order they will discuss their points II and III by considering the principles of recency, primacy, or complexity discussed earlier in this chapter.

ORGANIZING IDEAS BY PROBLEM AND SOLUTION

If you want to discuss why a problem exists or what its effects are, you will probably organize your speech according to cause and effect, as discussed in the previous section. However, if you want to emphasize how best to *solve* the problem, you will probably use a **problem-and-solution** pattern of organization.

Problem–Solution　Like causes and effects, problems and solutions can be discussed in either order. If you speak to an audience that is already fairly aware of a problem but uncertain how to solve it, you will probably discuss the problem first and then the solution(s), as in this example:

Purpose Statement:	At the end of my speech, the audience will be able to list and explain three ways in which crime on university campuses can be reduced.
Central Idea:	Crimes on university campuses can be reduced by implementing three safety measures.
Main Ideas:	I. (*Problem*): Crimes against both persons and property have increased dramatically on college campuses over the last few years.
	II. (*Solution*): Crimes could be reduced by stricter enforcement of the Student Right to Know and Campus Security Acts.
	III. (*Solution*): Crimes could be reduced by assigning student identification numbers that are different from their Social Security numbers.
	IV. (*Solution*): Crimes could be reduced by converting campus buildings to an integrated security system requiring key cards for admittance.[6]

Solution–Problem　If your audience knows about an action or program that has been implemented but does not know the reasons for its implementation, you might select instead a solution–problem pattern of organization. In the following example, the speaker knows that her listeners are already aware of a new business–school partnership program in their community but believes that they may be unclear about why it has been established:

Purpose Statement:	At the end of my speech, the audience will be able to explain how business–school partnership programs can

	help solve two of the major problems facing our public schools today.
Central Idea:	Business–school partnership programs can help alleviate at least two of the problems faced by public schools today.
Main Ideas:	I. (*Solution*): In a business–school partnership, local businesses provide volunteers, financial support, and in-kind contributions to public schools.
	II. (*Problem*): Many public schools can no longer afford special programs and fine-arts programs.
	III. (*Problem*): Many public schools have no resources to fund enrichment materials and opportunities.

ACKNOWLEDGING CULTURAL DIFFERENCES IN ORGANIZATION

Although the five patterns just discussed are typical of the way speakers in the United States are expected to organize and process information, they are not necessarily typical of all cultures.[7] In fact, each culture teaches its members patterns of thought and organization that are considered appropriate for various occasions and audiences. On the whole, U.S. speakers tend to be more linear and direct than speakers from Semitic, Asian, Romance, or Russian cultures. Semitic speakers support their main points by pursuing tangents that might seem "off topic" to many U.S. speakers. Asians may only allude to a main point through a circuitous route of illustration and parable. And speakers from Romance and Russian cultures tend to begin with a basic principle and then move to facts and illustrations that they only gradually connect to a main point. The models in Figure 10.2 illustrate these culturally diverse patterns of organization.

Of course, these are very broad generalizations. But as an audience member, recognizing the existence of cultural differences when you are listening to a speech can

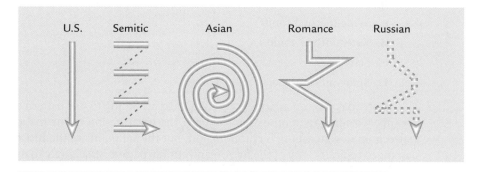

FIGURE 10.2 **Organizational Patterns by Culture**

From Lieberman, Devorah A., *Public Speaking in the Multicultural Environment* 2e. Published by Allyn & Bacon, Boston, MA. Copyright 1997 by Pearson Education. 2000. All rights reserved. Reprinted by permission of the publisher.

QUICK CHECK: *Organize Main Ideas*

- Chronologically
- Topically
- From simple to complex
- Spatially
- To show cause and effect
- To present problems and solutions

help you appreciate and understand the organization of a speaker from a culture other than your own. He or she may not be disorganized, but simply using organizational strategies different from the ones presented earlier in this chapter.

10.b Subdividing Your Main Ideas

After you have decided how to organize your main ideas, you may need to subdivide at least some of them. For example, if you give a how-to speech on dog grooming, your first main idea may be

1. Gather your supplies.

"Supplies" indicates that you need more than one piece of equipment, so you add subpoints that describe the specific supplies needed:

1. Gather your supplies.
  a. Soft brush
  b. Firm brush
  c. Wide-toothed comb
  d. Fine-toothed comb
  e. Scissors
  f. Spray-on detangler

Note that you can arrange your main ideas according to one pattern and your subpoints according to another. For example, the organization of the main ideas of this speech on dog grooming is chronological, but the subpoints of the first main idea are arranged topically. Any of the five organizational patterns that apply to main ideas can apply to subpoints as well.

Right now, don't worry about such outlining details as Roman numerals, letters, and margins. Your goal at this point is to get your ideas and information on paper. Keep in mind, too, that until you've delivered your speech, none of your decisions is etched in stone. You may add, regroup, or eliminate main ideas or subpoints at any stage in the preparation process, as you consider the needs, interests, and expectations of your audience. Multiple drafts indicate that you are working and reworking ideas to improve your speech and make it the best you can. They do not mean that you are a poor writer or speaker.

10.c Integrating Your Supporting Material

Once you have organized your main ideas and subpoints, you are ready to flesh out the speech with your supporting material.

WORD-PROCESSING FILES

If you have entered your supporting material into a word-processing file, you may want to print out a hard copy of this file so that you can have it in front of you while you work on your speech plan. When you determine where in the speech you need supporting material, find what you need on the hard copy and then go back into the word-processing file to cut and paste that supporting material electronically into your speech plan.

NOTE CARDS

If you have written or pasted supporting material on note cards, write each main idea and subpoint on a separate note card of the same size as the ones on which you recorded your supporting material. Arrange these note cards in the order in which you have organized your speech. Then go through your supporting-material note cards, one by one, and decide where in the speech you will use each one. The headings you wrote at the top of each card should help in this process. Place each supporting-material card behind the appropriate main-idea or subpoint card. You now have a complete plan for your speech on note cards.

PHOTOCOPIES

If most of your supporting material is photocopied, search these copies for what you need and then write or type this supporting material into your speech plan. Regardless of which strategy you use to integrate your supporting material, take care not to lose track of the source of the supporting material.

SMOOTH INCORPORATION OF SUPPORT MATERIAL

Once your supporting material is logically placed into your plan, your next goal is to incorporate it smoothly into your speech so as not to interrupt the flow of ideas. Notice how skillfully this goal is met by a speaker delivering a speech on the inherent dangers of discarded computer components:

Sample Integration of Supporting Material

Disposing of old computer products should become the joint responsibility of the manufacturer and the consumer. According to the *Seattle Times* of February 20, 2003, Representative Mike Cooper has proposed legislation to allow manufacturers to include the cost of disposal or recycling of their products into the sale price. In this way, the burden of recycling will then fall on the consumer who actually uses the product. . . .[8]

- State the point. The statement should be concise and clear, as it is here.
- Cite the source of the supporting material. As we noted in Chapter 4 in the discussion of oral citations, you should provide the author's name (if available) and the title and date of the publication.
- Present the supporting material. In this example, the supporting material is an explanation of proposed legislation.
- Explain how the supporting material substantiates or develops the point. Do not assume that audience members will automatically make the connection.

Your listeners may not remember many specific facts and statistics after a speech, but they should remember the important points. Connecting ideas and supporting material make it more likely that they will.

QUICK CHECK: *Integrate Supporting Material*

- State the point.
- Cite the source.
- Present the supporting material.
- Explain how the supporting material substantiates or develops the point.

10.d Organizing Your Supporting Material

Suppose you have decided what supporting material to use and identified the ideas in your speech that require support. Now you realize that in support of your second main idea you have an illustration, two statistics, and an opinion. In what order should you present these items?

You can sometimes use the five standard organizational patterns to arrange your supporting material, as well as your main ideas and subpoints. Illustrations, for instance, may be organized chronologically. In the following excerpt from a speech on childhood obesity, the speaker arranges several brief examples in a chronological sequence:

I can think of at least three moments in the past half century that dramatically shifted the course of America's medical and scientific history.

The first time came exactly 51 years ago today—March 26, 1953—when Jonas Salk called a press conference to announce the discovery of a polio vaccine.

The second time, amazingly, came just four weeks later, when Watson and Crick published their discovery of the double helix structure of DNA.

The third time was in 1964, when U.S. Surgeon General Luther Terry courageously reported that cigarette smoking does cause cancer and other deadly diseases. . . .

On March 9, 2004, the CDC Director declared that obesity is overtaking smoking and tobacco use as the number-one cause of preventable death in America.[9]

At other times, however, none of the five patterns may seem suited to the supporting materials you have. In those instances, you may need to turn to an organizational strategy more specifically adapted to your supporting materials. These strategies include (1) primacy or recency, (2) specificity, (3) complexity, and (4) "soft" to "hard" evidence.

PRIMACY OR RECENCY

We have already discussed how the principles of primacy and recency can determine whether you put material at the beginning or the end of your speech. These patterns are used so frequently to arrange supporting materials that we mention them again here. Suppose that you have several statistics to support a main point. All are relevant and significant, but one is especially gripping. In a recent speech, American Cancer Society CEO John Seffrin showed images of and described the following brief examples of international tobacco advertising:

The effort to build brand loyalty begins early. Here is an example of that in Africa—a young man wearing a hat with a cigarette brand logo. . . .

Look at this innocent baby wearing a giant Marlboro logo on his shirt. . . .

Notice how this ad links smoking to American values that are attractive to third world kids—wealth, sophistication, and urbanity. It also shows African Americans living the American Dream. If you're a poor kid in Africa, this image can be very powerful.

And finally, this one from Bucharest, Romania, which is my favorite. When the Berlin Wall came down, no one rushed into Eastern Europe faster than the tobacco industry. Here you can see the Camel logo etched in the street lights. In my opinion, this is one of the most disturbing examples of the public sector partnering with private industry to the detriment of its citizens.[10]

It is evident that Seffrin applied the principle of recency to his examples, as he identifies the final one as "my favorite" and "one of the most disturbing." The principle of primacy or recency can also be applied to groups of statistics, opinions, or any combination of supporting material.

SPECIFICITY

Sometimes your supporting material will range from very specific examples to more general overviews of a situation. You may either offer your specific information first and end with your general statement, or make the general statement first and support it with specific evidence.

Another application of specificity might be to compact or explode statistics. In her speech on unnecessary prescription drugs, Kristin begins with a sweeping statistic and then compacts it:

> Thirty percent of Americans have asked their doctor about a medicine they saw advertised on TV. And of those, . . . 44 percent received the prescription. That translates into one in eight Americans seeing a drug on TV and later picking it up at their local pharmacy.[11]

COMPLEXITY

We have already discussed organizing subtopics by moving from the simple to the complex. The same method of organization may also determine how you order your supporting material. In many situations, it makes sense to start with the simplest ideas that are easy to understand and work up to more complex ones. In her speech on solar radiation, Nichole first explains the most obvious effects of solar peaks—electrical blackouts and disruptions in radio broadcasts—and then goes on to the more complex effect, cosmic radiation:

> The sun produces storms on its surface in eleven-year cycles. During solar maximum, these storms will make their presence known to the land-bound public through electrical blackouts and disruptions in radio broadcasts. These storms cause the sun to throw off electrically charged ions that, combined with charged particles, enter the Earth's atmosphere from outer space. This is known collectively as cosmic radiation.[12]

SOFT EVIDENCE TO HARD EVIDENCE

Supporting material can also be arranged from "soft" to "hard." **Soft evidence** rests on opinion or inference. Hypothetical illustrations, descriptions, explanations, definitions, analogies, and opinions are usually considered soft. **Hard evidence** includes factual examples and statistics. Actually, it is more accurate to think of soft and hard as two ends of a continuum, with various supporting material falling somewhere between. The U.S. Surgeon General's analysis of the AIDS crisis, for example, would be placed nearer the hard end of the continuum than would someone's experience of seeing the NAMES Project AIDS Memorial Quilt, even though both would be classified as opinions. The Surgeon General is a more credible speaker, whose analysis is the result of his or her extensive knowledge of and research into the subject.

Soft-to-hard organization of supporting material relies chiefly on the principle of recency—that the last statement is remembered best. Notice how Jennifer moves from an illustration to a statistic in her speech on amusement park safety:

> Zipora Jacob waited in line for hours to ride the Indiana Jones Adventure. After leaving the 40-mph ride that jerks riders back and forth, Jacob complained of intense pressure on her head, and suffered a torn blood vessel that later threw her into a coma. She still experiences memory lapses and has a plastic tube running from her head to her abdomen draining excess fluid. What is far more startling than the details of Jacob's experience is that stories like hers are far too common. *The New York Times* of January 23, 2003, reports brain injuries from roller coaster rides increased 95 percent in less than five years.[13]

The speaker has arranged her supporting material from soft to hard.

QUICK CHECK: *Organizing Your Supporting Material*

Strategy	Description
Primacy	Most important material first
Recency	Most important material last
Specificity	From specific information to general overview or from general overview to specific information
Complexity	From simple to more complex material
Soft to hard evidence	From opinion or hypothetical illustration to fact or statistic

10.e Developing Signposts

Once you have organized your note cards, you have a logically ordered, fairly complete plan for your speech. But if you tried to deliver the speech at this point, you would find yourself frequently groping for some way to get from one point to the next. Your audience might become frustrated or even confused by your hesitations and awkwardness.

Your next organizational task is to develop **signposts**—words and gestures that allow you to move smoothly from one idea to the next throughout your speech, showing relationships between ideas and emphasizing important points. Three types of signposts can serve as glue to hold your speech together:

- Transitions
- Previews
- Summaries

TRANSITIONS

Transitions indicate that a speaker has finished discussing one idea and is moving to another. Transitions may be either verbal or nonverbal. Let's consider some examples of each type.

Verbal Transitions   A speaker can sometimes make a verbal transition simply by repeating a key word from an earlier statement or by using a synonym or a pronoun that refers to an earlier key word or idea. This type of transition is often used to make one sentence flow smoothly into the next. The previous sentence itself is an example: "This type of transition" refers to the sentence that precedes it. Other verbal transitions are words or phrases that show relationships between ideas. Note the italicized transitional phrases in the following examples:

- *In addition* to transitions, previews and summaries are *also* considered to be signposts.

- *Not only* does plastic packaging use up our scarce resources, it contaminates them *as well.*
- *In other words,* as women's roles have changed, they have *also* contributed to this effect.
- *In summary,* Fanny Brice is probably the best remembered star of Ziegfeld's Follies.
- *Therefore,* I recommend that you sign the grievance petition.

Simple enumeration (*first, second, third*) can also point out relationships between ideas and provide transitions.

Avoid Signaling the End of the Speech   One type of signpost that can occasionally backfire and do more harm than good is one that signals the end of a speech. *Finally* and *in conclusion* give the audience implicit permission to stop listening, and they often do. If the speech has been too long or has otherwise not gone well, the audience may even audibly express relief.

Better strategies for moving into a conclusion include repeating a key word or phrase, using a synonym or pronoun that refers to a previous idea, offering a final summary, or referring to the introduction of the speech. We will discuss the final summary in more detail later in this chapter.

Internal previews and summaries, which we will discuss shortly, are yet another way to provide verbal transitions from one point to the next in your speech. They have the additional advantage of repeating your main ideas, thereby enabling audience members to understand and remember them.

Repetition of key words or ideas, the use of transitional words or phrases, enumeration, and internal previews and summaries all provide verbal transitions from one idea to the next. You may need to experiment with several alternatives before you find the smooth transition you seek in a given instance. If none of these alternatives seems to work well, consider a nonverbal transition.

QUICK CHECK: *Verbal Transitions*

Strategy	Example
Repeating a key word or phrase or using a synonym or pronoun that refers to a key word or phrase	"These problems cannot be allowed to continue."
Using a transitional word or phrase	"In addition to the facts that I've mentioned, we need to consider one additional problem."
Enumerating	"Second, there has been a rapid increase in the number of accidents reported."
Using internal summaries	"Now that we have discussed the problems caused by illiteracy, let's look at some of the possible solutions."

Nonverbal Transitions   Nonverbal transitions can occur in several ways, sometimes alone and sometimes in combination with verbal transitions. A change in facial expression, a pause, an altered vocal pitch or speaking rate, or a movement all may indicate a transition.

For example, a speaker talking about the value of cardiopulmonary resuscitation began his speech with a powerful anecdote of a man who suffered a heart attack at a party. No one knew how to help, and the man died. The speaker then looked up from his notes and paused, while maintaining eye contact with his audience. His next words were "The real tragedy of Bill Jorgen's death was that it should not have happened." His pause, as well as the words that followed, indicated a transition into the body of the speech. Like this speaker, most good speakers use a combination of verbal and nonverbal transitions to move from one point to another through their speeches.

PREVIEWS

One significant difference between writing and public speaking is that public speaking is more repetitive. Audience-centered speakers need to remember that the members of their audiences, unlike readers, cannot go back to review a missed point. As its name indicates, a *preview* is a statement of what is to come. Previews help to ensure that audience members will first anticipate and later remember the important points of a speech. Like transitions, previews also help to provide coherence. Two types of previews are usually used in speeches:

- The preview statement, or initial preview
- The internal preview

Initial Previews   The preview statement is a statement of what the main ideas of the speech will be and is usually presented in conjunction with the central idea as a blueprint for the speech at or near the end of the introduction.

Speaking on illiteracy among athletes, Melody offers the following blueprint at the end of her introduction:

> Illiteracy among athletes must be stopped. In order to fully grasp the significance of this problem, we will look at the root of it, and then move to [its] effects, and finally, we will look at the solution.[14]

In this blueprint, Melody clearly previews her main ideas and introduces them in the order in which she will discuss them in the body of the speech.

Sometimes speakers enumerate their main ideas to identify them even more clearly:

> To solve this issue, we must first examine the problem itself. Second, we'll analyze the causes of the problem, and finally we'll turn to a number of solutions to the problem of children in the diet culture.[15]

Notice that both of the preceding examples consist of two sentences. A preview statement need not necessarily be one long, rambling sentence.

Internal Previews   In addition to using previews near the beginning of their speeches, speakers also use them at various points throughout. These internal previews introduce and outline ideas that will be developed as the speech progresses. As noted, internal previews also serve as transitions. The following speaker, for example, has just discussed the dangers associated with organic farming. She then provides this transitional preview into her next point:

> Having seen the dangers of our anti-pesticide attitude, we can now look to some solutions to stop the trend toward organic foods.[16]

Having heard this preview, her listeners expect her next to discuss solutions to the problems associated with organic farming. Their anticipation increases the likelihood that they will later remember the information.

Questions as Internal Previews   Sometimes speakers couch internal previews in the form of questions they plan to answer. Note how the question in this example provides an internal preview:

> Now that we know about the problem of hotel security and some of its causes and impacts, the question remains, what can we do, as potential travelers and potential victims, to protect ourselves?[17]

Just as anticipating an idea helps audience members remember it, so mentally answering a question helps them plant the answer firmly in their minds.

SUMMARIES

Like previews, summaries provide additional exposure to a speaker's ideas and can help ensure that audience members will grasp and remember them. Most speakers use two types of summaries:

- The final summary
- The internal summary

Final Summary   A final summary occurs just before the end of a speech, often doing double duty as a transition between the body and the conclusion. The final summary is the opposite of the preview statement. The preview statement gives an audience their first exposure to a speaker's main ideas; the final summary gives them their last exposure to those ideas.

Here is an example of a final summary from a speech on the U.S. Customs Service:

> Today, we have focused on the failing U.S. Customs Service. We have asked several important questions, such as "Why is Customs having such a hard time doing its job?" and "What can we do to remedy this situation?" When the cause of a serious problem is unknown, the continuation of the dilemma is understandable. However, the cause for the failure of the U.S. Customs Service is known: a lack of personnel. Given that fact and our understanding that Customs is vital to America's interests, it would be foolish not to rectify this situation.[18]

This final summary leaves no doubt as to the important points of the speech.

Internal Summary Internal summaries, as their name suggests, occur within and throughout a speech. They are often used after two or three points have been discussed, to keep those points fresh in the minds of the audience as the speech progresses. Susan uses this internal summary in her speech on the teacher shortage:

> So let's review for just a moment. One, we are endeavoring to implement educational reforms; but two, we are in the first years of a dramatic increase in enrollment; and three, fewer quality students are opting for education; while four, many good teachers want out of teaching; plus five, large numbers will soon be retiring.[19]

Like internal previews, internal summaries can help provide transitions. In fact, internal summaries are often used in combination with internal previews to form transitions between major points and ideas. Each of the following examples makes clear what has just been discussed in the speech as well as what will be discussed next:

> Now that we've seen how radon can get into our homes, let's take a look at some of the effects that it can have on our health once it begins to build.[20]

> So now we are aware of the severity of the disease and unique reasons for college students to be concerned, we will look at some steps we need to take to combat bacterial meningitis.[21]

> It seems as though everyone is saying that something should be done about NutraSweet. It should be retested. Well, now that it is here on the market, what can we do to see that it does get investigated further?[22]

QUICK CHECK: *Types of Signposts*

Verbal transitions
Nonverbal transitions
Preview statements
Internal previews
Final summaries

10.f Supplementing Signposts with Presentation Aids

Transitions, summaries, and previews are the "glue" that holds a speech together. Such signposts can help you achieve a coherent flow of ideas and help your audience remember those ideas. Unfortunately, however, you cannot guarantee that your audience will be attentive to your signposts. It is possible for your listeners to be so distracted by internal or external noise that they fail to hear or process even your most carefully planned verbal signposts.

One way you can increase the likelihood of your listeners' attending to your signposting is to prepare and use presentation aids to supplement your signposts. For example, you could display on an overhead transparency a bulleted or numbered outline of your main ideas as you initially preview them in your introduction, and again as you summarize them in your conclusion.

Some speakers like to use one transparency or PowerPoint slide for each main point. Transitions between points are emphasized as the speaker displays the next transparency or slide. Especially if your speech is long or its organization is complex, you can help your audience remember your organization if you provide visual support for your signposts.

Summary

- Speeches are organized for audiences, with the speaker keeping in mind at all times the unique needs, interests, and expectations of the particular audience.

- Organize your speech in a logical way so that audience members can follow, understand, and remember your ideas.

- Consider how best to organize your main ideas. Five common patterns of organization include chronological, topical, spatial, causal, and problem–solution.

- Main ideas are often subdivided. Organize subpoints so that audience members can readily grasp, understand, and remember them.

- Integrate your supporting material into your speech. It may help to begin by putting all main points, subpoints, and supporting material on note cards and then arranging those cards in order.

- Incorporate the supporting material smoothly into your speech. One strategy involves (1) stating the point, (2) citing the source, (3) presenting the supporting material, and (4) explaining how the supporting material substantiates or develops the point.

- When you have more than one piece of supporting material for a main idea or subpoint, organize the supporting material according to one of the five common patterns or according to such strategies as primacy, recency, specificity, complexity, or soft to hard.

- Various types of signposts can help you communicate your organization to your audience. Signposts include verbal and nonverbal transitions, previews, and summaries.

- Presentation aids increase the likelihood that your listeners will attend to your signposting.

Key Terms

cause-and-effect organization (p. 205)
chronological organization (p. 200)

complexity (p. 204)
hard evidence (p. 212)

A QUESTION OF ETHICS

You plan to give a speech about nuclear energy. Even though the process of producing energy this way is extremely complex, you will need to make your presentation very simple. How can you prevent your audience from assuming your topic is simple rather than complex? Should you let the audience know that you are oversimplifying the process? Explain your answer.

CHAPTER 11

Introducing Your Speech

T he opening seconds of a television commercial are carefully crafted to get your attention. The person who designed that message knows something you should know, too: The introduction of a message is vital to achieving your communication goal. Just as a trumpet fanfare signals the appearance of an important person, your speech introduction signals the arrival of your message to your listeners.

> *The average man thinks about what he has said; the above average man about what he is going to say.*
> **—Anonymous**

Although it makes up only about 10 percent of the total speech you deliver, the introduction provides audiences with important first impressions of speaker and speech. This is too important to the overall success of your speech to be left to chance or last-minute preparation.

Many speakers think the first task in preparing a speech is to start drafting your introduction. Actually, the introduction is more often the last part of the speech you develop. A key purpose of your introduction is to provide an overview of your message. How can you do that until you know what the message is going to be? Selecting patterns and strategies for organizing the body of your speech and using appropriate transitions, previews, and summaries should precede the crafting of the introduction to your speech. In this chapter we will further explore organization by discussing introductions.

11.a Purposes of Introductions

Within a few seconds of meeting a person, you form a first impression that is often quite lasting. So, too, do you form a first impression of a speaker and his or her message within the opening seconds of a speech. The introduction may convince you to listen carefully, because this is a credible speaker presenting a well-prepared speech, or it may send the message that the speaker is ill-prepared and the message not worth your time. In a ten-minute speech, the introduction will probably last no more than a minute and a half.

To say that the introduction needs to be well planned is an understatement, considering how important and yet how brief this portion of any speech is.

As a speaker, your task is to ensure that your introduction convinces your audience to listen to you. Specifically, a good introduction must perform five important functions:

- Get the audience's attention.
- Introduce the subject.
- Give the audience a reason to listen.
- Establish your credibility.
- Preview your main ideas.

Let's examine each of these five functions in more detail.

GET THE AUDIENCE'S ATTENTION

A key purpose of the introduction is to gain favorable attention for your speech. Because listeners form their first impressions of the speech quickly, if the introduction does not capture their attention and cast the speech in a favorable light, the rest of the speech may be wasted on them. The speaker who walks to the podium and drones, "Today I am going to talk to you about . . ." has probably lost most of the audience in those first few boring words. Some specific ways to gain the attention of audiences will be discussed later in this chapter.

We emphasize *favorable* attention for a very good reason. It is possible to gain an audience's attention but in so doing to alienate them or disgust them so that they become irritated instead of interested in what you have to say. For example, a student began a pro-life speech with a graphic description of the abortion process. She caught her audience's attention but made them so uncomfortable that they could hardly concentrate on the rest of her speech.

Another student gave a speech on the importance of donating blood. Without a word, he began by savagely slashing his wrists in front of his stunned audience. As blood spurted, audience members screamed, and one fainted. The blood was real blood, but it wasn't his. The speaker worked at a blood bank, and he was using the bank's blood. He had placed a device under each arm that allowed him to pump out the blood as if from his wrists. He certainly captured his audience's attention! But they never heard his message. The shock and disgust of seeing such a display made that impossible. He did not gain favorable attention.

The moral of our two tales: By all means, be creative in your speech introductions. But also use common sense in deciding how best to gain the favorable attention of your audience. Alienating them is even worse than boring them.

INTRODUCE THE SUBJECT

Perhaps the most obvious purpose of an introduction is to introduce the subject of a speech. Within a few seconds after you begin your speech, the audience should have a pretty good idea what you are going to talk about. Do not get so carried away with jokes or illustrations that you forget this basic purpose. Few things will frustrate your audience more than having to wait until halfway through your speech to figure out what you are talking about! The best way to ensure that your introduction does indeed introduce the subject of your speech is to include a statement of your central idea in the introduction. For example, in introducing his speech on the needs of the aged, this speaker immediately established his subject and central idea:

> If you take away just one thing from what I have to say, I hope you'll come to understand in the next few minutes that the exploding population of seniors demands a conscious, considered, and collaborative response to plan for the health, financial, and social implications of an older population.[1]

GIVE THE AUDIENCE A REASON TO LISTEN

Even after you have captured the attention of your audience and introduced the topic, you have to give the audience some reason to want to listen to the rest of your speech. An unmotivated listener quickly tunes out. You can help establish listening motivation by showing the members of your audience how the topic affects them directly.

One criterion for determining the effectiveness of your supporting material is proximity, the degree to which the information affects your listeners directly. Just as proximity is important to supporting materials, it is also important to speech introductions. "This concerns me" is a powerful reason to listen. Notice how Chandra involves her audience members in her speech on the hepatitis C risk inherent in tattooing:

> If you're one of the millions wanting to show your patriotism by getting a star-spangled banner tattooed across your back, ask questions regarding its potential risks.[2]

Sheena also uses proximity to motivate her audience to empathize with people who suffer from exposure to toxic mold:

> Headaches, fatigue, dizziness, and memory impairment seem like ailments that each person in this room has had at one point, right? You stay up late cramming for an exam. The next day, you are fatigued, dizzy, and cannot remember the answers.[3]

It does not matter so much how or when you demonstrate proximity. But it is essential that you, like Chandra and Sheena, do at some point establish that your topic is of vital personal concern to your listeners.

ESTABLISH YOUR CREDIBILITY

Credibility is a speaker's believability. A credible speaker is one whom the audience judges to be a believable authority and a competent speaker. A credible speaker is also someone the audience believes they can trust. We stress here that as you begin your speech, you should be mindful of your listeners' attitudes toward you. When thinking of your listeners, ask yourself, "Why should they listen to me? What is my background with respect to the topic? Am I personally committed to the issues about which I am going to speak?"

Many people have so much admiration for a political or religious figure, an athlete, or an entertainer that they sacrifice time, energy, and money to hear these celebrities speak. When the Pope travels abroad, people travel great distances and stand for hours in extreme heat or cold to celebrate Mass with him. But ordinary people cannot take their own credibility for granted when they speak. If you can establish your credibility early in a speech, it will help motivate your audience to listen.

One way to build credibility in the introduction is to be well prepared and to appear confident. Speaking fluently while maintaining eye contact does much to convey a sense of confidence. If you seem to have confidence in yourself, your audience will have confidence in you.

A second way to establish credibility is to tell the audience of your personal experience with your topic. Instead of considering you boastful, most audience members will listen to you with respect. In a speech to a group of women executives, the president of the St. Louis, Missouri, Board of Education offered this insight into her experience:

> If any of you have ever had the blessing of serving on a school board—and that's what I consider it to be, a blessing—you know how difficult it is. There are always too many needs to meet, never enough money to meet those needs, and a multitude of competing stakeholders who know exactly how you should allocate scarce resources: on the one thing that matters most to them, which is always different than what's important to the person standing next to them. And that's when times are good and things are going well.[4]

PREVIEW YOUR MAIN IDEAS

A final purpose of the introduction is to preview the main ideas of your speech. The preview statement usually comes near the end of the introduction, included in or immediately following a statement of the central idea. The preview statement allows your listeners to anticipate the main ideas of your speech, which in turn helps ensure that they will remember those ideas after the speech.

A preview statement is an organizational strategy called a *signpost.* Just as signs posted along a highway tell you what is coming up, a signpost in your speech tells the listeners what to expect by enumerating the ideas or points that you plan to present. If, for example, you were giving a speech about racial profiling, you might say:

> To end these crimes against color, we must first paint an accurate picture of the problem, then explore the causes, and finally establish solutions that will erase the practice of racial profiling.[5]

Identifying your main ideas helps organize the message and enhances listeners' learning.

The introduction to your speech, then, should get your audience's attention, introduce the subject, give the audience a reason to listen, establish your credibility, and preview your main ideas. All this—and brevity too—may seem impossible to achieve. But it isn't!

QUICK CHECK: *Does Your Introduction Accomplish Its Purpose?*

Does Your Introduction ...	To Make Sure It Does ...
Get the audience's attention?	Use an illustration, a startling fact or statistic, a quotation, humor, a question, a reference to an historical event or to a recent event, a personal reference, a reference to the occasion, or a reference to a preceding speech.
Introduce the subject?	Present your central idea to your audience.
Give the audience a reason to listen?	Tell your listeners how the topic directly affects them.
Establish your credibility?	Offer your credentials. Tell your listeners about your commitment to your topic.
Preview your main ideas?	Tell your audience what you are going to tell them.

11.b Effective Introductions

With a little practice, you will be able to write satisfactory central ideas and preview statements. It may be more difficult to gain your audience's attention and give them a reason to listen to you. Fortunately, there are several effective methods for developing speech introductions. Not every method is appropriate for every speech, but chances are that you can discover among these alternatives at least one type of introduction to fit the topic and purpose of your speech, whatever they might be. We will discuss ten ways of introducing a speech:

- Illustrations or anecdotes
- Startling facts or statistics
- Quotations
- Humor
- Questions
- References to historical events
- References to recent events
- Personal references
- References to the occasion
- References to preceding speeches

ILLUSTRATIONS OR ANECDOTES

Not surprisingly, because it is the most inherently interesting type of supporting material, an illustration or **anecdote** can provide the basis for an effective speech introduction. In fact, if you have an especially compelling illustration that you had planned to use in the body of the speech, you might do well to use it in your introduction instead. A relevant and interesting anecdote will introduce your subject and almost invariably gain an audience's attention. Former First Lady Barbara Bush opened her 1990 Wellesley College commencement address with this illustration:

> Wellesley, you see, is not just a place, but an idea, an experiment in excellence in which diversity is not just tolerated, but is embraced.
>
> The essence of this spirit was captured in a moving speech about tolerance given last year by the student body president of one of your sister colleges. She related the story by Robert Fulghum about a young pastor who, finding himself in charge of some very energetic children, hit upon a game called "Giants, Wizards, and Dwarfs." "You have to decide now," the pastor instructed the children, "Which you are . . . a giant, a wizard, or a dwarf?" At that, a small girl tugging on his pants leg asked, "But where do the mermaids stand?"
>
> The pastor told her there are no mermaids. "Oh yes there are," she said. "I am a mermaid."
>
> This little girl knew what she was and she was not about to give up on either her identity or the game. She intended to take her place wherever mermaids fit into the scheme of things.[6]

Barbara Bush's story both introduced the subject of her address and captured the attention of her audience.

STARTLING FACTS OR STATISTICS

A second method of introducing a speech is to use a startling fact or statistic. Startling an audience with the extent of a situation or problem invariably catches its members' attention and motivates them to listen further as well as helping them remember afterward what you had to say. Kristin's audience must have come to attention quickly when they heard these opening words:

> Frances Dodd is a 67-year-old grandmother. But it's not her two grandkids that make her special. Rather, what sets Frances Dodd apart is that she is a drug smuggler.[7]

Kristin went on to explain that the drugs in question are in fact prescription medications, for which Frances Dodd pays in Canada only a fraction of what they would cost her in the United States.

QUOTATIONS

Using an appropriate quotation to introduce a speech is a common practice. Often a past writer or speaker has expressed an opinion on your topic that is more authoritative, comprehensive, or memorable than what you can say. Terrika opened her speech on the importance of community with a quotation from poet Johari Kungufu:

> Sisters, Men
> What are we doin?
> What about the babies, our children?
> When we was real we never had orphans or children in joints.
> Come spirits
> drive out the nonsense from our minds and the crap from our dreams
> make us remember what we need, that children are the next life.
> bring us back to the real
> bring us back to the real

"The Real." Johari Kungufu, in her poem, specifically alludes to a time in African history when children were not confused about who they were.[8]

A different kind of quotation, this one from an expert, was chosen by another speaker to introduce the topic of the disappearance of childhood in America:

> "As a distinctive childhood culture wastes away, we watch with fascination and dismay." This insight of Neil Postman, author of *Disappearance of Childhood,* raised a poignant point. Childhood in America is vanishing.[9]

Because the expert was not widely recognized, the speaker included a brief statement of his qualifications. This authority "said it in a nutshell"—he expressed in concise language the central idea of the speech.

Although a quote can effectively introduce a speech, do not fall into the lazy habit of turning to a collection of quotations every time you need an introduction. There are so many other interesting, and sometimes better, ways to introduce a speech that quotes should be used only if they are extremely interesting, compelling, or very much to the point.

Like the methods of organization discussed in an earlier chapter, methods of introduction are not mutually exclusive. Very often, two or three are effectively combined in a single introduction. For example, Thad combined a quotation and an illustration for this effective introduction to a speech on the funeral industry:

> "Dying is a very dull, dreary affair. And my advice to you is to have nothing whatsoever to do with it." These lingering words by British playwright Somerset Maugham were meant to draw a laugh. Yet the ironic truth to the statement has come to epitomize the grief of many, including Jan Berman of Martha's Vineyard. In a recent interview with National Public Radio, we learn that Ms. Berman desired to have a home funeral for her mother. She possessed a burial permit and was legally within her rights. But when a local funeral director found out, he lied to her, telling her that what she was doing was illegal.[10]

HUMOR

Humor, handled well, can be a wonderful attention-getter. It can help relax your audience and win their goodwill for the rest of the speech. National Newspaper Publishers Association Editor-in-Chief George Curry told this humorous story to open his speech commemorating the 50th anniversary of the *Brown v. Board of Education* decision:

> To understand the significance of the *Brown v. Board of Education* Supreme Court decision, it's important to understand what life in the South was like at that time.

Civil rights leaders liked to tell the joke about a Chicago seminary student who was suddenly awakened at 3 a.m. by a voice imploring him: Go to Mississippi! Go to Mississippi!! Go to Mississippi!!! The student said, "Lord, you said that you will be with me always, even until the end of the earth. If I go to Mississippi, will you go with me?" The heavenly voice replied, "I'll go as far as Memphis."[11]

Another speaker used humor to express appreciation for being invited to speak to a group by beginning his speech with this story:

Three corporate executives were trying to define the word *fame.*

One said, "Fame is getting invited to the White House to see the President."

The second one said, "Fame is being invited to the White House and while you are visiting, the phone rings and he doesn't answer it."

The third executive said, "You're both wrong. Fame is being invited to the White House to visit with the President when his Hot Line rings. He answers it, listens a minute, and then says, 'Here, it's for you!' "

Being asked to speak today is like being in the White House and the call's for me.[12]

Subtle Humor   Humor need not always be the slapstick comedy of the Three Stooges. It does not even have to be a joke. It may take more subtle forms, such as irony or incredulity. When General Douglas MacArthur, an honor graduate of the U.S. Military Academy at West Point, returned to West Point in 1962, he delivered his now-famous "Farewell to the Cadets." He opened that speech with this humorous illustration:

As I was leaving the hotel this morning, a doorman asked me, "Where are you bound for, General?" And when I replied, "West Point," he remarked, "Beautiful place. Have you ever been there before?"[13]

MacArthur's brief illustration caught the audience's attention and made them laugh— in short, it was an effective way to open the speech.

Humor and Diversity   If your audience is linguistically diverse or composed primarily of listeners whose first language is not English, you may want to choose an introduction strategy other than humor. Because much humor is created by verbal plays on words, people who do not speak English as their native language may not perceive the humor in an anecdote or quip that you intended to be funny. And humor rarely translates well. Former President Jimmy Carter recalls speaking at a university near Kyoto, Japan, and being startled by unexpectedly hearty laughter in response to a short humorous anecdote he related. When he later asked his interpreter how he had translated the story so successfully, the interpreter finally admitted sheepishly, "I told them, 'President Carter has just told a funny story. Everyone laugh.' "[14]

Just as certain audiences may preclude your use of a humorous introduction, so may certain subjects. It would hardly be appropriate to open a speech on world hunger, for example, with a funny story. Nor would it be appropriate to use humor in a talk on certain serious crimes. Used with discretion, however, humor can provide a lively, interesting, and appropriate introduction for many speeches.

QUESTIONS

When using a question to open a speech, you will generally use a **rhetorical question**, the kind you don't expect an answer to. Nevertheless, your listeners will probably try to answer mentally. Questions prompt the audience's mental participation in your introduction. Such participation is an excellent way to ensure their continuing attention to your speech. Lisa opened her speech on geographic illiteracy with a series of questions:

> Can you name the states that border the Pacific Ocean? What country lies between Panama and Nicaragua? Can you name the Great Lakes?[15]

And Richard opened his speech on teenage suicide with this simple question:

> Have you ever been alone in the dark?[16]

Delivery   To turn questions into an effective introduction, the speaker must do more than just think of good questions to ask. He or she must also deliver the questions effectively. Effective delivery includes pausing briefly after each question, so that audience members have time to try to formulate a mental answer. After all, the main advantage of questions as an introductory technique is to "hook" the audience by getting them to engage in a mental dialogue with you. The speaker who delivers questions most effectively is also one who may look down at notes while he or she asks the question, but who then reestablishes eye contact with listeners. As we discuss in more detail in Chapter 15, eye contact signals that the communication channel is open. Establishing eye contact with your audience following a question provides additional motivation for them to think of an answer.

Audience Response   Although it does not happen frequently, an audience member may blurt out a vocal response to a question intended to be rhetorical. If you plan to open a speech with a rhetorical question, be aware of this remote possibility, and plan possible appropriate reactions. If the topic is light, a Jay Leno–style return quip may win over the audience and turn the interruption into an asset. If the topic is more serious or the interruption is inappropriate or contrary to what you expected, you might reply with something like "Perhaps most of the rest of you were thinking . . .," or you might answer the question yourself.

Questions with Other Introduction Methods   Questions are commonly combined with another method of introduction. For example, Beth opened her speech on the inadequacies of the current U.S. driver's license renewal system with three brief startling facts followed by a question:

> In 31 states, a blind man can be licensed to drive. In five states, just send in your check and they will send back your renewed license, no questions asked.
> In 1916 my grandfather got his license for the first time. No exam was required; no exam has been required since. Ever wonder why our highways seem a bit unsafe today?[17]

Either by themselves or in tandem with another method of introduction, questions can provide effective openings for speeches. Like quotations, however, questions can also be "crutches" for speakers who have not taken the time to explore other options. Unless you can think of a truly engaging question, work to develop one of the other introduction strategies.

REFERENCES TO HISTORICAL EVENTS

What American is not familiar with the opening line of Lincoln's classic Gettysburg Address: "Four score and seven years ago, our fathers brought forth on this continent a new nation, conceived in liberty, and dedicated to the proposition that all men are created equal"? Note that this opening sentence refers to the historical context of the speech. You, too, may find a way to begin a speech by making a reference to a historic event.

Every day is the anniversary of something. Perhaps you could begin a speech by drawing a relationship between an historic event that happened on this day and your speech objective. How do you discover anniversaries of historic events? You could consult Jane M. Hatch's *The American Book of Days;* this resource lists key events for every day of the year and also provides details of what occurred.[18] Another source, *Anniversaries and Holidays,* by Ruth W. Gregory, identifies and describes key holidays.[19] Finally, many newspapers have a section that identifies key events that occurred on "this day in history." If, for example, you know you are going to be speaking on April 6, you could consult a copy of a newspaper from April 6 of last year to discover the key events for that day.

We are not recommending that you arbitrarily flip through one of these sources to crank up your speech; your historical reference should be linked clearly to the purpose of your speech. Note how Boeing vice president and comptroller Laurette Koellner opened her remarks on career management to the Amelia Earhart Society in Long Beach, California:

> It is a great pleasure to address the Long Beach Chapter of the Amelia Earhart Society, and to honor people who—like the great Amelia—have exceeded expectations.
>
> Amelia Earhart had a brilliant career. She was the first to cross the Atlantic twice in an airplane and the second person ever to fly solo across the Atlantic. Like Amelia, each of us is responsible for managing his or her own career. We all have teammates, and we may have mentors. But, at the end of the day, planning and managing a career is the ultimate solo flight—for each of us.[20]

REFERENCES TO RECENT EVENTS

If your topic is timely, a reference to a recent event can be a good way to open your speech. An opening taken from a recent news story can take the form of an illustration, a startling statistic, or even a quotation, gaining the additional advantages discussed under each of those methods of introduction. Moreover, referring to a recent event increases your credibility by showing that you are knowledgeable about current affairs.

"Recent" does not necessarily mean a story that broke just last week or even last month. An event that occurred within the past year or so can be considered recent.

Even a particularly significant event that is slightly older can qualify. The key, says one speaker,

> is to avoid being your grandfather. No more stories about walking uphill both ways to school with a musket on your back and seventeen Redcoats chasing you. Be in the now, and connect with your audience.[21]

PERSONAL REFERENCES

A reference to yourself can take several forms. You might express appreciation or pleasure at having been asked to speak, as did this speaker:

> I would like, if I may, to start on a brief personal note. It is a great pleasure for me to be speaking in Cleveland, Ohio. This is where I grew up. Since then, I have traveled all over the world, but I have never stopped missing Ohio.[22]

Or you might share a personal experience, as did philanthropist Glenn Schaffer at the beginning of his speech at the dedication of the University of Iowa Writers' Workshop library:

> The celebrated Workshop spans 70 years, and has produced illustrious alumni whose pedigrees in the literary field are unrivaled. By another extra stroke of good fortune, I happened to be enrolled there in the middle 1970s alongside a cohort of ambitious, greatly talented writers, many of whom have since earned an honored place in the nation's literary pantheon: T. C. Boyle, Alan Gurganus, Jane Smiley, and Jorie Graham, to cite a few. In my own small way, I suspect, I served to hold down the Workshop's otherwise high achievement average.[23]

Although personal references take a variety of forms, what they do best, in all circumstances, is to establish a bond between you and your audience.

REFERENCES TO THE OCCASION

References to the occasion are often made at weddings, birthday parties, dedication ceremonies, and other such events. For example, when First Lady Laura Bush spoke at a recent White House Salute to America's Authors, she opened her remarks this way:

> Good afternoon. Welcome to the "White House Salute to America's Authors." This program, the second in a series on American authors, celebrates one of the richest literary periods in American history, the Harlem Renaissance, and the authors whose genius brought it to life.[24]

The reference to the occasion can also be combined with other methods of introduction, such as an illustration or a rhetorical question.

REFERENCES TO PRECEDING SPEECHES

If your speech is one of several being presented on the same occasion, such as in a speech class, at a symposium, or as part of a lecture series, you will usually not know until shortly before your own speech what other speakers will say. Few experiences will make your stomach sink faster than hearing a speaker just ahead of you speak on your topic. Worse still, that speaker may even use some of the same supporting materials you had planned to use. When this happens, you must decide on the spot whether referring to one of these previous speeches will be better than using the introduction you originally prepared. It may be wise to refer to a preceding speech when another speaker has spoken on a topic so related to your own that you can draw an analogy. In a sense, your introduction becomes a transition from that earlier speech to yours. Here is an example of an introduction delivered by a fast-thinking student speaker under those circumstances:

> When Juli talked to us about her experiences as a lifeguard, she stressed that the job was not as glamorous as many of us imagine. Today I want to tell you about another job that appears to be more glamorous than it is—a job that I have held for two years. I am a bartender at the Rathskeller.[25]

In summary, as you plan your introduction, remember that any combination of the methods just discussed is possible. With a little practice, you will become confident at choosing from several good possibilities as you prepare your introduction.

HOW TO: *Develop an Effective Introduction*

- Use an illustration or anecdote.
- Use a personal anecdote to establish your credibility.
- Present startling facts or statistics.
- Use an appropriate quotation.
- Use humor.
- Begin with a rhetorical question.
- Refer to historical events.
- Refer to recent events.
- Use personal references.
- Refer to the occasion.
- Refer to preceding speeches.

Summary

- It is important to begin your speech in a way that is memorable.
- A good introduction gets the audience's attention, introduces your subject, gives the audience a reason to listen, establishes your credibility, and previews your main ideas.

- You can introduce your subject and preview the body of your speech by including your central idea and preview statement in the introduction.

- You can gain favorable attention and provide a motivation for listening by using one or a combination of the following: illustrations, startling facts or statistics, quotations, humor, questions, references to historical events, references to recent events, personal references, references to the occasion, or references to preceding speeches, if there are any.

Key Terms

anecdote (p. 226)   rhetorical question (p. 229)
credibility (p. 223)

A QUESTION OF ETHICS

Michael and Julianne are in the same section of a public-speaking class. Michael has discovered an illustration that he thinks will make an effective introduction. When he tells Julianne about it, she is genuinely enthusiastic. In fact, she thinks it would make a great introduction for her own speech, which is on a different topic, but one that is nonetheless relevant to Michael's illustration. When the students are given schedules for their speeches, Julianne realizes that she will speak before Michael. She badly wants to use the introductory illustration that Michael has discovered. Is it ethical for her to do so if she cites the original source of the illustration in her speech?

CHAPTER 12

Concluding Your Speech

The closing seconds of a television commercial are just as important as the opening seconds. The closing seconds rename the product or service, summarize its virtues, and often suggest where you can purchase it. An effective conclusion is as vital to achieving your communication goal as an introduction. Just as most fireworks displays end with a grand finale, your speech should end, not necessarily with fireworks, but with a conclusion worthy of your well-crafted message.

> *A hard beginning maketh a good ending.*
> —**John Heywood**

12.a Purposes of Conclusions

Your introduction creates an important first impression; your conclusion leaves an equally important final impression. Long after you finish speaking, your audience is likely to remember the effect, if not the content, of your closing remarks.

Unfortunately, many speakers pay less attention to their conclusions than to any other part of their speeches. They believe that if they can get through the first 90 percent of a speech, they can think of some way to conclude it. Perhaps you have had the experience of listening to a speaker who failed to plan a conclusion. Awkward final seconds of stumbling for words may be followed by hesitant applause from an audience that is not even sure the speech is over. It is hardly the best way to leave people who came to listen to you.

An effective conclusion will serve four purposes. It will

- Summarize the speech.
- Reemphasize the main idea in a memorable way.
- Motivate the audience to respond.
- Provide closure.

Just as you learned ways to introduce a speech, you can learn how to conclude one. We begin by considering the purposes of conclusions and go on to study methods that can help you achieve those purposes.

SUMMARIZE THE SPEECH

A conclusion is a speaker's last chance to repeat his or her main ideas for the audience. John effectively summarized his speech on emissions tampering, casting the summary as an expression of his fears about the problem and the actions that could solve those fears:

> I'm frightened. Frightened that nothing I could say would encourage the 25 percent of emissions-tampering Americans to change their ways and correct the factors that cause their autos to pollute disproportionately. Frightened that the American public will not respond to a crucial issue unless the harms are both immediate and observable. Frightened that the EPA will once again prove very sympathetic to industry. Three simple steps will alleviate my fear: inspection, reduction in lead content, and, most importantly, awareness.[1]

Most speakers summarize their speech in the first part of the conclusion or perhaps even in a transition between the body of the speech and its conclusion.

REEMPHASIZE THE CENTRAL IDEA IN A MEMORABLE WAY

Another purpose of a conclusion is to restate the central idea of the speech in a memorable way. The conclusions of a number of famous speeches are among the most memorable statements we have. For example, General Douglas MacArthur's farewell to the nation at the end of his career concluded with these memorable words:

> "Old soldiers never die; they just fade away." And like the old soldier of that ballad, I now close my military career and just fade away—an old soldier who tried to do his duty as God gave him the light to see that duty. Good-bye.[2]

But memorable endings are not the exclusive property of great orators. With practice, most people can prepare similarly effective conclusions. As a preliminary example of the memorable use of language, here is how Noelle concluded her speech on phony academic institutions on the Internet:

> What we have learned from all this is that we, and only we, have the power to stop [fraudulent learning institutions]. So we don't get www.conned.[3]

This speaker's clever play on "dot.com" helped her audience remember her topic and central idea.

The end of your speech is your last chance to impress the central idea on your audience. Do it in such a way that they cannot help but remember it.

MOTIVATE THE AUDIENCE TO RESPOND

One of your tasks in an effective introduction is to motivate your audience to listen to your speech. Creating motivation is also a necessary function of an effective conclusion—not motivation to listen, but motivation to respond to the speech in some way. If your speech is informative, you may want the audience to think about the topic or to research it further. If your speech is persuasive, you may want your audience to take some sort of appropriate action—write a letter, buy a product, make a telephone call, or get involved in a cause. In fact, an *action* step is essential to the persuasive organizational strategy called the motivated sequence.

At the close of her speech on negligent landlords, Melanie included a simple audience response as part of her action step:

> By a show of hands, how many people in this room rely on rental housing? Look around. It's a problem that affects us all, if not directly, then through a majority of our friends. . . .[4]

Another speaker ended a speech on colon cancer with this conclusion:

> Let's join Katie Couric in the crusade to conquer this disease that so few of us like to talk about, but most definitely should.[5]

In both of the preceding examples, the speakers draw on the principle of proximity, discussed earlier, to motivate their audiences. If audience members feel that they are or could be personally involved or affected, they are more likely to respond to your message.

PROVIDE CLOSURE

Probably the most obvious purpose of a conclusion is to let the audience know that the speech has ended. Speeches have to "sound finished."

You can attain **closure** both verbally and nonverbally. Verbal techniques include using such transitions as "finally," "for my last point," and "in conclusion." Use care in signaling your conclusion, however. Such a cue gives an audience unspoken permission to tune out. (Notice what students do when their professor signals the end of the class. Books and notebooks slam shut, pens are stowed away, and the class generally stops listening.)

A concluding transition needs to be followed quickly by the final statement of the speech. We will discuss another verbal technique for closure—referring to the introduction—later in this chapter.

You can also signal closure with one or more nonverbal cues:

* Pausing between the body of your speech and its conclusion
* Slowing your speaking rate

QUICK CHECK: *Purposes of Your Speech Conclusion*
- Does it summarize your speech?
- Does it reemphasize the main idea in a memorable way?
- Does it motivate the audience to respond?
- Does it provide closure?

- Moving out from behind a podium to make a final impassioned plea to your audience
- Signaling with falling vocal inflection that you are making your final statement

12.b   Effective Conclusions

Effective conclusions may employ illustrations, quotations, personal references, or any of the other methods used for introductions.

- **Quotations.** Just as using an appropriate quotation to introduce a speech is a common practice, so too is using a quotation to conclude a speech. Often a past writer or speaker has expressed an opinion on your topic that is more authoritative, comprehensive, or memorable than what you can say, such as the quote

  > If you need inspiration, READ. Turn to the last page of *Black Boy* and read this:
  >   "I would hurl words into this darkness and wait for an echo, and if an echo sounded, no matter how faintly, I would send other words to tell, to march, to fight, to create a sense of the hunger for life that gnaws in us all, to keep alive in our hearts a sense of the inexpressibly human."
  > Keep reading, keep writing, and keep living the liberated life.[6]

- **Illustrations or anecdotes.** An illustration or anecdote can provide the basis for an effective conclusion. It can help the audience focus on the main point of your speech and hold their attention. A personal illustration used in a conclusion will also reinforce your credibility.

- **Startling facts or statistics.** Startling facts and statistics can help your audience remember afterward what you had to say.

- **Humor.** A humorous conclusion puts the audience in a relaxed frame of mind so that they leave with a sense of enjoyment of what you have told them and good-will toward you as the speaker.

- **Questions.** Just as using a rhetorical question to open a speech focuses the audience's attention, using a rhetorical question in your conclusion keeps your speech in the audience's mind as they try to answer the question.

In addition, there are at least three other distinct ways of concluding a speech: with references to the introduction, with inspirational appeals or challenges, and with appeals to action.

REFERENCES TO THE INTRODUCTION

In our discussion of closure, we mentioned referring to the introduction as a way to end a speech. Finishing a story, answering a rhetorical question, or reminding the audience of the startling fact or statistic you presented in the introduction are excellent ways to provide closure. Like bookends at either side of a group of books on your desk, a related introduction and conclusion provide unified support for the ideas in the middle.

Sonja's topic dealt with the health problems caused by the reprocessing of medical devices. She had opened her speech with an illustration of a 7-year-old Cub Scout named Timothy Anderson, who was killed when his heart was sliced by a reprocessed heart catheter. Her conclusion was this:

> Because while we all want our health care to be affordable, we need to resist the push to do so at the expense of our health. After all, Timothy Anderson will never build the model '57 Chevy he was to receive on his eighth birthday.[7]

John had begun his speech on the need for catastrophic health insurance by quoting Robert Browning:

> Grow old along with me!
> The best is yet to be,
> The last of life, for which the first was made.[8]

He concluded his speech by referring to that Browning quotation:

> Robert Browning tells us the last of life is as precious as the first. While the future will always hold uncertainty, with catastrophic health insurance we can more fully prepare for whatever is yet to be.[9]

Benjamin had introduced his speech by talking about the downfalls inevitably suffered by the heroes of Greek mythology. He drew an analogy between the risks they faced and the risks inherent in the use of antibiotics—the dangers of overuse. Here is how Benjamin ended his speech:

> The demise of Medusa carries with it one final message. With her death, Perseus received two drops of blood. One drop had the power to kill and spread evil; the other, to heal and restore well-being. Similarly, antibiotics offer us two opposite paths. As we painfully take stock in our hubris, in assuming that we can control the transformation of nature, we may ponder these two paths. We can either let antibiotics do the work of our immune systems and proper farm management, which may return us to the times when deathly plagues spread across the world, or we can save these miracle drugs for the times when miracles are truly needed.[10]

Each of the three examples just given is quite different. In the first, the speech opened and closed with an illustration; in the second, both introduction and conclusion centered on a quotation; and in the third, beginning and ending relied on an analogy between mythology and modern medicine. In all three speeches, the conclusion alluded to the introduction to make the speech memorable, to motivate the audience to respond, and to provide closure.

INSPIRATIONAL APPEALS OR CHALLENGES

Another way to end your speech is to issue an inspirational appeal or challenge to your listeners, rousing them to a high emotional pitch at the conclusion of the speech. The conclusion becomes the climax. One famous example comes from Martin Luther King Jr.'s "I Have a Dream" speech:

> From every mountainside, let freedom ring, and when this happens . . . when we allow freedom to ring, when we let it ring from every village and every hamlet, from every state and every city, we will be able to speed up that day when all of God's children, black men and white men, Jews and Gentiles, Protestants and Catholics, will be able to join hands and sing in the words of the old Negro spiritual, "Free at last! Thank God Almighty, we are free at last!"[11]

That King's conclusion was both inspiring and memorable has been affirmed by the growing fame of that passage through the years since he delivered the speech.

More recently, on September 15, 2001, George W. Bush delivered his weekly radio address—an address that was suddenly anything but routine, following the catastrophic terrorist attacks of September 11. He concluded his talk with this inspirational appeal:

> Great tragedy has come to us and we are meeting it with the best that is in our country, with courage and concern for others. Because this is America. This is who we are. This is what our enemies hate and have attacked. And this is why we will prevail.[12]

King's and Bush's inspiring conclusions reemphasized their central ideas in a memorable way, motivated their audiences to respond, and provided closure to their speeches.

APPEALS TO ACTION

As we noted earlier, persuasive speeches often include an appeal to action in their conclusions. In the conclusion of his investiture speech, Jake Schrum, president of Southwestern University in Georgetown, Texas, made this unique and effective call for action:

> Before I end my remarks, I invite all Southwestern alumni and all Southwestern students to stand and to remain standing for my final words.
>
> Years ago, I knew a woman named Audry Dillow who had been a school teacher all of her adult life. In her eighties when I met her, we often reflected on the attributes and beliefs of college students. Frankly, she was not as positive about the goodness of students as I was.
>
> One day, she asked me, "Jake, are there students today who truly care about someone other than themselves, who really care about the world, who are genuinely good at heart?" I said, "Yes." She said, "Who?" I said, "What do you mean, 'Who?'" She said, "Who—who are they? Give me their names."
>
> I said, "You want me to give you the actual names of people who will basically fight the world's fight?" She said, "Yes, I want names."
>
> If she were here today to ask me the same question, may I give her your name?
>
> The world is waiting for your reply.
>
> Your answer will change the world.[13]

HOW TO: *Develop an Effective Conclusion*

● Refer to the introduction.
● Create an inspirational appeal or challenge.
● Create an appeal to action.
● Use an illustration or anecdote.
● Use a personal anecdote to reinforce your credibility.
● Present startling facts or statistics.
● Use an appropriate quotation.
● Use humor.

Summary

- It is important to end your speech in a way that is memorable and that also provides the repetition audiences need.

- Concluding your speech well is just as important as introducing it well, for it is the conclusion that leaves the final impression.

- A conclusion should summarize your speech, reemphasize your central idea in a memorable way, motivate the audience to respond, and provide closure.

- Conclusions may employ any of the approaches used for introductions. In addition, you can refer to the introduction, make inspirational appeals or challenges, or make appeals to action.

Key Term

closure (p. 237)

A QUESTION OF ETHICS

An aide assigned to work with speakers and speeches during both the 1996 and the 2000 Republican National Conventions compared the relative freedom allowed speakers at the 2000 convention with the censorship imposed on the 1996 convention speeches. Speeches at the 1996 convention "were diligently reviewed and monitored by convention organizers, who insisted that speakers promise to stick to their script before allowing them to go on." Is such censorship a violation of the speakers' freedom of speech?

CHAPTER 13

Outlining and Editing Your Speech

A while ago, a family decided to spend a weekend near the Texas Gulf Coast. Soon after they left home on a hot, cloudless June morning, the air conditioning in their car broke down. By late afternoon, the car was very hot, the family was very tired, and the prospect of an air-conditioned motel room was very welcome. The husband was driving and the wife navigating as they approached their destination. Only a few more minutes, they thought, and they would relax in the cool quiet of their room. Imagine their frustration when, half an hour later, they were still searching for the motel.

"Let me see the map," demanded the exasperated husband.

"Here, if you think you can do better," snapped the wife. "This map is useless!"

Trying to remain cool and collected (no easy task with the temperature approaching 100°F), the husband studied the map. Sure enough, it looked as though they should be at the motel by now. In sweaty desperation, he finally stopped to ask for directions.

"Oh, you should've turned right four blocks back," explained a store clerk. The wife had been right. The map was useless, because it had not shown the necessary turn in the road.

This actually happened to our family. We experienced directly the frustration of having an inaccurate map. Just as we rely on maps to find our way on unfamiliar roads, so we rely on outlines to be "speech maps." In Chapter 10, you learned approaches to organizing your ideas and supporting materials. In Chapter 11, you learned how to introduce your speech effectively and memorably, and in Chapter 12, how to conclude it. In this chapter, we will discuss how to map, or outline, the organization of the speech you have developed and how to edit a speech that is too long.

Most speakers find that they need to proceed through three steps during this stage of the process: (1) developing a preparation outline, (2) editing the speech, and (3) developing a delivery outline and speaking notes. Let's examine the purposes and requirements of each of these steps.

> *Every discourse ought to be a living creature; having a body of its own and head and feet; there should be a middle, a beginning, and end, adapted to one another and to the whole.*
> —**Plato**

13.a Developing a Preparation Outline

One CEO notes,

> Unless you sit down and write out your thoughts and put them in a cogent order, you can't deliver a cogent speech. Maybe some people have mastered that art. But I have seen too many people give speeches they really haven't thought out.[1]

Although few speeches are written paragraph form, most speakers develop a detailed **preparation outline** that includes main ideas, subpoints, and supporting material. It may also include the specific purpose, introduction, blueprint, conclusion, and signposts.

THE PREPARATION OUTLINE

To begin your outlining task, you might try a technique known as **mapping**, or clustering. Write on a sheet of paper all the main ideas, subpoints, and supporting material for the speech. Then use geometric shapes and arrows to indicate the logical relationships among them, as shown in Figure 13.1.

Nationwide Insurance speechwriter Charles Parnell favors yet another technique for beginning an outline:

> I often start by jotting down a few ideas on the [computer] screen, then move them around as necessary to build some sort of coherent pattern. I then fill in the details as they occur to me.
>
> What that means is that you can really start anywhere and eventually come up with an entire speech, just as you can start with any piece of a puzzle and eventually put it together.[2]

Whatever technique you choose to begin your outline, your ultimate goal is to produce a plan that lets you judge the unity and coherence of your speech, to see how well the parts fit together and how smoothly the speech flows. Your finished preparation outline will help you make sure that all main ideas and subpoints are clearly and logically related and adequately supported.

The following suggestions will help you complete your preparation outline. However, keep in mind that different instructors may have different expectations for both outline content and format. Be sure to understand and follow your own instructor's guidelines.

Write Your Preparation Outline in Complete Sentences Unless you write complete sentences, you will have trouble judging the coherence of the speech. Moreover, complete sentences will help during your early rehearsals. If you write cryptic phrases, you may not remember what they mean.

Use Standard Outline Form Although you did not have to use standard outline form when you began to outline your ideas, you need to do so now. **Standard outline form** lets you see at a glance the exact relationships among various main ideas,

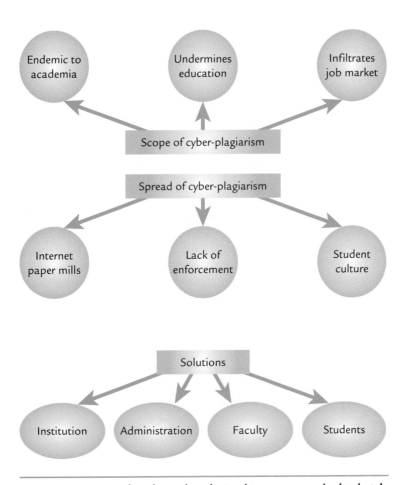

FIGURE 13.1   A map that shows the relationships among each of Valerie's three main ideas and their subpoints. Main ideas are enclosed by rectangles; subpoints, by ovals. Supporting material could be indicated by another shape and connected to the appropriate subpoints.

subpoints, and supporting material in your speech. It is an important tool for evaluating your speech, as well as a requirement in many public-speaking courses. An instructor who requires speech outlines will generally expect standard outline form. To produce a correct outline, follow the instructions given here.

Use Standard Outline Numbering   Logical and fairly easy to learn, outline numbering follows this sequence:

   I. First main idea

      A. First subpoint of I

    B. Second subpoint of I

        1. First subpoint of B

        2. Second subpoint of B

           a. First subpoint of 2

           b. Second subpoint of 2

II. Second main idea

Although it is unlikely that you will subdivide beyond the level of lowercase letters (a, b, etc.) in most speech outlines, next would come numbers in parentheses and then lowercase letters in parentheses.

Use at Least Two Subdivisions, if Any, for Each Point   Logic dictates that you cannot divide anything into one part. If, for example, you have only one piece of supporting material, incorporate it into the subpoint or main idea that it supports. If you have only one subpoint, incorporate it into the main idea above it. Although there is no firm limit to the number of subpoints you may have, if you have more than five, you may want to place some of them under another point. An audience will remember your ideas more easily if they are divided into blocks of no more than five.

Indent Main Ideas, Points, Subpoints, and Supporting Material Properly   Main ideas, indicated by Roman numerals, are written closest to the left margin. Notice that the periods following the Roman numerals line up, so that the first words of the main ideas also line up.

  I. First main idea

 II. Second main idea

III. Third main idea

Letters or numbers of subpoints and supporting material begin directly underneath the first *word* of the point above.

 I. First main idea

   a. First subpoint of I

If a main idea or subpoint takes up more than one line, the second line begins under the first *word* of the preceding line:

 I. Every speech has three parts.

   a. The first part, both in our discussion and in actual delivery, is the introduction.

The same rules of indentation apply at all levels of the outline.

Write and Label Your Specific Purpose at the Top of Your Preparation Outline   Unless your instructor directs you to do otherwise, do not work the specific purpose into the outline itself. Instead, label it and place it at the top of the outline. Your specific purpose can serve as a yardstick by which to measure the relevance of each main idea, subpoint, and piece of supporting material. Everything in the speech should contribute to your purpose.

Add the Blueprint, Key Signposts, and an Introduction and Conclusion to Your Outline Place the introduction after the specific purpose, the blueprint immediately following the introduction, the conclusion after the outline of the body of the speech, and other signposts within the outline. Follow your instructor's guidelines as to whether and how you should incorporate these elements into your numbering.

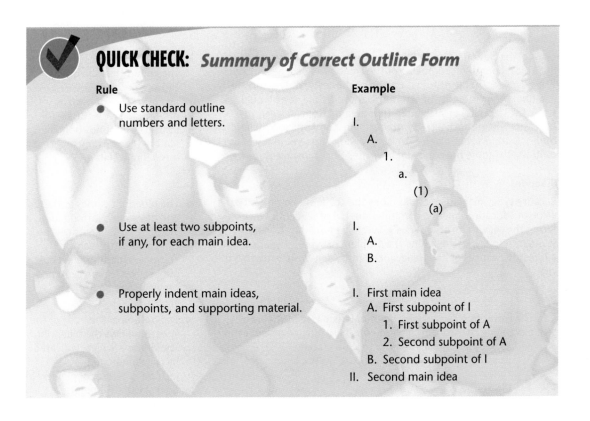

QUICK CHECK: *Summary of Correct Outline Form*

Rule	Example

● Use standard outline numbers and letters.	I.
	  A.
	    1.
	      a.
	        (1)
	          (a)

● Use at least two subpoints, if any, for each main idea.	I.
	  A.
	  B.

● Properly indent main ideas, subpoints, and supporting material.	I. First main idea
	  A. First subpoint of I
	    1. First subpoint of A
	    2. Second subpoint of A
	  B. Second subpoint of I
	II. Second main idea

SAMPLE PREPARATION OUTLINE

The sample outline that follows is for a ten-minute persuasive speech by student speaker Valerie Waldock.[3] Notice that in this example, the purpose, introduction, blueprint, signposts, and conclusion are separated from the numbered points in the body of the speech. Be sure to learn and follow your own instructor's specific requirements for how you should incorporate these elements.

SAMPLE PREPARATION OUTLINE

Purpose

By the end of my speech, the audience will be able to take several steps to combat cyber-plagiarism.

◄ Writing the purpose statement at the top of your outline helps you keep it foremost in mind.

Central Idea

We are facing the corruption of America's investment in educational standards.

◄ Your instructor may also ask you to write your central idea at the top of your outline.

Introduction

In 1999, the National Communication Association endorsed a Credo for Ethical Communication. One of the credo's major tenets includes, "We advocate that truthfulness, accuracy, honesty, and reason are essential to the integrity of communication." While none would argue the necessity of such integrity, students from all levels of education violate such a credo. According to the April 2002 *School Library Journal*, cyber-plagiarism is a growing virus, yet many of us continue to ignore the educational virtues that it disables.

◄ As Valerie prepares her speech, she knows that she must first capture her audience's attention. She does so by quoting the NCA's Credo for Ethical Communication, then stating the startling fact that it is being violated.

Blueprint

Because cyber-plagiarism undermines the academic community, the value of education, and the earning potential of students, we are facing the corruption of America's investment in educational standards. Today, let's examine the problem of cyber-plagiarism, address the causes of its spread, and identify solutions to disable this virus.

◄ The blueprint comes at the end of Valerie's introduction. The first sentence states the central idea (the same statement that is pulled out above). The second sentence previews the body of the speech.

Body

I. The corruption caused by cyber-plagiarism is identifiable by examining the scope of the problem, how it devalues education, and its negative implications for our job market.

◄ The outline of the body of the speech follows the blueprint. The first main idea, indicated by the Roman numeral I, includes an internal preview of the speech's subpoints.

    A. The outbreak of cyber-plagiarism is endemic to academia.

◄ Subpoint A states the scope of the problem.

        1. *Wired News*, May 4, 2001, reports that the University of Virginia nabs 122 students plagiarizing term papers.

        2. *Vancouver Sun*, January 7, 2002, reports that Simon Fraser University punishes 47 students who turn in virtually the same economics paper.

        3. *CNN Online News*, February 7, 2002, reveals that Christine Pelter of Piper, Kansas, flunks 28 students for plagiarizing a biology assignment.

◄ Subpoints 1, 2, and 3 offer supporting material for subpoint A. Compare Valerie's oral citations of her sources with the recommendations for such citations in Chapter 3.

Internal Summary

Clearly, cases of cyber-plagiarism are infecting academia.

◄ Valerie restates the scope of the problem.

  B. Additionally, we must understand how cyber-plagiarism undermines the value and importance of education.

◄ Subpoint B answers the question "So what?" It explains how cyber-plagiarism devalues education.

  1. Dr. Louis Bloomfield of the University of Virginia asserts in the aforementioned *Wired News* that a college degree should mean that students earn their degree honorably.
  2. Rice University expects its students to maintain the highest standards of conduct in their research.
  3. Professor Susan Jones of Parkland College points out in the previously cited *School Library Journal* that cyber-plagiarism enables students to graduate without learning essential skills such as research and writing.

◄ Subpoints 1, 2, and 3 offer supporting material for the value of honest and honorable education.

◄ The tournament at which this speech was delivered was held at Rice University. This mention of Rice subtly acknowledges the audience and the occasion.

Internal Summary

Do we really want our investment in education to produce copycat diplomas?

◄ Valerie summarizes her second subpoint with a rhetorical question aimed at the student members of her audience.

  C. Third, cyber-plagiarism infiltrates itself into our job market, both as employers and employees seeking positions.
  1. As reported by the January 6, 2003, *Chronicle of Higher Education*, editor of the *Atlantic Monthly* James Fallows can recount multiple instances in which his own work was plagiarized. In turn, we are also at risk of having others take advantage of our work.
  2. The September 15, 2002, *New York Times* also reports that employers are increasingly screening applicants for honesty, integrity, and ethics.

◄ Subpoint C states a negative result of cyber-plagiarism.

◄ Subpoints 1 and 2 offer support for subpoint C.

Internal Summary

Clearly, cyber-plagiarism is spreading, undermining the value of education and destroying the quality of our job market.

◄ Valerie summarizes subpoint C.

 II. Cyber-plagiarism continues to spread for three reasons: availability, lack of enforcement, and the culture of cyber-plagiarism.
  A. Internet paper mills provide thousands of research papers at the click of a mouse.
  1. According to the March 2, 2001, *Educause,* over 200 cheating sites are available, such as *123HelpMe* and *schoolsucks.*
  2. On the paper mill Web site *123HelpMe,* I easily found the paper "The Plague of Internet Plagiarism," that I could

◄ Now Valerie moves from her first main idea—the problem portion of her speech—to the second main idea—reasons the problem exists. The first reason, subpoint A, is that Internet papers are readily available. Subpoints 1, 2, and 3 offer supporting documentation.

(continued)

SAMPLE PREPARATION OUTLINE *(continued)*

purchase for $9.45 and receive the same day—but rest assured I did not.

   3. On the November 10, 2002, broadcast of *60 Minutes,* founders of *schoolsucks.com* report that with over a quarter of a million visitors each day on their Web site alone, students are relying on these easy access resources.

B. Second, lack of enforcement allows this virus to spread.

   1. As reported by the Winter 2001 *Library Trends,* campus environments that only casually address cheating actually encourage cheating.

   2. *Plagiarism.org,* an educational service to detect cyber-plagiarism that is updated daily and last accessed March 23, 2003, reports that 90 percent of students don't believe cheaters are caught or severely punished if they are caught.

   3. Unfortunately, these students are often right. According to the August 15, 2002, *Chronicle of Higher Education,* like many instructors, Dr. Vincent Moore of Tiffin University has reported cases of cyber-plagiarism. However, contradictory to his campus policy to flunk plagiarizers from the course, his administration protected the students from failing.

C. Finally, the student culture of cyber-plagiarism fuels this problem.

   1. Professor Don McCabe, founder of the Center for Academic Integrity, warns on the previously referenced *60 Minutes* that today's students don't see anything wrong with stealing material from the Internet. Rather, these students legitimize plagiarism by noting other students who cyber-plagiarize.

   2. Further, as explained by the aforementioned *Library Trends,* and in numerous communication journal articles, many students today have a consumer mentality and view education as the passport to a desired job instead of a learning experience.

Internal Summary

Overall, cyber-plagiarism continues to spread because of accessible resources, lack of enforcement, and the copycat culture.

III. On a spectrum ranging from elementary school to post-secondary education, we must combat cyber-plagiarism on an institutional, classroom, and individual level.

A. Initially, we should encourage our administrations to use a cyber-plagiarism detection service, such as *Turnitin.com.*

◀ The second reason for the problem, subpoint B, is that cheaters are not appropriately discouraged from cyber-plagiarism. Again, three sources (subpoints 1, 2, and 3) document the reason.

◀ A third reason the problem exists is the student culture. Valerie explains in subpoints 1 and 2 what she means by "the student culture of cyber-plagiarism."

◀ Valerie provides an internal summary of subpoint C, the reasons the problem of cyber-plagiarism exists.

◀ Valerie states her third and final main idea: the solution to the problem of cyber-plagiarism.

◀ Subpoint A suggests one solution that could be implemented on the institutional level.

1. At the cost of about fifty cents per student, these services compare submitted papers to Internet material and material in a print database.
2. As explained on *Turnitin.com,* updated daily and last accessed March 25, 2003, within 3 to 24 hours professors receive a report highlighting copied material, whether it is a simple phrase or multiple paragraphs.
3. According to the December 26, 2002, *New York Daily News,* at Hunter High in Manhattan, *Turnitin.com* has reduced rates of plagiarism by 85 percent.
4. *Turnitin.com* was also the service that allowed Christine Pelter of Piper, Kansas, to catch her 28 students plagiarizing.

◀ Subpoints 1–4 document the feasibility (cost, ease, and effectiveness) of using a cyber-plagiarism detection device (solution A).

B. In addition, our academic institutions should establish and enforce honor codes, such as having students pledge not to cheat. As reported by the November 18, 2002, *Salt Lake Tribune,* reports of cheating are as much as 50 percent lower on campuses that focus on honor codes than on those that do not.

◀ Subpoint B offers a second institutional solution, the use of honor codes.

C. Educators are in a direct position to emphasize the importance of academic integrity.
1. The University of Alberta library offers an online workshop encouraging educators to create focused assignments, require multiple drafts, and warn students that they will check papers for cyber-plagiarism.
2. As stated in the aforementioned *Salt Lake Tribune,* Professor Pat Matteson of Southern Utah University tells her students that it may take them 5 minutes to copy material from the Internet, but by using a search engine such as *Google,* it only takes her 5 minutes to find it.

◀ Subpoint C suggests solutions that educators can implement. Subpoints 1 and 2 provide examples of effective educator efforts.

D. Finally, as individuals, we can all combat cyber-plagiarism by teaching students that education is more than just a diploma. As students, we must hold ourselves to a higher standard. The solution is simple: Be ethical, and foster integrity in others.

◀ Valerie directs subpoint D to the student members of her audience.

Conclusion

Today, we have examined the problem of cyber-plagiarism, addressed causes of its prevalence, and identified solutions to reassert an academic standard that we must uphold, we must value, and we must teach. The National Communication Association created a credo of ethics that our academic communities should model and enforce. Despite the apparently priceless material available on the Internet, we must remember that in the end, the true value rests in a quality education. As commencement approaches, I like to believe that my fellow graduates have earned their degrees honorably. As students, instructors, and educated citizens in a prime position to combat cyber-plagiarism, clearly we have some homework to do.

◀ In her conclusion, Valerie summarizes her main ideas and refers back to the NCA credo that she mentioned at the beginning of the speech. Additional strategies for concluding a speech are discussed in Chapter 12.

◀ Valerie provides closure by identifying with the student members of her audience.

Once you have completed your preparation outline, you can use it to help analyze and possibly revise the speech. The following questions can help you in this critical thinking task.

- **Does the speech as outlined fulfill the purpose you have specified?** If not, you need to revise the specific purpose or change the direction and content of the speech itself.

- **Are the main ideas logical extensions (natural divisions, reasons, or steps) of the central idea?** If not, revise either the central idea or the main ideas. Like the first question, this one relates to the unity of the speech and is critical to making certain the speech "fits together" as a whole.

- **Do the signposts enhance the comfortable flow of each idea into the next?** If not, change or add previews, summaries, or transitions. If signposts are not adequate, the speech will lack coherence.

- **Does each subpoint provide support for the point under which it falls?** If not, then either move or delete the subpoint.

- **Is your outline form correct?** For a quick reference, refer to the earlier Quick Check box, Summary of Correct Outline Form, on page 247.

Having considered these five questions, you are ready to rehearse your speech, using the preparation outline as your first set of notes. See Chapter 15 for additional tips on effective rehearsal.

13.b Editing Your Speech

Audiences will forgive a speaker many speaking errors, but one of the hardest for audiences to forgive is speaking for too long. Although you want an appreciative audience, you don't want your listeners to break into applause when you intone, "And in conclusion, ..." Often when you rehearse using your preparation outline, you discover you've got too much information. You have to cut your speech. Here are a few tips to help you edit a speech that is too long.[4]

REVIEW YOUR SPECIFIC PURPOSE

Many speeches are too long because you are trying to accomplish too much. With your audience in mind, take a hard look at your specific purpose statement. If, for example, you want your audience to be able to list and describe five advantages of staying on standard time rather than switching to daylight savings time, you may have to decide on a less ambitious purpose and describe only three advantages—pick your best three.

CONSIDER YOUR AUDIENCE

You may be weary of this advice, but it is critical to consider your audience. What do audience members really need to hear? Go back over your speech outline and take a hard look at it. Which parts of your message will be most and least interesting to your listeners? Cut those portions that are of least potential interest.

SIMPLY SAY IT

You can cut some time from your speech if you just get to the point. Consider these suggestions. *Eliminate phrases that add no meaning to your message.* When he criticized Senator John Kerry's use of "pointless embellishments," political correspondent and author William Saletan demonstrated how Kerry could have deleted unnecessary words and phrases from this statement made in Los Angeles in May 2004:[5]

> Let me just ~~very quickly~~ say that the ~~horrifying~~ abuse of Iraqi prisoners ~~which the world has now seen~~ is ~~absolutely~~ unacceptable ~~and inexcusable~~. And the response of the administration—~~certainly the Pentagon~~—has been slow ~~and inappropriate~~.

Here are some additional phrases you could eliminate from your orations:

In my opinion (just state the opinion)

And all that (meaningless)

When all is said and done (just say it)

As a matter of fact (just state the fact)

Before I begin, I'd like to say (you've already begun—just say it)

Avoid narrating your speaking technique. There's no need to say, "Here's an interesting story that I think you will like." Just tell the story. Or why say, "I'd like to now offer several facts about this matter"? Just state the facts. Yes, it's useful to provide signposts and internal summaries throughout your message—redundancy is needed in oral messages—but be careful of providing cluttering narration about the techniques you're using.

HOW TO: *Avoid Long Phrases*

Instead of saying . . .	Say . . .
So, for that reason	So
But at the same time	But
In today's society	Today
Due to the fact	Because
In the course of	During
In the final analysis	Finally

KEEP ONLY THE BEST SUPPORTING MATERIAL

Your stories, illustrations, quotations, and other supporting material may be soaking up your time. Of course, stories and other types of supporting material help you make your point and maintain interest. So you don't want to reduce your speech to a bare-bones outline. But do you need two stories to make your point, or will one do? Is there a shorter, more pithy quotation that will add punch and power to your prose? Scan your speech for supporting material that can be cut.

ASK A LISTENER TO HELP YOU CUT

It's often easier to have someone else help you cut material. Ask a friend or roommate to listen to your speech and help you note parts that are less powerful, clear, or convincing.

LOOK AT YOUR INTRODUCTION AND CONCLUSION

Your introduction should generally take up about 10 percent of your speaking time; the same 10 percent estimate applies to your conclusion. If either your introduction or your conclusion exceeds this guideline, see if you can shorten an illustration or summarize more succinctly.

13.c Developing Your Delivery Outline and Speaking Notes

As you rehearse your speech, you will find that you need your preparation outline less and less. Both the structure and the content of your speech will become set in your mind. At this point, you are ready to prepare a **delivery outline**.

THE DELIVERY OUTLINE

A delivery outline, as the name implies, is meant to give you all you will need to present your speech in the way you have planned and rehearsed. However, it should not be so detailed that it encourages you to read it rather than speak to your audience. Here are a few tips:

- **Make the outline as brief as possible.** Write in single words or short phrases rather than complete sentences. That said, make certain the information is not so abbreviated that it becomes unclear. In August 2003, NASA blamed the loss of the Space Shuttle *Columbia* in part on the fact that an outline on possible wing damage was "so crammed with nested bullet points and irregular short forms that it was nearly impossible to untangle."[6]

- **Include the introduction and conclusion in much shortened form.** You may feel more comfortable if you have the first and last sentences written in full in front of you. Writing out the first sentence eliminates any fear of a mental block at the outset of your speech. And writing a complete last sentence ensures a smooth ending to your speech and a good final impression. However, aside from these two sentences, the remainder of your introduction and conclusion should be in the form of brief phrases, as in the sample delivery outline.

- **Include supporting material and signposts.** Write out statistics, direct quotations, and key signposts. Writing key signposts in full ensures that you will not grope awkwardly for a way to move from one point to the next. In the sample delivery outline that follows, notice the statistics and sources written out in the introduction and the transitions written out at key junctures—between IA and IB, IB and IC, IC and IIA, and IIA and IIB. After you have rehearsed the speech several times, you will know where you are most likely to falter and can add or omit written transitions as needed.

- **Do not include your purpose statement in your delivery outline.**

- **Use standard outline form.** This will allow you to easily find the exact point or piece of supporting material you are seeking when you glance down at your notes.

SAMPLE DELIVERY OUTLINE

Note that the following delivery outline for Valerie's speech on cyber-plagiarism does not include a statement of the purpose and that the introduction and conclusion appear in shortened and bulleted form. As you rehearse your speech, you will probably continue to edit the delivery outline. You may decide to cut further or to revise signposts. Your outline should provide just enough information to ensure smooth delivery. It should not burden you with unnecessary notes or tempt you to look down too often during the speech.

SAMPLE DELIVERY OUTLINE

Introduction

- 1999 NCA Credo for Ethical Communication: "We advocate that truthfulness, accuracy, honesty, and reason are essential to the integrity of communication."
- Students violate.
- *School Library Journal*, April 2002: CP a growing virus, yet many ignore educational virtues it disables.

◄ The introduction is shortened and uses bulleted phrases and abbreviations (such as NCA for National Communication Association and CP for cyber-plagiarism).

Blueprint

CP undermines
- Academic community
- Value of education
- Earning potential of students

= corruption of America's investment in educational standards.

The central idea is presented as a bulleted list, and the preview is a numbered list, to
◄ make it easy for Valerie to glance down and pick up major points.

SAMPLE DELIVERY OUTLINE *(continued)*

1. Examine problem
2. Address causes
3. Identify solutions

Body

I. Examine
  • Scope
  • How CP devalues education

> Both main ideas and subpoints are single words and short phrases. Lists or items in series are bulleted. In her editing process, Valerie cut the point about cyber-plagiarism infiltrating the job market, so she is careful to cut it from this statement of main idea I.

  A. Is endemic to academia
    1. *Wired News,* May 4, 2001: Univ. of VA nabs 122 students plagiarizing term papers
    2. *Vancouver Sun,* January 7, 2002: Simon Fraser Univ. punishes 47 students who turn in same economics paper
    3. *CNN Online News,* February 7, 2002: Christine Pelter, Piper, Kansas, flunks 28 students for plagiarizing biology assignment

> Sources are written out to ensure accuracy. Quoted material should be written verbatim.

Summary

Clearly, cases of CP are infecting academia.
  B. Undermines value and importance of education
    1. *Wired News:* Dr. Louis Bloomfield, Univ. of VA, college degree should mean students earn degree honorably
    2. Rice Univ. expects students to maintain highest standards of conduct in research
    3. *School Library Journal:* Prof. Susan Jones, Parkland Coll, CP enables students to graduate without learning research and writing skills

> Internal summaries are labeled so Valerie can find them easily. Writing them out in full ensures fluency.

Summary

Do we really want our investment in education to produce copycat diplomas?

Summary

Clearly, CP is spreading and undermining the value of education.
  II. Continues to spread for three reasons:

  • Availability
  • Lack of enforcement
  • Culture of CP

> Valerie cut the third point under main idea I. The editing did not affect the coherence of the speech.

> Three reasons are bulleted so Valerie can see them at a glance.

A. Internet paper mills—thousands of research papers at the click of a mouse
   1. *Educause,* March 2, 2001: over 200 cheating sites available
      - *123HelpMe*
      - *Schoolsucks*
   2. *123HelpMe:* Found "The Plague of Internet Plagiarism"—$9.45, same day (did not)
   3. *60 Minutes,* November 10, 2002: founders of *schoolsucks.com* report that with over a quarter of a million visitors each day on their Web site alone, students are relying on these easy access resources

◄ Another list is bulleted so Valerie can spot it easily.

B. Lack of enforcement
   1. *Library Trends,* Winter 2001: campus environments casually address, actually encourage cheating
   2. *Plagiarism.org,* updated daily, last accessed March 23, 2003: educational service to detect CP reports that 90% of students don't believe cheaters are caught or severely punished if caught
   3. *Chronicle of Higher Education,* August 15, 2002: Dr. Vincent Moore, Tiffin Univ., has reported CP, but despite campus policy to flunk plag., administration protected
C. Student culture
   1. *60 Minutes:* Prof. Don McCabe, founder of Center for Academic Integrity, today's students don't see anything wrong w/ stealing material from Internet. Legit. plag. by noting other students who CP
   2. *Library Trends* and numerous comm. journal articles: consumer mentality, view ed. as passport to job instead of learning experience

Summary

Overall, CP continues to spread because of
- Accessible resources
- Lack of enforcement
- Copycat culture

III. Must solve on
   - Institutional
   - Classroom
   - Individual levels
   A. Admin. should use CP detection service, such as *Turnitin.com*
      1. @ $.50/student—compare submitted papers to Internet material and paper database

Valerie continues to use ◄ abbreviations–here, "@" for *at,* and "$.50/student" for "fifty cents per student."

(continued)

SAMPLE DELIVERY OUTLINE *(continued)*

2. *Turnitin.com*, updated daily, last accessed March 25, 2003: 3–24 hrs., profs. receive report highlighting copied material, whether simple phrase or multiple ¶s

◄ Valerie substitutes the paragraph sign "¶" for the word *paragraph*.

3. *New York Daily News*, December 26, 2002: Hunter High in Manhattan, *Turnitin.com* reduced plag. by 85%

4. *Turnitin.com*: how Christine Pelter of Piper, Kansas caught her 28 students plagiarizing

B. Admin. should establish, enforce honor codes. *Salt Lake Tribune*, December 26, 2002: reports of cheating as much as 50% lower on campuses w/ honor codes

C. Educators should emphasize academic integrity

1. Univ. of Alberta library: online workshop encouraging educators
   - To create focused assignments
   - Require multiple drafts
   - Warn students they will check papers for CP

2. *Salt Lake Tribune:* Professor Pat Matteson, S. Utah Univ., it may take 5 min. to copy Internet material, but via *Google*, only takes her 5 min. to find it

D. Students must hold selves to higher standard:
   - Ethical
   - Foster integrity in others

Conclusion

1. Have examined problem of CP
2. Addressed causes
3. Identified solutions
   - Must uphold
   - Must value
   - Must teach
   - NCA credo–academic communities should model and enforce.
   - Must remember true value rests in quality education.
   - As commencement approaches, I like to believe that my fellow graduates have earned their degrees honorably. As students, instructors, and educated citizens in a prime position to combat cyber-plagiarism, clearly we have some homework to do.

◄ Like the introduction, the conclusion is written with numbered and bulleted lists.

◄ The final sentences are written out in full to ensure a fluent finish.

SPEAKING NOTES

Many speakers find paper difficult to handle quietly, so they transfer their delivery outlines to note cards. Note cards are small enough to hold in one hand, if necessary, and stiff enough not to rustle. Two or three note cards will give you enough space for a delivery outline; the exact number of cards you use will depend on the length of your speech. Type or print your outline neatly on one side, making sure that the letters and words are large enough to read easily. You may find it helpful to plan your note cards according to logical blocks of material, using one note card for the introduction, one or two for the body, and one for the conclusion. At any rate, plan so that you do not have to shuffle note cards midsentence. Number the note cards to prevent a fiasco if your notes get out of order.

Instead of using an outline, you might use an alternative format for your speaking notes. For example, you could use a map. Or you could use a combination of words, pictures, and symbols. Whatever form your notes take, they should make sense to *you.* A final addition to your speaking notes will be delivery cues and reminders, such as "Louder," "Pause," or "Move in front of podium." You could write your delivery cues in the margins by hand, or if the entire outline is handwritten, in ink of a different color. Several years ago, former President Gerald Ford accidentally read the delivery cue "Look into the right camera" during an address. Clearly differentiating delivery cues from speech content will help prevent such mistakes.

Summary

- The speech outlining process has three stages: (1) developing a preparation outline; (2) editing the speech; and (3) developing a delivery outline and speaking notes.

- A preparation outline includes your carefully organized main ideas, subpoints, and supporting material; it may also include your specific purpose, introduction, blueprint, internal previews and summaries, transitions, and conclusion.

- Write each of these elements in complete sentences and standard outline form. Use the preparation outline to begin rehearsing your speech.

- As you rehearse, consider whether your speech falls within the time limits allotted to you. If not, you may need to edit your speech.

- Strategies for editing a speech that is too long include reviewing your specific purpose, considering your audience, simply saying it, keeping only the best supporting material, asking a listener to help you cut, and looking again at your introduction and conclusion.

- After you have rehearsed several times from the preparation outline and edited your speech if necessary, prepare a delivery outline. This, with slight adjustments, becomes your final speaking notes.

- You need not include the purpose statement or central idea in your delivery outline. Note all other ideas and materials in only as much detail as you will need when delivering the speech. You may eventually transfer the delivery outline to note cards and add delivery cues.

Key Terms

delivery outline (p. 254)
mapping (p. 244)

preparation outline (p. 244)
standard outline form (p. 244)

A QUESTION OF ETHICS

In recent years, people have become increasingly conscious of the ways in which our language gives the impression that we are referring only to men when it is more appropriate to refer to both men and women. Has political correctness gotten out of hand? Are we becoming too sensitive to gender issues in our public dialogue? Or are we not sensitive enough? Explain your answer.

CHAPTER 14

Using Words Well: Speaker Language and Style

P eople lazily scanning the classified ads and headlines of their local newspapers must have rubbed their eyes in disbelief when they read the following:[1]

> *A speech is poetry; cadence, rhythm, imagery, sweep! A speech reminds us that words, like children, have the power to make dance the dullest beanbag of a heart.*
>
> **—Peggy Noonan**

FORECLOSURE LISTINGS
Entire state of NJ available. Deal directly with owners. 5–8 months before auction. Call 201-286-1156.

NEED Plain Clothes Security. Must have shoplifting experience. Apply between 8 A.M.–3 P.M. Mon.–Fri., at suite 207.

BABYSITTER
Looking for infant to babysit in my home. Excellent references.

Unemployment Not Working, Critics Say

FAMILY CATCHES FIRE JUST IN TIME, CHIEF SAYS . . .

The Richard Harder family Sunday returned home from church just in time, Lindsey Fire Chief Tom Overmyer said. The family . . . got back from church about 11:15 A.M. to find their kitchen table on fire and . . .

STORE CLERK BETTER AFTER BEING SHOT

These ads and headlines, from the "Headlines" files of comedian Jay Leno, are funny, as he notes, "because they were never intended to be funny in the first place. That they're checked and rechecked by a proofreader makes them funnier still." Certainly they illustrate that using language accurately, clearly, and effectively can be a challenge, even for professional wordsmiths!

For public speakers, the task is doubly challenging. One must speak clearly and communicate ideas accurately. At the same time, it is important to present those ideas in such a way that your audience will listen to, remember, and perhaps act on what you have to say.

In this chapter we will focus on the power of language. We will suggest ways to communicate your ideas and feelings to others accurately and effectively. We will also discuss how the choice of words and word structures can help give your message a distinctive style.

14.a Oral Versus Written Language Style

Your instructor has probably told you not to write your speech out word for word. The professor has said this because of the differences between speaking and writing. There are at least three major differences between oral and written language styles.

ORAL STYLE IS MORE PERSONAL THAN WRITTEN STYLE

When speaking, you can look your listeners in the eye and talk to them directly. If you see that they don't like or don't understand what you are saying, you can adjust your statements and explanations to gain greater acceptance. In other words, you and your audience can interact, something a writer and a reader cannot do. This interaction provides you, the public speaker, with personal contact and potentially the opportunity to experience the warm response of your audience, an experience not available to the writer working in seclusion.

That warmth and personal contact affect your speech and your verbal style. As a speaker, you are likely to use more pronouns (*I, you*) than you would in writing. You are also more likely to address specific audience members by name.

ORAL STYLE IS LESS FORMAL THAN WRITTEN STYLE

Written communication often uses rather formal language and structure. Note that memorized speeches usually sound as if they were written because the words and phrases are longer, more complex, and more formal than those used by most speakers. Spoken communication, by contrast, is usually less formal, characterized by shorter words and phrases and less complex sentence structures. Speakers generally use many more contractions and colloquialisms than writers. Oral language is also much less varied than written language, with only fifty words accounting for almost 50 percent of what English-speakers say.

Finally, spoken language is often less precise than written language. Speakers are more likely than writers to use somewhat vague quantifying terms, such as *many, much,* and *a lot.* The use of such terms may, in fact, be an asset to a speaker who wants to be thought of by his audience as "personal" and "connected." Walter Weintraub, a clinical professor of psychiatry at the University of Maryland Medical Center, once dubbed Bill Clinton a "mainstream" speaker, in part because of his "theatrical . . . use of such adverbial intensifiers as *really, very, so,* and *such.*"[2]

However, there are great variations within both oral and written styles. One speech may be quite personal and informal, whereas another may have characteristics more often associated with written style. For example, President George W. Bush used these simple words and short sentences in his December 13, 2000, election-victory speech:

> Republicans want the best for our nation. And so do Democrats. Our votes may differ, but not our hopes.[3]

Compare Bush's straightforward language and sentence structure with the more formal language and more complex sentence structures used by Al Gore to express a similar thought in his concession speech on that same evening:

> While we yet hold and do not yield our opposing beliefs, there is a higher duty than the one we owe to political party. This is America, and we put country before party.[4]

Regardless of whether the communication is written or oral, the personality of the speaker or writer, the subject of the discourse, the audience, and the occasion all affect the style of the language used.

ORAL STYLE IS MORE REPETITIVE THAN WRITTEN STYLE

When you don't understand something you are reading in a book or an article, you can stop and reread a passage, look up unfamiliar words in the dictionary, or ask someone for help. When you're listening to a speech, those opportunities usually aren't available. For this reason, an oral style is and should be more repetitive.

QUICK CHECK: *Oral Versus Written Style*

Oral Style	More personal, facilitating interaction between speaker and audience
	Less formal
	More repetitive
Written Style	Less personal, with no immediate interaction between writer and reader
	More formal
	Less repetitive

When you study how to organize a speech, you learn to preview main ideas in your introduction, develop your ideas in the body of the speech, and summarize these same ideas in the conclusion. You build in repetition to make sure that your listener will grasp your message. Even during the process of developing an idea, it is sometimes necessary to state it first, restate it in a different way, provide an example, and finally, summarize it.

14.b   Using Words Effectively

As a speaker, your challenge is to use words well so that you can communicate your intended message. Ideally, language should be specific and concrete, simple, and correct. We shall discuss each of these factors.

USE SPECIFIC, CONCRETE WORDS

If you were to describe your pet snake to an audience, you would need to do more than say it is a serpent. Instead, you would want to use the most specific term possible, describing your snake as a ball python or, if you were speaking to an audience of scientists, perhaps as a *Python regius*. Specific words or terms such as *ball python* refer to individual members of a class of more general things such as *serpent* or *snake*.

Specific words are often concrete words, which appeal to one of our five senses, whereas general words are often abstract words, which refer to ideas or qualities. A linguistic theory known as general semantics holds that the more concrete your words, the clearer your communication. Semanticists use a "ladder of abstraction" to illustrate how something can be described in either concrete or abstract language. Figure 14.1 shows an example. The words are most abstract at the top of the ladder and become more concrete as you move down the ladder.

Specific, concrete nouns create memorable images. At the September 14, 2001, Washington National Cathedral prayer service for victims of the September 11 terrorist attacks, George W. Bush said,

We have seen the images of fire and ashes and bent steel.[5]

The concrete nouns *fire, ashes,* and *steel* created much more specific images for Bush's listeners than abstract nouns such as *aftermath* or even *holocaust* would have.

Specific, concrete verbs can be especially effective. The late Representative Barbara Jordan of Texas, whose language skills one speechwriter describes as "legendary," recognized the power of concrete verbs.[6] For example, the first draft of a passage in her 1992 Democratic National Convention keynote stated,

The American dream is not dead. It is injured, it is sick, but it is not dead.

Jordan revised the line to read,

The American dream is not dead. It is gasping for breath, but it is not dead.

Abstract

Nature

Mammal

Dog

Pit Bull

Concrete

FIGURE 14.1 A "ladder of abstraction" is used by semanticists to show how a concept, idea, or thing can be described in either concrete or abstract terms.

The concrete verb phrase "gasping for breath" brings alive the image Jordan intended to create.

At the opposite end of the language spectrum from specific, concrete words is the cliché, an overused expression that may make listeners "start tuning out and completely miss the message."[7] A recent poll of 5,000 people from some 70 countries found that the most annoying cliché was "at the end of the day," followed by "at this moment in time." Also on the list were "24/7," "absolutely," "awesome," "ballpark figure," and "I hear what you're saying." Like most clichés, these phrases were at one time original and interesting, but their overuse has doomed them. Substitute specific, concrete words for clichés.

When searching for a specific, concrete word, you may want to consult a **thesaurus**. But in searching for an alternative word, do not feel that you have to choose the most obscure or unusual term to vary your description. Simple language can often evoke a vivid image for your listeners.

USE SIMPLE WORDS

The best language is often the simplest. Your words should be immediately understandable to your listeners. Don't try to impress them with jargon and pompous language. Instead, as linguist Paul Roberts advises,

> Decide what you want to say and say it as vigorously as possible . . . and in plain words.[8]

In his essay "Politics and the English Language," George Orwell lists rules for clear writing, including this prescription for simplicity:

> Never use a long word where a short one will do. If it is possible to cut a word out, always cut it out. Never use a foreign phrase, a scientific word, or a jargon word if you can think of an everyday English equivalent.[9]

Tape-record your practice sessions. As you play the tape back, listen for chances to express yourself with simpler and fewer words. Used wisely, simple words communicate with great power and precision.

USE WORDS CORRECTLY

> I was listening to the car radio one day when a woman reading the news referred to someone as a suede-o-intellectual. I pondered through three traffic lights until I realized she wasn't talking about shoes, but a pseudointellectual.[10]

A public speech is not the place to demonstrate your lack of familiarity with English vocabulary and grammar. In fact, your effectiveness with your audience depends in part on your ability to use the English language correctly. If you are unsure of the way to apply a grammatical rule, seek assistance from a good English usage handbook. If you are unsure of a word's pronunciation, use a dictionary.

Connotation and Denotation   Perhaps the greatest challenge to using words correctly is remaining aware of denotations as well as connotations. Language operates on two levels. The **denotation** of a word is its literal meaning, the definition you find in a dictionary. For example, the denotation of the word *notorious* is "famous." The **connotation** of a word is not usually found in a dictionary, but consists of the meaning we associate with the word, based on our past experiences. *Notorious* connotes fame resulting from some dire deed. *Notorious* and *famous* are not really interchangeable. It is just as important to consider the connotations of the words you use as it is to consider the denotations.

During times of war, politicians and members of the military consider the connotations of words carefully and deliberately. Wartime language

> must . . . enable combatants and noncombatants alike to see the other side as killable, to overcome the innate queasiness over the taking of human life.[11]

For example, soldiers use the word *enemy* instead of *person,* because enemy has "a fear-inducing connotation."

Sometimes connotations are private. For example, the word *table* is defined denotatively as a piece of furniture consisting of a smooth, flat slab affixed on legs. But when you think of the word *table,* you may think of the old oak table your grandparents used to have; *table* may evoke for you an image of playing checkers with your grandmother. This is a private connotation of the word, a unique meaning based on your own past experiences. Private meanings are difficult to predict, but as a public speaker you should be aware of the possibility of triggering audience members' private connotations. This awareness is particularly important when you are discussing highly emotional or controversial topics.

And finally, if your audience includes people whose first language is not English, to whom the nuances of connotation may not be readily apparent, it may be necessary to explain your intentions in more detail, rather than relying on word associations.

14.C Adapting Your Language Style to Diverse Listeners

To communicate successfully with the diverse group of listeners who comprise your audience, make sure your language is understandable, appropriate, and unbiased.

USE LANGUAGE THAT YOUR AUDIENCE CAN UNDERSTAND

Even if you and all your public-speaking classmates speak English, you probably speak many varieties of the language. Perhaps some of your classmates speak in an **ethnic**

vernacular, such as "Spanglish," the combination of English and Spanish often heard near the United States–Mexico border; Cajun, with its influx of French words, frequently spoken in Louisiana; or the African American language variety sometimes known as "Ebonics." Some of you may reflect where you grew up by your use of **regionalisms**, words or phrases specific to one part of the country but rarely used in quite the same way in other places. Others of you may frequently use **jargon**, the specialized language of your profession or hobby.

If you give a speech to others who share your ethnic, regional, or professional background, you can communicate successfully with them using these specialized varieties of English. However, if you give a speech to an audience as diverse as the members of your public-speaking class, where do you find a linguistic "common ground"? Not only public-speaking students struggle with this question. An analysis of former President Herbert Hoover's speeches reveals that Hoover's high vocabulary level and technical jargon were "not well suited for ordinary audiences."[12] The answer is to use standard U.S. English. **Standard U.S. English** is the language taught by schools and used in the media, business, and government in the United States. "Standard" does not imply that standard U.S. English is inherently right and all other forms are wrong, only that it conforms to a standard that most speakers of U.S. English will readily understand—even though they may represent a variety of ethnic, regional, and professional backgrounds.

USE APPROPRIATE LANGUAGE

Shortly after the September 11, 2001, terrorist attacks, U.S. Vice President Dick Cheney made remarks in which he referred to Pakistanis as "Paks." Although he was speaking admiringly of the Pakistani people, he was chided for his use of the term. The variation *Paki* is considered a slur, and *Pak* is only slightly less offensive. Columnist William Safire remarked, "Cheney probably picked up *Paks* in his Pentagon days, but innocent intent is an excuse only once; now he is sensitized, as are we all."[13]

A speaker whose language defames any subgroup—people of particular ethnic, racial, and religious backgrounds or sexual orientations; women; people with disabilities—or whose language might be otherwise considered offensive or risqué runs a great risk of antagonizing audience members. In fact, one study suggests that derogatory language used to describe people with disabilities adversely affects an audience's perceptions of the speaker's persuasiveness, competence, trustworthiness, and sociability.[14]

USE UNBIASED LANGUAGE

Even speakers who would never dream of using overtly offensive language may find it difficult to avoid language that more subtly stereotypes or discriminates. Sexist language falls largely into this second category.

For example, not many years ago, a singular masculine pronoun (*he, him, his*) was the accepted way to refer to a person of unspecified sex:

Everyone should bring his book to class tomorrow.

This usage is now considered sexist and unacceptable. Instead, you may include both a masculine and a feminine pronoun:

> Everyone should bring his or her book to class tomorrow.

Or, you may reword the sentence so that it is plural and thus gender neutral:

> All students should bring their books to class tomorrow.

Also now considered sexist is the use of a masculine noun to refer generically to all people. The editors of *The American Heritage Dictionary of the English Language, Fourth Edition,* consulted a usage panel of 200 writers and scholars on such questions as whether the word *man* was acceptable as meaning "human" in some instances.[15] Only 58 percent of the women on the panel found such usage appropriate. To put it another way: If you were speaking to an audience of these distinguished women, you would offend 42 percent of them by using a phrase such as "modern man." Although the word *man* is the primary offender, you should also monitor your use of such masculine nouns as *waiter, chairman, fireman,* and *Congressman.* Instead choose such gender-neutral alternatives as *server, chair, firefighter,* and *member of Congress.*

In addition to avoiding masculine nouns and pronouns to refer to all people, avoid sexist language that patronizes or stereotypes people:

Sexist	**Unbiased**
Barbara Bush, daughter of President George W. Bush and Laura, graduated from Yale University.	Barbara Bush, daughter of President and Mrs. Bush, graduated from Yale University. or Barbara Bush, daughter of George W. and Laura Bush, graduated from Yale University.
The policeman is an underpaid professional who risks his life daily.	Police are underpaid professionals who risk their lives daily.
The male nurse took good care of his patients. (Note: The phrase "male nurse" implies that nursing is a typically female profession. The pronoun *his* clarifies the sex of the nurse.)	The nurse took good care of his patients.

As noted earlier, it is not always easy to avoid biased language. Even with good intentions and deliberate forethought, you can find yourself at times caught in a double bind. For example, suppose that Dr. Pierce is a young, black, female M.D. If you don't mention her age, race, and gender when you refer to her, you may reinforce your listeners' stereotypical image of a physician as middle-aged, white, and male. But if you *do* mention these factors, you may be suspected of implying that Dr. Pierce's achievement is unusual. There is no easy answer to this dilemma or others like it. You will have to consider your audience, purpose, and the occasion in deciding how best to identify Dr. Pierce.

As women and members of racial, ethnic, and other minorities have become increasingly visible in such professions as medicine, law, engineering, and politics, the public has grown to expect unbiased, inclusive language from news commentators, teachers, textbooks, and magazines—and from public speakers. Language that does not reflect these changes will disrupt your ability to communicate your message to your audience, which may well include members of the minority group to which you are referring.

14.d Crafting Memorable Word Structures

The president of the United States is scheduled to make an important speech in your hometown. You attend the speech and find his thirty-minute presentation both interesting and informative. In the evening, you turn on the news to see how the networks cover his address. All three major networks excerpt the same ten-second portion of his speech. Why? What makes certain portions of a speech quotable or memorable? Former presidential speechwriter Peggy Noonan has said,

> Great speeches have always had great sound bites. . . . They sum up a point, or make a point in language that is pithy or profound.[16]

In other words, memorable speeches are stylistically distinctive. They create arresting images. And they have what a marketing-communication specialist has termed "ear appeal":

> "Ear appeal" phrases can be like the haunting songs of a musical that the members of the audience find themselves humming on the way home. Even if people want to forget them, they can't.[17]

Earlier in this chapter, we discussed the importance of using words that are concrete, unbiased, vivid, simple, and correct. In this section, we turn our attention to groups of words, or word structures—phrases and sentences that create the drama, figurative images, and cadences needed to make a speech memorable by giving it both "eye and ear appeal."[18]

CREATING FIGURATIVE IMAGES

One way to make your message memorable is to use figures of speech to create arresting images. A **figure of speech** deviates from the ordinary, expected meanings of words to make a description or comparison unique, vivid, and memorable. Common figures of speech include metaphors, similes, and personification.

Metaphors and Similes A **metaphor** is an implied comparison. In his presidential farewell address on January 18, 2001, Bill Clinton compared American diversity to a coat of many colors and admonished his fellow citizens,

> Remember that America cannot lead in the world unless here at home we weave the threads of our coat of many colors into the fabric of one America.[19]

In addition to using related words to create the metaphor—*weave, threads, coat,* and *fabric*—Clinton gives Biblical authority to his comparison by alluding to the coat of many colors worn by Joseph in the Old Testament.

A **simile** is a comparison that includes the word *like* or *as.* In his eulogy for Ronald Reagan, President George W. Bush noted that on Reagan, the title "President" *fit like a white Stetson.*[20]

Speakers often turn to metaphor and simile in times that are especially momentous or overwhelming—times when literal language seems insufficient. In the hours and days after the September 11, 2001, terrorist attacks on the United States, various speakers used such metaphorical phrases as "one more circle of Dante's hell," "nuclear winter," and "the crater of a volcano" to describe the site of the destroyed World Trade Center in New York.[21] Such language is often categorized as "crisis rhetoric."

Personification   **Personification** is the attribution of human qualities to inanimate things or ideas. Franklin Roosevelt personified nature as a generous living provider in this line from his first inaugural address:

> Nature still offers her bounty and human efforts have multiplied it. Plenty is at our doorstep.[22]

CREATING DRAMA

Another way you can make phrases and sentences memorable is to use them to create drama in your speech—to keep the audience in suspense or to catch them slightly off guard by saying something in a way that differs from the way they expected you to say it.

Use a Short Sentence to Express a Vitally Important Thought

We have already talked about the value of using short, simple words. Short, simple sentences can have much the same power. Columnist George F. Will recently pointed out that the most eloquent sentence in Lincoln's memorable second inaugural address is just four words long:[23]

> And the war came.

Other strategies for achieving drama in your speech include three stylistic devices: omission, inversion, and suspension.

Use Omission   Leave out a word or phrase that the audience expects to hear. When telegrams were a more common means of communication, senders tried to use as few words as possible, because they were charged by the word, and the more they could leave out, the cheaper the telegram was. But, of course, your listeners or readers must understand the words you have left out. For example, a captain of a World War II Navy destroyer used **omission** to inform headquarters of his successful efforts at sighting and sinking an enemy submarine. He spared all details when he cabled back to headquarters: "Sighted sub—sank same." Using as few words as possible, he communicated his message in a memorable way. About 2,000 years earlier, another military commander informed his superiors in Rome of his conquest of Gaul with the economical message: "I came, I saw, I conquered." That commander was Julius Caesar.

Use Inversion   Reverse the normal word order of a phrase or sentence. John F. Kennedy used **inversion** by changing the usual subject-verb-object sentence pattern to object-subject-verb in this brief declaration from his inaugural speech:

> This much we pledge. . . .[24]

More recently, President George W. Bush inverted the last two words of this statement in his 2003 eulogy for the seven astronauts of the Space Shuttle *Columbia:*

> To leave behind Earth and air and gravity . . . was a dream fulfilled.[25]

Use Suspension   Place a key word or phrase at the end of a sentence, rather than at the beginning. When you read a mystery novel, you are held in suspense until you reach the end and learn "who done it." The stylistic technique of verbal **suspension** does something similar. When Al Gore conceded the 2000 presidential election in December of that year, he told his audience,

> For the sake of our unity as a people and the strength of our democracy, I offer my concession.[26]

Advertisers use the technique of suspension frequently. A few years ago, the Coca-Cola Company used suspension as the cornerstone of its worldwide advertising campaign. Rather than saying, "Coke goes better with everything," the copywriter decided to stylize the message by making *Coke* the last word in the sentence. The slogan became "Things go better with Coke." Again, the stylized version was more memorable because it used language in an unexpected way.

CREATING CADENCE

Even very small children can memorize nursery rhymes and commercial jingles with relative ease. As we grow older, we may make up rhythms and rhymes to help us remember such facts as "Thirty days hath September,/April, June, and November" and "Red sky at night/A sailor's delight." Why? Rhythms are memorable. The public speaker can take advantage of language rhythms, not by speaking in singsong patterns, but by using such stylistic devices as parallelism, antithesis, repetition, and alliteration.

Parallelism   **Parallelism** occurs when two or more clauses or sentences have the same grammatical pattern. When he delivered the Phi Beta Kappa oration at Harvard in 1837, Ralph Waldo Emerson cast these simple expressions in parallel structures:

> We will walk on our own feet; we will work with our own hands; we will speak our own minds.[27]

In his 2004 State of the Union address, President George W. Bush described America's strength in the months and years following September 11, 2001:

> In grief, we have found the grace to go on. In challenge, we rediscovered the courage and daring of a free people. In victory, we have shown the noble aims and good heart of America.[28]

Bush's three parallel prepositional phrase-subject-verb-object structures added memorable rhythm to his statement.

Antithesis The word *antithesis* means "opposition." A sentence that uses **antithesis** has two parts with parallel structures but contrasting meanings. Speakers have long realized the dramatic potential of antithesis. In his first inaugural address, Franklin Roosevelt declared,

> Our true destiny is not to be ministered unto but to minister to ourselves and to our fellow men.[29]

Both in meaning and in structure, his words foreshadowed the more famous remark of John F. Kennedy nearly thirty years later:

> Ask not what your country can do for you; ask what you can do for your country.[30]

We will examine Kennedy's statement in greater detail later in this chapter.

Antithesis is not restricted to politicians. When William Faulkner accepted the Nobel Prize for literature in 1950, he spoke the now famous antithetical phrase,

> I believe that man will not merely endure: he will prevail.[31]

An antithetical statement is a good way to end a speech. The cadence it creates will make the statement memorable.

Repetition Repetition of a key word or phrase gives rhythm and power to your message and makes it memorable. At the climax of Patrick Henry's "Liberty or Death" speech in 1775 was this passionate use of repetition:

> The war is inevitable—and let it come! I repeat it, sir, let it come![32]

Twentieth-century speakers also recognized the power of repetition as a memorable stylistic device. In a speech honoring the Tuskegee Airmen and addressing issues of race in the modern U.S. military, former Deputy Secretary of Defense Rudy de Leon claimed that recruitment of minorities is only one part of the task facing the military:

> *Our job is not finished* if we fail to recognize that each generation has its own unique problems and perceptions when it comes to race and ethnicity.
>
> We can ensure our rules and regulations are clear and fair.
>
> But *our job is not finished* if people believe that those rules and regulations are not being enforced fairly.
>
> *Our job is not finished* if the rules and regulations work for those in uniform, but they do not reach people in our civilian workforce. [emphasis added][33]

The repeated mantra, "our job is not finished" rings in one's mind long after hearing or reading the passage.

Alliteration   **Alliteration** is the repetition of a consonant sound (usually an initial consonant) several times in a phrase, clause, or sentence. Alliteration adds cadence to a thought. Consider these examples:

Alliterative Phrase	Speaker	Occasion
discipline and direction	Franklin Roosevelt	first inaugural address[34]
confidence and courage	Franklin Roosevelt	first fireside chat[35]
disaster and disappointment	Winston Churchill	speech urging British resistence[36]
virility, valour, and civic virtue	Winston Churchill	speech to U.S. Congress[37]
conviction, not calculation	Dick Cheney	campaign speech[38]

Used sparingly, alliteration can add cadence to your rhetoric.

ANALYZING AN EXAMPLE OF MEMORABLE WORD STRUCTURE

We'd like to illustrate all seven techniques for creating drama and cadence with one final example.[39] If you asked almost anyone for the most quoted line from John F. Kennedy's speeches, that quote would probably be "Ask not what your country can do

---

QUICK CHECK: *Crafting Memorable Word Structures*

Word Structures with Figurative Imagery

Metaphor	Makes an implied comparison
Simile	Compares by using the word *like* or *as*
Personification	Attributes human qualities to inanimate things or ideas

Word Structures with Drama

Short sentence	Emphasizes an important idea
Omission	Boils an idea down to its essence by leaving out understood words
Inversion	Reverses the expected order of words and phrases
Suspension	Places a key word at the end of a phrase or sentence

Word Structures with Cadence

Parallelism	Uses the same pattern to begin several sentences or phrases
Antithesis	Uses parallel structures but opposing meanings in two parts of a sentence
Repetition	Repeats a key word or phrase several times for emphasis
Alliteration	Uses the same consonant sound several times in a phrase

for you; ask what you can do for your country," from his inaugural address. Besides expressing a noble thought, this line is so quotable because it uses all seven stylistic techniques.

- **Omission and inversion.** "Ask not . . ." is an example of omission. The subject, *you*, is not stated. "Ask not" is also an example of inversion. In casual everyday conversation, we would usually say "do not ask" rather than "ask not." The inversion makes the opening powerful and attention-grabbing.

- **Suspension.** The sentence also employs the technique of suspension. The key message of the phrase, "ask what you can do for your country," is suspended, or delayed, until the end of the sentence. If the sentence structure had been reversed, the impact would not have been as dramatic. Consider: "Ask what you can do for your country rather than what your country can do for you."

- **Parallelism and antithesis.** Kennedy uses parallelism and antithesis. The sentence is made up of two clauses with parallel construction, one in opposition to the other.

- **Repetition.** He also uses the technique of repetition. He uses a form of the word *you* four times in a sentence of seventeen words. In fact, he uses only eight different words in his seventeen-word sentence. Just one word in the entire sentence, *not*, occurs only once.

- **Alliteration.** Finally, Kennedy adds alliteration to the sentence with the words *ask, can,* and *country*. The alliterative *k* sound is repeated at more or less even intervals.

Although the sentence we have analyzed does not include any figurative images, the speech from which it comes does have some memorable figurative language, most notably metaphors such as "chains of poverty," "beachhead of cooperation," and "jungle of suspicion." Kennedy used figurative imagery, drama, and cadence to give his inaugural address "eye and ear appeal" and make it memorable—not just to those who heard it initially, but also to those of us who hear, read, and study it more than forty years later.

14.e Tips for Using Language Effectively

Having reviewed ways to add style and interest to the language of your speech, we must now consider how best to put those techniques into practice.

- Use distinctive stylistic devices sparingly. Even though we have made great claims for the value of style, do not overdo it. Including too much highly stylized language can put the focus on your language rather than on your content.

- Use stylistic devices at specific points in your speech. Save your use of stylistic devices for times during your speech when you want your audience to remember your key ideas or when you wish to capture their attention. Some kitchen mixers have a "burst of power" switch to help churn through difficult mixing chores with extra force. Think of the stylistic devices we have reviewed as opportunities to provide a burst of power to your ideas. Use them in your opening sentences, statements of key ideas, and conclusion.

- Short words are more forceful than long ones. Think of those monosyllabic commands—Sit! March! Stop! When a technical term is too unusual or cumbersome, find a way to describe the concept with another word, or use a simile or a metaphor. To talk about the process of *floccinaucinihilipilification* (the action or habit of estimating something as worthless) may make an interesting speech, but your audience will probably not remember the word itself.

- Use stylistic devices to economize. When sentences become too long or complex, see if you can recast them with antithesis or suspension. Also, remember the possibility of omission.

HOW TO: *Create Figurative Images, Drama, and Cadence*

- Make an implied comparison (metaphor).
- Compare by using the word *like* or *as* (simile).
- Attribute human qualities to inanimate things or ideas (personification).
- Use a short sentence to express a vitally important thought.
- Omit understood words to reduce an idea to its essence.
- Reverse the expected order of words and phrases (inversion).
- Place a key word or idea at the end of a sentence (suspension).
- Use the same pattern to begin several sentences or phrases (parallelism).
- Oppose one part of a sentence to another (antithesis).
- Repeat a key word or phrase several times for emphasis (repetition).
- Use the same initial consonant sound several times in a phrase or sentence (alliteration).

Summary

- Carefully select and use words to give your ideas maximum impact.
- Understand the differences between the way people talk and the way they write.
- Oral style is more personal, less formal, and more repetitious than written style.
- Words should be specific, concrete, and simple and should be used correctly. Understand the connotations of words, as well as their denotations.
- Adapt your language style to diverse listeners. Use language your listeners can understand, use appropriate language to avoid offending them, and use unbiased language to communicate in a sensitive way to subgroups.

- Create arresting images through such figures of speech as metaphors, similes, and personification. Create drama and cadence with structures such as short sentences, omission, inversion, suspension, parallelism, antithesis, repetition, and alliteration.

- Taking the time and effort to use words and sentence structures well can help you gain and maintain the attention of your audience and can help your audience understand your message and remember what you say.

Key Terms

alliteration (p. 273)
antithesis (p. 272)
connotation (p. 266)
denotation (p. 266)
ethnic vernacular (p. 266)
figure of speech (p. 269)
inversion (p. 271)
jargon (p. 267)
metaphor (p. 269)

omission (p. 270)
parallelism (p. 271)
personification (p. 270)
regionalism (p. 267)
repetition (p. 272)
simile (p. 270)
standard U.S. English (p. 267)
suspension (p. 271)
thesaurus (p. 265)

A QUESTION OF ETHICS

Louis Howe, aide to President Franklin D. Roosevelt, is now thought to have written the famous line from Roosevelt's first inaugural address: "The only thing we have to fear is fear itself." Is it ethical to credit Roosevelt with this line?

5

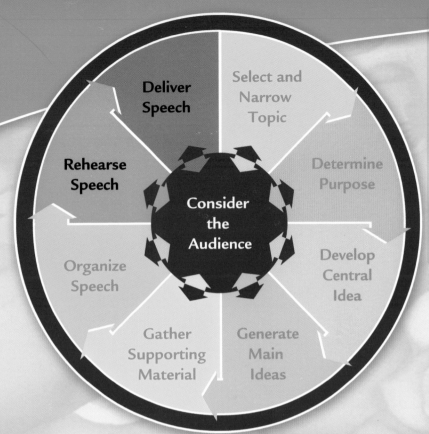

Deliver
Speech

Select and
Narrow
Topic

Rehearse
Speech

Determine
Purpose

Consider
the
Audience

Develop
Central
Idea

Organize
Speech

Gather
Supporting
Material

Generate
Main
Ideas

Delivering a
Speech

CHAPTER 15 Delivering Your Speech

Delivering a Speech

Delivering a Speech

15 Delivering Your Speech

➡ **The Power of Speech Delivery (p. 284)**
- Nonverbal communication such as eye contact, posture, vocal quality, and facial expression play a major role in the communication process.
- Listeners expect effective delivery.
  - When you speak to an audience, strive for a natural, conversational tone.
  - Have good eye contact with your listeners, and use appropriate gestures.
  - Be sure your voice has a natural, varied inflection (rather than a droning monotone) and an intensity that communicates that you're interested in your listeners.
  - There is not one "ideal" style of delivery or set of prescribed gestures that is appropriate for all audiences.

➡ **Methods of Delivery (p. 286)**
- Manuscript speaking may provide some insurance against forgetting a speech, but it is rarely done well enough to be interesting.
  - One advantage of manuscript speaking is that you can choose words very carefully when dealing with a sensitive and critical issue.
  - Be familiar enough with your manuscript that you can make as much eye contact with your audience as possible.
  - Use gestures and movement to add interest and emphasis to your message.
- Memorized speaking has the advantage of allowing you to have maximum eye contact with the audience.
  - Most memorized speeches sound stiff, stilted, and over-rehearsed.
  - You run the risk of forgetting parts of your speech and awkwardly searching for words in front of your audience.
- Impromptu speaking is often described as "thinking on your feet" or "speaking off the cuff."

- The advantage of impromptu speaking is that you can speak informally, maintaining direct eye contact with the audience.
- An impromptu speech usually lacks logical organization and thorough research.
- Extemporaneous speaking is speaking from a written or memorized general outline, but not having the exact wording in front of you or in memory.
  - An extemporaneous style is conversational; it gives your audience the impression that the speech is being created as they listen to it.
  - An extemporaneous speech sounds live rather than prepared.

➡ **Characteristics of Effective Delivery (p. 290)**
- Eye contact with your audience opens communication, makes you more believable, and keeps your audience interested.
  - Continued eye contact lets you know how your audience is responding to your speech.
  - Establish eye contact with the entire audience, not just with those in the front row or only one or two people.
- Give emphasis to your message by using appropriate gestures.
  - Gestures vary from culture to culture, so be aware of cultural expectations so you can make appropriate gestures.
  - Gestures can lend strength to or detract from your words by repeating, contradicting, substituting for, complementing, emphasizing, or regulating them,
- Your use of movement during your speech should make sense to your listeners.
  - Take care that your movement doesn't distract from your message.
  - Be mindful of physical barriers that exist between you and your audience.
  - Move closer to listeners as a primary way of communicating both physical and psychological closeness between you.
  - When changing from one topic to a new one, use movement to signal that your approach to the speaking situation is changing.
- Your posture communicates significant information, including intensity of emotion, and can affect your credibility.
  - Your posture should arise naturally from your topic and the context of your speech, but should not call attention to itself.
- Your audience sees your face before they hear your message.
  - Your facial expression should naturally vary to be consistent with your message.

- While rehearsing, consider standing in front of a mirror or, better yet, videotape yourself practicing your speech.
- Vocal delivery includes pitch, speaking rate, volume, pronunciation, articulation, pauses, and general variation of the voice.
- A speaker has at least two key vocal obligations to an audience: Speak to be understood, and speak with vocal variety to maintain interest.
  - Speak loudly enough that your audience can hear you.
  - Poor enunciation reflects negatively on your credibility as a speaker.
  - Articulate clearly and distinctly so that your audience can understand your words.
  - Pronounce words carefully. Mispronouncing words can detract from your credibility.
  - If your pronunciation of words is significantly distracting to your listeners, consider modifying your dialect.
  - To speak with variety, vary your pitch, speaking rate, and pauses.
  - Do not deliver your speech too quickly. One symptom of speech anxiety is that you tend to rush through your speech to get it over with.
  - Effective use of pauses, also known as *effective timing,* can greatly enhance the impact of your message.
  - Silence can be an effective tool in emphasizing a particular word or sentence. A well-timed pause coupled with eye contact can powerfully accent your thought.
- If you are inaudible or use a microphone awkwardly, your speech will not have the desired effect.
- Strategies for using a microphone effectively:
  - If you have a fully stationary microphone, you will need to remain behind the microphone with your mouth about the same distance from the mike at all times to avoid fluctuations in the volume of sound.
  - Microphones amplify sloppy habits of pronunciation and enunciation. Therefore, you need to speak clearly and crisply when using a mike.
  - If you must test a microphone, count or ask the audience whether they can hear you.
  - When you deliver your speech, speak directly into the microphone, making sure that your words are appropriately amplified.
- Personal appearance affects how your audience will respond to you and your message, particularly during the opening moments of your presentation.

At a Glance *(continued)*

➡️ **Audience Diversity and Delivery (p. 304)**
- You need to adapt your presentation to the expectations of your listeners, especially those from different cultural backgrounds.
  - Avoid an ethnocentric mindset.
  - Consider using a less dramatic style for predominantly high-context listeners.
  - Consult with other speakers who have presented to your audience.
  - Monitor your level of immediacy with your audience.
  - Monitor your expression of emotion.
  - Know the code.

➡️ **Rehearsing Your Speech: Some Final Tips (p. 305)**
- Effective public speaking is a skill that takes practice. Practicing takes the form of rehearsing.
  - Finish drafting your speech outline at least two days before your speech.
  - Before you prepare speaking notes, rehearse your speech aloud to help determine where you will need notes to prompt yourself.
  - Prepare your speaking notes. Use whatever system works best for you.
  - Rehearse your speech standing up so that you can get a feel for your use of gestures as well as your vocal delivery.
  - If you can, present your speech to someone else so that you can practice establishing eye contact.
  - If possible, tape-record or videotape your speech during the rehearsal stage so that you can observe your vocal and physical mannerisms and make necessary changes.
  - Rehearse using all your presentation aids.
  - Try to make sure that your final rehearsals re-create, as much as possible, the speaking situation you will face.
  - Practice good delivery skills while rehearsing.

➡️ **Delivering Your Speech (p. 306)**
- Get plenty of rest before your speech.
- Review the suggestions for becoming a confident speaker, such as to re-create the speech environment when you rehearse, use deep breathing techniques to help you relax, make sure you are especially familiar with your introduction and conclusion, and act calm to feel calm.
- Arrive early for your speaking engagement.
- Visualize success.

➡ **Adapting Your Speech Delivery for Television (p. 308)**

- If you need to adapt your speech delivery for television:
  - Tone down gestures. Keep your hands still, and don't fidget with pens, hair, or clothing.
  - Dress appropriately: nonwhite clothing, solid colors, simple styles and accessories.
  - Monitor your facial expressions.
  - Choose your words with care and style, but keep your message short.
  - Keep your target audience in mind.
  - Become familiar with the technology before you speak.

➡ **Responding to Questions (p. 311)**

- During a Q & A session, your delivery method changes to impromptu speaking. To make the Q & A period less challenging:
  - Prepare.
  - Repeat or rephrase the question.
  - Stay on message.
  - Ask yourself the first question.
  - Listen nonjudgmentally.
  - Neutralize hostile questions.
  - When you don't know, admit it.
  - Be brief.
  - Use organizational signposts.
  - Indicate when the Q & A period is concluding.

Delivering Your Speech

What's more important: what you say or how you say it? Delivery has long been considered an important part of public speaking. But is the delivery of your speech more important than the content of your message? Since ancient Greece, people have argued about the role of delivery in public speaking. More than 2,300 years ago, some thinkers held that delivery was not an "elevated" topic of study. In his classic treatise *Rhetoric,* written in 333 B.C., Aristotle claimed that "the battle should be fought out on the facts of the case alone; and therefore everything outside the direct proof is really superfluous." Writing in the first century, Quintilian, Roman rhetorician and author of the first book on speech training, acknowledged the importance of delivery when he said that the beginning speaker should strive for an "extempore," or conversational, delivery style. His countryman, the great orator Cicero, claimed that without effective delivery, "a speaker of the highest mental capacity can be held in no esteem, whereas one of moderate abilities, with this qualification, may surpass even those of the highest talent." Sixteen centuries later, the elocution movement carried the emphasis on delivery to an extreme. For elocutionists, speech training consisted largely of techniques and exercises for improving posture, movement, and vocal quality.

Speak the speech, I pray you, as I pronounced it to you, trippingly on the tongue.

—William Shakespeare

Today, communication teachers believe that both content and delivery contribute to speaking effectiveness. One survey suggested that "developing effective delivery" is a primary goal of most speech teachers.[1] Considerable research supports the claim that delivery plays an important role in influencing how audiences react to a speaker and his or her message. It is your audience who will determine whether you are successful. Delivery counts.

Although some courses on public speaking are offered in various countries throughout the world, most of the formal instruction on how to deliver a speech is offered in the United States. Our advice about speech delivery, therefore, is closely related to the discipline of communication here in the United States. It's not possible for us to provide a comprehensive compendium of each cultural expectation you may face as you give speeches in a variety of educational and professional settings, but throughout this chapter we will try to sample conventions and preferences of other cultures as we discuss speech delivery.

15.a   The Power of Speech Delivery

The way you hold your notes, your gestures and stance, and your impatient adjustment of your glasses all contribute to the overall effect of your speech. **Nonverbal communication** is communication other than through written or spoken language that creates meaning for someone. Nonverbal factors such as your eye contact, posture, vocal quality, and facial expression play a major role in the communication process. As much as 65 percent of the social meaning of messages is based on nonverbal expression.[2]

Why does your delivery have such power to affect how your audience will receive your message? One reason is that listeners expect a good speaker to provide good delivery. Your unspoken message is also how you express your feelings and emotions to an audience. And ultimately, an audience believes what it sees more than what you say.

LISTENERS EXPECT EFFECTIVE DELIVERY

In a public-speaking situation, nonverbal elements have an important influence on the audience's perceptions about a speaker's effectiveness. Communication researcher Judee Burgoon and her colleagues have developed a theory called **nonverbal-expectancy theory**. The essence of the theory is this: People have certain expectations as to how you should communicate.[3] If you don't live up to those expectations, your listeners will feel that you have violated their expectations. The theory predicts that if a listener expects you to have effective delivery, and your delivery is poor, you will lose credibility. There is evidence that although many speakers do not deliver speeches effectively, audiences nevertheless expect a good speech to be well-delivered.

As we have also emphasized, audience members with different cultural backgrounds will hold different assumptions about how a speech should be presented. In our discussion of delivery, we note how the cultural and ethnic background of your audience affects the delivery style your listeners prefer.

Platform Conversation   What do most people consider effective delivery today? Effective speech delivery for most North American listeners has been described as "platform conversation." When you speak to an audience, strive for a natural, conversational tone. More than 100 years ago, speakers were taught to deliver orations using a more formal style of speaking than most people prefer today. When you look at old newsreels of speakers during the early part of the twentieth century, their gestures and movement looked stilted and unnatural, because they were taught to use dramatic, planned gestures.

Effective delivery today includes having good eye contact with your listeners. It also includes using appropriate gestures, just as you do in your interpersonal conversations with your friends (but, of course, avoiding distracting mannerisms such as jingling change in your pockets or unconsciously playing with your hair). Effective delivery also means your voice has a natural, varied inflection (rather than a droning monotone) and an intensity that communicates that you're interested in your listeners.

Audience-Centered Delivery   Of course, different audiences prefer different styles of delivery; there is not one "ideal" style of delivery or set of prescribed gestures that is appropriate for all audiences. If you are speaking to an audience of a thousand people, using a microphone to reach the back of the auditorium, your listeners may expect a more formal delivery style. Your public-speaking class members would probably find it odd if you spoke to them using a formal oratorical style that resembles the way a politician would have addressed a political rally in 1910.

LISTENERS MAKE EMOTIONAL CONNECTIONS WITH YOU THROUGH DELIVERY

Nonverbal behavior is particularly important in communicating feelings, emotions, attitudes, likes, and dislikes to an audience. One researcher found that we communicate as little as 7 percent of the emotional impact of a message by the words we use.[4] About 38 percent hinges on such qualities of voice as inflection, intensity, or loudness, and 55 percent hinges on our facial expressions. Generalizing from these findings, we may say that we communicate approximately 93 percent of emotional meaning nonverbally. Although some scholars question whether these findings can be applied to all communication settings, the research does suggest that the manner of delivery provides important information about the speaker's feelings and emotions.[5] Audience expectations can help you match the amount of emotional expression you exhibit to your listeners.

Another reason to pay attention to how you communicate emotions when delivering a speech is that emotions are "contagious." *Emotional contagion theory* suggests that people tend to "catch" the emotions of others.[6] If you want your listeners to feel a certain emotion, then it's important for you to express that emotion yourself.

Have you ever noticed that when you watch a movie in a crowded movie theatre where others are laughing, you're more likely to laugh too? TV situation comedy producers use a laugh track or record the laughter of a live audience to enhance the emotional reactions of home viewers; these producers know that emotions are contagious.

Your delivery enhances the overall feelings that listeners have toward you and your speech. One study found that when a speaker's delivery was effective, the audience felt greater pleasure and had a more positive emotional response than when the same speaker had poor delivery.[7] In addition to these stronger emotional responses, listeners seemed to understand speakers better and to believe them more when their delivery was good. Clearly, if you want your audience to respond positively to both you and your message, it pays to polish your delivery.

LISTENERS BELIEVE WHAT THEY SEE

"I'm very glad to speak with you tonight," drones the speaker in a monotone, eyes glued to his notes. His audience probably does not believe him. When our nonverbal delivery contradicts what we say, people generally believe the nonverbal message. In this case, the speaker is communicating that he's *not* glad to be talking to this audience.

We usually believe nonverbal messages because they are more difficult to fake. Although we can monitor certain parts of our nonverbal behavior, it is difficult to control all of it consciously. Research suggests that a person trying to deceive someone may speak with a higher vocal pitch, at a slower rate, and with more pronunciation mistakes than normal.[8] Blushing, sweating, and changed breathing patterns also often belie our stated meaning. As the saying goes, "What you do speaks so loud, I can't hear what you say."

15.b Methods of Delivery

The style of delivery you choose will influence your nonverbal behaviors. There are four basic methods of delivery from which a speaker can choose: manuscript speaking, memorized speaking, impromptu speaking, and extemporaneous speaking. Let's consider each in some detail.

MANUSCRIPT SPEAKING

You have a speech to present and are afraid you will forget what you have prepared to say. So you write your speech and then read it to your audience.

Speech teachers frown on this approach, particularly for public-speaking students. Reading is usually a poor way to deliver a speech. Although it may provide some insurance against forgetting the speech, **manuscript speaking** is rarely done well enough to be interesting. You have probably attended a lecture that was read and wondered, "Why doesn't he just make a copy of the speech for everyone in the audience rather than reading it to us?"

Need for Careful Crafting   However, some speeches should be read. One advantage of reading from a manuscript is that you can choose words very carefully when dealing with a sensitive and critical issue. The president of the United States, for example, often finds it useful to have his remarks carefully scripted. There are times, however, when it is impossible to have a manuscript speech at hand. Minutes following the September 11, 2001, attacks on the World Trade Center and the Pentagon, George W. Bush offered unscripted comments to reporters, in which he promised to hunt down "those folks who committed this act." Three days later, he spoke more eloquently from a manuscript at the Washington National Cathedral, where he said, "We are here in the middle hour of our grief. So many have suffered so great a loss, and today we express our nation's sorrow."[9] His prepared comments were intended to offer comfort during an emotional period.

When possible, during times of crisis, statements to the press by government or business leaders should be carefully crafted rather than tossed off casually. An inaccurate or misspoken statement could have serious consequences.

Delivery Cues   Roger Ailes, a media consultant to Republican presidents and governors, suggests that if you do have to read from a manuscript, to ensure maximum eye contact, you should type your speech in short, easy-to-scan phrases on the upper two-thirds of the paper so that you do not have to look too far down into your text.[10] Make eye contact at the ends of sentences. He also recommends that you should not read a speech too quickly. Finally, use your index finger to keep your place in the manuscript.

The key to giving an effective manuscript speech is to sound as though you were not giving a manuscript speech. Speak with vocal variation—vary the rhythm, inflection, and pace of your delivery. Be familiar enough with your manuscript that you can make as much eye contact with your audience as possible. Use gestures and movement to add interest and emphasis to your message.

MEMORIZED SPEAKING

"All right," you think, "since reading a speech is hard to pull off, I'll write my speech out word for word and then memorize it." You're pretty sure that no one will be able to tell, because you won't be using notes. **Memorized speaking** also has the advantage of allowing you to have maximum eye contact with the audience.

Risks   The inherent differences between speaking and writing are evident in a memorized speech, just as they can be heard in a manuscript speech. Most memorized speeches sound stiff, stilted, and overrehearsed. You also run the risk of forgetting parts of your speech and awkwardly searching for words in front of your audience. And you won't be able to make on-the-spot adaptations to your listeners if your speech is memorized. For these reasons, speech teachers do not encourage their students to memorize speeches for class presentation.

Appropriate Use   If you are accepting an award, introducing a speaker, making announcements, or delivering other brief remarks, however, a memorized delivery style is sometimes acceptable. But, as with manuscript speaking, you must take care to make your presentation sound lively and interesting.

IMPROMPTU SPEAKING

You have undoubtedly already delivered many impromptu presentations. Your response to a question posed by a teacher in class or an unrehearsed rebuttal to a comment made by a colleague during a meeting are examples of impromptu presentations. The impromptu method is often described as "thinking on your feet" or "speaking off the cuff." The advantage of **impromptu speaking** is that you can speak informally, maintaining direct eye contact with the audience. But unless a speaker is extremely talented or has learned and practiced the techniques of impromptu speaking, the speech itself will be unimpressive. An impromptu speech usually lacks logical organization and thorough research.

There are times, of course, when you may be called on to speak without advance warning or to improvise when something goes awry in your efforts to deliver your planned message. This was the case when former President Clinton was delivering his first State of the Union address in 1993 and the teleprompter scrolled the wrong text of his speech for seven minutes. What did he do, as millions of people watched on television? He kept going. Drawing on his years of speaking experience, he continued to speak; no one watching knew about the error until afterward.

Clinton's efforts were somewhat more successful than was the performance given some years earlier by a friend of the authors, a man who is a Fellow at Cambridge University in England. Given the responsibility of conferring degrees on the graduates of his college, he had carefully memorized his Latin text, but found to his horror that his mind went blank when the moment arrived. Sheepishly, he admits, "I got through it by mumbling some bits of Latin I could remember, but I think I said something like 'Blessed be the fruit of thy womb.' "

Essential Preparation   What lesson should you draw from these examples? If you know you will be giving a speech, prepare and rehearse it. Don't just make mental notes or assume that you will find the words when you need them. It was Mark Twain who said, "A good impromptu speech takes about three weeks to prepare."

Reverend Jesse Jackson is known for his skill as an impromptu speaker. It's been reported that he got a D in his preaching class because he refused to write his sermons out word for word as his professor requested. He was able to deliver impromptu orations that skillfully and powerfully moved listeners to respond to his message. Once, knowing he was to speak next, after one of Jackson's charismatically delivered speeches, Martin Luther King Jr. allegedly developed a sudden case of laryngitis.[11] The Reverend Jackson certainly has speaking talent, but he also uses principles and skills that you can use to enhance your impromptu speaking ability.

Guidelines for Impromptu Speaking   When you are called on to deliver an improvised or impromptu speech, the following guidelines can help ease you through it.

- **Consider your audience.** Just as you have learned to do in other speaking situations, when you are called on for impromptu remarks, think first of your audience. Who are the members of your audience? What are their common characteristics and interests? What do they know about your topic? What do they expect you to say? What is the occasion of your speech? A quick mental review of these questions will help ensure that even impromptu remarks are audience-centered.

- **Be brief.** When you are asked to deliver an off-the-cuff speech, your audience knows the circumstances and will not expect or even want a lengthy discourse. One to three minutes is a realistic time frame for most impromptu situations. Some spur-of-the-moment remarks, such as press statements, may be even shorter.

- **Organize!** Even off-the-cuff remarks need not falter or ramble. Effective impromptu speakers still organize their ideas into an introduction, body, and conclusion. Consider organizing your points using a simple organizational strategy such as chronological order or a topical pattern. A variation on the chronological pattern is the past, present, future model of addressing an issue. This pattern is well known to students who compete in impromptu speaking contests. The speaker organizes the impromptu speech by discussing (1) what has happened in the past, (2) what is happening now, and (3) what may happen in the future.

- **Speak honestly, but with reserve, from personal experience and knowledge.** Because there is no opportunity to conduct any kind of research before delivering an impromptu speech, you will have to speak from your own experience and knowledge. Remember, audiences almost always respond favorably to personal illustrations, so use any appropriate and relevant ones that come to mind. Of course, the more knowledge you have about the subject to be discussed, the easier it will be to speak about it off the cuff. But do not make up information or provide facts or figures you're not certain about. An honest "I don't know" or a very brief statement is more appropriate.

- **Be cautious.** No matter how much knowledge you have, if your subject is at all sensitive or your information is classified, be careful when discussing it during your impromptu speech. If asked about a controversial topic, give an honest but noncommittal answer. You can always elaborate later, but you can never take back something rash you have already said. It is better to be cautious than sorry!

QUICK CHECK: *Impromptu Presentations*

- Consider your audience.
- Be brief.
- Organize ideas into an introduction, body, and conclusion.
- Speak honestly, but with reserve, from personal experience and knowledge.
- Be cautious about what you say.

EXTEMPORANEOUS SPEAKING

If you are not reading from a manuscript, reciting from memory, or speaking impromptu, what's left? **Extemporaneous speaking** is the approach most communication teachers recommend for most situations. When delivering a speech extemporaneously, you speak from a written or memorized general outline, but you do not have the exact wording in front of you or in memory. You have rehearsed the speech so that you know key ideas and their organization, but not to the degree that the speech sounds memorized.

An extemporaneous style is conversational; it gives your audience the impression that the speech is being created as they listen to it, and to some extent it is. Audiences prefer to hear something live rather than something canned. Even though you can't tell the difference between a taped or live performance when it is broadcast on TV, you would probably prefer seeing it live. Seeing something happening *now* provides added interest and excitement. An extemporaneous speech sounds live rather than as though it were prepared yesterday or weeks ago. The extemporaneous method reflects the advantages of a well-organized speech delivered in an interesting and vivid manner.

You develop an extemporaneous style by first rehearsing your speech, using many notes or perhaps looking at your preparation outline. As you continue to rehearse, try to rely less on your notes, but don't try to memorize your message word for word. After going over your speech a few times, you will find that you have internalized the overall structure of the speech, although the exact way you express your ideas may vary. You'll rely less on your notes and focus more on adapting your message to your listeners. The final draft of your speaking notes may be an abbreviated outline or a few key words and essential facts or statistics that you want to remember.

QUICK CHECK: *Methods of Delivery*

- Manuscript speaking: Reading your speech from a prepared text
- Memorized speaking: Giving a speech from memory without using notes
- Impromptu speaking: Delivering a speech without preparing in advance
- Extemporaneous speaking: Knowing the major ideas and speaking from a written or memorized general outline but without memorizing the exact wording

15.c   Characteristics of Effective Delivery

You have learned the importance of effective delivery and have identified four methods of delivery. You now know that, for most speaking situations, you should strive for a conversational style. But you still may have a number of specific questions about enhancing the effectiveness of your delivery. Typical concerns include "What do I do with my hands?" "Is it all right to move around while I speak?" "How can I make my voice sound interesting?" Although these concerns may seem overwhelming, presenting a well-prepared and well-rehearsed speech is the best antidote to jitters about delivery. Practice and a focus on communicating your message to your audience are vital for effective communication and great for your confidence.

To help answer specific questions about presenting a speech, we consider seven major categories of nonverbal behavior that affect delivery: eye contact, gestures, movement, posture, facial expression, vocal delivery, and personal appearance.

EYE CONTACT

Of all the delivery features discussed in this chapter, the most important one in a public-speaking situation for North Americans is eye contact. Eye contact with your audience opens communication, makes you more believable, and keeps your audience interested. Each of these functions contributes to the success of your delivery. Eye contact also provides you with feedback about how your speech is coming across.

Making eye contact with your listeners clearly shows that you are ready to talk to them. Most people start a conversation by looking at the person they are going to talk to. The same process occurs in public speaking.

Once you've started talking, continued eye contact lets you know how your audience is responding to your speech. You don't need to look at your listeners continuously. As the need arises, you should certainly look at your notes, but also look at your listeners frequently, just to see what they're doing.

Credibility   Most listeners will think you are capable and trustworthy if you look them in the eye. Several studies document a relationship between eye contact and increased speaker credibility.[12] Speakers with less than 50 percent eye contact are considered unfriendly, uninformed, inexperienced, and even dishonest by their listeners.

Another study showed that those audience members who had more than 50 percent eye contact with their speaker performed better in postspeech tests than did those who had less than 50 percent eye contact.[13] However, not all people from all cultures prefer the same amount of direct eye contact when listening to someone talk. In interpersonal contexts, people from Asian cultures, for example, prefer less direct eye contact when communicating with others than do North Americans.

Priority   Most audiences in the United States prefer that you establish eye contact with them even before you open your speech with your attention-catching introduction. When it's your time to speak, walk to the lectern or to the front of the audience, pause briefly, and look at your audience before you say anything. Eye contact nonverbally sends the message, "I am interested in you; tune me in; I have something I want to share with you." You should have your opening sentence well enough in mind that you can deliver it without looking at your notes or away from your listeners.

Inclusion   Establish eye contact with the entire audience, not just with those in the front row or only one or two people. Look to the back as well as the front and from one side of your audience to the other, selecting an individual to focus on and then moving on to someone else. You need not rhythmically move your head back and forth like a lighthouse beacon; it's best not to establish a predictable pattern for your eye contact. Look at individuals, establishing person-to-person contact with them—not so long that it will make a listener feel uncomfortable, but long enough to establish the feeling that you are talking directly to that individual. Don't look over your listeners' heads; establish eye-to-eye contact.

QUICK CHECK: *Benefits of Eye Contact*

- Lets your audience know you are interested in them and that you want to talk to them
- Permits you to monitor audience reaction to your message in order to determine whether your audience is responding to you
- Establishes your credibility
- Helps your audience maintain interest and remember more of your message

GESTURES

The next time you have a conversation with someone, notice how both of you use your hands and bodies to communicate. Important points are emphasized with gestures. You also gesture to indicate places, to enumerate items, and to describe objects. Gestures have the same functions for public speakers. Yet many people who gesture easily and appropriately in the course of everyday conversations aren't sure what to do with their hands when they find themselves in front of an audience.

Cultural Expectations　There is evidence that gestures vary from culture to culture. When he was mayor of New York City during the 1930s and 1940s, Fiorello La Guardia, fluent in Yiddish and Italian as well as in English, would speak the language appropriate for each audience. One researcher studied old newsreels of the mayor and discovered that with the sound turned off, viewers could still identify the language the mayor was speaking. How? When speaking English, he used minimal gestures. When speaking Italian, he used broad, sweeping gestures. And when speaking Yiddish, he used short and choppy hand movements.

Cultural expectations can help you make decisions about your approach to using gestures. Listeners from Japan and China, for example, prefer a quieter, less flamboyant use of gestures. One Web site that offers tips for people conducting business in India suggests "When you wish to point, use your chin or your full hand, but never just a single finger, as this gesture is used only with inferiors. The chin is not used to signal to superiors. The best way to point is with the full hand."[14] When one of your authors spoke in England, several listeners noted the use of "typical American gestures and movement." British listeners seem to prefer that the speaker stay behind a lectern and use relatively few gestures. Other Europeans agree they can spot an American speaker because Americans typically are more animated in their use of gestures, movement, and facial expressions than are European speakers.

Inappropriate Gestures　Public-speaking teachers often observe several unusual, inappropriate, and unnatural gestures among their students. One common problem is keeping your hands behind your back in a "parade rest" pose. We are not suggesting that you never put your hands behind your back, only that standing at parade rest during an entire speech looks awkward and unnatural and may distract your audience.

Another common position is standing with one hand on the hip in a "broken wing" pose. Worse than the "broken wing" is both hands resting on the hips in a "double broken wing." The speaker looks as though he or she might burst into a rendition of "I'm a Little Teapot." Again, we are not suggesting that you should never place your hands on your hips, only that to hold that one pose throughout a speech looks unnatural and will keep you from using other gestures.

Few poses are more awkward-looking than when a speaker clutches one arm, as if grazed by a bullet. The audience half expects the speaker to call out reassuringly, "Don't worry, Ma; it's only a flesh wound." Similarly, keeping your hands in your pockets can make you look as if you were afraid to let go of your change or your keys.

Some students clasp their hands and let them drop in front of them in a distracting "fig leaf clutch." Gestures can distract your audience in various other ways as well.

Grasping the lectern until your knuckles turn white or just letting your hands flop around without purpose or control does little to help you communicate your message.

Functions of Gestures If you don't know what to do with your hands, think about the message you want to communicate. As in ordinary conversation, your hands should simply help emphasize or reinforce your verbal message. Specifically, your gestures can lend strength to or detract from what you have to say by (1) repeating, (2) contradicting, (3) substituting, (4) complementing, (5) emphasizing, and (6) regulating.

- **Repeating.** Gestures can help you repeat your verbal message. For example, you can say, "I have three major points to talk about today," while holding up three fingers. Or you can describe an object as twelve inches long while holding your hands about a foot apart. Repeating what you say through nonverbal means can reinforce your message.

- **Contradicting.** Because your audience will believe what you communicate nonverbally sooner than what you communicate verbally, monitor your gestures to make sure that you are not contradicting what you say. It is difficult to convey an image of control and confidence while using flailing gestures and awkward poses. You don't want to display behavior that will conflict with your intended image or message, nor do you want to appear stiff and self-conscious. So the crucial thing to keep in mind while monitoring your own behavior is to *stay relaxed.*

- **Substituting.** Not only can your behavior reinforce or contradict what you say, but your gestures can also substitute for your message. Without uttering a word, you can hold up the palm of your hand to calm a noisy crowd. Flashing two fingers to form a V for "victory" or raising a clenched fist are other common examples of how gestures can substitute for a verbal message.

- **Complementing.** Gestures can also add further meaning to your verbal message. A politician who declines to comment on a reporter's question while holding up her hands to augment her verbal refusal is relying on the gesture to complement or provide further meaning to her verbal message.

- **Emphasizing.** You can give emphasis to what you say by using an appropriate gesture. A shaking fist or a slicing gesture with one or both hands helps emphasize a message. So does pounding your fist into the palm of your hand. Other gestures can be less dramatic but still lend emphasis to what you say. You should try to allow your gestures to arise from the content of your speech and your emotions.

- **Regulating.** Gestures can also regulate the exchange between you and your audience. If you want the audience to respond to a question, you can extend both palms to invite a response. During a question-and-answer session, your gestures can signal when you want to talk and when you want to invite others to do so.

Using Gestures Effectively Turn-of-the-century elocutionists taught their students how to gesture to communicate specific emotions or messages. Today, teachers of speech have a different approach. Rather than prescribe gestures for specific situations, they feel it is more useful to offer suitable criteria (standards) by which to judge effective gestures, regardless of what is being said. Here are some guidelines to consider when working on your delivery.

- **Stay natural.** Gestures should be *relaxed,* not tense or rigid. Your gestures should flow from your message. Avoid sawing or slashing through the air with your hands unless you are trying to emphasize a particularly dramatic point. The pounding fist or forefinger raised in hectoring style will not necessarily enhance the quality of your performance.

- **Be definite.** Gestures should appear *definite* rather than as accidental brief jerks of your hands or arms. If you want to gesture, go ahead and gesture. Avoid minor hand movements that will be masked by the lectern.

- **Use gestures that are consistent with your message.** Gestures should be *appropriate* for the verbal content of your speech. If you are excited, gesture more vigorously. But remember that prerehearsed gestures that do not arise naturally from what you are trying to say are likely to appear awkward and stilted.

- **Vary your gestures.** Strive for *variety* and versatility in your use of gesture. Try not to use just one hand or one all-purpose gesture. Gestures can be used for a variety of purposes, such as enumerating, pointing, describing, and symbolizing an idea or concept (for example, clasping your hands together to suggest agreement or a coming together).

- **Don't overdo it.** Gestures should be *unobtrusive;* your audience should focus not on the beauty or appropriateness of your gestures but on your message. Your purpose is to communicate a message to your audience, not to perform for your listeners to the extent that your delivery receives more attention than your message.

- **Coordinate gestures with what you say.** Gestures should be *well timed* to coincide with your verbal message. When you announce that you have three major points, your gesture of enumeration should occur simultaneously with your utterance of the word *three*. It would be poor timing to announce that you have three points, pause for a second or two, and then hold up three fingers.

QUICK CHECK: *Effective Gestures*

The most effective gestures are

- Natural and relaxed
- Definite
- Consistent with your message
- Varied
- Unobtrusive
- Coordinated with what you say
- Appropriate to your audience and situation

- **Make your gestures appropriate to your audience and situation.** Gestures must be adapted to the audience. In more formal speaking situations, particularly when speaking to a large audience, bolder, more sweeping, and more dramatic gestures are appropriate. A small audience in a less formal setting calls for less formal gestures.

In summary, keep one important principle in mind: Use gestures that work best for you. Don't try to be someone you are not. Jesse Jackson's style may work for him, but you are not Jesse Jackson. Your gestures should fit your personality. It may be better to use no gestures—to just put your hands comfortably at your side—than to use awkward, distracting gestures or to try to counterfeit someone else's gestures. Your nonverbal delivery should flow from *your* message.

MOVEMENT

Should you walk around during your speech, or should you stay in one place? If there is a lectern, should you stand behind it, or would it be acceptable to stand in front of it or to the side? Is it all right to sit down while you speak? Can you move among the audience, as Oprah Winfrey does on her TV show? You may well find yourself pondering one or more of these questions while preparing for your speeches. The following discussion may help you answer them.

Purpose, Not Distraction   You may want to move purposefully about while delivering your speech, but take care that your movement does not detract from your message. If the audience focuses on your movement rather than on what you are saying, it is better to stand still. An absence of movement is better than distracting movement. In short, your movement should be consistent with the verbal content of your message. It should make sense rather than appear as aimless wandering.

Physical Barriers   Robert Frost said, "Good fences make good neighbors." Professional speech coach Brent Filson says, however, "For my money, good fences make lousy speeches."[15] He recommends, as do we, that you eliminate physical barriers between you and the audience. For more formal occasions you will be expected to stand behind a lectern to deliver your message. But even on those occasions, it can be appropriate to move from behind the lectern to make a point, signal a change in mood, or move to another idea.

Immediacy   Your movement and other nonverbal cues can help you establish immediacy with your listeners. According to psychologist Albert Mehrabian, **immediacy** is "the degree of physical or psychological closeness between people."[16] **Immediacy behaviors** are those that enhance the quality of the relationship between a speaker and an audience. Moving closer to listeners is one primary way of communicating both physical and psychological closeness between you. There are some other immediacy behaviors as well:

- Using appropriate levels of eye contact
- Smiling while talking, and more specifically, smiling at individual audience members

- Using appropriate gestures
- Having an appropriately relaxed posture
- Moving purposefully

Over three decades of research on the immediacy cues used by teachers in North American classrooms clearly suggests that teachers who are more immediate enhance student learning, increase student motivation to learn, and have more favorable teacher evaluations.[17] It seems logical to suggest that public speakers who increase immediacy will have similar positive results. One cautionary note: Listeners—not the speaker—determine the appropriate amount of immediacy. Be vigilantly audience-centered as you seek the appropriate level of immediacy between you and your listeners.

Transitions   You may also signal the beginning of a new idea or major point in your speech with movement. As you make a transition statement or change from a serious subject to a more humorous one, movement can be a good way to signal that your approach to the speaking situation is changing.

Your use of movement during your speech should make sense to your listeners. Avoid random pacing and overly dramatic gestures. Temper our advice about proximity and other delivery variables by adapting to the cultural expectations of your audience.

POSTURE

Although there have been few formal studies of posture in relation to public speaking, there is evidence that the way you carry your body communicates significant information. One study even suggests that your stance can reflect on your credibility as a speaker.[18] Slouching over the lectern, for example, does not project an image of vitality and interest in your audience. Whereas your face and voice play the major role in communicating a specific emotion, your posture communicates the intensity of that emotion. If you are happy, your face and voice reflect your happiness; your posture communicates the intensity of your joy.[19]

Since the days of the elocutionists, few speech teachers or public-speaking texts have advocated specific postures for public speakers. Today, we believe that the specific stance you adopt should come about naturally, as a result of what you have to say, the environment, and the formality or informality of the occasion. For example, during a very informal presentation, it may be perfectly appropriate as well as comfortable and natural to sit on the edge of a desk. Most speech teachers, however, do not encourage students to sit while delivering classroom speeches. In general, avoid slouched shoulders, shifting from foot to foot, or drooping your head. Your posture should not call attention to itself. Instead, it should reflect your interest in the speaking event and your attention to the task at hand.

FACIAL EXPRESSION

Media experts today doubt that Abraham Lincoln would have survived as a politician in our appearance-conscious age of telegenic politicians. His facial expression, according to those who saw him, seemed wooden and unvaried.

Your face plays a key role in expressing your thoughts, and especially your emotions and attitudes.[20] Your audience sees your face before they hear what you are going to say. Thus, you have an opportunity to set the emotional tone for your message before you start speaking. We are not advocating that you adopt a phony smile that looks insincere and plastered on your face, but a pleasant facial expression helps establish a positive emotional climate. Your facial expression should naturally vary to be consistent with your message. Present somber news with a more serious expression. To communicate interest in your listeners, keep your expression alert and friendly.

Although humans are technically capable of producing thousands of different facial expressions, we most often express only six primary emotions: happiness, anger, surprise, sadness, disgust, and fear. But when we speak to others, our faces are a blend of expressions rather than communicators of a single emotion. According to cross-cultural studies by social psychologist Paul Ekman, the facial expressions of these emotions are virtually universal, so even a culturally diverse audience will be able to read your emotional expressions clearly.[21] When you rehearse your speech, consider standing in front of a mirror or, better yet, videotape yourself practicing your speech. Note whether you are allowing your face to help communicate the emotional tone of your thoughts.

VOCAL DELIVERY

Have you ever listened to a radio announcer and imagined what he or she looked like, only later to see a picture and have your image of the announcer drastically altered? Vocal clues play an important part in creating the impression we have of a speaker. Based on vocal clues alone, you make inferences about a person's age, status, occupation, ethnic origin, income, and a variety of other matters. As a public speaker, your voice is one of your most important delivery tools in conveying your ideas to your audience. Your credibility as a speaker and your ability to communicate your ideas clearly to your listeners will in large part depend on your vocal delivery.

Vocal delivery includes pitch, speaking rate, volume, pronunciation, articulation, pauses, and general variation of the voice. A speaker has at least two key vocal obligations to an audience: Speak to be understood, and speak with vocal variety to maintain interest.

Speaking to Be Understood To be understood, you need to consider four aspects of vocal delivery: volume, articulation, dialect, and pronunciation.

VOLUME. The fundamental purpose of your vocal delivery is to speak loudly enough that your audience can hear you. The **volume** of your speech is determined by the amount of air you project through your larynx, or voice box. More air equals more volume of sound. Your diaphragm, a muscle in your upper abdomen, helps control sound volume by increasing air flow from your lungs through your voice box.

If you put your hands on your diaphragm and say, "Ho-ho-ho," you will feel your abdominal muscles contracting and the air being forced out of your lungs. Breathing from your diaphragm—that is, consciously expanding and contracting your abdomen as you breathe in and out, rather than merely moving your chest as air flows into your lungs—can increase the volume of sound as well as enhance the quality of your voice.

ARTICULATION. The process of producing speech sounds clearly and distinctly is **articulation**. In addition to speaking loudly enough, say your words so that your audience can understand them. Without distinct enunciation, or articulation of the sounds that make up words, your listeners may not understand you or may fault you for simply not knowing how to speak clearly and fluently.

Here are some commonly misarticulated words:[22]

Dint	instead of	*didn't*
Lemme	instead of	*let me*
Mornin	instead of	*morning*
Seeya	instead of	*see you*
Soun	instead of	*sound*
Wanna	instead of	*want to*
Wep	instead of	*wept*
Whadayado	instead of	*what do you do*

Many errors in articulation result from simple laziness. It takes effort to articulate speech sounds clearly. Sometimes we are in a hurry to express our ideas, but more often we simply get into the habit of mumbling, slurring, and abbreviating. Such speech flaws may not keep your audience from understanding you, but poor enunciation does reflect on your credibility as a speaker.

The best way to improve your articulation of sounds is first to identify words or phrases that you have a tendency to slur or chop. Once you have identified them, practice saying the words correctly. Make sure you can hear the difference between the improper and proper pronunciation. A speech teacher can help you check your articulation.

DIALECT. Most newscasters in North America use what is called standard American pronunciation and do not typically have a strong dialect. A **dialect** is a consistent style of pronouncing words that is common to an ethnic group or a geographic region such as the South, New England, or the upper Midwest. In the southern part of the United States, people prolong some vowel sounds when they speak. And in the northern Midwest, the word *about* sometimes sounds a bit like "aboat."

It took a bit of adjustment for many U.S. citizens to get used to President John Kennedy's Bostonian pronunciation of Cuba as "Cuber" and Harvard as "Haaavahd." Lyndon Johnson's Texas twang was a sharp contrast to Kennedy's New England sound. And George W. Bush's Texas lilt also contrasts with the slight southern drawl of his predecessor, Bill Clinton.

Are dialects detrimental to effective communication with an audience? Although a speaker's dialect may pigeonhole that person as being from a certain part of the country, it won't necessarily affect the audience's comprehension of the information unless the dialect is so pronounced that the listeners can't understand the speaker's words. Research does suggest, however, that listeners tend to prefer a dialect similar to their own pronunciation style.[23] Many well-known and effective speakers have a distinct dialect; Jesse Jackson, Bill Clinton, Jesse Helms, Billy Graham, and Garrison Keillor are all known not only for their rhetorical skill but also for having some degree of a regional dialect. We don't recommend that you eliminate a mild dialect; but if your word pronunciation is significantly distracting to your listeners, you might consider modifying your dialect (although radically changing a dialect is difficult and time consuming).

Dialect includes four elements: intonation pattern, vowel production, consonant production, and speaking rate.

- **Intonation pattern.** A typical North American intonation pattern is predominantly a rising and falling pattern. The pattern looks something like this:

  "Good ^{morn} ing. How ^{are} you?"

  Intonation patterns of other languages, such as Hindi, may remain on almost exactly the same pitch level; some native North American listeners find the monotone pitch distracting.

- **Vowel production.** A second element in any dialect is the way vowel sounds are produced. Many people who speak English as a second language often clip, or shorten, the vowel sounds, which can make comprehension more challenging. Stretching or elongating vowels within words can be a useful skill for such speakers to develop. If this is a vocal skill you need to cultivate, consider taping your speech and then comparing it with the standard American pronunciation you hear on TV or radio.

- **Consonant production.** Consonant production, the third element in vocal dialects, varies depending on which language you are speaking. It is sometimes difficult to produce clear consonants that are not overdone. Consonants that are so soft as to be almost unheard may produce a long blur of unintelligible sound rather than a crisply articulated sound.

- **Speaking rate.** A fourth and final element in vocal dialect is speaking rate. People whose first language is not English sometimes speak at too fast a rate in the hope that this will create the impression of being very familiar with English. Slowing the rate just a bit often enhances comprehension for native English speakers listening to someone less familiar with English pronunciation. A rate that is too fast also contributes to problems with clipped vowels, soft or absent consonants, and an intonation pattern that is on one pitch level rather than comfortably varied.

PRONUNCIATION. Whereas articulation relates to the clarity of sounds, **pronunciation** concerns the degree to which the sounds conform to those assigned to words in standard English. Mispronouncing words can detract from a speaker's credibility.[24] Often, however, we are not aware that we are not using standard pronunciation unless someone points it out.

Some speakers reverse speech sounds, saying "aks" instead of "ask," for example. Some allow an *r* sound to intrude into some words, saying "warsh" instead of "wash," or leave out sounds in the middle of a word, as in "ackchally" instead of "actually" or "Febuary" instead of "February." Some speakers also accent syllables in nonstandard ways; they say *po'lice* instead of *po lice'* or *um'brella* rather than *um brel'la*.

If English is not your native language, you may have to spend extra time working on your pronunciation and articulation. Here are two useful tips to help you. First, make an effort to prolong your vowel sounds. Speeeeak tooooo prooooooloooong eeeeeeach vooooooowel sooooooound yooooooooou maaaaaaaake. Second, to reduce choppy-sounding word pronunciation, blend the end of one word into the beginning of the next. Make your speech flow from one word to the next, instead of separating it into individual chunks of sound.[25]

Speaking with Variety   To speak with variety is to vary your pitch, rate, and pauses. It is primarily through the quality of our voices, as well as our facial expressions, that we communicate whether we are happy, sad, bored, or excited. If your vocal clues suggest that you are bored with your topic, your audience will probably be bored also.

Appropriate variation in vocal pitch and rate as well as appropriate use of pauses can add zest to your speech and help maintain audience attention.

PITCH.   Vocal **pitch** is how high or low your voice sounds. You can sing because you can change the pitch of your voice to produce a melody. Lack of variation in pitch has been consistently identified as one of the most distracting characteristics of ineffective speakers. A monotone is boring.

Everyone has a habitual pitch. This is the range of your voice during normal conversation. Some people have a habitually high pitch, whereas others have a low pitch. The pitch of your voice is determined by how fast the folds in your vocal cords vibrate. The faster the vibration, the higher the pitch. Male vocal folds vibrate approximately 100 to 150 times each second; female vocal folds vibrate about 200 times per second, thus giving women a higher vocal pitch.

Your voice has **inflection** when you raise or lower the pitch as you pronounce words or sounds. Your inflection helps determine the meaning of your utterances. A surprised "ah!" sounds different from a disappointed "ah" or a questioning "ah?" Your vocal inflection is thus an important indicator of your emotions and gives clues as to how to interpret your speech.

In some cultures, vocal inflection plays a major role in helping people interpret the meaning of words. For example, Thai, Vietnamese, and Mandarin Chinese languages purposely use such inflections as monotone, low, falling, high, and rising.[26] If you are a native speaker of a language in which pitch influences meaning, be mindful that listeners do not expect this in many Western languages, although all languages rely on inflection to provide nuances of meaning.

The best public speakers vary their inflection considerably. We're not suggesting that you need to imitate a top-forty radio disk jockey when you speak. But variation in your vocal inflection and overall pitch helps you communicate the subtlety of your ideas.

Record your speech as you rehearse, and evaluate your use of pitch and inflection critically. If you are not satisfied with your inflection, consider practicing your speech with exaggerated variations in vocal pitch. Although you would not deliver your speech this way, it may help you explore the expressive options available to you.

RATE.   How fast do you talk? Most speakers average between 120 and 180 words per minute. There is no "best" speaking rate. The speaking skill of great speakers does not depend on a standard rate of speech. Daniel Webster purportedly spoke at about 90 words per minute, Franklin Roosevelt at 110, President Kennedy at a quick-paced 180. Martin Luther King Jr. started his "I Have a Dream" speech at 92 words a minute and was speaking at 145 words per minute during his conclusion.[27] The best rate depends on two factors: your speaking style and the content of your message.

A common fault of many beginning speakers is to deliver a speech too quickly. One symptom of speech anxiety is that you tend to rush through your speech to get it over with. Feedback from others can help you determine whether your rate is too rapid. Tape-recording your message and listening critically to your speaking rate can help you assess whether you are speaking at the proper speed.

Fewer speakers have the problem of speaking too slowly, but a turtle-paced speech will almost certainly make it more difficult for your audience to maintain interest. Remember, your listeners can grasp information much faster than you can speak it.

You need not deliver your entire speech at the same pace. It is normal to speak more rapidly when talking about something that excites you. You slow your speaking rate to emphasize key points or ideas. Speaking rate is another tool you can use to add variety and interest to your vocal delivery. The pace of your delivery, however, should make sense in terms of the ideas you are sharing with your listeners.

PAUSES.   It was Mark Twain who said, "The right word may be effective, but no word was ever as effective as a rightly timed pause." An appropriate pause can often do more to accent your message than any other vocal characteristic. President Kennedy's famous line, "Ask not what your country can do for you; ask what you can do for your country," was effective not only because of its language but also because it was delivered with a pause dividing the two thoughts. Try delivering that line without the pause; it just doesn't have the same power without it.

Effective use of pauses, also known as *effective timing,* can greatly enhance the impact of your message. Whether you are trying to tell a joke, a serious tale, or a dramatic story, your use of a pause can determine the effectiveness of your anecdote. Jay Leno, David Letterman, and Ellen Degeneres are masters at timing a punch line. Radio commentator Paul Harvey is known for his flair for vocal delivery. His dramatic pauses serve as meaningful punctuation in his talks.

Beware, however, of the vocalized pause. Many beginning public speakers are uncomfortable with silence, and so, rather than pausing where it seems natural and normal, they vocalize sounds such as "umm," "er," "you know," and "ah." We think you will agree that "Ask not, ah, what your, er, country can do, ah, for you; ask, you know, what you, umm, can do, er, for your, uh, country" just doesn't have the same impact as the unadorned original statement.

One research study counted how frequently certain people use "uhs."[28] Science professors in this study said "uh" about 1.4 times a minute; humanities professors timed in at 4.8 times a minute—almost 3.5 times more. Another psychologist counted the "ums" per minute of well-known speakers. *Wheel of Fortune* host Pat Sajak won the count with almost 10 "ums" per minute; David Letterman was a close second with 8.1. Former President Bill Clinton had only .79 vocalized pause per minute. Former Vice President Dan Quayle had only .1.

SILENCE. Silence can be an effective tool in emphasizing a particular word or sentence. A well-timed pause coupled with eye contact can powerfully accent your thought. Asking a rhetorical question of your audience, such as "How many of you would like to improve your communication skills?," will be more effective if you pause after asking the question rather than rushing into the next thought. Silence is a way of saying to your audience, "Think about this for a moment." Pianist Arthur Schnabel said this about silence and music: "The notes I handle not better than many pianists. But the pauses between the notes, ah, that is where the art resides.[29] In speech, too, an effective use of a pause can add emphasis and interest.

Using a Microphone   "Testing. Testing. One . . . two . . . three. Is this on?" These are not effective, attention-catching opening remarks. Yet countless public speakers have found themselves trying to begin their speech, only to be upstaged by an uncooperative public address system. No matter how polished your gestures or well-intoned your vocal cues, if you are inaudible or use a microphone awkwardly, your speech will not have the desired effect. There are three kinds of microphones, only one of which demands much technique.

LAVALIERE MICROPHONE.   The **lavaliere microphone** is the clip-on type often used by newscasters and interviewees. Worn on the front of a shirt or dress, it requires no particular care other than not thumping it or accidentally knocking it off.

BOOM MICROPHONE.   The **boom microphone** is used by makers of movies and TV shows. It hangs over the heads of the speakers and is remote-controlled, so the speaker need not be particularly concerned with it.

STATIONARY MICROPHONE.   The third kind of microphone, and the most common, is the **stationary microphone**. This is the type that is most often attached to a lectern, sitting on a desk, or standing on the floor. Generally, the stationary microphones used today are multidirectional. You do not have to remain frozen in front of a stationary mike while delivering your speech. However, you do need to take some other precautions when using one.

- First, if you have a fully stationary microphone, rather than one that converts to a hand mike, you will have to remain behind the microphone, with your mouth about the same distance from the mike at all times to avoid distracting fluctuations in the volume of sound. You can turn your head from side to side and use gestures, but you will have to limit other movements.

- Second, microphones amplify sloppy habits of pronunciation and enunciation. Therefore, you need to speak clearly and crisply when using a mike. Be especially careful when articulating such "explosive" sounding consonants as *B* and *P*; they can be overamplified by the microphone and produce a slight popping sound. Similarly, a microphone can intensify the sibilance of the *S* sound at the beginning or ending of words (such as in *hiss, sometime,* or *specials*). You may have to articulate these sounds with slightly less intensity to avoid creating overamplified, distracting noises.

- Third, if you must test a microphone, count or ask the audience whether they can hear you. Blowing on a microphone produces an irritating noise! Do not tap, pound, or shuffle anything near the microphone. These noises, too, will be heard by the audience loudly and clearly. If you are using note cards, quietly slide them aside as you progress through your speech. Notes on paper are more difficult to handle quietly, but do so with as little shuffling as you can manage.

- Finally, when you are delivering your speech, speak directly into the microphone, making sure that your words are appropriately amplified. Some speakers lower their volume and become inaudible when they have a microphone in front of them.

Under ideal circumstances, you will be able to practice with the type of microphone you will use before you speak. If you have the chance, figure out where to stand for the best sound quality and how sensitive the mike is to extraneous noise. Practice will accustom you to any voice distortion or echo that might occur so that these sound qualities do not surprise you during your speech.

QUICK CHECK: *Characteristics of Good Vocal Delivery*

Good Speakers	Poor Speakers
Speak with adequate volume	Speak too softly to be heard
Articulate speech sounds clearly and distinctly	Slur speech sounds
Pronounce words accurately	Mispronounce words
Have varied pitch	Have a monotonous pitch
Vary their speaking rate	Consistently speak too fast or too slowly
Pause to emphasize ideas	Rarely pause or pause too long

PERSONAL APPEARANCE

Most people have certain expectations about the way a speaker should look. One of your audience analysis tasks is to identify what those audience expectations are. This can be trickier than it might at first seem. John T. Molloy has written two books, *Dress for Success* and *Dress for Success for Women,* in an effort to identify what the well-dressed businessperson should wear. But as some of Molloy's research points out, appropriate wardrobe varies, depending on climate, custom, culture, and audience expectations. It may be improper to wear blue jeans to a business meeting, but it would be just as inappropriate to wear a business suit to a rodeo or a grade school picnic.

There is considerable evidence that your personal appearance affects how your audience will respond to you and your message, particularly during the opening moments of your presentation. If you violate their expectations about appearance, you will be less successful in achieving your purpose.

Styles and audience expectations change and are sometimes unpredictable. Therefore, a general rule of thumb to follow is this: When in doubt about what to wear, select something conservative. Also, take your cue from your audience. You need not always mirror their appearance, but if you know that the males in your audience wear suits and ties and the females wear dresses, you would be wise to avoid dressing more casually.

15.d   Audience Diversity and Delivery

Most of the suggestions we have offered in this chapter assume that your listeners will be expecting a typical North American approach to delivery. However, these assumptions are based on research responses from U.S. college students, who are mostly white and in their late teens or early twenties, so our suggestions are not applicable to every audience. As we have stressed throughout the book, you need to adapt your presentation to the expectations of your listeners, especially those from different cultural backgrounds. Consider the following suggestions to help you develop strategies for adapting both your verbal and your nonverbal messages for a culturally diverse audience.

Avoid an Ethnocentric Mindset   As you learned previously, *ethnocentrism* is the assumption that your own cultural approaches are superior to those of other cultures. When considering how to adapt your delivery style to your audience, try to view different approaches and preferences not as right or wrong but merely as different from your own.

Consider Using a Less Dramatic Style for Predominantly High-Context Listeners   A high-context culture places considerable emphasis on unspoken messages. Therefore, for a high-context audience, you need not be overly expressive. For example, for many Japanese people, a delivery style that included exuberant gestures, overly dramatic facial expressions, and frequent movements might seem overdone. A more subtle, less demonstrative approach would create less "noise" and be more effective.

Consult with Other Speakers Who Have Presented to Your Audience   Talk with people you may know who are familiar with the cultural expectations of the audience you will address. Ask specific questions. For example, when speaking in Poland, one of the authors expected the speech to start promptly at 11 a.m., as announced in the program and on posters. By 11:10 it was clear the speech would not begin on time. In Poland, it turns out, all students know about the "academic quarter." This means that most lectures and speeches begin at least 15 minutes, or a quarter hour, after the announced starting time. If the author had asked another professor about the audience's expectations, he would have known this custom in advance. As you observe or talk with speakers who have addressed your target audience, ask the following questions:

* What are audience expectations about where I should stand while speaking?
* Do listeners like direct eye contact?
* When will the audience expect me to start and end my talk?
* Will listeners find movement and gestures distracting or welcome?

Monitor Your Level of Immediacy with Your Audience   Speaker immediacy involves how close you are to your listeners, the amount of eye contact you display, and whether you speak from behind or in front of a lectern. North Americans seem to prefer immediacy behaviors from teachers. Some cultures may expect less immediacy; the key is not to violate what listeners expect.[30] For example, we've been told that Japanese audiences don't expect speakers to move from behind a lectern and stand very close to listeners. Even in small seminars, Japanese speakers and teachers typically stay behind the lectern.

Monitor Your Expression of Emotion   Not all cultures interpret and express emotions the same way. People from the Middle East and the Mediterranean are typically more expressive and animated in their conversation than are Europeans.[31] People from a high-context culture—a culture in which nonverbal messages are exceptionally important (such as Japanese or Chinese culture)—place greater emphasis on your delivery of a message than do people from a low-context culture (such as North Americans).[32]

Remember, however, that even though you may be speaking to an audience from a low-context culture—a culture that places a high value on verbal messages—you do not have license to ignore how you deliver a message. Delivery is always important. But audience members from a high-context culture will rely heavily on your unspoken message to help them interpret what you are saying.

Know the Code   Communication occurs when both speaker and listener share the same code system—both verbal and nonverbal. One of the authors of this book embarrassed himself with a Caribbean audience because he used a circled thumb and finger gesture to signal "okay" to compliment a student. Later he discovered that this was an obscene gesture—like extending a middle finger to a North American audience. Even subtle nonverbal messages communicate feelings, attitudes, and cues about the nature of the relationship between you and your audience, so it is important to avoid gestures or expressions that would offend your listeners.

Although we cannot provide a comprehensive description of each cultural expectation you may face in every educational and professional setting, we can remind you to keep cultural expectations in mind when you rehearse and deliver a speech. We are not suggesting that you totally abandon your own cultural expectations about speech delivery. Rather, we urge you to become sensitive and responsive to cultural differences. There is no universal dictionary of nonverbal meaning, so spend some time asking people who are from the same culture as your prospective audience about what gestures and expressions your audience will appreciate.

15.e   Rehearsing Your Speech: Some Final Tips

Just knowing some of the characteristics of effective speech delivery will not make you a better speaker unless you can put these principles into practice. Effective public speaking is a skill that takes practice. Practicing takes the form of rehearsing. As indicated in

HOW TO: *Make the Most of Your Rehearsal Time*

● Finish drafting your speech outline at least two days before your speech performance. The more time you have to work on putting it all together, the better.

● Before you prepare the speaking notes to use in front of your audience, rehearse your speech aloud to help determine where you will need notes to prompt yourself.

● Revise your speech as necessary to keep it within the time limits set by your instructor or whoever invited you to speak.

● Prepare your speaking notes. Use whatever system works best for you. Some speakers use pictorial symbols to remind themselves of a story or an idea. Others use complete sentences or just words or phrases in an outline pattern to prompt them. Most teachers advocate using note cards for speaking notes.

● Rehearse your speech standing up. This will help you get a feel for your use of gestures as well as your vocal delivery. Do not try to memorize your speech or choreograph specific gestures. As you rehearse, you may want to modify your speaking notes to reflect appropriate changes.

● If you can, present your speech to someone else so you can practice establishing eye contact. Seek feedback from your captive audience about both your delivery and your speech content.

● If possible, tape-record or videotape your speech during the rehearsal stage so that you can observe your vocal and physical mannerisms and make necessary changes. If you don't have a video camera, you may find it useful to practice before a mirror so you can observe your body language—it's low-tech, but it still works.

● Rehearse using all your presentation aids. Don't wait until the last minute to plan, prepare, and rehearse with flipcharts, slides, overhead transparencies, or other aids that you will need to manipulate as you speak.

● Your final rehearsals should re-create, as much as possible, the speaking situation you will face. If you will be speaking in a large classroom, find a large classroom in which to rehearse your speech. If your audience will be seated informally in a semicircle, then this should be the context in which you rehearse your speech. The more realistic the rehearsal, the more confidence you will gain.

● Practice good delivery skills while rehearsing. Remember this maxim: Practice *makes* perfect if practice *is* perfect.

Figure 15.1, rehearsing your speech helps you prepare to deliver your speech to an audience. The suggestions above can help you make the most of your rehearsal time.

Do you want to make a good grade on your next speech? Research suggests that one of the best predictors of the effectiveness of a speech is the amount of time you spend preparing and rehearsing it; instructors gave higher grades to students who spent more time rehearsing their speeches and gave lower grades to students who spent less time preparing and rehearsing.[33]

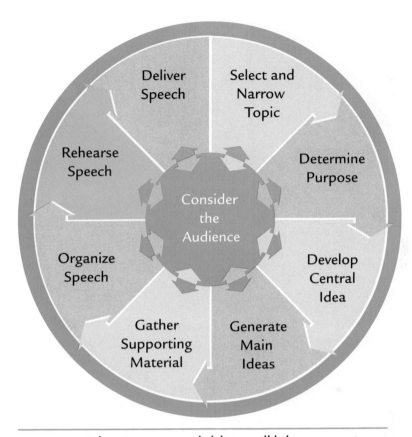

FIGURE 15.1 **Rehearsing your speech delivery will help you present your speech with confidence.**

15.f Delivering Your Speech

You've worked hard on your speech, and you are ready. Using information about your audience as an anchor, you have developed a speech with an interesting topic and a fine-tuned purpose. Your central idea is clearly identified. You have gathered interesting and relevant supporting material (examples, illustrations, statistics) and organized it well. Your speech has an appropriate introduction, a logically arranged body, and a clear conclusion that nicely summarizes your key theme. You have rehearsed your speech several times; it is not memorized, but you are comfortable with the way you express the major ideas. Your last task is calmly and confidently to communicate with your audience. You are ready to deliver your speech.

As the time for presenting your speech to your audience approaches, consider the following suggestions to help you prepare for a successful performance (see Figure 15.2).

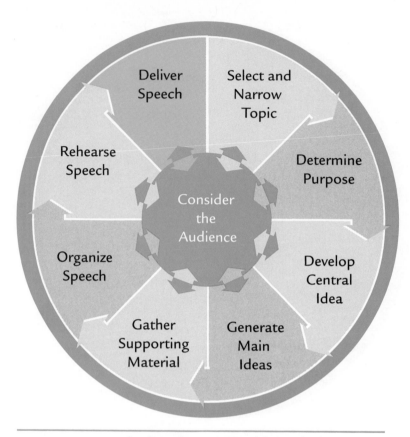

FIGURE 15.2 **You need to be audience-centered during the final step of the speechmaking process—delivering the speech.**

- Get plenty of rest before your speech. Last-minute, late-night final preparations can take the edge off your performance. Many professional public speakers also advocate that you watch what you eat before you speak; a heavy meal or too much caffeine can have a negative effect on your performance.

- Review the suggestions in Chapter 2 for becoming a confident speaker. It is normal to have prespeech jitters. But if you have developed a well-organized, audience-centered message on a topic of genuine interest to you, you're doing all the right things to make your speech a success. Remember some of the other tips for developing confidence. Re-create the speech environment when you rehearse. Use deep breathing techniques to help you relax. Also, make sure you are especially familiar with your introduction and conclusion. Act calm to feel calm.

- Arrive early for your speaking engagement. If the room is in an unfamiliar location, give yourself plenty of time to find it. You may want to rearrange the furniture or make other changes in the speaking environment. If you are using audiovisual equipment, check to see that it is working properly and set up your support material carefully. You might even project a slide or two to make sure they are in the tray right side up. Relax before you deliver your message; budget your time so you do not spend the moments before you speak hurriedly looking for a parking place or frantically trying to attend to last-minute details.

- Visualize success. Picture yourself delivering your speech in an effective way. Also, remind yourself of the effort you have spent preparing for your speech. A final mental rehearsal can boost your confidence and help ensure success.

Even though we have identified many time-tested methods for enhancing your speech delivery, keep in mind that speech delivery is an art rather than a science. The manner of your delivery should reflect your personality and individual style.

15.9 Adapting Your Speech Delivery for Television

You may not plan to be a newscaster or a politician whose messages are routinely broadcast on local or national radio or TV, but you may have an opportunity to be interviewed for a news story or find that a speech you deliver is also going to be videotaped. And with the advent of satellite video teleconferences and the increasing use of video software on the Internet, it is becoming common for messages to be televised and transmitted electronically to an audience that is not physically present.

Should you use a different style of speaking when speaking to the media? When your message is telecast to others, use the principles and skills we've discussed already, and keep the following additional specific guidelines in mind.

CONSIDER TONING DOWN GESTURES

Most newscasters use head nods and facial expressions rather than pronounced gestures to help emphasize their points. Keep your hands still, and don't fidget with pens, hair, or clothing. Also, keep your hands away from your face. Of course, if your primary audience are those who are physically present when you present your speech, they are the audience to whom you adapt your style of speaking. But if the target audience is watching on monitors elsewhere, tone down the gestures a bit.

In January, 2004, Democratic presidential hopeful Howard Dean delivered a screeching, arm-waving outburst to supporters after he finished third in the Iowa Caucus. A few days later, Dean defended the speech as appropriate to the "3,500 kids waving American flags who'd worked their hearts out for us for three weeks."[34] Unfortunately, Dean's emotionalism did not come across well to the television audience that was also watching, and some people believe it cost Dean the nomination.

DRESS FOR TV SUCCESS

White clothing sometimes creates a glare on TV. Men who do not plan to wear a jacket may want to wear a light blue rather than a white dress shirt, and women should consider nonwhite clothing. You may also want to avoid black or dark gray—these colors can look too somber. Also, avoid large patterns, jangling or shiny jewelry, and overly frilly or complicated necklines. Solid colors look best. Also remember that the camera can add five to ten pounds to your appearance. No, you don't need to go on a crash diet before a TV appearance, but do wear clothes that make you look and feel your best.

MONITOR YOUR FACIAL EXPRESSIONS

Be aware that TV amplifies facial expressions. Your listeners are seeing your expression up close rather than from a distance, as they would in a live public-speaking context. Therefore, if you have a tendency to use exaggerated or exceptionally dramatic expressions, realize that they will be seen from the camera's perspective rather than from an audience perspective. Smile appropriately, but make sure you're not smiling at inappropriate times. If you are asked a serious question but you have a big grin on your face when the camera cuts to you, it will appear that you are insensitive to the question.

KEEP YOUR TARGET AUDIENCE IN MIND

If your message will be broadcast to many people, remind yourself whom you are trying to reach. If you're giving a persuasive presentation, realize that you do not necessarily want to persuade everyone in "TV land" who sees you.

KEEP IT SHORT

If you are giving a political speech or a presentation that you hope will be picked up by the media, realize that you will only be given a few seconds of air time for a news broadcast. Editors look for sound bites.

CHOOSE YOUR WORDS WITH CARE AND STYLE

The sound bites that get quoted or broadcast are those phrases that are particularly attention catching or that communicate the essence of your message in a memorable way. Review the strategies discussed in Chapter 14 for creating drama (omission, inversion, suspension) or creating cadence (parallelism, antithesis, repetition, alliteration).

When we recently served as consultants to a political candidate, we were asked to review a draft of her speech declaring her candidacy for the U.S. House of Representatives. The speech was good but had no obvious attention-catching, stylized phrases that would lend themselves to good quotes for the media. We suggested she add some repetition, alliteration, and parallelism. Sure enough, the phrases quoted in the media were those she had taken special care to stylize.

BECOME FAMILIAR WITH THE TECHNOLOGY BEFORE YOU SPEAK

If you are being taped or broadcast in a studio, be sure to arrive in plenty of time so that you won't have to rush around making last-minute adjustments to your microphone.

15.h Responding to Questions

It's possible that a speech you deliver will be followed by a question-and-answer (Q & A) session. These sessions can be especially challenging, because although you may not know the questions in advance, you will still be expected to deliver your answers thoughtfully and smoothly. During a Q & A session, your delivery method changes to impromptu speaking. In addition to the suggestions for impromptu speaking we offered earlier, here are additional tips to make the Q & A period less challenging.[35]

- **Prepare.** One of the best ways to prepare for a Q & A session is to anticipate what questions you may be asked. How do you anticipate questions? You analyze your audience. Think of possible questions those particular listeners might ask you, and then rehearse your answers. Prior to presidential debates, candidates have their staff members pepper them with questions so the candidates can practice responding. Perhaps your friends can ask you questions after you've rehearsed your speech for them.

- **Repeat or rephrase the question.** Repeating a question helps in four ways. First, your paraphrase makes sure that everyone can hear the question. Second, paraphrasing ensures that you understand the question before you go charging off with your answer. Third, by paraphrasing, you can succinctly summarize rambling questions. And finally, repeating the question gives you just a bit of time to think about your answer.

- **Stay on message.** Sometimes listeners may ask questions unrelated to your talk. If so, you'll want to find a way to gently guide your questioner back to the message you have prepared. Keep bringing the audience back to your central idea. Your answers, rather than the questions, are what are important. We're not suggesting that you dodge questions; you should address the question asked, but re-emphasize the key points you have made. Some seasoned speakers suggest that you save a bit of your speech to deliver during the Q & A session. It's called giving a "double-barreled" talk.[36] You present your speech, and then, during the Q & A period, you give your second, much briefer speech.

- **Ask yourself the first question.** One way to prime the audience for the Q & A session is to ask yourself a challenging question first. For example, you might say, "As we move into Q & A, a number of you may be wondering . . . ." State the question and answer it. Doing this also gives you a comfortable way to make a transition between the speech and the Q & A period. Asking yourself a tough question tells the audience that you're open for serious questions, and it snaps them to attention as well.

- **Listen nonjudgmentally.** Use the effective listening skills that we discussed in Chapter 5. Keep your eyes focused on the person asking the question, lean forward slightly, and give your full attention to the questioner. Audience members expect speakers to be polite and attentive. If you think the question is stupid, don't say so. Just listen and respond courteously. Audience members can judge for themselves whether a question was appropriate or not. Don't wince, grimace, or scowl at the questioner. You'll gain more credibility by keeping your cool than by losing your composure.

- **Neutralize hostile questions.** Every hostile question gives you an opportunity to score points with your listeners. You'll have your listeners' attention; use that attention to your advantage. The following strategies can help.

   Restate the question. If the question was a lengthy attack, focus on the essence of the issue. If the question is, "Your ideas are just wrong! I'm angry that you have no clue as to how to proceed. Your proposal has been a disaster in the past. Why are you still trying to make it work?" a paraphrase could be, "You're asking me why I'm still trying to implement a program that hasn't been successful. From your perspective, the program has failed."

   Acknowledge emotions. For example, you could say, "I can understand why you are angry. I share your anger and frustration. It's because of my frustration that I want to give my proposal more time to work."

   Don't make the issue personal. Even if the hostile questioner has made you the villain, don't attack the person who asked the question. Keep the conversation focused on issues, not on personalities.

   Get to the heart of the issue. Respond directly to a hostile question. Consider restating the evidence you presented in your speech. Or provide new insights to support your position.

- **When you don't know, admit it.** If you've been asked a question to which you don't know the answer, just say so. You can promise to find out more information and then get back to the person later. (If you make such a promise, follow through on it. Ask for the person's business card or e-mail address at the end of the Q & A session.)

- **Be brief.** Even if you've anticipated questions and have a "double-barreled" talk, make it short and to the point.

- **Use organizational signposts.** Quickly organize your responses. If you have two responses to a question, let your listeners know it. Then use a verbal signpost (a statement that clues your audience in to how you're organizing your message) by saying, "I have two responses. First . . . ." When you get to your second point, say, "My second point is . . . ." These signposts will both help you stay organized and impress your listeners with your clarity.

- **Indicate when the Q & A period is concluding.** Tell your audience, "I have time for two more questions." Let them know that the Q & A session will soon conclude. Even if you have someone helping you moderate the discussion, you should remain in charge of concluding the session.

Summary

- The way you deliver your speech plays a major role in the successful communication of your thoughts and emotions to an audience.

- Audiences will believe what they see more readily than what they hear.

- Of the four methods of delivery—manuscript, memorized, impromptu, and extemporaneous—the extemporaneous method is most desirable in most situations.

- Speak from an outline without memorizing the exact words.

- Your gestures and movements should appear natural and relaxed, definite, consistent with your message, varied, unobtrusive, and coordinated with what you say. They should also be appropriate to your audience and situation.

- Eye contact is the single most important delivery variable: Looking at your audience helps control communication, establishes your credibility, maintains audience interest, and provides feedback about how your speech is coming across.

- Your facial expressions and vocal cues are the primary ways in which you communicate your feelings and emotions to an audience.

- How loudly you speak, how clearly you articulate, and whether you correctly pronounce the words you use determine how well your audience will understand your thoughts; your vocal pitch, rate, and use of pauses help provide variation to add interest to your talk.

- Leave at least two days to focus on your speech delivery and develop your speaking notes.

- As much as possible, re-create the speech environment when you rehearse.

- During a Q & A session, your delivery method changes to impromptu speaking.

Key Terms

articulation (p. 298)
boom microphone (p. 302)
dialect (p. 298)
extemporaneous speaking (p. 289)
immediacy (p. 295)
immediacy behaviors (p. 295)
impromptu speaking (p. 287)
inflection (p. 300)
lavaliere microphone (p. 302)

manuscript speaking (p. 286)
memorized speaking (p. 287)
nonverbal communication (p. 284)
nonverbal-expectancy theory (p. 284)
pitch (p. 300)
pronunciation (p. 299)
stationary microphone (p. 302)
volume (p. 297)

A QUESTION OF ETHICS

Brenda, who is from a rural area in Kentucky, is now a student at a prestigious college in Boston, Massachusetts. She has to deliver a speech to her classmates. Is it ethical for her to deliver her speech using the Boston dialect even though she uses her original speech patterns with friends and when she returns to Kentucky? Why or why not?

6

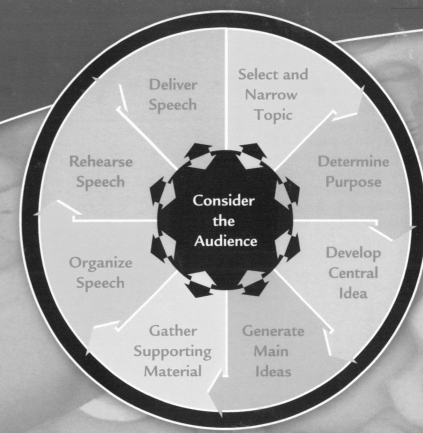

Consider the Audience

Select and Narrow Topic

Determine Purpose

Develop Central Idea

Generate Main Ideas

Gather Supporting Material

Organize Speech

Rehearse Speech

Deliver Speech

Presentation Aids

Presentation Aids

Presentation Aids

16 Designing and Using Presentation Aids

➡ **The Value of Presentation Aids (p. 321)**
- A presentation aid is any object that reinforces your point visually so that your audience can better understand it.
  - Presentation aids enhance understanding.
  - Presentation aids enhance memory.
  - Presentation aids help listeners organize ideas.
  - Presentation aids help gain and maintain attention.
  - Presentation aids help illustrate a sequence of events or procedures.

➡ **Types of Presentation Aids (p. 323)**
- Three-dimensional presentation aids used to illustrate a talk include objects, models, and people.
  - Objects add interest because they are tangible. They can be touched, smelled, heard, and even tasted, as well as seen.
  - If you cannot bring the object you would like to show, consider bringing a model.
  - If you use a person, choose a trusted individual, and do so before your presentation so that you can explain what needs to be done. Rehearse your speech using your living presentation aid.
- The most common presentation aids are two-dimensional: drawings, photographs, slides, maps, graphs, charts, flipcharts, chalkboards, and overhead transparencies.
  - Drawings are used often because they are easy and inexpensive to make.
  - Photographs show objects or places that cannot be illustrated with drawings or that an audience cannot view directly.
  - Slides can help illustrate your talk if you have access to a screen and a slide projector.

At a Glance *(continued)*

- Most maps are designed to be read from a distance of no more than two feet. As with photographs, the details on most maps won't be visible to your audience unless you are able to enlarge them.
- Graphs are pictorial representations of statistical data in an easy-to-understand format.
- Charts summarize and present a great deal of information in a small amount of space.
- A flipchart is a large pad of paper resting on an easel. You can either prepare your visual aids before your speech or draw on the paper while speaking.
- Chalkboards and whiteboards are inexpensive, simple to use, and low-tech, so you don't need to worry about extension cords or special training.
- Overhead transparencies, images drawn on clear sheets of plastic, can be projected onto a screen so that the images can be seen by a large group.
- Audiovisual aids join sound and sight to communicate ideas.
  - You can use videotapes and movies to help communicate your ideas by showing brief scenes from rented movies, excerpts from training videos, or custom-made videos.
  - The files on CDs can be displayed in combination with a large-screen video projector or an LCD panel connected to an overhead projector.
  - Digital video disks (DVDs) can be stopped and started at a precise place, so you know that your movie or video will start exactly where you want it to.
  - Music on tapes or compact disks (CDs) can complement a visual display
- Computer-generated graphics are images, words, charts, and graphs designed and presented with the help of a computer and special computer software.

➡ **Guidelines for Developing Presentation Aids (p. 333)**
- Prepare your presentation aids well in advance of your speaking date so that you can make them as attractive and polished-looking as possible.
- Make them easy to see.
- Keep them simple.
- Group related elements into visual units.
- Establish a consistent graphic theme.
- Choose a typeface with care.
- Vary fonts and font sizes with care.
- Use color to create a mood and sustain attention.
- Use black and white effectively.
- Don't detract from your message.
- Show numerical data graphically.
- Select the right presentation aids.

Guidelines for Using Presentation Aids (p. 339)

- Do not use dangerous or illegal presentation aids.
- Rehearse with your presentation aids.
- Make eye contact with your audience, not with your presentation aids.
- Explain your presentation aids.
- Do not pass objects among members of your audience.
- Use animals with caution.
- Use handouts effectively.
- Time the use of visuals to control your audience's attention.
- Use technology effectively.
- Remember Murphy's law.

17 Using Presentation Software

Presentation Software (p. 347)

- A graphics presentation program can assist you in making professional-looking visual aids, including transparencies, slides, handouts, and posters.
- Microsoft's PowerPoint, Persuasion by Adobe, and Lotus's Freelance Graphics are three of the best-known and most used tools for producing graphics.

Using Presentation Software (p. 348)

- The various presentation software packages are designed to let you easily include a variety of aids in your presentation. However, the images or clips that you choose must help develop your central idea; otherwise, do not include them.
  - Keep sights and sounds simple.
  - Repeat visual elements to unify your presentation.
  - Choose a typeface with care.
  - Make informed decisions about using color.
  - Allow plenty of time to prepare your presentation aids.

At a Glance (continued)

➡ **Preparing a Presentation with PowerPoint® (p. 350)**
- When you first open PowerPoint, the program displays a dialog box with four options—AutoContent Wizard, Template, Blank Presentation, and Open an Existing Presentation.
  - The AutoContent Wizard provides suggestions and ideas for your presentation and guides you through the design and layout process by asking specific questions about your presentation.
  - Templates are provided that contain color schemes, slide and title masters with custom formatting, and styled fonts designed for a particular "look."
  - A blank presentation has neither suggested content nor design. Choosing Blank Presentation enables you to create your own slide design.
  - You can also open, edit, or view existing presentations in many different locations.
  - You can save a presentation, whether it's new or has been saved before. You can also save it with a different name or in a different location and in HTML format.
- There are several different ways you can view the presentation aids you create.
  - In slide view, you can see an entire slide or zoom in to magnify a portion of the slide for detailed work.
  - Outline view displays text in an outline format so that you can see how your main points flow from slide to slide.
  - Master view enables you to include items as a company logo or particular formatting on every slide, notes page, or handout by making your changes on the appropriate master.
  - In slide sorter view, you see miniature versions of all the slides in your entire presentation so that you can easily add, delete, and reorder slides.
  - When you switch to black-and-white view, the objects in your presentation appear on screen and print in shades of black and white.
  - Notes page view allows you to type speaker notes to use during your presentation.
- Create a consistent look using design templates, the slide master, the title master, and color schemes.
  - The slide master controls the format and placement of the titles and text you type on slides.
  - The title master controls the format and placement of the title slide and any other slide you designate as a title slide.
  - Color schemes are sets of eight balanced colors designed to be used as the main colors of a slide presentation—for text, background, fill, accents, etc.

- Create a distinctive look.
  - Add text by typing directly into any placeholder on the slide.
  - Insert pictures using the Clip Gallery, which contains professionally designed images.
  - Insert charts and graphs, scanned pictures, and equations.
- You can print your entire presentation— the slides, outline, speaker's notes, and audience handouts—in either color or black and white.
- You can create notes pages while you're creating your presentation and then use these pages as speaker notes when you give a slide show. You can also create handouts of slides for the audience.
- Using special effects such as transitions and animations sparingly can add interest to your presentation, help highlight important points, and control the flow of information.

CHAPTER 16

Designing and Using Presentation Aids

F razier walked to the front of the class and dramatically pulled a two-foot papier-mâché model of a cockroach out of a sack. He attached a string to the "bug" and suspended it from the ceiling. Then he began his speech about how to rid a home of pests. The trouble was, no one listened to Frazier's message. His audience was obsessed with the creature dangling in midair.

> *The soul never thinks without a picture.*
> —**Aristotle**

The intention was good, but the execution was bad. Frazier had failed to use his presentation aid effectively. Presentation aids—especially visual aids—are powerful tools. They can help communicate your ideas with greater clarity and impact than can words alone, but they can also overwhelm your speech. For maximum effectiveness, follow the guidelines described in this chapter.

A **presentation aid** is any object that reinforces your point visually so that your audience can better understand it. Charts, photographs, posters, drawings, graphs, slides, movies, and videos are just some of the types of presentation aids that we will discuss. Some of these, such as movies and videos, call on sound as well as sight to help you make your point.

In this chapter, we look at presentation aids as an important communication tool and also examine several kinds. Toward the end of the chapter, we suggest guidelines for using presentation aids in your speeches.

16.a The Value of Presentation Aids

Presentation aids are invaluable to an audience-centered speaker. They help your audience understand and remember your message, communicate the organization of your ideas, gain and maintain attention, and illustrate a sequence of events or procedures.[1]

PRESENTATION AIDS ENHANCE UNDERSTANDING

Of your five senses, you learn more from sight than from all the others combined. In fact, it has been estimated that more than 80 percent of all information comes to you through sight.[2] To many people, seeing is believing. We are a visually oriented society. For example, most of us learn the news by seeing it presented on TV. Because your audience is accustomed to visual reinforcement, it is wise to consider how you can increase their understanding of your speech by using presentation aids.

For example, President George W. Bush often speaks against a backdrop inscribed with the theme of the day, such as "A Better America," "Working toward Independence," or "Corporate Responsibility."[3]

PRESENTATION AIDS ENHANCE MEMORY

Your audience will not only have an improved understanding of your speech, but will also better remember what you say as a result of visual reinforcement.[4] It is well known that you remember most what you understand best. Researchers estimate that you remember 10 percent of what you read, 20 percent of what you hear, 30 percent of what you see, and 50 percent of what you simultaneously hear and see. For example, in your speech about the languages spoken in Africa, your audience is more likely to remember words in Arabic, Swahili, and Hausa if you display the words visually, rather than just say them.

PRESENTATION AIDS HELP LISTENERS ORGANIZE IDEAS

Most listeners need help understanding the structure of a speech. Even if you clearly lay out your major points, use effective internal summaries, and make clear transition statements, your listeners will welcome additional help. Listing major ideas on a chart, a poster, or an overhead transparency can add clarity to your talk and help your audience grasp your main ideas. Visually presenting your major ideas during your introduction, for example, can help your audience follow them as you bring them into the body of your speech. You can display key ideas during your conclusion to help summarize your message succinctly.

PRESENTATION AIDS HELP GAIN AND MAINTAIN ATTENTION

Keshia began her speech about poverty in the United States by showing a photo of the face of an undernourished child. She immediately had the attention of her audience. Chuck began his speech with the flash of his camera to introduce his photography lecture. He certainly alerted his audience at that point. Midway through her speech about the lyrics in rap music, Tomoko not only spoke the words but also displayed a giant poster of the song lyrics so that her audience could read the words and sing along. Presentation aids not only grab the attention of your listeners but also keep their interest when words alone might not.

PRESENTATION AIDS HELP ILLUSTRATE A SEQUENCE OF EVENTS OR PROCEDURES

If your purpose is to inform an audience about a process—how to do something or how something functions—you can do this best through actual demonstrations or with a series of visuals. Whether your objective is instructing people on how to make a soufflé or how to build a greenhouse, demonstrating the step-by-step procedures helps your audience understand them.[5] If you wish to explain how hydroelectric power is generated, a series of diagrams can help your listeners understand and visualize the process.

When demonstrating how to make something, such as your prize-winning cinnamon rolls, you can prepare an example of each step of the process ahead of time and show the audience each example as you describe the relevant step; for example, you might have the dough already mixed and ready to demonstrate how you sprinkle on the cinnamon. A climax to your speech could be to unveil a finished pan of rolls still warm from the oven. If time does not permit you to demonstrate how to prepare your rolls, you could have on hand a series of diagrams and photographs to illustrate each step of the procedure.

Today's audiences expect visual support. Contemporary audiences are quite different from those over a century ago when Thomas Edison invented the kinetoscope, a precursor of the movie camera. Edison said, "When we started out it took the average audience a long time to assimilate each image. They weren't trained to visualize more than one thought at a time."[6] Times have changed. The predominance of visual images—on TV, in movies, on the Internet, and even on our phones—attests to how central images are in the communication of information to modern audiences.

QUICK CHECK: *The Value of Presentation Aids*

- They help your audience understand your message.
- They help your audience remember your message.
- They communicate the organization of your message.
- They gain and maintain audience attention.
- They illustrate a sequence of events or procedures.

16.b   Types of Presentation Aids

The first question many students ask when they learn they are required to use presentation aids is, "What type of presentation aid should I use?" We will discuss various kinds, grouped into classes: three-dimensional, two-dimensional, audiovisual, and computer generated.

THREE-DIMENSIONAL PRESENTATION AIDS

Three-dimensional presentation aids used to illustrate a talk include objects, models, and people.

Objects　You have played the trombone since you were in fifth grade, so you decide to give an informative speech about the history and function of this instrument. Your trombone is an obvious presentation aid, which you can show to your audience as you talk about how it works. Perhaps you might play a few measures to demonstrate its sound and your talent.

Objects add interest because they are tangible. They can be touched, smelled, heard, and even tasted, as well as seen. Objects are real, and audiences like the real thing. If you use an object to illustrate an idea, make sure that you can handle the object with ease. If an object is too large, it can be unwieldy and difficult to show. Tiny objects can only be seen close up. It will be impossible for your listeners to see the detail on your antique thimble, the intricate needlework on your cross-stitch sampler, or the attention to detail in your miniature log cabin. Other objects can be dangerous to handle. One speaker, for example, attempted a demonstration of how to string an archery bow. He made his audience extremely uncomfortable when his almost-strung bow flew over the heads of his listeners. He certainly got their attention, but he lost his credibility.

Models　If you cannot bring the object you would like to show your audience, consider showing them a **model**. You cannot bring a World War II fighter plane to class, so buy or build a scale model instead. To illustrate a lecture about human anatomy, one student brought a plastic model of a skeleton. An actual human skeleton would have been difficult to get and carry to class. Similarly, most colleges and universities do not allow firearms on campus. A drawing that shows the features of a gun is much safer than a real gun as a presentation aid. If you need to show the movable parts of a gun, perhaps a papier-mâché, plastic, or wood model would serve. Make sure, however, that any model you use is large enough to be seen by all members of your audience.

People　At least since Ronald Reagan, U.S. presidents have often used people as visual aids during their State of the Union addresses—usually relating a poignant story and then asking the protagonist of the story, seated in the balcony, to stand and be recognized. One speechwriter noted that George W. Bush used this strategy to especially good effect, finding it "a way of coming down from the stage, as it were, and mingling with the crowd."[7]

In classroom speeches, too, people can serve as presentation aids. For example, Amelia wanted to illustrate an intricate Latin folk dance, so she arranged to have a dancer attend her speech to demonstrate the dance.

Using people to illustrate your message can be tricky, however. It is usually unwise to ask for spur-of-the-moment help from volunteers while you are delivering your speech. Instead, choose a trusted friend or colleague, and do so before your presentation so that you can fully inform him or her about what needs to be done. Rehearse your speech using your living presentation aid.

Also, it is distracting to have your support person stand beside you doing nothing. If you don't need the person to demonstrate something during your opening remarks, wait and introduce the person to your audience when needed.

Finally, do not allow your assistants to run away with the show. For example, don't let your dancer perform longer than necessary to illustrate your point about technique.

Nor should you permit your models to prance about too provocatively while displaying your dress designs. And don't allow your buddy to throw you when you demonstrate the wrestling hold that made you the district wrestling champ. Remember, your presentation aids are always subordinate to your speech. You must remain in control.

Generally, *you* can serve as a presentation aid to demonstrate or illustrate major points. If you are talking about tennis, you might bring your racquet to class so that you can illustrate your superb backhand or simply show novices the proper way to hold it. If you are a nurse or an emergency room technician giving a talk about medical procedures, by all means wear your uniform to establish your credibility.

TWO-DIMENSIONAL PRESENTATION AIDS

Although three-dimensional objects, models, and people can be used to illustrate a talk, the most common presentation aids are two-dimensional: drawings, photographs, slides, maps, graphs, charts, flipcharts, chalkboards, and overhead transparencies. Today, you can use computer software to generate many of these forms, as we will discuss later.

Drawings   Drawings are popular and often-used presentation aids because they are easy and inexpensive to make. Drawings can be tailored to your specific needs. To illustrate the functions of the human brain, for example, one student traced an outline of the brain and labeled it with large block letters to indicate where brain functions are located. Another student wanted to show the different sizes and shapes of leaves of trees in the area, so she drew enlarged pictures of the leaves, using appropriate shades of green.

You don't have to be a master artist to develop effective drawings. As a rule, large and simple line drawings are more effective for stage presentations than are detailed images. If you have absolutely no faith in your artistic skill, you can probably find a friend or relative who can help you prepare a useful drawing, or you may be able to use computer software to generate simple line drawings.

Photographs   Photographs can be used to show objects or places that cannot be illustrated with drawings or that an audience cannot view directly. The problem with photos, however, is that they are usually too small to be seen clearly from a distance. Passing a photograph among your listeners is not a good idea either; it creates competition for your audience's attention.

The only way to be sure that a printed photograph will be effective as a presentation aid for a large audience is to enlarge it. Some photo shops will produce poster-size color laser photocopies at a modest cost. You can also take a picture of your photograph with slide film and project the image onto a large screen. Or, using a scanner or digital camera, you can incorporate your image into a computer program such as PowerPoint and project your image using a TV monitor or video projection system. Later in the chapter we will discuss using computer images in your speeches.

Slides   Because of the increased use of computer-graphics programs such as Power-Point®, fewer speakers are using slides. However, slides can help illustrate your talk if you have access to a screen and a slide projector. Charts and graphs that you develop on a computer can be made into slides. Automatic programming and remote-control features on many modern projectors help you change from one slide to the next without relying on anyone else for help. And audiences generally enjoy illustrated talks, which have an inherent attention factor that a speaker can use to advantage.

Working with slides can also present problems. Projector bulbs can burn out, and slides can jam in the projector. Moreover, with the lights out, you are less able to receive nonverbal feedback, and you cannot maintain eye contact with your audience.

Giving a slide lecture, therefore, requires considerable preparation. First, be sure the slides are right side up and in the order in which you want to show them during your speech. Second, know in which direction the slide carousel moves as it feeds the projector so that you will know how to load it. Third, know how to operate the programming feature or the remote-control switch so that you can move back and forth among your slides.

Maps   Most maps are designed to be read from a distance of no more than two feet. As with photographs, the details on most maps won't be visible to your audience. You could use a large map, however, to show general features of an area. Or you can use a magnified version of your map. Certain copiers can enlarge images as much as 200 percent. It is possible, using a color laser copier, to enlarge a standard map of Europe enough for listeners in the last row to see the general features of the continent. Using a black marker, one speaker highlighted the borders on a map of Europe to indicate the countries she had visited the previous summer (see Figure 16.1). She used a green marker to show the general path of her journey.

Graphs   A **graph** is a pictorial representation of statistical data in an easy-to-understand format. Because statistics are abstract summaries of many examples, most listeners find that graphs help make the data more concrete. Graphs are particularly effective in showing overall trends and relationships among data. The four most common types of graphs are bar graphs, pie graphs, line graphs, and picture graphs. Many of today's computer presentation programs can easily convert statistics into visual form.

- **Bar graphs.** A bar graph uses flat areas—bars—of various lengths to represent information. The bar graph in Figure 16.2 clearly shows the number of people who work from home. This graph makes the information clear and immediately visible to an audience. By comparison, words and numbers are more difficult to assimilate, especially in something as ephemeral as a speech.

- **Pie graphs.** A pie graph shows the general distribution of data. The pie graph in Figure 16.3, on page 328, shows what people would do if they had three extra hours of free time. Pie graphs are especially useful in helping your listeners to see quickly how data are distributed in a given category or area.

- **Line graphs.** Line graphs show relationships between two or more variables. Like bar graphs, line graphs organize statistical data to show overall trends (Figure 16.4, page 328). A line graph can cover a greater span of time or numbers than a bar graph without looking cluttered or confusing. As with other types of presentation aids, a simple line graph communicates better than a cluttered one.

- **Picture graphs.** In place of either a line or a bar, you can use pictures to represent the data you are summarizing (Figure 16.5, page 329). **Picture graphs** look

FIGURE 16.1   A map can be an effective visual aid, especially if the speaker personalizes it by highlighting the relevant information.

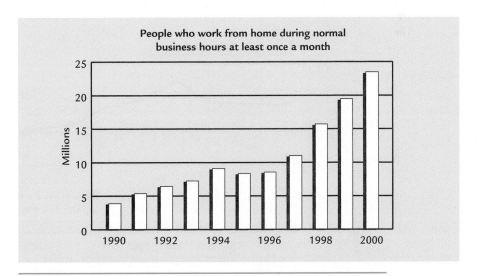

FIGURE 16.2   Bar graphs can help summarize statistical information clearly so that the information is immediately visible to your audience.
Source: Joanne H. Pratt Associates.

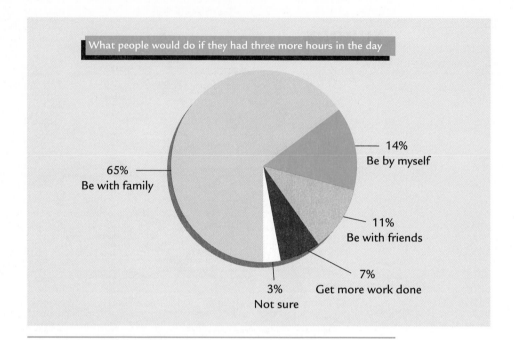

FIGURE 16.3 **A pie graph shows general distribution of data.**

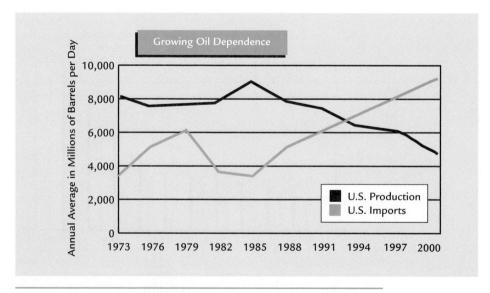

FIGURE 16.4 **Line graphs show relationships between two or more variables.**

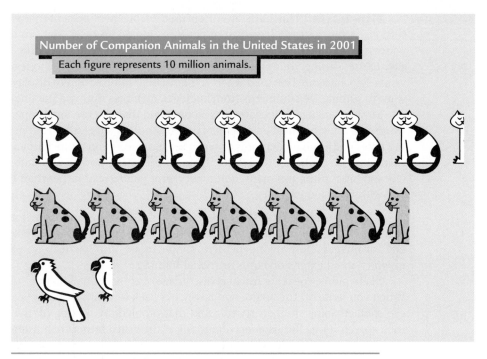

FIGURE 16.5 **Consider adding visual symbols to enhance your presentation of statistics.**

somewhat less formal and less intimidating than other kinds of graphs. One of the advantages of picture graphs is that they use few words or labels, which makes them easier for your audience to read.

Charts Charts summarize and present a great deal of information in a small amount of space. They have several advantages. They are easy to use, reuse, and enlarge. They can also be displayed in a variety of ways. You can use a flipchart, a poster, or an overhead projector, which can project a giant image of your chart on a screen. As with all other presentation aids, charts must be simple. Do not try to put too much information on one chart.

The key to developing effective charts is to prepare the lettering of the words and phrases you use very carefully. If the chart contains too much information, audience members may feel it is too complicated and ignore it. If your chart looks cramped or crowded, divide the information into several charts and display each as needed. Do not handwrite the chart; a hand-lettered chart may seem unprofessional. Consider using a computer that has the software capability to prepare large charts or graphs. Make sure your letters are large enough to be seen clearly in the back row. Use simple words or phrases, and eliminate unnecessary words.

Flipcharts   Flipcharts are often used in business presentations and training sessions. A flipchart is a large pad of paper resting on an easel. You can either prepare your visual aids before your speech or draw on the paper while speaking. Flipcharts are easy to use. During your presentation, you need only flip the page to reveal your next visual. Flipcharts are best used when you have brief information to display or when you want to summarize comments from audience members during a presentation.

Most experienced flipchart users recommend that you use lined paper to keep your words and drawings neat and well organized. Another suggestion is to pencil in speaking notes on the chart that only you can see. Brief notes on a flipchart are easier to use than notes on cards or a clipboard. If you do use notes, however, be sure that they are few and brief; using too many notes will tempt you to read rather than have eye contact with your audience.

Chalkboards and Whiteboards   Chalkboards and whiteboards are often used to offer visual support for spoken words. Chalkboards and whiteboards have several advantages: They are inexpensive, simple to use, and low-tech, so you don't need to worry about extension cords or special training.

Many public-speaking teachers discourage overuse of chalkboards, however. Why? When you write on the board, you have your back to your audience; you do not have eye contact! Some speakers try to avoid that problem by writing on the board before their speech starts. But listeners often look at the visual rather than listen. Also, chalkboards and whiteboards, which have been around for a long time, are not particularly effective at getting or holding audience attention. Use a board only for brief phrases or for very simple line diagrams that can be drawn in just a few seconds.

Overhead Transparencies   An overhead projector projects images drawn on clear sheets of plastic, called *transparencies,* onto a screen so that the images can be seen by a large group. Although computer-generated presentations are replacing overheads in many settings, overhead projectors remain popular because they have several advantages. They allow you to maintain eye contact with your audience, yet still see your visual. Unlike a traditional slide projector, the overhead doesn't require that you turn off the lights in the room to ensure that the projected image is visible. You may wish to dim the lights a bit, but most images can be seen clearly in normal room light. Overhead projectors also permit you to prepare your transparency ahead of time and to mark on it during your presentation. If you do write during your speech, limit yourself to a few short words or to underlining key phrases.

AUDIOVISUAL AIDS

Perhaps the most exciting presentation aids are those that join sound and sight to communicate ideas. You are probably familiar with movies, videotapes, CD-ROMs, and DVDs, as well as with audio aids such as tapes and compact disks. Now you can consider these familiar media in a new context. Instead of being passively entertained or instructed by them, you may use them actively to support your ideas.

Videotapes and Movies   With the ready availability of video cassette recorders (VCRs) and cameras, more public speakers are using videotapes to help com-

HOW TO: *Use an Overhead Projector*

- If possible, practice with the overhead projector in the room in which you will be delivering your speech. That way you can be certain that the projector is the proper distance from the screen and that your image will be large enough to be seen.

- When you are not showing a visual, turn the overhead projector off so it does not detract from your speech.

- Do not put too much information on one transparency. Use no more than seven lines on one sheet. Do not use a full page of typewritten material as a transparency.

- Align the projector so that the head beams the image directly onto the screen. If the image is too low, it will get projected up and suffer a distortion called a *keystone effect,* which makes the image seem larger at the top and smaller at the bottom. Besides making sure the projector is properly aligned, you can tilt the projector screen forward if it is mounted high on a wall.

- When you use an overhead projector, you may need to increase the volume of your voice. The fan's motor, which keeps the high-intensity projector bulb cool, can be noisy.

- When developing your transparency, consider using a large type size. Using 18-point, 24-point, or even larger type will make your words easier to read. Because most students develop written materials using a computer, it is very easy simply to increase the size of the type, even if it means putting your information on more than one transparency. Bigger is better.

- Reveal one line of text at a time by blocking out the text below it with a sheet of paper. This helps hold the audience's interest.

- If possible, leave the bottom fourth of your transparency blank. Images projected low on the screen often are not visible to audience members in the back.

- Consider using color. Colored acetate sheets are available from most bookstores. You can also use different colors of markers to highlight key points.

- For ease of handling, place the transparency in a cardboard frame. These are available wherever acetate sheets are sold. A frame lessens the likelihood that transparencies will stick together or become torn along the edges.

municate their ideas by showing brief scenes from a rented movie, excerpts from training videos, or custom-made videos. High-quality VCRs permit stop-action, freeze-frame viewing, and some have a slow-motion function. You can also play and replay a scene several times if you want your audience to watch subtle movement or action.

A 25-inch screen is generally visible to an audience of twenty-five or thirty people. For larger audiences, you will need several TV monitors or a large projection TV system. You can use a large-screen video projector to display your video. Or, if one is available, you could use a liquid crystal display (LCD) panel connected to an overhead projector to project your image.

Before you decide to use a movie, however, think about whether it will really enhance your speech. Although movies can dramatically capture and hold your audience's attention, they are not really designed as supporting material for a speech. Usually, they are conceived as self-contained packages, and unless you show only short excerpts, they can quickly overwhelm your speech. Of course, if you are a skilled moviemaker, you will probably have enough control over your medium to tame it and make it serve your purpose. Be sure to rehearse with the equipment until you can handle it smoothly.

CDs   One technology finding its way into classrooms, corporate meetings, training sessions, and lecture halls is the compact disk, or **CD**. CDs can include words, images, and audio or video clips. The files on CDs are read by the CD drive in a personal computer and can be displayed by linking the computer to a large-screen video projector or an LCD panel connected to an overhead projector. All the information can be retrieved instantly because it is stored digitally; one disk can contain hundreds of images, sound bites, or an entire encyclopedia.

While giving a lecture about Elizabeth Cady Stanton, you could click the computer mouse a couple of times to project her picture or hear an actress read one of her speeches. Or, if you want your audience to hear the dramatic opening four notes of Beethoven's *Fifth Symphony,* you can click the mouse to retrieve his famous "Da, da, da, daaaaah" while simultaneously showing Beethoven's music manuscript in his own handwriting. A CD's key advantage is the ease and speed with which a speaker can retrieve audio or visual information. Increasingly, information that is stored on CDs is also available on the Internet.

Digital Video Disks (DVDs)   Because you can stop and start a **digital video disk**, or **DVD**, at a precise place, you can be confident that your movie or video will start exactly where you want it to start when you are ready to show it to an audience. Now that DVD recorders are readily available, it's easy to use DVDs to record video images and audio clips to support speech ideas. But because newer DVD recorders may use a format that is not compatible with DVD players that are even a couple of years old, it would be wise to be certain that your self-recorded DVD will be usable on the equipment that will be available when you deliver your presentation. You may, for example, have recorded something using a DVD-RW format, and the DVD player may only play DVD-R or DVD+RW. It pays to double-check the compatibility of the equipment well in advance of your presentation.

Audio Aids   Tapes or audio compact disks (CDs) can complement a visual display—you might play a tape or CD recording of a few measures of Bach's *Toccata and Fugue in D Minor* to illustrate a point. While showing slides of her recent Caribbean vacation, a student used a recording of steel drum music as a soft introductory background for her talk. Another student interviewed students on campus about local parking problems. Rather than reading quotes from irate drivers who couldn't find a place to park, he played a few excerpts of taped interviews.

Probably the easiest and least expensive audio aid to use is a tape recorder that uses cassettes. It is small enough to handle easily, can be held up to a microphone to amplify the sound for a large audience, and can be cued to start exactly where you want it to. Mini CD recorders can record either voices or music; their small size makes them easy to handle, and the digital quality produces crystal-clear sound.

A compact disk has excellent fidelity, and it can be cued to start at a certain passage. Some CD players need a separate amplifier and speakers to take full advantage of the improved sound quality. But an average-size "boom box" will do the job nicely unless you have a very large audience. A CD burner permits you to record selected tracks of music either from another CD or from music you legally download from the Internet.

As with movies and videos, use audio aids sparingly. You do not want your speech's electronic soundtrack to interfere with your message.

COMPUTER-GENERATED PRESENTATION AIDS

Computer-generated graphics are images, words, charts, and graphs designed and presented with a computer and graphics software. Although computer-generated graphics can be overused and can distract from your message if used improperly, they open up professional-looking possibilities for illustrating your speech.

Using a presentation program such as PowerPoint, you can design and create complete presentation aids on your personal computer. You can then use the computer to display the presentation aid to your audience by connecting it to a special projector. You can run the program manually using a mouse (some computers are even equipped with a wireless mouse) or the keyboard to advance the images as you speak, or you can set the program to run automatically. Even if you don't have access to a computer to use for your presentation, you can create the graphic images you need using a computer at a commercial copy center or campus computer lab and then transfer the images to slides or overhead transparencies. Or you can print the images on paper and develop dazzling posters to display on an easel.

16.c Guidelines for Developing Presentation Aids

The following guidelines offer commonsense and research-based strategies that can help you prepare effective presentation aids for your speeches.[8]

ALLOW PLENTY OF TIME TO PREPARE YOUR PRESENTATION AIDS

Prepare your presentation aids well in advance of your speaking date so that you can make them as attractive and polished-looking as possible. Avoid late-night, last-minute construction of your presentation aids. A sloppy, amateurish presentation aid will convey the impression that you are not a credible speaker, even if you have spent many hours preparing the verbal part of your speech. If you haven't used computer-generated graphics before, don't expect to whip out the software manual and produce professional-looking images the night before your presentation. Focus your final hours on rehearsing, not on learning a computer program.

MAKE THEM EASY TO SEE

Without a doubt, the most violated principle of using presentation aids in public speaking is "Make it big!" Countless speeches have been accompanied by a chart or graph that contains writing too small to read, an overhead projector image not large enough to be legible, or a graph on a flipchart that simply can't be deciphered from the back row.

Make your presentation aid large enough to be seen by all in your audience; write big or use a font that even those in the back of the room will be able to read easily.

KEEP THEM SIMPLE

Simple presentation aids usually communicate best. Resist trying to make your visuals complicated. Indeed, *any* complexity is too much. Words should be limited to key words or phrases. Lengthy dissertations on poster board or an overhead transparency usually do more harm than good.

Presentation aids *support* your message; they are not your message. Or, as CEO John W. Roe wisely expressed, "Visual aids should be made to steer, not to row."[9] What are techniques for keeping your visual message simple? Consider these ideas:

- Use no more than seven lines of text on any single visual.
- Use bullet points in parallel structure (such as beginning each bulleted phrase with the same word, as we are doing in this list).
- Use the heading of each slide to summarize the essential point of the visual; if listeners only read the headings of your visuals, they should still be able to follow the key points of the story you're telling.[10]

If your presentation contains dry or complex information that might be tedious to absorb in large amounts, consider breaking up the pace by using drawings or pictures instead of text on some of your presentation aids. Your audience will find your presentation more understandable and enjoyable if you vary the types of graphics that you show. However, when you incorporate a drawing or picture into your presentation, be careful to ensure that the image you display complements the mental image created by your spoken words.

GROUP RELATED ELEMENTS INTO VISUAL UNITS

By grouping related points, you can help your audience grasp key concepts and understand relationships as you convey information. Grouping points frees up space. This space, in turn, highlights the text blocks and also provides a resting place for the eye.

The alignment you choose for your text and images also affects the open space on the visual aid and directs the reader's gaze. Alignment can be flush left, flush right, or centered. Centered alignment is often effective for titles, but centered body text can look ragged and disorderly. A flush left or flush right alignment makes the text look crisp and allows the eye to flow easily from point to point.

ESTABLISH A CONSISTENT GRAPHIC THEME

Choose a basic design and color scheme and use it throughout your presentation. If you are designing a series of graphics, try to repeat a word, a symbol, styles, or a font throughout the presentation to convey a sense of unity. To carry out a consistent theme, choose a symbol other than a round bullet to use for emphasis, maintain a consistent color scheme, and use consistent spacing.

Repetition, however, can be boring, so you may want to vary your visuals a little, but keep in mind that a consistent theme will help your audience process and remember complex information.

CHOOSE A TYPEFACE WITH CARE

Although software packages vary, generally you'll be able to choose from among dozens of typefaces and fonts. A **typeface** is a set of fonts that have common characteristics; the typeface Helvetica, for example, comes in a variety of sizes and styles, including roman, italic, and boldface. Each typeface has a name, and typefaces vary in weight and spacing. A **font** is a collection of all uppercase and lowercase letters, numbers, symbols, and punctuation of a particular typeface size. For example, 9-point Helvetica bold, 12-point Helvetica, and 16-point Palatino italic are all examples of fonts.

Make an informed choice rather than just using a typeface because it strikes your fancy at the moment. Graphic designers divide typefaces into four different classes: serif, sans serif, script, and decorative. You'll see each of these classes illustrated in Figure 16.6. Serif typefaces, like the ones you are reading in this book, are easier to read

Serif	**Sans Serif**
Times New Roman	Arial
Bookman Old Style	Franklin Gothic Book
Americana	Tahoma
Garamond	Century Gothic
Script	**Decorative**
Ashley Script MT	Whimsy
Freestyle	CRITTER
Brush Script	
School Script	

FIGURE 16.6 **Classes of Typefaces and Examples**

for longer passages because the little lines at the top and bottom of the letters (called *serifs*) help guide the eye from one letter to the next. Sans serif typefaces (*sans* means "without") do not have the extra lines. Script typefaces are designed to look like handwriting, but they should be used sparingly because they are harder to read than serif and sans serif type. And use decorative typefaces only when you want to communicate a particular tone or mood. Regardless of which typeface or font you use, don't use more than one or two typefaces on a single visual; if you do use two, designers suggest they should be from different font categories.

Of course, designers do sometimes violate these guidelines to achieve special effects. There is no law that says you cannot use a serif typeface in a title and a sans serif typeface in the text. Just be sure that your audience will be able to read and understand your message.

VARY FONTS AND FONT SIZES WITH CARE

A font is a typeface of a particular size and style. Font size is measured in points; a point is 1/72 of an inch. The larger the point size, the larger the letters. It is easy to get carried away by all of the possibilities, but if you combine typefaces carelessly, you will soon discover that your choices conflict instead of complement one another. The strategies discussed below should help you avoid conflict in your design.

You also need to think about readability when you decide what size to use for the various elements in your graphics. Your visuals must be big enough to be seen by people in the back row of your audience. How big is big enough? Microsoft offers some general guidelines for visual aids. They recommend using 44-point type for titles, 32-point type for subtitles or for text if there is no subtitle, and 28-point type for the text if there is also a subtitle. The Microsoft designers reason that it is better for a presentation aid to be too big than too small. If you are not sure your font is large enough, try looking at your visual aid in the setting where you will be making your presentation. Figure 16.7 illustrates a range of point sizes.

Avoid using all uppercase letters for emphasis, except in short titles. Longer stretches of text in all caps are hard to read, because our eyes are accustomed to seeing contrasting letter shapes. When we read, we recognize not only the individual letters, but also the shapes of the words. For example, when you drive along a highway, you can probably recognize the words on the sign for your exit long before you are close enough to make out the individual letters because you recognize the shape of the words.

USE COLOR TO CREATE A MOOD AND SUSTAIN ATTENTION

Graphic designers have long known that warm colors (oranges and reds) communicate excitement and interest (which is why most fast-food restaurant chains use red, yellow, and orange in their color schemes; they literally want to make you hungry and catch your attention). Cooler colors such as green and blue have a more calming effect on viewers. Warm colors tend to come forward and jump out at the viewer, whereas cool

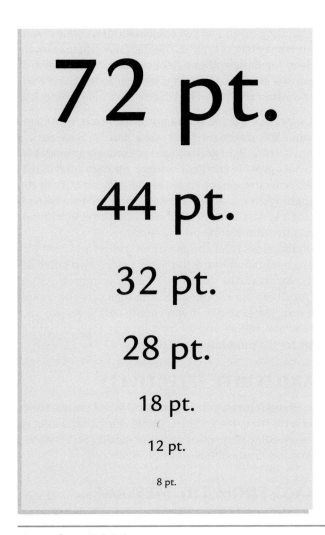

FIGURE 16.7   **Point Sizes**

colors recede into the background. What are the implications of the power of color to communicate? Consider using warm colors for positive messages (for example, "Profits are up") and cooler colors for more negative messages ("We're losing money").

    Avoid Conflicting Colors   It is also important to choose colors for backgrounds and text or graphics that contrast with one another but do not conflict. The use of yellow against a blue background is effective; the colors are contrasting yet harmonious. The use of purple against a blue background, on the other hand, is not effective because both colors are dark and the purple letters do not stand out from the background.

Be cautious about using green and red combinations in your visual aids. Some of your audience members may have a type of color blindness that makes these two colors indistinguishable. Even for those without color blindness, this combination is not effective. Red type against a green background is difficult to read. The colors are not harmonious and do not contrast effectively, making the text and graphics hard on the eyes.

Design for Contrast If you're designing overheads, consider using dark text on a light background. You might use black, dark blue, or dark red text that would stand out crisply from a white, light gray, or light yellow background. Each color would be distinctive and would provide excellent contrast for high readability. If your visual aids will be computer-generated and projected as slides, on an LCD, or through another projection system, light text on a dark background will produce better results. Yellow and white text on a black, dark blue, or dark green background will produce the contrast you need for an attention-getting presentation.

Attractive and harmonious color combinations will get and hold your listeners' attention. But resist the temptation to use too many colors. Two different colors of text on one background color should be sufficient. To unify your presentation, consider using the same color for all of your backgrounds, and then vary the complementary colors you use for the text. For example, if you choose dark green for your background color, you could use white, yellow, and a very light gray for text. Save your most dramatic color contrasts for the most important point.

USE BLACK AND WHITE EFFECTIVELY

If your budget or equipment limits you to black and white presentation aids, you can still use contrast to create attractive graphics. By choosing contrasting typefaces, spacing text widely or more compactly, using larger or smaller text, and using both bold and lightface text, you can create differences in textual color.

DON'T DETRACT FROM THE MESSAGE

Presentation graphics should be simple and uncluttered. As you begin to work with sophisticated layout and design tools, you may be tempted to load up your graphics with fancy fonts, clip art, and outlandish colors. Resist that temptation. Such visuals can quickly become distracting and hard to read. Instead of supporting your presentation, they will actually confuse your audience and detract from your message.

Each element in your visual aid should serve a clear and specific purpose that is appropriate to your audience, topic, and setting.

SHOW NUMERICAL DATA GRAPHICALLY

If you need to supply complex numerical data or information to illustrate a point or provide essential background information to your listeners, consider showing this information graphically. A well-drawn graph can often convey the information that you wish to present without requiring your audience to absorb and interpret complex numerical data.

HOW TO: *Select the Right Presentation Aids*

- Consider your audience. Factors such as audience size dictate the size of the visual you select. If you have a large audience, do not choose a presentation aid unless everyone can see it clearly. The age, interests, and attitudes of your audience also affect your selection of audiovisual support.
- Think of your speech objective. Don't select a presentation aid until you have decided on the purpose of your speech.
- Take into account your own skill and experience. Use only equipment with which you are comfortable or have had practical experience.
- Know the room in which you will speak. If the room has large windows with no shades and no other way to dim the lights, do not consider using visuals that require a darkened room.

The type of data you have and the message that you wish to convey will help you determine which type of graph is the most appropriate for your purposes. If your audience requires detailed numerical information in addition to what you present in your graphs, consider supplying it in a handout that they will be able to study in detail at their leisure.

16.d Guidelines for Using Presentation Aids

Now that we have offered strategies for developing effective presentation aids, here are some tips to help you use them for maximum audience impact.

DO NOT USE DANGEROUS OR ILLEGAL PRESENTATION AIDS

Earlier, we described a speaker who accidentally caused an archery bow to fly over the heads of his startled audience. Not only did he lose credibility because he was not able to string the bow successfully, he also endangered his audience. Dangerous or illegal presentation aids may either shock your audience or physically endanger them. These types of aids will also detract from your message. They are never worth the risk of a ruined speech or an injured audience member. If your speech seems to call for a dangerous or illegal object or substance, substitute a model, picture, chart, or other representational device.

REHEARSE WITH YOUR PRESENTATION AIDS

Jane nervously approached her speech teacher ten minutes before class. She wondered whether class could start immediately, because her presentation aid was melting. She had planned to explain how to get various stains out of clothing, and her first demonstration would show how to remove chewing gum. But she had forgotten the gum, so she had to ask for a volunteer from the audience to spit out his gum, so she could use it in her demonstration. The ice she had brought to rub on the sticky gum had by this time melted. All she could do was dribble some lukewarm water on the gummed-up cloth in a valiant but unsuccessful effort to demonstrate her cleaning method. It didn't work. To make matters worse, when she tried to set her poster in the chalkboard tray, it kept falling to the floor. She ended up embarrassed and on the edge of tears. It was obvious that she had not rehearsed with her presentation aids.

Unlike Jane, Marti knew she had an important presentation the next day, and she was well prepared. Because she was going to use PowerPoint computer graphics in her presentation, she carefully developed each visual to coordinate with her talk. She rehearsed her speech in the same room in which she would be speaking; she also practiced her presentation using the same computer that she would use for her speech. She competently sailed through her presentation without a hitch. Although the unexpected can always happen, Marti's thorough preparation and rehearsal boosted both her confidence and her credibility with her listeners.

Your appearance before your audience should not be the first time you deliver your speech while holding up your chart, turning on the overhead projector, operating the slide projector, or using the flipchart. Practice with your presentation aids until you feel at ease with them.

MAKE EYE CONTACT WITH YOUR AUDIENCE, NOT WITH YOUR PRESENTATION AIDS

You may be tempted to talk to your presentation aid rather than to your audience. Your focus, however, should remain on your audience. Of course, you will need to glance at your visual to make sure that it isn't upside down or that it is the proper one. But do not face it while giving your talk. Keep looking your audience in the eye.

EXPLAIN YOUR PRESENTATION AIDS

Some speakers believe that they need not explain a presentation aid. They think it's enough just to show it to their audience. Resist this approach. When you exhibit your chart showing the overall decline in the stock market, tell your audience what point you are trying to make.

Visual support performs the same function as verbal support. It helps you communicate an idea. Make sure that your audience knows what that idea is. Don't just unceremoniously announce, "Here are the recent statistics on birth rates in the United States" and hold up your visual without further explanation. Tell the audience how to interpret the data. Always set your visuals in a verbal context.

DO NOT PASS OBJECTS AMONG MEMBERS OF YOUR AUDIENCE

You realize that your marble collection will be too small to see, so you decide to pass some of your most stunning marbles around while you talk. Bad idea. While you are excitedly describing some of your cat's-eye marbles, you have provided a distraction for your audience. People will be more interested in seeing and touching your marbles than in hearing you talk about them.

What can you do if your object is too small to be seen without passing it around? If no other speaker follows your speech, you can invite audience members to come up and see your object when your speech is over. If your audience is only two or three rows deep, you can even hold up the object and move in close to the audience to show it while you maintain control.

USE ANIMALS WITH CAUTION

Most actors are unwilling to work with animals—and for good reason. At best, they may steal the show. And most often, they are unpredictable. You may think you have the smartest, best-trained dog in the world, but you really do not know how your dog will react to a strange environment and an unfamiliar audience. The risk of having an animal detract from your speech may be too great to make planning a speech around one worthwhile.

A zealous student at a midwestern university a few years ago decided to give a speech on cattle. What better presentation aid, he thought, than a cow? He brought the cow to campus and led her up several flights of stairs to his classroom. The speech in fact went well. But the student had neglected to consider one significant problem: Cows will go up stairs but not down them.

Another student had a handsome, well-trained German shepherd guard dog. The class was enjoying his speech and his demonstrations of the dog's prowess until the professor from the next classroom poked his head in the door to ask for some chalk. The dog lunged, snarling and with teeth bared, at the unsuspecting professor. Fortunately, he missed—but the speech was concluded prematurely. These and other examples emphasize our point: Use animals with care, if at all.

USE HANDOUTS EFFECTIVELY

Many speech instructors believe that you should not distribute handouts during a speech. Handing out papers during your presentation will only distract your audience. However, many audiences in business and other types of organizations expect a summary of your key ideas in written form. If you do find it necessary to use written material to reinforce your presentation, keep the following suggestions in mind.

- Don't distribute your handout during the presentation unless your listeners must refer to the material while you're talking about it. Do not distribute handouts that have only a marginal relevance to your verbal message. They will defeat your purpose.

- If you do need to distribute a handout and you see that your listeners are giving the written material more attention than they are giving you, tell them where in the handout you want them to focus. For example, you could say, "I see that many of you are interested in the second and third pages of the report. I'll discuss those items in just a few moments. I'd like to talk about a few examples before we get to page 2."

- After distributing your handouts, tell audience members to keep the material face down until you're ready to talk about the material; this will help listeners not be tempted to peek at your handout instead of keeping their focus on you and your message.

- Make sure you clearly number the pages on your handout material. This will make it easy for you to direct audience members to specific pages in your handouts.

- To make sure your listeners know what page of your handouts you want them to focus on, prepare overhead transparencies of each page of your handout. You'll be able to display the specific page you're talking about. Even if the words are too small for audience members to read, they will be able to glance up and see what page you're on if they miss your verbal description of where you are in the material. With a transparency you can also quickly point to the paragraph or chart on the page you want them to focus on. It's not a good idea, however, to economize by only displaying material designed to be used as handouts on an overhead projector and not providing handouts. The print will undoubtedly be too small to be seen clearly.

- If your listeners do not need the information during your presentation, tell them that you will distribute a summary of the key ideas at the end of your talk. Your handout might refer to the specific action you want your audience to take, as well as summarize the key information you have discussed.

TIME THE USE OF VISUALS TO CONTROL YOUR AUDIENCE'S ATTENTION

A skillful speaker knows when to show a supporting visual and when to put it away. For example, it's not wise to begin your speech with all your charts, graphs, and drawings in full view unless you are going to refer to them in your opening remarks. Time the display of your visuals to coincide with your discussion of the information contained in them.

Jessica was extremely proud of the huge replica of the human mouth that she had constructed to illustrate her talk on the proper way to brush one's teeth. It stood over two feet tall and was painted pink and white. It was a true work of art. As she began her speech, she set her mouth model in full view of the audience. She opened her speech with a brief history of dentistry in America. But her listeners never heard a word. Instead, they were fascinated by the model. Jessica would have done better to cover her presentation with a cloth and then dramatically reveal it when she wanted to illustrate proper tooth brushing.

Here are a few more suggestions for timing your presentation aids.

- Remove your presentation aid when you move to your next point, unless the information it contains will also help you communicate your next idea.

- Have your overhead transparency already in place on the projector. When you are ready to show your visual, simply turn on the projector to reveal your drawing. Change to a new visual as you make your next point. Turn the projector off when you are finished with your visual support.

- Consider asking someone beforehand to help you hold your presentation aid, turn the pages of your flipchart, or change the slides on the projector. Make sure you rehearse with your assistant so that all goes smoothly during your presentation.

USE TECHNOLOGY EFFECTIVELY

You may be tempted to use some of the new technologies we have described because of their novelty rather than because of their value in helping you communicate your message. Most of them, however, are expensive. And some novice speakers are tempted to overuse presentation aids simply because they can quickly produce eye-catching visuals. Resist this temptation. Also consider that many classrooms and lecture rooms are not equipped with the necessary hardware. And realize that to project images from large-screen projectors or LCD panels, you may have to dim the lights or turn the overhead lights completely off. As we have noted, when you use audiovisual equipment that requires a dark room, you lose vital visual contact with your listeners.

REMEMBER MURPHY'S LAW

According to Murphy's Law, if something can go wrong, it will. When you use presentation aids, you increase the chances that problems or snags will develop when you present your speech. The chart may fall off the easel, you may not find any chalk, or the bulb in the overhead projector may burn out. We are not saying that you should be a pessimist, just that you should have backup supplies and a backup plan in case your best-laid plans go awry.

HOW TO: *Use Presentation Aids Effectively*

- Rehearse with your presentation aids until you feel at ease with them.
- Make eye contact with the audience, not with your presentation aid.
- Explain your presentation aids; always set your visuals in a verbal context.
- Do not pass objects among members of your audience
- Use animals with caution.
- Use handouts effectively.
- Time the use of your visuals to control your audience's attention.
- Use technology effectively.
- Remember Murphy's Law.

If something doesn't go as you planned, do your best to keep your speech on track. If the chart falls over, simply pick it up and keep talking; don't offer lengthy apologies. If you can't find the chalk you will need and it is your turn to speak, quietly ask a friend to go on a chalk hunt in another room. A thorough rehearsal, a double-check of your equipment, and extra supplies such as extension cords, projector bulbs, or masking tape can help repeal Murphy's Law.

Summary

- Presentation aids are tools to help you communicate your ideas more dramatically than words alone can.

- Presentation aids help improve your listeners' understanding and recollection of your ideas. They also help you communicate the organization of your ideas, gain and maintain the audience's attention, and illustrate a sequence of events or procedures.

- Three-dimensional presentation aids include objects, models, and people.

- Two-dimensional presentation aids include drawings, photographs, slides, maps, graphs, charts, flipcharts, chalkboards, and projected transparencies.

- Audiovisual aids include videotapes, movies, CDs, and DVDs. Audio aids such as tapes and compact disks can also be used to help communicate ideas to your listeners.

- Software graphics packages can be used to produce many presentation aids inexpensively and efficiently.

- Simple, well-designed, and well-planned drawings and pictures can be valuable additions to your presentation.

- When preparing your presentation aids, make sure your visuals are large enough to be seen clearly by all of your listeners.

- Choose a basic design and color scheme and use it throughout your presentation. If you are designing a series of graphics, you can repeat a word, symbol, style, or font throughout the presentation to convey a sense of unity.

- Typefaces can be divided into four classes: serif, sans serif, script, and ornamental or decorative.

- When you choose colors, think about how you want your audience to react to your visual aid. It is also important to choose colors for backgrounds and text or graphics that contrast with one another but do not conflict.

- Each element in your visual aid should serve a clear and specific purpose that is appropriate to your audience, topic, and setting.

- A well-drawn graph can often convey the numerical message that you wish to present so that your audience need not absorb and interpret complex numerical data.

- Your visual aids should enhance your message, not deliver it for you. Each visual aid should also make sense on its own.

- Prepare your visuals well in advance, and make sure they are not illegal or dangerous to use.

- As you present your speech, be sure to look at your audience, not at your presentation aid; talk about your visual, don't just show it; avoid passing objects among your audience; use handouts to reinforce the main points in your speech; time the use of your visuals carefully; and be sure to have backup supplies and a contingency plan.

- No matter what medium you plan to use, you should give your audience enough time to absorb what you place in front of their eyes and to listen carefully to your verbal information before asking them to shift their attention to another image.

Key Terms

bar graph (p. 326)
CD (p. 332)
chart (p. 329)
computer-generated graphics (p. 333)
digital video disk (DVD) (p. 332)
font (p. 335)
graph (p. 326)

line graph (p. 326)
model (p. 324)
picture graph (p. 326)
pie graph (p. 326)
presentation aid (p. 321)
typeface (p. 335)

A QUESTION OF ETHICS

Tom is preparing a speech on driver safety. He plans to begin his speech with a series of graphic pictures showing traffic accident victims who were maimed or killed because they did not use safety belts. Is it ethical to show graphic images that arouse audience fears?

CHAPTER 17

Using Presentation Software

M any audiences, especially those in corporate America, have come to expect to see speeches accompanied by computer-generated presentations created with such popular software as PowerPoint. Although computer-generated presentations can be overused and, like any presentation aid, can distract from your message if used improperly, they nonetheless open up professional-looking possibilities for illustrating your speech.

> *We will draw the curtain and show you the picture.*
> —**William Shakespeare**

17.a Presentation Software

Some of the best tools for producing visual aids today are graphics presentation programs. These programs can assist you in making professional-looking visual aids, including transparencies, slides, handouts, and posters. You can also display the visual aids you produce with these programs on a computer screen or project them onto a large screen using a projection system, for larger audiences. These programs enable you to adapt your designs to suit a wide variety of settings without having to redo the visual aids each time.

Microsoft's PowerPoint, Persuasion® by Adobe, and Lotus's Freelance Graphics® are three of the best-known and most used tools for producing graphics. Using one of these programs, you can design and create complete presentation aids on your personal computer.

Even if you don't have access to a computer to use for your in-class presentation, you can create the graphic images you need using a computer at a commercial copy center or campus computer lab and then transfer the images to slides or overhead transparencies. Or you can print the images on paper and develop dazzling posters to display on an easel.

17.b Using Presentation Software

The various presentation software packages are designed to let you easily include a variety of aids in your presentation. For instance, you can develop a key word or phrase outline to emphasize your main points as you speak. You can incorporate computer-generated graphs, charts, or drawings into the presentation to display statistical information or illustrate particular points. You can also use a scanner to convert any photograph or drawing into digital format, which you can then incorporate as a visual image in your presentation.

If you have the necessary equipment, you can even incorporate video or audio clips into your presentation. As with any presentation aid, the images or clips that you choose must help develop your central idea; otherwise, do not include them.

There is an art to developing an effective computer-generated presentation. But you don't have to be a professional artist. That's the advantage of using presentation software—virtually anyone can use it to craft professional-looking presentations. In addition to learning the mechanics of the software program, keep the following tips in mind when designing computer-generated presentations.[1]

KEEP SIGHTS AND SOUNDS SIMPLE

Simple is better. Even though you can use fancy fonts and can add as many images as you like to your visual, don't. Keep in mind that presentation aids support your message; they are not your message.

Most graphics software lets you add sound effects to highlight your message. But the sound of a zooming racecar zipping across the computer screen or a typewriter sound as letters pop in place can detract from your speech. Cute sounds often lose their novelty after the first slide or two and can become irritating. We suggest that you be the soundtrack, not your computer.

REPEAT VISUAL ELEMENTS TO UNIFY YOUR PRESENTATION

Use a common visual element, such as a bullet or visual symbol, at the beginning of each word or phrase on a list. Use common color schemes and spacing to give your visuals coherence. Also, avoid mixing and matching different fonts. You get a professional, polished look when you use a similar visual style for each of your images.

Both color and black-and-white images are available as clip art. Clip art consists of pictures and images that either are in printed form or are stored as electronic images in a computer file. You can incorporate these images into your visuals. Clip art (as shown in Figure 17.1) can give your visuals and graphics a professional touch, even if you did not excel in art class. Repeating the visual image can provide a consistent look and feel to your presentation.

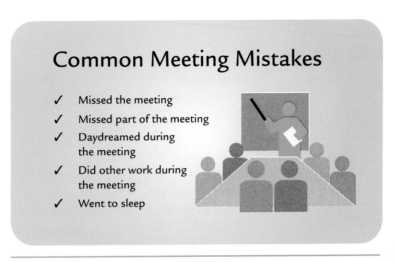

Common Meeting Mistakes

✓ Missed the meeting
✓ Missed part of the meeting
✓ Daydreamed during the meeting
✓ Did other work during the meeting
✓ Went to sleep

FIGURE 17.1 **Clip art can be used to illustrate visuals.**

CHOOSE A TYPEFACE WITH CARE

Make an informed choice rather than just using a font because it strikes your fancy at the moment. As noted in Chapter 16, serif typefaces are easier to read for longer passages because the serifs at the tops and bottoms of the letters help guide the eye from one letter to the next. Sans serif typefaces do not have the extra lines.

Script typefaces are designed to look like handwriting; although interesting and dramatic, they should be used sparingly because they are harder to read. And use decorative typefaces only when you want to communicate a certain special tone or mood. Regardless of which typeface or font you use, don't use more than one or two typefaces on a single visual; if you do use two, designers suggest they should be from different font categories.

MAKE INFORMED DECISIONS ABOUT USING COLOR

Color communicates. Think about the topic and purpose of your speech, and choose colors that will support and reinforce those. But don't get carried away using color. To unify your presentation, use the same background color on all visuals and no more than two colors for words. Using a dark background with lighter-colored words can have a pleasing effect and can be easy to see.

ALLOW PLENTY OF TIME TO PREPARE YOUR PRESENTATION AIDS

Prepare your presentation aids well in advance of your speaking date so that you can make them as attractive and polished-looking as possible. Avoid late-night, last-minute

HOW TO: *Develop Effective Visuals*

Make visuals simple	• Use bullets
	• Use parallel structure
	• Limit the use of sound
Make visuals unified	• Use a common visual image on each slide
	• Use a common font
	• Use common color schemes and spacing
Choose fonts carefully	• Use serif fonts to increase ease of reading
	• Use script and sans serif fonts sparingly
	• Do not use more than one or two typefaces on a single visual
	• Use decorative fonts only for dramatic impact
Choose colors carefully	• Use the same background color on all visuals
	• Use no more than two colors for words
	• Use a dark background with lighter text to catch attention
Prepare your visuals well in advance of your presentation	• Use your time to integrate your verbal message with your visual aids
	• Practice using your visuals when you rehearse your speech

presentation-aid construction. A sloppy, amateurish presentation aid will convey the impression that you are not a credible speaker, even if you have spent many hours preparing the verbal part of your speech.

If you haven't used presentation software before, don't expect to whip out the manual and produce professional-looking images the night before your presentation. Focus your final hours on rehearsing, not on learning a computer program.

17.C Preparing a Presentation with PowerPoint

There are many powerful and user-friendly graphics presentation programs available for both Windows and Macintosh computers. PowerPoint is the industry leader, and you will probably encounter it if you enter the business world. Here is an overview of its features.

When you first open PowerPoint, the program displays a dialog box with four options—AutoContent Wizard, Template, Blank Presentation, and Open an Existing Presentation.

AUTOCONTENT WIZARD

You can create a new presentation in several ways. You can start by working with the **AutoContent Wizard**, which provides suggestions and ideas for your presentation. The AutoContent Wizard guides you through the design and layout process by asking specific questions about your presentation. It also provides you with a variety of sample presentations from which to choose, such as a presentation on project status or one thanking a speaker.

The AutoContent Wizard asks you how your presentation will be used and what type of output you want—slides, overheads, handouts, etc. Once you provide this information, the AutoContent Wizard sets up an outline for titles, subtitles, main points, and subpoints and displays a slide design.

TEMPLATE

Another way to create a presentation is to select **Template**. PowerPoint comes with a variety of professional presentations as well as professionally designed templates that contain color schemes, slide and title masters with custom formatting, and styled fonts designed for a particular "look." Different versions of PowerPoint provide different selections and numbers of templates. Click on a template to preview it; then choose one you like.

BLANK PRESENTATION

You can also begin with an outline you import from another application, such as Microsoft Word, or with a **blank presentation** that has neither suggested content nor design. Choosing Blank Presentation enables you to create your own slide design. You choose a layout, colors, graphics, fonts, and how the content is organized.

OPEN AN EXISTING PRESENTATION

With PowerPoint you can also open, edit, or view existing presentations in many different locations—including on your hard drive, on a network drive that you are connected to, or on an Internet site.

SAVING A PRESENTATION

You can save a presentation, whether it's new or has been saved before. You can also save it with a different name or in a different location. You can save a presentation in HTML format so it can be viewed and used on the Internet. You can also save a presentation so that whenever you open it, it always starts as a slide show.

VIEWING A PRESENTATION

There are several different ways you can view the presentation aids you create: slide view, outline view, master view, slide sorter view, black-and-white view, and notes page view.

Slide View   In **slide view**, you can see an entire slide or zoom in to magnify a portion of the slide for detailed work. You can add both text and art to individual slides.

Outline View   **Outline view** displays text in an outline format so you can see how your main points flow from slide to slide. Use outline view when you need to organize and develop the content of your presentation.

Master View   To add items such as a company logo or formatting that you want to appear on every slide, notes page, or handout, use **master view** and make your changes on the appropriate master. The master text determines the format of text on all slides. If you make a change to the slide master, the change affects all slides in your presentation that are based on that master.

Slide Sorter View   In **slide sorter view**, you see miniature versions of all the slides in your entire presentation so you can easily add, delete, and reorder slides. You can also add transitions and animation effects and set the timings for electronic slide shows.

Black-and-White View   When you're creating a presentation in color, you might want to print handouts in black and white. When you switch to **black-and-white view**, the objects in your presentation appear on screen and print in shades of black and white.

Notes Page View   To display the notes page for selected slides, switch to **notes page view**, where you can type speaker notes to use during your presentation. You can also move or resize the slide image and the notes box and print a copy of your notes for reference.

CREATING A CONSISTENT LOOK

PowerPoint is designed to give your presentations a consistent appearance. In addition to the menu of design templates, you can use the program's slide master and color schemes features to control the look of your slides.

Slide Master   The **slide master** controls the format and placement of the titles and text you type on slides, while the **title master** controls the format and placement of the title slide and any other slide you designate as a title slide. Masters also hold background items such as graphics that you want to appear on every slide. Any change you make to a slide master is reflected on each slide.

Color Schemes   **Color schemes** are sets of eight balanced colors designed to be used as the main colors of a slide presentation—for text, background, fill, accents, and so on. Each different element on a slide is automatically given a color in the scheme. You can pick a color scheme for an individual slide or for an entire presentation.

If you create unique slides—for example, slides with backgrounds that differ from the master or fill colors that aren't part of the master color scheme—these slides retain their unique features even when you change the master. If you change your mind later, you can always restore slides you altered to the master format.

CREATING A DISTINCTIVE LOOK

Adding Text   The easiest way to add text to a slide is to type directly into any placeholder on the slide. When you want to add text outside a placeholder or shape, you can use the Text Box tool on the Drawing toolbar. Added text can be made to wrap around other visual elements if desired.

To add text to an AutoShape (a basic shape provided in PowerPoint), just click the shape and type the text. The text attaches to the shape and moves or rotates with the shape as the shape moves or rotates. You can add text to most AutoShapes, except to lines, connectors, and free forms.

Inserting Pictures   PowerPoint comes with its own set of pictures in the **Clip Gallery**, a collection of a wide variety of clip art that makes it easy for you to dress up your presentations with professionally designed images.

Select a picture by clicking Insert Clip Art, and then clicking the Clip Art or Pictures tab. The Clip Gallery includes a handy Find feature to help you locate just the right images for your presentation.

The AutoClipArt command on the Tools menu searches your presentation for concepts and then suggests images in the Clip Gallery you might use to express your ideas.

You can also insert pictures and scanned photographs from other programs and locations. To insert a picture from another program, point to Picture on the Insert menu, and then click From File. When you select a picture, the Picture toolbar appears with tools you can use to crop or recolor the picture, add a border to it, and adjust its brightness and contrast. To insert a scanned photograph, point to Picture on the Insert menu, and then click From Scanner.

You can also draw your own pictures using PowerPoint drawing tools.

Inserting Charts and Graphs   PowerPoint includes programs you can use to add charts, scanned pictures, and equations to your presentations. Organization Chart, Graph, Photo Editor, and Equation Editor all create embedded objects that you can insert into a presentation. By **embedding** data in a document, you can edit it in your document without having to return to the source files.

PRINTING A PRESENTATION

You can print your entire presentation— the slides, outline, speaker's notes, and audience handouts—in either color or black and white. To print your presentation, open the file and choose whether you want to print slides, handouts, notes pages, or an outline. Then identify the slides to be printed and the number of copies you want.

You can also make color or black-and-white overhead transparencies or create 35mm slides. When you print handouts, you can print one, two, three, or six slides on a page; or you can use the Microsoft Word Send To command (under the File menu), and then use Word to print other layout variations.

CREATING SPEAKER NOTES AND HANDOUTS

You can create notes pages while you're creating your presentation and then use these pages as speaker notes when you give a slide show. You can also create handouts of slides for the audience.

In addition, you can send your notes and slide images to Microsoft Word and use Word features to enhance their appearance, or you can send them there to become the starting point for a more detailed handout, such as a training manual.

When you want to show only the content of the slides, use handouts. Use notes pages when you want to include the speaker notes with the slides.

USING SPECIAL EFFECTS

Transitions and animations, when used sparingly, can add interest to your presentation, help highlight important points, and control the flow of information. PowerPoint comes with music, sounds, and videos you can play during your slide shows. You can also animate text, graphics, and other objects. You can insert a sound or video clip on a slide where you want it to play during a slide show. However, you will need special equipment on your computer to play music, sounds, and videos.

You can change the order and timing of animations and set them to occur automatically. Text can appear one letter, one word, or one paragraph at a time. Graphic images and other objects can appear progressively; the elements of a chart can be animated; the order in which objects appear on a slide can be altered; and you can set timings for each object.

QUICK CHECK: *Be Prepared*

- Save all files you create for your visual aids.
- Save your presentation on the hard drive, but also make backup disks.
- Keep the size of your files manageable.
- Plan to rehearse the presentation on the equipment that you will actually use for your presentation.
- Bring copies of the backup disk for your presentation.
- Check the equipment before you begin your presentation to ensure that it works correctly.
- Have a backup plan in case there are problems; either make a set of transparencies that you can show on an overheard projector, or print your slides and use them as handouts.

Summary

- Using a presentation program, you can design and create complete presentation aids on your personal computer.

- The images or clips that you choose to display must help develop your central idea; otherwise, do not include them.

- Keep sights and sounds simple.

- Repeat visual elements to unify your presentation.

- Choose a typeface with care.

- Make informed decisions about using color.

- Prepare your presentation aids well in advance of your speaking date so that you can make them as attractive and polished-looking as possible.

- There are several different ways you can view the presentation aids you create with PowerPoint: in slide view, outline view, master view, slide sorter view, black-and white view, and notes page view.

- There are three ways to control the look of your slides—with masters, color schemes, and design templates.

- PowerPoint comes with its own set of pictures in the Clip Gallery.

- PowerPoint includes programs you can use to add charts, scanned pictures, and equations to your presentations.

- You can print your entire presentation: the slides, outline, speaker's notes, and audience handouts. You can also make color or black-and-white overhead transparencies or create 35mm slides.

- You can create notes pages while you're creating your presentation and then use these pages as speaker notes when you give a slide show. You can also create handouts of slides for the audience.

- Transitions and animations, when used sparingly, can add interest to your presentation, help highlight important points, and control the flow of information.

Key Terms

AutoContent Wizard (p. 351)
black-and-white view (p. 352)
blank presentation (p. 351)
Clip Gallery (p. 353)
color schemes (p. 352)
embedding (p. 353)
master view (p. 352)

notes page view (p. 352)
outline view (p. 352)
slide master (p. 352)
slide sorter view (p. 352)
slide view (p. 352)
template (p. 351)
title master (p. 352)

A QUESTION OF ETHICS

If a speaker has a statistic that offers overwhelming evidence of the severity of a given problem, is it ethical for the speaker to save that statistic for last, or should the speaker reveal immediately to the audience how severe the problem really is? In other words, is there an ethical distinction between primacy and recency? Discuss your answer.

7

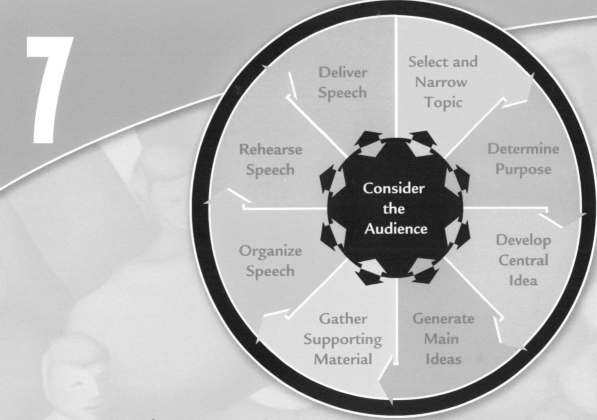

Deliver Speech

Select and Narrow Topic

Rehearse Speech

Consider the Audience

Determine Purpose

Organize Speech

Develop Central Idea

Gather Supporting Material

Generate Main Ideas

Types of Speeches

Types of Speeches

Types of Speeches

18 Speaking to Inform

➡ **Goals of Informative Speaking (p. 366)**
- To enhance understanding: Understanding occurs when a listener accurately interprets the intended meaning of a message.
- To maintain interest: If audience members feel they will benefit from your speech in some way, your speech will interest them.
- To be remembered: Being organized, using internal summaries and a final summary, and relating the message to listeners' interests are all useful methods of helping your audience increase their retention.

➡ **Types of Informative Speeches (p. 367)**
- A speech about an object might be about anything tangible—anything you can see or touch.
- A speech about a procedure discusses how something works or describes a process that produces a particular outcome.
- A speech about a person could be about someone famous or someone obscure, someone you've researched or someone you know personally.
- A speech about a major event should describe the event in concrete, tangible terms so as to bring the experience to life for your audience.
- A speech about ideas is usually more abstract than the other types of speeches.

➡ **Strategies to Enhance Audience Understanding (p. 373)**
- Speak with clarity.
- Preview your main ideas in your introduction.
- Tell your listeners how what you present relates to a previous point.
- Frequently summarize key ideas.
- Provide a visual outline to help listeners follow your ideas.
- Provide a handout prior to your talk with the major points outlined. Leave space on your outline so that listeners can jot down key ideas.
- Stay on message.

- Don't present too much information too quickly.
- Use principles and techniques of adult learning.
  - Give audience members information they can use immediately.
  - Actively involve them in the learning process.
  - Connect their life experiences with the new information you give them.
  - Explain how the new information is relevant to their needs and busy lives.
  - Give them information that helps them understand and solve problems.
- Clarify complex processes.
- Use effective visual reinforcement.

➡ **Strategies to Maintain Audience Interest (p. 377)**
- Establish a motive for your audience to listen to you.
- Tell a story.
- Present information that relates to your listeners.

➡ **Strategies to Enhance Audience Recall (p. 379)**
- Build in redundancy.
- Pace your information flow.
- Reinforce key ideas verbally.
- Reinforce key ideas nonverbally with gestures to accent or emphasize key phrases and well-placed pauses.

19 Understanding Principles of Persuasive Speaking

➡ **Persuasion Defined (p. 385)**
- Persuasive speaking is the process of changing or reinforcing attitudes, beliefs, values, or behavior.

➡ **How Persuasion Works (p. 387)**
- There are two ways listeners can be persuaded. They can be persuaded directly by the logic, reasoning, arguments, and evidence presented to them. The second way is to be persuaded by the credibility of the speaker or the overall emotional tone of the message.

- The need to restore balance to their lives and avoid stress, the need to avoid pain, and the desire to increase pleasure have been documented as influencing audiences' attitudes, beliefs, values, and behavior.

➡ **How to Motivate Listeners (p. 388)**
- Motivation is the underlying internal force that drives people to achieve their goals. Persuasion works because listeners are motivated to respond to a message.
- Motivate listeners by presenting information that will help them solve their problems or otherwise meet their needs.
- Convince the audience that good things will happen to them if they follow your advice or that bad things will occur if they don't.

➡ **How to Develop Your Persuasive Speech (p. 395)**
- The process of developing a persuasive speech follows the same audience-centered path you would take to develop any speech.
  - Consider the audience.
  - Select and narrow your persuasive topic.
  - Determine your persuasive purpose.
  - Develop your central idea and main ideas.

➡ **Putting Persuasive Principles into Practice (p. 401)**
- When persuading an audience, it is important to have an accurate understanding of listeners' likes and dislikes, beliefs about what is true or false, and perceptions of good or bad.
- Develop persuasive messages that help listeners avoid inconsistent or dissonant feelings.
- Tell listeners how your proposal will help solve a problem that is creating dissonance for them.
- Show how your ideas will address listeners' needs or result in positive, pleasurable outcomes or help them to avoid negative consequences.
- When using fear appeals, you have an ethical responsibility to make sure that the threat to listeners' well-being is an actual one.

20 Using Persuasive Strategies

➡ **Establishing Credibility (p. 405)**
- Credibility is the audience's perception of a speaker's competence, trustworthiness, and dynamism.
- Credibility is based on the listeners' mindset regarding the speaker.
- To be credible, a speaker should be considered informed, skilled, or knowledgeable about the subject he or she is talking about.
- A second aspect of credibility is a speaker's trustworthiness.
- Another factor in credibility is the speaker's dynamism, or energy. Dynamism is often projected through delivery. Charisma is a form of dynamism.

➡ **Enhancing Your Credibility (p. 407)**
- There are three phases of speaker credibility.
  - Initial credibility: the impression your audience has before you speak. Giving careful thought to your appearance and establishing eye contact before you begin your talk enhance your initial credibility.
  - Derived credibility: the perception your audience forms as you present yourself and your message.
  - Terminal credibility, or final credibility: the perception listeners have when you finish your speech.

➡ **Using Logic and Evidence to Persuade (p. 408)**
- Using words as well as statistical information to develop logical arguments can make your persuasive efforts more convincing.
- You must present evidence and then use appropriate reasoning to lead your listeners to the conclusion you advocate.
- There are three major ways to structure an argument to reach a logical conclusion: inductively, deductively, and causally.
  - Inductive reasoning: reasoning that arrives at a general conclusion from specific instances or examples.
  - Deductive reasoning: reasoning from a general statement or principle to reach a specific conclusion.
  - Causal reasoning: relating two or more events in such a way as to conclude that one or more of the events caused the others.

- You have an ethical responsibility to use your skill to construct arguments that are well supported with logical reasoning and sound evidence. Many persuaders use inappropriate techniques called fallacies.
  - Causal fallacy: making a faulty causal connection.
  - Bandwagon fallacy: arguing that "everybody thinks it's a good idea, so you should too."
  - Either/or fallacy: arguing that there are only two approaches to a problem in an effort to oversimplify the issue.
  - Hasty generalization: reaching a conclusion from too little evidence or nonexistent evidence.
  - Ad hominem: also known as attacking the person; this approach involves attacking irrelevant personal characteristics about the person who is proposing an idea rather than attacking the idea itself.
  - Red herring: attacking an issue by using irrelevant facts or arguments as distractions.
  - Appeal to misplaced authority: use of testimony by an expert in a certain field to support an argument on a topic on which the person has no particular expertise.
  - Non sequitur: an argument that does not logically relate to or follow from previous ideas or evidence.

➡ **Using Emotion to Persuade (p. 419)**
- The three dimensions of pleasure, arousal, and dominance are believed to form the bases of all emotional responses.
- When using emotion to persuade:
  - Use concrete examples that help your listeners visualize what you describe.
  - Use emotion-arousing words.
  - Use nonverbal behavior to communicate your emotional response.
  - Use visual images to evoke emotions.
  - Use appropriate metaphors and similes.
  - Use appropriate fear appeals.
  - Consider using appeals to several emotions.
  - Tap audience members' beliefs in shared myths.
- Regardless of which emotions you use to motivate your audience, you have an obligation to be ethical and forthright.

➡ **Strategies for Adapting Ideas to People and People to Ideas (p. 423)**
- To persuade a receptive audience:
  - Identify with your audience.
  - Clearly state your speaking objective.
  - Tell your audience exactly what you want them to do.
  - Ask listeners for an immediate show of support.
  - Use emotional appeals effectively.
  - Make it easy for your listeners to act.
- To persuade a neutral audience:
  - Capture your listeners' attention early in your speech.
  - Refer to beliefs that many listeners share.
  - Relate your topic not only to your listeners but also to their families, friends, and loved ones.
  - Be realistic about what you can accomplish.
- To persuade an unreceptive audience:
  - Don't immediately announce that you plan to change their minds.
  - Begin your speech by noting areas of agreement before you discuss areas of disagreement.
  - Don't expect a major shift in attitude from a hostile audience.
  - Acknowledge the opposing points of view that members of your audience may hold.
  - Establish your credibility.
  - Consider making understanding rather than advocacy your goal.

➡ **Strategies for Organizing Persuasive Messages (p. 427)**
- If you feel that your audience may be hostile to your point of view, advance your strongest arguments first.
- Do not bury key arguments and evidence in the middle of your message.
- If you want listeners to take action, tell them what you want them to do at the end of your speech.
- When you think your listeners are well informed and are familiar with the disadvantages of your proposal, present both sides of an issue, rather than just the advantages of your position.
- Make some reference to the counterarguments, and then refute them with evidence and logic.
- Four organizational patterns that can be used to organize persuasive speeches are problem–solution, refutation, cause and effect, and the motivated sequence.

- Problem–solution: The most basic organizational pattern for a persuasive speech is to make the audience aware of a problem and then present a solution that clearly solves it.
- Refutation: Another way to persuade an audience to support your point of view is to prove that the arguments against your position are false—that is, to refute them.
- Cause–effect method: Begin with an effect, or problem, and then identify the causes of the problem in an effort to convince your listeners that the problem is significant. You can also begin by noting a problem and then spelling out the effects of the problem.
- The motivated sequence is a five-step organizational plan. The five steps are attention, need, satisfaction, visualization, and action.

21 Special-Occasion Speaking

➡ **Public Speaking in the Workplace (p. 441)**
- Workplace presentations may be a routine aspect of meeting management or may take the form of reports to company executives, training seminars within the company, or public-relations speeches to people outside the company.
  - The general purpose of a report is to communicate information or policy; sometimes reports end with a persuasive appeal to try some new course of action.
  - Public-relations speeches are designed to inform the public and improve relations with them.

➡ **Ceremonial Speaking (p. 443)**
- Ceremonial speeches make up a broad class of speeches delivered on many kinds of occasions.
  - In an introductory speech, the speaker provides information about the main speaker and arouses interest in the speaker and his or her topic.
  - A toast is a brief salute to a momentous occasion, usually accompanied by a round of drinks and immediately followed by the raising or clinking together of glasses or goblets.

- Award presentations are somewhat like introducing a speaker or a guest: Remember that the audience did not come to hear you, but to see and hear the winner of the award. A presentation speech refers to the occasion, talks about the history and significance of the award, and names the person who is to receive the award.
- Nomination speeches involve noting the occasion and describing the purpose and significance of the office to be filled.
- Acceptance speeches are given by anyone who receives an award or nomination.
- Keynote addresses are usually presented at or near the beginning of a meeting or conference. The keynote emphasizes the importance of the topic or the purpose of the meeting, motivates the audience to learn more or work harder, and sets the theme and tone for other speakers and events.
- Commencement addresses must praise the graduating class and turn graduates toward the future.
- Commemorative addresses and tributes are those delivered during special ceremonies held to celebrate some past event and are often combined with tributes to the person or persons involved.
- Eulogies are delivered when someone has died. When you deliver a eulogy, you should linger on the unique achievements of the person to whom you are paying tribute and, of course, express a sense of loss.

➡ **After-Dinner Speaking: Using Humor Effectively (p. 451)**
- After-dinner speeches may present information or persuade, but their primary purpose is to entertain.
  - Tell humorous stories. Humorous stories should be simple. Successful humorous speakers also need a broad repertoire. Finally, it is important to know one's anecdotes very well.
  - Use humorous verbal strategies such as plays on words using devices such as puns, spoonerisms, malapropisms, hyperbole, understatement, verbal irony, or wit.
  - Create humor using such nonverbal cues as posture, gesture, and voice.

CHAPTER 18

Speaking to Inform

A s you participate in your company's management training classes, the group facilitator turns to you and asks you to summarize your team's discussion about the importance of leadership.

Your sociology professor requires each student to give an oral report describing the latest findings from the U.S. census.

At the conclusion of your weekly staff meeting, your boss turns to you and asks for a brief report summarizing the new product you and your team are developing.

> Not only is there an art in knowing a thing, but also a certain art in teaching it.
>
> —*Cicero*

In each of these situations, your task is to give information to someone. Whether you are having spontaneous conversation or delivering a rehearsed speech, you will often find that your speaking purpose is to inform, or teach someone something you know. One survey of both speech teachers and students who had taken a speech course found that the single most important skill taught in a public-speaking class is how to give an informative speech.[1]

A **speech to inform** shares information with others to enhance their knowledge or understanding of the information, concepts, and ideas you present. When you inform someone, you assume the role of a teacher by defining, illustrating, clarifying, or elaborating on a topic.

Conveying information to others is a useful skill in most walks of life. You may find that informing others will be an important part of your job. As a regional manager of a national corporation, you may have to report sales figures every fiscal quarter; as an accountant, you may have to teach your administrative assistant how to organize your files. Other activities, such as teaching a Chinese cooking class or chairing monthly meetings of the Baker Street Irregulars, can also require you to provide information.

In this chapter, we will suggest ways to build on your experience and enhance your skill in informing others. We will discuss goals of informative speaking, examine different types of informative tasks, and discuss specific ways to inform others. Finally, we will present some general principles for making your informative presentations memorable.

18.a Goals of Informative Speaking

Speaking to inform others can be a challenging task. As a student, you know from first-hand experience that you don't always soak up knowledge like a sponge just because a teacher presents information. Informing or teaching others is a challenge because of a simple fact: Presenting information does not mean that communication has occurred. Communication happens when the listeners make sense of the information.

When trying to help listeners make sense of information, speakers often have one or more of the following goals in mind: to enhance understanding, to gain and maintain interest, or to ensure that listeners can remember what was said. Let's explore each of these three important informative-speaking goals.

SPEAKING TO ENHANCE UNDERSTANDING

Understanding occurs when a listener accurately interprets the intended meaning of a message. Given the fragile nature of meaning, our words and nonverbal expressions are often misunderstood by others. Even when your speaking goal is to enhance understanding, the words you select to improve understanding may actually hinder the listener from accurately interpreting your meaning.

Someone once noted that the 500 most common words in the English language have over 14,000 different dictionary definitions! And these dictionary definitions do not include the personal or private meanings for words we use. Given the potential for misunderstanding, it's amazing we interpret meaning as well as we do.

When your speaking goal is to enhance understanding, you must first make sure you are using words that your listeners will interpret in the same way as you do. How do you do this? Be audience-centered. If you are using words that require unique background or knowledge your listeners don't have, your meaning will be muddled. The stories you tell, the examples you use, and the statistics you cite will only make sense to listeners if you and they have a common understanding for the words you speak. Otherwise, the job would be like trying to write a term paper on a computer with software designed to keep track of your checkbook rather than to write sentences. Without a common framework, your message won't make sense.

SPEAKING TO MAINTAIN INTEREST

You may have carefully selected words, examples, and illustrations that your listeners understand, but if your listeners are bored and not focusing on your message, you won't achieve your informative-speaking goal.

People may be interested in you and your topic for a variety of reasons. They often listen to what affects them directly, adds to their knowledge, satisfies their curiosity, or entertains them. These reasons are not mutually exclusive. For example, if you were talking to a group of businesspeople about the latest changes in local tax policies, you would be discussing something that directly affects them, adds to their knowledge, and satisfies their curiosity. But your listeners' primary interest would be in how local taxes affect them.

By contrast, if you were giving a lecture on fifteenth-century Benin sculpture to a middle-class audience at the YMCA, your listeners would be interested because your talk would add to their knowledge, satisfy their curiosity, and entertain them. Such a talk can also affect your listeners directly by making them more interesting to others. The commonality in these two speaking situations is the focus on listeners' interests and needs. If your audience members feel they will benefit from your speech in some way, your speech will interest them. And an interesting speech commands attention as well as respect.

SPEAKING TO BE REMEMBERED

You may recall that one day after hearing a presentation, most audience members will remember only about half of what they were told. And they will recall only about 25 percent two weeks later. Your job as an informative speaker is to improve on those statistics. Just because listeners do not typically remember what a speaker says, your listeners are not necessarily doomed to a similar fate.

Throughout this book we've offered strategies and suggestions to help you help listeners remember information. Being organized, being appropriately redundant by using internal summaries and a final summary, and relating the message to listeners' interests are all useful methods of helping your audience increase their retention of the message you've worked so hard to develop. Later in the chapter we'll offer additional suggestions for increasing audience recall of messages.

QUICK CHECK: *Goals of Informative Speeches*
- Enhance understanding
- Gain and maintain interest
- Ensure that listeners can remember what was said

18.b Types of Informative Speeches

Informative speeches can be classified according to the subject areas they cover. Classifying your speech can help you decide how to organize the information you want to present. As you will see in the following discussion, the demands of your purpose often dictate a structure for your speech.

As you look at these suggestions about structure, however, remember that good organization is only one factor in your audience's ability to process your message. In the next section, we will discuss additional strategies for ensuring that your listeners will *understand* the information in your speech.

SPEECHES ABOUT OBJECTS

A speech about an object might be about anything tangible—anything you can see or touch. You may or may not show the actual object to your audience while you are talking about it. Almost any kind of object could form the basis of an interesting speech:

Something from your own collection (rocks, compact disks, antiques, baseball cards, and so on)

Sports cars

Cellos

Personal digital assistants (PDAs)

Digital video cameras

WWII Memorial

Toys

Antique Fiestaware

Staffordshire dogs

The time limit for your speech will determine the amount of detail you can share with your listeners. Even in a 30- to 45-minute presentation, you cannot talk about every aspect of any of the objects listed. So you will need to focus on a specific purpose. Here's a sample outline for a speech about an object:

TOPIC: Dead Sea Scrolls

GENERAL PURPOSE: To inform

SPECIFIC PURPOSE: At the end of my speech, my audience should be able to describe how the Dead Sea Scrolls were found, why they are important to society, and the key content of the ancient manuscripts.

I. How the Dead Sea Scrolls were found

    A. The scrolls were found in caves near the Dead Sea.

    B. The scrolls were first discovered by a shepherd in 1947.

    C. In the late 1940s and early 1950s, archeologists and Bedouins found ten caves that contained Dead Sea Scrolls.

II. Why the Dead Sea Scrolls are important to society

    A. The Dead Sea Scrolls are the oldest known manuscripts of any books of the Bible.

    B. The Dead Sea Scrolls give us a look at Jewish life in Palestine over 2000 years ago.

III. The primary content of the Dead Sea Scrolls

    A. The Dead Sea Scrolls include all the books of the Old Testament except the book of Esther.

    B. The Dead Sea Scrolls include fragments of the Septuagint, the earliest Greek translation of the Old Testament.

C. The Dead Sea Scrolls include a collection of hymns used by the inhabitants of the Qumran Valley.

Speeches about objects may be organized topically, chronologically, or spatially. The speech about the Dead Sea Scrolls is organized topically. It could, however, be revised chronologically. The first major idea could be Jewish life in Palestine 2000 years ago. The second point could present information about how the scrolls were found in the 1940s and 1950s. The final major idea could be the construction of the museum in Jerusalem that houses the famous scrolls. Or the speech could be organized spatially, describing the physical layout of the caves in which the scrolls were found.

SPEECHES ABOUT PROCEDURES

A speech about a procedure discusses how something works (for example, the human circulatory system) or describes a process that produces a particular outcome (such as how grapes become wine). At the close of such a speech, your audience should be able to describe, understand, or perform the procedure you have described. Here are some examples of procedures that could be the subjects of effective informative presentations:

How state laws are made

How the U.S. patent system works

How a rotary engine works

How to refinish furniture

How to select an inexpensive stereo system

How to plant an organic garden

How to use the Internet

Notice that all these examples start with the word *how*. A speech about a procedure usually focuses on how a process is completed or how something can be accomplished. Speeches about procedures are often presented in workshops or other training situations in which people learn skills.

Anita, describing how to develop a new training curriculum in teamwork skills, used an organizational strategy that grouped some of her steps together like this:

I. Conduct a needs assessment of your department.

A. Identify the method of assessing department needs.

1. Consider using questionnaires.

2. Consider using interviews.

3. Consider using focus groups.

B. Implement the needs assessment.

II. Identify the topics that should be presented in the training.

A. Specify topics that all members of the department need.

B. Specify topics that only some members of the department need.

III. Write training objectives.

    A. Write objectives that are measurable.

    B. Write objectives that are specific.

    C. Write objectives that are attainable.

IV. Develop lesson plans for the training.

    A. Identify the training methods you will use.

    B. Identify the materials you will need.

Anita's audience will remember the four general steps much more easily than they would have if each aspect of the curriculum-development process were listed as a separate step.

Many speeches about procedures include visual aids. Whether you are teaching people how to hang wallpaper or how to give a speech, showing them how to do something is almost always more effective than just telling them how to do it.

SPEECHES ABOUT PEOPLE

A biographical speech could be about someone famous or someone obscure, someone you know through your research or someone you know personally. Most of us enjoy hearing about the lives of real people, whether famous or not, living or dead, who had some special quality. The key to presenting an effective biographical speech is to be selective. Don't try to cover every detail of your subject's life. Relate the key elements in the person's career, personality, or other significant life features so that you are building to a particular point rather than just reciting facts about an individual. Perhaps your grandfather was known for his generosity, for example. Mention some notable examples of his philanthropy. If you are talking about a well-known personality, pick information or a period that is not widely known, such as the person's childhood or private hobby.

One speaker gave a memorable speech about his neighbor:

> To enter Hazel's house is to enter a combination greenhouse and zoo. Plants are everywhere; it looks and feels like a tropical jungle. Her home is always warm and humid. Her dog Peppy, her cat Bones, a bird named Elmer, and a fish called Frank can be seen through the philodendron, ferns, and pansies. While Hazel loves her plants and animals, she loves people even more. Her finest hours are spent serving coffee to her friends and neighbors, playing Uno with family until late in the evening, and just visiting about the good old days. Hazel is one of a kind.

Note how the speech captures Hazel's personality and charm. Speeches about people should give your listeners the feeling that the person is a unique, authentic individual.

One way to talk about a person's life is in chronological order—birth, school, career, marriage, achievements, death. However, if you are interested in presenting a specific theme, such as "Winston Churchill, master of English prose," you may decide instead to organize those key experiences topically. First you would discuss Churchill's achievements as a brilliant orator whose words defied Germany in 1940 and then trace the origins of his skill to his work as a cub reporter in South Africa during the Boer War of 1899–1902.

SPEECHES ABOUT EVENTS

Where were you on September 11, 2001? Chances are that you clearly remember where you were and what you were doing on that and other similarly fateful days. Major events punctuate our lives and mark the passage of time.

A major event can form the basis of a fascinating informative speech. You can choose to talk about either an event you have witnessed or one you have researched. Your goal is to describe the event in concrete, tangible terms and to bring the experience to life for your audience. Were you living in Miami when Hurricane Andrew struck? Have you witnessed the inauguration of a president, governor, or senator? Have you experienced the ravages of a flood or earthquake? Or you may want to re-create an event that your parents or grandparents lived through. What was it like to be in Pearl Harbor on December 7, 1941?

Make the Event Come Alive   You may have heard a recording of the famous radio broadcast of the explosion and crash of the dirigible *Hindenburg*. The announcer's ability to describe both the scene and the incredible emotion of the moment has made that broadcast a classic. As that broadcaster was able to do, your purpose as an informative speaker describing an event is to make that event come alive for your listeners and to help them visualize the scene.

Organize for Effect   Most speeches built around an event follow a chronological arrangement. But a speech about an event might also describe the complex issues or causes behind the event and be organized topically. For example, if you were to talk about the Civil War, you might choose to focus on the three causes of the war:

I. Political

II. Economic

III. Social

Although these main points are topical, specific subpoints may be organized chronologically. However you choose to organize your speech about an event, your audience should be enthralled by your vivid description.

SPEECHES ABOUT IDEAS

Speeches about ideas are usually more abstract than the other types of speeches. The following principles, concepts, and theories might be topics of idea speeches:

Principles of communication

Freedom of speech

Evolution

Theories of aging

Islam

Communal living

Trickle-down theory of economics

Most speeches about ideas are organized topically (by logical subdivisions of the central idea) or according to complexity (from simple ideas to more complex ones). The example at the top of the facing page illustrates how one student organized an idea topic into an informative speech:

✔ **QUICK CHECK:** *Types of Informative Speeches*

Speech Type	Description	Typical Organizational Patterns	Sample Topics
Objects	Presents information about tangible things	Topical Spatial Chronological	The Rosetta Stone Museums International space station Voting machines
Procedures	Reviews how something works or describes a process	Chronological Topical Complexity	How to . . . Fix a carburetor Operate a nuclear-power plant Buy a quality used car Trap lobsters
People	Describes either a famous person or a personal acquaintance	Chronological Topical	Sojourner Truth Nelson Mandela Indira Gandhi Your granddad Your favorite teacher
Events	Describes an event that either has happened or will happen	Chronological Topical Spatial	The 2005 Southeast Asian tsunami Inauguration Day Cinco de Mayo
Ideas	Presents abstract information or discusses principles, concepts, theories, or issues	Topical Complexity	Communism Success Buddhism Reincarnation

TOPIC: Communication theory

GENERAL PURPOSE: To inform

SPECIFIC PURPOSE: At the end of my speech, the audience should be able to identify and describe three functions and three types of communication theory.

I. Communication theory has three important functions.

    A. Communication theory helps us explain how communication functions.

    B. Communication theory helps us make predictions about how people will communicate with others.

    C. Communication theory helps us be more in control of communication situations because we can explain and predict communication behavior.

II. There are several types of communication theory.

    A. Communication systems theory helps explain the transactive nature of communication.

    B. Rhetorical-communication theory helps explain and predict how public speakers influence others.

    C. Functional group-communication theory identifies the important group-communication behaviors that can enhance group communication.

18.c Strategies to Enhance Audience Understanding

The skill of teaching and enhancing understanding is obviously important to teachers, but it's also important to virtually any profession. Whether you're a college professor, chief executive officer of a Fortune 500 company, or a parent raising a family, you will be called on to teach and explain. At the heart of creating understanding in someone is the ability to describe both old and new ideas to the person. Just because an idea, term, or concept has been around for centuries doesn't mean that it is easy to understand. A person hearing an old idea for the first time goes through the same process he or she would experience in learning about the latest cutting-edge idea. How do you enhance someone's knowledge or understanding? We can suggest several powerful strategies.

SPEAK WITH CLARITY

To speak with clarity is to express ideas so that the listener understands the intended message accurately. Speaking clearly is an obvious goal of an informative speaker. What is not so obvious is *how* to speak clearly. As a speaker you may think you're being clear, but only the listener can tell you whether he or she has received your message. The most effective speakers (those whose message is both understood and appropriately acted on) build in success by consciously developing and presenting ideas with the listener in mind, rather than flinging information at listeners and hoping some of it

HOW TO: *Enhance Message Clarity*

- **Preview your main ideas in your introduction.** Let your listeners know what's coming.

- **Tell your listeners how what you present relates to a previous point.** People learn best by relating what they already know to new information.

- **Frequently summarize key ideas.** Sprinkling several summaries throughout your talk helps those listeners who may have tuned out now and then.

- **Provide a visual outline to help listeners follow your ideas.** Use Power-Point slides, an overhead projector, or some other presentation aid. Some people learn better by seeing ideas rather than by hearing them.

- **Provide a handout prior to your talk with the major points outlined.** Leave space on your outline so that listeners can jot down key ideas. Provide just enough structure so that your listeners can follow your ideas, but don't provide too much of your content in writing; having all the information in advance may decrease their reason for listening.

- **Once you announce your topic and outline, stay on message.** Don't go off on tangents.

- **Don't present too much information too quickly.** Remember the 30/70 principle we talked about in Chapter 5: 30 percent of your speaking time should be spent presenting information, and 70 percent should be spent supporting that information.

sticks. Communication researcher Joseph Chesebro has summarized several research-based strategies you can use to enhance message clarity.[2]

USE PRINCIPLES AND TECHNIQUES OF ADULT LEARNING

Most public-speaking audiences you face will consist of adults. Perhaps you've heard of **pedagogy,** the art and science of teaching children. The word *pedagogy* is based on the Greek words *paid,* which means "child," and *agogus,* which means "guide." Thus, pedagogy is the art and science of teaching children.

Adult learning is called **andragogy.**[3] *Andr* is the Greek word that means "adult." Andragogy is the art and science of teaching adults. Researchers and scholars have found andragogical approaches that are best for adults. (By "adults" we don't just mean people who are over 30; if you're a college student over the age of 18, you probably fit the characteristics of an adult learner.) What are andragogical, or adult-learning, principles? Here are some of the most important ones.

Adults Like to Be Given Information They Can Use Immediately

Most people who work in business have an in-basket on their desk to receive letters that must be read and work that must be done. Each of us also has a kind of mental in-basket, an agenda for what we want or need to accomplish. If you present adult listeners with information that they can apply immediately to their "in-basket," they are more likely to focus on and understand your message.

Adult Learners Like to Be Actively Involved in the Learning Process Rather than having your listeners sit passively as you speak, consider asking them questions to think about or, in some cases, to respond to on the spot.

Adult Learners Like to Connect Their Life Experiences with the New Information Adult listeners are more likely to understand your message if you help them connect the new information with their past experiences. The primary way to do this is to know the kinds of experiences that your listeners have had and then refer to those experiences as you present your ideas.

Adult Learners Like to Know How New Information Is Relevant to Their Needs and Busy Lives Most adults are busy—probably, if pressed, most will say they are *too* busy for their own good. So when speaking to an adult audience, realize that any information or ideas you share will more likely be heard and understood if you relate what you say to their chock-full-of-activity lives. People who are working, going to school, raising families, and involved in their community need to be shown how the ideas you share relate to their lives.

Adult Learners Are Problem-Oriented Learners Most people have problems and are looking for solutions to them. People will be more likely to pay attention to information that helps them better understand and solve their problems. Note the cover stories on many magazines; typical stories help people lose weight, avoid stress, enhance their love lives, or be healthy. When presenting information, seek ways to relate the ideas you share to listeners' problems. Doing so will help you solve the problem of how to get people to listen to you.

CLARIFY COMPLEX PROCESSES

If you are trying to tell your listeners about a complex process, you will need more than definitions to explain what you mean. Research suggests that you can demystify a complex process if you first provide a simple overview of the process with an analogy, model, picture, or vivid description.[4]

Before going into great detail, first give listeners the "big picture," or convey the gist of the process.[5] *Analogies* (comparisons) are often a good way to do this.[6] For example, if you are describing how a personal computer works, you could say that it stores information as a filing cabinet does or that computer software works like a piano roll on an old-fashioned player piano. In addition to using an analogy, consider using a model or other visual aid to show relationships among the parts of a complex process, following the guidelines we presented in Chapter 16.

You can also *describe* the process, providing more detail than you do when you just define something. Descriptions answer questions about the who, what, where, why, and when of the process. Who is involved in the process? What is the process, idea, or event that you want to describe? Where and when does the process take place? Why does it occur, or why is it important to the audience? (Of course, not all of these questions apply to every description.)

Or, you can clarify a process with a *word picture*. Word pictures are lively descriptions that help your listeners form a mental image by appealing to their senses of sight, taste, smell, sound, and touch. The following suggestions will help you construct effective word pictures.

- **Form a clear mental image of the person, place, or object before you try to describe it.**

- **Describe the appearance of the person, place, or object.** What would your listeners see if they were looking at it? Use lively language to describe the flaws and foibles, bumps and beauties of the people, places, and things you want your audience to see. Make your description an invitation to the imagination—a stately pleasure dome into which your listeners can enter and view its treasures with you.

- **Describe what your listeners would hear.** Use colorful, onomatopoeic words, such as *buzz, snort, hum, crackle,* or *hiss*. These words are much more descriptive than the more general term *noise*. Imitate the sound you want your listeners to hear mentally. For example, instead of saying, "When I walked in the woods, I heard the sound of twigs breaking beneath my feet and wind moving the leaves above me in the trees," you might say, "As I walked in the woods, I heard the crackle of twigs underfoot and the rustle of leaves overhead."

- **Describe smells, if appropriate.** What fragrance or aroma do you want your audience to recall? Such diverse subjects as Thanksgiving, nighttime in the tropics, and the first day of school all lend themselves to olfactory imagery. No Thanksgiving would be complete without the rich aroma of roast turkey and the pungent, tangy odor of cranberries. A warm, humid evening in Miami smells of salt air and gardenia blossoms. And the first day of school evokes for many the scents of new shoe leather, unused crayons, and freshly painted classrooms. In each case, the associated smells greatly enhance the overall word picture.

- **Describe how an object feels.** Use words that are as clear and vivid as possible. Rather than saying that something is rough or smooth, use a simile, such as "the rock was rough as sandpaper" or "the pebble was as smooth as a baby's skin." These descriptions appeal to both the visual and the tactile senses.

- **Describe taste, one of the most powerful sensory cues, if appropriate.** Thinking about your grandmother may evoke for you memories of her rich homemade noodles; her sweet, fudgy, nut brownies; and her light, flaky, buttery pie crust. Descriptions of these taste sensations would be welcomed by almost any audience, particularly your fellow college students subsisting mainly on dormitory food or their own cooking! More important, such descriptions can help you paint an accurate, vivid image of your grandmother.

- **Describe the emotion that a listener might feel if he or she were to experience the situation you relate.** If you experienced the situation, describe your own emotions. Use specific adjectives rather than general terms such as *happy* or *sad.* One speaker, talking about receiving her first speech assignment, described her reaction with these words:

> My heart stopped. Panic began to rise up inside. Me? . . . For the next five days I lived in dreaded anticipation of the forthcoming event.[7]

Note how effectively her choices of such words and phrases as "my heart stopped," "panic," and "dreaded anticipation" describe her terror at the prospect of making a speech—much more so than if she had said simply, "I was scared." The more vividly and accurately you can describe emotion, the more intimately involved in your description the audience will become.

USE EFFECTIVE VISUAL REINFORCEMENT

Research about learning styles suggests that many of your listeners are more likely to remember your ideas if you can reinforce them with presentation aids. As we noted in Chapter 16, pictures, graphs, posters, and computer-generated graphics can help you gain and maintain audience members' attention, as well as increase their retention. Today's audiences are exposed daily to a barrage of messages conveyed through TV and the Internet, both of which are highly visual electronic media. Modern audiences have grown to depend on more than words alone to help them remember ideas and information. When you present summaries of data, a well-crafted line graph or colorful pie chart can quickly and memorably reinforce the words and numbers you cite.

HOW TO: *Enhance Audience Understanding*

- Define ideas clearly.
- Use principles and techniques of adult learning.
- Clarify complex processes.
- Use effective visual reinforcement.
- Clarify the process with a word picture.
- Form a clear mental image of the person, place, or object before you try to describe it.

18.d Strategies to Maintain Audience Interest

Before you can inform someone, you must gain and maintain his or her interest. No matter how carefully crafted your definitions, skillfully delivered your description of a process, or visually reinforcing your presentation aid, if your listeners aren't paying attention, you won't achieve your goal of informing them. Strategies for gaining and holding interest are vital in achieving your speaking goal.

In discussing how to develop attention-catching introductions, we itemized several specific techniques for gaining your listeners' attention. The following strategies build on those techniques.

ESTABLISH A MOTIVE FOR YOUR AUDIENCE TO LISTEN TO YOU

Most audiences will probably not be waiting breathlessly for you to talk to them. You will need to motivate them to listen to you.

Some situations have built-in motivations for listeners. A teacher can say, "There will be a test covering my lecture tomorrow. It will count as 50 percent of your semester grade." Such threatening methods may not make the teacher popular, but they certainly will motivate the class to listen. Similarly, a boss might say, "Your ability to use these sales principles will determine whether you keep your job." Your boss's statement will probably motivate you to learn the company's sales principles. However, because you will rarely have the power to motivate your listeners with such strong-arm tactics, you will need to find more creative ways to get your audience to listen to you.

Don't assume that your listeners will be automatically interested in what you have to say. Pique their interest with a rhetorical question. Tell them a story. Tell them how the information you present will be of value to them. As the British writer G. K. Chesterton once said, "There is no such thing as an uninteresting topic; there are only uninterested people."[8]

TELL A STORY

Good stories with interesting characters and riveting plots have fascinated listeners for millennia; the words "Once upon a time . . ." are usually a sure-fire attention-getter. A good story is inherently interesting. Stories are also a way of connecting your message to people from a variety of cultural backgrounds.[9]

The characteristics of a well-told tale are simple yet powerful. Here we elaborate on some ideas about storytelling. A good story includes conflict, incorporates action, creates suspense, and may also include humor.

- **A good story includes conflict.** Stories that pit one side against another and that include descriptions of opposing ideas and forces in government, religion, or personal relationships foster attention. The Greeks learned long ago that the essential ingredient for a good play, be it comedy or tragedy, is conflict.

- **A good story incorporates action.** An audience is more likely to listen to an action-packed message than to one that listlessly lingers on an idea too long. Good stories have a beginning that sets the stage, a heart that moves to a conclusion, and then an ending that ties up all the loose ends. The key to holding audience interest is a plot that moves along.

- **A good story creates suspense.** TV dramas and soap operas long ago proved that the way to ensure high ratings is to tell a story with the outcome in doubt. Suspense is created when the characters in the story may do one of several things.

Keeping people on the edge of their seats because they don't know what will happen next is another element in good storytelling.

- **A good story may incorporate humor.** A fisherman went into a sporting-goods store. The salesperson offered the man a wonderful lure for trout: It had beautiful colors, eight hooks, and looked just like a rare Buckner bug. Finally, the fisherman asked the salesperson, "Do fish really like this thing?"

    "I don't really know," admitted the salesperson, "I don't sell to fish."

    We could have simply said, "It's important to be audience-centered." But using a bit of humor makes the point while holding the listener's attention. Not all stories have to be funny. Stories may be sad or dramatic without humor. But adding humor at appropriate times usually helps maintain interest and attention.

QUICK CHECK: *What Makes a Good Story?*

- A good story includes conflict.
- A good story incorporates action.
- Good stories have a beginning that sets the stage, a heart that moves to a conclusion, and then an ending that ties up all the loose ends.
- A good story creates suspense.
- A good story may incorporate humor.

PRESENT INFORMATION THAT RELATES TO YOUR LISTENERS

Throughout this book, we have encouraged you to develop an audience-centered approach to public speaking. Being an audience-centered informative speaker means being aware of information that your audience can use. If, for example, you are going to teach your audience pointers about trash recycling, be sure to talk about specific recycling efforts on your campus or in your own community. Adapt your message to the people who will be in your audience.

18.e Strategies to Enhance Audience Recall

Think of the best teacher you ever had. He or she was probably a good lecturer with a special talent for being not only clear and interesting but also memorable. The very fact that you can remember your teacher is a testament to his or her talent. Like teachers, some speakers are better than others at presenting information in a memorable way. In this final section, we review strategies that will help your audiences remember you and your message.

BUILD IN REDUNDANCY

It is seldom necessary for writers to repeat themselves. If readers don't quite understand a passage, they can go back and read it again. When you speak, however, it is useful to repeat key points. Audience members generally cannot stop you if a point in your speech is unclear or if their minds wander.

How do you make your message redundant without insulting your listeners' intelligence? We've already mentioned several techniques in this book. Permit us some redundancy here to make our point.

* A clear preview at the beginning of your talk as well as a summary statement in your conclusion are the most straightforward ways to make sure listeners get your points.

* Including internal summaries—short summaries after key points during your speech—is another technique to help audiences remember key ideas.

* Using numeric signposts (numbering key ideas verbally by saying, "My first point is . . ., My second point is . . ., And now here's my third point . . .") is another way of making sure your audience can identify and remember key points.

* A reinforcing visual aid that displays your key ideas can also enhance recall. If you really want to ensure that listeners come away from your speech with essential information, consider preparing a handout or an outline of key ideas. (When using a handout, make sure the audience is focusing on you, not on your handout.)

PACE YOUR INFORMATION FLOW

Organize your speech so that you present an even flow of information, rather than bunching up a number of significant details around one point. If you present too much new information too quickly, you may overwhelm your audience. Their ability to understand may falter.[10]

You should be especially sensitive to the flow of information if your topic is new or unfamiliar to your listeners. Make sure that your audience has time to process any new information you present. Use supporting materials both to help clarify new information and to slow down the pace of your presentation.

Again, do not try to see how much detail and content you can cram into a speech. Your job is to present information so that the audience can grasp it, not to show off how much you know.

REINFORCE KEY IDEAS VERBALLY

You can reinforce an idea by using such phrases as "This is the most important point" or "Be sure to remember this next point; it's the most compelling one." Suppose you have four suggestions for helping your listeners avoid a serious sunburn, and your last suggestion is the most important. How can you make sure your audience knows that? Just tell them. "Of all the suggestions I've given you, this last tip is the most important one. The higher the SPF level on your sunscreen, the better." Be careful not to overuse this technique. If you claim that every other point is a key point, soon your audience will not believe you.

REINFORCE KEY IDEAS NONVERBALLY

You can also signal the importance of a point with nonverbal emphasis. Gestures serve the purpose of accenting or emphasizing key phrases, as italics do in written communication.

A well-placed pause can provide emphasis to set off and reinforce a point. Pausing just before or just after making an important point will focus attention on your thought. Raising or lowering your voice can also reinforce a key idea.

Movement can help emphasize major ideas. Moving from behind the lectern to tell a personal anecdote can signal that something special and more intimate is about to be said. Your movement and gestures should be meaningful and natural, rather than seemingly arbitrary or forced. Your need to emphasize an idea can provide the motivation to make a meaningful movement.

QUICK CHECK: *Enhance Audience Recall*

- Build in redundancy.
- Pace your information flow.
- Reinforce key ideas verbally.
- Reinforce key ideas nonverbally.

Summary

- To inform is to teach someone something you know. Public speakers use specific goals, principles, and strategies to inform others.
- Informative speeches have three goals—to enhance understanding, to maintain interest, and to be remembered.
- Speeches about objects discuss tangible things.
- Speeches about procedures explain a process or describe how something works.
- Speeches about people can be about either the famous or the little known.
- Speeches about events describe major occurrences or personal experiences.
- Speeches about ideas are often abstract and generally discuss principles, concepts, or theories.
- To enhance your listeners' understanding of a message, (1) define ideas clearly, (2) use principles and techniques of adult learning, based on andragogical rather than pedagogical educational assumptions, (3) clarify complex processes and use de-

scriptions effectively, and (4) use effective visual reinforcement of your ideas when appropriate.

- To gain and maintain interest in your informative talk, establish a motive for your audience to listen to you. Next, tell a story; a well-told story almost always works to keep listeners focused on you and your message. Finally, present information that relates to your listeners' interest; in essence, be audience-centered.

- Help your listeners remember what you told them by being redundant as appropriate to foreshadow or restate the key ideas of your message.

- Pacing the flow of your information helps listeners recall your ideas.

- Reinforcing your ideas verbally and nonverbally can also help your audience members remember important points you make.

Key Terms

andragogy (p. 374)   speech to inform (p. 365)
pedagogy (p. 374)

A QUESTION OF ETHICS

The American Tobacco Institute has hired a physician to represent the organization at a meeting to discuss the relationship between tobacco and diseases. The physician has been instructed to support the institute's position. Is it ethical for the physician not to mention that the institute is paying him or her? Explain your answer.

SAMPLE INFORMATIVE SPEECH *Choosing a Speech Topic*

by Roger Fringer[11]

Today I'd like to talk to you about [pause] tables. Tables are wood . . . usually . . . and they are. . . . How often do we sit in a class and feel the intelligence draining out of us? In a speech class, we are given the opportunity to add to that feeling or to add to the intelligence. Selecting a meaningful speech topic will make our speeches interesting, important, as well as being informative. As students, we've all been in the situation of being more anxious than necessary because we are talking about an unfamiliar or uninteresting speech topic. In our public speaking class, we spend a number of hours giving speeches and listening to them. If we have four days of speeches, at what—seven speech topics, that equals 28 hours spent listening to speeches. Let's not forget that we are paying to listen to those speeches. If our tuition is, say, $15,000 a year, that's $875 that we have spent listening to those 28 hours of speeches. We work hard for our tuition, so we should spend it wisely. Spending it wisely means we don't waste our time. We don't waste our own time on preparing and giving the speeches, and we don't waste our classmates' time who have to listen to our speeches. The solution is simple if we take choosing our topic seriously.

◀ Roger cleverly captures attention by purposefully starting with an unimaginative topic and using halting delivery that makes listeners wonder, "What's this really about?"

◀ Roger establishes a common bond with his listeners by relating to them as fellow students who are often confronted with the same problem: how to select a topic for a speech.

◀ Rather than just saying we waste time and money when listening to speeches, Roger uses statistics specifically adapted to the audience to whom he is speaking; this is a good example of being audience-centered.

I recommend that we choose topics following *The Three I's* to guide us. The first *I* is to make speeches *interesting*. By doing so, we can alleviate the boredom that so often permeates the public speaking classroom. If the topic is interesting to us, we will present it in a manner that shows our interest. We will also keep our audience's attention when we know, as students, they can be thinking about a million other things. Choosing an interesting topic will also alleviate some of the angst, anxiety we feel while giving the speech topic.

◀ He clearly previews his major ideas and links each idea together by beginning each point with a word that begins with *I*.

The second *I* is to make the speech *important*. The speech should not only be interesting but important to us. It should be relevant to our lives now or in the future.

◀ Here he uses a signpost by clearly noting he's moved to his second point.

The third *I* is to make the speech *informative*. Let's not waste our tuition money by not learning anything new in those 28 hours of class time. This is our opportunity to learn from each other's experiences and expertise.

◀ Again, he uses a verbal signpost to indicate that this is his third point.

(continued)

SAMPLE INFORMATIVE SPEECH *(continued)*

Now, just picture yourself putting these ideas into practice. Imagine sitting in a classroom, listening to your classmates talk about issues or ideas that are important to them. They are so excited that you can't help but be excited about the topic with them. You're learning from their life experiences, experiences that you would not have had the opportunity to learn about if it had not been for their speech. Then, imagine being able to talk about the experiences and knowledge that are important to you. Sometimes you only have seven minutes to express what is most important to you. Besides that, it's to a captive audience that has no choice but to listen to you. There are few times in our lives when we can have an impact on someone else's life, and we have only a short amount of time to do it. But in our public speaking class, we can have that chance. Let's all think about how we use our time and energy in our public speaking class. I don't want to waste my time or have any unnecessary stress over [pause] tables. I would like all of us to use our opportunities wisely by choosing topics that are interesting, important, and informative.

◄ Although Roger's primary purpose is to inform, he uses a hypothetical example to tell the audience how the information he has given them will help them solve a problem—how to find a good speech topic.

◄ Roger provides closure to his message by making a reference to the example he used in his introduction.

CHAPTER 19

Understanding Principles of Persuasive Speaking

Efforts to persuade you occur at an average rate of once every two and a half minutes each day.[1] Because persuasion is such an ever-present part of your life, it is important for you to understand how it works.

In this chapter, we are going to discuss how persuasion works. Such information can help you sharpen your own persuasive skills and can also help you become a more informed receiver of the persuasive messages that come your way. We will define persuasion and discuss the psychological principles underlying all or most efforts at persuading others. We will also discuss some tips for choosing a persuasive speech topic and developing arguments for your speeches.

The purposes of informing and persuading are interrelated. Information alone has the potential to convince others, but if information is coupled with strategies to persuade, the chances of success increase. Persuasive speakers try to influence the listeners' points of view or behavior. If you want your listeners to respond to your persuasive appeal, you will need to think carefully about the way you structure your message to achieve your specific purpose.

In a persuasive speech, the speaker explicitly asks the audience to make a choice, rather than just informing them of the options. As a persuasive speaker, you will do more than teach; you will ask your listeners to respond to the information you share. Audience analysis is crucial to achieving your goal.

> . . . the power of speech, to stir men's blood.
>
> —William Shakespeare

19.a   Persuasion Defined

Persuasion is the process of changing or reinforcing attitudes, beliefs, values, or behavior. Although knowing your listeners' attitudes, beliefs, and values can help you craft any message, these three variables are especially important to consider when designing and delivering a persuasive message.

ATTITUDES

Our attitudes represent our likes and dislikes. An **attitude** is a learned predisposition to respond favorably or unfavorably toward something.[2] In a persuasive speech, you might try to persuade your listeners to favor or oppose a new shopping mall, to like bats because of their ability to eat insects, or to dislike an increase in sales tax. Attitudes are easier to change than either beliefs or values. Today we may approve of the president of the United States; tomorrow we may disapprove of him because of a recent action he has taken. For example, we may still believe that the country is financially stable because of the president's programs, and we may still value a democratic form of government, but our attitude toward the president has changed because of this particular policy decision.

BELIEFS

A persuasive speech could also change or reinforce a belief. A **belief** is something you understand to be true or false. If you believe in something, you are convinced that it exists or is true. Beliefs are typically based on past experiences. If you believe the sun will rise in the east again tomorrow, or that nuclear power is safe, you base these beliefs either on what you've directly experienced or on the experience of someone you find trustworthy. Beliefs are usually based on evidence, but we hold some beliefs based on faith—we haven't directly experienced something, but we believe anyway. A belief is more susceptible to change than a value is, but it is still difficult to alter. Beliefs are changed by evidence. Usually it takes a great deal of evidence to change a belief and alter the way your audience structures reality.

VALUES

A persuasive speech could also seek to change or reinforce a value. A **value** is an enduring concept of right or wrong, good or bad. If you value something, you classify it as good or desirable, and you tend to think of its opposite as bad or wrong. If you do not value something, you are indifferent to it. Values form the basis of your life goals and the motivating force behind your behavior. Understanding what your listeners value can help you refine your analysis of them and adapt the content of your speech to those values. Most of us acquired our values when we were very young and have held on to them into adulthood. Our values, therefore, are generally deeply ingrained. It is not impossible to change the values of your listeners, but it is much more difficult than trying to change a belief or an attitude. Political and religious points of view, which are usually based on long-held values, are especially difficult to modify.

Why is it useful to make distinctions among attitudes, beliefs, and values? Since the essence of persuasion is to change or reinforce these three kinds of predispositions, it is very useful to know exactly which one you are targeting.

Values are the most deeply ingrained; of the three predispositions, they change least frequently. Beliefs change, but not as much as attitudes. Trying to change attitudes is easier than attempting to change values. We suggest that you think carefully about your purpose for making a persuasive speech. Know with certainty whether your objective is to change or reinforce an attitude, a belief, or a value. Then decide what you have to do to achieve your objective.

Persuasive messages often attempt to do more than change or reinforce attitudes, beliefs, or values—they may attempt to change behavior. Getting listeners to eat less, to not smoke tobacco, to not consume drugs, to not drink and drive, or to exercise more are typical goals of persuasive messages that we hear. It seems logical that knowing someone's attitudes, beliefs, and values will let us precisely predict how that person will behave. But we are complicated creatures, and human behavior is not always neatly predictable. Sometimes our attitudes, beliefs, and values may not appear consistent with how we act. For example, you may know that if you're on a low-carb diet, you should avoid that second helping of Dad's homemade chocolate cake; but you cut off a slice and gobble it up anyway.

19.b How Persuasion Works

Now that you know what persuasion is and how attitudes, beliefs, and values influence your behavior, you may still have questions about how persuasion works. The **elaboration likelihood model (ELM) of persuasion** has a long name but is actually a simple idea that explains how you are persuaded to do or think about something.[3] The theory suggests that there are two ways you can be persuaded. First, you can be persuaded directly by the logic, reasoning, arguments, and evidence presented to you. For example, you buy a high-speed Internet connection for your home because you are convinced you will save time downloading information; you've read the literature and have made a logical, rational decision.

A second way you can be persuaded, according to the ELM, is more indirect. You can be persuaded by such peripheral strategies as catchy music used in an advertisement or by simply liking the salesperson who is selling you a product; it's not the logic or content of the argument that persuades you, it's the overall feeling you have about the product or the salesperson that triggers your purchase. When hearing a speech, you may be persuaded by the appearance of the speaker (he looks nice; I trust him), the sheer number of research studies in support of the speaker's proposal (there are so many reasons to buy this product, I think I'll take it), or the speaker's use of an emotionally charged story (I can't let that little girl starve; I'll donate 50 cents a day to save her). Aristotle noted that in addition to logical persuasive strategies, you can be persuaded by the credibility of the speaker (*ethos*), or by the overall emotional response you have to a message or messenger (*pathos*). Along with logical persuasive strategies, we will explore ways of bolstering credibility and using emotion in Chapter 20.

Which is best, the direct or the indirect approach to persuading others? As you might suspect, the answer is "it depends on your audience." Some listeners are more prone to being persuaded with logic and evidence. Others are persuaded by less logical forms of support. The best advice is to use all available ethical means of persuasion: appeals to logic, credibility, and emotion. Among the factors that determine whether you are more likely to be persuaded by a direct route (with logic) or a more indirect, peripheral route (with credibility or emotion) is the concept of motivation. **Motivation** is the internal force that drives people to achieve their goals. Our motives explain why we do things.[4] Several factors motivate people to respond to persuasive messages: the need to restore balance to their lives and avoid stress, the need to avoid pain, and the desire to increase pleasure have been documented as influencing attitudes, beliefs, values, and behavior.

19.c How to Motivate Listeners

It's late, and you're watching your favorite talk show before going to bed. The program is interrupted by a commercial extolling the virtues of a well-known brand of ice cream. Suddenly, you remember that you have some of the advertised flavor in your own freezer. You apparently hadn't realized how hungry you were for ice cream until the ad reminded you of the lip-smacking goodness of the cool, creamy, smooth treat. Before you know it, you are at the freezer, helping yourself to a couple of scoops of ice cream.

If the maker of that commercial knew how effective it had been, he or she would be overjoyed. The ad was persuasive and changed your behavior because the message was tailor-made for you. What principles explain why you were motivated to dig through the freezer at midnight for a carton of ice cream? At the heart of the persuasion process is the audience-centered process of motivating listeners to respond to your message.

Persuasion works because listeners are motivated to respond to a message. An audience is more likely to be persuaded if you help members solve their problems or otherwise meet their needs. They can also be motivated if you convince them that good things will happen to them if they follow your advice or that bad things will occur if they don't.

USE DISSONANCE

Dissonance theory is based on the principle that people strive to solve problems and manage stress and tension in a way that is consistent with their attitudes, beliefs, and values.[5] According to the theory, when you are presented with information inconsistent with your current attitudes, beliefs, values, or behavior, you become aware that you have a problem; you experience a kind of discomfort called **cognitive dissonance**. The word *cognitive* has to do with our thoughts. *Dissonance* means "lack of harmony or agreement." When you think of a dissonant chord in music, you probably think of a collection of sounds that are unpleasant or not in tune with the melody or other chords Cognitive dissonance means that you are experiencing a way of thinking that is inconsistent and uncomfortable.

Most people seek to avoid problems or feelings of dissonance. If, for example, you smoke cigarettes and a speaker reminds you that smoking is unhealthy, this reminder creates dissonance. You can restore balance and solve the problem either by no longer smoking or by rejecting the message that smoking is harmful.

The need to restore balance is common. We have all experienced it at one time or another. If you are walking down a flight of stairs too fast and start to lose your balance, you will probably grab for the handrail so you won't fall. This is similar to the process that, according to dissonance theory, occurs psychologically when information you hear causes you discomfort.

Creating dissonance with a persuasive speech can be an effective way to change attitudes and behavior. The first tactic in such a speech is to identify an existing problem or need. For example, a speaker seeking to ban aerosol sprays could begin her speech by focusing on a need we all generally share, such as the need to preserve the environment. The speaker could then point out that the continued use of aerosol sprays depletes the ozone layer, which protects us from the sun's harmful rays.

By doing so, the speaker is deliberately creating dissonance. She knows that people in her audience appreciate the convenience of aerosol sprays, so their attitudes about protecting the environment *conflict with* their feelings about getting housework done easily or styling their hair effectively. Next, the speaker would aim at restoring the audience's sense of balance. She could claim that her solution—using nonaerosol sprays—can resolve the conflict. Using this strategy, the speaker may motivate the audience to change their behavior. The change is the speaker's objective.

Political candidates use a similar strategy. A mayoral candidate usually tries first to make his or her audience aware of problems in the community, then blames the current mayor for most of the problems. Once dissonance has been created, the candidate then suggests that these problems would be solved, or at least managed better, if he or she were to be elected as the city's next mayor. Using the principles of dissonance theory, the mayoral candidate first upsets the audience, then restores their feeling of balance and comfort by providing a solution to the city's problem: his or her election as mayor.

How Listeners Cope with Dissonance   Effective persuasion requires more than simply creating dissonance and then suggesting a solution to the problem. When your listeners confront dissonant information, a number of options are available to them besides following your suggestions. You need to be aware of other ways your audience may react before you can reduce their cognitive dissonance.[6]

- **Listeners may discredit the source.** Instead of believing everything you say, your listeners could choose to discredit you. Suppose you drive a Japanese-made car and you hear a speaker whose father owns a Chevrolet dealership advocate that all Americans should drive cars made in the United States. You could agree with him, or you could decide that the speaker is biased because of his father's occupation. Instead of selling your Japanese-made car and buying an American-made car, you could simply suspect the speaker's credibility and ignore the suggestion to buy American automobiles. As a persuasive speaker, you need to ensure that your audience will perceive you as competent and trustworthy so that they will accept your message.

- **Listeners may reinterpret the message.** A second way your listeners may overcome cognitive dissonance and restore balance is to hear what they want to hear. They may choose to focus on the parts of your message that are consistent with what they already believe and ignore the unfamiliar or controversial parts. Your job as an effective public speaker is to make your message as clear as possible so that your audience will not reinterpret your message. If you tell a customer looking at a new kind of computer software that it takes ten steps to get into the word-processing program, but that the program is easy to use, the customer might focus on those first ten things and decide that the software is too hard to use. Choose your words carefully, and use simple, vivid examples to keep listeners focused on what's most important.

- **Listeners may seek new information.** Another way that listeners cope with cognitive dissonance is to seek more information on the subject. Your audience members may look for additional information to negate your position and to refute your well-created arguments. For example, as the owner of a minivan, you would experience dissonance if you heard a speaker describe the recent rash of safety problems with minivans. You might turn to your friend and whisper, "Is this true? Are minivans really dangerous? I've always heard they were safe." You would request new information to validate your ownership of a minivan. Similarly, when listeners hear a political speech that tries to change their view, they may seek new information to help justify their own stand on the issues.

- **Listeners may stop listening.** Some messages are so much at odds with listeners' attitudes, beliefs, and values that the audience may decide to stop listening. Most of us do not seek opportunities to hear or read messages that oppose our opinions. It is unlikely that a staunch Democrat would attend a fund-raiser for the state Republican party.

  The principle of selective exposure suggests that we tend to pay attention to messages that are consistent with our points of view and to avoid those that are not. When we do find ourselves trapped in a situation in which we are forced to hear a message that doesn't support our beliefs, we tend to tune the speaker out. We stop listening to avoid the dissonance. Being aware of the existing attitudes, beliefs, and values of the audience can help you ensure that they won't tune you out.

- **Listeners may change their attitudes, beliefs, values, or behavior.** A fifth way an audience may respond to dissonant information is to do as the speaker wishes them to. As we have noted, if listeners change their attitudes, they can reduce the dissonance that they experience. You listen to a life-insurance salesperson tell you that when you die, your family will have no financial support. This creates dissonance; you'd prefer to think of your family as happy and secure. So you decide to take out a $100,000 policy to protect your family. This action restores your sense of balance. The salesperson has persuaded you successfully. The goals of advertising copywriters, salespeople, and political candidates are similar: They want you to experience dissonance so that you will change your attitudes, beliefs, values, or behavior.

USE LISTENER NEEDS

Need is one of the best motivators. The person who is looking at a new car because he or she needs one is more likely to buy one than the person who is just thinking about how nice it would be to drive the latest model. The more you understand what your listeners need, the greater the chances are that you can gain and hold their attention and ultimately get them to do what you want. The classic theory that outlines basic human needs was developed by Abraham Maslow.[7]

Maslow suggests that there is a hierarchy of needs that motivates everyone's behavior. Basic physiological needs (such as for food, water, and air) have to be satisfied before we can be motivated to respond to higher-level needs. Figure 19.1 illustrates Maslow's five levels of needs, with the most basic at the bottom. When attempting to persuade an audience, a public speaker tries to stimulate these needs in order to change or reinforce attitudes, beliefs, values, or behavior. Let's examine these needs in some detail.

Physiological Needs   The most basic needs for all humans are physiological: We all need air, water, and food. According to Maslow's theory, unless those needs are met, it will be difficult to motivate a listener to satisfy other needs. If your listeners are hot, tired, and thirsty, it will be more difficult to persuade them to vote for your candidate, buy your insurance policy, or sign your petition in support of local pet-leash laws. As a public speaker, you should be sensitive to the basic physiological needs of your audience so that your appeals to higher-level needs will be heard.

Safety Needs   Once basic physiological needs are met, your listeners are concerned about their safety. We have a need to feel safe, secure, and protected, and we need to be able to predict that our own and our loved ones' need for safety will be met. The classic sales presentation from insurance salespeople includes appeals to our need for safety and security. Many insurance sales efforts include photos of wrecked cars, anecdotes of people who were in ill health and could not pay their bills, or tales of the head of a household who passed away, leaving the basic needs of his or her family un-

FIGURE 19.1   **Maslow's Hierarchy of Needs**

met. Appeals to use safety belts, stop smoking, start exercising, and use condoms all play to our need for safety and security.

In a speech titled "Emissions Tampering: Get the Lead Out," John appealed to his listeners' need for safety and security when he began his speech with these observations:

> A major American producer is currently dumping over 8,000 tons of lead into our air each year, which in turn adversely affects human health. The producers of this waste are tampering with pollution control devices in order to cut costs. This tampering escalates the amount of noxious gases you and I inhale by 300 to 800 percent. That producer is the American motorist.[8]

Social Needs   We all need to feel loved and valued. We need contact with others and reassurance that they care about us. According to Maslow, these social needs translate into our need for a sense of belonging to a group (a fraternity, a religious organization, a circle of friends). Powerful persuasive appeals are based on our need for social contact. We are encouraged to buy a product or support a particular issue because others are buying the product or supporting the issue. The message is that to be liked and respected by others, we must buy the same things they do or support the same position they support.

Self-Esteem Needs   The need for self-esteem reflects our desire to think well of ourselves. Jesse Jackson is known for appealing often to the self-worth of his listeners by inviting them to chant, "I am somebody." This is a direct appeal to his listeners' need for self-esteem. Advertisers also appeal to our need for self-esteem when they encourage us to believe that we can be noticed by others or stand out in the crowd if we purchase their product. Commercials promoting luxury cars usually invite you to picture yourself in the driver's seat with a beautiful person next to you while you receive looks of envy from those you pass on the road. The powerful need for self-esteem fuels many persuasive messages.

Self-Actualization Needs   At the top of Maslow's hierarchy is the need for **self-actualization**. This is the need to fully realize one's highest potential. For many years, the U.S. Army used the slogan "Be all that you can be" to tap into the need for self-actualization. Calls to be the best and the brightest are appeals to self-actualization. According to Maslow's assumption that our needs are organized into a hierarchy, needs at the other four need levels must be satisfied before we can be motivated to satisfy the highest-level need.

USE POSITIVE MOTIVATION

Positive motivational appeals are statements suggesting that good things will happen if the speaker's advice is heeded. A key to using positive motivational appeals effectively is to know what your listeners value. Knowing what audience members view as desirable, good, and virtuous can help you select the benefits of your persuasive proposal that best appeal to them.

What do most people value? A comfortable, prosperous life; stimulating, exciting activity; a sense of accomplishment; world, community, and personal peace; and happiness are some of the many things people value. How can you use these values in a persuasive speech? When identifying reasons for your audience to think, feel, or behave as you want them to, review the values just listed to determine what benefits would accrue to your listeners. If, for example, you advocate that your listeners enroll in a sign-language course, what are the benefits to the audience? You could stress the sense of accomplishment, contribution to society, or increased opportunities for friendship that would develop if they learned this new skill. A speech advocating that recording companies print the lyrics of all songs on the label of a recording could appeal to family values.

Most salespeople know that it is not enough just to identify, in general terms, the features of their product. They must translate those features into an obvious benefit that enhances the customer's quality of life. It is not enough for the real-estate salesperson to say, "This floor is the new no-wax vinyl." It is more effective to add, "And this means that you will never have to get down on your hands and knees to scrub another floor." When using positive motivational appeals, be sure your listeners know how the benefits of your proposal can improve their quality of life or the lives of their loved ones.

USE NEGATIVE MOTIVATION

"If you don't stop what you're doing, I'm going to tell Mom!" Whether he or she realizes it or not, the sibling who threatens to tell mom is using a persuasive technique called a *fear appeal*. One of the oldest methods of trying to change someone's attitude or behavior, the use of a threat is also one of the most effective. In essence, the appeal to fear takes the form of an "if–then" statement. If you don't do X, then awful things will happen to you. A persuader builds an argument on the assertion that a need will not be met unless the desired behavior or attitude change occurs.

The principal reason that appeals to fear continue to be made in persuasive messages is that they work. A variety of research studies support the following principles for using fear appeals.[9]

- **A strong threat to a loved one tends to be more successful than a fear appeal directed at the audience members themselves.** A speaker using this principle might say, "Unless you get your children to wear safety belts, they could easily be injured or killed in an auto accident."

- **The more competent, trustworthy, or respected the speaker, the greater the likelihood that an appeal to fear will be successful.** A speaker with less credibility will be more successful with moderate threats. The U.S. Surgeon General will be more successful in convincing people to use condoms to lessen the risk of AIDS than you will.

- **Fear appeals are more successful if you can convince your listeners that the threat is real and will probably occur unless they take the action you are advocating.** For example, you could dramatically announce, "Last year, thousands of smokers developed lung cancer and eventually died. Unless you stop smoking, there is a high probability that you could develop lung cancer, too."

- **In general, increasing the intensity of a fear appeal increases the chances that the fear appeal will be effective.** This is especially true if the listener can take some action (the action the persuader is suggesting) to reduce the threat.[10] In the past, some researchers and public-speaking textbooks reported that if a speaker creates an excessive amount of fear and anxiety in listeners, the listeners may find the appeal so strong and annoying that they stop listening. More comprehensive research, however, has concluded that there is a direct link between the intensity of the fear appeal and the likelihood that audience members will be persuaded by the message. Fear appeals work. Strong fear appeals seem to work even better than mild ones, assuming that evidence backs up the threat made by a credible speaker. The speaker who uses fear appeals has an ethical responsibility to be truthful and not exaggerate when trying to arouse listeners' fear.

- **Fear appeals are more successful if you can convince your listeners that they have the power to make a change that will reduce the fear-causing threat.** As a speaker, your goal is not only to arouse audience members' fear, but also to empower them to act. When providing a solution to the fear-inducing problem, make sure that there is something your listeners can do to reduce the threat.[11] If, for example, you tell your listeners that unless they lose weight, they will die prematurely, they may want to shed pounds but think it's just too hard to do. You'll be a more effective persuader if you couple your fear-arousing message (lose weight or die early) with a strategy to make weight loss achievable (here's a diet plan that you can follow; it is simple, and it works). The audience-centered principle again applies here. You may think the solution is evident, but will your listeners think the same thing? View the solution from their point of view.

QUICK CHECK: *Using Fear Appeals to Persuade*

- Fear appeals involving loved ones are often more effective than appeals involving audience members themselves.
- The greater your credibility, the more likely it is that your fear appeal will be effective.
- You must convince your audience that the threat is real and could actually happen.
- Strong fear appeals are more effective than mild fear appeals if there is evidence to support the threat made by the speaker.
- Empower your listeners to act, as well as arousing their fear.

The effectiveness of fear appeals is based on the theories of cognitive dissonance and Maslow's hierarchy of needs. The fear aroused creates dissonance, which can be reduced by following the recommendation of the persuader. Appeals to fear are also based on targeting an unmet need. Fear appeals depend on a convincing insistence that a need will go unmet unless a particular action or attitude change occurs.

Cognitive dissonance, needs, and appeals to the emotions, both positive and negative, can all persuade listeners to change their attitudes, beliefs, values, and behavior. Realize, however, that persuasion is not as simple as these approaches may lead you to believe. There is no precise formula for motivating and convincing an audience. Attitude change occurs differently in each individual; there are no magic words, phrases, or appeals. Persuasion is an art that draws on science. Cultivating sensitivity to listeners' emotions and needs and ethically using public-speaking strategies you have learned will help you make your persuasive messages effective.

19.d How to Develop Your Persuasive Speech

The process of developing a persuasive speech follows the same audience-centered path you would take to develop any speech.

As illustrated by the center of our model of the speechmaking process in Figure 19.2, you first consider your audience, especially when attempting to persuade listeners.

CONSIDER THE AUDIENCE

Although being audience-centered is important in every speaking situation, it is vital when your objective is to persuade. It would be a challenge to persuade someone without knowing something about his or her interests, attitudes, beliefs, values, and behaviors.

One essential aspect of being audience-centered is being sensitive to the culturally diverse nature of most contemporary audiences. In our multicultural society, how persuasion works for one cultural group is different from how it works for others. North Americans, for example, tend to place considerable importance on direct observations and verifiable facts. Our court system places great stock in eyewitness testimony. People in some Chinese cultures, however, consider such evidence unreliable because they believe that what people observe is always influenced by personal motives. In some African cultures, personal testimony is also often suspect; it is reasoned that if you speak up to defend a person or friend, you have an ulterior motive and therefore the observation is discounted.[12] Although your audience may not always include listeners from Africa or China, given the growing diversity of Americans, that possibility is increasing. Or, you may have listeners from other cultures with different perspectives.

Don't design a persuasive message using strategies that would be effective only for you or those from your cultural background. The wise persuader consciously thinks about the persuasive strategies that will be effective for his or her listeners. An effective communicator is especially sensitive to cultural differences between himself or herself and the audience, while at the same time being cautious not to make stereotypical assumptions about an audience based only on cultural factors.

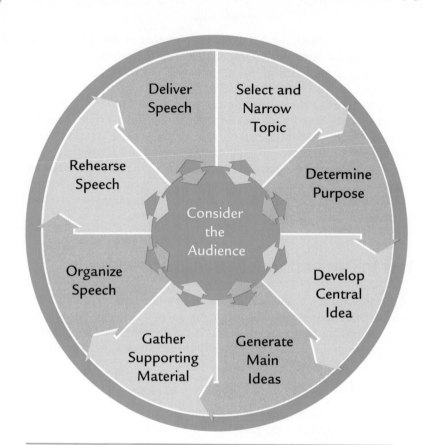

FIGURE 19.2 **Considering the audience is central to the speechmaking process.**

SELECT AND NARROW YOUR PERSUASIVE TOPIC

Deciding on a persuasive speech topic sometimes stumps beginning speakers. In Appendix C, we offer a few ideas to get you thinking about persuasive speech topics. But rather than just picking the first idea that pops into your mind, select a persuasive speech topic that is important to you.

What are you passionate about? What issues stir your heart and mind? You'll present a better speech if you've selected a topic you can speak about with sincere conviction. In addition to your interests, always reflect on your audience's passions and convictions. The ideal topic speaks to a need, concern, or issue of the audience as well as to your interests and zeal.

Controversial Issues   Controversial issues make excellent sources for persuasive topics. A controversial issue is a question about which people disagree. In choosing a controversial topic, you need to be audience-centered—to know the local, state, national, or international issues that interest your listeners. In addition, the best persuasive-speech topics focus on important rather than frivolous issues.

Media and Internet Resources   Pay attention to the media and the Internet to stay current on the important issues of the day. Read at least one newspaper every day, especially the editorial page. Also take a look at a national news magazine such as *Time, Newsweek,* or *U.S. News and World Report* to keep in touch with issues and topics of interest.

Another interesting source of controversial issues is talk radio programs. Both national and local radio call-in programs may give you ideas that are appropriate for a persuasive speech. You might also monitor chat rooms on the Internet or peruse the homepages of the Web sites of print and broadcast media for ideas. Even if you already have a clear idea of your speech topic, keeping up with the media and the Internet can give you additional ideas to help narrow your topic or can help you find interesting and appropriate supporting material.

DETERMINE YOUR PERSUASIVE PURPOSE

When your goal is to persuade, you've already decided on your general purpose: You want the members of your audience to change or reinforce their attitudes, beliefs, values, or behavior. But you still must develop your specific purpose.

When you persuade others, you don't always have to strive for dramatic changes in their attitudes, beliefs, values, and behavior. People rarely make major life changes after hearing just one persuasive message. Your persuasive speaking goal may be to move listeners *a bit closer* to your ultimate persuasive objective. **Social judgment theory** suggests that when listeners are confronted with a persuasive message, their responses can be classified into one of three categories: latitude of acceptance (they generally agree with the speaker), latitude of rejection (they disagree), or latitude of noncommitment (they're not sure how to respond).[13] If most of your listeners' attitudes and beliefs are in the latitude of rejection toward your position (for example, you're in favor of gay marriage and they are against it), it's going to be difficult to move them to a latitude of acceptance in one ten-minute speech. If you can get them to be less rejecting of the message and at least move toward being noncommited, you've made progress toward your goal. Although your goal is to have your listeners fully accept your message, that may be unrealistic. It's important to know where they stand on an issue (their latitude of acceptance, rejection, or noncommitment) before you craft your message so that you can ethically adapt to them.

DEVELOP YOUR CENTRAL IDEA AND MAIN IDEAS

The overall structure of your speech flows from your central idea and the main ideas that support your central idea. Your central idea, as you recall, is a one-sentence summary of your speech. When persuading others, most speakers find it useful to state their central idea in the form of a proposition. A **proposition** is a statement with which you want your audience to agree. In the following list, note how the propositions are actually the central ideas of speeches:

All students should be required to take a foreign language.

Organic gardening is better for the environment than gardening using chemicals.

The United States should not provide economic aid to other countries.

There are three categories of propositions: propositions of fact, propositions of value, and propositions of policy. Determining which category your persuasive proposition fits into can not only help you clarify your central idea but also give you an idea of how to select specific persuasive strategies that will help you achieve your specific purpose.

Proposition of Fact   A **proposition of fact** focuses on whether something is true or false, on whether it did or did not happen. Al Gore received more votes nationwide than George W. Bush in the 2000 presidential election. The Chicago White Sox won the 2005 World Series. Texas is bigger than Poland. Each of these statements is a proposition of fact that can be verified simply by consulting an appropriate reference or source. Other propositions of fact will take more time and skill—perhaps an entire persuasive speech—to prove. Here are examples of more controversial propositions of fact:

Talk radio is directly responsible for violence against U.S. government agencies.

When women joined the military, the quality of the military improved.

Children who were abused by their parents are more likely to abuse their own children.

Global warming is not occurring in our atmosphere.

To prove each of these propositions, a speaker would need to provide specific supporting evidence. To persuade listeners to agree with a proposition of fact, the speaker must focus on changing or reinforcing their beliefs. A belief, as you recall, is the way in which a person structures reality to accept something as either true or false. Most persuasive speeches that focus on a proposition of fact begin by identifying one or more reasons that the proposition is true.

The following persuasive speech outline on the topic of low-carb diets is based on a proposition of fact:

TOPIC:	Low-carbohydrate diets
GENERAL PURPOSE:	To persuade
PROPOSITION:	Low-carbohydrate diets are safe and effective.
SPECIFIC PURPOSE:	At the end of my speech, audience members will agree that low-carb diets are safe and effective.
MAIN IDEAS:	I. Carbohydrates are a significant part of our diets.
	A. Many people eat a significant amount of fast food that is laden with carbohydrates.
	B. Lunches provided in elementary school cafeterias include significant amounts of carbohydrates.
	C. Many people eat a significant amount of highly processed, carb-rich foods.

II. Carbohydrates are making people fat and unhealthy.

    A. A diet rich in carbohydrates leads to obesity.

    B. A diet rich in carbohydrates leads to Type II diabetes.

III. Low-carb diets are a safe and effective way to lose weight and maintain your health.

    A. Research supports the safety of such low-carb diets as the South Beach diet or the Atkins diet.

    B. Research supports the effectiveness of such low-carb diets as the South Beach diet or the Atkins diet.

Proposition of Value   A **proposition of value** is a statement that calls for listeners to judge the worth or importance of something. Values, as you recall, are enduring concepts of good and bad, right and wrong. Value propositions are statements that assert that something is either good or bad or that one thing or course of action is better than another thing or action. Note these examples:

It is wrong to turn away immigrants who want to come to the United States.

Democracy is a better form of government than Communism.

Speech communication is a better major than home economics.

A private-school education is more valuable than a public-school education.

Capital punishment is good for the country.

It is better for citizens to carry concealed weapons than to let criminals rule society.

Each of these propositions either directly states or implies that something is better than something else. Value propositions often compare two things directly and suggest that one of the options is better than the other.

Manny's speech was designed to convince his audience that contemporary rock music is better than classical music.

TOPIC:	Rock music
GENERAL PURPOSE:	To persuade
PROPOSITION:	Rock music is better than classical music for three reasons.
SPECIFIC PURPOSE:	After listening to my speech, the audience should listen to rock music more often than they listen to classical music.
MAIN IDEAS:	I. More people listen to rock music than to classical music.
	II. Rock music can increase worker productivity, whereas classical music is more likely to put people to sleep.
	III. Rock music is more sophisticated than classical music.

Proposition of Policy   The third type of proposition, a **proposition of policy**, advocates a specific action—changing a policy, procedure, or behavior. Note how all the following propositions of policy include the word *should*; this is a tip-off that the speaker is advocating a change in policy or procedure.

Our community should set aside one day each month as "Community Cleanup Day."

Senior citizens should pay for more of their medical costs.

Each student at our school should receive a new personal computer.

In a speech based on a proposition of policy, Paul aimed to convince his audience that academic tenure for college professors should be abolished. He organized his speech topically, identifying reasons academic tenure is no longer a sound policy for most colleges and universities. To support his proposition of policy, he used several propositions of fact. Note, too, that Paul's specific purpose involved specific action on the part of his audience.

TOPIC:	Academic tenure
GENERAL PURPOSE:	To persuade
PROPOSITION:	Our college, along with other colleges and universities, should abolish academic tenure.
SPECIFIC PURPOSE:	After listening to my speech, audience members should sign a petition calling for the abolition of academic tenure.
MAIN IDEAS:	I. Academic tenure is outdated.
	II. Academic tenure is abused.
	III. Academic tenure contributes to ineffective education.

Here's another example of an organization scheme for a persuasive speech based on a proposition of policy. Again, note how the major ideas are propositions of fact used to support the proposition of policy.

TOPIC:	Computer education
GENERAL PURPOSE:	To persuade
PROPOSITION:	Every person in our society should know how to use a personal computer.
SPECIFIC PURPOSE:	After listening to my speech, all audience members who have not had a computer course should sign up for one.
MAIN IDEAS:	I. Most people who own a personal computer do not know how to use most of the features.
	II. Computer skills will help you with your academic studies.
	III. Computer skills will help you get a good job, regardless of your major or chosen profession.

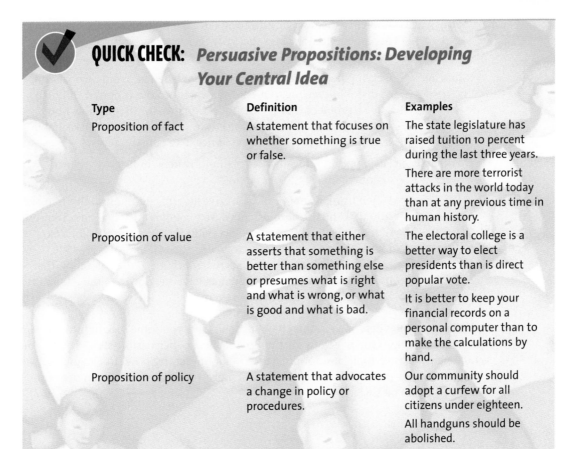

QUICK CHECK: *Persuasive Propositions: Developing Your Central Idea*

Type	Definition	Examples
Proposition of fact	A statement that focuses on whether something is true or false.	The state legislature has raised tuition 10 percent during the last three years.
		There are more terrorist attacks in the world today than at any previous time in human history.
Proposition of value	A statement that either asserts that something is better than something else or presumes what is right and what is wrong, or what is good and what is bad.	The electoral college is a better way to elect presidents than is direct popular vote.
		It is better to keep your financial records on a personal computer than to make the calculations by hand.
Proposition of policy	A statement that advocates a change in policy or procedures.	Our community should adopt a curfew for all citizens under eighteen.
		All handguns should be abolished.

19.e Putting Persuasive Principles into Practice

We have identified some of the factors that can motivate an audience and have provided some clues for formulating a proposition for your speech. We conclude this chapter by discussing three general principles to help you link the theory of persuasion with the practice of persuasion.

Principle: Audience members' attitudes, beliefs, and values help predict how they will respond to a persuasive message.

Practice: When persuading an audience, it is important to have an accurate understanding of listeners' likes and dislikes, beliefs about what is true or false, and perceptions of good or bad. You can do a better job of finding out what motivates an audience if you know their attitudes, beliefs, and values.

Principle: Audience members are motivated to avoid dissonance, to have their needs met, to do things that give them pleasure, and to avoid things that create pain.

Practice: Develop persuasive messages that help listeners avoid inconsistent or dissonant feelings. Or tell listeners how your proposal will help solve a problem that is creating dissonance for them. Show how your ideas will address their needs or result in positive, pleasurable outcomes or help them to avoid negative consequences.

Principle: Fear appeals, ethically used, can motivate your listeners to take action.

Practice: When using fear appeals, you have an ethical responsibility to make sure that the threat to listeners' well-being is an actual one. Your use of fear appeals will be more successful if (1) the threat is directed toward a loved one, (2) the source of the fear appeal is credible, (3) the threat is real and will actually occur, (4) there is action that listeners can take, and (5) listeners have the power to put a plan into action to reduce the threat to them or their loved ones.

The principles described in this chapter should give you some insight into the way persuasion works. Our overview of the approaches to persuasion should help you choose a persuasive topic and formulate a specific speech purpose. In Chapter 20, we will build on the principles reviewed here and suggest specific strategies for developing your persuasive message.

Summary

- Various theories explain how persuasion works to change or reinforce attitudes, beliefs, and values, which are the determinants of behavior.

- Persuasion is the process of changing or reinforcing attitudes, beliefs, values, or behavior.

- Attitudes are learned predispositions to respond favorably or unfavorably toward something.

- A belief is a person's understanding of what is true and what is false.

- A value is a concept of right and wrong.

- To motivate listeners, use cognitive dissonance, the human tendency to strive for balance or consistency in our thoughts. When a persuasive message invites us to change our attitudes, beliefs, values, or behavior, we respond by trying to maintain intellectual balance, or cognitive consistency.

- Maslow identified a five-level hierarchy of needs—physiological, safety, social, self-esteem, and self-actualization—that can be stimulated to motivate an audience to respond to persuasion.

- Positive motivational appeals can help you develop a persuasive message by encouraging listeners to respond favorably to your message.

- Fear can motivate people to respond favorably to a persuasive suggestion. To avoid pain or discomfort, we may follow the recommendation of a persuasive speaker.

- Preparing and presenting a persuasive speech require the same approaches as preparing any other kind of speech.

- Speakers can apply broad principles of persuasion to prepare a persuasive speech.

Key Terms

attitude (p. 385)
belief (p. 386)
cognitive dissonance (p. 388)
elaboration likelihood model (ELM) of
   persuasion (p. 387)
motivation (p. 387)
persuasion (p. 385)

proposition (p. 397)
proposition of fact (p. 398)
proposition of policy (p. 400)
proposition of value (p. 399)
self-actualization (p. 392)
social judgment theory (p. 397)
value (p. 386)

A QUESTION OF ETHICS

Markita wants to convince her classmates, a captive audience, that they should join her in a twenty-four-hour sit-in at the university president's office to protest the recent increase in tuition and fees. The president has made it clear that any attempt to occupy her office after closing hours will result in arrests. Is it appropriate for Markita to use a classroom speech to encourage her classmates to participate in the sit-in? Explain your answer.

CHAPTER 20

Using Persuasive Strategies

T he ancient Greek philosopher Aristotle defined rhetoric as the process of discovering the "available means of persuasion." What are these "available means" that can help you persuade an audience? In this chapter, we will discuss methods that can help you prepare your persuasive speech. Specifically, we will suggest how to gain

> *Speech is power:*
> *Speech is to persuade,*
> *to convert, to compel.*
> —**Ralph Waldo**
> **Emerson**

credibility, develop well-reasoned arguments, and move your audience with emotion. We will also discuss how to adapt your specific message to your audience, and we will end with some suggestions for organizing your persuasive message.

20.a Establishing Credibility

If you were going to buy a new car, to whom would you turn for advice? Perhaps you would ask a trusted family member, or you might seek advice from *Consumer Reports,* a monthly publication that reports studies of various products on the market, among them automobiles. In other words, you would probably turn to a source that you consider knowledgeable, competent, and trustworthy—a source you think is credible.

Credibility is the audience's perception of a speaker's competence, trustworthiness, and dynamism. As a public speaker, especially one who wishes to persuade an audience, you hope that your listeners will have a favorable attitude toward you. Current research points clearly to a relationship between credibility and speech effectiveness: The more believable you are to your listener, the more effective you will be as a persuasive communicator.

Aristotle used the term **ethos** to refer to a speaker's credibility. He thought that to be credible, a public speaker should be ethical, possess good character, have common sense, and be concerned for the well-being of the audience. Quintilian, a Roman teacher of public speaking, believed that an effective public speaker also should be a person of good character. Quintilian's advice was that a speaker should be "a good person speaking well." The importance to a speaker of a positive public image has been recognized for centuries. But don't get the idea that credibility is something that a speaker literally possesses or lacks. Credibility is based on the listeners' mindset regarding the speaker. Your listeners, not you, determine whether you have credibility or lack it.

Credibility is not just a single factor or a single view of you on the part of your audience. It encompasses many factors and many views. Aristotle's speculations as to the factors that influence a speaker's credibility have been generally supported by modern experimental studies.

One clear factor in credibility is **competence**—to be credible, a speaker should be considered informed, skilled, or knowledgeable about the subject he or she is talking about. If a used-car salesman sings the virtues of a car on his lot, you want to know what qualifies him to give believable information about the car.

Do competent speakers always get positive results? Although there are no absolutes, one comprehensive study found that the candidates for U.S. president who emphasized policy proposals more than their own character in their campaign speeches were more likely to win elections.[1] Although audiences are certainly swayed by a variety of issues, they seem to highly value solid ideas that enhance competence.

When you give a speech, you will be more persuasive if you convince your listeners that you are knowledgeable about your topic. If, for example, you say it would be a good idea for everyone to have a medical checkup each year, your listeners might mentally ask, "Why? What are your qualifications to make such a proposal?" But if you support your conclusion with medical statistics showing how having a physical exam each year leads to a dramatically prolonged life, you enhance the credibility of your suggestion. Thus, one way to enhance your competence is to cite credible evidence to support your point.

A second major factor that influences your audience's response to you is **trustworthiness**. You trust people whom you believe to be honest. While delivering your speech, you have to convey honesty and sincerity. Your audience will be looking for evidence that they can trust you, that you are believable.

Earning an audience's trust is not something that you can do simply by saying, "Trust me." You earn trust by demonstrating that you have had experience dealing with the issues you talk about. Your listeners would be more likely to trust your advice about how to travel around Europe on $50 a day if you had been there than they would if you took your information from a tour book you bought from the bargain table at the bookstore. Your trustworthiness may be suspect if you advocate something that will result in a direct benefit to you. That's why salespeople and politicians are often stereotyped as being untrustworthy; if you do what they say, they will clearly benefit from a sales commission if you buy a product, or gain power and position if you give them your vote.

A third factor in credibility is a speaker's **dynamism**, or energy. Dynamism is often projected through delivery. **Charisma** is a form of dynamism. A charismatic person possesses charm, talent, magnetism, and other qualities that make the person attractive and energetic. Many people considered Presidents Franklin Roosevelt and Ronald Reagan charismatic speakers.

20.b Enhancing Your Credibility

Speakers establish their credibility in three phases.

INITIAL CREDIBILITY

Initial credibility is the impression of your credibility your listeners have even before you speak. Giving careful thought to your appearance and establishing eye contact before you begin your talk will enhance both your confidence and your initial credibility. It is also wise to prepare a brief description of your credentials and accomplishments so that the person who introduces you can use it in his or her introductory remarks. Even if you are not asked for a statement beforehand, be prepared with one.

DERIVED CREDIBILITY

Derived credibility is the perception of your credibility your audience forms as you present yourself and your message. Most of this book presents principles and skills that help establish your credibility as a speaker. Several specific research-supported skills for enhancing your credibility as you speak include establishing common ground with your audience, supporting your key arguments with evidence, and presenting a well-organized and well-delivered message.

You establish common ground by indicating in your opening remarks that you share the values and concerns of your audience. To begin to persuade an audience that she understands why budget cuts upset parents, a politician might speak of her own children. If you are a student persuading classmates to enroll in an economics class, you could stress that understanding economic issues will be useful as they face the process of interviewing for a job. Of course, you have an ethical responsibility to be truthful when outlining the common goals you and your audience share.

Having evidence to support your persuasive conclusions strengthens your credibility.[2] Margo was baffled as to why her plea for donations for the homeless fell flat. No one offered any financial support for her cause when she concluded her speech. Why? She offered no proof that there really were any homeless people in the community. If she had provided well-documented evidence that there was a problem and that the organization she supported could effectively solve the problem, she would have been more likely to gain support for her position.

Presenting a well-organized message also enhances your credibility as a competent and rational advocate.[3] Rambling, emotional requests rarely change or reinforce listeners' opinions or behavior. We will present specific organizational strategies for persuasive messages later in the chapter. Regardless of the organizational pattern you use, it is crucial to ensure that your message is logically structured and uses appropriate internal summaries, signposts, and enumeration of key ideas.

Your delivery also affects your derived credibility. For most North Americans, frequent eye contact, varied vocal inflection, and appropriate attire have positive influences on your ability to persuade listeners to respond to your message.[4] Why does delivery affect how persuasive you are? Researchers suggest that if your listeners expect you to be a good speaker and you aren't, they are less likely to do what you ask them to do.[5] So don't violate their expectations by presenting a poorly delivered speech. Effective delivery also enhances your ability to persuade, because it helps gain and maintain listener attention and affects whether listeners will like you.[6] If you can arouse listeners' attention and if they like you, you'll be more persuasive than if you don't gain their attention and they don't like you.

TERMINAL CREDIBILITY

The last phase of credibility, called **terminal credibility**, or final credibility, is the perception of your credibility your listeners have when you finish your speech. Again we emphasize the value of eye contact. Also, don't start leaving the lectern or the speaking area until you have finished your closing sentence. Even if there is no planned question-and-answer period following your speech, be ready to respond to questions from interested listeners.

20.C Using Logic and Evidence to Persuade

"The reason we need to cut taxes is to improve the economy," claimed the politician on a Sunday-morning talk show. "The stock market has lost 300 points this month. People aren't buying things. A tax cut will put money in their pockets and give the economy a boost." In an effort to persuade reluctant members of her political party to support a tax cut, this politician was using a logical argument supported with evidence that stock prices were dropping. Logic is a formal system of rules for making inferences. Because wise audience members will be listening, persuasive speakers need to give careful attention to the way they use logic to reach a conclusion. Aristotle called logic **logos**, which literally means "the word." Using words as well as statistical information to develop logical arguments can make your persuasive efforts more convincing. It can also clarify your own thinking and help make your points clear to your listeners. Logic is central to all persuasive speeches.

Aristotle said that any persuasive speech has two parts: First, you state your case. Second, you prove your case. In essence, he was saying that you must present evidence and then use appropriate reasoning to lead your listeners to the conclusion you advocate. Reasoning is the process of drawing a conclusion from evidence. Evidence consists of the facts, examples, statistics, and expert opinions that you use to support the points you wish to make. When advancing an argument, it is your task to prove your point. Proof consists of the evidence you offer plus the conclusion you draw from it. The Sunday-morning talk-show politician reached the conclusion that a tax cut was necessary; the evidence supporting her claim was lower stock-market values and fewer people buying things. The conclusion: We need a tax cut to stimulate the economy. Let's consider the two key elements of proof in greater detail.

UNDERSTANDING TYPES OF REASONING

Developing well-reasoned arguments for persuasive messages has been important since antiquity. If your arguments are structured in a rational way, you have a greater chance of persuading your listeners. There are three major ways to structure an argument to reach a logical conclusion: inductively, deductively, and causally.

Inductive Reasoning   Reasoning that arrives at a general conclusion from specific instances or examples is known as **inductive reasoning**. Using this classical approach, you make a **generalization**—an all-encompassing statement—based on specific examples, facts, statistics, and opinions. You may not know for a certainty that the specific instances prove that the conclusion is true, but you decide that in all probability, the specific instances support the general conclusion. According to contemporary logicians, you reason inductively when you claim that an outcome is probably true because of specific evidence.

For example, if you were giving a speech attempting to convince your audience that foreign cars are unreliable, you might use inductive reasoning to make your point. You could announce that you recently bought a foreign car that gave you trouble. Your cousin also bought a foreign car that kept stalling on the freeway. Finally, your English professor told you her foreign car has broken down several times in the past few weeks. Based on these specific examples, you ask your audience to agree with your general conclusion: Foreign cars are unreliable.

HOW TO: *Judge the Validity of a Generalization*

- **Are there enough specific instances to support the conclusion?** Are three examples of problems with foreign cars enough to prove your point that all foreign cars are unreliable? Of the several million foreign cars manufactured, three cars, especially if they are of different makes, are not a large sample. If those examples were supported by additional statistical evidence that more than 50 percent of foreign-car owners complained of serious engine malfunctions, the evidence would be more convincing.

- **Are the specific instances typical?** Are the three examples you cite representative of all foreign cars manufactured? How do you know? What are the data on the performance of foreign cars? Also, are you, your cousin, and your professor typical of most car owners? The three of you may be careless about routine maintenance of your autos.

- **Are the instances recent?** If the foreign cars you are using as examples of poor reliability are more than three years old, you cannot reasonably conclude that today's foreign cars are unreliable products. Age alone may explain the poor performance of your sample.

   The logic in the example of the problematic foreign cars, therefore, is not particularly sound. The speaker would need considerably more evidence to prove his or her point.

Testing the Validity of Inductive Reasoning As a persuasive speaker, your job is to construct a sound argument. That means basing your generalization on evidence. When you listen to a persuasive message, notice how the speaker tries to support his or her conclusion.

Reasoning by Analogy Reasoning by analogy is a special type of inductive reasoning. An *analogy* is a comparison. This form of reasoning compares one thing, person, or process with another, to predict how something will perform and respond. When you observe that two things have a number of characteristics in common and that a certain fact about one is likely to be true of the other, you have drawn an analogy, reasoning from one example to reach a conclusion about the other. If you try to convince an audience that mandatory safety-belt laws in Texas and Florida have reduced highway deaths and therefore should be instituted in Kansas, you are reasoning by analogy. But as with reasoning by generalization, there are questions that you should ask to check the validity of your conclusions.

- **Do the ways in which the two things are alike outweigh the ways they are different?** Could other factors besides the safety-belt laws in Texas and Florida account for the lower automobile accident death rate? Maybe differences in the speed limit or the types of roads in those states can account for the difference.

- **Is the assertion true?** Is it really true that mandatory safety-belt laws in Texas and Florida have reduced auto highway deaths? You will need to give reasons the comparison you are making is valid and evidence that will prove your conclusion true.

Deductive Reasoning According to a centuries-old perspective, reasoning from a general statement or principle to reach a specific conclusion is called **deductive reasoning**. This is just the opposite of inductive reasoning. Contemporary logic specialists add that when the conclusion is certain rather than probable, you are reasoning deductively. The certainty of your conclusion is based on the validity or truth in the general statement that forms the basis of your argument.

Deductive reasoning can be structured in the form of a syllogism. A **syllogism** is a way of organizing an argument into three elements: a major premise, a minor premise, and a conclusion. To reach a conclusion deductively, you start with a general statement that serves as the **major premise**. In a speech attempting to convince your audience that the communication professor teaching your public-speaking class is a top-notch teacher, you might use a deductive reasoning process. Your major premise is "All communication professors have excellent teaching skills." The certainty of your conclusion hinges on the soundness of your major premise. The **minor premise** is a more specific statement about an example that is linked to the major premise. The minor premise in the argument you are advancing is "John Smith, our teacher, is a communication professor." The **conclusion** is based on the major premise and the more specific minor premise. In reasoning deductively, you need to ensure that both the major premise and the minor premise are true and can be supported with evidence. The conclusion to our syllogism is "John Smith has excellent teaching skills." The persuasive power of deductive reasoning derives from the fact that the conclusion cannot be questioned if the premises are accepted as true.

Here's another example you might hear in a speech. Ann was trying to convince the city council not to approve a building permit for Mega-Low-Mart, a large chain discount store that wants to move into her town. She believes the new store would threaten her downtown clothing boutique. Here's the deductive structure of the argument she advanced:

Major premise:	Every time a large discount store moves into a small community, the merchants in the downtown area lose business and the town loses tax revenue from downtown merchants.
Minor premise:	Mega-Low-Mart is a large discount store that wants to build a store in our town.
Conclusion:	If Mega-Low-Mart is permitted to open a store in our town, the merchants in the downtown area will lose business and the city will lose tax revenue.

The strength of Ann's argument rests on the validity of her major premise. Her argument is sound if she can prove that the presence of large chain discount stores does, in fact, result in a loss of business and tax revenue for merchants in nearby towns. (Also note Ann's efforts to be audience-centered; addressing the city council, she argues that not only will she lose money but that the city will lose tax revenue as well—something in which city council members are deeply interested.) In constructing arguments for your persuasive messages, assess the soundness of the major premise on which you build your argument. Likewise, when listening to a persuasive pitch from someone using a deductive argument, critically evaluate the accuracy of the major premise.

HOW TO: *Test the Truth of an Argument*

- **Is the major premise (general statement) true?** In our example about communication professors, is it really true that all communication professors have excellent teaching skills? What evidence do you have to support this statement? The power of deductive reasoning hinges in part on whether your generalization is true.

- **Is the minor premise (the particular statement) also true?** If your minor premise is false, your syllogism can collapse right there. In our example, it is easy enough to verify that John Smith is a communication professor. But not all minor premises can be verified as easily. For example, it would be difficult to prove the minor premise in this example:

> All gods are immortal.
>
> Zeus is a god.
>
> Therefore, Zeus is immortal.

We can accept the major premise as true because immortality is part of the definition of *god.* But proving that Zeus is a god would be very difficult. In this case, the truth of the conclusion hinges on the truth of the minor premise.

Causal Reasoning   A third type of reasoning is called **causal reasoning**. When you reason by cause, you relate two or more events in such a way as to conclude that one or more of the events caused the others. For example, you might argue that having unprotected sex causes the spread of AIDS.

There are two ways to structure a causal argument. First, you can reason from cause to effect, moving from a known fact to a predicted result. You know, for example, that interest rates have increased in the past week. Therefore, you might argue that because the rates are increasing, the Dow Jones Industrial Average will decrease. In this case, you move from something that has occurred (rising interest rates) to something that has not yet occurred (decrease in the Dow). Weather forecasters use the same method of reasoning when they predict the weather. They base a conclusion about tomorrow's weather on what they know about today's meteorological conditions.

A second way to frame a causal argument is to reason backward, from known effect to unknown cause. You know, for example, that a major earthquake has occurred

QUICK CHECK: *Comparing Inductive, Deductive, and Causal Reasoning*

	Inductive Reasoning	Deductive Reasoning	Causal Reasoning
Reasoning begins with...	Specific examples	A general statement	Something known
Reasoning ends with...	A general conclusion	A specific conclusion	A speculation about something unknown, based on what is known
Conclusion of reasoning is that something is...	Probable or improbable	True or false	Likely or not likely
Goal of reasoning is...	To reach a general conclusion or discover something new	To reach a specific conclusion by applying what is known	To link something known with something unknown
Example	When tougher drug laws went into effect in Kansas City and St. Louis, drug traffic was reduced. The United States should therefore institute tougher drug laws, because these decrease drug traffic nationwide.	All bachelors are unmarried men. Frank is a bachelor. Therefore, Frank is an unmarried man.	Since the 70-mile-per-hour speed limit was reinstated, traffic deaths have increased. The increased highway speed has caused an increase in highway deaths.

(known effect). To explain this event, you propose that the cause of the earthquake was a shift in a fault line (unknown cause). You cannot be sure of the cause, but you are certain of the effect. A candidate for president of the United States may claim that the cause of current high unemployment (known effect) is mismanagement by the present administration (unknown cause). He then constructs an argument to prove that his assertion is accurate. To prove his case, he needs to have evidence that the present administration mismanaged the economy. The key to developing strong causal arguments is in the use of evidence to link something known with something unknown. An understanding of the appropriate use of evidence can enhance inductive, deductive, and causal reasoning.

PERSUADING THE DIVERSE AUDIENCE

Effective strategies for developing your persuasive objective will vary depending on the background and cultural expectations of your listeners. Rhetoricians from the United States typically use a straightforward, factual-inductive method of supporting ideas and reaching conclusions.[7] First, they identify facts and link them to support a specific proposition or conclusion. For example, in a speech to prove that the government spends more money than it receives, a speaker could cite year-by-year statistics on income and expenditures to document the point. North Americans also like debates involving a direct clash of ideas and opinions. Our low-context culture encourages people to be more direct and forthright in dealing with issues and disagreement than do high-context cultures.

Not all cultures assume a direct, linear, methodical approach to supporting ideas and proving a point.[8] People from high-context cultures, for example, may expect that participants in debates will establish a personal relationship before debating issues. Some cultures use a deductive pattern of reasoning, rather than an inductive pattern. Speakers in these cultures begin with a general premise and then link it to a specific situation when they attempt to persuade listeners.

Speakers in Middle Eastern cultures usually do not use standard inductive or deductive structures. They are more likely to use narrative methods to persuade an audience. They tell stories that evoke feelings and emotions and use extended analogies, examples, and illustrations, allowing their listeners to draw their own conclusions by inductive association.[9]

Although this book stresses the kind of inductive reasoning that will be persuasive to most North Americans, you may need to use alternative strategies if your audience is from another cultural tradition. Consider the following general principles to help you construct arguments that a culturally diverse audience will find persuasive.

Evidence   According to intercultural communication scholars Myron Lustig and Jolene Koester, "There are no universally accepted standards about what constitutes evidence."[10] They suggest that for some Muslim and Christian audiences, parables or stories are a dramatically effective way to make a point. A story is told and a principle is derived from the lesson of the story. For most North Americans and Europeans, a superior form of evidence is an observed fact. A study by two communication scholars reported that both African Americans and Hispanic Americans found statistical evidence more persuasive than stories alone.[11] Statistics, said the listeners, are more believable and verifiable; stories can more easily be modified. What may be convincing evidence to you may not be such an obvious piece of evidence for others. If you are uncertain whether your listeners will perceive your evidence as valid and reliable, you could test your evidence on a small group of people who will be in your audience before you address the entire group.

Appeals to Action   In some high-context cultures, such as in Japan and China, the conclusion to your message can be stated indirectly. Rather than spell out the precise action explicitly, you can imply what you'd like your listeners to do. In a low-context culture such as the United States, listeners may generally expect you to more directly state the action you'd like your audience members to take.

Message Structure   North Americans often like a well-organized message with a clear, explicit link between the evidence used and the conclusion drawn. North Americans also are comfortable with a structure that focuses on a problem and then offers a solution, or a message in which the causes are identified and the effects are specified. Audiences in the Middle East, however, would expect less formal structure and greater use of a narrative style of message development. The audience may be left to infer the point, or the speaker may conclude by making the point clear. In some situations, it's better to get a message out of someone than to put a message into someone. Being indirect or implicit may sometimes be the best persuasive strategy. Not all audiences expect a speech to sound like the summation of an attorney making a legal case loaded with evidence. In fact, some lawyers decide, after "reading" their jury, that the best way to conclude their case is to tell a story rather than to present a litany of the facts and evidence.

Persuasive Communication Style   We've placed a considerable emphasis on logos by emphasizing logical structure and the use of evidence. But another cultural factor that influences how receptive listeners are to a message is the presentation style of the speech. A speaker's overall style includes the use of emotional appeals, delivery style, language choice, and rhythmic quality of the words and gestures used. Some Latin American listeners, for example, expect speakers to express more emotion and passion when speaking than North American listeners are accustomed to. If you focus only on analyzing and adapting to the audience's expectations about logic and reasoning, without also considering the overall impression you make on your audience, you may present compelling arguments but still not achieve your overall goal. The best way to assess the preferred speaking style of an audience with which you're not familiar is to observe other successful speakers addressing the audience you will face. Or talk with audience members before you speak to identify expectations and communication-style preferences.

SUPPORTING YOUR REASONING WITH EVIDENCE

You cannot simply state a conclusion without proving it with evidence. Evidence in persuasive speeches consists of facts, examples, statistics, and expert opinions. When attempting to persuade listeners, it is useful to make sure that your evidence logically supports the inductive, deductive, or causal reasoning you are using to reach your conclusion.

Facts   When using facts to persuade, make sure your fact is really a fact. A *fact* is something that has been directly observed to be true or can be proved to be true. The shape of earth, the number of women CEOs, the winner of the 2004 presidential election have all been directly observed or measured. Without direct observation or measurement, we can only make an inference. An inference is a conclusion based on available evidence, or partial information.

Examples   Examples are illustrations that are used to dramatize or clarify a fact. Only valid, true examples can be used to help prove a point. For example, one speaker, in an effort to document the increased violence in children's television programs, told her audience, "Last Saturday morning as I watched cartoons with my daughter, I was shocked by the countless times we saw examples of beatings and even the death of the cartoon characters in one half-hour program." The conclusion she wanted her audience to reach: Put an end to senseless violence in children's television programs.

Hypothetical Examples   A hypothetical example, one that is fabricated to illustrate a point, should not be used to reach a conclusion. It should be used only to clarify. David encouraged his listeners to join him in an effort to clean up the San Marcos River. He wanted to motivate his audience to help by asking them to "imagine bringing your children to the river ten years from now. You see the river bottom littered with cans and bottles." His example, while effective in helping the audience to visualize what might happen in the future, does not prove that the river ecosystem will deteriorate. It only illustrates what might happen if action isn't taken.

Opinions   *Opinions* can serve as evidence if they are expressed by an expert, someone who can add credibility to your conclusion. The best opinions to use in support of a persuasive argument are those expressed by someone known to be unbiased, fair, and accurate. If the U.S. Surgeon General has expressed an opinion regarding drug testing, his or her opinion would be helpful evidence. Even so, opinions are usually most persuasive if they are combined with other evidence, such as facts or statistics that support the expert's position.

Statistics   A *statistic* is a number used to summarize several facts or samples. In an award-winning speech, Jeffrey Jamison used statistics effectively to document the serious problem of alkali batteries polluting the environment. He cited evidence from *The New York Times* that documents ". . . each year we are adding 150 tons of mercury, 130 tons of lead, and 170 tons of cadmium to the environment."[12] Without these statistics, Jeffrey's claim that alkali batteries are detrimental to the environment would not have been as potent.

Does the type of evidence you use make a difference in whether your listeners will support your ideas? One research study found that examples and illustrations go a long way in helping to persuade listeners.[13] Additional research documents the clear power of statistical evidence to persuade.[14] And yet another research study concluded that using both statistics and specific examples is especially effective in persuading listeners.[15]

Poignant examples may touch listeners' hearts, but statistical evidence appeals to their intellect. Because we believe that messages should be audience-centered rather than source-centered, we suggest that you consider your listeners to determine the kind of evidence that will be the most convincing to them.

If you are using an inductive-reasoning strategy (reasoning from specific examples to a general conclusion), you need to make sure you have enough facts, examples, statistics, and credible opinions to support your conclusion. If you reason deductively (from a generalization to a specific conclusion), you need evidence to document the truth of your initial generalization. When developing an argument using causal reasoning, evidence is also vital as you attempt to establish that one or more events caused something to happen.

AVOIDING FAULTY REASONING: ETHICAL ISSUES

We have emphasized the importance of developing sound, logical arguments supported with appropriate evidence. You have an ethical responsibility to use your skill to construct arguments that are well supported with logical reasoning and sound evidence. Not all people who try to persuade you will use sound arguments to get you to vote for them, buy their product, or donate money to their cause. Many persuaders use inappropriate techniques called fallacies. A **fallacy** is false reasoning that occurs when someone attempts to persuade without adequate evidence or with arguments that are irrelevant or inappropriate. You will be both a better and more ethical speaker and a better listener if you are aware of the following fallacies.

Causal Fallacy   The Latin term for the causal fallacy is *post hoc, ergo propter hoc,* which translates as "after this, therefore, because of this." The **causal fallacy** is making a faulty causal connection. Simply because one event follows another does not mean that the two are related. If you declared that your school's football team won this time because you sang your school song before the game, you would be guilty of a causal fallacy. There are undoubtedly other factors that explain why your team won, such as good preparation or facing a weaker opposing team. For something to be a cause, it has to have the power to bring about a result. "That howling storm last night knocked down the tree in our backyard" is a logical causal explanation for the noise that disturbed your sleep and the mess you found in the morning. Here are more examples of causal fallacies:

> The increased earthquake and hurricane activity is caused by the increase in violence and war in our society.
>
> As long as you wear this lucky rabbit's foot, you will never have an automobile accident.
>
> The decline of morals in this country is caused by excessive government spending.

In each instance, there is not enough evidence to support the cause–effect conclusion.

Bandwagon Fallacy   Someone who argues that "everybody thinks it's a good idea, so you should too" is using the **bandwagon fallacy**. Simply because "everyone" is "jumping on the bandwagon," or supporting a particular point of view, does not make the point of view correct. Sometimes speakers use the bandwagon fallacy in more subtle ways in their efforts to persuade:

> Everybody knows that talk radio is our primary link to a free and democratic society.
>
> Most people agree that we spend too much time worrying about Medicare.
>
> Everybody agrees with me that we need a change in Congress.

Beware of sweeping statements that include you and others without offering any evidence that the speaker has solicited opinions.

Either/Or Fallacy Someone who argues that there are only two approaches to a problem is trying to oversimplify the issue by using the **either/or fallacy**. "It's either vote for higher property taxes or close the library," asserts Daryl at a public hearing on tax increases. Such a statement ignores a variety of other solutions to a complex problem. The following are additional examples of inappropriate either/or simplistic reasoning:

> Either mothers should stay home and spend less time at work, or juvenile delinquency will increase.
>
> Either television violence is reduced, or we have an increase in child and spouse abuse.
>
> Either more people start volunteering their time to work for their community, or your taxes increase.

Hasty Generalization A person who reaches a conclusion from too little evidence or nonexistent evidence is making a **hasty generalization**. For example, simply because one person became ill after eating the meat loaf in the cafeteria does not mean that everyone eating in the cafeteria will develop food poisoning. Here are some additional hasty generalizations:

> It's clear that our schools can't educate children well, because my niece went to school for six years and she still can't read at her grade level.
>
> The city does a terrible job of taking care of the elderly—my grandmother lives in a city-owned nursing home, and the floors there are always filthy.
>
> We don't need mandatory lawn-watering rules in our city, because the people I know do their best to conserve water.

Ad Hominem Also known as *attacking the person,* an **ad hominem** (Latin for "to the man") approach involves attacking irrelevant personal characteristics about the person who is proposing an idea rather than attacking the idea itself. A statement such as "We know Janice's idea won't work because she has never had a good idea yet" does not really deal with the idea, which may be perfectly valid. Don't dismiss an idea solely because you have been turned against the person who presented it. Here are some more examples of ad hominem attacks:

> Anyone who is a talk-radio host certainly has no idea how to develop a plan to reduce the deficit.

She was educated in a foreign country and could not possibly have good ideas for improving education in our community.

Tony is an awful musician and is not sensitive enough to chair such an important committee.

Red Herring   The **red herring** fallacy is used when someone attacks an issue by using irrelevant facts or arguments as distractions. This fallacy gets its name from an old trick of dragging a red herring (a particularly pungent dried fish) across a trail to divert the dogs that may be following. Speakers use a red herring when they want to distract an audience from the real issues. For example, a politician who had been accused of taking bribes while in office calls a press conference. During the press conference, he talks about the evils of child pornography, rather than addressing the charge against him. He is using the red herring technique to divert attention from the real issue—did he or did he not take the bribe? Or, consider another example of a fallacious argument using the red herring method, from a speech against gun control:

The real problem is not eliminating handguns; the real problem is that pawnshops that sell guns are controlled by the Mafia.

Appeal to Misplaced Authority   When ads use baseball catchers to endorse automobiles and TV stars to sell political candidates or an airline or hotel, we are faced with the fallacious **appeal to misplaced authority**. Although we have great respect for these people in their own fields, they are no more expert than we are in the areas they are advertising. As both a public speaker and a listener, you must recognize what is valid expert testimony and what is not. For example, a physicist who speaks on the laws of nature or the structure of matter could reasonably be accepted as an expert. But if the physicist speaks on politics, the opinion expressed is not that of an expert and is no more significant than your own. The following examples are appeals to misplaced authority:

Former Congressman Smith endorses the new art museum, so every business should get behind it, too.

Our history professor recommended that we stay at the Frontier Place in Orlando, so it must be good.

Katie Couric thinks this cookie recipe is the best, so you should try it too.

Non Sequitur   If you argue that a new parking garage should not be built on campus because the grass has not been mowed on the football field for three weeks, you are guilty of a **non sequitur** (Latin for "it does not follow"). Grass growing on the football field has nothing to do with the parking problem. Your conclusion simply does not follow from your statement. The following are examples of non sequitur conclusions:

We should not give students condoms, because TV has such a pervasive influence on our youth today.

You should endorse me for Congress, because I have three children.

We need more parking on our campus, because we are the national football champions.

You should help pick up trash in our community, because our new cable-TV studio is now in operation.

20.d Using Emotion to Persuade

Roger Ailes, a political communication consultant, has nominated several memorable moments as outstanding illustrations of speakers using emotional messages powerfully and effectively.[16]

> Martin Luther King, announcing his vision of brotherhood and equality at the Lincoln Memorial in 1963, extolled, "I have a dream!"

> General Douglas MacArthur, in announcing his retirement before a joint session of Congress, April 19, 1951, closed his speech with "Old soldiers never die; they just fade away. And like the old soldier of that ballad, I now close my military career and just fade away."

> British Prime Minister Winston Churchill in his 1940 speech to the House of Commons in preparing his people for war intoned, "Let us therefore brace ourselves to our duties, and so bear ourselves that, if the British Empire and its Commonwealth last for a thousand years, men will still say, 'This was their finest hour.'"

Emotion is a powerful way to move an audience and support your persuasive purpose. Aristotle used the term **pathos** to refer to the use of appeals to emotion. An appeal to emotion can be an effective way to achieve a desired response from an audience. Whereas logical arguments may appeal to our reason, emotional arguments generally appeal to nonrational sentiments. Often we make decisions based not on logic, but on emotion.

One theory suggests that emotional responses can be classified along three dimensions—pleasure, arousal, and dominance.[17] First, you respond with varying degrees of *pleasure* or *displeasure*. Pleasurable stimuli consist of such things as images of smiling, healthy babies or daydreams about winning millions in a sweepstakes. Stimuli causing displeasure may be TV news stories of child abuse or dreadful images of terrorism.

A second dimension of emotional responses exists on a continuum of *arousal–nonarousal*. You become aroused emotionally, for example, by seeing a snake in your driveway, or you may be lulled into a state of nonarousal by a boring lecture.

The third dimension of emotional responses is one's feeling of *dominance or powerlessness* when confronted with some stimulus. When thinking about the destructive force of nuclear weapons or the omnipotence of God, you may feel insignificant and powerless. Or perhaps you feel a sense of power when you imagine yourself conducting a symphony or winning an election.

These three dimensions—pleasure, arousal, and dominance—are believed to form the bases of all emotional responses. Theory predicts that if listeners feel pleasure and are also aroused by something, such as a political candidate or a product, they will tend to form a favorable view of the candidate or product. A listener's feeling of being dominant has to do with being in control and having permission to behave as he or she wishes. A listener who feels dominant is more likely to respond to the message.

As a public speaker trying to sway your listeners to your viewpoint, your job is to use emotional appeals to achieve your goal. If you wanted to persuade your listeners that capital punishment should be banned, you would try to arouse feelings of displeasure and turn them against capital punishment. Advertisers selling soft drinks typically strive to arouse feelings of pleasure in those who think of their product. Smiling people, upbeat music, and good times are usually part of the formula for selling soda pop.

TIPS FOR USING EMOTION TO PERSUADE

Although the underlying theory of emotions may help you understand how emotions work, as a public speaker your key concern is "How can I ethically use emotional appeals to achieve my persuasive purpose?" Let's consider several methods.

Use Concrete Examples That Help Your Listeners Visualize What You Describe Using a concrete example of an emotionally moving scene can create a powerful response in your audience. Describing what the town of Saragosa, Texas was like after a tornado destroyed it can evoke strong emotions. The images used to evoke the emotions can also help communicate the power of nature and the value of taking proper precautions when a storm warning is sounded.

> The town is no more. No homes in the western Texas town remain standing. The church where twenty-one people perished looks like a heap of twisted metal and mortar. A child's doll can be seen in the street. The owner, four-year-old Maria, will no longer play with her favorite toy; she was killed along with five of her playmates when the twister roared through the elementary school.

Use Emotion-Arousing Words Words and phrases can trigger emotional responses in your listeners. *Mother, flag, freedom,* and *slavery* are among a large number of emotionally loaded words. Patriotic slogans, such as "Remember Pearl Harbor" or "Remember 9/11," can produce strong emotional responses.

Use Nonverbal Behavior to Communicate Your Emotional Response The great Roman orator Cicero believed that if you want your listeners to experience a certain emotion, you should first model that emotion for them. If you want an audience to feel anger at a particular law or event, you must display anger and indignation in your voice, movement, and gesture. As we have already noted, delivery plays the key role in communicating your emotional responses. If you want your audience to become excited about and interested in your message, you must communicate that excitement and interest through your delivery.

Use Visual Images to Evoke Emotions In addition to nonverbal expressions, pictures or images of emotion-arousing scenes can amplify your speech. An image of a lonely homeowner looking out over his waterlogged house following a ravaging flood in Houston, Texas, can communicate his sense of despair. A picture of children in war-torn Macedonia can communicate the devastating effects of violence with greater impact than mere words can. In contrast, a photo of a refugee mother and child reunited after an enforced separation can communicate the true meaning of joy. You can use similar images as visual aids to evoke your audience's emotions, both positive and negative. Remember, however, that when you use visual images, you have the same ethical responsibilities as you do when you use verbal forms of support: Make sure your image is from a credible source and that it has not been altered or taken out of context.

Use Appropriate Metaphors and Similes A metaphor is an implied comparison between two things. The person who says, "Our lives are quilts upon which we stitch the patterns of our character. If you don't pay attention to the ethical dimension of the decisions you make, you will be more likely to make a hideous pattern in your life quilt," is using a metaphor. A simile makes a direct comparison between two things using the word *like* or *as*. Here's an example of a simile: "Not visiting your academic counselor regularly is like being a gambler in a high-stakes poker game; you're taking a big chance that you're taking the right courses." Several research studies have found that speakers who use appropriate and interesting metaphors and similes are more persuasive than those who don't use such stylistic devices.[18] Metaphors and similes can create a fresh, emotional perspective on a persuasive point; they can both enhance your credibility and develop an emotional image in a way that nonmetaphorical language can't.[19]

Use Appropriate Fear Appeals The threat that harm will come to your listeners unless they follow your advice is an appeal to fear. Listeners can be motivated to change their behavior if appeals to fear are used appropriately. Research suggests that high fear arousal ("You will be killed in an auto accident unless you wear a safety belt") is more effective than moderate or low appeals if you are a highly credible speaker.[20]

Consider Using Appeals to Several Emotions Appealing to the fears and anxieties of your listeners is one of the most common types of emotional appeals used to persuade, but you could also elicit several other emotions to help achieve your persuasive goal.

- **Hope.** Listeners could be motivated to respond to the prospect of a brighter tomorrow. When Franklin Roosevelt said, "The only thing we have to fear is fear itself," he was invoking hope for the future.

- **Pride.** "The pride is back" is a slogan used to sell cars. An appeal to pride can also be used to motivate listeners in a persuasive speech. The persuasive appeal to achieve an objective based on pride in oneself or one's country, state, or hometown can be very powerful.

- **Courage.** Challenging your audience to take a bold stand or to step away from the crowd can emotionally charge your listeners to take action. Referring to courageous men and women as role models can help motivate your listeners to take similar actions. Patrick Henry's famous "Give me liberty, or give me death!" speech appealed to his audience to take a courageous stand on the issues before them.

- **Reverence.** The appeal to the sacred and the revered can be an effective way to motivate. Supporting your persuasive message by referring to sacred traditions, revered institutions, or cherished and celebrated individuals can inspire your audience to change or reinforce attitudes, beliefs, values, or behavior. The late Mother Teresa, holy writings, and the Congress of the United States are examples of people, things, or institutions that your listeners may perceive as sacred. As an audience-centered speaker, however, you need to remember that what may be sacred to one individual or audience may not be sacred to another.

Tap Audience Members' Beliefs in Shared Myths   Often people talk about a "myth" as something that is untrue. The Easter Bunny, the Tooth Fairy, and Santa Claus are often labeled myths. But in a rhetorical sense, a **myth** is a belief held in common by a group of people and based on their values, cultural heritage, and faith. A myth may, in fact, be factual—or it may be based on a partial truth that a group of people believes to be true. Myths are the "big stories" that give meaning and coherence to a group of people or a culture. The myth of the "Old West" is that the pioneers of yesteryear were strong, adventurous people who sacrificed their lives in search of a better tomorrow. Similarly, our parents, grandparents, and great-grandparents belonged to "the greatest generation" because they overcame a devastating economic depression and were triumphant in two world wars. The myth of the 1950s was that U.S. families were prosperous and lived like Ward and June Cleaver and their sons, Wally and "The Beaver," in the TV program *Leave It to Beaver*. Religious myths are beliefs shared by a group of faithful disciples. So, a myth is not necessarily "false"—it is a belief that a group of people share and that provides emotional support for the way they view the world.

As a public speaker, you can draw on the myths you and your audience members share to provide emotional and motivational support for your message. Referring to a shared myth is a way to identify with your listeners and help them see how your ideas support their ideas; it can help you develop a common bond with audience members. In trying to convince his listeners to vote, Ron argued, "We can't let down those who fought for our freedom. We must vote to honor those who died for the privilege of voting that we enjoy today." He was drawing on the powerful myth that people have died for our freedoms. To gain parent support for a new high school, Cynthia said, "Our parents and grandparents lived through the Great Depression and the world wars of the past century so that we can send our children to the best public schools in the world. Vote for the new high school." She was appealing to the myth that the previous generation sacrificed, so we also have a responsibility to sacrifice for our children. Again we reemphasize that myth does not mean "false" or "made up"—people really did die for our freedom, and our parents and grandparents did live through the Depression and tragic world wars. Some myths are powerful because the audience knows that particular events did occur. Myth becomes a powerful underlying story that evokes an emotional response to the message.

Politicians use myth when they show pictures of themselves surrounded by their families. The underlying myth is "I cherish what you cherish—to live in a country that supports and nurtures the family values we hold dear." Appealing directly or indirectly to the commonly held myths of an audience is a powerful way to evoke emotional support for your message. But as with any form of support, especially emotional support, you have an ethical responsibility to use this strategy wisely and not to exploit your listeners.

USING EMOTIONAL APPEALS: ETHICAL ISSUES

Regardless of which emotions you use to motivate your audience, you have an obligation to be ethical and forthright. Making false claims, misusing evidence to arouse emotions, or relying only on emotions without any evidence to support a conclusion violates ethical standards of effective public speaking.

A **demagogue** is a speaker who attempts to gain power or control over others by using impassioned emotional pleas and appealing to listeners' prejudices. The word *demagogue* comes from the Greek word *demagogos,* meaning "popular leader." Speakers who become popular by substituting emotion and fallacies in place of well-supported reasoning are guilty of demagoguery. During the early 1950s, Wisconsin Senator Joseph McCarthy sought to convince the nation that Communists had infiltrated government, education, and the entertainment industry. This was at the height of the Cold War, and anything or anyone remotely connected to Communism elicited an immediate negative emotional response. For a time, McCarthy was successful in his effort to expose the unpatriotic Communists among us. His evidence, however, was scanty, and he relied primarily on scaring his listeners about the potential evil of alleged Communists. His trumped-up evidence and unethical use of fear appeals eventually undermined his credibility and earned him a reputation as a demagogue. You have an ethical responsibility not to misuse emotional appeals when persuading others.

Your credibility, reasoning, and emotional appeals are the chief ways to persuade an audience. Your use of these persuasive strategies depends on the composition of your audience. As we have observed several times before, an early task in the public-speaking process is to analyze your audience. This is particularly important in persuasion. Audience members are not just sitting there waiting to respond to every suggestion a speaker makes.

HOW TO: *Use Emotion to Persuade*

- Use concrete examples.
- Use emotion-arousing words.
- Use nonverbal behavior to communicate your emotional response.
- Use visual images.
- Use appropriate metaphors and similes.
- Use appropriate fear appeals.
- Use appeals to a variety of emotions such as hope, pride, courage, or reverence.
- Tap audience members' beliefs in shared myths.

20.e Strategies for Adapting Ideas to People and People to Ideas

One definition of persuasive communication nicely summarizes the importance of adapting your message to your audience. "Rhetoric," suggested Donald C. Bryant, "is the process of adjusting ideas to people and people to ideas."[21] Your appeals to reason, emotion, and your own credibility are all dependent on the attitudes, beliefs, and values of your listeners.

Audience members may hold differing views of you and your subject. Your task is to find out whether there is a prevailing viewpoint held by a majority of your listeners. If they are generally friendly toward you and your ideas, you need to design your speech differently from the way you would if your listeners were neutral, apathetic, or hostile. Research studies as well as seasoned public speakers can offer some useful suggestions to help you adapt your approach to your audience. We will discuss three general responses your audience may have to you: receptive, neutral, and unreceptive.

PERSUADING THE RECEPTIVE AUDIENCE

It is always a pleasure to face an audience that already supports you and your message. In speaking to a receptive group, you can explore your ideas in greater depth than otherwise. Here are some suggestions that may help you make the most of your speaking opportunity.

Identify with Your Audience   To establish common ground with her audience of fellow students, Rita told them, "Just like most of you, I struggle to pay my way through college. That's why I support expanding the campus work-study program." Like Rita, if you are a college student speaking to other college students with similar backgrounds and pressures, point to your similar backgrounds and struggles. Emphasize the similarities between you and your audience. What other common interests do you have? The introductory portion of your speech is a good place to mention your common interests and background.

Clearly State Your Speaking Objective   When speaking to a group of her campaign workers, mayoral candidate Maria Hernandez stated early in her speech, "My reason for coming here today is to ask each of you to volunteer three hours a week to help me become the next mayor of our city." We have stressed several times how important it is to provide an overview of your major point or purpose. This is particularly so when speaking to a group who will support your point of view.[22]

Tell Your Audience Exactly What You Want Them to Do   Besides telling your listeners what your speaking objective is, you can also tell them how you expect them to respond to your message. Be explicit in directing your listeners' behavior.

Ask Listeners for an Immediate Show of Support   Asking for an immediate show of support helps to cement the positive response you have developed during your speech. For example, Christian evangelists usually speak to receptive audiences. Evangelist Billy Graham always asks those who support his Christian message to come forward at the end of his sermon.

Use Emotional Appeals Effectively   You can usually move a receptive audience to action with strong emotional appeals while also reminding them of the evidence that supports your conclusion. If the audience already supports your position, you need not spend a great deal of time on lengthy, detailed explanations or factual information. You can usually assume that your listeners are already in possession of much of that material.

Make It Easy for Your Listeners to Act   It is a good idea not only to tell your listeners precisely what you want them to do and ask for an immediate response, but also to make sure that what you're asking them to do is clear and easy. If you're asking them to write or e-mail someone, hand out postcards already addressed to the recipient, or distribute an e-mail address printed on a card for handy reference. If you want the recipient to call someone, make sure each person has the phone number— it's even better if you can give a toll-free number.

PERSUADING THE NEUTRAL AUDIENCE

Think of how many lectures you go to with an attitude of indifference. Probably quite a few. Many audiences will fall somewhere between wildly enthusiastic and unreceptive; they will simply be neutral or indifferent. They may be neutral because they don't know much about your topic or because they just can't make up their minds whether to support your point of view. They may also be indifferent because they don't see how the topic or issue affects them. Regardless of the reason for your listeners' indifference, your challenge is to make them interested in your message. Let's look at some approaches to gaining their attention and keeping their interest.

Capture Your Listeners' Attention Early in Your Speech   "Bill Farmer died last year, but he's about to fulfill his lifelong dream of going into space."[23] In a speech about the high cost of funerals, Karmen's provocative opening statement effectively captures the attention of her listeners.

Refer to Beliefs That Many Listeners Share   When speaking to a neutral audience, identify common concerns and values that you plan to address. Martin Luther King's "I Have a Dream" speech (Appendix D) includes references to his listeners' common beliefs.

Relate Your Topic Not Only to Your Listeners But Also to Their Families, Friends, and Loved Ones   You can capture the interest of your listeners by appealing to the needs of people they care about. Parents will be interested in ideas and policies that affect their children. People are generally interested in matters that may affect their friends, neighbors, and others with whom they identify, such as members of their own religion or economic or social class.

Be Realistic About What You Can Accomplish   Don't overestimate the response you may receive from a neutral audience. People who start with an attitude of indifference are probably not going to become as enthusiastic as you are after hearing just one speech. Persuasion does not occur all at once or at a first hearing of arguments.

PERSUADING THE UNRECEPTIVE AUDIENCE

One of the biggest challenges in public speaking is to persuade audience members who are against you or your message. If they are hostile toward you personally, your job is to seek ways to enhance your acceptability and persuade them to listen to you. If they are unreceptive to your point of view, there are several approaches that you can use to encourage them to listen to you.

Don't Immediately Announce That You Plan to Change Their Minds   Paul wondered why his opening sales pitch ("Good morning. I plan to convince you to purchase this fine set of knives at a cost to you of only $250") was not greeted enthusiastically. If you immediately and bluntly tell your listeners that you plan to change their opinions, it can make them defensive. It is usually better to take a more subtle approach when announcing your persuasive intent.[24]

Begin Your Speech by Noting Areas of Agreement Before You Discuss Areas of Disagreement   In addressing the school board, one community member began his persuasive effort to convince board members they should not raise taxes by stating, "I think each of us here can agree on one common goal: We want the best education for our children." Once you help your audience understand that there are issues on which you agree (such as agreeing that the topic you will discuss is controversial), your listeners may be more attentive when you explain your position.

Don't Expect a Major Shift in Attitude from a Hostile Audience   Set a realistic limit on what you can achieve. A realistic goal might be to have your listeners hear you out and at least consider some of your points.

Acknowledge the Opposing Points of View That Members of Your Audience May Hold   Summarize the reasons individuals may oppose your point of view. Doing this communicates that you at least understand the issues.[25] Your listeners will be more likely to listen to you if they know that you understand their viewpoint. Of course, after you acknowledge the opposing point of view, you will need to cite evidence and use arguments to refute the opposition and support your conclusion. Early in his speech to a neighborhood group about the possibility of building a new airport near their homes, City Manager Anderson acknowledged, "I am aware that a new airport brings unwanted changes to a neighborhood. Noise and increased traffic are not the type of challenges you want near your homes." He went on to identify the actions the city would take to minimize the problems a new airport would cause.

Establish Your Credibility   Being thought credible is always an important goal of a public speaker, and it is especially important when talking to an unreceptive audience. Let your audience know about the experience, interest, knowledge, and skill that give you special insight into the issues at hand.

Consider Making Understanding Rather Than Advocacy Your Goal   Sometimes your audience disagrees with you because its members just don't understand your point. Or they may harbor a misconception about you and your message. For example, if your listeners think that AIDS is transferred though kissing or other casual contact rather than through unprotected sexual contact, you'll first have to acknowledge their beliefs and then construct a sound argument to show how inaccurate their assumptions are. To change misconceptions and enhance accurate understanding, experienced speakers use a four-part strategy.[26]

- **Summarize the common misconceptions about the issue or idea you are discussing.** "Many people think that AIDS can be transmitted through casual contact such as kissing or that it can easily be transmitted by your dentist or physician."

- **State why these misconceptions may seem reasonable.** Tell your listeners why it is logical for them to hold that view or identify "facts" they may have heard that would lead them to their current conclusion. "Since AIDS is such a highly contagious disease, it may seem reasonable to think it can be transmitted through such casual contact."

- **Dismiss the misconceptions and provide evidence to support your point.** Here you need sound and credible data to be persuasive. "In fact, countless medical studies have shown that it is virtually impossible to be infected with the AIDS virus unless you have unprotected sexual contact or use unsterilized hypodermic needles that have also been used by someone who has AIDS." In this instance, you would probably cite specific results from two or three studies to lend credibility to your claim.

- **State the accurate information that you want your audience to remember.** Reinforce the conclusion you want your listeners to draw from the information you presented, with a clear summary statement such as "According to recent research, the most common factor contributing to the spread of AIDS is unprotected sex. This is true for individuals of both sexes and all sexual orientations."

20.f Strategies for Organizing Persuasive Messages

Is there one best way to organize a persuasive speech? The answer is no. Specific approaches to organizing speeches depend on audience, message, and desired objective. But how you organize your speech does have a major effect on your listeners' response to your message.

Research suggests that there are some general principles to keep in mind when preparing your persuasive message.[27]

- If you feel that your audience may be hostile to your point of view, advance your strongest arguments first. If you save your best argument for last, your audience may have already stopped listening.

- Do not bury key arguments and evidence in the middle of your message. Your listeners are more likely to remember information presented first and last.[28] In speaking to his fraternity about the evils of drunk driving, Frank wisely began his speech with his most powerful evidence: The leading cause of death among college-age males is alcohol-related automobile accidents. He got their attention with his sobering fact.

- If you want your listeners to take some action, it is best to tell them what you want them to do at the end of your speech. If you call for action in the middle of your speech, it won't have the same power as including it in your conclusion.

- Make some reference to the counterarguments, and then refute them with evidence and logic. It may be wise to compare the proposal you are making with an alternative proposal, perhaps one offered by someone else. By comparing and contrasting your solution with another recommendation, you can show how your proposal is better.[29]

There are special ways to organize persuasive speeches. Here we present four organizational patterns: problem–solution, refutation, cause and effect, and the motivated sequence.

PROBLEM–SOLUTION

The most basic organizational pattern for a persuasive speech is to make the audience aware of a problem and then present a solution that clearly solves it. Almost any problem can be phrased in terms of something you want more of or less of. The problem–solution pattern works best when a clearly evident problem can be documented and a solution can be proposed to deal with the evils of the well-documented problem.

If you are speaking to an apathetic audience, or if listeners are not aware that a problem exists, a problem–solution pattern works nicely. Your challenge will be to provide ample evidence to document that your perception of the problem is accurate. You'll also need to convince your listeners that the solution you advocate is the most appropriate one to resolve the problem.

Many political candidates use a problem–solution approach. Problem: The government wastes your tax dollars. Solution: Vote for me and I'll see to it that government waste is eliminated. Problem: We need more and better jobs. Solution: Vote for me and I'll institute a program to put people back to work.

Note in the following outline of Jason Fruit's speech, "The Dangers of Electromagnetic Fields," how he plans to first document a clear problem and then recommend strategies for managing the problem.

PROBLEM:

I. Power lines and power stations around the country emit radiation and are now being shown to increase the risk of cancer.

   A. Childhood leukemia rates are higher in children who live near large power lines.

   B. The International Cancer Research Institute in Lyon, France, published a report linking electromagnetic fields and childhood cancer.

SOLUTION:

II. Steps can be taken to minimize our risk of health hazards caused by electromagnetic energy.

   A. The federal government should establish enforceable safety standards for exposure to electromagnetic energy.

   B. Contact your local power company to make sure its lines are operated safely.

   C. Stop using electric blankets.

   D. Use protective screens for computer-display terminals.

The problem–solution arrangement of ideas applies what you learned about cognitive dissonance in Chapter 19: It identifies and documents a concern that calls for change, and then suggests specific behaviors that can restore cognitive balance.

REFUTATION

Another way to persuade an audience to support your point of view is to prove that the arguments against your position are false—that is, to refute them. To use refutation as a strategy for persuasion, you first identify objections to your position that your listeners might raise and then refute or overcome those objections with arguments and evidence. You would be most likely to use refutation as your organizational strategy when your position was being attacked. Or, if you know what your listeners' chief objections are to your persuasive proposal, you could organize your speech around the arguments your listeners hold.

Research suggests that in most cases it is better to present both sides of an issue rather than just the advantages of the position you advocate. Even if you don't acknowledge arguments your listeners have heard, they will probably think about them anyway.

Suppose, for example, you plan to speak to a group of real-estate developers and advocate a new zoning ordinance that would reduce the number of building permits granted in your community. Your listeners will undoubtedly have some concerns about how the ordinance will affect new housing starts and the overall economic forecast. You could organize your presentation to this group using those two obvious concerns as major issues to refute. Your major points could be as follows:

I. The new zoning ordinance will not cause an overall decrease in the number of new homes built in our community.

II. The new zoning ordinance will have a positive effect on economic growth in our community.

If, after making a persuasive presentation using a refutation strategy, there is a question-and-answer forum, you should be prepared to answer questions. Credible evidence, facts, and data will be more effective than emotional arguments alone when you are attempting to persuade an audience that you know is not in favor of your persuasive objective. In your postspeech session, you can use your refutation skills to maintain a favorable audience response to your message in the face of criticism or attacks on the soundness of your logic.

CAUSE AND EFFECT

Like the problem–solution pattern to which it is closely related, the cause-and-effect approach is a useful organizational strategy. One way to use the cause–effect method is to begin with an effect, or problem, and then identify the causes of the problem in an effort to convince your listeners that the problem is significant. A speech on the growing problem of gangs might focus on poverty, drugs, and a financially crippled school system.

You could also organize a message by noting the problem and then spelling out the effects of the problem. If you identify the problem as too many unsupervised teenagers roaming your community's streets after 11 p.m., you could organize a speech noting the effects this problem is having on your fellow citizens.

The goal of using cause-and-effect organization for a persuasive speech is to convince your listeners that one event caused another. As we noted earlier, you argue that something known caused something else to happen. For example, you may try to reason that students in your state have low standardized test scores because they had poor teachers. Of course, you must prove that there are no other factors responsible for the low test scores. It may not be the teachers who caused the low test scores; perhaps it was the lack of parent involvement, or one of a number of other factors.

The challenge in using a cause-and-effect organizational strategy is to prove that one event caused something else to occur. Simply because two events occurred at the same time or in close succession does not prove that there is a cause-and-effect relationship. Earlier we noted the causal fallacy ("after this, therefore because of this," or *post hoc, ergo propter hoc*). As an example of the challenge in documenting a cause-and-effect relationship, consider a study that found that people who spend several hours a day on the Internet are also psychologically depressed. This finding does not necessarily prove that Internet use causes depression—other factors could cause the depression. Perhaps people who are depressed are more likely to use the Internet, or psychologically depressed people may find general comfort and security in using technology.

Here's an example of how a persuasive speech could be organized using a cause-and-effect strategy:

I. There is high uncertainty about whether interest rates will increase or decrease. (cause)

II. Money markets are unstable in Asia, Eastern Europe, and Latin America. (cause)

III. There has been a rise in unemployment. (cause)

IV. In the late 1920s in the United States, these three conditions were followed by a stock-market crash. Thus, because of today's similar economic uncertainty, you should decrease the amount of money you have invested in stocks; if you don't, you will lose money. (effect)

THE MOTIVATED SEQUENCE

The motivated sequence is a five-step organizational plan that has proved successful for several decades. Developed by Alan Monroe, this simple yet effective strategy for organizing speeches incorporates principles that have been confirmed by research and practical experience.[30] Based on the problem–solution pattern, it also uses the cognitive-dissonance approach: First, disturb your listeners, and then point them toward the specific change you want them to adopt. The five steps are attention, need, satisfaction, visualization, and action.

1. Attention. Your first goal is to get your listeners' attention. Remember the particular benefits of using a personal or hypothetical example, a startling statement, an unusual statistic, a rhetorical question, or a well-worded analogy. The attention step is, in essence, the introduction to your speech. James Chang began his prize-winning speech titled "Sustainable Giving" with this riveting, attention-catching introduction:

> Beatrice Biira, a nine-year-old girl in Uganda, lives in abject poverty. Living in a shanty home where the rain seeps through the roof every night, neither she nor any of her siblings has ever stepped foot in a school. Her story, sadly, is not unique. The World Bank in 2001 concluded that nearly 3 billion people live on less than two dollars a day.[31]

2. Need. After getting the attention of your audience, establish why your topic, problem, or issue should concern your listeners. Arouse dissonance. Tell your audience why the current program, politician, or whatever you're attempting to change is not working. Convince them there is a need for a change. You must also convince your listeners that this need for a change affects them directly. During the need step, you should develop logical arguments backed by ample evidence to support your position.

To document the need for increased charitable giving to support the world's most impoverished people, James provided specific evidence to describe the problem.

> The UN Food and Agricultural Organization reports in the 2002 assessment of the state of food insecurity in the World that more than 840 million people in the world are malnourished and more than 150 million of them are under the age of five. Six million children die every year as a result of hunger.[32]

3. Satisfaction. After you present the problem or need for concern, you next identify how your plan will satisfy the need. What is your solution to the problem? At this point in the speech, you need not go into great detail. Present enough information so that your listeners have a general understanding of how the problem may be solved.

James suggests that the solution to the problem of world hunger is to donate money to the Heifer Project—an organization that helps the world's poor by teaching them how to use contemporary farming techniques. Here's how he introduced the satisfaction step:

> The old adage goes, "give a man a fish, and you feed him for a day; teach a man to fish, and you feed him for a lifetime." It was the belief of the founders in the simple premise that people should have the ability to feed themselves that was the foundation for the Heifer Project. Heifer International operates Animals to Families as sustainable gifts. The families raise the animals, benefiting from the products of those animals and selling them as a source of revenue.[33]

4. Visualization. Now you need to give your audience a sense of what it would be like if your solution were or were not adopted. You could take a positive-visualization approach: Paint a picture with words to communicate how wonderful the future will be if your solution is adopted. You could take a negative-visualization approach: Tell your listeners how awful things will be if your solution is not adopted. If they think things are bad now, just wait; things will get worse. Or, you could present both a positive and a negative visualization of the future: The problem will be solved if your solution is adopted, and the world will be a much worse place if your solution is not adopted.

To encourage his audience to visualize the benefits of providing sustainable resources to help families climb out of poverty, James describes how one family was able to take out a small loan in order to start a small business.

> Irma Hernandez, a woman from Honduras, joined with four other women in taking out a loan for $120 from the Adelante Foundation. . . . Her husband worked full-time as a farm laborer, but because work was not always available, the income was simply too low and too unstable to support the five children that they had. With the money that Irma borrowed, she was able to buy the necessary tools to start a clothes-making business that brought a steady second income to the family.[34]

James could have made his visualization step even stronger by noting not only what happens when people benefit from the proposal he advocates, but also what happens when people do not receive help. Using both a positive and a negative visualization approach demonstrates how your solution (satisfaction step) directly addresses the problem you have described (need step).

Martin Luther King Jr. drew on visualization as a rhetorical strategy in his moving "I Have a Dream" speech (Appendix D). Note how King powerfully and poetically paints a picture with words that continue to provide hope and inspiration today.

> I have a dream that one day this nation will rise up and live out the true meaning of its creed, "We hold these truths to be self-evident, that all men are created equal."
>
> I have a dream that one day on the red hills of Georgia the sons of former slaves and the sons of former slaveowners will be able to sit down together at the table of brotherhood.
>
> I have a dream that one day even the state of Mississippi, a state sweltering with the heat of injustice, sweltering with the heat of oppression, will be transformed into an oasis of freedom and justice.
>
> I have a dream that my four little children will one day live in a nation where they will be judged not by the color of their skin but by the content of their character. I have a dream today.
>
> I have a dream that one day, down in Alabama, with its vicious racists, with its governor having his lips dripping with the words of interposition and nullification, one day right there in Alabama little black boys and black girls will be able to join hands with little white boys and white girls as sisters and brothers. I have a dream today.
>
> I have a dream that one day every valley shall be exalted, every hill and mountain shall be made low, the rough places will be made plain and the crooked places will be made straight, and the glory of the Lord shall be revealed, and all flesh shall see it together.[35]

5. Action. This last step forms the basis of your conclusion. You tell your audience the specific action they can take to implement your solution. Identify exactly what you want your listeners to do. Give them simple, clear, easy-to-follow steps to achieve your goal. For example, you could give them a phone number to call for more information, provide an address so that they can write a letter of support, hand them a petition to sign at the end of your speech, or tell them for whom to vote. Outline the specific action you want them to take.

QUICK CHECK: *Organizational Patterns for Persuasive Messages*

Type	Definition	Example
Problem–solution	Present the problem; then present the solution	I. The national debt is too high. II. We need to raise taxes to lower the debt.
Refutation	Anticipate your listeners' key objections to your proposal and then address them.	I. Even though you may think we pay too much tax, we are really undertaxed. II. Even though you may think the national debt will not go down, tax revenue will lower the deficit.
Cause-and-effect	First present the cause of the problem; then note how the problem affects the listeners. Or identify a known effect; then document what causes the effect.	I. The high national debt is caused by too little tax revenue and too much government spending. II. The high national debt will increase both inflation and unemployment.
Motivated sequence	Use a five-step pattern of organizing a speech, whose steps include attention, need, satisfaction, visualization, and action.	I. Attention: Imagine a pile of $1000 bills 67 miles high. That's our national debt. II. Need: The increasing national debt will cause hardships for our children and grand-children. III. Satisfaction: We need higher taxes to reduce our debt. IV. Visualization: Imagine our country in the year 2050; it could have low inflation and full employment or be stuck with a debt ten times our debt today. V. Action: If you want to lower the debt by increasing tax revenue, sign my petition that I will send to our senators.

In his "Sustainable Giving" speech, James describes a specific action for his listeners to take to help solve the problem he has described:

> The most important question that should then remain is how you personally can help out. On an institutional level, the United States Agency for International Development, USAID, is one of the leaders in fighting global poverty and should be encouraged to strengthen and increase its sustainable programs. Information about USAID and the ability to contact the agency can be found on its Web site at usaid.org.[36]

James concluded by making a specific appeal to his listeners to donate money to USAID, the Heifer Project, or other organizations dedicated to eradicating world hunger. Note that he directed his listeners to a specific Web address; the best action step precisely spells out the next step your audience should take.

You can modify the motivated sequence to suit the needs of your topic and audience. If, for example, you are speaking to a receptive audience, you do not have to spend a great deal of time on the need step. They already agree that the need is serious. They may, however, want to learn about some specific actions that they can take to implement a solution to the problem. Therefore, you would be wise to emphasize the satisfaction and action steps.

Conversely, if you are speaking to a hostile audience, you should spend considerable time on the need step. Convince your audience that the problem is significant and that they should be concerned about the problem. You would probably not propose a lengthy, detailed action.

If your audience is neutral or indifferent, spend time getting their attention and inviting their interest in the problem. The attention and need steps should be emphasized.

The motivated sequence is a guide, not an absolute formula. Use it and the other suggestions about speech organization to help you achieve your specific objective. Be audience-centered; adapt your message to your listeners.

Summary

- Means of persuasion are techniques that can help you convince your listeners to follow your recommendations.

- You can persuade with credibility, logic, and emotion.

- Credibility is a listener's view of a speaker. The three factors contributing to credibility are competence, trustworthiness, and dynamism. Specific strategies can enhance your credibility before you speak, while you speak, and after you speak.

- The effectiveness of logical arguments hinges on the proof you employ.

- Proof consists of evidence plus the reasoning that you use to draw conclusions from evidence.

- Three types of reasoning are inductive reasoning, which moves from specific instances or examples to reach a general, probable conclusion; deductive reasoning, which moves from a general statement to reach a specific, more certain conclusion; and causal reasoning, relating two or more events so as to be able to conclude that one or more of the events caused the others.

- You can use four types of evidence: facts, examples, opinions, and statistics. Avoid using fallacious arguments.

- Emotion theory has identified three dimensions of emotional response to a message: pleasure–displeasure, arousal–nonarousal, and dominance–powerlessness.

- Specific suggestions for appealing to audience emotions include using examples, emotion-arousing words, nonverbal behavior, visual images, metaphors and similes, selected appeals to fear, and appeals to such emotions as hope, pride, courage, or reverence.

- To persuade skillfully, you need to adapt your message to receptive, neutral, and unreceptive audiences.

- Four patterns for organizing a persuasive speech are problem–solution, refutation, cause-and-effect, and the motivated sequence.

- The five steps of the motivated sequence are attention, need, satisfaction, visualization, and action. Adapt the motivated sequence to your specific audience and persuasive objective.

Key Terms

ad hominem (p. 417)
appeal to misplaced authority (p. 418)
bandwagon fallacy (p. 416)
causal fallacy (p. 416)
causal reasoning (p. 412)
charisma (p. 406)
competence (p. 406)
conclusion (p. 410)
credibility (p. 405)
deductive reasoning (p. 410)
demagogue (p. 423)
derived credibility (p. 407)
dynamism (p. 406)
either/or fallacy (p. 417)
ethos (p. 405)
example (p. 415)

fallacy (p. 416)
generalization (p. 409)
hasty generalization (p. 417)
inductive reasoning (p. 409)
initial credibility (p. 407)
logos (p. 408)
major premise (p. 410)
minor premise (p. 410)
myth (p. 422)
non sequitur (p. 418)
pathos (p. 419)
red herring (p. 418)
syllogism (p. 410)
terminal credibility (p. 408)
trustworthiness (p. 406)

A QUESTION OF ETHICS

Roya plans to give a persuasive speech to convince her classmates that term limits should be imposed for senators and members of Congress—even though she is personally against term limits. Is it ethical to develop a persuasive message based on a proposition with which you personally disagree?

SAMPLE PERSUASIVE SPEECH *Medical Mayhem*

by Alyssa Horn[37]

In a hypothetical situation in a very real world, Bob, a forty-something blue-collar worker, suffers from gastrointestinal distress. Finally, he can no longer stand the discomfort. Bob jumps on to his computer and searches the Internet until he comes across www.livingbetter.com, a Web site sponsored by Procter and Gamble Pharmaceuticals. In the "Understand Your Disease" section, Bob learns about ulcerative colitis, an inflammation of the lining of the colon and the rectum. The symptoms listed are very similar to the ones that he is experiencing. On every page that he visits, there is a graphic linking to prescription information for Azacol, a drug produced by Procter and Gamble to abate the symptoms of ulcerative colitis. Bob immediately calls his clinic to schedule an appointment with his physician to discuss a prescription of Azacol.

◀ Alyssa captures the attention of her listeners with an opening hypothetical example.

Now, can you detect the problem inherent in this scenario? The patient, who has limited knowledge regarding even basic medical procedures, demands a specific drug from a trained doctor. Obviously, the patient had to get the idea from somewhere. And in this example, as in many cases, it's pharmaceutical companies utilizing a direct-to-consumer advertising, also known as DTC advertising. Although there are many ramifications of using direct-to-consumer marketing that reach far beyond the patient—for example, to doctors as well as insurance agencies—no one is more directly affected than the patient. It's important that we, as consumers, do our part to educate ourselves regarding the financial and medical ramifications of direct-to-consumer advertising so that we can make good decisions regarding our own physical well-being.

◀ Notice how Alyssa uses a rhetorical question to move from her introductory example and introduce the key problem she is addressing.

Today, we will first visit the problems inherent in direct-to-consumer practices. Second, we will examine a potential solution to the identified problems. Let's start by looking at the problems. In my research, I have discovered that DTC marketing primarily harms the patient in two ways: financially and physically. First, from the

◀ Because she has analyzed her audience as generally supportive of her key ideas, Alyssa presents a clear overview of her major points.
◀ If she thought her audience was hostile to her ideas, she would not have provided an explicit preview of her persuasive goal.

financial point of view, pharmaceutical companies spend billions—billions!—on advertising in order to increase their sales. According to a 2001 research report from the National Institute for Health Care Management Foundation, pharmaceutical companies spent $2.5 billion in the year 2000 on DTC advertising. The National Institute for Health Care Management Foundation, an independent research firm, indicates that this spending has increased each year: $791 million in 1996; $1.8 billion in 1999; and $2.5 billion in the year 2000. This report also states that the drugs most heavily advertised are also the drugs that bring in the most profit. Sales increased in the 1999–2000 fiscal year by $20.8 billion. Almost half of that increase was produced by the fifty most heavily DTC-marketed drugs. While the drug companies research in order to provide drugs that supposedly improve the quality of life of physically impaired individuals, the rationale for this substantial increase of drug use must be questioned. What do drug companies do with all of these profits? In addition to paying their stockholders, most profits are used to generate additional profits, not improving products. According to a 2000 report, "Profit and Pills: A Primer on Prescription Drug Prices," produced by the Alliance for Retired Americans, drug manufacturers spend only 12 percent of overall profits on research and development; 18 percent of profits are used to gain greater financial power; and 30 percent, the summation of the previous two resource reservoirs, are spent on DTC marketing.

◄ To support her analysis of the problem, Alyssa uses statistics from sources that her audience will find credible.

What is the bottom line? Direct-to-consumer marketing is financially profitable. However, consumers are financially harmed, mostly through higher prices. The 2002 article "Do Ads Really Drive Pharmaceutical Sales?" in the American Marketing Association's *Marketing Health Services* journal answers its own question by asserting that there is "strong circumstantial evidence that ad spending is one of the many important elements driving the sharp rise in pharmaceutical sales to consumers." DTC marketing does inflate the cost of drugs. In the previously mentioned ARA report, a personal example is given about Ms. F. M. of Rossville, Georgia, who is 73 and widowed. Her annual prescription drug costs are about $4200, or $350 per month, but her income is only $608 a month. Ms. F. M. has had both a heart attack and a hiatal hernia. She has lost her insurance coverage and used her savings to pay for prescriptions until she doesn't have enough to pay for her Medicare premiums.

◄ Again, she uses a rhetorical question to lead into the key point the audience should remember from the statistical evidence she has shared.

Not only does DTC advertising hurt us financially, it can also harm us physically, which leads to the second major problem with DTC advertising: This practice hurts the patient physically. How? After all, aren't the drug companies just giving us information, information that has the potential to benefit the consumer? How can this

◄ Using an effective internal summary, Alyssa then provides a transition to her next major point.

(continued)

SAMPLE PERSUASIVE SPEECH *(continued)*

information possibly be dangerous? Well, that's what the drug companies argue. And that's what I also thought, but as I continued my research, I found the error in thinking of the patient as a consumer in search of a commodity rather than recognizing the individual as an ill person in search of health. Thinking of the patient as a consumer allows the mentality that anything the patient wants, the patient can get, and that's a dangerous assumption, especially in the medical world. Accordingly, as in the case with our friend Bob, a result of DTC advertising is patient self-diagnosis. Patients, or consumers in search of a commodity, then proceed to the doctors armed with the information from an advertisement and the knowledge that this brand name medication will help ease their symptoms and improve their quality of life. The physician, after the patient's 12- to 18-minute appointment, prescribes the medication the patient has requested. The Federal Drug Administration, also known as the FDA, researched this phenomenon in 1983 and concluded that direct-to-the-public prescription advertising was not in the public's interest. Yet, the drug companies continue to advertise to the public. Many people elect to take Bob's route, believing an ad that promotes the medication and demanding a prescription from their physician. However, this may endanger your health. This actually happened to a friend of mine a couple of years ago. Her parents requested that she be prescribed Prozac. After three weeks on the medication, the remnants of a previously prescribed medication interacted with the components of the Prozac and lodged themselves inside of her muscle fibers, causing her three trips to the emergency room, immense pain, and semi-paralysis.

Another problem that influences the health of the patient is what Woloshin calls the "medicalization of America." Because DTC advertising often suggests to "see your doctor," we are encouraged to go see the doctor over very ordinary experiences. Not only does this create more demand on our doctors' time, driving up medical costs, every drug has physical ramifications and potential side effects.

So now I have shown you that DTC marketing is detrimental to us financially and physically. So what is the solution to this prescribed medicated mess? Well, there seem to be two solutions. The first solution we can implement immediately. The second one will involve a change in state policy. The first solution is to use generic drugs whenever possible. Generic drugs don't add to advertised brand name revenues, and that gives pharmaceutical companies less profit to work with and eases the financial burden on patients and insurance agencies. According to the Governmental Employees' Health Association, generic equivalents cost 30 percent to 50 percent

◀ Alyssa now moves into her solution, again using a rhetorical question to move to her next point.

less than their brand name counterparts. They have exactly the same ingredients in exactly the same proportions. While the inactive ingredients, things like fillers and coatings and the like, differ to some degree, they don't influence the overall effectiveness of the drug. With reduced revenues, perhaps pharmaceutical companies would place their emphasis on research and development instead of on advertising and increasing their profits. The only way to talk to a for-profit industry is to yell loudly by reducing their profits.

The second solution also talks to pharmaceutical companies' bottom line by looking into the future. The second solution is a change in Minnesota's policy regarding pharmaceutical companies. As indicated in the December 2001 *New York Times* article written by Freudenheim and Petersen, there is no clear federal plan for dealing with rising drug prices. Therefore, states are taking on the responsibilities themselves. Alaska, Idaho, Montana, Oregon, Washington, Maine, Vermont, Florida, and California have all taken it upon themselves to protect their citizens from DTC marketing and the increased costs of drugs. I'm advocating that Minnesota join those states in protecting their citizens. As Minnesota citizens, I ask that you support those senators and representatives that support the investigation of how Minnesota citizens have been impacted by DTC marketing and the increased costs of drugs. Vote for those who advocate a change in public policy based on those investigations. My hope is that these two solutions will create both short- and long-term effects.

◄ Since her audience is primarily other citizens from Minnesota, Alyssa links her own background with her listeners to establish common ground.

In conclusion, direct-to-consumer advertising places an unnecessary burden on the patient, forcing the patient into the role of a consumer desiring a commodity, and therefore hurting the patient financially and physically—both of which endanger the patient's health. The solution we can most quickly act on is to ask for generic drugs whenever possible. And, long term, we need to encourage our state legislature to create policies that weaken the pharmaceutical companies' negative impact on our state's physical health.

◄ Alyssa again states her central idea as she begins her conclusion.

Oh, and by the way, Bob from the introduction got the prescription he wanted. He discussed his doctor's appointment with his buddy, Pete, over a beer and a large meat-lover's pizza. To his surprise, Pete was also on Azacol for ulcerative colitis and Zyban to help him quit smoking, Meridia to help him lose weight, Propecia to help stop his male-pattern baldness, Claritin for allergies, and Techzem for high blood pressure, as well as Lipitor for cholesterol.

◄ To provide closure, Alyssa makes a reference to her opening example and then drives home the point by extending the example.

CHAPTER 21

Special-Occasion Speaking

There is money in public speaking. Many of the ex-presidents, generals, athletes, and entertainment personalities who speak professionally earn five- or even six-figure fees for a single talk. Former President Gerald Ford earns $60,000 per speech, and former President Bush, $80,000. In the $100,000-plus range are former President Bill Clinton and former U.S. Senator John Glenn.[1]

Although most of us will never be rewarded with such lucrative contracts for our public-speaking efforts, it is likely that we will at some time be asked to make a business or professional presentation or to speak on some occasion that calls for celebration, commemoration, inspiration, or entertainment. Special occasions are important enough and frequent enough to merit study, regardless of the likelihood of resulting wealth or fame for the speaker.

In this chapter, we will discuss the various types of speeches that may be called for on special occasions and examine the specific and unique audience expectations for each. First, we will discuss two speaking situations that are likely to occur in the workplace. We will then turn our attention to several types of ceremonial speeches and the after-dinner speech.

> *Historians agree that the greatest banquet speech in history was the one by the ancient Greek philosopher Socrates moments after he drank hemlock. "Gack," he said, falling face-first into his chicken. The other Greeks applauded like crazy.*
>
> **—Dave Barry**

21.a Public Speaking in the Workplace

Nearly every job requires some public-speaking skills. In many careers and professions, public speaking is a daily part of the job. Workplace audiences may range from a group of three managers to a huge auditorium filled with company employees. Presentations may be a routine aspect of meeting management or may take the form of reports to company executives, training seminars within the company, or public-relations speeches to people outside the company. The occasions and opportunities are many, and chances are good that you will be asked or expected to do some on-the-job public speaking in the course of your career.

REPORTS

One of the most common types of on-the-job presentation is the **report**. You may be asked to report on how to increase sales in the next quarter or to present a market survey conducted by your division in the past several months. Whatever the specific objective of the report, the general purpose is to communicate information or policy; sometimes reports end with a persuasive appeal to try some new course of action.

Most successful reports include the following structural elements:

* When you are presenting your report, keep in mind that your audience is there to hear you address a particular need or problem. Begin by briefly acknowledging that situation.

* If you are reporting on a particular project or study, first discuss what your research group decided to do to explore the problem. Then explain how you gathered the information.

* Finally, present the possible solutions you have come up with. For some reports, the most important part is this outline of new courses of action or changes in present policy. In addition, tell your audience what's in it for them—what benefits will accrue to them directly as a result of the new proposal. One business consultant suggests,

> Tune your audience into radio station WIIFM—What's In It For Me. Tell your listeners where the benefits are for them, and they'll listen to everything you have to say.[2]

In addition to listening to the presentation, audience members usually receive a hard copy or email attachment of the report.

PUBLIC-RELATIONS SPEECHES

People who work for professional associations, government agencies, universities, churches, or charitable institutions, as well as commercial enterprises, are often called on to speak to audiences about what their organization does or about a special project the organization has taken on. These speeches can be termed **public-relations speeches**. They are designed to inform the public and improve relations with them—either in general, or because a particular program or situation has raised some questions.

Discuss the Need or Problem   Like the person presenting a report, the public-relations speaker first discusses the need or problem that has prompted the speech. Then he or she goes on to explain how the company or organization is working to meet the need or solve the problem, or why the organization's decision makers believe there is no problem.

Anticipate Criticism   It is important in public-relations speaking to anticipate criticism, whether it comes from the audience as a whole or from a minority contingent. The speaker may suggest and counter potential problems or objections, especially if past presentations have encountered some opposition to the policy or program. The speaker should emphasize the positive aspects of the policy or program and take care not to become defensive. He or she wants to leave the impression that the company or organization has carefully worked through potential pitfalls and drawbacks.

It should be noted that not all public-relations speeches make policy recommendations. Many simply summarize information for those who need to know. For example, local developer Jack Brooks is very aware that many of those present at the city council meeting are opposed to his developing an area of land within the popular Smythson Creek greenbelt. Rather than ignore the objections, he deliberately and carefully addresses them:

> Many of you here tonight played in the Smythson Creek greenbelt as children. It was there that you learned to swim and that you hiked with your friends. I, too, share memories of those experiences.
>
> I want to assure you that my proposed development will actually help to preserve the greenbelt. We will dedicate in perpetuity an acre of unspoiled greenbelt for each acre we develop. Further, we will actively seek to preserve that unspoiled land by hiring an environmental specialist to oversee its protection. As things stand now, we risk losing the entire greenbelt to pollution and unmanaged use. I can promise a desirable residential development, plus the preservation of at least half the natural environment.

21.b   Ceremonial Speaking

Ceremonial speeches make up a broad class of speeches delivered on many kinds of occasions. We will explore nine types of ceremonial speeches: introductions, toasts, award presentations, nominations, acceptances, keynote addresses, commencement addresses, commemorative addresses and tributes, and eulogies.

INTRODUCTIONS

Most of us have heard poor introductions. A nervous speaker making a **speech of introduction** stands up and mispronounces the main speaker's name. Or the introducer speaks for five or ten minutes before yielding the floor to the main speaker.

An introductory speech is much like an informative speech. The speaker delivering the introduction provides information about the main speaker to the audience. The ultimate purpose of an introduction, however, is to arouse interest in the speaker and his or her topic.

When you are asked to give a speech of introduction for a featured speaker or an honored guest, your purposes are similar to those of a good opening to a speech: You need to get the attention of the audience, build the speaker's credibility, and introduce the speaker's general subject. You also need to make the speaker feel welcome while revealing some of his or her personal qualities to the audience so that they can feel they know the speaker more intimately.

There are two cardinal rules of introductory speeches: be brief and be accurate.

- **Be brief.** The audience has come to hear the main speaker or to honor the guest, not to listen to you.

- **Be accurate.** Nothing so disturbs a speaker as having to begin by correcting the introducer. If you are going to introduce someone at a meeting or dinner, ask that person to supply you with relevant biographical data beforehand. If someone else provides you with the speaker's background, make sure the information is accurate. Be certain that you know how to pronounce the speaker's name and any other names or terms you will need to use.

This short speech of introduction adheres to the two criteria we have just suggested: It's brief and it's accurate.

> This evening, friends, we have the opportunity to hear one of the most innovative mayors in the history of our community. Mary Norris's experience in running her own real-estate business gave her an opportunity to pilot a new approach to attracting new businesses to our community, even before she was elected mayor in last year's landslide victory. She was recently recognized as the most successful mayor in our state by the Good Government League. Not only is she a skilled manager and spokesperson for our city, but she is also a warm and caring person. I am pleased to introduce my friend, Mary Norris.

Finally, keep the needs of your audience in mind at all times. If the person you are introducing truly needs no introduction to the group, do not give one! Just welcome the speaker and step aside. "Friends" (or "Ladies and gentlemen"), "please join me in welcoming our guest speaker for tonight, the former chairman of this club, Mr. Daniel Jones." Note that the President of the United States is always introduced simply: "Ladies and gentlemen, the President of the United States."

QUICK CHECK: *Introduce a Speaker*

- Relate the speaker's background to the speaking occasion.
- Correctly identify the speaker's title.
- Pronounce the speaker's name correctly.
- Verify the speaker's credentials ahead of time.
- Be brief.

TOASTS

Most people are asked at some time or another to provide a toast on some momentous occasion—a wedding, a celebration, the birth of a new baby, a reunion of friends, or a successful business venture. A **toast** is a brief salute to such an occasion, usually accompanied by a round of drinks and immediately followed by the raising or clinking together of glasses or goblets. The custom is said to have taken its name from the old custom of tossing a bit of bread or a crouton into a beverage for flavoring.[3] "Drinking the toast" was somewhat like enjoying a dunked doughnut.

The modern toast is usually quite short—only a few sentences at most. Some toasts are very personal, as, for example, one given by a wedding guest who is a close friend of both the bride and the groom:

> I would like to say a few words about this couple. You see, I knew Rachel and Ben before they were a couple—when they were friends. I first met Rachel when we were freshmen in high school. Her sarcastic sense of humor has kept me laughing ever since.[4]

In contrast, a toast made by someone who does not know the primary celebrants as intimately may be more generic. Here is an example of such a generic wedding toast:

> When the roaring flames of your love have burned down to embers, may you find that you've married your best friend.[5]

If you are asked to make an impromptu toast, let your audience and the occasion dictate what you say. Sincerity is more important than wit. At a dinner the authors attended in Moscow, Russia, a few years ago, all the guests were asked to stand at some point during the meal and offer a toast. Although this Russian custom took us by surprise, one of our friends gave a heartfelt and well-received toast that went something like this:

> We have spent the past week enjoying both the natural beauty and the man-made marvels of your country. We have visited the exquisite palaces of the czars and stood in amazement before some of the world's great art treasures. But we have also discovered that the most important national resource of Russia is the warmth of her people. Here's to new and lasting friendships.

Our Russian hosts were most appreciative. The rest of us were impressed. Mary's toast was a resounding success because she spoke sincerely about her audience and the occasion.

AWARD PRESENTATIONS

Presenting an award is somewhat like introducing a speaker or a guest: Remember that the audience did not come to hear you, but to see and hear the winner of the award. Nevertheless, delivering a **presentation speech** is an important responsibility, one that has several distinct components.

Refer to the Occasion   First, when presenting an award, you should refer to the occasion of the presentation. Awards are often given to mark the anniversary of a special event, the completion of a long-range task, the accomplishments of a lifetime, or high achievement in some field.

Talk About the History and Significance of the Award   Next, you should talk about the history and significance of the award. This section of the speech may be fairly long if the audience knows little about the award; it will be brief if the audience is already familiar with the history and purpose of the award. Whatever the award, a discussion of its significance will add to its meaning for the person who receives it.

Name the Person   The final section of the award presentation will be naming the person to whom it has been given. The longest part of this segment is the description of the achievements that elicited the award. That description should be given in glowing terms. Hyperbole is appropriate here.

If the name of the person getting the award has already been made public, you may refer to him or her by name throughout your description. If you are going to announce the individual's name for the first time, you will probably want to recite the achievements first and leave the person's name for last. Even though some members of the audience may recognize from your description the person you are talking about, you should still save the drama of the actual announcement until the last moment.

NOMINATIONS

Nomination speeches are similar to award presentations. They, too, involve noting the occasion and describing the purpose and significance of, in this case, the office to be filled. The person making the nomination should explain clearly why the nominee's skills, talents, and past achievements serve as qualifications for the position. And the actual nomination should come at the end of the speech. When Senate Minority Leader Everett Dirksen nominated Barry Goldwater for the Republican presidential candidacy in 1964, he emphasized those personal qualities of the admittedly controversial candidate that he thought would appeal to the audience:

> Whether in commerce or finance, in business or industry, in private or public service, there is such a thing as competence. What is it but the right vision, the right touch, in the right way, at the right time? What man could be a jet pilot without this touch? But Barry Goldwater has demonstrated it over and over in his every activity. As Chief of Staff of his state National Guard, he brought about its desegregation shortly after World War II and long before Civil Rights became a burning issue. He brought integration to his own retail enterprises. For his own employees he established the five-day week and a health and life insurance plan. All this was done without fanfare or the marching of bands.[6]

And Dirksen ended his speech with the nomination itself:

> I nominate my friend and colleague, Barry Goldwater of Arizona, to be the Republican candidate for President of the United States.

ACCEPTANCES

Anyone who receives an award or nomination usually responds with a brief **acceptance speech**. Acceptance speeches have received something of a bad name because of the lengthy, emotional, rambling, and generally boring speeches delivered annually on prime-time TV by the winners of the film industry's Oscars. As the late humorist Erma Bombeck once wryly noted,

> People exchange wedding vows in under thirty seconds. . . . You only get thirty seconds to come up with the final "Jeopardy" answer. My kids can demolish a pizza in thirty seconds. So how long does it take to say, "Thank you?"[7]

The same audience who may resent a lengthy oration will readily appreciate a brief, heartfelt expression of thanks. In fact, brief acceptance speeches can actually be quite insightful, even inspiring, and can leave the audience feeling no doubt that the right person won the award. Two months before he died in 1979, John Wayne accepted an honorary Oscar with these touching words:

> Thank you, ladies and gentlemen. Your applause is just about the only medicine a fella would ever need. I'm mighty pleased I can amble here tonight. Oscar and I have something in common. Oscar first came on the Hollywood scene in 1928. So did I. We're both a little weatherbeaten, but we're still here and plan to be around a whole lot longer.[8]

If you ever have to give an acceptance speech, it may be impromptu, because you may not know that you have won until the award is presented. A fairly simple formula should help you compose a good acceptance speech on the spur of the moment.

First, you should thank the person making the presentation and the organization that he or she represents. It is also gracious to thank a few people who have contributed greatly to your success—but resist thanking a long list of everyone you have ever known, down to the family dog.

Next, you should comment on the meaning or significance of the award to you. PLO leader Yasser Arafat interpreted his 1994 Nobel Peace Prize as a catalyst for continuing efforts toward peace in the Middle East:

> I realize that this award, which is of ultimate significance and gesture, was not granted to me and to my two partners . . . to crown an endeavor that we have completed but rather to encourage us to continue a road which we have started, continue in wider steps and deeper consciousness in order to convert the option of peace—the peace of the brave—from mere theory to a practice in reality.[9]

You may also wish to reflect on the larger significance of the award to the people and ideals it honors. Elie Wiesel, Holocaust survivor, author, and lifelong advocate of human rights, began his eloquent acceptance speech for the 1986 Nobel Peace Prize with these words:

> It is with a profound sense of humility that I accept the honor you have chosen to bestow upon me. I know your choice transcends me. This both frightens and pleases me.
>
> It frightens me because I wonder: Do I have the right to represent the multitudes who have perished? Do I have the right to accept this great honor on their behalf? I do not. That would be presumptuous. No one may speak for the dead, no one may interpret their mutilated dreams and visions.
>
> It pleases me because I may say that this honor belongs to all the survivors and their children, and through us, to the Jewish people with whose destiny I have always been identified.[10]

Finally, try to find some meaning the award may have for your audience—people who respect your accomplishments and who may themselves aspire to similar achievements. In what has become one of the most often quoted acceptance speeches ever made, novelist William Faulkner dedicated his 1950 Nobel Prize for Literature to

> the young men and women already dedicated to the same anguish and travail, among whom is already that one who will some day stand here where I am standing.[11]

HOW TO: *Give an Acceptance Speech*

- Give a brief, heartfelt expression of thanks.
- Thank the person making the presentation and the organization that he or she represents.
- Thank a few people who have contributed greatly to your success.
- Comment on the meaning or significance of the award to you.
- Reflect on the larger significance of the award to the people and ideals it honors.
- Try to find some meaning the award may have for your audience.

KEYNOTE ADDRESSES

A **keynote address** is usually presented at or near the beginning of a meeting or conference. The keynote emphasizes the importance of the topic or the purpose of the meeting, motivates the audience to learn more or work harder, and sets the theme and tone for other speakers and events.

The hardest task the keynote speaker faces is being specific enough to arouse interest and inspire the audience. One way in which a keynote speaker can succeed in his or her task is to incorporate examples and illustrations to which the audience can relate. The late Texas congresswoman Barbara Jordan delivered two Democratic National Convention keynote addresses, one in 1976 and the other in 1992. Note how she used specific examples in this excerpt from the 1992 keynote:

> The American dream . . . is slipping away from too many. It is slipping away from too many black and brown mothers and their children; from the homeless of every color and sex; from the immigrants living in communities without water and sewer systems. The American dream is slipping away from the workers whose jobs are no longer there because we are better at building war equipment that sits in warehouses than we are at building decent housing.[12]

COMMENCEMENT ADDRESSES

Cartoonist Garry Trudeau has said that **commencement addresses** "were invented largely in the belief that outgoing college students should never be released into the world until they have been properly sedated."[13] Unfortunately, most commencement speeches deserve Trudeau's assessment. They are often oblivious to the audience on an occasion that demands and deserves audience-centeredness. To be audience-centered, a commencement speaker must fulfill two important functions.

First, the commencement speaker should praise the graduating class. Because the audience includes the families and friends of the graduates, the commencement speaker can gain their goodwill (as well as that of the graduates themselves) by pointing up the significance of the graduates' accomplishments. Author Kurt Vonnegut congratulated the 1998 graduates of Rice University in the opening seconds of his commencement address:

> God bless you and those who made it possible for you to study at this great American university. By becoming informed and reasonable and capable adults, you have made this a better world than it was before you got here.[14]

A second function of an audience-centered commencement speaker is to turn graduates toward the future. A commencement address is not the proper forum in which to bemoan the world's inevitable destruction or the certain gloomy economic future of today's graduates. Rather, commencement speakers should suggest bright new goals and try to inspire the graduates to reach for them, as writer Toni Morrison did when she told the 2004 graduates of Wellesley College,

> I see your life as already artful, waiting, just waiting and ready for you to make it art.[15]

Commencement speakers who want to be audience-centered can learn from former Hewlett Packard CEO Carly S. Fiorina. In the spring of 2000 Fiorina consulted by email with the graduating class of the Massachusetts Institute of Technology, whom she was scheduled to address. She discovered that students wanted a speech based on life experience, not theory, and advice on how to make the decisions needed to live life. And, Fiorina adds, "On one point there was complete unanimity: Please don't run over your time."[16]

COMMEMORATIVE ADDRESSES AND TRIBUTES

Commemorative addresses—those delivered during special ceremonies held to celebrate some past event—are often combined with tributes to the person or persons involved. For example, a speech given on the Fourth of July both commemorates the signing of the Declaration of Independence and pays tribute to those who signed it. Your town's sesquicentennial celebrates both the founding and the founders of the town. And if you were asked to speak at the reception for your grandparents' fiftieth wedding anniversary, you would probably relate the stories they've told you of their wedding day and then go on to praise their accomplishments during their fifty years together.

The speaker who commemorates or pays tribute is, in part, an informative speaker. He or she needs to present some facts about the event and/or people being celebrated. Then the speaker builds on those facts, urging the audience to let past accomplishments inspire them to achieve new goals. Speaking at Pointe du Hoc, France, during June 1994 ceremonies to commemorate the fifty-year anniversary of D-Day, Bill Clinton paid tribute to the assembled veterans:

> We are the children of your sacrifice. We are the sons and daughters you saved from tyranny's reach. We grew up behind the shield of the strong alliances you forged in blood upon these beaches, on the shores of the Pacific and in the skies above us. We flourished in

the nation you came home to build. The most difficult days of your lives bought us fifty years of freedom.[17]

His tribute completed, Clinton added this challenge:

Let us carry on the work you began here. You completed your mission here, but the mission of freedom goes on; the battle continues.

EULOGIES

Speeches of tribute delivered when someone has died are an especially difficult form of commemorative address. When you deliver a **eulogy**, you should mention—indeed, linger on—the unique achievements of the person to whom you are paying tribute and, of course, express a sense of loss. At the funeral of former First Lady Jacqueline Kennedy in 1994, Senator Edward Kennedy remembered his sister-in-law in this way:

She was a blessing to us and to the nation, and a lesson to the world on how to do things right, how to be a mother, how to appreciate history, how to be courageous.

No one else looked like her, spoke like her, wrote like her, or was so original in the way she did things.[18]

It is also proper in a eulogy to include personal and even humorous recollections of the person who has died. In his June 11, 2004 eulogy for Ronald Reagan, former President George H.W. Bush related this incident:

Oh, how President Reagan loved a good story. When asked, "How did your visit go with Bishop Tutu?" he replied, "So-so." It was typical. It was wonderful.[19]

Finally, turn to the living, and encourage them to transcend their sorrow and sense of loss and feel instead gratitude that the dead person had once been alive among them. In eulogizing his sister, Diana, the Princess of Wales, Earl Spencer affirmed,

Today is our chance to say thank you for the way you brightened our lives, even though God granted you but half a life. We will all feel cheated, always, that you were taken from us so young, and yet we must learn to be grateful that you came along at all.[20]

HOW TO: *Deliver a Eulogy*

- Keep your emotions under control.
- Focus on the person and not the circumstances of his or her death.
- Express a sense of loss.
- Emphasize the person's positive qualities.
- Mention family members and friends of the deceased by name.
- Mention the unique achievements of the person to whom you are paying tribute.
- Include personal, but tasteful humorous recollections of the person who has died.
- Encourage the living to transcend their sorrow and sense of loss.

21.C

After-Dinner Speaking: Using Humor Effectively

> If you are a human being or even a reasonably alert shrub, chances are that sooner or later a club or organization will ask you to give a speech. The United States is infested with clubs and organizations, constantly engaging in a variety of worthwhile group activities such as (1) eating lunch; (2) eating dinner; (3) eating breakfast; and of course (4) holding banquets. The result is that there is a constant demand for post-meal speakers, because otherwise all you'd hear would be the sounds of digestion.[21]

With typically irreverent wit, columnist Dave Barry thus begins his observations of the activity known as after-dinner speaking. Certainly he is right about one thing: the popularity of mealtime meetings and banquets among business and professional organizations and service clubs. And with such meetings inevitably comes the requirement for an **after-dinner speech.**

Interestingly, not only is the after-dinner speech not always after *dinner* (as Barry points out, the meal is just as likely to be breakfast or lunch), but it is also not always *after* anything. The after-dinner speech may also be delivered before the meal or even between courses. Former First Lady Barbara Bush preferred to schedule speeches first and dinner later during state dinners. In another variation, Librarian of Congress James Billington, at a dinner in honor of philosopher Alexis de Tocqueville, served up one speech between each course, "so that one had to earn the next course by listening to the speech preceding it."[22] Regardless of the variation, the after-dinner speech is something of an institution, and one with which a public speaker should be prepared to cope.

After-dinner speeches may present information or persuade, but their primary purpose is to entertain—arguably the most inherently audience-centered of the three general purposes for speaking discussed in Chapter 7. And when it comes to after-dinner speaking, to entertain is to make people laugh. Communication researcher John Meyer explains that it is the audience that "gives attempts at humor their success or failure."[23] Because humor is listener-centered, the essential question for the after-dinner speaker must be this: What do audiences find funny?

Speakers, actors, and comedians frequently employ the following strategies to make audiences laugh.

HUMOROUS STORIES

Chances are that if you have found an experience or event funny, an audience will, too. The Comedy Gym in Austin, Texas, a school for aspiring stand-up comedians, advocates that one of the best ways to create humor is to start with what speakers know—"themselves, their lives, what makes them laugh."[24] And audiences almost always enjoy stories in which the speaker pokes fun at himself or herself. Comedy writer John Macks points out that self-deprecating humor is "an instant way to establish a rapport with an audience."[25]

Humorous stories should be simple. Complicated stories and jokes are rarely perceived by audiences as funny. Jay Leno claims that "jokes work best when they're easy to understand."[26]

Successful humorous speakers also need a broad repertoire. One successful after-dinner speaker says that she tries

> to get about 25 to 30 jokes, anecdotes or one-liners before I write the speech. This will be reduced to the best and most appropriate 6 or 7, but one needs as much material as possible to begin with.[27]

Finally, it is important to know one's anecdotes very well. Nothing deflates a humorous story more than getting halfway through and then saying, "Oh, and I forgot to tell you . . . . " Only if you know the material can you hope to deliver it with the intonation and timing that will make it funny.

HUMOROUS VERBAL STRATEGIES

Either a humorous anecdote or a shorter "one-liner" may rely on one of the following verbal strategies for humorous effect.

Plays on Words Most of us are familiar with the use of such verbal devices as **puns**, which rely on double meanings, to create humor. For example, the old joke in which an exasperated speaker tries to explain the meaning of "hide" by shouting, "Hide! Hide! A cow's outside!" provokes the response, "I'm not afraid of cows." The joke relies on the pun on the words *hide* and *outside*.

Another play on words is the spoonerism, named for William Spooner, a professor at Oxford University in the 1930s, who frequently used it (inadvertently, in his case). A **spoonerism** occurs when someone switches the initial sounds of words in a single phrase: "sublic peaking" instead of "public speaking," for example. In one joke that relies on a spoonerism, the Chattanooga Choo-choo becomes the "cat who chewed the new shoes." Many parodies and satires employ spoonerisms to avoid charges of libel or copyright infringement; a spoonerism might be employed to name a boy wizard "Perry Hotter."

A third play on words is the malapropism, named for the unfortunate Mrs. Malaprop in Richard Brinsley Sheridan's eighteenth-century play *The School for Scandal*. A **malapropism** is the mistaken use of a word that sounds much like the intended word: "destruction" for "instruction," for example. Archie Bunker, on the 1970s TV series *All in the Family,* achieved much of his humor through malapropisms.

Hyperbole **Hyperbole**, or exaggeration, is often funny. In an after-dinner speech on "The Alphabet and Simplified Spelling," Mark Twain claimed,

> Simplified spelling brought about sun-spots, the San Francisco earthquake, and the recent business depression, which we would never have had if spelling had been left all alone.[28]

Of course, spelling could not have caused such catastrophes, but by using hyperbole, Twain makes his point in a humorous way.

Understatement The opposite of hyperbole, **understatement** involves downplaying a fact or event. Not usually renowned for his modesty, Twain noted at a luncheon in his honor,

> My books have had effects, and very good ones, too, here and there, and some others not so good.[29]

Verbal Irony   A speaker who employs **verbal irony** says just the opposite of what he or she really means. Student Chris O'Keefe opens his speech on reading Shakespeare with the following statement:

> At a certain point in my life, I came to the realization that I wanted to spend my life's effort to become a great playwright.[30]

Chris reveals the verbal irony of the statement when he continues,

> It has been about an hour and a half now and the feeling is still going strong.

Wit   One of the most frequently used verbal strategies for achieving humor is the use of **wit**: relating an incident that takes an unexpected turn at the end. In an after-dinner speech on the weather, Twain related this brief incident:

> You make up your mind that the earthquake is due; you . . . take hold of something to steady yourself, and the first thing you know you get struck by lightning.[31]

The wit occurs in the final phrase, "You get struck by lightning," which catches off-guard the audience anticipating some detail related to earthquakes.

HUMOROUS NONVERBAL STRATEGIES

Sometimes thought of as "clown humor," physical slapstick is the strategy employed by such classic comic actors as Charlie Chaplin, Laurel and Hardy, and Lucille Ball, and by such contemporary ones as Jim Carrey.

Although after-dinner speakers are unlikely to employ exaggerated physical slapstick, they often create humor through such nonverbal cues as posture, gesture, and voice. Well-timed pauses are especially crucial delivery cues for after-dinner speakers to master. One experienced after-dinner speaker advocates "a slight pause before the punch line, then pause while the audience is laughing."[32]

It is true that some people seem to be "naturally" funny. If you are not one of them—if, for example, you struggle to get a laugh from even the funniest joke—you

QUICK CHECK: *Strategies for Achieving Humor in After-Dinner Speeches*

- Relate humorous stories and funny anecdotes.
- Play on words with puns, hyperbole, and intentional errors such as spoonerisms and malapropisms.
- Understate or downplay a fact or event.
- Use verbal irony, saying just the opposite of what you mean.
- Use wit or include an unexpected turn at the end of a fact or incident.
- Use humorous nonverbal physical or vocal elements such as posture, gestures, pauses, and intonations.

may still be able to use the strategies outlined above to prepare and deliver an after-dinner speech that is lighthearted and clever, if not uproariously funny. Such a speech can still be a success.

Summary

- Chances are that at some time you will be called on to speak in a business or professional setting, or for some occasion that calls for celebration, commemoration, inspiration, or entertainment.

- Special-occasion speeches are critical-thinking activities that require the speaker to synthesize and apply his or her speaking skills to unique situations.

- Public-speaking skills are used frequently in the workplace, from making report presentations to representing your company or profession before the public. These two professional speaking challenges each have unique requirements.

- Ceremonial speeches include introductions, toasts, award presentations, nominations, acceptances, keynote addresses, commencement addresses, commemorative addresses and tributes, and eulogies.

- After-dinner speaking is an established institution in which speakers entertain through the use of humorous stories, verbal strategies, and nonverbal strategies.

Key Terms

acceptance speech (p. 446)
after-dinner speech (p. 451)
commemorative address (p. 449)
commencement address (p. 448)
eulogy (p. 450)
hyperbole (p. 452)
keynote address (p. 448)
malapropism (p. 452)
nomination speech (p. 446)
presentation speech (p. 445)

public-relations speech (p. 442)
pun (p. 452)
report (p. 442)
speech of introduction (p. 443)
spoonerism (p. 452)
toast (p. 444)
understatement (p. 452)
verbal irony (p. 453)
wit (p. 453)

A QUESTION OF ETHICS

Even during times of intense personal crisis—for example, following the death of a family member—the press relentlessly pursues celebrities to try to elicit impromptu statements. Is this an ethical practice? Does the public's right to know justify the invasion of privacy?

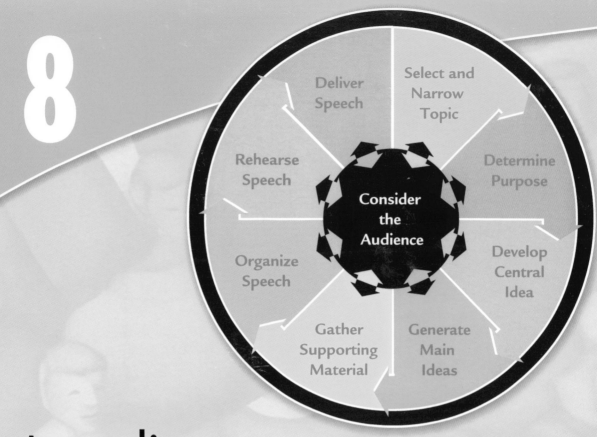

Appendices

Appendices

Appendix A

Speaking in Small Groups

➡ **Small Group Communication (p. 459)**
- Small group communication is interaction among from three to twelve people who share a common purpose, feel a sense of belonging to the group, and influence one another.
- Working in groups has several advantages compared to working on projects alone.
  - Groups usually have more information available.
  - Groups are often more creative; the very presence of others can spark innovation.
  - When you work in groups, you're more likely to remember what you discussed, because you're actively involved in processing information.
  - Group participation usually results in group members being more satisfied with their results than if someone just told them what to do.
- Although working in groups can be a positive experience, working in groups can also be challenging.
  - Group members may use excessive pressure to get others to conform to their point of view.
  - One person may dominate the discussion.
  - Group members may rely too much on others and may not do their part.

➡ **Solving Problems in Groups and Teams (p. 460)**
- Problem solving is a means of finding ways of overcoming obstacles to achieve a desired goal.
  - Identify and define the problem.
  - Analyze the problem by examining the causes, effects, symptoms, history, and other background information that will help the group eventually reach a solution.
  - Generate possible solutions.

- Select the best solution that meets the criteria and solves the problem.
- Test and implement the solution.

➡ **Participating in Small Groups (p. 463)**
- To be an effective group participant, you have to understand how to manage the problem-solving process. But knowing the steps is not enough.
  - Come prepared for group discussions.
  - Do not suggest solutions before analyzing the problem.
  - Evaluate evidence.
  - Help summarize the group's progress.
  - Listen and respond courteously to others.
  - Help manage conflict.

➡ **Leading Small Groups (p. 464)**
- Group members typically need a leader to help the group collaborate effectively and efficiently.
  - Authoritarian leaders assume positions of superiority, giving orders and assuming control of the group's activity.
  - Democratic leaders involve group members in the decision-making process rather than dictating what should be done.
  - Laissez-faire leaders allow group members complete freedom in all aspects of the decision-making process.
  - Transformational leaders are good communicators who support and encourage rather than demean or demand.

➡ **Managing Meetings (p. 466)**
- To be effective, a meeting should have two characteristics: structure and interaction.
- Give meetings structure by identifying the goals of the meeting and developing an agenda.
- Foster meeting interaction by serving as a gatekeeper and making quality contributions.

➡ **Planning a Group Presentation (p. 467)**
- Make sure each group member understands the task or assignment, and work together to identify a topic.
- If your group assignment is to solve a problem or to inform the audience about a specific issue, try brainstorming to develop a topic or problem question.
- Give group members individual assignments.
- Develop a group outline.
- Decide on your presentation approach.

- Rehearse the presentation.
- Incorporate principles and skills of effective audience-centered public speaking when giving the group presentation.

➡ **Making a Group Presentation (p. 468)**

- Clarify your purpose.
- Use presentation aids effectively.
- Choose someone to serve as coordinator or moderator.
- Be ready to answer questions.

Speaking in Small Groups

Groups are an integral part of our lives. Work groups, family groups, therapy groups, committees, and class-project groups are just a few of the groups in which we may participate at one time or another. Chances are that you have had considerable experience in communicating in small groups.

In this appendix you will learn some key communication principles and skills to help you work as a productive member of a small group. Specifically, you will learn what small group communication is, ways to improve group problem solving, and how to be an effective group participant or group leader.[1]

> *Never doubt that a small group of thoughtful concerned citizens can change the world. Indeed, it's the only thing that ever has.*
>
> —**Margaret Mead**

Small Group Communication

What is **small group communication**? It is interaction among from three to twelve people who share a common purpose, feel a sense of belonging to the group, and influence one another. In groups larger than twelve, communication more closely resembles public speaking.

Working in groups has several advantages compared to working on projects alone. Groups typically make better-quality decisions than do individuals for several reasons:[2]

- Groups usually have more information available.

- Groups are often more creative; the very presence of others can spark innovation.

- When you work in groups, you're more likely to remember what you discussed, because you're actively involved in processing information.

- Group participation usually results in group members being more satisfied with their results than if someone just told them what to do.

Although working in groups can be a positive experience, working in groups can also be challenging. Here are some of the potential disadvantages of working in groups:[3]

- Group members may use excessive pressure to get others to conform to their point of view.
- One person may dominate the discussion.
- Group members may rely too much on others and may not do their part.

This chapter concentrates on increasing the advantages and decreasing the disadvantages of working with others.

Solving Problems in Groups and Teams

A central purpose of many groups and teams is solving problems. Problem solving is a means of finding ways of overcoming obstacles to achieve a desired goal: How can we raise money for the new library? What should be done to improve the local economy? How can we make higher education affordable for everyone in our state? Each of these questions implies that there is an obstacle (lack of money) blocking the achievement of a desired goal (new library, more local income, affordable education).

Imagine that you have been asked to suggest ways to make a college education more affordable. The problem: The high cost of higher education keeps many people from their goal of attending college. How would you begin to organize a group to solve this problem? In 1910, John Dewey, a philosopher and educator, identified the way most individuals tackle a problem. He called his method of problem solving **reflective thinking**. Here are his suggestions: (1) Identify and define the problem, (2) analyze the problem, (3) generate possible solutions, (4) select the best solution, and (5) test and implement the solution. Although not every problem-solving discussion has to follow these steps, reflective thinking does provide a helpful blueprint that can relieve some of the uncertainty that exists when groups try to solve problems.

IDENTIFY AND DEFINE THE PROBLEM

Groups work best when they define their problem clearly and early in their problem-solving process. To reach a clear definition, the group should consider the following questions:

- What is the specific problem that concerns us?
- What terms, concepts, or ideas do we need to understand in order to solve the problem?
- Who is harmed by the problem?
- When do the harmful effects occur?

Policy questions can help define a problem and identify the course of action that should be taken to solve it. Policy questions begin with phrases such as "What should be done about" or "What could be done to improve." Here are some examples:

- What should be done to improve security at U.S. airports?
- What should be done to improve the tax base in our state?
- What steps can be taken to improve the U.S. trade balance with other countries?

If your group were investigating the high cost of pursuing a college education, for example, after defining key terms as "higher education" and "college" and gathering statistics about the magnitude of the problem, you could phrase your policy question this way: "What could be done to reduce the high cost of attending college?"

ANALYZE THE PROBLEM

Ray Kroc, founder of McDonald's, said, "Nothing is particularly hard if you divide it into small jobs." Once the group understands the problem and has a well-worded question, the next step is to analyze the problem. **Analysis** is a process of examining the causes, effects, symptoms, history, and other background information that will help a group eventually reach a solution. When analyzing a problem, a group should consider the following questions:

- What is the history of the problem?
- How extensive is the problem?
- What are the causes, effects, and symptoms of the problem?
- Can the problem be subdivided for further definition and analysis?
- What methods do we already have for solving the problem, and what are their limitations?
- What new methods can we devise to solve the problem?
- What obstacles might keep us from reaching a solution?

To analyze the problem of the high cost of attending college, your discussion group will have to use a library or the Internet to research the history of the problem and existing methods of solving it.

Included in the process of analyzing the problem is identifying criteria. **Criteria** are standards for identifying an acceptable solution. They help you recognize a good solution when you discover one; criteria also help the group stay focused on its goal. Typical criteria for an acceptable solution specify that the solution should (1) be implemented on schedule, (2) be agreed to by all group members, (3) be achieved within a given budget, and (4) remove the obstacles causing the problem.

GENERATE POSSIBLE SOLUTIONS

When your group has identified, defined, and analyzed the problem, you will be ready to generate possible solutions using group brainstorming. Use the following guidelines:

- **Set aside judgment and criticism.** Criticism and faultfinding stifle creativity. If group members find withholding judgment difficult, have individual members write suggestions on paper first and then share the ideas with the group.

- **Think of as many possible solutions to the problem as you can.** All ideas are acceptable, even wild and crazy ones. Piggyback off one another's ideas. All members must come up with at least one idea.

- **Have a member of the group record all the ideas that are mentioned.** Use a flipchart or chalkboard, if possible, so that all group members can see and respond to all the ideas.

- **After a set time has elapsed, evaluate the ideas, using criteria the group has established.** Approach the solutions positively. Do not be quick to dismiss an idea, but do voice any concerns or questions you might have. The group can brainstorm again later if it needs more creative ideas.

Some groups have found it useful to use technology to help them generate options and possible solutions.[4] For example, group members can brainstorm possible solutions to a problem individually, then e-mail their list of ideas to each other. Or the group's leader could collect all of the ideas, eliminate duplicate suggestions, and then share them with the group. Research suggests that groups can generate more ideas if group members first generate ideas individually and then collaborate.[5]

SELECT THE BEST SOLUTION

Next, the group needs to select the solution that best meets the criteria and solves the problem. At this point, the group may need to modify its criteria or even its definition of the problem.

Research suggests that after narrowing the list of possible solutions, the most effective groups carefully consider the pros and the cons of each proposed solution.[6] Groups that don't do this often make poor decisions because they haven't carefully evaluated the implications of their solution; they haven't looked before they leaped. To help in evaluating the solution, consider the following questions:

- Which of the suggested solutions deals best with the obstacles?

- Does the suggestion solve the problem in both the short term and the long term?

- What are the advantages and disadvantages of the suggested solution?

- Does the solution meet the established criteria?

- Should the group revise its criteria?

- What is required to implement the solution?

- When can the group implement the solution?

- What result will indicate success?

If the group is to reach agreement on a solution, some group members will need to abandon their attachment to their individual ideas for the overall good of the group. Experts who have studied how to achieve **consensus**—support for the final decision by all members—suggest that it helps to summarize frequently and keep the group oriented toward its goal. Emphasizing where group members agree, clarifying misunderstandings, writing down known facts for all members to see, and keeping the discussion focused on issues rather than on emotions are also strategies that facilitate group consensus.[7]

TEST AND IMPLEMENT THE SOLUTION

The group's work is not finished when it has identified a solution. "How can we put the solution into practice?" and "How can we evaluate the quality of the solution?" have yet to be addressed. The group may want to develop a step-by-step plan that describes the process for implementing the solution, a time frame for implementation, and a list of individuals who will be responsible for carrying out specific tasks.

Participating in Small Groups

To be an effective group participant, you have to understand how to manage the problem-solving process. But knowing the steps is not enough; you also need to prepare for meetings, evaluate evidence, effectively summarize the group's progress, listen courteously, and be sensitive to conflict.

COME PREPARED FOR GROUP DISCUSSIONS

To contribute to group meetings, you need to be informed about the issues. Prepare for group discussions by researching the issues. If the issue before your group is the use of asbestos in school buildings, for example, research the most recent scientific findings about the risks of this hazardous material. Use the library and the resources of the Internet to gather information to prepare for group deliberations. Bring your research notes to the group; don't just rely on your memory or your personal opinion to carry you through the discussion. Without research, you will not be able to analyze the problem adequately.

DO NOT SUGGEST SOLUTIONS BEFORE ANALYZING THE PROBLEM

Research suggests that you should analyze a problem thoroughly before trying to zero in on a solution.[8] Resist the temptation to settle quickly on one solution until your group has systematically examined the causes, effects, history, and symptoms of a problem.

EVALUATE EVIDENCE

One study found that a key difference between groups that make successful decisions and those that don't lies in the ability of the group members to examine and evaluate evidence.[9] Ineffective groups are more likely to reach decisions quickly without considering the validity of evidence (or sometimes without any evidence at all). Such groups usually reach flawed conclusions.

HELP SUMMARIZE THE GROUP'S PROGRESS

Because it is easy for groups to get off the subject, group members need to summarize frequently what has been achieved and to point the group toward the goal or task at hand. One research study suggests that periodic overviews of the discussion's progress can help the group stay on target.[10] Ask questions about the discussion process rather than about the topic under consideration: "Where are we now?" "Could someone summarize what we have accomplished?" and "Aren't we getting off the subject?"

LISTEN AND RESPOND COURTEOUSLY TO OTHERS

The suggestions for improving listening skills that were offered earlier in the book are useful when you work in groups, but understanding what others say is not enough. You also need to respect their points of view. Even if you disagree with someone's ideas, keep your emotions in check and respond courteously. Being closed-minded and defensive usually breeds group conflict.

HELP MANAGE CONFLICT

In the course of exchanging ideas and opinions about controversial issues, disagreements are bound to occur.[11] You can help prevent conflicts from derailing the problem-solving process by doing the following:

- Keep the discussion focused on issues, not on personalities.
- Rely on facts rather than on personal opinions for evidence.
- Seek ways to compromise; don't assume that there must be a winner and a loser.
- Try to clarify misunderstandings in meaning.
- Be descriptive rather than evaluative and judgmental.
- Keep emotions in check.

If you can apply these basic principles, you can help make your group an effective problem-solving team.

Leading Small Groups

Group members typically need a leader to help the group collaborate effectively and efficiently, and a leader needs followers in order to lead. In essence, **leadership** is the process of influencing others through communication. Some see a leader as one individual empowered to delegate work and direct the group. In reality, however, group leadership is often shared.

LEADERSHIP RESPONSIBILITIES

Leaders are needed to help get tasks accomplished and to maintain a healthy social climate for the group. Rarely does one person perform all these leadership responsibilities, even a leader who is formally appointed or elected. Most often a number of individual group members assume some specific leadership task, based on their personalities, skills, sensitivity, and the group's needs.

If you determine that the group needs a clearer focus on the task or that maintenance roles are needed, be ready to influence the group appropriately to help get the job done in a positive, productive way.

LEADERSHIP STYLES

Leaders can be described by the types of behavior, or leadership styles, that they exhibit as they influence the group to help achieve its goal. When you are called on to lead, do you give orders and expect others to follow you? Or do you ask the group to vote on the course of action to follow? Or maybe you don't try to influence the group at all. Perhaps you prefer to hang back and let the group work out its own problems. These strategies describe three general leadership styles: *authoritarian, democratic,* and *laissez-faire.*[12] Authoritarian leaders assume positions of superiority, giving orders and assuming control of the group's activity. Although authoritarian leaders can usually organize group activities with a high degree of efficiency and virtually eliminate uncertainty about who should do what, most problem-solving groups prefer democratic leaders.

Having more faith in their groups than do authoritarian leaders, democratic leaders involve group members in the decision-making process rather than dictating what should be done. Democratic leaders focus more on guiding discussion than on issuing commands.

Laissez-faire leaders allow group members complete freedom in all aspects of the decision-making process. They do little to help the group achieve its goal. This style of leadership (or nonleadership) often leaves a group frustrated because it lacks guidance and has to struggle with organizing the work

What is the most effective leadership style? No single style is effective in every group situation. Sometimes a group needs a strong authoritarian leader to make decisions quickly so that the group can achieve its goal. Although most groups prefer a democratic leadership style, leaders sometimes need to assert their authority to get the job done. The best leadership style depends on the nature of the group task, the power of the leader, and the relationship between the leader and his or her followers.

One contemporary approach to leadership is transformational leadership. Transformational leadership is not so much a particular style of leadership as it is a quality or characteristic of relating to others.[13] **Transformational leadership** is the process of influencing others by building a shared vision of the future, inspiring others to achieve, developing high-quality individual relationships with others, and helping people see how what they do is related to a larger framework or system. To be a transformational leader is not just to perform specific tasks or skills, but to have a philosophy of helping others see "the big picture" and inspiring them to make the vision of the future reality.[14] Transformational leaders are good communicators who support and encourage rather than demean or demand.

Managing Meetings

You will spend a major part of your work time in small groups. Up to 15 percent of a typical organization's total personnel budget is spent on group work. Middle managers generally spend up to 35 percent of their time working in groups. Most senior managers work in groups for up to 60 percent of their working day.[15] Even though millions of meetings take place each day, most people don't like them.

One research team found that what bothers people the most about meetings are discussions that drift off the subject; lack of goals or an agenda; inconclusive, disorganized, rambling meetings that start late; meetings that last too long; and meetings with no follow-up.[16]

If these are the key meeting problems, what are the solutions? The short answer is a simple one: Don't do these things. You may, however, need more direction than that, so here are a few suggestions to help you manage group meetings with skill.

To be effective, a meeting should have two characteristics: structure and interaction. *Structure* involves such attributes as an organized agenda and a logical, rational approach to discussing the issues. A meeting with too much structure resembles a speech. When there is a minimum of interaction and only one or two people do all the talking, participants may wonder why there is a need for a meeting; the information could have been distributed by memo. *Interaction* includes the dynamic process of managing the talk and group discussion. A meeting with too much interaction and not enough structure rambles and digresses and has no clear purpose. The key to managing a meeting is to strike a proper balance between structure and interaction.

GIVING MEETINGS STRUCTURE

The two most important things you can do to ensure that a meeting has appropriate structure are to identify the goals of the meeting and to develop a useful agenda to achieve the goals.[17]

Identify the Goals Most meetings have one or more of the following goals: to share information, to discuss issues, or to take action by making decisions or solving a problem.

Your meeting goal is like your purpose when giving a speech: It serves as a guide to what you include in or exclude from the meeting agenda.

Develop an Agenda The most powerful tool you have to give a meeting structure is an **agenda**, a brief list or description of what the group will discuss during the meeting.[18] Consider organizing your agenda around the three major goals of the meeting: information, discussion, and action. Often groups spend too much time on early agenda items and give less attention to those scheduled for late in the meeting (when most people want to leave). Therefore, do not schedule important items for the end of the meeting. Cover vital issues early, and use the end of the meeting to determine what needs to happen at the next meeting, to summarize the action that needs to be taken, and to determine who will do what.

If you are a meeting leader, keep your eye on two things: the clock and the agenda. Think of your agenda as the map—where you want to go. Think of the clock as your gas gauge—the amount of fuel you have to get where you want to go. If you are running low on fuel (time), you will either need to budget more or recognize that you will not get where you want to go.

FOSTERING MEETING INTERACTION

A meeting is not a speech by the leader to which the rest of the group listens. Leaders and participants should ensure that a meeting is interactive. By being a gatekeeper and making quality contributions to the discussion, a group participant can help ensure that meetings include an appropriate amount of interaction.

Serve as a Gatekeeper   A gatekeeper helps control who talks and who doesn't. Draw out quiet members by calling them by name and asking for their opinions. Ask more talkative members to hold their comments until all have contributed to the discussion. Another strategy for encouraging participation and keeping the discussion on track is to periodically summarize group members' contributions.

Make Quality Contributions   You don't have to be the elected or appointed meeting leader to enhance the quality of group discussion during a meeting. One research team made the following recommendations for meeting participants:[19]

- Organize your contributions, and make one point at a time. Rambling and disorganized comments increase the likelihood that the meeting will stray from the agenda.

- Support your ideas with evidence. Facts, statistics, and well-selected examples help keep the group focused on the task.

- Listen actively and monitor your nonverbal messages. Check your understanding of group members' comments by summarizing or paraphrasing, and watch your own body language.

Planning a Group Presentation

Working in groups takes a coordinated team effort. If you are used to developing reports and speeches on your own, it may be a challenge to work with others on a group assignment. Consider these suggestions to enhance teamwork:

- Make sure each group member understands the task or assignment, and work together to identify a topic. Take a few moments to verbalize the goals and objectives of the assignment. Don't immediately plunge in and try to start dividing up the work just so you can hurry off to your next class or responsibility.

- If your group assignment is to solve a problem or to inform the audience about a specific issue, try brainstorming to develop a topic or problem question. Then assess your audience's interests as well as group members' interests and talents to help you choose among your ideas.

- Give group members individual assignments. After you decide on your group's presentation topic, divide up the tasks involved in investigating the issues. Also, devise a plan for keeping in touch with one another frequently to share information and ideas.

- Develop a group outline. After group members have researched key issues, begin drafting an outline of your group presentation, following the steps of the reflective-thinking process we presented earlier in this chapter.

- Decide on your presentation approach. Determine whether you will use a symposium, forum, or panel presentation, or some combination of these approaches. Make decisions about who will present which portions of your outline and how to integrate them. Your presentation should have an introduction and a definite ending that reflect your group's work as an integrated problem-solving team.

- Rehearse the presentation, just as you would an individual speech. If you are using visual aids, be sure to incorporate them in your rehearsal. Also, be sure to time your presentation when you rehearse.

Making a Group Presentation

Because of the increased challenge of coordinating your communication efforts with other group or team members, keep the following tips in mind as you offer conclusions or recommendations.

- Clarify your purpose. Just as with an individual speech, it's important for listeners to know what your speaking goal is and to understand why you are presenting the information to them. It's also important for each group member to be reminded of what the overall goal is. It would be helpful if the first speaker could ensure that the group has a good understanding of its purpose. If your group is responding to a specific discussion question, it may be useful to write the question or purpose of the presentation on a chalkboard, whiteboard, flipchart, or overhead transparency.

- Use presentation aids effectively. You can use presentation aids not only to clarify your purpose, but also to summarize key findings and recommendations. Visual aids can serve the important function of unifying your group presentation. If your group is using PowerPoint visuals, consider having each group member use the same template and typefaces to add to the coordinated look and feel of your presentation.

- Choose someone to serve as coordinator or moderator. Groups need a balance between structure and interaction. Without adequate structure, conversation can bounce from person to person without a clear focus. A moderator can help provide needed structure to a group presentation by introducing both the topic and the group members. A moderator can also help keep track of time and ensure that one or more people don't dominate the discussion or speak too little.

- Incorporate principles and skills of effective audience-centered public speaking when giving the group presentation.

- Armed with a well-planned outline, present your findings to your audience. If you are using a symposium format, each group presentation is essentially a mini-speech. A panel or forum presentation is more extemporaneous and may even have an impromptu quality, but your delivery and comments should still be well organized. In addition, your visual aids should enhance your presentation by being clear and attractive.

- Be ready to answer questions. Communication is more than just giving people information; it also includes responding to feedback and questions from listeners. Group presentations often include a question-and-answer session (a forum format) following the presentation. Besides being informed about your topic, it's a wise idea to have thoroughly read any written report the group has distributed.

You may face some questioners who offer pointed or hostile questions. How do you handle those? First, keep your composure. Second, you could try to rephrase a very negative question to defuse the sting embedded in it.

If someone asks a question that has just been asked and answered, or asks an irrelevant or poorly worded question, don't criticize the questioner. Be polite, tactful, and gracious. Rather than saying, "That's a dumb question" or "Someone just asked that," calmly provide an answer and move on. If you don't understand a question, just ask for more clarification. Also, don't let a questioner start making a speech. If it looks like a questioner is using the question-and-answer period to give an oration, gently ask: "And what is your question?" or "How can we help you?" Such questions should result in a question that you can then address and return the communication process back to the control of the group.

Summary

- Effective group members prepare for meetings, evaluate evidence, summarize the group's progress, listen well, and help manage group conflict.

- Leaders organize the work, help to achieve the task, and maintain the social climate of the group.

- Leaders of small groups adopt one or more of three styles: authoritarian, democratic, or laissez-faire.

- The best style depends on the group's task, the leader's authority, and the leader's relationship with other group members.
- Meeting leaders are responsible for preparing and distributing an agenda, keeping the meeting on track, and making sure there is balanced participation by meeting members.
- Group members should ensure that their contributions are well-organized, relevant, and understood by others.
- Listening and monitoring the nonverbal messages of others can also promote effectiveness.

Key Terms

agenda (p. 466)
analysis (p. 461)
consensus (p. 462)
criteria (p. 461)

leadership (p. 464)
reflective thinking (p. 460)
small group communication (p. 459)
transformational leadership (p. 465)

A QUESTION OF ETHICS

Karl is working in a group with four other people. One group member, Jose, seems to have taken charge and is making assignments for other group members. Although Jose's leadership skills are helping to get a lot accomplished, Karl resents his overly zealous efforts to take charge. Should Karl keep quiet and just go along with Jose, or should he speak up and express his concerns about Jose's actions?

The Classical Tradition of Rhetoric

by Thomas R. Burkholder

Preparing and delivering a speech always seems to be a very personal task. You must research your own topic. You must analyze and attempt to adapt to the particular audience you will face. You must find a way to cope with your own nervousness. When you confront those problems, it is sometimes helpful to remember that countless others have done so before you. And for as long as people have been giving speeches, they have been looking for ways to make them better. In fact, the study of speeches and speechmaking, or the study of rhetoric, dates back to the earliest years of Western civilization, hundreds of years before the birth of Christ. So in a way, your own efforts are a continuation of that classical tradition.

Speechmaking is probably as old as language itself. And speech criticism is probably as old as listening! But perhaps the earliest recorded evidence of "rhetorical consciousness," the awareness of excellence in speechmaking, appears in the epic poetry of Homer, the ancient Greek poet. His *Iliad,* composed before 700 B.C., contains numerous well-organized speeches or orations. They appear in scenes depicting debates between humans and gods, in councils of military leaders, and so forth. And they demonstrate that the ancient Greeks had a clear sense of rhetorical excellence.

The Earliest Teachers of Rhetoric

We will probably never know who first offered advice to another person who was preparing to deliver an oration. But many ancient writers credit a teacher named Corax with the "invention" of rhetoric sometime around 476 B.C. Corax was a resident of the city of Syracuse on the island of Sicily. He developed a "doctrine of general probability," to be used by speakers in the courts. Imagine a small man being brought into court and accused of beating a much larger, stronger man. According to the doctrine of general probability, the small man should defend himself by saying something like "It is surely unlikely (not probable) that I would beat this man. After all, he is much larger and stronger than I. I would be crazy to risk making him angry by hitting him." But the larger man could resort to the same doctrine in response: "Of course people would think it unlikely that he would hit me. That is exactly why he felt safe in doing it!"

Another similar exchange was the basis of the most famous story about Corax and his student Tisias. Tisias refused to pay Corax for his lessons in rhetoric, so Corax sued him in court. Corax addressed the judges: "Tisias must pay me regardless of your decision. If he wins the case, that proves the lessons I taught him were valuable and I deserve payment. And if he loses, the court will force him to pay. So either way, he must pay." But Tisias responded, "I shall pay nothing. If I lose the case, that will prove the training I received from Corax was worthless and he does not deserve payment. But if I win the case, the court will decree that I owe him nothing. So either way, I shall not pay." The judges quickly tired of such banter and threw the case out of court with the admonition "Mali corvi malum ovum," or "A bad egg from a bad crow!" Legend has it that Tisias promptly left Syracuse and opened his own school of rhetoric in Greece.

Beginning of the Greek Tradition: The Sophists

Whether Tisias actually went to Greece is unknown. But by the middle of the fifth century B.C., schools of rhetoric flourished in the Greek city states. Citizens often spoke in the assemblies or legislatures, and because there were no lawyers, they presented their own cases in the courts. It was soon apparent that the most skilled speakers prevailed in the assembly and won in court. Speech teachers were in great demand. The Greeks called these teachers "Sophists," a term that literally means "wisdom bearer." The rhetorical training offered by these teachers varied greatly. Some, such as Antiphon (480–411 B.C.) and Lysias (459–380 B.C.), were actually logographers. They merely wrote speeches to be delivered by their clients and made no effort to provide training in rhetoric. Others, like Protagoras (481–411 B.C.) and Gorgias (485–380 B.C.), advertised themselves as teachers of eloquence, or the art of effective speaking.

Protagoras is often considered to be the originator of academic debating, because he required his students to argue opposing sides of issues. He believed that each side of important questions had merit, and that humans could never be certain of the "truth." Thus, he encouraged his students to build the strongest possible case for the side of the issue they were assigned to debate. Such training, he felt, would best prepare his students to conduct their affairs in the assembly and the courts. Gorgias was perhaps the first teacher of rhetoric to encourage careful use of language. He believed that speakers would be more persuasive if their speaking style was embellished. He encouraged the use of stylistic devices familiar to modern writers, such as assonance, alliteration, antithesis, and parallelism.

One of the most famous Sophists was Isocrates (436–338 B.C.). Unlike Protagoras and Gorgias, who taught only rhetoric, Isocrates claimed to train citizens to be statesmen. He made rhetoric the center of a more fully developed course of study designed to make his students wise as well as eloquent. Isocrates believed that three qualities were necessary for a person to be a great orator and statesman. First, that person must possess natural ability. Second, that ability must be developed and refined through practice and experience. Finally, to be a great orator and statesman, a person must be well educated, not just in rhetoric, but in philosophy as well. While no one can teach natural ability, Isocrates endeavored to provide his students with practice, experience, and philosophical education.

Although the Sophists attracted many students, and many Sophists became wealthy from their teaching efforts, they were not without their critics. Many felt that the training provided by the Sophists was worthless, if not dangerous. Teachers like Gorgias were accused of providing worthless training by emphasizing florid language with no regard for substance. Teachers like Protagoras were accused of training speakers to "make the worse case appear the better" by urging speakers to develop strong speeches on both sides of any issue. And Sophists in general were often criticized for failing to make their students better, more virtuous people. Without question, the most severe critic of the Sophists was the great Greek philosopher Plato (427–347 B.C.).

Plato

Plato was the student of Socrates (469–399 B.C.), and he went on to become one of the most profound and influential thinkers in history. In 385 B.C., Plato founded the famous Academy in Athens. The Academy attracted the best and brightest students and teachers in all of Greece and remained in operation for almost nine hundred years. Plato's writings were a major influence in the development of Western philosophy and culture. His *Republic* was a blueprint for the ideal political state ruled over by a philosopher-king. His other writings covered a wide variety of subjects, including psychology, logic, and rhetoric. Most of his writings were "dialogues," which resembled plays in which the characters discussed important issues. In many of Plato's dialogues, Socrates was the chief character.

In a typical dialogue, Plato had Socrates attempt to determine the truth relevant to the issue at hand by engaging other characters in a series of questions and answers. That approach is now frequently called the "Socratic method" or the "Platonic method." It illustrated the process of "dialectic," which Plato believed was the means of discovering truth. The dialogues were often named after the characters who opposed Socrates in the discussion. Two of the dialogues, *Gorgias* and *Phaedrus,* named after those Sophists, dealt explicitly with rhetoric.

Plato's dialogues are complicated and often difficult to understand fully. Scholars have debated their meaning for centuries. Some have argued that *Gorgias* and *Phaedrus* presented inconsistent and conflicting views of rhetoric; that Plato condemned rhetoric in *Gorgias* and then praised it in *Phaedrus.* In fact, when taken together, the two dialogues presented Plato's clear and coherent view of the nature and function of rhetoric.

In *Gorgias,* Plato, through the character of Socrates, condemned rhetoric as practiced by many Sophists of his day. He said that the rhetoric of the Sophists was merely a "knack," or a form of flattery, intended only to please the ears of listeners much like cookery pleases the palate. He condemned the Sophists for using florid language, pleasant to the ear, to "make the worse case appear the better." And he accused them of first claiming to impart wisdom and thus to make their students more just and virtuous, and then of failing to do so. But these charges were leveled at rhetoric as the Sophists practiced it, not at rhetoric itself.

In *Phaedrus,* once again through the character of Socrates, Plato praised rhetoric as it ought to be practiced. The Sophists focused their attention on speaking in assemblies and courts. But Plato saw the true rhetoric as a means of using language to influence the minds of listeners, wherever they might be. Going further, he saw rhetoric as a means of influencing the very souls of listeners, thus making them more virtuous. The difference between the Sophistic and Platonic ideas of rhetoric grew from Plato's understanding of "truth."

In Plato's view, truth, or knowledge, existed on several levels. The lowest, least reliable, yet most common level was called *doxa*. This sort of knowledge was the product of the human senses, of what people observed. It was least reliable because it was so easily corrupted; the senses were easily misled. Thus, Plato's condemnation of the rhetoric of the Sophists grew from its aim of pleasing (and often, he felt, misleading) the senses of listeners. On the other end of Plato's scale was *episteme,* or true knowledge. It was the product not of sensory observation, but rather of philosophical inquiry. For Plato, rhetoric as it ought to be practiced was grounded in episteme. Only this "true" rhetoric could be trusted to influence the souls of listeners.

The idea of rhetoric based on truth is appealing. But before we award too much praise to Plato, we must know also that he thought most people were not capable of achieving true knowledge. Only philosophers could attain true knowledge, and thus, in the ideal political state described in his *Republic,* only the philosopher-king was allowed to use rhetoric, for the good of the state. Such uses of rhetoric are frightening. Seen in that light, the Sophists' idea that both sides of important issues should be debated in public seems preferable indeed.

Aristotle

Plato's most famous student was Aristotle (384–322 B.C.). Of all ancient scholars, including Plato, no other was more influential than Aristotle. He wrote extensively on subjects as diverse as philosophy, drama, natural science, and rhetoric. Like his teacher, Aristotle had a profound effect on the development of Western culture.

Throughout his life, Aristotle was directly associated with the most brilliant and important people of his time. His father, Nicomachus, was physician in the court of Amyntas II, king of Macedon and father of Philip the Great. When Aristotle was seventeen, he was sent to Athens to study in the Academy. There he remained until Plato's death. In 343 B.C., he was summoned back to Macedon to become tutor to Philip's son, Alexander the Great. Aristotle returned to Athens in 335 B.C. and eventually founded his own school, the Lyceum. After the death of Alexander in 323 B.C., he came under suspicion in Athens because of his prior close association with Macedon. Aristotle fled to the city of Chalcis where he died the next year.

Aristotle's *Rhetoric* is the earliest systematic discussion of speechmaking of which we have record. It probably existed first as his own notes for lectures he gave to students in the Lyceum. Legend has it that his students edited and published those notes after Aristotle's death. His approach to rhetoric was influenced by the philosophy of Plato. But his practical suggestions for speakers demonstrate that Aristotle was influenced by the Sophists as well. In effect, he was able to transcend both Plato and the Sophists and form a distinctive theory of rhetoric. The impact of his work continues today. Indeed, much of what appears earlier in this textbook originated with Aristotle.

Like Plato, Aristotle believed in true or ultimate knowledge. Also like Plato, he believed that only through philosophical inquiry, which was beyond the ability of most people, could true knowledge be attained. But Plato viewed rhetoric as a means through which, for the good of the state, philosopher-kings might manipulate those incapable of gaining true knowledge. Aristotle took a very different position. He believed that even those who could not attain true knowledge could, nevertheless, be persuaded to the good. Thus, persuasion was an acceptable, although inferior, substitute for true knowledge. In Plato's ideal state, only the philosopher-king could employ rhetoric because in the hands of the unenlightened, rhetoric could do great harm. In contrast, Aristotle believed that rhetoric was a morally neutral art. He did not restrict the use of rhetoric to rulers alone because he believed that, in any dispute, good would prevail provided both sides were equally well prepared; that is, provided both sides were equally well trained in rhetoric.

Aristotle envisioned rhetoric as an art, as a system that could be taught. He defined rhetoric as "the faculty of discovering, in any given case, the available means of persuasion." These means of persuasion he classified into three types: *ethos,* or ethical appeals, based on the degree of credibility awarded to a speaker by listeners; *logos,* or logical appeals; and *pathos,* or appeals to listeners' emotions. The *Rhetoric* offered speakers extremely detailed suggestions for discovering, understanding, and implementing each means of persuasion.

Aristotle also classified the different situations, or "given cases," in which speeches might be given. Those were deliberative, or legislative speaking; forensic, or speaking in the courts; and epideictic, or what he called the "ceremonial oratory of display." Today, we would call that last type "special-occasion" speaking. According to Aristotle, those types were determined by the role listeners must play in each case; by the sort of "decision" they must make after hearing a particular speech. In that regard, Aristotle took an "audience-centered approach" to speechmaking.

In Aristotle's system of classification, those who heard deliberative speeches were asked to render a decision regarding the most expedient course for future action. Those who heard forensic speeches were asked to judge the justice or injustice of a person's past action. And those who heard epideictic speeches were asked to award either praise or blame to the subject (usually a person) of the speech, and to judge the orator's skill as well. The *Rhetoric* offered speakers detailed suggestions for demonstrating the expediency or inexpediency of proposed courses of action, the justice or injustice of a person's deeds, and those qualities worthy of praise or blame. Aristotle also allowed for considerable overlap between the three types, indicating that although one type would predominate, elements of all three might appear in a single speech.

His discussions of expediency, justice, and qualities worthy of praise or blame made Aristotle's *Rhetoric* more than a simple "handbook" for speakers. Those discussions provided a philosophical or ethical foundation for speechmaking. But its practical suggestions made the *Rhetoric* an extremely useful manual for public speaking as well.

The Roman Tradition

The Greek tradition of rhetoric had its most immediate, and perhaps its greatest, influence in the Roman educational system. In the second century B.C., Rome's military might extended the Republic to the east. There, Romans became familiar with Greek culture and the Greek educational system. Much of what they discovered was incorporated into Roman society, and that included training in rhetoric. In fact, rhetorical training eventually became the center of Roman education.

The Roman education system was designed to prepare citizens to participate in the affairs of the state. Primarily, that meant citizens must be prepared to speak in the legislatures and the courts. Rhetorical instruction began in the Roman grammar schools. There, students engaged in a progressive series of written and spoken exercises called the Progymnasmata. The lessons built on each other, with each more difficult than the one that preceded it. Near the end of the program of instruction, students were assigned a thesis which required them to develop arguments on a given theme, such as whether it was more noble to be a soldier or a lawyer. The series of lessons culminated in exercises in which students were required to speak for and against an existing law.

With grammar-school instruction completed, most students moved on to schools of rhetoric. Instruction there was more broad in scope, but it continued to focus on preparing students to be productive citizens of Rome; that is, to be effective speakers. Students were required to learn a vast body of rhetorical theories and concepts based on centuries of oratorical study. They were taught that the art of rhetoric consisted of five separate arts: invention, which involved gathering and analyzing facts and physical evidence; arrangement, or organization; style, or the eloquent and effective use of language; memory, or recollection of the speech for presentation; and delivery. These five classical "canons" of rhetoric are familiar to today's students of public speaking. The exercises in which students in Roman times participated were of two types, *suasoria* and *controversia*. Suasoria were exercises in legislative speaking. Students debated hypothetical questions of public policy, laws, and so forth. Controversia were exercises in forensic or legal speaking. Students argued opposing sides of hypothetical court cases, much as present-day law students do in "moot court" contests.

Following their training in schools of rhetoric, Roman students were often apprenticed to practicing rhetoricians, such as legislators or lawyers. There the students were given opportunities to learn by observing other speakers in legislative and judicial situations. Thus, the entire Roman educational system was designed to prepare citizens to assume roles as orators in the society. Rome produced many scholars who contributed to the rhetorical tradition. Two of the most important were Cicero (106–43 B.C.) and Quintilian (A.D. 35–95).

Marcus Tullius Cicero was the child of an upper-middle-class family from central Italy. Social custom dictated that he pursue his education in Rome, where he studied with the leading rhetoricians of his day. According to many, he became the greatest orator in all Rome. His most famous works on the theory and practice of rhetoric were *De Inventione*, written when he was approximately twenty years old; *De Oratore*, published in 55 B.C.; and *Brutus* and *Orator*, both written in approximately 46 B.C. Cicero's aim in these works was to gather, synthesize, and expand on the greatest teachings of previous Greek and Roman rhetoricians. He was appalled by the emphasis given to style and delivery in some schools of rhetoric and felt the true orator should be a fully educated person. Cicero saw rhetoric as far more than courtroom pleading. Rather, he believed that the ideal orator was the learned philosopher-statesman, who used his talent for the good of the state. In his view, the true orator should be able to speak with eloquence and wisdom on any important subject.

Marcus Fabius Quintilianus was born in the part of the Roman Empire that is now Spain. Like Cicero, he was the product of a traditional Roman education. But unlike Cicero, Quintilian lived in a time when oratory began to be repressed. Tyrants ruled the Roman Empire; the legislative speaking and even the legal speaking that had characterized Cicero's time were greatly restricted. Despite that fact, or perhaps because of it, Quintilian's aim as a teacher of rhetoric was to educate the perfect orator. His most famous rhetorical treatise was *Institutio Oratoria,* which emphasized the moral and ethical uses of rhetoric. For Quintilian, the ideal orator was "a good man speaking well." Unfortunately, that dictum has been much abused by many modern rhetorical scholars, often to justify the study of the speaking and speeches of only highly successful political figures who were usually white and male. In fact, Quintilian urged those who would become great orators to pursue not only eloquence, but excellence in morality and ethical character as well—qualities that are certainly not limited to, or perhaps even characteristic of, successful politicians!

Conclusion

The rhetorical tradition that began with the ancient Greeks and Romans has been a significant influence in Western civilization. Their theories and guidelines for successful rhetorical practice have been analyzed, refined, and extended by countless scholars for thousands of years. This book is a part of that tradition. Many of the rhetorical principles and suggestions for effective speechmaking that appear in this book can be traced through the ages back to such classical rhetoricians as Isocrates, Plato, Aristotle, Cicero, and Quintilian. Throughout history, other rhetorical scholars have made important contributions as well. As you work to prepare your own speeches to be delivered in class or in other settings, it is interesting and perhaps even comforting to know that your efforts are a continuation of a classical tradition of rhetoric as old as Western culture.

REFERENCES

Aristotle. *Rhetoric and Poetics.* Translated by W. Rhys Roberts and Ingram Bywater. New York: Modern Library, 1954.

Black, Edwin. "Plato's View of Rhetoric." *Quarterly Journal of Speech* 44 (Dec. 1958): 361–74.

Clark, Donald Lemen. *Rhetoric in Greco–Roman Education.* New York: Columbia UP, 1957.

Guthrie, W. K. C. *The Sophists.* Cambridge, England: Cambridge UP, 1971.

Hamilton, Edith, and Huntington Cairns, eds. *The Collected Dialogues of Plato*. Princeton: Princeton UP, 1961.

Kauffman, Charles. "The Axiological Foundations of Plato's Theory of Rhetoric." *Central States Speech Journal* 33 (Summer 1982): 353–66.

Kennedy, George. *The Art of Persuasion in Greece*. Princeton: Princeton UP, 1963.

Murphy, James J., ed. *A Synoptic History of Classical Rhetoric*. Davis, CA: Hermagoras, 1983.

Murphy, James J., ed. *Quintilian on the Teaching of Speaking and Writing. Translations from Books 1, 2, and 10 of Institutio Oratoria*. Carbondale: Southern Illinois UP, 1987.

Watson, J. S., trans. *Cicero on Oratory and Orators*. Carbondale: Southern Illinois UP, 1970.

Suggested Speech Topics

O ne of the more challenging tasks for beginning speakers is deciding what to talk about. We identified several suggestions in Chapter 6 to help you select and narrow your topic. Specifically, we suggested that you should

1. Consider the audience.
2. Consider the demands of the occasion.
3. Consider yourself.

We also described several techniques to help you with your topic-selection hunt:

1. Brainstorm—free-associate topics until you have a long list before you start to critique your topics.
2. Read and pay attention to the media; keep current on the news of the day.
3. Scan lists and indexes.
4. Use Internet search engines.

To help prime your creative pump, we have included the following list of topics. Most of the topics presented here are appropriate for an informative speech. Depending on your point of view, they could also be adapted for persuasive speech topics.

Informative Speech Topics

Why go to graduate school?

The history and significance of the Panama Canal

What's happening in Afghanistan [or another country]?

Why are so many dot.com companies going broke?

What exactly happened on Black Monday?

What's the current role of health education?

What's going on with nuclear energy?

What is the privacy act?

Is censorship going on in the United States?

What's involved in being an organ donor?

What are the standards banks use to approve people for credit cards?

The history of the situation in Bosnia

We thank Professor Russell Wittrup, Austin Community College, for sharing his speech-topic ideas with us.

The evolution of the musician as a popular hero

What are the facts on world hunger?

What are the facts on the homeless in the United States?

Who is a powerful contemporary writer?

What is subliminal advertising?

The social/economic problems in Mexico [or another country]

The history of the gay-rights movement

What the experts say about choosing a career

Present trends in animal conservation

What goes into making a compact disk?

What's the United States doing about littering?

How is technology affecting education?

Which diets really work?

What is socialized medicine?

What do primary elections tell us?

What are the goals of general education courses?

The facts on child abuse

What the experts say predicts a good marriage

New discoveries in health care

What's the current status on finances for U.S. education?

What's happening with solar energy?

The facts on religious cults

What is the current status of the military draft?

What are the rights of adopted children?

The facts about legalized prostitution

How happy are marriages without children?

What is involved in being a blood donor?

What has the 70-mph speed limit done for safety?

What's being done to save national parks?

Who gets guaranteed student loans and why?

What are new methods in waste disposal?

Why people become vegetarians

Tips on bicycle safety and protection

The implications of the Internet for education

What is the electoral college?

Is there life on other planets?

What exactly are money-market funds?

What the experts say about crime prevention

The previous decade in the Middle East

How do we choose a president in the United States?

How does the stock market work?

What's being done to find a cure for AIDS?

What's being done to make reparations to Native Americans?

Rap music as cultural expression

Do we have any ecological crises?

What measures are in place to protect us from bioterrorism?

What are the job forecasts for the future?

What's the background of the problems of Ireland?

What's the media's role in shaping the news?

What's the New Age movement?

The latest in genetic engineering

Technology in the twenty-first century

The changing job market

What is sexist language?

New trends in advertising

What does "English as an official language" mean?

How are movie ratings determined?

What are the facts about legalized gambling?

Are there any new concepts in mass transportation?

What is the role of the ACLU?

The impact of the instant replay in sports

How are maps made?

What is the latest in stereo technology?

How is the rate of inflation determined?

How is a loudspeaker made?

The effect of telephone deregulation

The history of the [name of] River

The history of the [name of] building

The history of blue laws

How can you test your own blood-alcohol level?

What's being done about TV violence?

What a chiropractor can/cannot do for you

What is the foreign-exchange-student program?

What kinds of work do volunteers do?

Tips on fire prevention in dorms

The facts about diet pills

What happens in drug-therapy clinics?

The history of jazz [or another type of music]

What is electroshock therapy?

The history of cable TV

How do unions work?

Living together

Success of designated-smoking-area laws

The history of cremation customs

How does cloning work?

What is stem-cell research?

What are the current child-custody laws?

Multiple births

The facts about teenage alcoholism

New breakthroughs for the disabled

What is the Consumer Protection Agency?

How are scholarships awarded?

What is the "Sunset Law" for government agencies?

What is the impact of the new immigration laws?

What has been the impact of recycling centers?

Reasons for changes in marriage and divorce rates

Sexual harassment: what it is and how to deal with it if it happens to you

Is there a "glass ceiling" for working women?

Persuasive Speech Topics

We should reduce our fat intake.

We should reduce our body weight.

Spend more leisure time doing [something].

Volunteer for [something].

The electoral-college system for electing presidents should be changed.

Every U.S. citizen should spend two years in mandatory community service.

State drug laws should be changed.

The income-tax system should be changed.

All undergraduate courses should be graded on a pass/fail basis only.

Everyone should study a foreign language.

Everyone should read a weekly news magazine regularly.

Couples should [or should not] live together before marriage.

We devote too much attention to college athletics.

Don't [or do] invest in the stock market.

The United States should have a tougher trade policy.

All farmers should be given low-interest loans.

The government should provide health care for all.

Divorce laws should be changed.

Spend less time watching TV.

Casino gambling should [or should not] be legalized in this state.

Birth-control pills should [or should not] be dispensed by state-supported schools.

The federal court system needs to be changed.

A college education should be available to all citizens at no cost.

Teachers should be paid more.

Nuclear-power plants should [or should not] be phased out.

Developing alternative energy sources must become a national priority.

School choice should [or should not] be promoted.

Affirmative action is the best way to overcome discrimination.

What working mothers and fathers need from their employers.

Why a national health-care system will [or won't] work.

College students should [or shouldn't] be given the opportunity to pay off their tuition through public service.

The use of animals in research should be fully regulated.

It's time to put an end to violence on television.

All students should be required to take a public-speaking course.

The United States should [or should not] invest in the stock market to save Social Security.

Stem-cell research is a good [or bad] thing.

We should increase drilling for oil in national parks and forests.

The United States should [or should not] drastically change its foreign policy in response to the events of September 11, 2001.

Speeches for Analysis and Discussion

I Have a Dream*

by Martin Luther King Jr., Washington, D.C., August 28, 1963

I am happy to join with you today in what will go down in history as the greatest demonstration for freedom in the history of our nation.

Five score years ago, a great American, in whose symbolic shadow we stand today, signed the Emancipation Proclamation. This momentous decree came as a great beacon light of hope to millions of Negro slaves, who had been seared in the flames of withering injustice. It came as a joyous daybreak to end the long night of their captivity.

But one hundred years later, the Negro is still not free. One hundred years later, the life of the Negro is still sadly crippled by the manacles of segregation and the chains of discrimination. One hundred years later, the Negro lives on a lonely island of poverty in the midst of a vast ocean of material prosperity. One hundred years later, the Negro is still languishing in the corners of American society and finds himself an exile in his own land. And so we've come here today to dramatize a shameful condition.

In a sense we've come to our nation's Capitol to cash a check. When the architects of our republic wrote the magnificent words of the Constitution and the Declaration of Independence, they were signing a promissory note to which every American was to fall heir. This note was a promise that all men—yes, black men as well as white men— would be guaranteed the inalienable rights of life, liberty, and the pursuit of happiness.

It is obvious today that America has defaulted on this promissory note insofar as her citizens of color are concerned. Instead of honoring this sacred obligation, America has given the Negro people a bad check—a check which has come back marked "insufficient funds."

But we refuse to believe that the bank of justice is bankrupt. We refuse to believe that there are insufficient funds in the great vaults of opportunity of this nation. And so we've come to cash this check—a check that will give us upon demand the riches of freedom and the security of justice.

---

*Reprinted by arrangement with the Heirs of the Estate of Martin Luther King Jr., c/o Joan Daves Agency as agent for the proprietor. Copyright © 1963 by Martin Luther King Jr., copyright renewed 1991 by Coretta Scott King.

We have also come to this hallowed spot to remind America of the fierce urgency of now. This is no time to engage in the luxury of cooling off or to take the tranquilizing drug of gradualism. Now is the time to make the real promises of democracy. Now is the time to rise from the dark and desolate valley of segregation to the sunlit path of racial justice. Now is the time to lift our nation from the quicksands of racial injustice to the solid rock of brotherhood. Now is the time to make justice a reality for all of God's children.

It would be fatal for the nation to overlook the urgency of the moment. This sweltering summer of the Negro's legitimate discontent will not pass until there is an invigorating autumn of freedom and equality. Nineteen sixty-three is not an end, but a beginning. Those who hope that the Negro needed to blow off steam and will now be content will have a rude awakening if the nation returns to business as usual. There will be neither rest nor tranquility in America until the Negro is granted his citizenship rights. The whirlwinds of revolt will continue to shake the foundations of our nation until the bright day of justice emerges.

But there is something that I must say to my people, who stand on the warm threshold which leads into the palace of justice. In the process of gaining our rightful place, we must not be guilty of wrongful deeds. Let us not seek to satisfy our thirst for freedom by drinking from the cup of bitterness and hatred.

We must forever conduct our struggle on the high plane of dignity and discipline. We must not allow our creative protest to degenerate into physical violence. Again and again we must rise to the majestic heights of meeting physical force with soul force.

The marvelous new militance which has engulfed the Negro community must not lead us to a distrust of all white people. For many of our white brothers, as evidenced by their presence here today, have come to realize that their destiny is tied up with our destiny. They have come to realize that their freedom is inextricably bound to our freedom. We cannot walk alone.

As we walk, we must make the pledge that we shall always march ahead. We cannot turn back. There are those who are asking the devotees of civil rights, "When will you be satisfied?" We can never be satisfied as long as the Negro is the victim of the unspeakable horrors of police brutality. We can never be satisfied as long as our bodies, heavy with the fatigue of travel, cannot gain lodging in the motels of the highways and hotels of the cities. We cannot be satisfied as long as the Negro's basic mobility is from a smaller ghetto to a larger one. We can never be satisfied as long as our children are stripped of their selfhood and robbed of their dignity by signs stating "For Whites Only." We cannot be satisfied as long as a Negro in Mississippi cannot vote and a Negro in New York believes he has nothing for which to vote. No, no, we are not satisfied, and we will not be satisfied until justice rolls down like waters, and righteousness like a mighty stream.

I am not unmindful that some of you have come here out of great trials and tribulations. Some of you have come fresh from narrow jail cells. Some of you have come from areas where your quest for freedom left you battered by the storms of persecution and staggered by the winds of police brutality. You have been the veterans of creative suffering. Continue to work with the faith that unearned suffering is redemptive.

Go back to Mississippi, go back to Alabama, go back to South Carolina, go back to Georgia, go back to Louisiana, go back to the slums and ghettos of our Northern cities, knowing that somehow this situation can and will be changed. Let us not wallow in the valley of despair.

I say to you today, my friends, so even though we face the difficulties of today and tomorrow, I still have a dream. It is a dream deeply rooted in the American dream.

I have a dream that one day this nation will rise up and live out the true meaning of its creed, "We hold these truths to be self-evident, that all men are created equal."

I have a dream that one day on the red hills of Georgia the sons of former slaves and the sons of former slaveowners will be able to sit down together at the table of brotherhood.

I have a dream that one day even the state of Mississippi, a state sweltering with the heat of injustice, sweltering with the heat of oppression, will be transformed into an oasis of freedom and justice.

I have a dream that my four little children will one day live in a nation where they will not be judged by the color of their skin but by the content of their character. I have a dream today.

I have a dream that one day, down in Alabama, with its vicious racists, with its governor having his lips dripping with the words of interposition and nullification, one day right there in Alabama little black boys and black girls will be able to join hands with little white boys and white girls as sisters and brothers. I have a dream today.

I have a dream that one day every valley shall be exalted, every hill and mountain shall be made low, the rough places will be made plain and the crooked places will be made straight, and the glory of the Lord shall be revealed, and all flesh shall see it together.

This is our hope. This is the faith that I go back to the South with. With this faith we will be able to hew out of the mountain of despair a stone of hope. With this faith we will be able to transform the jangling discords of our nation into a beautiful symphony of brotherhood. With this faith we will be able to work together, to pray together, to struggle together, to go to jail together, to stand up for freedom together knowing that we will be free one day.

This will be the day—this will be the day when all of God's children will be able to sing with new meaning, "My country 'tis of thee, sweet land of liberty, of thee I sing. Land where my fathers died, land of the Pilgrims' pride, from every mountainside, let freedom ring." And if America is to be a great nation, this must become true.

So let freedom ring from the prodigious hilltops of New Hampshire. Let freedom ring from the mighty mountains of New York. Let freedom ring from the heightening Alleghenies of Pennsylvania!

Let freedom ring from the snowcapped Rockies of Colorado! Let freedom ring from the curvaceous slopes of California!

But not only that. Let freedom ring from Stone Mountain of Georgia!

Let freedom ring from Lookout Mountain of Tennessee!

Let freedom ring from every hill and molehill of Mississippi. From every mountainside, let freedom ring.

And when this happens, when we allow freedom to ring—when we let it ring from every village and every hamlet, from every state and every city—we will be able to speed up that day when all of God's children, black men and white men, Jews and Gentiles, Protestants and Catholics, will be able to join hands and sing, in the words of the old Negro spiritual, "Free at last! Free at last! Thank God almighty, we are free at last!"

Making Democracy Work: Your Responsibility to Society

by Cynthia Opheim, Professor and Chair, Department of Political Science,
Southwest Texas State University

President Supple, Regent Flores, and members of the platform party, colleagues, friends and families of our graduates, my family, graduates. Les felicito por este logro! I congratulate you for this achievement! You've made it! After concentrated effort, sacrifice, and expense, you've accomplished a distinct achievement: a graduate education.

Let's take a moment to celebrate this achievement. Only 7.5 percent of the adult population in this country earn graduate degrees; only 6.5 percent of the adult population in Texas (only 4.5 in Arkansas, but who's comparing?). Today, the average difference in annual income between those with a Bachelor's versus those with a Master's degree is almost $11,000. Your educational accomplishments have officially placed you into a category that my colleagues, political scientists, refer to as "elites." (I prefer the term "meritocracy.")

While you enjoy your new status as the educated elite (or the meritocracy), you must know that it places new responsibilities on you. It is up to you, even more than others, to make our democracy work! I do feel a little guilty giving you this message; you've worked very hard for months and years and now I'm telling you that your responsibilities are greater than ever! "Give me a break," you say. Well, I can't; the stakes are too high.

Democracies are not automatically self-sustaining. Samuel Huntington, a prominent scholar, notes that there have been three great waves of democracy in the last 200 years, that is, three historical periods where democracies have emerged: a long slow wave from 1828 to 1926; a post–World War II wave, from 1945 to 1964; and the present wave beginning in 1976. The first two waves ended with a reverse wave of democratic breakdowns during which some of the new or reestablished democracies collapsed. Will the new century bring a third reverse wave? If so, how will the reversals occur? It has been said that "the death of democracy is not likely to be an assassination from ambush. It will be a slow extinction from apathy, indifference, and undernourishment."

This evening I'd like to lay out two strategies for making our democracy work, a basic recipe that you, as the most educated members of our society, should think about. The first is informed participation in public life. Participation in political or public life is the most basic corollary of democracy. I challenge you to organize a group, circulate a petition, attend a public hearing, run for the school board, volunteer in a hospital, e-mail your congressional representative, speak out at a city council meeting, organize a meals-to-the-elderly program. As the most educated members of our society, you should play a leading role in civic life.

Notice, however, there is an additional responsibility attached to participating: staying informed. In one of my favorite quotes, Thomas Jefferson said, "Ignorant participation is not democratic." Staying informed should be easier for you than for many—you would not be sitting here if you didn't already know how to cultivate the discipline and love for learning you've had in graduate school. Continue these habits: read at least one or two articles from the international section of the newspaper; take the time to decipher both sides of an issue; listen (really listen) to someone whose point of view is different from your own (I tell my students, if you're a liberal, turn on Rush Limbaugh; if you're a conservative, listen to one of Jesse Jackson's speeches— tough challenges no doubt); try to think about the interest of the broader community. Apply the principles of informed democracy in your work and in your life; if you are a manager or administrator, be aggressive about seeking advice.

Above all, THINK about the responsibility you as elites have to make our democracy work. Prove Adolf Hitler wrong when he said, "What luck for rulers that men do not think."

The second strategy for making our democracy work is to carefully select and then respect our political leaders. It's this second part of the recipe that is the greatest challenge. Fewer people are voting; less than half of those eligible voted in the last presidential election. Yet our responsibility for selecting the right leaders is as crucial to the success of our democracy as participation in the process itself.

Your educational training has given you the capacity to analyze important public issues and tie those issues to candidates and public officials. Thus, you have a special commitment to do so.

Once we select our leaders, it's crucial that we have at least some trust in them. This is the most difficult challenge of all in America. Americans have always distrusted power and those who hold power. In my political science classes I always tell my students that we have an antipolitical political tradition. We have always embraced a culture of individualism and dissent, never more so than today as the media lays bare the weaknesses and failures of our leaders.

The very procedures of open democratic decision-making encourage our suspicion of those who engage in it. Democracy is messy; it is not efficient. We often witness our leaders discussing, arguing, amending, compromising, and it frustrates us. Most of us believe Mark Twain was right when he said there are two things you should never watch being made: sausage and legislation.

But at some point we must trust our leaders. Why? Because it gives them greater flexibility to deal with difficult issues. It's important that they possess a reserve of mass confidence that allows them to call on citizens to make short-term sacrifices for long-term goals. School board members may ask permission from the public to borrow money through the sale of bonds to improve the schools. Congress may have to reduce funding for a popular program to direct funds to something more important. When trust is low, leaders are pressured to make short-sighted decisions at the expense of a healthy future.

Many of you, the meritocracy, have been and will be selected as leaders. To those of you selected, I ask that you always remember how crucial it is to maintain the trust of those you lead. There is likely to be intense scrutiny of you and your actions. Be aware that these days, you must not only act ethically, you must maintain the appearance of acting ethically. Always remember you build trust over time; you lose it quickly.

So tonight while we celebrate your achievement, and it is an extraordinary achievement, remember your special responsibility to our society. It is you I think of now when I read the comments Alexander Hamilton made about our new constitutional system in 1789. He's describing the great experiment in democracy that is America when he states that "... it is reserved to the people of this country, by their conduct and example, to decide the important question, whether societies of men are really capable or not of establishing good government from reflection and choice, or whether they are forever destined to depend on accident and force."

Be involved, stay informed, select your leaders carefully, nurture trust in your own leadership, and help make our great experiment a success!

Congratulations!

Have a happy and productive life.

Van Gogh's Incredible Life

by Kristy Shaw

When you hear the name Vincent van Gogh, does the picture of an insane artist who cut off his ear come to mind? That's what I first thought about him until I learned more about his life. And now I feel to remember him that way is to deny him the genius of his work and the fascinating details of his life.

Though Van Gogh's life was short—he was only 37 when he killed himself—his life was marked by depression, madness, loneliness, and lost love. According to the 1992 Carol Strickland's book, *The Annotated Mona Lisa*, Van Gogh once said, "I'd rather die of passion instead of boredom." Van Gogh's certainly was a life of passion. He experienced outbursts of intense joy, brotherly love, and creative spurts that produced brilliant artwork that we still admire to this day. During this speech, I will walk you through this fascinating man's life. I will tell you about his beginnings; the troubled teen years where he bounced around trying to find his niche in the world; and the creative middle years where he decided to be an artist and throws himself into the field; and finally, the last two years of his life that marked his rapid demise into madness and eventually drove him to commit suicide.

According to the Van Gogh Museum Web site entitled "Van Gogh's Life and Times," Van Gogh was born in 1853 on March 30th in the Netherlands. He was the eldest of six children, and his favorite brother, Theo, was born four years later. Theo would be his financial and emotional supporter throughout his life. Van Gogh attempted two careers in his lifetime. The first was an apprenticeship at Goupil & Cie, an international art dealership with which he joined after he dropped out of school at the age of sixteen. He worked at a branch office there for seven years until, at the age of 23, he was fired. After becoming disillusioned with the art trade, he reportedly told customers they were buying junk. Between the ages of 23 and 27, Van Gogh attempted to be a minister. He was driven by a desire to help the common man, and he wanted to be a clergyman. Soon, he became obsessed with evangelical Christianity, and he even tried to enroll in the Amsterdam Theology School, but he failed the entrance exam. Therefore, he became a lay minister. He worked among impoverished miners. He slept on the floor, gave away all his possessions, and preached to them. Finally, the church ended up dismissing him due to his overzealous commitments.

After two failed careers, at the age of 27, Van Gogh's mental health is suffering. He's in acute poverty. He's in the middle of a spiritual crisis. He's a failure in the eyes of his family. He has no job, no income, and he's searching for something to dedicate his life to. It is in 1880 that Van Gogh discovers art. He feels it's a way to express himself and God and to also get income from his work. Between the years 1880 and 1887, Van Gogh funnels his time and enthusiasm into being an artist. At the age of 27, Van Gogh begins to study watercolor and oils. In 1883, he begins to paint bleak landscapes and peasant worker pictures. He completes 40 painted studies of peasants and gives them to Theo to sell. An example is the 1885 piece, Potato Eaters. As you can see, he begins to use dark colors in his painting. However, at this time, Van Gogh and Theo have personal tensions between them. Van Gogh accuses Theo of not selling his work. And Theo explains that Van Gogh's style, which is dark colors, does not meet the current style, which is bright, lively colors. And therefore, his painting won't sell.

During this time, Van Gogh also hits a series of love disasters in his lifetime. First, he falls in love with his cousin, Kee Vos-Stricker. Van Gogh disgraces his family with this unacceptable affair. And to top it all off, Vos-Stricker rejects him. Two years later in 1882, Van Gogh again scandalizes his family by bringing a pregnant prostitute named Sien Hoornik and her 11-year-old daughter into his household. Now, initially, Van Gogh wanted Hoornik to pose for his art, but she refuses. Eventually, she is thrown out of the household for causing too much trouble. But Van Gogh contracts gonorrhea during this time.

Between the age of 32 and 34, Van Gogh begins to blend his creativity and vision to form his own unique style. While visiting Theo in Paris, he is introduced to impressionistic style of painting. He likes the light colors and the short brush strokes. And he begins to use colors to symbolize emotions. He also experiments with many different types of hues and changes to the lighter palette. According to the Think Quest Web site entitled "Van Gogh in Essence," Van Gogh said, "Instead of trying to reproduce exactly what's before my eyes I use color more arbitrarily to express myself more forcibly."

Lawrence and Elizabeth Hanson's 1955 book, *Passionate Pilgrim*, states that Van Gogh becomes unlucky in love once again. This time he falls in love with his neighbor, Margot Begemann. Begemann is a spinster who is 10 years older than he. And even though his feelings are reciprocated at this time and they plan to marry, his parents don't approve of the marriage, and they won't let them. Begemann poisons herself in protest. And even though she survives, her parents take her away. And she and Van Gogh never see each other again. Van Gogh slips into depression over another lost love.

The last few years of Van Gogh's life are marked by creative brilliance, but also by mental instability that eventually leads him to commit suicide. When Van Gogh is 35 years old he is worn down by his activities in Paris. He retreats to a province in France; rents a studio with little distractions; he begins to paint. As far as art goes, he enters a period of sustained creativity where he paints more than 200 canvases including Sunflowers in the Vase. As you can see, this painting features light colors as opposed to the dark colors of Potato Eaters. Van Gogh, however, cannot sell any of his paintings, and he lives in poverty, relying solely on Theo for money and support. Soon, he begins to suffer from fits of madness, depression, and hallucinations. But one good thing in Van Gogh's life is that he is eagerly awaiting his friend and mentor, Paul Gaugin. Gaugin visits him in the fall, and for nine months, they paint side by side and have wonderful art discussions. But soon, personal tensions grow between the two men, and Van Gogh threatens Gaugin with a razor blade. Now Gaugin is unharmed, but this is the infamous incident where Van Gogh cuts off his left earlobe. He wraps the earlobe in paper and gives it to a prostitute as a present, as recorded in Hansons' book.

At the age of 36, the Van Gogh Museum Web site states that Van Gogh is admitted into a psychiatric hospital. He's subject to attacks ranging from depression to frantic bursts of energy. But he is able to find some solace in the asylum's structured days. But there is one episode where he eats paint in a failed attempt to commit suicide. While at the asylum, Van Gogh finds inspiration in its long gardens, and he paints more than 150 paintings while there, including Starry Night, for which he receives favorable reviews. The Van Gogh Museum Web site records Van Gogh as saying, "I feel happier here with my work than I could be on the outside. By staying here a good, long time I shall have learned regular habits. And in the long run there will be more order in my life."

Van Gogh was released from the hospital under a physician's care and moves near Paris to be closer to Theo. When Van Gogh is 37 years old, he begins to feverishly paint producing a painting a day for the next two months. His paintings focus on portraits and nearby landscapes. But mentally, Van Gogh's passion for art begins to fade. He feels like a failure. And when informed that Theo is beginning to start his own business, and therefore, money will be short, he becomes concerned about his financial situation and worries about becoming a greater burden. According to Think Quest Web site, Van Gogh states, "I feel a failure. That's it as far as I'm concerned. I feel that this is the destiny that I must accept. And that will never change." On July 27th, 1890, Van Gogh walks into a field and shoots himself in the stomach with a pistol. He stumbles back to the house and dies two days later with Theo at his side. Van Gogh's dying words were "Who would believe their life could be so sad?"

Van Gogh's life was not an easy one. He experienced troubled teen years where he struggled to find what he wanted to do with his life; middle years that were full of creativity; and finally, the last years of his life where mental illness took over and eventually drove him to commit suicide. Despite an unhappy life marked by turmoil, depression, and loneliness, Van Gogh managed to leave a lasting impression on the world by expressing himself the only way he knew how—through his paintings. According to Strickland, Van Gogh once said, "I have risked my life for my work. And my mind has half floundered." It is these paintings that are the legacy of Van Gogh. Though marked by personal tragedy and despair, Van Gogh was always driven to paint. It was the only thing he knew how to do. Hansons' book cites a passage from a letter

Van Gogh wrote to his brother; in it, Van Gogh writes, "A white worm must eat salad roots to attain its transformation. And I think that a painter must paint. Perhaps there'll be something after that."

REFERENCES

Hanson, L. & Hanson, E. (1995). *Passionate pilgrim: The life of Vincent van Gogh.* New York: Random House.

Strickland, C. (1992). *The annotated Mona Lisa.* Kansas City, MO: Universal Press Syndicate Company.

Van Gogh at Etten–sketches and billboards. (n.d.). *Think Quest,* http://library. thinkquest.org/C001734/eng/textonly.html.

Van Gogh's life and times. (n.d.). *Van Gogh Museum, Amsterdam,* http://www. vangoghmuseum.nl/bisrd/top-1-2-2-4-1.html.

The Electoral College

by Nathan Harrington

George Bush, 50,456,169; Al Gore, 50,996,116. Al Gore is our president, right? Wrong. Although he did not receive the majority of the popular vote, George Bush received 271 electoral votes to Al Gore's 266. The election of 2000 focused renewed attention and criticism on the role of the Electoral College in selecting our president. In this speech, I will discuss the Electoral College, specifically its history, current issues, and future changes that have been proposed. Hopefully informing you about this topic will help you understand the importance of electoral votes in the upcoming presidential election.

According to William Kimberling, the Deputy Director of the Federal Election Commission, our country's founders faced a number of problems in establishing a way to elect a president. People wanted a way to select the president without political parties because many believed they were corrupt at the time. They also did not want national campaigns. There were four million people at the time, and they had no system to count the votes. The country was also very rural and the population was scattered. The original 13 states carefully guarded their own powers and distrusted the national government.

A committee of our Founders rejected several ideas of choosing the president, such as having Congress choose, having the state legislatures vote, or relying just on the popular vote. With the popular vote, there was fear that people wouldn't have enough information about candidates and would vote with regional preferences, so no candidate would win a majority. They were also concerned that larger states would have more power. A committee came up with the idea of the original Electoral College.

Each state had a group of electors, which were the number of senators plus the number of U.S. representatives. The electors would be the individuals from the state who were most capable of choosing a deserving president. The process of choosing electors was left up to the particular state. Each elector was required to cast two votes for president. One of these had to be for a candidate from outside the elector's own state. This was an attempt to get away from the "favorite son" bias. Kimberling notes that the Electoral College function is comparable to the way the Roman Catholic Church uses the Cardinals to choose a Pope. The Electoral College was later adjusted with the 12th Amendment, which required each elector to cast one vote for president and a separate vote for vice president, instead of just designating the runner-up as vice president. The amendment also stated that if no candidate received a clear majority vote, the House of Representatives would vote, with each state having only one vote.

The current structure of the Electoral College is that with only a couple of exceptions, states choose their electors in a statewide election. The presidential candidate who wins the popular vote in a state takes all of the state's electors. To be elected president, a candidate must receive 270 electoral votes out of 538. It is possible to win the popular vote and lose the election. Four times in our history, the person who lost the popular vote has become president: 1824: John Quincy Adams; 1876, Rutherford B. Hayes; 1888: Benjamin Harrison; and 2000: George Bush, Jr. Al Gore won the popular vote by over a half a million votes; however, Bush had more electoral votes. As you can see, Bush obviously won more states; however, Al Gore focused his attention on the larger states with more electoral votes. Bush was declared the winner by the Supreme Court after weeks of dispute over Florida's 25 electoral votes. After the final count, only 537 out of 5,000,000 votes separated the two candidates.

The election of 2000 focused attention on faulty voting procedures and their impact in close elections. An editorial in *The Little Rock Gazette* argues that the Electoral College should not be blamed for the states' failures to handle their votes properly. However, there have been calls for reform of these procedures and also for change in the Electoral College itself.

One idea is to use only the popular vote to elect the president. Those who advocate the popular vote point out that people could become apathetic about voting if they think that their vote does not count. Ledbetter and Prior argue in *The Little Rock Gazette* that the Electoral College can violate the basic premise of democracy and that it is hypocritical of the U.S. to push democracy on other countries when we are not practicing true democracy here. William Benoit, a communication professor, suggests in "Let's Abolish the Electoral College" that voters feel powerless. Benoit also argues that the Electoral College encourages candidates to ignore certain states and to target their efforts to win the necessary electoral votes, setting up "battleground" states.

Others argue that we should keep the current system. Those who think we should keep the Electoral College, as reported by Ben Silver in *The Boston Globe,* maintain that the Electoral College is a way of making sure that the elected candidate represents the whole country, not just one region. With the popular vote, you could have a case in which an extreme candidate would win heavily in a region and become president. Albert Southwick notes that abolishing the Electoral College could set up a multi-party system in which no one candidate would get a majority of the vote. This might require a run-off election if, for example, no candidate received at least 40 percent of the vote. Another benefit from keeping the current system is if a candidate would die after being elected in November but before the January inauguration, the Electoral College has the authority to substitute someone else.

The purpose of my speech was to inform you about the complex process we use to choose the president. I discussed the historical context, current issues, and future ideas that have been proposed. Hopefully, my speech has helped you understand this process, and it is my hope that you apply this understanding in analyzing future elections.

REFERENCES

Benoit, W. "Let's abolish the Electoral College." *New York Newsday,* April 20, 2004. http://web.lexisnexis.com/universe/document?_m=37731f34502a1216a1bd8c3alce7d43.

"Here we go again. What's right with the Electoral college." Editorial. *Arkansas Democrat-Gazette,* February 18, 2004. http://web.lexisnexis.com/university/document?_m=37731f34502a1216a1bd8c3alce7d43.

Kimberling, W. C. *The Electoral College.* http://www.fec.gov/pdf/eleccoll.pdf.

Ledbetter, C. R., and D. Pryor, "Time for 21st century changes in Electoral College." *Arkansas Democrat-Gazette,* February 9, 2004. http://web.lexisnexis.com/universe/document?_m=37731f34502a1216a1bd8c3alce7d43.

Silver, B. "Good reasons for the Electoral College." *Boston Globe,* April 27, 2004. http://web.lexisnexis.com/university/document?_m=37731f34502a1216a1bd8c3alce7d43.

Southwick, A. B. "Electoral College remains an important part of system." *Worcester Telegram and Gazette,* November 9, 2003. http://web.lexisnexis.com/universe/document?_m=37731f34502a1216a1bd8c3alce7d43.

The Dirty Secret

by Ben Johnson, University of Nevada, Reno

For Armilda Mesa, the job was like a dream come true. It allowed her to stay close to home and finally start the family that she'd always dreamed of having. After 20 years of working, she was able to build a life for herself. Everything was finally perfect for the 40-year-old mother of two. That's why it came as a complete shock when the test results came back positive. You see, Armilda did not fit any of the traditional risk factors for disease. According to the American Cancer Society's *Facts and Figures Guide for 2002,* Hispanic women have a low exposure rate, and childbearing further decreases the risk of disease. Armilda did not smoke or drink and had no history of the disease in her family. It's almost a mystery that Armilda's doctor would break the terrible news to her one day in 1984. That's until you learn that Armilda Mesa was a worker in a high-tech factory clean room. The Intel Web site, last accessed January 20, 2003 and updated daily, states that clean rooms are where the computer chips are manufactured. However, workers in these so-called clean rooms are constantly put in contact with highly dangerous chemicals and fumes. This sector of industry has often gone unnoticed and under-regulated, the deadly consequences of which are finally starting to surface. When

Armilda watched more than 10 of her coworkers, friends, and now potentially herself die from cancer, she realized it wasn't her dream job after all.

In order to gain a better understanding of this crisis, we will begin by discussing the problem behind clean rooms. Next we will examine the underlying issues that continue to fuel this problem. Finally we will uncover some possible solutions to put a stop to clean room illnesses and death. According to the March/April 2002 issue of *Mother Jones*, over 300,000 people work in semiconductor plants in the United States. Additionally there are over 1 million semiconductor workers worldwide. The June 27, 2002 issue of the *Pittsburgh Post Gazette* explains that clean rooms are areas in high-tech operations that aim to keep the workplace contaminant-free. Workers wear booties, latex gloves, and other protective coverings to maintain the "clean" environment. These rooms demand cleanliness because the tiniest speck of dust can completely ruin a computer chip. The process begins with workers taking wafers of silicon and use acids to etch patterns into them. Then other chemicals are used to clean and smooth the chips, such as arsenic, benzene, trichloroethylene, and phenols, only to name a few. But the list goes on and on. A single manufacturing plant uses anywhere from 500 to 1,000 chemicals every day. Many of these chemicals appear on the American Cancer Society's list of industrial carcinogens. Exposure to these chemicals occurs in two ways: dermal and inhalation. Dermal exposure occurs when workers come in direct physical contact with the chemicals, often due to inadequate gloves or clothing. The second type, inhalation, is caused because air in clean rooms is recirculated to keep the damaging particles away, but the filtration system doesn't remove toxic fumes, leaving employees breathing chemical vapors over long periods of time. According to the *Journal of the American Medical Association* on March 24, 1999, a study was conducted on 125 women who had been exposed to industrial solvents. Out of the group, 13 gave birth to children with major congenital malformations. A second study conducted on women who were not exposed to chemicals showed that only 1 out of 125 women gave birth to a child with defects. The study also concluded that women exposed to chemical solvents were at a much higher risk for miscarriage. The *Recorder* states on June 3, 2002 that former clean room employees have filed over 250 lawsuits against Intel, IBM, and several major chemical suppliers and that number is expected to grow. So if these rooms are so clean, then why are the workers turning up ill? For this answer we must look at the cause of this terrible problem.

Toxic clean rooms continue to pose a serious health risk for workers for two reasons: industry inaction and lax governmental regulation. The May 26, 2002 *Minneapolis Star Tribune* states that "clean rooms" is a misnomer. The rooms may be clean of dust, but the safety practices of chip manufacturers jeopardize the health of employees. Armilda Mesa explains "The gloves we were wearing were sort of sticky when we'd wash the chemicals off the chips. Sometimes, we didn't wear the gloves because they just didn't work. We'd just put our hands in and pull the stuff out." Industry officials also ignored warnings about the hazards of these chemicals. According to the previously cited issue of *Mother Jones*, one IBM chemist wrote an internal memo to company officials warning of the high proportion of cancer among workers. However, the company refused to take action. Additionally, in 1996, Faye Calton and Michael Ruffing sued IBM after their son Zachary was born with severe skeletal deformities. IBM quickly settled the case before it went to trial and as part of the deal, parties aren't allowed to discuss the details. A statement issued by IBM says, "We firmly believe, based upon state-of-the-art science, that we had no liability in this case and that we did not act wrongfully in any matter." IBM also stated in the February 26, 2002 issue of *USA Today,* "We feel deep compassion for any employee suffering from an illness, but it is important to remember that no scientific and statistical evidence exists linking these health issues to our clean rooms." This completely ignores the fact that the semiconductor industry has repeatedly blocked attempts to study the health hazards of their chemicals.

The second cause of this problem comes from a lack of governmental regulation. The Occupational Safety and Health Administration, or OSHA's Web site, last updated September 13, 2002, states "Workers in this industry should be made aware of the known hazards and use the best available measures to reduce these dangers." Yet despite this statement, OSHA has not issued any specific regulations aimed toward the semiconductor industry. Instead, computer chip manufacturers fall under general industrial regulations. But this industry is constantly changing and as a result these regulations may not cover the new chemicals used in the plants. The May 28, 2002 issue of the Scripps Howard News Service reports that OSHA issued a notice that it planned to set exposure limits and held hearings in the early 1990s but no regulations were ever adopted. By the time that regulations are put into place and enforced, it may be too late for hundreds or even thousands of clean room workers.

Now that we have discussed the problem and the cause of clean rooms, we are finally ready to examine some possible solutions. Steps need to be taken on a governmental, corporate, and individual level to help stop the growing problem of clean room safety. First, on a governmental level, the Department of Labor and OSHA need to set specific standards and guidelines for the semiconductor industry. The longer this industry goes unregulated, the more people are going to succumb to toxic exposure. After guidelines have been put in place, they need to be rigorously enforced with strict penalties for violations. Nothing will change if these companies know they can get away with it. Next, on a corporate level, semiconductor manufacturers need to ensure that all employees are properly trained. Companies like IBM must monitor employees to ensure that safety precautions are taken at all times. And how can we invoke these changes? That's where the individual level comes in. Although it may sound cliché, contact the Department of Labor and OSHA telling them to develop stricter regulations for computer chip manufacturers. Finally, you can also write to your congressional delegation to let them know you are concerned about this problem. Demand that they work towards tougher regulation of this industry.

You can begin by joining the Silicon Valley Toxics Coalition at www.svtc.org. As a member you will join the Campaign for Responsible Technology and fight to make manufacturers responsible for their actions. A tax-deductible donation goes toward publicizing the dangerous mess that these companies don't want you to know about. By visiting the Web site you can also find out about volunteer activities to help stop toxic exposure. The microchip industry is only 20 years old but already it has exploded into a multibillion-dollar business. But somewhere along the way personal safety has been forgotten in favor of profit. Today we have discussed the problem of clean rooms and how employees are facing life-threatening illnesses because of poor industry practice. Next we examined the cause of this problem and have seen that an unregulated industry is allowed to perpetuate. And finally we offered some possible solutions to help stop this unnecessary exposure. Armilda Mesa reflects that "company officials told us that, number one, they would always look out for you as an individual," and she recalls "we trusted them totally." It's time that we made clean rooms safe for the workers, not just the computer chips they produce.

Binge Drinking on College Campuses

by Ali Heidarpour, University of Oklahoma

A skier since age five, Scott Kreuger knew he had a good shot at becoming the next captain of his university's ski team. Thrilled at the possibility, Scott braced himself. According to the *Christian Science Monitor* of May 8, 2000, at the day of the competition he had an early pasta lunch to settle his stomach, and then he went for it. Scott and twelve other members of his ski team gathered that night around a keg in his basement while friends and girlfriends stood by. At countdown, they began chugging one beer a minute. The last one to throw up would become captain. Finally with an alcohol blood level of .22, Scott lost it at twelve beers. He didn't even make junior captain. If Scott Kreuger were the only student to die from overdrinking, his story would be an isolated incident of lost potential. But in fact, college binge drinking is more of an issue that ever. Yet the fact is that at least two out of every five U.S. college students binge drink, and according to the *New York Times* of March 24, 2002, this results each year in approximately fourteen hundred student deaths, a distressing number of assaults and rapes, a shameful amount of vandalism, and countless cases of suicide. So today, in order for us to stop this alcohol haze, we will need to first examine the extent of binge drinking on college campuses; then, explore why this problem continues to persist; and finally, provide some practical solutions on both the institutional and personal level.

So first, let us examine the extent of binge drinking on college campuses. The College Alcohol Study released by Harvard University in 2001 defines binge drinkers as male students who had five or more and female students who had four or more drinks in a row at least once in a two-week period. In other words, binge drinking is drinking to get drunk. The study went on to define a frequent binge drinker as a student who binged three or more times in a two-week period. Overall, some 44 percent of college students had binged at least once during the past two weeks of this survey.

Binge drinking is also a women's health issue. Because of differences in metabolism, women are more heavily affected by alcohol than men. Heavy alcohol use, coupled with inexperience with drinking, puts young women in serious jeopardy for sexual assault. Female students who binge drink are more than three times as likely to be forced to have intercourse than those who do not binge drink. The *Oakland Tribune* of January 4, 2003, estimate that each year more than a hundred thousand college women between the ages of 18 and 24 are forced to engage in sex while they are intoxicated and therefore unable to give consent.

The problem of binge drinking and its effects points to a deeply ingrained culture of student drinking in America—a culture that spends $5.5 billion on alcohol each year, more than they spend on soft drinks, tea, milk, juice, coffee, and textbooks combined. A culture that still poses the question, why does this crisis continue to persist?

The Christian Science Monitor on May 21, 2002 reports that efforts to curb binge drinking so far have often sent mixed messages. For example, Maryland State University and Johns Hopkins University converted a dining hall into a bar in an effort to control how much students drink and keep them from driving after drinking. *The Boston Globe* of May 11, 2002 reports that local bars around campuses cater to students' needs with nickel pitchers of beer and even have shuttles to round up students from campuses. Some schools create ads in cooperation with alcohol manufacturers that emphasize responsible drinking. But if you tell someone to drink responsibly, you are still telling them to drink, thus creating the perception that drinking is completely common.

This perception is another major reason for the persistence of alcohol abuse, even though it is not correct. According to CNN.com, survey after survey of college students have told us that these populations regularly overestimate the behavior of their peers with regard to consumption of alcohol. This overestimate of risk-taking behavior suggests that social norms shape our behavior. The study also went on to say that this false norm creates a baseless, but powerful, peer pressure among students that encourages them to override their own personal attitudes to match what they perceive is expected of them. Simply put, it encourages them to drink up to the false norm. So now that we understand why this problem continues to persist, let us discuss some possible solutions on both the institutional and personal level.

While there are no easy solutions for this issue, an increasing number of campuses are trying a new approach. *US News & World Report* of January 26, 1998 reports that Northern Illinois University had a 44 percent reduction in binge drinking after nine years. Santa Clara University had a 28 percent reduction in binge drinking after three years. So what led to their reduction in binge drinking? A social norm campaign was in place. Social norms marketing shows what is actually happening and discredits what most students are thinking. The goal of this campaign is to replace the false norm with the true information about most students' moderate and responsible behavior regarding alcohol. As a result, the imagined peer pressure to drink to excess will decrease over time, as the true norm because known and accepted. These programs are all funded by grants from various organizations, including the U.S. Department of Education and Center for Substance Abuse Prevention. Therefore, colleges must acknowledge that an alcohol problem exists and must not cooperate with the purveyors of alcohol. Rather, administrators should request these grants from the Department of Education or Center for Substance Abuse Prevention. The grant should heavily emphasize the creation of social norms campaigns.

Next, on a personal level, the only way that the social norms campaign will be effective is by widely publicizing the true norm, that most students do not binge drink. Therefore, I challenge everyone in this room to do two things. First, write a letter to the editor of your school's newspaper to inform the campus community about the problem of binge drinking on your campus. Make sure your voice is heard. Also, meet with your student body president and inform him or her about this epidemic and propose implementing a social norms campaign on your campus. When talking to your student body president, ensure the clubs and organizations are involved in the social norms campaign as well.

Finally, and this is as simple as it gets—Don't drink, and, in particular, don't binge drink and remind your friends to be responsible and safe as well.

In the past few minutes we have examined the extent of binge drinking on college campuses; then, explored why this problem continues to persist; and finally, discussed some possible solutions on the institutional and personal level. *The Washington Post* of January 1, 2003 reports that Melinda Somers, 19 years old, died after she fell from an eighth-floor dormitory window. Her blood alcohol was .21 percent. *USA Today* of March 24, 2002 reports that Benjamin Wayne, 20 years old, died after a night out on the town. His blood alcohol level was .58. The fact that so many U.S. college students binge drink indicates a failure not only of our best and brightest but also of higher education, and to some extent our own attitudes. Imagine one of your loved ones or classmates, just fresh out of high school, eager to get a sense of freedom. They attend the college of their choice and one week later end up like Scott Kreuger, or Melinda Somers, or Benjamin Wayne—another college student fallen at the hands of alcohol.

Curtailing the Contemporary College Counseling Crisis

by Sonja Ralston, Texas Tech University

During her sophomore year at MIT, pushed by her own obsession with perfectionism and the institution's extreme pressure to succeed, 19-year-old Elizabeth Shin fell over the edge. Elizabeth's tragedy, however, is not just one of teen mental anguish, but more importantly, one of the university systems that failed to help her. University records report that starting in the late fall of 1999, she took herself repeatedly to the campus mental health clinic, but each time she went to discuss her suicidal thoughts, she met with a different counselor, few of whom were certified psychologists. When her friends and dorm master rushed her to the emergency clinic on April 8, 2000 after she had tried to stab herself, yet another new campus counselor released her over the phone. Two days later, Elizabeth locked her door and set herself on fire. She died April 14, and now, according to the *New York Times* of April 28, 2002, her parents are suing MIT for negligence. This tragedy has brought much-needed national attention to the growing college counseling crisis. The National Institute for Mental Health, or NIMH, reports on its Web site, last updated on March 14, 2003, that suicide is the single leading cause of death for college students and nearly one in four students will suffer from a mental illness serious enough to need professional help at some point during college. But even if they are lucky enough to recognize the need for help, as Elizabeth Shin did, the previously cited *New York Times* explains that those services will most likely be unavailable or dangerously inadequate. Because today's students are tomorrow's leaders, it is imperative for us all, inside and outside the academy, to turn our attention to this crisis by first, examining its impact on our campuses; second, explaining why it continues to grow; and third, exploring what can be done to improve the situation.

A study from Kansas State University, published in the *New York Times* of February 3, 2003, explains this crisis as a simple problem of demand outpacing supply: Colleges and universities are supporting mental health counseling today at about the same level as they were twenty years ago, despite the fact that nearly three times as many students need their help. This discrepancy between what students need and what schools are providing has three serious, detrimental effects: It is difficult for students to get help, the help is rarely consistent, and they are often helped by under-qualified individuals. First, National Public Radio of August 13, 2002 says students often feel "shortchanged," because almost all centers are now limiting the number of times a student can meet with a counselor—some as few as four visits in an academic year. *USA Today* of January 25, 2002 reported that the average wait for an initial visit is two weeks. Second, University Wire of March 14, 2002 explained the common problem of never seeing the same counselor twice. A Yale student relayed the experience "I felt like the person I was talking to wasn't really there." When students are forced to meet with a new counselor every time, they are pushed back to square one and it becomes difficult to get the help they need because successful therapy relies on building a relationship between patient and counselor. Finally, a number of national surveys alluded to a fact confirmed by the University of Texas Student Counseling Center in a personal interview on April 17, 2003, that since centers are underfunded and understaffed, it is a common practice for psychology graduate students to act as counselors. Now, nothing against grad students, but they simply aren't yet qualified to assess a patient's needs on their own—we don't let first-year medical students treat patients without supervision. So, we have a nation of struggling students seeking help and not enough help to go around. But how did counseling centers go from deserted to demanded almost overnight?

There are two main causes for the college counseling crisis: More students need more help, and universities are reluctant to provide it. First, the experts all agree with Dr. Hara Marano of *Psychology Today* when she explained the "Prozac payoff" in the May 2002 issue of "Blues Buster." Students with serious mental problems, who could not have functioned well enough to get into college 20 years ago, are now an increasingly large part of the college demographic, thanks to psychotropic drugs like Prozac, yet they still need continuous counseling. Also, examples of what the August 12, 2002 *Daily News of Los Angeles* called "pressure-cooker academics" are more prevalent than ever as students experience increasing pressure associated with succeeding in school and the tight job market. The *London Guardian* of December 3, 2002 notes several other contributing factors, including the willingness of today's students to seek therapy for their problems and that ages 18–25 are when we are most at risk for serious mental illness. These factors combine to explain why counseling centers are more important than ever and bring us to the second cause: Universities are not providing enough funding for mental health services. When there is an increase in demand, an increase in supply should naturally follow, but as the *Boston Globe* of February 13, 2002, explained, most universities are facing serious general budget restraints and counseling centers have faced static or decreasing budgets. Interestingly enough though, not a single campus health clinic has been cut back. While tragic, only a handful of students will die each year from infectious diseases like meningitis—but remember, NIMH tells us that suicide is the single leading cause of death for students and depression is the most common illness. In the *Wisconsin State Journal* of October 5, 2002 the National Alliance for the Mentally Ill labels this disparate treatment of physical and mental illnesses a sign of the "chilling" and pervasive stigma against mental illness held by most Americans.

It should come as no surprise then that the solution to this problem must begin with a change in our attitudes, because until we realize that mental illness and physical illness are much the same, other solutions can have limited efficacy at best. The National Mental Health Awareness Campaign explains on their Web site, last updated December 19, 2002, that we should combat the stigma of mental illness every day by thinking and talking about brain disorders the same way we do heart disease and by refusing to use negative stereotypes and labels. This is especially important for college communities where a higher percentage of the population need help. Second, there are several options for universities to improve their counseling situations. MIT recently raised tuition to hire four new certified psychologists and extend clinic hours, according to the *Boston Globe* on April 25, 2002. Other schools, including the universities of South Carolina, Nevada at Reno, and Texas A&M, have eased the burden on their counseling centers in a less expensive manner, according to *US News & World Report* of February 18, 2002. They have implemented mandatory, in-depth seminars on the transition to college to help students develop good mentoring relationships with professors and older students and to ease stress, therefore improving overall mental health. *Newsweek* of October 7, 2002 tells of how changes in the Vanderbilt University center have improved services for students without adding cost. Basically, they reorganized the center to respond more like a hospital triage unit where every patient is seen within 30 minutes, not two weeks, to evaluate their condition and recommend further treatment. Finally, on a personal level, if someone you know starts to exhibit signs of depression, talk with them, ask them to get help, and encourage them to speak with their parents, as NIMH reports that students who discuss mental health issues with their parents have an 80 percent increased change of full recovery. Also, don't feel limited to campus, as many communities also offer free nonprofit clinics and there are national hotlines for crisis situations—all available in your local phone book. Clearly, nothing can be done to bring back Elizabeth Shin, but together we can prevent others from sharing her fate by improving college counseling centers.

In the days before her death, Elizabeth sent a desperate plea for help via e-mail to an instructor, a professor, and a dean, none of whom did anything to help her. As a whole, we each have the responsibility as members of a campus community, as faculty, staff, students and community members, to take this crisis more seriously, change our attitudes, and do something about it. After all, college counseling centers were designed to pull students back from the edge, not push them over it.

Notes

Chapter 1 Introduction to Public Speaking

1. Louis Nizer, *Reflections Without Mirrors,* quoted in Jack Valenti, *Speak Up with Confidence: How to Prepare, Learn, and Deliver Effective Speeches* (New York: Morrow, 1982) 34.
2. James C. Humes, *The Sir Winston Method: Five Secrets of Speaking the Language of Leadership* (New York: Morrow, 1991) 13–14.
3. Charles Schwab, as quoted in Brent Filson, *Executive Speeches: Tips on How to Write and Deliver Speeches from 51 CEOs* (New York: Wiley, 1994) 45.
4. Dee-Ann Durbin, "Study: Plenty of Jobs for Graduates in 2000," *Austin American-Statesman* 5 Dec. 1999: A28.
5. Dan B. Curtis, Jerry L. Winsor, and Ronald D. Stephens, "National Preferences in Business and Communication Education," *Communication Education* 38 (Jan. 1989) 6–14. See also Iain Hay, "Justifying and Applying Oral Presentations in Geographical Education," *Journal of Geography in Higher Education* 18.1 (1994): 44–45.
6. National Archives and Records Administration, *Kennedy's Inaugural Address of 1961* (1987) 6.
7. Melinda Henneberger, "In Speech Process Reversal, Gore Wrote, Aides Whittled," *The New York Times* 18 Aug. 2000: A1.
8. L. M. Boyd, syndicated column, *Austin American-Statesman* 8 Aug. 2000: E3.
9. Herman Cohen, *The History of Speech Communication: The Emergence of a Discipline: 1914–1945* (Annandale, VA: Speech Communication Association, 1994) 2.
10. Mark Twain, *The Adventures of Tom Sawyer,* 1876, ed. Stephen Railton and the U of Virginia Library. 2000. 4 July 2001 <http://etext.virginia.edu/railton/about/srchmtf.html>.
11. George W. Bush, address to the nation on 11 Sept. 2001, *The New York Times* 22 Sept. 2001: A4.
12. Adetokunbo F. Knowles-Borishade, "Paradigm for Classical African Orature," *Diversity in Public Communication: A Reader,* Christine Kelly et al. (Dubuque, IA: Kendall-Hunt, 1995) 100.
13. Patricia A. Sullivan, "Signification and African-American Rhetoric: A Case Study of Jesse Jackson's 'Common Ground and Common Sense' Speech," *Communication Quarterly* 41.1 (1993): 1–15.
14. Toni Morrison, "Commencement address to the Wellesley College Class of 2004." 28 May 2004. 4 June 2004 <www.wellesley.edu/PublicAffairs/Commencement/2004/morrison.html>.

Chapter 2 Speaking with Confidence

1. Survey conducted by R. H. Bruskin and Associates, *Spectra* 9 (Dec. 1973): 4; D. Wallechinsky, Irving Wallace, and Amy Wallace, *The People's Almanac Presents the Book of Lists* (New York: Morrow, 1977).
2. Steven Booth-Butterfield, "Instructional Interventions for Reducing Situational Anxiety and Avoidance," *Communication Education* 37 (July 1988): 214–23; also see Michael Motley, *Overcoming Your Fear of Public Speaking: A Proven Method* (New York: McGraw-Hill, 1995).
3. Joe Ayres and Theodore S. Hopf, "The Long-Term Effect of Visualization in the Classroom: A Brief Research Report," *Communication Education* 39 (1990): 75–78.
4. John Burk, "Communication Apprehension Among Masters of Business Administration Students: Investigating a Gap in Communication Education," *Communication Education* 50 (Jan. 2001): 51–58; Lynne Kelly and James A. Keaten, "Treating Communication Anxiety: Implications of the Communibiological Paradigm," *Communication Education* 49 (Jan. 2000): 45–57; Amber N. Finn, Chris R. Sawyer, and Ralph R. Behnke, "Audience-Perceived Anxiety Patterns of Public Speakers," *Communication Quarterly* 51 (Fall 2003): 470–81.

5. Maili Porhola, "Orientation Styles in a Public-Speaking Context," paper presented at the National Communication Association convention, Seattle, Washington, Nov. 2000; Ralph R. Behnke and Michael J. Beatty, "A Cognitive-Physiological Model of Speech Anxiety," *Communication Monographs* 48 (1981): 158–63.

6. Amy M. Bippus and John A. Daly, "What Do People Think Causes Stage Fright? Naïve Attributions About the Reasons for Public-Speaking Anxiety," *Communication Education* 48 (January 1999): 63–72.

7. Yang Lin and Andrew S. Rancer, "Sex Differences in Intercultural Communication Apprehension, Ethnocentrism, and Intercultural Willingness to Communicate," *Psychological Reports* 92 (2003): 195–200.

8. Michael J. Beatty, James C. McCroskey, and A. D. Heisel, "Communication Apprehension as Temperamental Expression: A Communibiological Paradigm," *Communication Monographs* 65 (1998): 197–219; Michael J. Beatty and Kristin Marie Valencic, "Context-Based Apprehension Versus Planning Demands: A Communibiological Analysis of Anticipatory Public Speaking Anxiety," *Communication Education* 49 (Jan. 2000): 58–71.

9. Kelly and Keaten, "Treating Communication Anxiety."

10. Maili Porhola, "Arousal Styles During Public Speaking," *Communication Education* 51 (Oct. 2002): 420–38.

11. Kelly and Keaten, "Treating Communication Anxiety."

12. Leon Fletcher, *How to Design & Deliver Speeches* (New York: Longman, 2001) 3.

13. Ralph R. Behnke and Chris R. Sawyer, "Public-Speaking Procrastination as a Correlate of Public-Speaking Communication Apprehension and Self-Perceived Public-Speaking Competence," *Communication Research Reports* 16 (1999): 40–47.

14. Peter D. MacIntyre and J. Renee MacDonald, "Public-Speaking Anxiety: Perceived Competence and Audience Congeniality," *Communication Education* 47 (Oct. 1998): 359–65.

15. Melanie Booth-Butterfield, "Stifle or Stimulate? The Effects of Communication Task Structure on Apprehensive and Non-Apprehensive Students," *Communication Education* 35 (October 1986): 337–48.

16. Joe Ayres, Tim Hopf, and Elizabeth Peterson, "A Test of Communication-Orientation Motivation (COM) Therapy," *Communication Reports* 13 (Winter 2000): 35–44.

17. Joe Ayers and Theodore S. Hopf, "Visualization: A Means of Reducing Speech Anxiety," *Communication Education* 34 (October 1985): 318–23.

18. Joe Ayres and Brian L. Heuett, "An Examination of the Impact of Performance Visualization," *Communication Research Reports* 16 (1999): 29–39.

19. Penny Addison, Ele Clay, Shuang Xie, Chris R. Sawyer, and Ralph R. Behnke, "Worry as a Function of Public Speaking State Anxiety Type," *Communication Reports* 16 (Summer 2003): 125–31.

20. MacIntyre and MacDonald, "Public-Speaking Anxiety"; Peter D. MacIntyre and K. A. Thivierge, "The Effects of Audience Pleasantness, Audience Familiarity, and Speaking Contexts on Public-Speaking Anxiety and Willingness to Speak," *Communication Quarterly* 43 (1995): 456–66; Peter D. MacIntyre, K. A. Thivierge, and J. Renee MacDonald, "The Effects of Audience Interest, Responsiveness, and Evaluation on Public-Speaking Anxiety and Related Variables," *Communication Research Reports* 14 (1997): 157–68.

21. MacIntyre and MacDonald, "Public-Speaking Anxiety"; R. B. Rubin, A. M. Rubin, and F. F. Jordan, "Effects of Instruction on Communication Apprehension and Communication Competence," *Communication Education* 46 (April 1997): 104–14.

22. Lisa M. Schroeder, "The Effects of Skills Training on Communication Satisfaction and Communication Anxiety in the Basic Speech Course," *Communication Research Reports* 19 (2002): 380–88.

23. Alain Morin, "History of Exposure to Audiences as a Developmental Antecedent of Public Self-Consciousness," *Current Research in Social Psychology* 5 (March 2000): 33–46.

Chapter 3 The Audience-Centered Speechmaking Process

1. The late Waldo Braden, long-time professor of speech communication at Louisiana State University, presented a memorable speech at the 1982 Florida Speech Communication Association in which he emphasized "The audience writes the speech" to indicate the importance and centrality of being an audience-centered speaker.

2. Clifford Stoll, as cited by Kevin A. Miller, "Capture: The Essential Survival Skill for Leaders

Buckling Under Information Overload, *Leadership* (Spring 1992): 85.

3. Greg Winter, "The Chips Are Down: Frito-Lay Cuts Costs with Smaller Servings," *Austin American-Statesman* 2 Jan. 2001: A6.

4. We thank Barbara Patton of Texas State University for sharing her speech outline with us.

5. Sample speech written by Pao Yang Lee, "Our Immigration Story," in Tasha Van Horn, Lori Charron, and Michael Charron, *Allyn & Bacon Video II User's Guide,* 2002.

Chapter 4 Ethics and Free Speech

1. Bill Carter and Felicity Barringer, "Patriotic Time, Dissent Is Muted," *The New York Times* 28 Sept. 2001: B8.

2. National Communication Association, "NCA Credo for Communication Ethics." 1999. 27 June 2001 <http://www.natcom.org/ conferences/Ethics/ethicsconfcredo99.htm>.

3. Samuel Walker, *Hate Speech* (Lincoln: U of Nebraska P, 1994) 162.

4. "Libel and Slander," *The Ethical Spectacle* 1 June 1997, 1 June 1998 <http://www.spectacle.org/ freespch/musm/libel.html>.

5. "Three Decades Later, Free Speech Vets Return to UC Berkeley," *Sacramento Bee* 3 Dec. 1994: A1.

6. James S. Tyre, "Legal Definition of Obscenity; Pornography." 1 June 1997, 1 June 1998 <http://internet.ggu.edu/university_library/reg/ _legal_obscene.html>.

7. "Supreme Court Rules: Cyberspace Will be Free! ACLU Hails Victory in Internet Censorship Challenge," *American Civil Liberties Union Freedom Network* 26 June 1997. 1 June 1998 <http:// www.aclu.org/news/no62697a.html>.

8. Sue Anne Pressley, "Oprah Winfrey Wins Case Filed by Cattlemen," *Washington Post* 27 Feb. 1998. 1 June 1998 <http://www.washingtonpost. com/wp-srv/WPlate/1998-02/27/1001022798-idx. html>.

9. Associated Press, "Free-Speech, Other Groups File Briefs Opposing Patriot Act." 4 November 2003. 13 June 2004 <http:// firstamendmentcenter.org/news.aspx?id=12174>.

10. Carter and Barringer, "Patriotic Time."

11. Walker, *Hate Speech,* 2.

12. Scott Smallwood, "A Weblog Starts a Fire," *The Chronicle of Higher Education* 7 November 2003: A11.

13. Edwin R. Bayley, *Joe McCarthy and the Press* (Madison: Wisconsin UP, 1981) 29.

14. Tom Wicker, "Improving the Debates," *The New York Times* 21 June 1991: A16.

15. Bill Bradley, "Race and the American City," address delivered in the U.S. Senate, 26 Mar. 1992, reprinted in *Representative American Speeches, 1991–92,* edited by Owen Peterson (New York: Wilson, 1992) 139.

16. Kathy Fitzpatrick, "U.S. Public Diplomacy," *Vital Speeches of the Day* (15 April 2004): 412–17.

17. Peg Tyre, "Improving on History," *Newsweek* 2 July 2001: 34.

18. *Publication Manual of the American Psychological Association,* 4th ed. (Washington, DC: American Psychological Association, 1994) 294.

19. Todd Holm, "Public Speaking Students' Perceptions of Cheating," *Communication Research Reports* (Winter 2002): 70.

20. Harold Barrett, *Rhetoric and Civility: Human Development, Narcissism, and the Good Audience* (Albany: SUNY, 1991) 154.

21. Kenneth L. Woodward, "Heard Any Good Sermons Lately?" *Newsweek* 4 Mar. 1996: 51.

22. Patricia Sullivan, "Signification and African-American Rhetoric: A Case Study of Jesse Jackson's 'Common Ground and Common Sense' Speech," *Communication Quarterly* 41.1 (1993): 11.

23. Richard M. Weaver, "A Responsible Rhetoric," speech delivered at Purdue University, 29 Mar. 1955, edited by Thomas Clark and Richard Johannesen for *The Intercollegiate Review* (Winter 1976–77): 82.

Chapter 5 Listening to Speeches

1. Study conducted by Paul Cameron, as cited in Ronald B. Adler and Neil Town, *Looking Out/ Looking In: Interpersonal Communications* (New York: Holt, Rinehart and Winston, 1981) 218.

2. L. Boyd, syndicated column, *Austin American-Statesman* 7 Dec. 1995: E7.

3. John T. Masterson, Steven A. Beebe, and Norman H. Watson, *Invitation to Effective Speech Communication* (Glenview, IL: Scott, Foresman, 1989) 4.

4. Frank E. X. Dance, *Speaking Your Mind: Private Thinking and Public Speaking* (Dubuque, IA: Kendall/Hunt Publishing Company, 1994).

5. Ralph G. Nichols and Leonard A. Stevens, "Six Bad Listening Habits," in *Are You Listening?* (New York: McGraw-Hill, 1957).

6. M. Fitch-Hauser, D. A. Barker, and A. Hughes, "Receiver Apprehension and Listening Comprehension: A Linear or Curvilinear Relationship?" *Southern Communication Journal* (1988): 62–71.

7. Fitch-Hauser, Barker, and Hughes, "Receiver Apprehension and Listening Comprehension."

8. Joseph L. Chesebro, "Effects of Teacher Clarity and Nonverbal Immediacy on Student Learning, Receiver Apprehension, and Affect," *Communication Education* 52 (April 2003): 135–47.

9. Albert Mehrabian, *Nonverbal Communication* (Hawthorne, NY: Aldine, 1972).

10. Paul Ekman and Wallace Friesen, "Head and Body Cues in the Judgement of Emotion: A Reformulation," *Perceptual and Motor Skills* 25 (1967): 711–24.

11. Nichols and Stevens, "Six Bad Listening Habits."

12. Paul Rankin, "Listening Ability: Its Importance, Measurement and Development," *Chicago Schools Journal* 12 (Jan. 1930): 177–79.

13. Kitty W. Watson, Larry L. Barker, and James B. Weaver, *The Listener Style Inventory* (New Orleans: LA SPECTRA, 1995).

14. S. L. Sargent and James B. Weaver, "Correlates Between Communication Apprehension and Listening Style Preferences," *Communication Research Reports* 14 (1997): 74–78.

15. M. D. Kirtley and J. M. Honeycutt, "Listening Styles and Their Correspondence with Second Guessing," *Communication Research Reports* 13 (1996): 174–82.

16. John N. Gardner and A. Jerome Jewler, *Your College Experiences: Strategies for Success*, 2nd ed. (Belmont, CA: Wadsworth, 1995) 104.

17. Mike Allen, Sandra Berkowitz, Steve Hunt, and Allan Louden, "A Meta-Analysis of the Impact of Forensics and Communication Education on Critical Thinking," *Communication Education* 48 (Jan. 1999): 18–30.

18. Cited by Marie Hochmuth, ed., A *History and Criticism of American Public Address,* vol. 3 (New York: Longmans, Green, 1955) 4; and by James R. Andrews, *The Practice of Rhetorical Criticism* (New York: Macmillan, 1983) 3–4.

19. Andrews, *The Practice of Rhetorical Criticism.*

20. Masterson, Beebe, and Watson, *Invitation to Effective Speech Communication.*

21. Robert Rowland, *Analyzing Rhetoric: A Handbook for the Informed Citizen in a New Millennium* (Dubuque, IA: Kendall/Hunt Publishing Company, 2002) 17–28.

Chapter 6 Analyzing Your Audience

1. For an excellent review of gender and persuasability research, see Daniel J. O'Keefe, *Persuasion: Theory and Research* (Newbury Park,

CA: Sage, 1990) 176–77. Also see James B. Stiff, *Persuasive Communication* (New York: Guilford, 1994) 133–36.

2. O'Keefe, *Persuasion.*

3. O'Keefe, *Persuasion.*

4. Gregory Herek, "Study Offers 'Snapshot' of Sacramento-Area Lesbian, Gay, and Bisexual Community." 23 July 2001 <http://psyweb.ucdavis.edu/rainbow/html/sacramento_study.html>. For an excellent review of literature about sexual orientation and communication, see T. P. Mottet, "The Role of Sexual Orientation in Predicting Outcome Value and Anticipated Communication Behaviors," *Communication Quarterly* 48 (2000): 233–39.

5. The research summarized here is based on pioneering work by Geert Hofstede, *Culture's Consequences: International Differences in Work-Related Values* (Beverly Hills, CA: Sage, 1984). Also see Edward T. Hall, *Beyond Culture* (New York: Doubleday, 1976).

6. M. E. Ryan, "Another Way to Teach Migrant Students," *Los Angeles Times* March 31, 1991: B20, as cited by M. W. Lustig and J. Koester, *Intercultural Competence: Interpersonal Communication Across Cultures* (Boston: Allyn & Bacon, 2003) 11.

7. G. Chen and W. J. Starosta, "A Review of the Concept of Intercultural Sensitivity," *Human Communication* 1 (1997): 7.

8. Eric Schmitt, "Whites in Minority in Largest Cities, the Census Shows," *The New York Times* 30 Apr. 2001: A1.

9. Genaro C. Armas, "Early Census Results Show an Increase in County's Diversity," *Austin American-Statesman* 9 Mar. 2001: A7.

10. David W. Kale, "Ethics in Intercultural Communication," in *Intercultural Communication: A Reader,* 6th ed., edited by Larry A. Samovar and Richard E. Porter (Belmont, CA: Wadsworth, 1991) 423; also see the discussion in Lustig and Koester, *Intercultural Competence.*

11. Donald E. Brown, "Human Universals and Their Implications," in *Being Humans: Anthropological Universality and Particularity in Transdisciplinary Perspectives,* edited by N. Roughley (New York: Walter de Gruyter, 2000). For an applied discussion of these universals, see Steven Pinker, *The Blank Slate: The Modern Denial of Human Nature* (London: Penguin Books, 2002).

12. Larry A. Samovar and Richard E. Porter, *Communication Between Cultures* (Stamford, CT: Wadsworth and Thomson Learning, 2001) 29.

13. Henry Sweets, "Mark Twain in India," *The Fence Painter: Bulletin of the Mark Twain Boyhood Home Associates* 26 (Winter 1996): 1.

14. For an excellent discussion of how to adapt to specific audience situations, see Jo Sprague and Douglas Stuart, *The Speaker's Handbook* (Fort Worth: Harcourt, Brace, Jovanovich, 1992) 345.
15. Leonard Spinrad and Thelma Spinrad, *Speaker's Lifetime Library* (West Nyack, New York: Parker Publishing Company, 1979).
16. Devorah Lieberman, *Public Speaking in the Multicultural Environment* (Boston: Allyn & Bacon, 2000). Also see Edward T. Hall, *The Silent Language* (Greenwich, CT: Fawcett, 1959); and Edward T. Hall, *The Hidden Dimension* (Garden City, NJ: Doubleday, 1966).

Chapter 7 Developing Your Speech

1. L. M. Boyd, syndicated column.
2. Roger Fringer, "Choosing a Speech Topic," in Tasha Van Horn, Lori Charron, and Michael Charron, *Allyn & Bacon Video II User's Guide,* 2002.
3. Bruce Gronbeck, from his presidential address, delivered at the annual conference of the Speech Communication Association, ts., November 1994.
4. Henry H. Sweets III, "Mark Twain's Lecturing Career Continuation—Part II," *The Fence Painter* (Winter 2000–2001).
5. Alex F. Osborn, *Applied Imagination* (New York: Scribner's, 1962).
6. Monique Russo, "The 'Starving Disease' or Anorexia Nervosa," student speech, University of Miami, 1984.
7. Brian Sosnowchik, "The Cries of American Ailments," *Winning Orations 2000* (Mankato, MN: Interstate Oratorical Association, 2000) 114.
8. Judith Humphrey, "Taking the Stage: How Women Can Achieve a Leadership Presence," *Vital Speeches of the Day* 1 May 2001: 437.
9. Adapted from Erin Gallagher, "Upholstered Furniture Fires: Sitting in the Uneasy Chair," *Winning Orations 2000* (Mankato, MN: Interstate Oratorical Association, 2000) 99–101.
10. NASA, "Past Shuttle Missions." 2 February 2004. 14 June 2004 <www.spaceflight.nasa.gov/shuttle/archives/>.
11. Adapted from Nicole Tremel, "The New Wasteland: Computers," *Winning Orations 2000* (Mankato, MN: Interstate Oratorical Association, 2000).
12. Erin Kane, "Alternative Defense," *Winning Orations 1995* (Mankato, MN: Interstate Oratorical Association, 1995) 82.

Chapter 8 Gathering Supporting Material

1. Elizabeth Kirk, "Practical Steps in Evaluating Internet Resources." 7 May 2001. 22 May 2001 <http://milton.mse.jhu.edu:8001/research/education/practical.html>.
2. Paul Gorski, "A Multicultural Model for Evaluating Educational Web Sites." Dec. 1999. 22 May 2001 <http://curry.edschool. virginia.edu/go/multicultural/net/comps/model.html>.
3. Matthew Mirapaul, "Making Federal Web Sites Friendly to Disabled Users," *The New York Times* 11 June 2001: B2.

Chapter 9 Supporting Your Speech

1. Bettijane Levine, "Fighting the Giant," *Los Angeles Times* 10 Aug. 1994: E-1.
2. Eric Quinones, "It Was a Dark and Stormy Sales Pitch, and Maybe It Worked," *The New York Times* 1 Aug. 1999: BU4.
3. Wendy Waite, "Staying a Professional Journalist," *Vital Speeches of the Day* 15 April 2004.
4. Kathleen Ligocki, "Middle Earth, Motown and Mo' Better Blues," *Vital Speeches of the Day* 15 February 2004.
5. Carrie A. Lydon, "Higher Exploitation: Universities Profiting from Sweatshop Labor," *Winning Orations 2000* (Mankato, MN: Interstate Oratorical Association, 2000) 34.
6. Professor Frazer White, University of Miami, personal communication.
7. George W. Bush, "Speech at the 60th Anniversary D-Day ceremony, 6 June 2004." *The Tocqueville Connection* 6 June 2004. 6 June 2004 <www.ttc.org/200406061205.i56c5hp2962.1.htm>.
8. Edwin Pittock, "America's Crisis in Aging," *Vital Speeches of the Day* 1 February 2004.
9. Dayna Kloeber, "Nursing Shortage," *Winning Orations 2003* (Mankato, MN: Interstate Oratorical Association, 2003) 1.
10. Shannon Burger, "Will It Hurt?" *Winning Orations 1994* (Mankato, MN: Interstate Oratorical Association, 1994) 89.
11. Manuel Goni, "Hazing: When Rites Become Wrongs," *Winning Orations 2001* (Mankato, MN: Interstate Oratorical Association, 2001) 1.
12. Barbara Bush, "Choices and Change," *Contemporary American Public Discourse,* edited by Halford Ross Ryan (Prospect Heights, IL: Waveland Press, 1992) 382.

13. Stephen Dannhauser, "Enlarged European Union," *Vital Speeches of the Day* 15 April 2004.

14. Elizabeth Cady Stanton, "Address to the First Women's Rights Convention (1848)," *A Treasury of the World's Great Speeches,* edited by Houston Peterson (New York: Simon & Schuster, 1965) 388–92.

15. Eric B. Wolff, untitled speech, *Winning Orations 1994* (Mankato, MN: Interstate Oratorical Association, 1994) 67.

16. Cal Darden, "The Sustainable Promise of Globalization," *Vital Speeches of the Day* 15 April 2004.

17. Ajay Krishnan, "Is Mr. Goodwrench Really Mr. Rip Off?" *Winning Orations 1998* (Mankato, MN: Interstate Oratorical Association, 1998) 120.

18. "Sorry, You've Got the Wrong Number," *The New York Times* 26 May 2001: A17.

19. "The Texas Miracle," *CBSNews.com*. 7 January 2004. 7 January 2004 <www.cbsnews.com/stories/2004/01/06/60II/main591676. shtml>.

20. George W. Bush, address to a joint session of Congress on 27 Feb. 2001, *Congressional Quarterly Weekly* 3 Mar. 2001: 497.

21. Sam Dillon, "Reflections on War, Peace, and How to Live Vitally and Act Globally," *The New York Times* 1 June 2003: A28.

22. Pittock, "America's Crisis in Aging."

23. Dena Craig, "Clearing the Air About Cigars," *Winning Orations 1998* (Mankato, MN: Interstate Oratorical Association, 1998) 13.

24. Walter Harrison, "Race, College Admissions," *Vital Speeches of the Day* 1 April 2004.

25. Kristin Lewis, "The Terrorists' Greatest Victory," *Winning Orations 2003* (Mankato, MN: Interstate Oratorical Association, 2003) 78.

26. Jessica Nordquist, "The American Inferno," *Winning Orations 2003* (Mankato, MN: Interstate Oratorical Association, 2003) 71.

27. Zach Fort, untitled speech, *Winning Orations 2003* (Mankato, MN: Interstate Oratorical Association, 2003) 62.

Chapter 10 Organizing Your Speech

1. Adapted from Bill Gallagher, "E-911: A 'Call' for Reform," *Winning Orations 1999* (Mankato, MN: Interstate Oratorical Association, 1999) 113–15.

2. Information in this example comes from the National Institutes of Health, "Stem Cells: A Primer," May 2000. 19 July 2001 <http://www.nih.gov/news/stemcell/primer.htm>.

3. Adapted from John Kuehn, untitled speech, *Winning Orations 1994* (Mankato, MN: Interstate Oratorical Association, 1994) 83–85.

4. Adapted from Vonda Ramey, "Can You Read This?" *Winning Orations 1985* (Mankato, MN: Interstate Oratorical Association, 1985) 32–35.

5. Adapted from Laurel Johnson, "Where There's a Will There's a Way," *Winning Orations 1986* (Mankato, MN: Interstate Oratorical Association, 1986) 59–62.

6. Adapted from Amy Stewart, untitled speech, *Winning Orations 1994* (Mankato, MN: Interstate Oratorical Association, 1994) 47–49.

7. The following information is adapted from Devorah A. Lieberman, *Public Speaking in the Multicultural Environment,* 2nd ed. (Englewood Cliffs, NJ: Prentice Hall, 1997).

8. Adapted from Steven Chang, "Warning: Your Computer May Be Hazardous to Yao Hong's Health," *Winning Orations 2003* (Mankato, MN: Interstate Oratorical Association, 2003) 73.

9. Risa Lavizzo-Mourey, "Childhood Obesity," *Vital Speeches of the Day* 15 April 2004.

10. John Seffrin, "The Worst Pandemic in the History of the World," *Vital Speeches of the Day* 1 April 2004.

11. Kristin Rose Cipolla, "Unnecessary Prescription Drugs: A Real Medical Emergency," *Winning Orations 2003* (Mankato, MN: Interstate Oratorical Association, 2003) 10.

12. Nichole Olson, "Flying the Safer Skies," *Winning Orations 2000* (Mankato, MN: Interstate Oratorical Association, 2000) 122.

13. Jennifer Helmers, "Roller Coaster Roulette," *Winning Orations 2003* (Mankato, MN: Interstate Oratorical Association, 2003) 41.

14. Melody Hopkins, "Collegiate Athletes: A Contradiction in Terms," *Winning Orations 1986* (Mankato, MN: Interstate Oratorical Association, 1986) 111.

15. Linh Thu Q. Do, "Children of the Diet Culture," *Winning Orations 1999* (Mankato, MN: Interstate Oratorical Association, 1999) 122.

16. Arwen Williams, "Organic Farming: Why Our Pesticide Paranoia Is Starving the World," *Winning Orations 2000* (Mankato, MN: Interstate Oratorical Association, 2000) 145.

17. Molly A. Lovell, "Hotel Security: The Hidden Crisis," *Winning Orations 1994* (Mankato, MN: Interstate Oratorical Association, 1994) 18.

18. Neela Latey, "U.S. Customs Procedures: Danger to Americans' Health and Society," *Winning Orations 1986* (Mankato, MN: Interstate Oratorical Association, 1986) 22.

19. Susan Stevens, "Teacher Shortage," *Winning Orations 1986* (Mankato, MN: Interstate Oratorical Association, 1986) 27.

20. Heather Green, "Radon in Our Homes," *Winning Orations 1986* (Mankato, MN: Interstate Oratorical Association, 1986) 5.

21. Ben Crosby, "The New College Disease," *Winning Orations 2000* (Mankato, MN: Interstate Oratorical Association, 2000) 133.
22. Lori Van Overbeke, "NutraSweet," *Winning Orations 1986* (Mankato, MN: Interstate Oratorical Association, 1986) 58.

Chapter 11 Introducing Your Speech

1. Edwin Pittock, "America's Crisis in Aging," *Vital Speeches of the Day* 1 February 2004.
2. Chandra Palubiak, "To Tattoo or Not to Tattoo," *Winning Orations 2002* (Mankato, MN: Interstate Oratorical Association, 2002) 11.
3. Sheena Holliday, "Uninvited Visitor," *Winning Orations 2003* (Mankato, MN: Interstate Oratorical Association, 2003) 84.
4. Darnetta Clinkscale, "The Other Crisis in Our Schools," *Vital Speeches of the Day* 1 April 2004.
5. Jennifer Sweeney, "Racial Profiling," *Winning Orations 2000* (Mankato, MN: Interstate Oratorical Association, 2000) 1.
6. Barbara Bush, "Choices and Change," *Vital Speeches of the Day* 1 July 1990: 549.
7. Kristin Rose Cipolla, "Unnecessary Prescription Drugs: A Real Medical Emergency," *Winning Orations 2003* (Mankato, MN: Interstate Oratorical Association, 2003) 9.
8. Terrika Scott, "Curing Crisis with Community," *Winning Orations 1995* (Mankato, MN: Interstate Oratorical Association, 1995) 11.
9. Theresa Clinkenbeard, "The Loss of Childhood," *Winning Orations 1984* (Mankato, MN: Interstate Oratorical Association, 1984) 4.
10. Thad Noyes, "Dishonest Death Care," *Winning Orations 1999* (Mankato, MN: Interstate Oratorical Association, 1999) 73.
11. George E. Curry, *"Brown v. Board of Education—50 Years Later,"* *Vital Speeches of the Day* 1 March 2004.
12. Joe Griffith, *Speaker's Library of Business Stories, Anecdotes, and Humor* (Englewood Cliffs, NJ: Prentice Hall, 1990) 335.
13. Douglas MacArthur, "Farewell to the Cadets," address delivered at West Point, 12 May 1962. Reprinted in Richard L. Johannesen, R. R. Allen, and Wil A. Linkugel, eds., *Contemporary American Speeches*, 7th ed. (Dubuque, IA: Kendall/Hunt, 1992) 393.
14. "Insert Funny Story Here," *Austin American-Statesman* 7 Apr. 2001: A14.
15. Lisa M. Kralik, "Geographical Illiteracy," *Winning Orations 1987* (Mankato, MN: Interstate Oratorical Association, 1987) 76.
16. Richard Propes, "Alone in the Dark," *Winning Orations 1985* (Mankato, MN: Interstate Oratorical Association, 1985) 22.
17. Beth Moberg, "Licensed to Kill," *Winning Orations 1985* (Mankato, MN: Interstate Oratorical Association, 1985) 89.
18. Jane M. Hatch, *The American Book of Days* (New York: Wilson, 1978).
19. Ruth W. Gregory, *Anniversaries and Holidays* (Chicago: American Library Association, 1975).
20. Laurette Koellner, "Managing Your Career: The Ultimate Solo Flight," *Vital Speeches of the Day* 15 January 2001: 213.
21. Adam Winegarden, "The After-Dinner Speech," in Tasha Van Horn, Lori Charron, and Michael Charron, eds., *Allyn & Bacon Video II User's Guide*, 2002.
22. Larry Cox, "A Vision of a New World Made New," *Vital Speeches of the Day* 1 February 2004.
23. Glenn Schaffer, "Philanthropy," *Vital Speeches of the Day* 15 February 2004.
24. Laura Bush, remarks at Harlem Renaissance event. *The White House Web site.* 13 March 2002. 11 March 2004 <www.whitehouse.gov/news/releases/2002/03/20020313-11.html>.
25. Student speech, University of Miami, 1981.

Chapter 12 Concluding Your Speech

1. John Ryan, "Emissions Tampering: Get the Lead Out," *Winning Orations 1985* (Mankato, MN: Interstate Oratorical Association, 1985) 63.
2. Douglas MacArthur, "Farewell to the Cadets," address delivered at West Point, 12 May 1962. Reprinted in Richard L. Johannesen, R. R. Allen, and Wil A. Linkugel, eds., *Contemporary American Speeches*, 7th ed. (Dubugue, IA: Kendall-Hunt, 1992) 396.
3. Noelle Stephens, "The WWW.CON of Higher Education," *Winning Orations 1999* (Mankato, MN: Interstate Oratorical Association, 1999) 12.
4. Melanie Loehwing, untitled speech, *Winning Orations 2003* (Mankato, MN: Interstate Oratorical Association, 2003) 23–24.
5. David Naze, "Colon Cancer: The Insidious Disease," *Winning Orations 1999* (Mankato, MN: Interstate Oratorical Association, 1999) 32.
6. Ronald Williams, "Hurling Words into the Darkness," *Vital Speeches of the Day* 15 April 2004.
7. Sonja Ralston, "Medical Reprocessing," *Winning Orations 2000* (Mankato, MN: Interstate Oratorical Association, 2000) 131.
8. Robert Browning, "Rabbi Ben Ezra," *Dramatis Personae* (1864), quoted by John Mietus, Jr.,

"The Best Is Yet to Be," *Winning Orations 1987* (Mankato, MN: Interstate Oratorical Association, 1987) 54.

9. Mietus, "The Best Is Yet to Be" 57.

10. Benjamin P. Berlinger, "Health and the Hubris of Human Nature: The Tragic Myth of Antibiotics," *Winning Orations 1987* (Mankato, MN: Interstate Oratorical Association, 1987) 35.

11. Martin Luther King Jr., "I Have a Dream," in Richard L. Johannesen, R. R. Allen, and Wil A. Linkugel, eds., *Contemporary American Speeches*, 7th ed. (Dubuque, IA: Kendall/Hunt, 1992) 369.

12. George W. Bush, weekly radio address delivered on 15 Sept. 2001. Reprinted in *The New York Times* 16 Sept. 2001: A5.

13. Jake B. Schrum, investiture speech as President of Southwestern University, Georgetown, Texas, 4 April 2001.

Chapter 13 Outlining and Editing Your Speech

1. John O'Brien, quoted in Brent Filson, *Executive Speeches: Tips on How to Write and Deliver Speeches from 51 CEOs* (New York: Wiley, 1994) 144–45.

2. Charles Parnell, "Speechwriting: The Profession and the Practice," *Vital Speeches of the Day* 15 January 1990: 56.

3. The sample outlines in this chapter are adapted from Valerie Waldock, "Disabling the Virus of Cyber-Plagiarism," *Winning Orations 2003* (Mankato, MN: Interstate Oratorical Association, 2003) 39–41.

4. Our discussion of how to edit speeches relies heavily on information in Brent Filson, *Executive Speeches*, 150–53.

5. William Saletan. "Kerryism of the Day," *Slate* 18 May 2004. 19 May 2004 <slate.msn.com/toolbar.asapx?action=print&id=2100720>.

6. Clive Thompson, "PowerPoint Makes You Dumb," *The New York Times Magazine* 14 December 2003: 88.

Chapter 14 Using Words Well: Speaker and Language Style

1. Advertisements and headlines compiled by Jay Leno, *Headlines* (New York: Wing Books, 1992).

2. "President's Body Language Loud and Clear," *The Sun* (Baltimore) 10 Aug. 1994: 1D.

3. George W. Bush, presidential victory speech, delivered at Austin, Texas. 13 Dec. 2000. 14 Dec. 2000 <http://dailynews. yahoo.com/h/ap/20001214/el/recount_bush_text_1.html>.

4. Al Gore, "The Common Good of All Americans" (presidential election concession speech), *Vital Speeches of the Day* 1 January 2001: 163.

5. George W. Bush, remarks delivered on 14 Sept. 2001, at the Washington National Cathedral prayer service for victims of the September 11, 2001, terrorist attacks. Reprinted in *The New York Times* 15 Sept. 2001: A6.

6. Max Woodfin, "Three Among Many Lives Jordan Touched," *Austin American-Statesman* 20 Jan. 1996: A13.

7. John Lister, quoted in "At the End of the Day, It Annoys." The Associated Press. 24 March 2004 <www.cbsnews.com/stories/2004/03/24/world/printable608391.shtml>.

8. Paul Roberts, "How to Say Nothing in Five Hundred Words," in William H. Roberts and Gregoire Turgeson, eds., *About Language* (Boston: Houghton Mifflin, 1986) 28.

9. George Orwell, "Politics and the English Language," in Roberts and Turgeson, *About Language,* 282.

10. Erma Bombeck, "Missing Grammar Genes Is, Like, the Problem," *Austin American-Statesman* 3 Mar. 1992.

11. Robin Tolmach Lakoff, "From Ancient Greece to Iraq, the Power of Words in Wartime." *The New York Times Online.* 18 May 2004. 21 May 2004 <www.nytimes.com/2004/05/18/science/18LANG.html>.

12. Martin Carcasson, "Herbert Hoover and the Presidential Campaign of 1932: The Failure of Apologia," *Presidential Studies Quarterly* (Spring 1998).

13. William Safire, "Words at War," *The New York Times Magazine* 30 Sept. 2001: Section 6.

14. John S. Seiter, Jarrod Larsen, and Jacey Skinner, " 'Handicapped' or 'Handicapable?': The Effects of Language About Persons with Disabilities on Perceptions of Source Credibility and Persuasiveness," *Communication Reports* 11:1 (1998): 21–31.

15. Edward Rothstein, "Is a Word's Definition in the Mind of the User?" *The New York Times* 25 Nov. 2000: A21.

16. Peggy Noonan, *What I Saw at the Revolution* (New York: Random House, 1990) 71.

17. Michael M. Klepper, *I'd Rather Die Than Give a Speech* (New York: Carol Publishing Group, 1994) 45.

18. For several examples used in our discussion of language style we acknowledge William Jordan, "Rhetorical Style," *Oral Communication Handbook* (Warrensburg, MO: Central Missouri State U, 1971–1972) 32–34.

19. Bill Clinton, "Farewell Address," *Vital Speeches of the Day* 1 February 2001: 229.
20. George W. Bush, eulogy for Ronald Reagan, delivered at the National Cathedral 11 June 2004. CNN.com. 11 June 2004. 13 June 2004 <www.cnn.com/2004/ALLPOLITICS/06/11/bush.transcript>.
21. Michiko Kakutani, "Struggling to Find Words for a Horror Beyond Words," *The New York Times* 13 Sept. 2001: E1.
22. Franklin Roosevelt, Inaugural address of 1933 (Washington, DC: National Archives and Records Administration, 1988) 22.
23. George F. Will, " 'Let Us . . .'? No, Give It a Rest," *Newsweek* 22 Jan. 2001: 64.
24. John F. Kennedy, Inaugural address (20 Jan. 1961), in Bower Aly and Lucille F. Aly, eds., *Speeches in English* (New York: Random House, 1968) 272.
25. George W. Bush, "Bush's Speech at the Houston Memorial Service for Shuttle's Crew," *The New York Times* 5 Feb. 2003: A17.
26. Gore, "The Common Good" 162.
27. Ralph Waldo Emerson, "The American Scholar," speech delivered 31 Aug. 1837, in Glenn R. Capp., ed., *Famous Speeches in American History* (Indianapolis: Bobbs-Merrill, 1963) 84.
28. George W. Bush, State of the Union Address. The White House Web site. 20 January 2004. 21 January 2004 <www.whitehouse.gov/news/releases/2004/01/print/200401207.html>.
29. Roosevelt, Inaugural address of 1933.
30. Kennedy, Inaugural address 275.
31. William Faulkner, speech in acceptance of the Nobel Prize for literature, delivered 10 Dec. 1950, in Houston Peterson, ed., *A Treasury of the World's Great Speeches* (New York: Simon & Schuster, 1965) 814–15.
32. Patrick Henry, "Liberty or Death," speech delivered 23 Mar. 1775, in Capp, *Famous Speeches in American History,* 22.
33. Rudy deLeon, "The Tuskegee Airmen," *Vital Speeches of the Day* 1 November 2000: 43.
34. Roosevelt, Inaugural address of 1933.
35. Franklin D. Roosevelt, first fireside chat on 12 Mar. 1933, in Peterson, *Treasury,* 751–54.
36. Winston Churchill, "finest hour" address, delivered 18 June 1940, in Peterson, *Treasury,* 754–60.
37. Winston Churchill, address to the Congress of the United States, delivered on 26 Dec. 1941, in Aly and Aly, *Speeches in English,* 233.
38. Dick Cheney, acceptance speech for the Republican vice-presidential nomination, delivered 2 Aug. 2000, *The New York Times* 3 Aug. 2000: A24.
39. Adapted from Jordan, *Oral Communication Handbook,* 34.

Chapter 15 Delivering Your Speech

1. James W. Gibson, John A. Kline, and Charles R. Gruner, "A Reexamination of the First Course in Speech at U.S. Colleges and Universities," *Speech Teacher* 23 (September 1974): 206–14.
2. Ray Birdwhistle, *Kinesics and Context* (Philadelphia: U of Pennsylvania, 1970).
3. Judee K. Burgoon and Beth A. Le Poire, "Nonverbal Cues and Interpersonal Judgments: Participant and Observer Perceptions of Intimacy, Dominance, Composure, and Formality," *Communication Monographs* 66 (1999): 105–24; Beth A. Le Poire and Stephen M. Yoshimura, "The Effects of Expectancies and Actual Communication on Nonverbal Adaptation and Communication Outcomes: A Test of Interaction Adaptation Theory," *Communication Monographs* 66 (1999): 1–30.
4. Albert Mehrabian, *Nonverbal Communication* (Hawthorne, NY: Aldine, 1972).
5. D. Lapakko, "Three Cheers for Language: A Closer Examination of a Widely Cited Study of Nonverbal Communication," *Communication Education* 46 (1997): 63–67.
6. Elaine Hatfield, J. T. Cacioppo, and R. L. Rapson, *Emotional Contagion* (New York: Cambridge University Press, 1994); also see John T. Cacioppo, Gary G. Berntson, Jeff T. Larsen, Kirsten M. Poehlmann, and Tiffany A. Ito, "The Psychophysiology of Emotion," in Michael Lewis and Jeannette M. Haviland-Jones, eds., *Handbook of Emotions,* 2nd ed. (New York: Guilford Press, 2004), 173–91.
7. Steven A. Beebe and Thompson Biggers, "The Effect of Speaker Delivery upon Listener Emotional Response," paper presented at the International Communication Association meeting, May 1989.
8. Paul Ekman, Wallace V. Friesen, and K. R. Schere, "Body Movement and Voice Pitch in Deception Interaction," *Semiotica* 16 (1976): 23–27; Mark Knapp, R. P. Hart, and H. S. Dennis, "An Exploration of Deception as a Communication Construct," *Human Communication Research* 1 (1974): 15–29.
9. Adam Clymer, "Defining a Leader First by His Words," *The New York Times* 16 Sept. 2001: 12 (Section 4).
10. Roger Ailes, *You Are the Message* (New York: Doubleday, 1989) 37–38.
11. David Gates, "Prince of the Podium," *Newsweek* June 14, 1996: 82.
12. Steven A. Beebe, "Eye Contact: A Nonverbal Determinant of Speaker Credibility," *Speech Teacher*

23 (Jan. 1974): 21–25; Steven A. Beebe, "Effects of Eye Contact, Posture and Vocal Inflection upon Credibility and Comprehension, *Australian Scan Journal of Nonverbal Communication* 7–8 (1979–1980): 57–70; Martin Cobin, "Response to Eye Contact," *Quarterly Journal of Speech* 48 (1963): 415–19.

13. Beebe, "Eye Contact" 21–25.

14. Khera Communications, Inc., "Business Tips for India." *More Business*. 2001. 8 June 2004 <www.morebusiness.com/ running_your_business/management/d930585271.brc?highlightstring=Business+Tips+for+India>.

15. Brent Filson, *Executive Speeches: Tips on How to Write and Deliver Speeches from 51 CEOs* (New York: John Wiley & Sons, Inc., 1994).

16. Albert Mehrabian, *Silent Messages* (Belmont, CA: Wadsworth, 1971).

17. See Virginia P. Richmond, Joan Gorham, and James C. McCroskey, "The Relationship Between Selected Immediacy Behaviors and Cognitive Learning," in M. McLaughlin, ed., *Communication Yearbook 10* (Beverly Hills, CA: Sage, 1987), 574–90; Joan Gorham, "The Relationship Between Verbal Teacher Immediacy Behaviors and Student Learning," *Communication Education* 37 (1988): 40–53; Diane M. Christophel, "The Relationship Among Teacher Immediacy Behaviors, Student Motivation, and Learning," *Communication Education* 39 (1990): 323–40; James C. McCroskey, Virginia P. Richmond, Aino Sallinen, Joan M. Fayer, and Robert A. Barraclough, "A Cross-Cultural and Multi-Behavioral Analysis of the Relationship Between Nonverbal Immediacy and Teacher Evaluation," *Communication Education* 44 (1995): 281–90; Timothy P. Mottet and Steven A. Beebe, "Relationships Between Teacher Nonverbal Immediacy, Student Emotional Response, and Perceived Student Learning," *Communication Research Reports* (January 2002).

18. Michael J. Beatty, "Some Effects of Posture on Speaker Credibility," library paper, Central Missouri State U, 1973.

19. Albert Mehrabian and M. Williams, "Nonverbal Concomitants of Perceived and Intended Persuasiveness," *Journal of Personality and Social Psychology* 13 (1969): 37–58.

20. Paul Ekman, Wallace V. Friesen, and S. S. Tomkins, "Facial Affect Scoring Technique: A First Validity Study," *Semiotica* 3 (1971).

21. Paul Ekman and Wallace Friesen, *Unmasking the Face* (Englewood Cliffs, NJ: Prentice Hall, Inc., 1975).

22. Adapted from Lester Schilling, *Voice and Diction for the Speech Arts* (San Marcos: Southwest Texas State U, 1979).

23. Mary M. Gill, "Accent and Stereotypes: Their Effect on Perceptions of Teachers and Lecture Comprehension," *Journal of Applied Communication* 22 (1994): 348–61.

24. Kenneth K. Sereno and G. J. Hawkins, "The Effects of Variations in Speakers' Nonfluency upon Audience Ratings of Attitude Toward the Speech Topic and Speakers' Credibility," *Speech Monographs* 34 (1967): 58–74; Gerald R. Miller and M. A. Hewgill, "The Effect of Variations in Nonfluency on Audience Ratings of Source Credibility," *Quarterly Journal of Speech* 50 (1964): 36–44; Mehrabian and Williams, "Nonverbal Concomitants of Perceived and Intended Persuasiveness."

25. These suggestions were made by Jo Sprague and Douglas Stuart, *The Speaker's Handbook* (Fort Worth, TX: Harcourt Brace Jovanovich, 1992) 331, and were based on research by Patricia A. Porter, Margaret Grant, and Mary Draper, *Communicating Effectively in English: Oral Communication for Non-Native Speakers* (Belmont, CA: Wadsworth, 1985).

26. James W. Neuliep, *Intercultural Communication: A Contextual Approach* (Boston: Houghton Mifflin, 2000) 247.

27. Stephen Lucas, *The Art of Public Speaking* (New York: Random House, 1986) 231.

28. Research cited by Leo Fletcher, *How to Design & Deliver Speeches* (New York: Addison Wesley Longman, 2001) 73.

29. "Comment," *The New Yorker* 1 Mar. 1993.

30. For an excellent review of the effects of immediacy in the classroom, see Mehrabian, *Silent Messages;* and James C. McCroskey, Aino Sallinen, Joan M. Fayer, Virginia P. Richmond, and Robert A. Barraclough, "Nonverbal Immediacy and Cognitive Learning: A Cross-Cultural Investigation," *Communication Education* 45 (1996): 200–11.

31. Larry A. Samovar and Richard E. Porter, *Communication Between Cultures* (Stamford, CT: Thomson Learning, 2001) 166.

32. William B. Gudykunst, *Bridging Differences: Effective Intergroup Communication* (Thousand Oaks, CA: Sage, 1998) 12.

33. Kent E. Menzel and Lori J. Carrell, "The Relationship Between Preparation and Performance in Public Speaking," *Communication Education* 43 (194): 17–26.

34. Patricia Wilson, "Dean Jokes About 'Screeching' in Iowa." *Reuters News Service*. 22 January 2004 <news.yahoo.com/news?tmpl=story2+cid=564&u=/nm/20040122/ts_nm/campaign_dean_dc_4&printer=1>.

35. Filson, *Executive Speeches*.

36. Filson, *Executive Speeches*.

Chapter 16 Designing and Using Presentation Aids

1. Emil Bohn and David Jabusch, "The Effect of Four Methods of Instruction on the Use of Visual Aids in Speeches," *The Western Journal of Speech Communication* 46 (Summer 1982): 253–65.
2. J. S. Wilentz, *The Senses of Man* (New York: Crowell, 1968).
3. "Watch His Back," *Time* 29 July 2002: 15.
4. Michael E. Patterson, Donald F. Dansereau, and Dianna Newbern, "Effects of Communication Aids and Strategies on Cooperative Teaching," *Journal of Educational Psychology* 84 (1992): 453–61.
5. Richard E. Mayer and Valerie K. Sims, "For Whom Is a Picture Worth a Thousand Words? Extensions of a Dual-Coding Theory of Multimedia Learning," *Journal of Educational Psychology* 86 (1994): 389–401.
6. Brent Filson, *Executive Speeches: Tips on How to Write and Deliver Speeches from 51 CEOs* (New York: John Wiley & Sons, Inc., 1994), 212.
7. Andrew Wilson, "In Defense of Rhetoric," *The Toastmaster* 70.2 (February 2004): 8–11.
8. We acknowledge Dan Cavanaugh's excellent supplement *Preparing Visual Aids for Presentation* (Boston: Allyn & Bacon/Longman, 2001) as a source for many of our tips and suggestions.
9. Brent Filson, *Executive Speeches.*
10. For a good discussion of how to develop and use PowerPoint visuals, see Jerry Weissman, *Presenting to Win: The Art of Telling Your Story* (Upper Saddle River, NJ: Financial Times/ Prentice Hall, 2003).

Chapter 17 Using Presentation Software

1. We acknowledge Dan Cavanaugh's excellent supplement *Preparing Visual Aids for Presentation* (Boston: Allyn & Bacon/Longman, 2001) as a source for many of our tips and suggestions.

Chapter 18 Speaking to Inform

1. John R. Johnson and Nancy Szczupakiewicz, "The Public Speaking Course: Is It Preparing Students with Work-Related Public Speaking Skills?" *Communication Education* 36 (April 1987): 131–37.
2. Joseph L. Chesebro, "Effects of Teacher Clarity and Nonverbal Immediacy on Student Learning, Receiver Apprehension, and Affect," *Communication Education* 52 (April 2003): 135–47.
3. Malcolm Knowles, *Self-Directed Learning* (Chicago: Follett, 1975).
4. Katherine E. Rowan, "A New Pedagogy for Explanatory Public Speaking: Why Arrangement Should Not Substitute for Invention," *Communication Education* 44 (1995): 236–50.
5. Rowan, "A New Pedagogy for Explanatory Public Speaking."
6. Michael A. Boerger and Tracy B. Henley, "The Use of Analogy in Giving Instructions," *Psychological Record* 49 (1999): 193–209.
7. Marcie Groover, "Learning to Communicate: The Importance of Speech Education in Public Schools," *Winning Orations 1984* (Mankato, MN: Interstate Oratorical Association, 1984) 7.
8. As cited by Eleanor Doan, *The New Speaker's Sourcebook* (Grand Rapids, MI: Zondervan, 1968).
9. C. S. Lewis, "On Stories," *Essays Presented to Charles Williams,* C. S. Lewis, ed. (Oxford: Oxford University Press, 1947); also see Walter R. Fisher, *Communication as Narration: Toward a Philosophy of Reason, Value, and Action* (Columbia: University of South Carolina Press, 1987).
10. D. K. Cruickshank and J. J. Kennedy, "Teacher Clarity," *Teaching & Teacher Education* 2 (1986): 43–67.
11. Roger Fringer, "Choosing a Speech Topic," in Tasha Van Horn, Lori Charron, and Michael Charron, *Allyn & Bacon Video II User's Guide,* 2002.

Chapter 19 Understanding Principles of Persuasive Speaking

1. Alvin Toffler, *Future Shock* (New York: Bantam Books, 1970) 3.
2. Martin Fishbein and I. Ajzen, *Belief, Attitude, Intention, and Behavior: An Introduction to Theory and Research* (Reading, MA: Addison-Wesley, 1975).
3. For a discussion of the elaboration likelihood model, see R. Petty and D. Wegener, "The Elaboration Likelihood Model: Current Status and Controversies," in S. Chaiken and Y. Trope, eds., *Dual Process Theories in Social Psychology* (New York: Guilford, 1999), 41–72; also see R. Petty and J. T. Cacioppo, *Communication and Persuasion: Central and Peripheral Routes to Attitude Change* (New York: Springer-Verlag, 1986).

4. For a discussion of motivation in social settings, see Douglas T. Kenrick, Steven L. Neuberg, and Robert B. Cialdini, *Social Psychology: Unraveling the Mystery* (Boston, MA: Allyn & Bacon, 2002).

5. Leon Festinger, *A Theory of Cognitive Dissonance* (Evanston, IL: Row, Peterson, 1957).

6. For additional discussion, see Wayne C. Minnick, *The Art of Persuasion* (Boston: Houghton Mifflin, 1967).

7. Abraham H. Maslow, "A Theory of Human Motivation," in *Motivation and Personality* (New York: Harper & Row, 1954), chap. 5.

8. John Ryan, "Emissions Tampering: Get the Lead Out," *Winning Orations 1985* (Mankato, MN: Interstate Oratorical Association, 1985) 50.

9. For a discussion of fear appeal research, see Irving L. Janis and Seymour Feshback, "Effects of Fear Arousing Communications," *Journal of Abnormal and Social Psychology* 48 (Jan. 1953): 78–92; Frederick A. Powell and Gerald R. Miller, "Social Approval and Disapproval Cues in Anxiety-Arousing Situations," *Speech Monographs* 34 (June 1967): 152–59; and Kenneth L. Higbee, "Fifteen Years of Fear Arousal: Research on Threat Appeals, 1953–68," *Psychological Bulletin* 72 (Dec. 1969): 426–44.

10. Paul A. Mongeau, "Another Look at Fear-Arousing Persuasive Appeals," in Mike Allen and Raymond W. Preiss, eds., *Persuasion: Advances Through Meta-Analysis* (Creskill, NJ: Hampton Press, 1998) 65.

11. K. Witte, "Putting the Fear Back into Fear Appeals: The Extended Parallel Process Model," *Communication Monographs* 59 (1992): 329–47.

12. See discussions in Myron W. Lustig and Jolene Koester, *Intercultural Competence: Interpersonal Communication Across Cultures* (Boston, MA: Allyn & Bacon, 2003) 347; Larry A. Samovar and Richard E. Porter, *Communication Between Cultures* (Stamford, CT: Wadsworth and Thomson Learning, 2001) 29.

13. C. W. Sherif, M. Sherif, and R. E. Nebergall, *Attitudes and Attitude Change: The Social Judgment-Involvement Approach* (Philadelphia: Saunders, 1965).

Chapter 20 Using Persuasive Strategies

1. William L. Benoit, "Topic of Presidential Campaign Discourse and Election Outcome," *Western Journal of Communication* 67 (Winter 2003): 97–112.

2. J. C. Reinard, "The Empirical Study of the Persuasive Effects of Evidence: The Status after Fifty Years of Research," *Human Communication Research* 15 (1988): 3–59.

3. James C. McCroskey and R. S. Rehrley, "The Effects of Disorganization and Nonfluency on Attitude Change and Source Credibility," *Speech Monographs* 36 (1969): 13–21.

4. For an excellent meta-analysis of forty-nine studies examining the influence of delivery variables and persuasion, see Chris Segrin, "The Effects of Nonverbal Behavior on Outcomes of Compliance Gaining Attempts," *Communication Studies* 44 (1993): 169–87.

5. Judee K. Burgoon, T. Birk, and M. Pfau, "Nonverbal Behaviors, Persuasion, and Credibility," *Human Communication Research* 17 (1990): 140–69.

6. Segrin, "The Effects of Nonverbal Behavior on Outcomes of Compliance Gaining Attempts."

7. For an excellent discussion of the influence of culture on public speaking, see Devorah A. Lieberman, *Public Speaking in the Multicultural Environment* (Englewood Cliffs, NJ: Prentice Hall, 1994) 10.

8. Devorah Lieberman and G. Fisher, "International Negotiation," in Larry A. Samovar and Richard. E. Porter, eds., *Intercultural Communication: A Reader* (Belmont, CA: Wadsworth, 1991) 193–200.

9. Lieberman and Fisher, "International Negotiation."

10. Myron W. Lustig and Jolene Koester, *Intercultural Competence: Interpersonal Communication Across Cultures* (New York: Harper-Collins, 1996) 223.

11. K. Ah Yun and L. L. Massi, "The Differential Impact of Race on the Effectiveness of Narrative versus Statistical Appeals to Persuade Individuals to Sign an Organ Donor Card," paper presented at the meeting of the Western States Communication Association, Sacramento, CA; cited by Lisa L. Massi-Lindsey and Kimo Ah Yun, "Examining the Persuasive Effect of Statistical Messages: A Test of Mediating Relationships," *Communication Studies* 54 (Fall 2003): 306–21.

12. Jeffrey E. Jamison, "Alkali Batteries: Powering Electronics and Polluting the Environment," *Winning Orations 1991* (Mankato, MN: Interstate Oratorical Association, 1991) 43.

13. H. B. Brosius and A. Bathelt, "The Utility of Exemplars in Persuasive Communications," *Communication Research* 21 (1994): 48–78.

14. Massi-Lindsey and Ah Yun, "Examining the Persuasive Effect of Statistical Messages"; D. C. Kazoleas, "A Comparison of the Persuasive Effectiveness of Qualitative versus Quantitative Evidence: A Test of Explanatory Hypotheses,"

Communication Quarterly 41 (1993): 40–50; also see M. Allen and R. W. Preiss, "Comparing the Persuasiveness of Narrative and Statistical Evidence Using Meta-Analysis," *Communication Research Reports* (1997): 125–31.

15. Franklin J. Boster, Kenzie A. Cameron, Shelly Campo, Wen-Ying Liu, Janet K. Lillie, Esther M. Baker, and Kimo Ah Yun, "The Persuasive Effects of Statistical Evidence in the Presence of Exemplars," *Communication Studies* 51, 3 (Fall 2000): 296–306; also see E. J. Baesler and Judee K. Burgoon, "The Temporal Effects of Story and Statistical Evidence on Belief Change," *Communication Research* 21 (1994): 582–602.

16. Roger Ailes, *You Are the Message* (New York: Doubleday, 1989).

17. Albert Mehrabian and J. A. Russell, *An Approach to Environmental Psychology* (Cambridge: MIT Press, 1974); T. Biggers and B. Pryor, "Attitude Change as a Function of Emotion Eliciting Qualities," *Personality and Social Psychology Bulletin* 8 (1982): 94–99; Steven A. Beebe and T. Biggers, "Emotion-Eliciting Qualities of Speech Delivery and Their Effect on Credibility and Comprehension," paper presented at the annual meeting of the International Communication Association, New Orleans, May 1989.

18. John W. Bowers and Michael M. Osborn, "Attitudinal Effects of Selected Types of Concluding Metaphors in Persuasive Speeches," *Speech Monographs* 33 (1966): 147–55; James C. McCroskey and W. H. Combs, "The Effects and the Use of Analogy on Attitude Change and Source Credibility," *Journal of Communication* 19 (1969): 333–39; N. L. Reinsch, "An Investigation of the Effects of the Metaphor and Simile in Persuasive Discourse," *Speech Monographs* 38 (1971): 142–45.

19. Pradeep Sopory and James Price Dillard, "The Persuasive Effects of Metaphor: A Meta-Analysis," *Human Communication Research* 28 (July 2002): 382–419.

20. See Irving Janis and S. Feshback, "Effects of Fear-Arousing Communication," *Journal of Abnormal and Social Psychology* 48 (1953): 78–92; Fredric A. Powell, "The Effects of Anxiety-Arousing Message When Related to Personal, Familial, and Impersonal Referents," *Speech Monographs* 32 (1965): 102–6.

21. Donald C. Bryant, "Rhetoric: Its Functions and Its Scope," *Quarterly Journal of Speech* 39 (Dec. 1953): 26.

22. William L. Benoit, "Forewarning and Persuasion," in Mike Allen and Raymond W. Preiss, eds., *Persuasion: Advances Through Meta-Analysis* (Cresskill, NJ: Hampton Press, 1998) 139–54.

23. Karmen Kirtley, "Grave Matter: The High Cost of Living," *Winning Orations 1997* (Mankato, MN: Interstate Oratorical Association, 1997).

24. Benoit, "Forewarning and Persuasion."

25. Mike Allen, "Comparing the Persuasive Effectiveness of One-and Two-Sided Messages," in Mike Allen and Raymond W. Preiss, eds., *Persuasion: Advances Through Meta-Analysis* (Cresskill, NJ: Hampton Press, 1998) 87–98.

26. Katherine E. Rowan, "A New Pedagogy for Explanatory Public Speaking: Why Arrangement Should Not Substitute for Invention," *Communication Education* 44 (1995): 236–50.

27. Carl I. Hovland, Arthur A. Lunsdaine, and Fred D. Sheffield, "The Effects of Presenting 'One Side' versus 'Both Sides' in Changing Opinions on a Controversial Subject," in *Experiments on Mass Communication* (Princeton: Princeton U, 1949). Also see Arthur Lunsdaine and Irving Janis, "Resistance to 'Counter-Propaganda' Produced by a One-Sided versus a Two-Sided 'Propaganda' Presentation," *Public Opinion Quarterly* (1953): 311–18.

28. N. Miller and Donald T. Campbell, "Recency and Primacy in Persuasion as a Function of the Timing of Speeches and Measurements," *Journal of Abnormal and Social Psychology* 59 (1959): 1–9; Adrian Furnham, "The Robustness of the Recency Effect: Studies Using Legal Evidence," *The Journal of General Psychology* 113 (1986): 351–57; R. Rosnow, "Whatever Happened to the 'Law of Primacy'?" *Journal of Communication* 16 (1966): 10–31.

29. Robert B. Ricco, "Analyzing the Roles of Challenge and Defense in Argumentation," *Argumentation and Advocacy* 39 (Summer 2002): 1–22.

30. Douglas Ehninger, Bruce E. Gronbeck, Ray E. McKerrow, and Alan H. Monroe, *Principles and Types of Speech Communication* (Glenview, IL: Scott, Foresman 1986) 15.

31. James Chang, "Sustainable Giving," *Winning Orations 2003* (Mankato, MN: Interstate Oratorical Association, 2003) 3.

32. Chang, "Sustainable Giving" 3.

33. Chang, "Sustainable Giving" 3.

34. Chang, "Sustainable Giving" 3.

35. Martin Luther King Jr., "I Have a Dream" (28 Aug. 1963), in Houston Peterson, ed., *A Treasury of the World's Great Speeches* (New York: Simon & Schuster, 1965) 835–39.

36. Chang, "Sustainable Giving" 3.

37. Following are sources of the information that appears in the sample speech on pages 436–439: Adams, C. "FDA to Review Policy Allowing Drugs on TV." *Wall Street Journal,* March 28, 2001, B1.

Alliance for Retired Americans. "Profits in Pills: A Primer on Prescription Drug Prices," March 2000, http://www. retiredamericans.org/news_theprofitinpills.htm.

American Broadcasting Corporation. "Pills, Profits and Public Health: America's Billion Dollar Pharmaceutical Industry" (P. Jennings, Executive Producer), *ABC News*, May 30, 2002, http://abcnews.go.com/sections/community/DailyNews/chat_pharmaceuticals020530.html.

Diede, M. L., & Liliedahl, R. "Getting on the Right Track," *Managed Care*, February 2002, http://www.managedcaremag.com/archives/0202/0202.edge.html.

Findlay, S. "Do Ads Really Drive Pharmaceutical Sales?" *Marketing Health Services*, 22(1) (2002): 20–26.

Lieberman, B. "When DTC Is DOA." *Pharmaceutical Executive* 36(4) (2001): 80–82.

National Institute for Health Care Management, "Prescription Drugs and Mass Media Advertising," November, 2001, http://www.nihcm.org/DTCbrief2001.pdf.

Petersen, M. "Increased Spending on Drugs Is Linked to More Advertising," *New York Times*, November 21, 2001, C1.

Wilkes, M. S., Bell, R. A., & Kravitz, R. L. "Direct to Consumer Prescription Drug Advertising: Trends, Impact and Implications," *Health Affairs* 19(2) (2000): 110–128.

Woloshin, S., Schwartz, L. M., Tremmel, J., & Welch, H. G. "Direct to Consumer Advertisements for Prescription Drugs: What Are Americans Being Sold?" *Lancet* 358 (2001): 1141–46.

Chapter 21 Special-Occasion Speaking

1. Leslie Wayne, "In World Where Talk Doesn't Come Cheap, Former Officials Are Finding Lucrative Careers," *The New York Times* 10 March 2004: A14.
2. Roger E. Flax, "A Manner of Speaking," *Ambassador* (May–June 1991): 37.
3. Slainte! Toasts, Blessings, and Sayings. March 1998. June 28, 1998 <http://zinnia.umfacad.maine.edu/~donaghue/toasts.html>.
4. Sarah Husberg, "A Wedding Toast," in Tasha Van Horn, Lori Charron, and Michael Charron, eds., *Allyn & Bacon Video II User's Guide*, 2002.
5. Jeff Brooks, *Wedding Toasts*. March 1998. June 29, 1998 <http://zinnia.umfacad.maine.edu/~donaghue/toasts07.html>.
6. Everett M. Dirksen, "Nominating Speech for Barry Goldwater" (15 July 1964), in James R.

Andrews and David Zarefsky, eds., *Contemporary American Voices* (New York: Simon & Schuster, 1965) 815.
7. Erma Bombeck, "Abbreviated Thank-You's Allow Us More Time to Study Danson's Head," *Austin American-Statesman* 22 June 1993: F3.
8. Cindy Pearlman, "Oscar Speeches: Statues in Their Hands, Feet in Their Mouths," *Austin American-Statesman* 24 Mar. 1997: E8.
9. "Arafat Calls for Speedier Peace in Nobel Speech," Reuter News Agency 10 Dec. 1994.
10. Elie Wiesel, "Acceptance of the 1986 Nobel Peace Prize," *The New York Times* 11 Dec. 1986: A8.
11. William Faulkner, "Acceptance of the Nobel Prize for Literature" (10 Dec. 1950), in Houston Peterson, ed., *A Treasury of the World's Great Speeches* (New York: Simon & Schuster, 1965) 815.
12. Barbara Jordan, "Change: From What to What?" *Vital Speeches of the Day* 15 August 1992: 651.
13. David Abel, "Commencement Addresses Leave Audiences Lost," *The Boston Globe* 5 June 2000: B4.
14. Kurt Vonnegut. "Title: I have no name for it, and hope nobody else comes up with one," speech delivered at Rice University commencement. 9 May 1998. 29 June 1998 <http://www.ruf.rice.edu/~presiden/Speakers/Commence98.html>.
15. Toni Morrison, commencement address to the Wellesley College class of 2004, Wellesley College Web site. 28 May 2004. 4 June 2004 <www.wellesley.edu/PublicAffairs/Commencement/2004/morrison.html>.
16. Abel, "Commencement Addresses Leave Audiences Lost," B4.
17. Bill Clinton, speech at Pointe du Hoc, France (June 1994), as quoted in David Shribman, "President, a Child of World War II, Thanks a Generation," *Boston Globe* 7 June 1994: 1.
18. Edward Kennedy, eulogy for Jacqueline Kennedy Onassis (May 1994), as quoted in "The Texts of Personal Tributes and Poems at the Services for Mrs. Onassis," *The New York Times* 24 May 1994: A10.
19. George Bush, eulogy for Ronald Reagan 11 June 2004, quoted in "Excerpts from the Eulogies: Recollections of Hope, Humor and One Very Big Heart," *The New York Times* 12 June 2004: A8.
20. Earl Spencer, "Eulogy for Diana, Princess of Wales, September 1997." *Britannia*. 29 June 1998 <http://www.britannia.com/ diana/article4.html>.
21. Dave Barry, "Speak! Speak!" *Austin American-Statesman* 2 June 1991: C4.

22. Sarah Booth Conroy, "State Dinners Offer Speech as First Course," *Austin American-Statesman* 10 November 1989.

23. John C. Meyer, "Humor as a Double-Edged Sword: Four Functions of Humor in Communication," *Communication Theory* 10 (3) (August 2000): 311.

24. Debi Martin, "Laugh Lines," *Austin American-Statesman* 20 May 1988: D1.

25. Jon Macks, *How to Be Funny* (New York: Simon & Schuster, 2003).

26. Joe Queenan, "How to Tell a Joke," *Reader's Digest* Sept. 2003: 73.

27. Alison White, "Writing a Humorous Speech." 3 June 2004 <www.bizinternet.com.au/StGeorges/humour.html>.

28. Mark Twain, "The Alphabet and Simplified Spelling," address at the dedication of the New York Engineers' Club, December 9, 1907. *Mark Twain's Speeches; with an Introduction by William Dean Howells,* Electronic Text Center, University of Virginia Library. 4 June 2004 <etext.lib. Virginia.edu>.

29. Mark Twain, address at the Pilgrims' Club Luncheon, London, June 25, 1907. *Mark Twain's Speeches; with an Introduction by William Dean Howells,* Electronic Text Center, University of Virginia Library. 4 June 2004 <etext.lib.Virginia. edu>.

30. Chris O'Keefe, untitled speech, in John K. Boaz and James Brey, eds., *1987 Championship Debates and Speeches* (Speech Communication Association and American Forensic Association, 1987) 99.

31. Mark Twain, "The Weather," address at the New England Society's seventy-first Annual Dinner, New York City. *Mark Twain's Speeches; with an Introduction by William Dean Howells,* Electronic Text Center, University of Virginia Library. 4 June 2004 <etext.lib.Virginia.edu>.

32. Susan Wallace, "Seriously, How Do I Write a Humorous Speech?" as reported by Mike Dicerbo, Leadership in Action 1 November 2000. 2 June 2004 <www.angelfire.com/az2/D3tmLeadership3/NewsNovSusanWallace.html>.

Appendix A Speaking in Small Groups

1. Group communication principles presented in this chapter are adapted from Steven A. Beebe and John T. Masterson, *Communicating in Small Groups. Principles and Practices,* 8th ed. (Boston: Allyn & Bacon, 2006).

2. For a discussion of the advantages and disadvantages of working in small groups, see Norman R. F. Maier, "Assets and Liabilities in Group Problem Solving: The Need for an Integrative Function," *Psychological Review* 74 (1967): 239–49; Michael Argyle, *Cooperation: The Basis of Sociability* (London: Routledge, 1991).

3. Maier, "Assets and Liabilities in Group Problem Solving;" Argyle, *Cooperation.*

4. H. Barki, "Small Group Brainstorming and Idea Quality: Is Electronic Brainstorming the Most Effective Approach?" *Small Group Research* 32, 2 (2001): 158–205; B. A. Nijstad, W. Stroebe, and H. F. M. Lodewijkx, "Cognitive Stimulation and Interference in Groups: Exposure Effects in an Idea Generation Task," *Journal of Experimental Social Psychology* 38 (2002): 535–44.

5. K. L. Dugosh, P. B. Paulus, E. J. Roland, and H. C. Yang, "Cognitive Stimulation in Brainstorming," *Journal of Personality and Social Psychology* 79, 5 (2000): 722–35.

6. R. Y. Hirokawa and A. J. Salazar, "Task-Group Communication and Decision-Making Performance," in L. Frey, ed., *The Handbook of Group Communication Theory and Research* (Thousand Oaks, CA: Sage, 1999) 167–91; D. Gouran and R. Y. Hirokawa, "Functional Theory and Communication in Decision-Making and Problem-Solving Groups: An Expanded View," in R. Y. Hirokawa and M. S. Poole, eds., *Communication and Group Decision Making* (Thousand Oaks, CA: Sage, 1996) 55–80.

7. C. A. VanLear and E. A. Mabry, "Testing Contrasting Interaction Models for Discriminating Between Consensual and Dissentient Decision-Making Groups," *Small Group Research* 30 (1999): 29–58; also see T. J. Saine and D. G. Bock, "A Comparison of the Distributional and Sequential Structures of Interaction in High and Low Consensus Groups," *Central States Speech Journal* 24 (1973): 125–39.

8. Randy Y. Hirokawa and Roger Pace, "A Descriptive Investigation of the Possible Communication-Based Reasons for Effective and Ineffective Group Decision Making," *Communication Monographs* 50 (Dec. 1983): 363–79.

9. Randy Y. Hirokawa, "Group Communication and Problem-Solving Effectiveness: An Investigation of Group Phases," *Human Communication Research* 9 (Summer 1983): 291–305.

10. Dennis S. Gouran, "Variables Related to Consensus in Group Discussion of Questions of Policy," *Speech Monographs* 36 (Aug. 1969): 385–91.

11. For a summary of research about conflict management in small groups, see S. M. Farmer and J. Roth, "Conflict-Handling Behavior in Work

Groups: Effects of Group Structure, Decision Processes, and Time," *Small Group Research* 29 (1998): 669–713; also see Beebe and Masterson, *Communicating in Small Groups.*

12. Ralph White and Ronald Lippitt, "Leader Behavior and Member Reaction in Three 'Social Climates,'" in Darwin Cartwright and Alvin Zander, eds., *Group Dynamics,* 3rd ed. (New York: Harper & Row, 1968) 319.

13. Peter M. Senge, "Leading Learning Organizations," in Richard Beckhard et al., eds., *The Leader of the Future* (San Francisco: Jossey-Bass, 1996); Bernard M. Bass and M. J. Avolio, "Transformational Leadership and Organizational Culture," *International Journal of Public Administration* 17 (1994): 541–54; Lynn Little, "Transformational Leadership," *Academic Leadership* 15 (Nov. 1999): 4–5.

14. Francis J. Yammarino and Alan J. Dubinsky, "Transformational Leadership Theory: Using Levels of Analysis to Determine Boundary Conditions," *Personnel Psychology* 47 (1994): 787–809.

15. Roger K. Mosvick and Robert B. Nelson, *We've Got to Start Meeting Like This!* (Glenview, IL: Scott, Foresman, 1987).

16. Mosvick and Nelson, *We've Got to Start Meeting Like This!*

17. For a comprehensive discussion of meeting agendas, see Beebe and Masterson, *Communicating in Small Groups.*

18. Suggestions about organizing meeting agendas are based on Michael Doyle and David Straus, *How to Make Meetings Work* (New York: Playboy Press, 1976); Mosvick and Nelson, *We've Got to Start Meeting Like This!;* Gay Lumsden and Donald Lumsden, *Communicating in Groups and Teams: Sharing Leadership* (Belmont, CA: Wadsworth, 1993); Dan B. Curtis, James J. Floyd, and Jerry L. Winsor, *Business and Professional Communication* (New York: HarperCollins, 1992); Dennis A. Romig and Laurie J. Romig, *Breakthrough Teamwork* (Chicago: Irwin, 1996); Thomas A. Kayser, *Mining Group Gold* (El Segundo, CA: Serif Publishing, 1990); John E. Tropman and Gershom Clark Morningstar, *Meetings: How to Make Them Work for You* (New York: Van Nostrand Reinhold, 1985) 56; John E. Tropman, *Making Meetings Work* (Thousand Oaks, CA: Sage 1996).

19. Mosvick and Nelson, *We've Got to Start Meeting Like This!*

Glossary

acceptance speech: A speech of thanks for an award, nomination, or other honor (p. 446)

accommodation: Sensitivity to the feelings, needs, interests, and backgrounds of other people (p. 52)

ad hominem: An attack on irrelevant personal characteristics of the person who is proposing an idea, rather than on the idea itself (p. 417)

after-dinner speech: An entertaining speech, usually delivered in conjunction with a mealtime meeting or banquet (p. 451)

agenda: A written list or description of the items and issues that a group will discuss during a meeting (p. 466)

alliteration: The repetition of a consonant sound (usually the first consonant) several times in a phrase, clause, or sentence (p. 273)

analogy: A comparison; also, a special type of inductive reasoning that compares one thing, person, or process with another to predict how something will perform and respond (p. 178)

analysis: Examination of the causes, effects, and history of a problem to understand it better (p. 461)

andragogy: The art and science of teaching adults (p. 374)

anecdote: An illustration or brief story (p. 226)

antithesis: Opposition, such as that used in two-part sentences whose parts have parallel structures but contrasting meanings (p. 272)

appeal to misplaced authority: Use of the testimony of an expert in a given field to endorse an idea or product for which the expert does not have the appropriate credentials or expertise (p. 418)

articulation: The production of clear and distinct speech sounds (p. 298)

attend: To focus on incoming information (p. 64)

attitude: A learned predisposition to respond favorably or unfavorably toward something; a like or dislike (p. 105)

audience adaptation: The process of ethically using information about an audience in order to adapt one's message so that it is clear and achieves the speaking objective (p. 95)

audience analysis: The process of examining information about those who are expected to listen to a speech (p. 93)

AutoContent Wizard: In PowerPoint, a feature that provides suggestions and ideas for the new presentation being created (p. 351)

bandwagon fallacy: Reasoning that suggests that because everyone else believes something or is doing something, then it must be valid or correct (p. 416)

bar graph: A graph in which bars of various lengths represent information (p. 326)

behavioral objective: Statement of the specific purpose of a speech, expressed in terms of desired audience behavior at the end of the speech (p. 136)

belief: An individual's perception of what is true or false (p. 106)

black-and-white view: In PowerPoint, a function that allows a user to view and print items in a presentation in black and white (p. 352)

blank presentation: In PowerPoint, a feature that enables a user to create a slide design by choosing layout, colors, graphics, fonts, and organization of content (p. 351)

517

blueprint: The central idea of a speech plus a preview of main ideas (p. 143)

bookmark: A browser feature that allows a user to save a URL for future reference (p. 149)

Boolean search: An advanced Web-searching technique that allows a user to narrow a subject or key word search by adding various requirements (p. 150)

boom microphone: A microphone that is suspended from a bar and moved to follow the speaker; often used in movies and TV (p. 302)

brainstorming: A problem-solving technique used to generate many ideas (p. 131)

brief illustration: An unelaborated example, often only a sentence or two long (p. 172)

browser: Software that accesses Web sites and Web pages (p. 149)

card catalog: A file of information about the books in a library; may be an index-card filing system or a computerized system (p. 153)

causal fallacy: A faulty cause-and-effect connection between two things or events (p. 416)

causal reasoning: Reasoning in which the relationship between two or more events leads you to conclude that one or more of the events caused the others (p. 412)

cause-and-effect organization: Organization that focuses on a situation and its causes or a situation and its effects (p. 205)

CD: A compact disk used for storing electronic files of images, words, and sounds (p. 332)

central idea: A one-sentence summary of a speech (pp. 34, 138)

channel: The visual and auditory means by which a message is transmitted from sender to receiver (p. 12)

charisma: A form of dynamism characteristic of a talented, charming, attractive speaker (p. 406)

chart: A display that summarizes information by using words, numbers, or images (p. 329)

chronological organization: Organization by time or sequence (p. 200)

Clip Gallery: In PowerPoint, a collection of clip art that can be used in presentations (p. 353)

closure: The quality of a conclusion that makes a speech "sound finished" (p. 237)

code: A verbal or nonverbal symbol for an idea or image (p. 11)

cognitive dissonance: The sense of mental discomfort that prompts a person to change when new information conflicts with previously organized thought patterns (p. 388)

color schemes: In PowerPoint, sets of balanced colors that can be applied to presentations (p. 352)

commemorative address: A speech delivered during ceremonies held in memory of some past event and often the person or persons involved (p. 449)

commencement address: A speech delivered at a graduation or commencement ceremony (p. 448)

competence: An aspect of a speaker's credibility that reflects whether the speaker is perceived as informed, skilled, or knowledgeable (p. 406)

complexity: Arrangement of the ideas in a speech from the simplest to the more complex (p. 204)

computer-generated graphics: Images, words, charts, and graphs designed and presented using a computer and graphics software (p. 333)

conclusion: The logical outcome of a deductive argument, which stems from the major premise and the minor premise (p. 410)

connotation: The meaning listeners associate with a word, based on past experience (p. 266)

consensus: The support and commitment of all group members to the decision of the group (p. 462)

context: The environment or situation in which a speech occurs (p. 12)

credibility: An audience's perception of a speaker as competent, trustworthy, knowledgeable, and dynamic (pp. 108, 223)

criteria: Standards for identifying an acceptable solution to a problem (p. 461)

critical listening: Evaluating the quality of information, ideas, and arguments put forth by a speaker (p. 77)

critical thinking: Making judgments about the conclusions presented in what you see, hear, and read (p. 77)

culture: A learned system of knowledge, behavior, attitudes, beliefs, values, and norms that is shared by a group of people (p. 98)

declamation: The delivery of an already famous speech (p. 15)

decode: To translate verbal or nonverbal symbols into ideas and images that constitute a message (p. 12)

deductive reasoning: Reasoning that moves from a general statement or principle to a specific, certain conclusion (p. 410)

definition: A statement of what a term means or how it is applied in a specific instance (p. 177)

definition by classification: A "dictionary definition," constructed by first placing a term in the general class to which it belongs and then differentiating it from all other members of that class (p. 177)

delivery outline: Condensed and abbreviated outline from which speaking notes are developed (p. 254)

demagogue: A speaker who gains control over others by using unethical emotional pleas and appeals to listeners' prejudices (p. 423)

demographic audience analysis: Analyzing an audience by examining demographic information so as to develop a clear and effective message (p. 97)

demographics: Statistics on population characteristics such as age, sexual orientation, race, gender, educational level, and religious views (p. 91)

denotation: The literal meaning of a word (p. 266)

derived credibility: The perception of a speaker's credibility that an audience forms during a speech (p. 407)

description: A word picture of something (p. 175)

dialect: A consistent style of pronouncing words that is common to an ethnic group or geographic region (p. 298)

digital video disk (DVD):   An electronic storage mode similar to a CD-ROM but capable of storing much more information and displaying it with exceptional clarity and fidelity (p. 332)

disposition: The orderly organization and arrangement of ideas and illustrations in a speech (p. 37)

dynamism: An aspect of a speaker's credibility that reflects whether the speaker is perceived as energetic (p. 406)

either/or fallacy: The oversimplification of an issue into a choice between only two outcomes or possibilities (p. 417)

elaboration likelihood model (ELM) of persuasion: The theory that listeners can be persuaded directly, by logic, reasoning, and evidence, or indirectly, by the overall emotional impact of the message (p. 387)

elocution: The expression of emotion through posture, movement, gestures, facial expression, and voice (p. 15)

embedding: In PowerPoint, the insertion of charts, pictures, equations, or other objects into a presentation (p. 353)

empowerment: Influence and potential leadership, gained in part by speaking with competence and confidence (p. 7)

encode: To translate ideas and images into verbal or nonverbal symbols (p. 11)

ethics: The beliefs, values, and moral principles by which people determine what is right or wrong (p. 47)

ethnic vernacular: A variety of English that includes words and phrases used by a specific ethnic group (p. 266)

ethnicity: That portion of a person's cultural background that relates to a national or religious heritage (p. 98)

ethnocentrism: The attitude that one's own culture and cultural perspectives and methods are superior to those of others (p. 98)

ethos: The term Aristotle used to refer to a speaker's credibility (p. 405)

eulogy: A speech of tribute to someone who has died (p. 450)

evidence: The facts, examples, opinions, and statistics that a speaker uses to support a conclusion (p. 78)

example: An illustration used to dramatize or clarify a fact (p. 415)

expert testimony: An opinion offered by someone who is an authority on the subject under discussion (p. 184)

explanation: A statement of how something is done or why it exists in its present form or existed in its past form (p. 175)

extemporaneous speaking: Speaking from a written or memorized speech outline without having memorized the exact wording of the speech (p. 289)

extended illustration: A detailed example that resembles a story (p. 172)

external noise: Physical sounds that interfere with communication (p. 12)

fact: Information that has been proven to be true through direct observation or that can be proved to be true (p. 77)

fallacy: False reasoning that occurs when someone attempts to persuade without adequate evidence or with arguments that are irrelevant or inappropriate (p. 416)

feedback: Verbal and nonverbal responses provided by an audience to a speaker (p. 12)

figurative analogy: A comparison between two essentially dissimilar things that share some feature on which the comparison depends (p. 179)

figure of speech: Language that deviates from the ordinary, expected meaning of words to make a description or comparison unique, vivid, and memorable (p. 269)

First Amendment: The amendment to the U.S. Constitution that guarantees free speech; the first of the ten amendments to the U.S. Constitution known collectively as the Bill of Rights (p. 48)

font: A collection of upper- and lowercase letters, as well as numbers, symbols, and punctuation, of a particular typeface size. (p. 335)

free speech: Legally protected speech or speech acts (p. 47)

full-text database: An indexing system, available on the World Wide Web or on CD-ROM, that provides not only bibliographic data but also full texts of entries (p. 156)

gender: The culturally constructed and psychologically based perception of one's self as feminine or masculine (p. 97)

general purpose: The overarching goal of a speech—to inform, to persuade, or to entertain (pp. 33, 135)

generalization: An all-encompassing statement (p. 409)

graph: A pictorial representation of statistical data (p. 326)

hard evidence: Factual examples and statistics (p. 212)

hasty generalization: A conclusion reached without adequate evidence (p. 417)

hyperbole: Exaggeration (p. 452)

hyperlink: Image, icon, or colored and underlined text on a Web page that connects the user with another Web page or Web site (p. 149)

hypothetical illustration: An example that might happen but that has not actually occurred (p. 173)

illustration: A story or anecdote that provides an example of an idea, issue, or problem the speaker is discussing (p. 172)

immediacy: The degree of physical or psychological closeness between people (p. 295)

immediacy behaviors: Nonverbal expressions of closeness to and liking for an audience, made through such means as physical approach or eye contact (p. 295)

impromptu speaking: Delivering a speech without advance preparation (p. 287)

inductive reasoning: Reasoning that uses specific instances or examples to reach a general, probable conclusion (p. 409)

inference: A conclusion based on partial information or an evaluation that has not been directly observed (p. 77)

inflection: The variation of the pitch of the voice (p. 300)

initial credibility: The impression of a speaker's credibility that listeners have before the speaker starts a speech (p. 407)

internal noise: Anything physiological or psychological that interferes with communication (p. 12)

Internet: A vast collection of hundreds of thousands of computers accessible to millions of people around the world (p. 148)

invention: The development or discovery of new ideas and insights (p. 34)

inversion: Reversal of the normal word order of a phrase or sentence (p. 271)

jargon: The specialized language of a profession (p. 267)

keynote address: A speech that sets the theme and tone for a meeting or conference (p. 448)

lavaliere microphone: A microphone that can be clipped to an article of clothing or worn on a cord around the neck (p. 302)

lay testimony: An opinion or description offered by a nonexpert who has firsthand experience of something (p. 185)

line graph: A graph that uses lines or curves to show relationships between two or more variables (p. 326)

listening styles: Preferred ways of making sense out of spoken messages (p. 73)

literal analogy: A comparison between two similar things (p. 179)

literary quotation: An opinion or description by a writer, expressed in a memorable and often poetic way (p. 185)

logic: A formal system of rules used to reach a conclusion (p. 78)

logos: Literally, "the word"; the term Aristotle used to refer to logic—the formal system of using rules to reach a conclusion (p. 408)

main ideas: The key points of a speech; subdivisions of the central idea (pp. 34, 141)

major premise: A general statement that is the first element of a syllogism (p. 410)

malapropism: The mistaken use of a word that sounds like the intended word (p. 452)

manuscript speaking: Reading a speech from a written text (p. 286)

mapping: Use of geometric shapes to sketch how all the main ideas, subpoints, and supporting material of a speech relate to the central idea and to one another (p. 244)

master view: In PowerPoint, a function that allows a user to view text or images that are to appear on every slide, notes page, or handout (p. 352)

memorized speaking: Delivering a speech word for word from memory without using notes (p. 287)

message: The content of a speech plus the way it is said (p. 11)

metaphor: An implied comparison between two things or concepts (p. 269)

minor premise: A specific statement about an example that is linked to the major premise; the second element of a syllogism (p. 410)

model: A small object that represents a larger object (p. 324)

motivation: An internal force that drives people to achieve their goals (p. 387)

myth: A belief based on the shared values, cultural heritage, and faith of a group of people (p. 422)

nomination speech: A speech that officially recommends someone as a candidate for an office or position (p. 446)

non sequitur: Latin for "it does not follow"; an idea or conclusion that does not logically relate to or follow from the previous idea or conclusion (p. 418)

nonverbal communication: Communication other than written or spoken language that creates meaning (p. 284)

nonverbal-expectancy theory: A communication theory suggesting that if listeners' expectations about how communication should be expressed are violated, listeners will feel less favorable toward the communicator of the message (p. 284)

notes page view: In PowerPoint, a function that allows a user to view and work on speaker notes for a presentation (p. 352)

omission: Leaving out a word or phrase the listener expects to hear (p. 270)

operational definition: A definition that explains how something works or what it does or that describes procedures for observing or measuring the concept being defined (p. 177)

opinion: Testimony or a quotation that expresses someone's attitudes, beliefs, or values (p. 184)

oral citation: The oral presentation of such information about a source as the author, title, and year of publication (p. 55)

outline view: In PowerPoint, a function that allows a user to view text in outline form while organizing and developing content (p. 352)

parallelism: Use of the same grammatical pattern for two or more clauses or sentences (p. 271)

pathos: Term used by Aristotle to refer to appeals to emotion (p. 419)

pedagogy: The art and science of teaching children (p. 374)

periodical: General-interest magazines and trade and professional journals (p. 154)

periodical index: A listing of bibliographical data for articles published in a group of magazines and/or journals during a given time period (p. 154)

personification: The attribution of human qualities to inanimate things or ideas (p. 270)

persuasion: The process of changing or reinforcing a listener's attitudes, beliefs, values, or behavior (p. 385)

picture graph: A graph that uses images or pictures to symbolize data (p. 326)

pie graph: A circular graph divided into wedges that show the distribution of data (p. 326)

pitch: The highness or lowness of voice sounds (p. 300)

plagiaphrasing: Using someone else's phrases in a speech without acknowledging the source (p. 53)

plagiarize: To present someone else's ideas as though they were one's own (p. 53)

prejudice: Preconceived opinions, attitudes, and beliefs about a person, place, or thing (p. 67)

preliminary bibliography: A list of potential resources to be used in the preparation of a speech (p. 163)

preparation outline: A detailed outline that includes main ideas, subpoints, and supporting material and that may also include a speech's specific purpose, introduction, blueprint, internal previews and summaries, transitions, and conclusion (p. 244)

presentation aid: Anything tangible (drawings, charts, graphs, video images, photographs, posters, music) that helps communicate an idea to an audience (p. 321)

presentation speech: A speech that accompanies the presentation of an award (p. 445)

primacy: Arrangement of the ideas in a speech from the most to the least important (p. 203)

primary source: The original collector and interpreter of information or data (p. 181)

problem-and-solution organization: Organization that focuses on a problem and various solutions or a solution and the problems it would solve (p. 206)

pronunciation: The proper use of sounds to form words clearly and accurately (p. 299)

proposition: A statement with which a speaker wants an audience to agree (p. 397)

proposition of fact: A proposition that focuses on whether something is true or false or whether it did or did not happen (p. 398)

proposition of policy: A proposition that advocates a change in a policy, procedure, or behavior (p. 400)

proposition of value: A proposition that calls for a listener to judge the worth or importance of something (p. 399)

psychological audience analysis: Analyzing the attitudes, beliefs, values, and other psychological information about an audience in order to develop a clear and effective message (p. 105)

public-relations speech: A speech designed to inform the public, to strengthen alliances with them, and in some cases to recommend policy (p. 442)

pun: A verbal device that uses double meanings to create humor (p. 452)

race: A person's biological heritage (p. 98)

reasoning: The process of drawing a conclusion from evidence (p. 79)

receiver: A listener or an audience member (p. 12)

receiver apprehension: The fear of misunderstanding or misinterpreting the spoken messages of others (p. 68)

recency: Arrangement of the ideas in a speech from the least to the most important (p. 201)

red herring: Irrelevant facts or information used to distract someone from the issue under discussion (p. 418)

reflective thinking: A method of structuring a problem-solving discussion that involves (1) identifying and defining the problem, (2) analyzing the problem, (3) generating possible solutions, (4) selecting the best solution, and (5) testing and implementing the solution (p. 460)

regionalism: A word or phrase used uniquely by speakers in one part of a country (p. 267)

remember: To recall ideas and information (p. 64)

repetition: Use of a key word or phrase more than once for emphasis (p. 272)

report: A presentation, often oral as well as written, of information or policy related to the workplace (p. 442)

rhetoric: The use of words and symbols to achieve a goal (p. 14)

rhetorical criticism: The process of using a method or standards to evaluate the effectiveness and appropriateness of messages (p. 79)

rhetorical question: A question intended to provoke thought, rather than elicit an answer (p. 229)

rhetorical strategies: Methods and techniques used by speakers to achieve their goals (p. 82)

search engine: A Web site that works much like a traditional card catalog, allowing access to the World Wide Web through a subject or key word search (p. 149)

secondary source: An individual, organization, or publication that reports information or data gathered by another entity (p. 181)

select: To single out a message from several competing ones (p. 64)

self-actualization: The need to achieve one's highest potential (p. 392)

signpost: A verbal or nonverbal signal that a speaker is moving from one idea to another (p. 213)

simile: A comparison between two things that uses the word *like* or *as* (p. 270)

situational audience analysis: Examining the time and place of a speech, the audience size, and the speaking occasion in order to develop a clear and effective message (p. 108)

slide master: In PowerPoint, the function that controls the format and placement of titles and text on slides (p. 352)

slide sorter view: In PowerPoint, a function that allows a user to view miniature versions of all slides in a presentation so that slides can be added, deleted, or reordered (p. 352)

slide view: In PowerPoint, a function that allows a user to view an entire slide or a portion of a slide while working on it (p. 352)

small group communication: Interaction among from three to twelve people who share a common purpose, feel a sense of belonging to the group, and influence one another (p. 459)

social judgment theory: The theory that listeners' responses to persuasive messages fall in the latitude of acceptance, the latitude of rejection, or the latitude of noncommitment (p. 397)

socioeconomic status: A person's perceived importance and influence based on factors such as income, occupation, and education level (p. 101)

soft evidence: Supporting material based on opinion or inference; includes hypothetical illustrations, descriptions, explanations, definitions, analogies, and opinions (p. 212)

source: The public speaker (p. 11)

spatial organization: Arrangement of ideas in a speech according to location or position (p. 204)

specific purpose: A concise statement of what you want your listeners to know, feel, or be able to do when you finish speaking (pp. 33, 136)

speech act: A behavior, such as burning a flag, that is viewed by law as nonverbal communication and is subject to the same protections and limitations as verbal speech (p. 49)

speech of introduction: A speech that provides information about another speaker (p. 443)

speech to inform: A speech that shares information with others about ideas, concepts, principles, or processes in order to enhance their knowledge or understanding (p. 365)

speech topic: The key focus of the content of a speech (p. 32)

spoonerism: A play on words involving the switching of the initial sounds of the words in a phrase (p. 452)

stacks: The collection of books in a library (p. 153)

standard outline form: Numbered and lettered headings and subheadings arranged hierarchically to indicate the relationships among parts of a speech (p. 244)

standard U.S. English: The English taught by schools and used in the media, business, and government in the United States (p. 267)

stationary microphone: A microphone attached to a podium, sitting on a desk, or standing on the floor (p. 302)

statistics: Numerical data that summarize facts or samples (p. 180)

suspension: Withholding a key word or phrase until the end of a sentence (p. 271)

syllogism: A three-part way of developing an argument, using a major premise, a minor premise, and a conclusion (p. 410)

symbols: Words, images, and behaviors that create meaning for someone (p. 82)

target audience: A specific segment of an audience that you most want to influence (p. 103)

template: In PowerPoint, a model containing color schemes, slide and title masters with custom formatting, and fonts, all of which can be customized for a particular type of presentation (p. 351)

terminal credibility: The final impression listeners have of a speaker's credibility, after a speech concludes (p. 408)

thesaurus: A list of words and their synonyms (p. 265)

title master: In PowerPoint, a function that controls the format and placement of any slide(s) designated as title slide(s) (p. 352)

toast: A brief salute to a momentous occasion (p. 444)

topical organization: Organization of the natural divisions in a central idea on the basis of recency, primacy, complexity, or the speaker's preference (p. 203)

transformational leadership: The process of influencing others by building a shared vision of the future, inspiring others to achieve, developing high-quality individual relationships with others, and helping people see how what they do is related to a larger framework or system (p. 465)

trustworthiness: An aspect of a speaker's credibility that reflects whether the speaker is perceived as believable and honest (p. 406)

typeface: A set of fonts that have characteristics in common; for example, Helvetica, Palatino, Brush Script, and Whimsy are all typefaces (p. 335)

understand: To assign meaning to the stimuli to which you attend (p. 64)

understatement: Downplaying a fact or event (p. 452)

URL: Uniform resource locator; the address of a Web site or Web page (p. 149)

value: An enduring concept of right and wrong, good and bad (p. 106)

verbal irony: A statement that expresses the exact opposite of the intended meaning (p. 453)

volume: The softness or loudness of a speaker's voice (p. 297)

Web directory: A Web site that allows access to the World Wide Web by offering the user ever-more-specific categories of information from which to select (pp. 133, 149)

Web page: An individual file or screen that is part of a Web site (p. 149)

Web site: A location on the World Wide Web that includes a number of related Web pages (p. 149)

wit: A statement that concludes in an unexpected way (p. 453)

Index